THE FOUNTAIN OF PEACE

The International Library of Poetry

Megan C. Olsen, Editor
Robert W. Hartman, Assistant Editor

The Fountain of Peace

Library of Congress
Cataloging in Publication Data

ISBN 1-58235-135-X

Proudly manufactured in the United States of America by
Watermark Press
One Poetry Plaza
Owings Mills, MD 21117

The International Library of Poetry
poetry.COM

FOREWORD

Throughout life, we store information collected from experiences and try in some way to make sense of it. When we are not able to fully understand the things that occur in our lives, we often externalize the information. By doing this, we are afforded a different perspective, thus allowing us to think more clearly about difficult or perplexing events and emotions. Art is one of the ways in which people choose to externalize their thoughts.

Within the arts, modes of expression differ, but poetry is a very powerful tool by which people can share sometimes confusing, sometimes perfectly clear concepts and feelings with others. Intentions can run the gamut as well: The artists may simply want to share something that has touched their lives in some way, or they may want to get help to allay anxiety or uncertainty. The poetry within *The Fountain of Peace* is from every point on the spectrum: every topic, every intention, every event or emotion imaginable. Some poems will speak to certain readers more than others, but it is always important to keep in mind that each verse is the voice of a poet, of a mind that needs to make sense of this world, of a heart that feels the effects of every moment in this life, and perhaps of a memory that is striving to surface. Nonetheless, recalling our yesterdays gives birth to our many forms of expression.

Melisa S. Mitchell
Senior Editor

Editor's Note

*"Those who have courage to love
should have courage to suffer."*—Anthony Trollope

Human beings are social creatures. As basic as the need for food and water is the human instinct to find a mate. Since the beginning of time, humankind has been driven by the need to find a partner with whom to share the pain and splendor of life. Ironically, though, the greatest pain on this Earthly journey is, oftentimes, that which comes from having a partner, and it is this kind of suffering that fosters the depth of emotion needed to create the kind of poetry that is universally recognizable.

When a relationship does go sour, anything and everything can act as a painful reminder of things gone wrong. In her poem, "Clams" (1), Julianne Nason uses the process of preparing and cooking clams as a metaphor both for her current relationship and for men in general. The poem has a very "immediate" feel to it, in the sense that the persona is defining her emotional experience through her dealings with the clams: Her handling of the clams is helping to define her feelings. Since the reader is with the persona as she prepares and cooks the clams, he becomes a part of the emotional experience.

Throughout the poem, the action parallels the persona's level of emotion. The opening stanza begins with the persona's soaking the clams, and here, Nason forms the first tie between the clams and her relationship. "They lie in my tub like the lazy man / I just dusted off, who dug them." The clams simply lie, and the persona, by way of mild revelation, notices the similarities between the clams and her partner. The poet's clever play on words in the first line also serves as early indication of her feelings toward men: Men lie. The action progresses to a state of subdued aggression, with the persona washing the clams over and over. This progression to an almost manic repetition of washing matches the rise in the extremity of emotion felt by the persona. Where the clams used to simply lie, the persona now perceives them as "Still, lazy men in a gritty tub spitting / griping, extruding slime."

Nason points out in the first stanza that her persona's main source of pain comes from her failed effort to mold men into what she expects them to be. The washing of the clams, who represent the men in her life, is the persona's metaphorical attempt to change the men from her past. The fact that this has been done over and over not only proves the futility—because the men stay the same—but also subtly alludes to the idea that the persona's repeatedly failed attempts at control are pushing her closer to the figurative edge.

The second stanza mirrors the first in the way the action and the emotions run parallel. The stanza begins with the persona's cooking clams:

> *Flames light the pot.*
> *I fight to type at my desk.*
> *The water warms.*

The mild action in the stanza's first few lines is again matched by the lack of emotional intensity in Nason's persona, which is understood through her actions: "I wait. I listen." The stanza moves on, much like the first, with the action of the clams mirroring the rising hostility of the persona, and this rise shows itself through her increasingly frantic behavior:

> *They start*
> *dancing with heat. I hear*
> *their shells tap and crack. I crack, tapping the maddest letter. . . .*

The parallels between emotion and action are not the only tool Nason uses to evidence the growing anger of her persona. The deliberate word choice in reference to typing the letter clearly shows the rise in emotion, as well. In line 13, she fights "to type"; in line 18, she is "tapping the maddest letter." This careful word choice along with her showing a rise in emotion furthers the notion from the first stanza that the persona is being pushed to the limits of rational thought because of her struggles with relationships.

In the first stanza, the persona's useless attempts at control led to almost manic behavior. The poem ends with "the maddest letter" going to "a man who's never mad." The fact that her partner is never mad implies a lack of emotion, and this aspect of him that she cannot change—much like the changes she hasn't been able to bring about in her past partners—keeps Nason's persona caught in a seemingly endless cycle: Her futile efforts at control result only in increased frustration.

Pain from relationships occurs for many reasons. Nason deals with the pain brought from not being able to mold a partner to one's expectations. In Ellaraine Lockie's "Commonplace" (1), the woman's frustration doesn't come from her partner's not being what she wants, but from her relationship's not holding the passion that it used to.

The poem begins, "She's nude in the kitchen." The choice of the word "nude" is an artistic and non-sexual reference to her nakedness. This implies that the woman in the relationship has regressed to being merely an object, whereas in the past, she was the focus of passion. The following lines continue to describe how the relationship, now, is a spark-less version of earlier days:

> *When he walks through her to grab a beer*
> *Ghost of an earlier time*
> *When he'd do a double-take*
> *Drink the beer later, lukewarm then*
> *Like their worn-out bodies. . . .*

The visual imagery and pace in these lines build a solid idea of how the relationship used to be. In the lines where the "double-take" results in "worn-out bodies," the action and the sexual reference are deliberate and strong. The careful word choice creates a mood of intense passion, which is carried on in the next few lines with the woman's

> *Ability to flick his switch*
> *And generate instant thermal energy*
> *Spontaneous combustion.*

Lockie makes it clear that the lack of passion is a drastic change from the past. Her ability to create, through words, a fire that feels so genuine allows the poem's progression to the lackluster present to be a true loss, both for the characters in the poem and for the reader drawn into it.

The relationship degenerated

Until she became everyday invisible
Familiarity fostered immunity
Injected over years of routine
Dangerous as the disease
It was meant to prevent
Extramarital epidemic extraordinary.

Once again, clever word choice tells the story of the relationship in a multi-layered fashion: Earlier, the fires of passion were made real with the repeated use of "heat" references— "lukewarm," "thermal energy," and "spontaneous combustion." In describing the demise of the relationship, Lockie employs a repetition of medical terms—"immunity," "injected," "disease," and "epidemic." These medical allusions create a mood of sterility and emotional detachment. In a hospital room, any human touch is out of necessity, rather than desire, and it is to this sad state that the relationship in "Commonplace" has regressed.

One similarity between the women in "Clams" and in "Commonplace" is that both personas crave a level of control. The persona in "Clams" is pushed to her wits' end by her not having the ability to create the man she wants. The woman in "Commonplace" also "craves that kind of power / [and the] ability to flick his switch." By the end of the poem the reader understands that the woman uses her sexual power more in an effort to prevent "extramarital epidemic" than as an expression of love. This ill-fated attempt at control through physical intimacy results in her ironically becoming "everyday invisible," and this loss of true passion is worse than losing the man she loves altogether.

Perhaps the greatest pain from relationships—greater than not being able to mold a partner, greater than the loss of passion—is the pain that comes from having to carry on after the death of a spouse. Christopher Hicks' "Sunday Afternoon at the Old Country Buffet" (1) is the melancholic telling of just such a fate.

The first line of the poem indicates that there is something wrong: "He sits at a table for two." From this somber beginning, Hicks goes on to tell the story of a man who has no other option but to carry on.

The restaurant serves as an integral part of the poem, with minute aspects explained in great detail. It is a metaphorical representation of what role the man's wife played in his life. The restaurant, in one way or another, is represented throughout the whole poem, which is evidence of the somber truth that the absent wife may have been the man's whole life, making his loss of her even more devastating. Parts of the restaurant actually become his dearly missed wife:

His dinner companion is an empty chair,
which stares at him with vacant leather-button eyes.
It had not always been this way.
Once the chair had a name,
had a voice . . . .

Hicks uses the restaurant-atmosphere and the metaphor to reference the happy times the couple had there together: "Once the chair would have asked for a taste / then would steal a bite before he could reply." These happy memories contribute to the overall mood Hicks creates of "not letting go." Every facet of the dining experience is a painful reminder of the once-happy relationship. From the empty chair to the bite-not-stolen, the man seems unwilling to move on with his life, and this reluctance to move on only keeps him in the pain of the loss.

Much of the most effective poetry is considered such because the words chosen offer an uninhibited view into the poet's soul. It is this kind of honesty that creates poetry whose story, though unique to the poet, communicates an emotional experience to which anyone who has ever felt true pain or bliss can relate. Please take some time to enjoy some of my favorites from the pages within where the poet offers a genuine glimpse into his or her soul: Jacqueline De Freitas' "Message on a Paper Napkin" (3), "All Yours" (4) by Hannah Slovek, Theresa McGoff's "Beacon" (4), Dried Funeral Flowers" (6) by Traci Mullins, Rebecca Harth's "Thinking Late" (9), "For the Player" (10) by Juliette Hwang, and Elizabeth Ament's "Glass Bottle" (15).

I would like to thank every poet who contributed to the wide range of material collected in this anthology. Your willingness and ability to share a part of your self has helped to create a piece of art that will have a lasting impact on its readers throughout time. Best wishes for continued success in all of your future creative endeavors.

The publication of this anthology has been the culmination of the efforts of many individuals. Judges, editors, assistant editors, customer service representatives, graphic artists, layout artists, office administrators, data entry staff, and mail room personnel have all contributed to this anthology's production. I am thankful for their assistance and support.

John C. Sullivan, Editor

Cover Art: Vic Thomas, "Nature's Natural Big Bang"

Clams

They lie in my tub like the lazy man
I just dusted off, who dug them,
nothing to do but spit:
mucus, sand, salt, cornmeal grit.
Over and over I wash them--
still, lazy men in a gritty tub, spitting,
griping, extruding slime.
I worry about the hot weather,
the price of meat,
and whether I can eat anything so live,
so like a man.
They come in all sizes,
parts lolling now from unzipped shells.

I cook a few; the dripping,
smallest ones I can handle.
Flames light the pot.
I fight to type at my desk.
The water warms. I wait, I listen.
No one's murdering pots of men.
They start dancing with heat.
I hear their shells tap and crack.
I crack, tapping the maddest letter
to a man who's never mad.

Julianne Nason

Sunday Afternoon
at the Old Country Buffet

He sits at a table for two.
His hair is the color of
the mashed potatoes piled on his plate,
with splotches of mushroom gravy over his ears.
His dinner companion is an empty chair,
which stares at him with vacant leather-button eyes.
It had not always been this way.
Once the chair had a name,
had a voice,
had an appetite for the cherry cobbler
which sits beside his plate.
Once the chair would have asked for a taste,
then would steal a bite before he could reply.
Now his companion only stares at him.
The chair doesn't know what it's missing.
The roast beef is really good today.

Christopher Hicks

Commonplace

She's nude in the kitchen
Her solution to icing-spared silk
When he walks through her to grab a beer
Ghost of an earlier time
When he'd do a double take
Drink the beer later, lukewarm then
Like their worn-out bodies
She craves that kind of power
Ability to flick his switch
And generate instant thermal energy
Spontaneous combustion
Until she became everyday invisible
Familiarity fostered immunity
Injected over years of routine
Dangerous as the disease
It was meant to prevent
Extramarital epidemic extraordinary
As oblivious to him
As her immaculate clothes

Ellaraine Lockie

Message on a Paper Napkin

Spilled my heart on a paper napkin
While I waited for you at the coffee shop
Because you can't take my messages
Home with you
And we hardly have time to say everything
When we meet on our way to work
In the morning
We sat in my car in the parking lot
And I watched as you sipped your coffee
Through a straw
Silent as you read my heart
And then you asked me
Whether I wouldn't mind kissing you
With coffee on your breath
I watched you walk to your car
And pondered the symbolism
As you crumpled my ink stained napkin
And together with your empty coffee cup
Tossed my heart

Jacqueline De Freitas

Poetry

Poetry whips
Through the air,
A wind that
Knocks me flat.
But it rushes past the
Staunch trees
With a congenial tip of its hat.

It moves debris.
It moves me.
But the walls still stand tall.

Or maybe they creak
Just a bit
And the trees sway a little
And the birds soar
And boats drift
As the wind passes by.

Sonja Likness

Faith

The seasons come and go in their graceful rhythms of change
Each one arriving and then fading into the next in perfect agreement
Nature shares a deep awareness of the invisible workings of creation
Each element belonging to itself and to the timelessness that
supports all life
Why then do we try to hold ourselves apart from the
primordial stream that continues to carry us despite our
foolhardy efforts to resist
It takes profound faith and courage to live in this world
with all its harsh realities that change us
and yet remain in harmony with all that is
Release your attachment to impose your small-mindedness
on yourself or others
Open your heart to embrace the life you are living
Become strong, throw away the idea of your own self-importance
and live wholeheartedly
There is a time for everything,
Even that which you thought too late to happen

Madelyn Warner

Aftermath, after Gabrielle

I knew I shouldn't have gone there with her,
But she's just too gorgeous to ignore.
I let myself fall in way over my head,
Definitely heart over brain.
She found her man on her own,
And now she's serving up that black coffee at night,
While I'm hating myself for ever having the total audacity to care.

E. Richard Lucas

Turning Down the TV News

"He must have changed his mind
They always do. . . ."

The doctor looked around
at the broken chair
and torn up walls,
the last war zone,
the broken room.

I had heard him scratching
Like a huge cat trying
to get in the house,
Or out.
But the breath of animal
And gravity in battle
Just made this kind of shuffle. . . .

And now when stone hits stone
and cracks a scull
A car backfires and kills a soldier,

I think about by noisy neighbor
hanging.

John Wetteland

Untitled

Helium balloons held tight at a funeral,
Earth so high and mighty prepares to return a child to her bosom,
Children play leap frog over frozen headstones,
Lives are now filled with dreamless sleeps,
My house is the home for the flags of the fallen,
Dancing on the brown dirt,
Your tears remind me of thunderstorms,
So honored,
So revered,
I wish to be held by you,
Just a bit longer,
I am captured in the trees,
Day long ventures in the mind,
Questioning my actions,
On one knee before the king,
His magicians are forecasting the speeding future,
For all their power,
They fail to notice,
Me falling for you (again?)

Jay Ehrmann

I had a flash of dirty thought of you,
But it went away
Like the sweeping of a stranger before me.
I put back the magazine,
No longer hiding my red face from
Anyone who dared hear my thoughts scream,
Including the discontented name-tagged lady,
Who drummed her dragon nails impatiently
As I wrote a check
At the supermarket checkout.

Christine DeSimone

Untitled

Upon sitting in a recital hall
in celebration of a dead guy's birthdays
as the metallic sounds of a harpsichord
give birth to electric fireflies that swarm the room, our ears, our heads,
we breathe them in and they buzz inside
our stomachs, relentless insects of sound and color.

When the music stops,
they die between our hands.

Mary Vasiltsova

Firefly Ballet

Firefields dance at sunset dawns
In tribal costumes made of moonlight.
Round and round the fire they go,
Dancing to rhythms too rapid to hear.
Holding the essence of time beneath their wings,
Allowing the glow to reach my eyes,
But never catching the attention of the clock.
Rocks in water have put out the fire,
But it matters not to them.
Now the rain may fall,
The sun may shine
For the fireflies have finished their dance
With the essence of time.

    Jill Palmer Naiman

All Yours

went to the rooftop
to dance with your soul
like yesterday
when the rain bounced off our faces
and your laugh was symphonic
gazing at the evening city-scape
with the stars laid out like a map above us
and the cars rushing by below
your kiss was like marmalade
everything perfect
now tears leave my eyes
for I know it shall never be that way again

    Hannah Slovek

Butterfly Whispered

poetry did not come upon me like the embrace of Apollo,
but crept in
on slow and sneaky feet—
one step, then more.
it had no appointment to keep with me,
no woman crying my destiny in the road,
no fanfare, trumpets, drum,
no foreshadowing dream of laurel and bay—
only a flicker, lick of flame in the mind
like something you had known, but forgotten,
a memory of wings and pine, healing,
the brief sight of something,
like a butterfly wing, disappearing behind a tree
so quick
you aren't even sure it was there,
and you are subsumed in scientific thoughts
of class and species
forgetting about the actual creature
until it flies into your face as you are looking the other way
and blinds you with the sun.

    Erin Shoemate

Beacon

The cat paws
the clothes hamper
stretches to sniff
scented air

He looks for your
scent here
and in the shoes left
with dangling laces

Shirts unchosen by you
hang still in the closet
my fingers snag in the weave
as if I, too, were a thread

This journey
this story
has no place for us
except for the beacon of your calls

    Theresa Mcgoff

Barefoot

August's honeysuckle breath
Ripples the sleeves of your shirt,
Flings your hair in front of your eyes.
You wink.

Your eyelashes,
Trimmed with gold,
Brush my cheek
Beneath my left eye.
Above us the clouds swell
And the heavens open.

I want to run for cover,
But you are my cover.
So we stay outside,
Splashing together under the showering sky.
I think I hear the footsteps of Aphrodite.

    Gailor Large

Ego

her name on his lips
limply crumbles—
a microcosmic
avalanche
of confectioner's sugar,
a bad actor on take two
sans Cyrano.

his ruptured plea thrashes
into itself like a starving
wench
jerking out the
Samba
in her flea infested
shanty
with only dirt
and hot, sticky air
for a partner.

    Cindy Ramos

Breathe

Facts of the matter scatter about the landscape,
God's hands shape the soil.
As people throw away weak dreams to crumble
Like tin foil.
All hopes and dreams are torn at the seams,
Questions and wishes are food for the fish.
We all swim in a lake of anger,
How long will it take for us to drown?
Killed and pulled down to the depth
Our last cries never left our mouths
in a world so vain in what pain do I believe.
I'm going insane from the pain.
It's getting hard to breathe!

    Anthony Martinez

The Cherry Tree

I stood beneath the Cherry Tree, danced along its branches
Tall, and above the world.
I wore these strapped red shoes, the way they made me feel.
Soft velvet against skin, like my lips to yours,
They dangled like a kiss.
We danced among the stars, bleeding cherries
staining the velvet with a darker, sweeter new hue.
That night beneath the cherry tree,
that silent perfect night we danced with the wind.
How I flowed in the shoes that made me part of the world,
But unique, and beautiful, clinging to my body like a sleeker,
prettier new skin.
Two drifting petals playing in the wind.

    Cassidy Healzer

Rooms

She walks through the dark and cluttered rooms of my mind
Picking at the bits and pieces of the broken pottery of my life.
From time to time, she pauses, to study a shard.
She kneels, sifting through the rubble for a matching piece.
Room to room she wanders, looking for one still whole.
She sees a light through a door, and knows she has found life.
Entering, she gazes around to see what it may contain.
But to her dismay, she sees herself in endless profusion.
Images of herself look back at her from every nook.
No two are the same, each differing from the one beside it.
Slowly, passing from one to the next, she understands.
She has found a shrine, one dedicated to herself.
And of far more importance, she has found a home.
Contentment filling her breast at last, she finds a nook and sits.
Awaiting the next time she crosses my mind,
another image coming home.

David Bates

Sunfish

My brother and I with bamboo poles, my father
lighting his cigarettes off the sun, casting so far
we thought he might drag the horizon in.
All my brother and I pulled in that day
were sunfish, Dad reaching into each tiny mouth to
dislodge our hooks until there were dozens
of scraps from the sun swimming in our cooler.

I can still see the cigarette balanced between his lips,
the smoke like fog rising from his voice,
as he worked a half-eaten glow worm back onto
my hook, his hands trembling with excitement
for us, as if all his internalized love
would shake itself free.

Here I am, thirty years old, and snagged
on a morning when I was six, so far
I had to reach for a decent memory of him. And a small
one at that, a sunfish really, in this lake
where I cast, again and again.

Stevw Gehrke

A Date for Breakfast

"We have a date for breakfast"
her words, his mind
two people unified but
completely separate on
the issue of
sugar

A date for breakfast
down through the years
past the memories of croissants
and exotic breakfast dishes she
could not pronounce
and long, leisurely touch
skeletons in the closet dance

Imagine . . . one night of passion
fire, fluid, hot and sticky
sweet rolls
ending only in breakfast

What would you make me for breakfast?

Natalie Collins

Kansas

A sorry state
the cornrowed-colored eyes of old men
spitting poppycock into sorry slop pans
of once there was
but never is
who drowsy hear
the mourning dove over cereal
and evergreen.

Susan Mardirosian

Bus Station Thoughts

marking time by passing trains
another hour to kill . . . again . . .
half of getting anywhere is waiting.

toothpaste in my bookbag
a tea bag between my fingers,
the water running hot, I, cold
as the ticker spits out warnings.
even the doors have stickers
to warn they're automatic.
"Don't try to touch me"
I guess is the message.

marking time by passing trains
another hour to kill . . . again . . .
half of getting anywhere is waiting.

Kathryn Kieran

Stratford-upon-Avon Calling

Shakespeare knew how to ride time warps.

He would stand barefoot in certain
spots and quote himself,
which would flip him in and out of
centuries
like a casting director
looking for new faces.

You didn't know it, but he
passed through here on his way
to Egypt yesterday.

I saw the notes he took on the
shape of your smile.

The rest, of course, is history.

Daniel Abel

Flight 127

Sinatra blares from the cocktail lounge
every thirty minutes or so.
I'm daydreaming about the open spaces
of twirling and dipping and fanciful stepping,

How beautiful it is in the movies.
Who's looking? No one knows me anyway.
Never again will I know the nakedness of the Newark Airport.

"Best Airline 1996,"
The banners read. The signs flash.
The patrons sleeping on benches agree.

A graveyard shift worker pushes his cart,
rubber wheels out of alignment,
down the polished and trod terrazzo
of the lonely concourse.

The cocktail lounge has its gates pulled down;
the servers have all gone home,
but the music's still loud ,
and where once was a crowd
is now just me dancing alone.

Echo Bartlett

Green Shirt

Shower off.
Dripping wet,
I slide a towel around my waist
then realize within a breath
I'd rather slip inside his shirt—
my favorite shirt,
the one striped green
that plants the envy in my sigh
and taunts my lips
without a blush
with brazen strokes upon his chest
as he walks by.

Sharon Sloane

The Old Flour Mill

The old flour mill still sits on the hill
Near the creek that flows through our town.
The window panes are broken and the glass lies on the ground.
The flour has molded
and the white sacks have turned brown.
The shingles on the roof have blown out of place
And the cobwebs have covered the staircase.
The gutters are filled with leaves from the near by trees.
And the sun rays and moon beams
Play peek-a-boo among the eves.
And you can still hear the chatter and laughter
From the echoes from among the rafters,
As the kids slid down the hill
and on across the frozen creek bed on their sleds,
On snowy days you could find rabbit tracks in the back,
Seeking feed for their need be,
From the empty feed sacks and further back near the rail road track
Wild strawberries grew and were picked by people you knew.
But still it's the only mill for miles around that still sets on a hill
And in all its stillness, it still graces my home town.

    E. Russell Gray

Duluth

North is coming down from the big bay,
all bracken and muskeg.
He walks through the forest,
shedding his coat and putting on
fir and fern and flower.
See how he stands on tiptoe, seeking his love,
who is warmth and moisture, all floral and succulent.
He moves over iron and granite and birch,
steps down the gentle hill and kneels at Superior.
Before he sips, he looks up to see you and
knowing that winter is over, he blows you a warm kiss.

    Brent Christianson

Library Books Like Tombstones

Library books like tombstones
lined in a row still await
the visit of a family member,
a friend, or even a stranger
to pay homage to a restless soul.

Titles on library volumes,
like names engraved on a stone,
recite the record of voices
calling from the depth of the Earth
to be saved from the wrath of oblivion.

Though many will visit the graveyard,
and many will read out the names,
only a few will discover
the messages waiting entombed
in the cemetery of stones without graves.

    Emil Jacob

Remembering You

The silence here is an echo;
pebbles dropping into the deep
with a plunk, and a slow decent
to the bottom, a silty bed of memories
suddenly stirred into a swirling ballet;
micro-fine images dancing
in the heavy cold alone, and then
together in the darkness,
before the music stops,
and weighted by truth,
they spiral toward the bottom,
settling into stillness once more.

    C. Wright

Thinking Late

At three AM. I realize our love
is not champagne and caviar
served on a silver tray
or the yellow rose thrown into the breeze
floating back, again and again.
There is silence between us—
the quiet kiss, a sealing off.

My chipped eyes stay pried open
like a mannequin in the dark
when the store closes.
The moonlight sifts through
the bare wooden slits of your bamboo shade.
Your cheek smells like baby powder
and the pulse of the clock
could go on all my life.

Thick with dreams
you rock me in your reaching arms as if
I am your lost childhood blanket,
the one they cut up gradually, gradually
until one day you whispered, it is gone.

    Rebecca Harth

Niña

She sits Indian-style,
brown knees almost touching the thinly
paved road like lanky unselfconscious
street dogs lapping up the
watermelon sunset.
I glance, broken.
Ask what she is doing.
"Pintando"
Painting the curb, evening's canvas,
Barrio stick illustrations.
She dips into cheap watercolor ovals,
filling in cracks, initials, hearts that
belonged to someone else before
the concrete dried.
Now they are her messy petroglyphs,
her self-possessed fingerprints and
link to the wind.
I glance, broken.
Ask if I can be seven again,
if I can please dress up the sidewalk too.

    Jori-Michelle Rambo

An Illusion of the Heart

Walking a path colored with glass
his reflection is caught a thousand times
in fleeting brilliance
with tiny beams of intertwining light
and lovely patterns of delicacy
which seem to infiltrate my body
and envelope my heart
in a moment of euphoric uncertainty
I am his possession
as he does always carry my heart
yet unfathomable is the actual levity
of consciously holding love in one's hands
and so the path must narrow
and the exquisite rays must diminish
as his ethereal figure moves calmly away
leaving a trail of mirrored shards behind
I listen, captivated by the paradoxical splendor,
as my pulse fades with his footsteps
until silence captures my eyes
and the glass ceases to exist

    Melissa Dibble

Just a Pup to Me

Dedicated to Bud Dawson

"He came out of the 60's, walked through three decades
just to say to me, "The truth, I want the truth,
before it's too late, before I die, you must tell the truth to me."
And I sat looking beyond thirty years,
I saw the jowls lessen, the lines decrease,
the hair turn dark and thick, the expression soften,
the eyes begin to twinkle,
I saw the bloom, and I could have said
something smart like, "The truth! You can't handle the truth!"
or, "What is truth? A word! And what is a word? A puff of air!"
But instead I said, "I can see that you're bigger,
and I know that you've grown older,
but what looks like an old man to
the rest of the world is still a flower
child, just a pup to me."
And I led my friend by the hand to the garden
to show him one red bloom.
I said, "It arrives every spring. It reminds me of you."
To which he asked, "Is that the truth?"
I answered, "It is to me."

Marianne Beasley

Captiva Mourning

I followed your trace to the island's north shore,
imagining the imprints your feet had made
before the tide rose and washed them away.

I sat on the beach and watched the sun set.
The sun blazed red and lingered,
taking one final view before the water consumed it.
The sand was damp beneath me in the spring dusk.

You, who once gazed at the same green gulf,
no longer know the wonder of twilight,
no longer hear the rhythms of oceans,
no longer taste the salt in the air.

Your death closed the chasm through which we passed into being.
We, like the sky after sunset,
are too late for the day,
too soon for the stars.
We wait, awe-struck and orphaned,
for darkness to come and a sad moon to rise.

William Lowe

Headlands

Sand dunes and
thistle, heather
and shells strewn
along an Erie lake
made wavy enough by
gentle winds and jet skis.

Bathers and babes,
splashing arrhythmically,
convey a sharkless safety that
swimmers can sink their teeth into.
Guard stations lie capsized,
seized by outstretched epidermis
inviting the errant volleyball—
a simple reminder that there still is
life after tan.

The only thing missing is salt,
but for the yellow-clad girl
with her mushroomed umbrella
just mining her business.

Marilyn Cristi

She Is Called Spring

Mother Nature now a youth, barefoot and
free, sundressed and rainbow ribbons.
Rambling through meadows, wind-tousled hair,
cheeks rouged, lips crimsoned by the sun.

Lying on verdant new grass, crocus all
ablaze—Enraptured with pride surveying
the beauty and wonder about her. Her
brushes splashing brilliant splendor, she
making the world new and fresh—an
exquisite array of rebirth.

Mating calls, loves sweet beckoning, fill
the air. She smiles her approval of the
unending ritual. She breathes the
sweetness of this fleeting moment, and
beams with deep satisfaction; For now—
She is called Spring!!

Larry Patterson

Time Brings Change

the gentle flow of your hair in the breeze.
you bring peace that covers. your breath comes to me
as your head lays quiet on my lap.
the busy outer world knows nothing
of this feeling, caught in the madness of going,
I'm staying. for times past we were far from this.
you stepped in the water when it touched the edge
of your dress you pulled up; i was the water.
you dreamed all night long when the whisper came
in your ear to rise, you sighed, maybe i spoke too loud.
you walked miles every night when the moon was hidden you
complained. sometimes i have to stay hidden. somehow i never
got to you, the distance was short but the feelings were
miles. a burden you had, one you wouldn't share. i screamed
into the dark night. what did i want? answers
for peace, peace i could have at a moment. so i
finally relaxed my chair and rested. i fell
asleep to the blowing wind. when i woke, your
head was there. i ran to find the answers only to
find them strapped to my back

Ian Snyder

Untitled

city-breath held against your back
as we pass the Lower East Side
this is one of those rare walks;
we'll never lose sight of each other

right there on the waterfront
do I reach for your hand

this day makes us say things like:
I have been here before
on days without you
and the water then seemed green to me
this is all I can give you:
Where has the madness gone?

Not somewhere else in this city
is it easy to spell out
every day possible
How can I convince you:
I meant for life to go on

Lia Munch

Unrested

can you hear
monday morning
slowly crawl
through your hair
and sleep in your ear
fill you
with unrest

Sharon Klebba

Music Teacher

As you get older and your eccentricities
become more prominent,
and as the dogs and cats and a tornado
sweep the house—
everything looks quite mad except the
Steinway.
The icons and mandalas on your walls are
just like lover's palms that you delouse.

If Chopin lilts and Mozart tumbles,
the weeping cherries nod in tune—
this is a restless woman's ballroom
gone out whale-watching in mid-June.

Tomorrow there will be more students
staring at space like students do—
the silent windows
are witness to how much a long, long time ago
he was in love with you.

Angie Angel

Magic Charms

Dripping skin
like August-melted chocolate,
time slows down
for the swimming pool
kids. I held your hand
and buttoned down
your red shirt, revealing
a sunburned stomach.
Let this tender teardrop salve soothe.

Disconnect all our simple sayings,
tied in knots
tightly to keep our words
safe. I could never read
your cursive words, written on scented
paper, folded sideways, sealed,
and sent. My chicken scratch
scrawl against your girl-curved words.
Handwritten last lines linger, than leave.

James Brubaker

Rain at 2 AM

streetlights
on the window
make stars
out of raindrops.

behind me
shadows waver:
countless fractures
in the wall.

I hear rain
on the roof;
it is paper
crumpled, softly.

Uriah Anderson

Two Images

Gold jewelries Aaron melted once
After his people begged, make Gods
To go before us. He complied,
To later voice, out came this calf
The golden God for which they cried.

Two images desire casts
Self-power strong, self-glory bright both worshiped.
Hear each human shout as every psyche,
Bound, bows low to gold or silver self come out.

D. Ward Kyle

[Untitled]

The Japanese had the right idea.
Instead of divine revelations
Or enlightened arguments
Or prolific tragedies,
They wrote three lines:
One about the wind
Blowing through a bonsai branch
Bending just slightly.

Where once I saw trees
Now I spy you
Hiding in the branches.
I try to write of you
And find it like trying to
Write of my pulse.
Or an ocean.
Or the wind:
You blow gently here
Through a gnarled and weathered branch
Bending to the right.

Joseph Wycoff

The Diagnosis

I think I thanked the doctor
Habit being what it is
And grace still a small part of what I
Had left of me when he closed that door
So loudly
And I shattered into pieces on the floor

A nurse came in shortly thereafter
To brief me during what must have been
My third alternate lifetime
To sweep little parts of me
Into the dust pan designated by my HMO
For occasions just like this one

Occasions where one stares in the mirror
And wonders,

"Who will have my eyes?"

Greg Mucha

Mexico

The Mexico that I know is a chimera.

Romantic, Potemkin village, restorations;
Bright waters ringed with worshipers
Prostrate, dulled with food and lust:
Torpid, mesmerized tourist-priests.

Brazen cats haunting breezy palapas
Demanding fresh portions, cleanly carved
And offered by painted fingers
Heavy with gaudy baubles,
Freshly mountain-mined.

Only when we stop in a dusty town
And wander to the empty church
(Except for toothless beggars at the door)
And see the agonized Christ forever dying,
Do I catch a fleeting glimpse

Of your true mystery, your tragedy,
Mexico.

Veronica Snyder

For Everything and Nothing

The lines on the road
laugh at her,
because parking meters
have more time than her coffee cup.
When passion has to be this quiet,
desire is clicking
with spelling mistakes
as she melts
and he waits
for the traffic light to change.

Jennifer A. Long

What Am I to Do When Someone Dies?

Call the relatives. Prepare the coffin.
Send the flowers. Contact the cemetery.
Find the funeral home. Say I'm sorry.
Send a card. Whisper my condolences?

Is it enough to give a hug?

To send a hundred dollar memoriam,
Their name to be hailed in prayer?
Is it enough to say "Fear No More . . ."?
Or "He but doth suffer a sea change"?

Shall I sit and drink my coffee,
Black, one sugar, and stare—stare?
What is one death when there
Was Auschwitz, Tiananmen Square?

One death. One Death? A universe gone!

To eternity. To Eternity? What solace, that.
The photo album rots with time.
Memories fade. Hearts deny, forget. Forget, but for our words—
Our words—limitless repository of history and love,

One death and Tiananmen Square.
  Anna T. Balash

Blue

It's not as if the snow means anything or the sky
is significant. They are only part of the landscape,
like everyone gathered here with nothing left to say.

Later, the lilies are orange, yellow, in a vase;
there are lumps of sugar, a pitcher full of cream.
Everything is still and carefully arranged.

And the snow stops falling; the mourners
fall away. What did they mean: The people,
the fragments of music, the clouds and hours

that merged and separated? We are left with
the deep hush after church bells, the quiet
pulse of living blood, your vacant place.
  Lisa Christina Powell

Old Friends

Words, like juicy grapes
Roll slowly forth
Drop into the bowl
Of conversation
Years have piled up
Like stacks of paper currency
Large denomination spent,
We are left with dollar bills
And an occasional ten spot of laughter
  Margo Koller

Immobile

For weeks I beg tagged trees to take in their energy,
send it back to Earth, store their power elsewhere.
Can they perceive me, mosquito like, darting about their bases?
The county has decreed a wider road in this arid land.
What is it like to stand immobile before fate,
to feel saws cutting off neighbors and not run.
Rootedness is not paralysis I remind myself.
A chance to understand surrender?

All of dry June I drive skidding white gravel
bleak and dusty—even saved trees have died.
For a time I don't see sunflowers at disturbed edges
till one day they astound with their color
softening the scars we all carry.
  Christina Husted

No Daisies Left to Pick

for bug . . .
i think of you with wine and a cigarette.
i think of you in bed,
laying there just tangled in skin
thinking of what we might have brought to tomorrow.
Sunday mornings still greet me,
only this time you're not walking through them.
breakfast never sets a table,
yet i still can smell you sitting across from me.
the Sunday sun shines itself down on my Hollywood morning,
questioning if i can make it without the old routine.
in a far away place, the same sun finds you.
slowly both of us find our shifts in the wind.

i look in all the familiar places. . . .
where are the flowers?
i still find myself wanting to pick you daisy's,
trying to build some castle without seeds.
  Christiana Frank

Grasshopper Summer

The summer we were thirteen,
brown and mosquito-scarred,
we rode one-speeds down gravel roads
through green corn-tunnels,
put on dusty theater in the haymow
to assemblies of barn cats
and raftered pigeons,
and learned to sew sun dresses
on the Singer treadle,
your mother sighing
at the puckers and thread-messes.
We talked hours
in the crooked arms of apple trees,
heard in the hot afternoons
grasshopper whispers in the fields,
and watched the long, white arms
of summer lightning,
feeling in ourselves the rising
sugar maples feel in early spring.
  Joan Peronto

The Projects

Down in Atlanta, dusty barefoot children
carry jelly jars
to hold their dreams for the night.
Women in aprons pick up pecans
from red earth, packed down shiny.
Men stand smoking
hand rolled Prince Alberts,
Humphrey Bogart hats tilted back.
Old folks sit quietly
on concrete front steps.
Might be a child molester
or just some soul gentled by loss.
Rain blows down
sheets pinned to lines,
criss cross, maps of lives
waiting to rise,
sucking up bobby pins
flip flops, broom-handled horses,
black tar bibles, empty pots,
lost spoons, and broken plastic.
  Sharon O'Sullivan

Summer Afternoon

The fantastic drowse of perpetual noon
Drapes the landscapes in velvets so heavy and sweet
And silhouetted by sunlight, birds carry the tune
Of the bittersweet pleasure of red-weather heat.
A certain slant of languid light
Flows like molasses through the trees
Whose arms sway, eternally to left and to right,
and whose emerald green flames flicker in the breeze.
The whispered songs of Sundays past
Flow on a thick and gentle drift
Of noontime's breath, and carries passed
The scent of sleep and natures gift.
A hum of sounds from years ago
Of children's laughter and falling tears
Swell and fade as the breezes flow
And bring memories to sleeping ears.
So go the passing days of magic
Who flow so slowly as an invisible tune
Save for these days; how sweet, and how tragic
The song of summer's afternoon.

Jessica Rabito

"For He Who Finds Me, Finds Life:" Proverbs

I pursue you in thin sheets,
washed with small words.
I pursue you in auditoriums,
where ancient bones are chewed and
chewed, and swallowed
by those with the stomach for it.
I look for you in the well-fed faces
of young men who got over sin
the way I got over acne,
and the busy bodies of young women,
who put you on, like an apron.
I listen for you in the voices
of old women who speak splinters,
and old men, who hold theirs
between cheek and gum, for a memory.
Sometimes I think this is a scavenger-hunt;
Other times, that we are all assassins, and
there is a price on your head.

Caitilin Cagney

Night Dreams

softly the night whispers
makes round notes
full of sultry silence
softly the veil rustles
like the wind, which kisses leaves
as a lady's fingertips
softly the moon warbles
filling silver cisterns
with grateful songs
of night blooming jasmine
softly the song
surrenders to the songbirds
every new verse another fallen star
kissing the purple hem
of night's garment
steal away with me
into the mist-shrouded river
of my seldom dreams
and touch me
in the night blooming jasmine

Donna Gifford

Untitled

In the days of being a good little Maxwell House wife
we were supposed to marry and live
happily ever after
We didn't,
and armies of us,
ill-prepared for the reality
of careers,
flooded the market
Taking jobs
that were only jobs,
marrying again,
not for love
but for survival,
and wondering
why in those days
of Donna Reed and Harriet Nelson,
Wally and the Beave,
nobody ever warned us
that happy endings were only in fiction

Roslyn Weinstein

Recollections of "Innocence Lost"

Her fingers dance on ivory keys,
As her head bends humbly down.
She plays with passionate, unspoken pleas,
A saddening, melodic sound.

This is her song of "Innocence Lost,"
She had written years before.
I ask myself "How high was the cost?"
That inspired this soulful score.

'Tis a song of a girl, coming-of-age,
Blossoming a little too soon.
Like a sheltered bird, escaping her cage,
Into a chaotic monsoon.

Listening to her play,
While watching her sway,
I realize she is a stranger.

Seeing her strain,
To this song of pain,
I pray this world doesn't change her.

Harvard Reynolds

Reign of Winter Dragon

In misty sky
Pale sun, his eye
Glares coldly o'er
Both mount and moor,
Surveying kingdom near and far.
Dust's commonplace
With crystal lace
And darker hues
In ice subdues,
With frostings thick enmantled.
Stems golden tall
In argent fall,
Defining path
Of chilling wrath.
Beware: cruel blast of icy breath!
Still water freezes
As it pleases,
Flawed mirrors to form
Which crack with warmth,
Reflecting rule soon to be ended.

Neville Starick

The Dreamcatcher

Tell me your thoughts uncut.
Don't censor the dreams you've captured
in dreamcatchers adorned with faux feathers.
Tell me the things you feel without allowing
the thieves of political correctness to steal your unspoken truths.
Don't hide your feelings from me; don't hide your pain.
Show me your guilt and tell me about your shame.
Don't listen to those fools listed in the credits.
They'll ask you to wait till the lighting's just right
before you cross that picturesque Sahara.
Your dreams will end up on a cutting room floor,
with lighting and sound guys pasting together your life.
Don't let that happen to your thoughts of me.
Take what you need from me and give me what you can.
Then run, just go away.
But leave behind that dreamcatcher,
the one with the faded faux feathers.
It's held your uncensored thoughts of me forever,
and I want to peek inside.
Michelle Caldwell

Memories

She was not as tall as the lilac bush,
Wearing a hand-made dress all rosebuds and smocking,
Her short, sturdy legs planted on the muddy ground
In bright red boots.
She'd buttoned her grandmother-made sweater
By herself, unevenly,
And the breeze stirred the soft hair toddlers have,
The sort a mother can't resist stroking off a forehead.
Zigzagging across the lawn like an aimless bee,
She was intent on picking every dandelion she could find
To add to the wilting bunch she held in her hands,
Fingers sticky with the milky sap.
When I blinked my eyes, I didn't know
Whether it was this spring
Or those afternoons years ago
When I made my own dandelion rings
And tilted buttercups under my sister's tipped chin.
If spring is the time for renewal,
It is memory that makes it more so.
Karla Hutchens

Relative Procession

Stucco clings like yellow paper peeling in wet April sun.
I see a smooth-skin, mustached face
past these frail houses and lawns.
My own father is here, bobbing in a black Lincoln interior.
It seems like I'm the only one who hears him say
in this knot-like, leathery openness,
"My father was a railroad man;
I am a railroad man's son."

We slide through the old neighborhood,
light cloth soft and shadowy.
We pass the 24th Ave. Bakery, pass Dick's
boxed-up barbershop, and I'm telling you
I can see my grandfather shooting pool in
that bar at the bridge. He's with the old
M&S boys talking about the warm weather and
about how the unions just aren't the same.
We are driving through it all, and I can see perfectly
how sometimes we're so proud.
Sometimes we are grounded to the root, and it can feel so good.
Joshua Hauser

After the Storm

Six AM, we started late today,
probably the weight of our proud, American luggage
slowing us down.
Half an hour ago the sun rose
above the twisted streets, their curves
carrying stories of barefoot children,
uneducated women, and men hauling
fruits and crabs and cow stomachs
to market.

I step onto the bus and place myself
next to my pale-skinned and yellow-haired companion.
The bus is large and full. It sputters
out of the city, into the stories of the campo,
and leaves its own trail of thick smoke
lounging behind.

A representative of the machismo society
has no qualms leaning over me or my yellow-haired companion.
His breath may as well be my own, since there is not
enough room anymore for us both.

And we hit another arduous bump.
Kayrl Stead

Sandstorm

he held himself like a newborn god
high on borrowed glory
walked the streets like a drunk coyote
took what he wanted and devil-be-damned
covered his feet with the painted Earth
running across the world.

he held out hope like a wedding ring
promise, and punishment too
took to a tan like a deep-shade beer
lifted the sun on a back made for lifting
covered the sky with yelling and cussing
left like he had somewhere to be.

he held this whole town like a breathless girl
bathed in the desert with cactus soap
rinsed himself off with lizard tongues
swallowed every dust storm
jumped into the panting heat.
that boy, he won't come back.
Kris Larson

Glass Bottle

You called me naive—
Innocence preserved
In a glass bottle
Balanced on the top shelf.
I was skipping through the winter paradise
Searching for my cave of comfort.
Thoughts danced inside my tainted mind,
Dressing up in different personalities
As my judgment slumps to the ground
With the thrust of a zipper.
I am the essence of pointillism.
Don't get too close.
Blending shades of sexual insecurity
Clash with intellectual confidence
And create that beautiful blue
So familiar to you.
Elizabeth Ament

A Love That Lasts a Lifetime . . .

To Dan and Meg with love . . .
A love that lasts a lifetime . . .
To feel as though you can move the sun,
chase the moon and catch the stars.
To lose yourself for days,
just by looking into each other's eyes . . .
To close your eyes and escape to a far off place together,
while sitting at opposite ends of a crowded room . . .
To look up a night sky, wrapped in each other's arms . . .
To know in your heart, that you share the same dreams
and that out of that sea of stars . . .
you've wished on the same star . . .
A love that lasts a lifetime,
cannot be measured by things that set us apart . . .
A love that lasts a lifetime,
is only measured by our soul and with our heart.

Kelley Sykes

My Retreat

Honey Harbour, place of rock and trees,
Sparkling water, and a western breeze,
Six thousand islands in that Huron Sea,
One little corner is my legacy.

Georgian waters, sometimes clear and bright,
Sometimes a gale with a stinging bite,
Dark, cool nights and whispering sounds,
With glittering stars the sky abounds.

Rugged Juniper, tough old pine,
Trembling aspen and a wild grape vine.
Little cottage on that Beausoleil isle,
I hope to linger for a long, long while.

Alma T. Wilson

What Is a Foster Child?

What is a foster child you ask?
We are children that come from broken homes.
We could be doctors, nurses, lawyers,
teachers, mothers, fathers, etc.
We could be high school grads,
We could have collage degrees.
We may not have our foster families last name,
But we are humans with feelings too.
We may not be rich or poor,
But we are proud of who we are.
We are people who have feelings like others.
We are proud to hold our heads high,
And say we made our way in life.
So please look at me as one of you
Because we have worked hard,
At what we have done for ourselves.

Gladys Den Boen

Captive Heart

Even from the
instant of conception
the mission was rescue.
Get in get hold get out.
But diplomacy unveiled desire
and my quarry twined herself around my heart,
swirled about my thoughts,
ensnared reason her fluid silken fragrant yielding,
And at once
liberator became captive,
quarry became captor,
and desire gave shape to the mission
which from the
instant of conception
was surrender.

Barbara Lighter

Missing Yesterday

How would I feel standing in your place.
Years gone so fast, in pictures I see your face.
Where would I be if it had not been for you.
Tears, laughter, change-there to see me through.

I remember a place so warm and full of light.
My eyes filled with admiration
Take me with you, just for tonight!

You were my world, my truth and my guide
Often times, though, you pushed me aside.
In my childlike mind you could have hung the moon.
How it still hurts, leaving me so soon.

Tanis Weinberger

Forgetting

You crossed my mind in the red brick garden
where sun paints shadows among the ferns,
your habit of coming and going
while tinkling piano notes
drift haltingly on the wind.
Now you stay still and silent
like the stone unicorn kneeling
over some blue flower,
the name I am forgetting.

Marie Serdynska

Why Do You Hurt Me?

I really don't understand why?
I really want to know!
But you will not speak to me.
You shut me out and will not let me in.
Oh, but why?
My feelings are no more.
I do stupid things and can't remember why.
I really want to know!
I have stood by you in thick and thin.
I have given you one hundred percent.
I know you can give only a little.
I know I'm not the easiest to live with.
If I don't know, then how can I help.
I really want to know!
Your hurt not only yourself, but everyone around you.
Open your eyes my dear and see what is out there.
I can only help if asked.
I really want to know!

Avril Harvey

A Mother's Prayer

As I look at my children, my love overflows.
They are my tomorrow, happiness and woes.
I pray for their future, please let them find peace.
To sleep ever safely, wonders never to cease.
They are so trusting, everything they behold
is new and wondrous their world is gold
No secrets they harbor, their complete faith in me.
I pray they discover how sweet life can be.
Ashley and Marley, my whole meaning in life
I want only to keep them from heartache and strife
I know their own mistakes they must make
May I soften their falls, let downs, heartache
I've made so many mistakes through the years
I've cried streams and rivers of heartbroken tears
But the sunniest days, the days of most charms
Were the days I held my new Babes in my arms
So fresh and beautiful, so innocent and sweet
You are my great pride. God's sweetest treat.
I pray for the strength to be there for you
To love you as only a mother can do!

Cindy Cole

Do You Know What You Did?

I was filled with joy and with your words you tore me right down.
For one small moment I was bright-eyed and looking forward
And with one glance you razed my heart and soul, sending me
Backward to the day long ago, when first a widow I became.

You walked away when you saw me coming toward you.
Perhaps, you felt uncomfortable and would know not what to say.
So, you turned into a store front or walked the other way,
Not knowing that what I saw would pierce the mask I wear.

Oh, how I wish I could convey the feelings deep within
That spring up when cross words are said or glaring eyes are met.
You have no idea what you cause within the depth of my being
When you speak with striking honesty, or criticize with care.

You may be right, you may be wrong, but it really does not matter.
I simply, at this point in time, find it difficult to deal with you,
Your ideas, thoughts or comments, when my world has come apart,
And need only love, charity and compassion to wrap my world.

Please take the time to think before you speak your mind and
React to how you would act if you were in my situation.
You see you are not, and, I pray, you never will experience
The terror of widowhood and the words and faces of "friends."

Joyce L. Kaestner

Stars at Night

Every night I look up in the sky
The moon so bright, stars twinkling likewise
Clouds forming into beautiful shapes
I see animals, people and places

Wishing I could fly, not just in dreams
Not just in memories nor tonight
I will start low, then I will fly high
I look to each star, I wish I was
I can, I will be the brightest star

Prayers will be answered I can smile
Every journey may start a li'l' while
My time have come, I will glow, I grow
No more hopeless moments nor sorrow
With my will to be, I am winning

I find the strength in me and nature
Weakness I left behind yesterday
Times have changed, I have grown, I matured
Tears will fall, but they will disappear
Nothing would stop me now, I am here

Champion Moonwind Avecilla

'Neath the Magnolia Tree

Lay me to rest 'neath the magnolia tree,
Where my loved ones may quietly think there of me.
Providing sweet shade in the hot southern day,
I'll repose there and listen to what they might say.

"A free spirit!" "An artist!"
"Oh, and of course—we remember her best riding her horse!"
"A sweet child of God laid to her rest
Beneath this old tree that she cherished as blessed."

The faithful old tree like a rock in the wind,
Protecting the treasure beneath its strong limbs.
Each day it spies down on the visitors there,
Bowing its crown so it too may hear.

When the moon beams light down where the people have sat,
The tree and the lady have their own private chat.
"Thank you for covering me here every day."
"You're welcome, dear lady; I like it this way.

When the Lord comes again, and you meet in the air,
Would you ask Him if He has need of a tree way up there?"
"Yes, I will," spoke the lady, "and He'll take you along,
Up to His throne where the faithful belong."

Barry Bazzell

You Are the Catalyst

You are the catalyst that lights my fire,
You're my one true burning desire,
You spark the flame that burns within,
You set my heart ablaze again.

You wrote the song I long to sing,
You sang it back to me again,
What more can I do?
You know I'd give my love to you.

Your lips are warm and tender;
They bid my heart to surrender,
As into your arms I did fall,
Now by your side I feel so tall.

Content to lie there by your side,
And rest awhile on your bed wide
Awaiting morning's light to shine,
Now I know that you are mine.

And when we kiss and touch afresh,
That's the time we both love best,
You are the catalyst that lights my fire,
You are still my true desire.

David Watkins

He Said

Be still my child, the Lord did say.
My love for you, will never stray.
The pain you feel is not of here.
Your time to come, is ever near.

Faith is all that's really needed.
Take my hand, with you I've leaded.
Gospel in your every word.
Soon is the time you will be heard.

Dear child, you must always remember.
Your birth was gentle, in early September.
My tests for you, a few more steps.
Each growing harder, and gaining depth.

Please do not take your life at hand.
To rush right now will never stand.
Your strength is growing everyday.
My lessons taught, this is the way.

I have prepared a spot for you.
Your place my child, is still not due.
I'll stand and wait at heaven's gate.
We'll walk hand in hand and celebrate.

Bonny Atkins

Sweet Sorrow

How can three weeks seem like a lifetime?
How can three weeks bring love and security?

How can you in three weeks inspire me in ways
Some were unable to in three years?
Afraid! Yes! Why?
Afraid I'll wake up! And my roses
And memories will have dried and died
With my tears and I'll spend years . . .
Waiting for another you . . . in sweet sorrow.

Lisa Ginyard

Trust Leteral Twinmates / Intimate Trust

Trueness to thyself and our partner
Resisting any and all wrongful temptations
Unconditional love and understanding
Spiritual and journeying through external life together
Telling each other and believing you are each other's best friend
Intimacy a very private world
That only two people share with secrecy

Kathleen Sangillo

A Seed

I was a seed and I knew what I was to do
When the gardener planted me into his nice garden
After a shower, I felt my energy on the go
Soon I pierced my way out of the ground
My roots begun to anchor deep in the rich soil
After I elevated higher and my leaves grew bountiful
My beautiful and healthy babies sprouted all over me
My green leaves broadened, shaded children from sun
The gardener weeded and cared for all of us tenderly
When my children ripened by the time of the harvest
A smile, on gardener's face, as he gathered my children
And carefully placed them in a big wicker basket

    Marshall N. Butler

Awaking of Spring

Spring is a time of change and rebirth
from bare trees to green leafs to the beauty of the flower trees.
From brown grass to green.
From bare ground to snowdrops crocuses,
tulips, hyacinths, Irises,
popping through the ground,
as well as wild flowers in the fields growing.
The smell of flowers in the air
With mother birds flying about making there nest.
Chipmunks and squirrels running about.
Mother rabbits digging there holes to make a nest
to give birth to their baby bunnies.
The Earth has come alive again.
Spring is a beautiful happy time of the year.

    Janet Millian

Old Oak Tree

Much water has gone under the bridge
Since an acorn sprouted on my ridge
Here North and South fired their muskets
I've seen collectors filling buckets
With live and spent shell they have dug up
Pierced buckles and buttons then shot up
In winter a no leaf skeleton
Catching snow the wind has blown on
When summer green the squirrels frolic in
Seemingly flying from limb to limb
Nothing grows in its forty foot shade
Its root network turns back any spade
I sometimes dream of what it could say
Of decades of men that have passed this way
Farmer, merchant, soldier and slave
Perhaps Andrew Jackson returned their wave
He knew John Overtons one block west
Now a Civil War shrine—Traveler's Rest

    Albert M. Maier

Music for the Spirits in Us

If I were to take one violin hair,
thread it through worn-torn days we spent,
making sense again of feelings being ripped apart,
wearing our emotions out and in, that way,
into any stage presence given, without notice,
of thoughts, words, and deeds,
escalating into the bottom-end of day.
I would try again, as seamstress-turned-musician
of forgiving heart beating with its ongoing message,
to diffuse the argument, somehow.
To use the fabric of its compromise,
to let us warm those places,
with me blocked out, or vice versa,
until time mends on its own two feet,
letting us enter that world again
as we were once together in this form of being,
clasping love's warm, mink eyes as a healthy diet,
to our constant securing togetherness
in its changing habits, somehow.

    Patricia Fritsche

Seasonal Ballet

Sun reflecting on gentle snowflakes
glistens in opalescence.
Wonderland of beauty does this make
Feathered fairy tale of frost on the window.
Leaves of gold cradle each flurry with gentleness.
Fall's cool breeze carrying a leaf,
gliding with no intent or direction.
Fall's seasonal cycle finished,
Replaced by a look of jeweled lace,
A seasonal ballet.

    Pattie L. Logar

To My Talented Father

My inspiration to write poetry to
My dearly beloved father.
He was always reciting it.
As kids we didn't mind it a bit

In his country he performed in a theater.
His talent included writing little skits.
Also a little stand-up comedy too.
There wasn't anything he couldn't do.

To entertain and please his audience.
He also played his Portuguese guitar,
At home, parties, just for fun
He was always on the run.

Music was his second love
Along with our traditional chamarita
Which he also called to his delight,
To make people happy all of the night.

I've tried my best to copy him again and again,
But there's no way I can do that.
So to my famous father I take my shot
And also I dedicate my love and heart to him.

    Isabelle Mattos

Stillness

The silence is almost lost,
Thoughts run wild through her mind,
Voices of things to do and what has to be done,
But underneath it all lies one massive thought.
Not knowing where to turn, not knowing who to tell,
She hides her eyes in comfort.
What is not seen is better off unsaid.
She chose what she wanted but it's not hers.
A simple past, a complex future, and a lonely present.

    Catrina Tchor

Rationale for Late Sleepers

The head is a house of dreams
That float through waves of night
Sending the sober mind of day
Off in a soaring flight.

Sometimes to a misty land
Of orchids and vague hope
Sometimes to the swamps of Freud,
Where murky infants grope.

But those who dream sometimes see truth,
That wise, sweet, distant sigh
Or some sudden avalanche of facts
That pierce the armored lie.

To stay in bed and dream and dream
Is to waste one's life, they say,
But why greet hate and greed and war
In the nightmare of the day?

    Mary Coddington

A Spider and a Fly

Interpretation from Russian by Mikhail Fridman
Some spider, heart-breaker, and a beautiful fly
Both buzzed into my ear, and quite for a while.

The fly nearly bagged me: "My friend, do it fast,
Describe our love that will be ever last!"

"But old Russian writer has done it already,"
I told her, "Go on, if you feel going steady."

The spider has added: "The old man's review
Had been unacceptable, fully not true."

The fly was insisting with tears in her eyes:
"My love is beyond other spiders and flies!"

"All spiders are killers, poor flies, they are prey.
She's subject to danger, "would everyone say.

My beautiful fly is so blind in her love, she's willing to die,
Like flame-aimed butterfly.

So, what can I do now, what can I say?
Unable to help her, I can only pray.

The young lovely flies are so naive and pretty,
That I just can't help with my feeling of pity.

Beware of the spiders and their strong nets!
And this is "The End," or in Russian: "Konetz."

Leonid Tsygan

If God Should Ever Go on Strike

It's a good thing God above has never gone on strike.
Because He wasn't treated fair,
Or things He didn't like.
If God ever sat down and said,
"That's it—I'm through!
I've had enough of those on Earth,
So this is what I'll do:
I'll give my orders to the sun,
Cut off your heat supply,
And to the moon:
"Give no more light and run the oceans dry."
Do you know He'd be justified,
If fairness were the game.
For no one has been more abused,
Or treated with disclaim.
We don't care who we hurt or harm,
To gain the things we like.
But what a mess we'd all be in,
If God should ever go on strike.

Ann Hurley

A Breezy Summer Eve

I am the shining silky water
Of the grey-green lake on a breezy summer eve.
My brothers are the deep pounding echoes,
Bounding from stone to stone,
In our bass filled bay.

My sisters are the deftly dancing foam
Swiftly sweeping the shore at the end of day.
Flaming Sun sinking to the distant shore
Sends its fingers of reflected light shimmering
Into the quickly nearing dark of night.

My brothers tossing it round their rocks
Place a golden blanket against the growing chill.
My sisters fold foam-laced edges fast around me
As I, swooshing a deeply felt sigh or two
Softly sink into soothing sleep.

Betty Ryen Breinin

The Wonder of it All

As I stood alone in the forest
Admiring the wonder of the Lord
My voice rang out with His praises
And I heard the great trees applaud!

How small I feel here in the forest
Dwarfed by trees towering over my head
For a moment I'm no longer in the forest
I find myself in a cathedral instead

A sudden hush settled all about me
I felt the presence of someone quite near
A warm glow swept over my body
Removing all my doubt and fears

A choir of birds singing in the tree tops
Filled the air with the sweetest melodies
And I thanked the good Lord for His blessing
While the breeze murmured "Amen" with me

Helen D. Sullivan

Reflections

So, what are old friends for?
A casual chat? A cocktail hour or two?
Ah, no. Old friends are meant for bridging gaps
between what's old and new,
for warm remembering beside the fire
on long, cold evenings when the sun goes down,
for recollections shared, to stem the tide
of all that crowds in when the night comes 'round.

New friends are fine.
If they become the answer for the present, that is well.
But old friends have a quality
that's rare as virgin pearls within the Oyster shell,
knowing the worst yet true and steadfast still,
ready to fight the battle, come what will.
Lucky are those who have their friends of yore
to keep the enemy without the door.

Phyllis W. Reinauer

Heart on the Altar

My chest has been torn open again,
Exposing my heart.
Here, Lord,
I have placed it on the altar
And I offer it up to you.
Would you take care of it for me?
I have not cared for it myself very well.

I made my breast plate from drive and pride.
Had I forged it with righteousness,
Your righteousness,
The pain, the loss
Would not be so great.
The righteousness would have given
My heart to you freely.

Judith Schaefer

Arriving Soon

A brand new life will shortly begin,
born innocent and free of sin.
What will it be—a girl, a boy?
It matters not for it will bring much joy!
A whole new being filled with great promise;
to laugh, to love, to walk among us.
Enriching those lives with whom it touches,
while hopefully avoiding harmful clutches.
Already loved though not yet born,
bringing much hope like a brand new morn.
So we joyfully await that happy day,
ready to welcome the sun's newest ray.

Anna Lyons

One Lover to Another

If you love me, show that you do
Not just by words alone
Show me by actions you mean to be true
Let your voice have a gentle tone
Little things count so much you see
I need to know that you care
We'll learn from each other, you'll let me be me
We'll kiss and moment by moment we'll share
You'll make me queen of your heart
I'll make you my king, O' love
Endearing words are just a start
Aren't the words charming above?
The action sweet one remains to be seen,
It's where we're going, not where we've been.

Delores Brown Harding

Sister, Dearest Sister

To me you have been a mother,
A sister, and a friend;
You have walked life's road of hard knocks
With me to the bitter end.

I knew that I could depend on you,
Through the good times and the bad,
To pick me up when I was down,
Make me feel happy when I was sad.

And when my days seem to be darkest,
When I am in my deepest despair,
Things will surely become brighter
Because you are always there.

So on this, your birthday,
May God bless and keep you, always.
And in the oncoming years,
Grant you many more happy birthdays,

Louis L. Williams

Mnemosyne's Shrine

Your fingers flutter
as a wave of inspiration washes through your limbs
temporarily setting the monitors to a furious scratching
but then they return to their lambdas and upsilons
and your eyes drift in a sea of nereids
whose scales caress and whose tails
lift you so you can't drink the water
but sometimes you steal a sip from one's cheek
or another's ear and from those tastes
you see the angels dancing on the shoulders
of the water and the arms of the sun trembling
as Hyperion reaches to cradle you and his smile
is what warms you as the salt dries on your body
but it is in the arms of Morpheus that you find salvation
for you are the truth in dreams that will not manifest

Megan Hodge

Learning

Learned to surf off Waikiki with a ten foot board;
to use the body for the same purpose at beaches o'er the Pali.

Learned to hula, play ukulele, and sing the songs;
to hustle tourists and tell tepid jokes to drunks in a nightclub.

Learned to spend weekends on the beach;
roast pig, swim in the surf, sing;
watch the stars until dawn swept through.

Learned the boy cannot go back when he has seen swaying palms,
eaten poi, felt the caress of the entwining breeze.

Learned my father was right when he went to Paree in seventeen
and couldn't stay down on the farm.

Aaron W. Hillman

Peaceful Dreamer

Last night I dreamt about God.
Sleep now, awaken, awaken from this peaceful slumber
Night has risen above the clouds, too dark, too bright
Look away into the darkness.

Feel the closeness of the light. Listen, hear the echoes
of his voice, so sweet, so low.
Awaken my child, and be not afraid, for I am, I am the tear
You cry, weep unto me.

Arise, arise, for I am the night, come unto me
Sweet, sweet, aroma, I am, I am the air you breathe.

What is this mist? My eyes cannot see. God awake me from
This dream. For I cannot find the way.
The light, it comes and goes, it fades.
Darkness at last, the morning awaits. I cried out loud,
Wiped sweat from my brow.
Look what my eyes see, God has truly blessed me.
No pain in sight . . . I had a dream about God last night!

Sandra Estelle

Diane, My Friend:

This is for Diane Yennes, I miss her, she made me laugh.
It all begins with life; it seems to be so full of endless strife.
Materialism is abounding, greediness that's so astounding.
I then walk through where I will be one day, I am embarrassed,
And I am afraid.
Isolation is everywhere. The memories seem to stare.
I bend in quiet desperation to feel, and smell this clean earth.
Then I begin to think of my rebirth.
The past seems to have never been, so is my future my end?
I have faith and I sincerely pray, but sadness has come to me
In the passing of a friend today.
She really suffered in unspeakable ways.
So now all I have left is hope for a kinder judgement day.

Susan Toba

Beautiful Hours Are Here

Our hour has come for peace, love and unity
The new millennium will show us how to live,
Expressing the desire and dreams to receive and give.
The Earth was filled with plenty for all,
In the spring, summer and fall.
God did not specify race creed or color,
To stand a distance from each other.
Our hour has come to let our children see,
What nature meant for us to be.
Shed off the old dear ones and put on the new.
Then we all can be honest and true.
What are your dreams, hopes and desires?
Name them to the world one by one and day to day.
Then when it's our time to go away,
Step off life's boat with a desire no longer to stay.

Edythe M. Sims

And Eternal

Again, the memory, years before of rejoice,
Of that small cry, giving a sign
Of a life's voice.
Apprehension, a mother's question,
Was it worthwhile,
All disappearing, upon seeing,
The baby's first smile.

Thomas Ford Mailloux

Lost within Myself

Sometimes I sit here all alone,
Just wondering if I have the strength to make it on my own.

Sometimes I think all I know is pain,
Although when you have nothing to lose
You have everything to gain.

I feel like I'm trapped in a maze,
And my whole life's gone by in one big blaze.

Nothing can help the loneliness I feel inside,
It's something I've tried and tried to hide.

Please hear my cries, and help me erase all the lies
Just take me in your arms and tell me it will be okay,

Tell me that you love me,
Help me find the way.

I've gone through my whole life,
Thinking I'm not good enough

The emptiness cuts me like a knife,
Whatever happened to my life?

Jessica Scott

With Six Seconds . . .

He rests his white hands on the rail
trying to find the words to tell me
that it ain't like he thought
and Miami, she keeps clapping her hands
steady rhythm now understood
he wasn't meant for me
don't go
but I can't say the words
eyes too heavy with tears as he walks away
I feel the sun bulging, pulsating in my throat
unable to formulate a command that would
send him back
and Miami does not warn me
of the approaching storm
a hurricane that I feel might not ever end
and in six seconds . . .
I'm destroyed beyond recognition
waiting to be rescued from a nightmare
I thought I was prepared for

Alissa Stone

In the Blink of an Eye

Going through the motions in my world
With no feeling to push me higher.
In the blink of an eye, I am living
With passion and desire.

Turning the pages of my life,
Nothing distinct do I hear.
In the blink of an eye, a chorus
Of sounds become crystal-clear.

Watching my adventures,
The scenes are black-and-white.
In the blink of an eye, vibrant colors appear
That bleed into the night.

Such joy and pain I've tasted
Through this tiny view.
But in the blink of an eye, I must return
To that which I once knew.

Cindy DeDanaan

Soul Mates

Our souls were promised before we were made.
Our lives were set up to coincide one day.
Mistakes were made, problems followed.
Never would we believe, we were made for each other.
Time passed, each life lived a part.
Never knowing our souls were destined to become one.
Love blossomed, only to die.
Believing true love would only pass us by.
Then the moment came to pass.
Our spirits met and the connection began.
First there was confusion, even guilt on both sides.
Yet we had forgotten God made our lives.
Our souls were promised before we were made.
Our lives were meant to coincide one day.
That day has arrived and we shall begin to truly
Fulfill our lives, soul mates until the end.

Leah Lynch

Her

For her who I once called lover, it now no longer even friend.
Isn't it so God-damned sad how quickly some things come to an end?
You'll never know how much your presence I do miss.
Nor; do you know you have broken my heart,
and scattered the pieces so far apart.
It's so difficult to put those pieces back together again.
My only answer to this problem is this;
stopping to think of you as I often will.
It will take me forever, and forever I shall stay blue.

Deborah Vespia

We Were There

We were there that day the Babe was born.
We breathed over him to keep him warm.
We knelt there in the fragrant hay,
And felt the blessing of the day.

We were there the night the shepherds came,
Worshiping Him and praising his name.
His glory shown around about us all,
As we gathered there in that humble stall.

The Maji came from lands afar,
Guided by that brilliant star.
They brought rare gifts to this Holy child,
Born of Mary, meek and mild.

We animals there in our lowly stall
Saw the greatest Miracle of all.
This holy Child of Mary, born
Upon that cold December morn.

Frances E. Stroup

My Children

I love my children and they love me.
As wide as the oceans and deep as the sea.
I care for their needs as I am able.
The perfect "MOM" is but just a fable.
I haven't been home for much of this year.
My children are feeling this ominous fear.
I tell them I'll be there and give them a sigh.
Even though I want to lay down and die.
My children will hurt because of this trauma.
Suicide they say was the death of their Mama.
Can I inflict on my children this pain?
When I feel the same again and again.
Lord give me the strength to suppress this urge.
The thoughts in my head, please will you purge?
I love my children and their love I can see.
It's the love in their hearts that will sustain me.

Julie Inman

Mississippi Black Gal

Black is the color in which I was born,
I hear a ton of criticism and bale of scorn,
I did not choose how I came onto this Earth,
But I can choose the course that I'll take after birth.

I can blame circumstances for a lot of things,
But how I react is the key to my dreams,
I refuse to let circumstances hold me back,
I'll seek another way and stay on the right track.

Building a strong bridge is difficult indeed,
I'll keep striving for the best, as I sow my seed,
A strong and loving family plays a gigantic role,
I consider myself blessed to be a part of this fold.

I am proud of who I am, and where I come from,
The back roads of Mississippi, cotton fields and red plums,
Where I go from here, is strictly up to me,
I can sigh and give up, or strive to be free.

I'll build my bridge strong, so my children can see,
It doesn't matter where I began,
The real test is where I'll end,
And that is strictly up to me and my God.

    Lucy Johnson

Storm Clouds

You gaze at the sky, see nothing but black.
Feel lost and alone, can't find your way back.
Bare your eyes, my brave child;
Find the hope that you lack.
Just search harder . . .
When storm clouds roll by.

Days once filled with joy seem shrouded in pain.
Where once there was light, now darkness and rain.
Bare your smile, my brave child;
Your bad days soon shall wane.
Just smile harder . . .
When storm clouds roll by.

A world so unlike the one you once knew,
Where dreams come up dry and goals are past due.
Bare your mind, my brave child;
Someday wishes come true.
Just dream harder . . .
When storm clouds roll by.

    Gary Vinturella

Perusal from a Patio

Distant toll of communal church bells, intermittently
accompanied by varying sounds of blackbird, robin and
indignant magpies with petite Jenny wren.

Swerving in and out of creviced weather-worn Brittany
granite, amazing how they sing with beak fulls of
discarded dog hair and sheep's wool.

Stark leafless oak trees fading into the low grey
passive clouds, whilst lichen and moss similar to
saffron Spanish paella, splattered over the Breton
stonework, sounds of nature divine Holy orison.

Shadows more sombre, darken under overhanging hand
chipped local tiles, with gaping crevices and cavity
forever increase, due to decaying mortar, at one time
so very sound and so plushly full.

Metaphorically a dentist's paradise, for him to
meticulously prise and probe, scrape out, and with
numerous care drill and extra filling.

Irregular pockets of dolphin-blue swimming in a nearly
static grey and swirling sea, the overhead sky seems
so oppressively dull.

    Joseph Dobson

No Peace for Ancient Woodlands

Next to The Spinney, this ancient woodland,
Where twenty-four houses may yet be built,
There is a ghetto of empty nesters.
What national folly that builds afresh,
Takes no account of unoccupied creche
That extrapolates singles for double, flit
of those who, for tax evading reason,
Would not disown the fathers of their sons.

Britain has no housing problem, simply
She lacks the political will to use
Fully the housing she already has.
False homelessness kills off our native birds.
Arsenic, cyanide, and asbestos
Landfill and bring pollution to once clear streams.
High Court injunctions, eco-warriors,
We groan for peace in this ancient woodland.

    Mildred Bateman

An Ode to My Dream Girl

I've loved you since the day we met, as you can plainly see.
You're everything I've dreamed about or ever hoped you'd be.
My shining star, my guiding light, my strength in time of stress,
My living doll of pulchritude, of gorgeous loveliness.

All my dreams are all in vain, dear if I can't have you,
The nicest girl in all the world, so loyal and true blue.
A girl so warm, so sweet and pure, perfect in every way,
That every time I think of you, you really make my day!

There's no one else that can ever mean the things you mean to me,
And no one else can take your place throughout eternity.
So please my darling, please be kind, and never let me go,
Without you dear I would be lost, because I love you so!

Distance was the only thing that kept us both apart,
But everyday in every way, you live within my heart.
There never was another girl, so gracious or so sweet,
And there will never be another like "My Angel," Marguerite!

    Everett H. Buck

Fire-Breathing Giant

Mt. Rainier towers over mountain peaks,
A sleeping giant full of fire inside.
He belches smoke and ashes as he speaks.
He'll send hot lava down the mountain side.

Seattle grew where sea and land provide;
The forests, mountain ores, and fish abound.
The riches called to people far and wide;
They came to build their homes on slopes around.

The giant guards the seas of puget sound.
Seattle rests upon its mighty shore.
Its wealth and bounty immigrants had found.
Mt. Rainier's riches last forever more.

The giant threatens death with lava flows.
The Mother Earth is only one who knows.

    Genevieve Campbell

Untitled

When I lay in my lonely bed
I look up at the ceiling
And wonder where all of my people have gone
Once this was a happy home
But now I'm all alone
With wonderful memories
So now I wait until I join them
In the great beyond
Where there is a place prepared for me
Oh, happy day I'm 83
It's getting closer you see.

    Dorothy C. Palmer

The Mind of a Poet

A cry from the darkness,
a scream from the deep.
Confusion and chaos infest this world;
sanity has been exterminated.
Contorted visions sliver,
sanctified images whither.
As I look for a place of peace,
I fall deeper into a black cavernous hole.
Yet, all I can feel is the rhythm of my soul,
I lose control, I feel cold.
All is numb.
I close my eyes.
Evil dwells; my eyes swell to see,
nothing, but reality.
To wonder where this distorted world lies;
Behind a poet's eyes.

Lisette Delvitt

Ignoring Mother Nature

Nature surrounds us, and nature is there,
it is needed discreetly everywhere.
The joys of love and the terrors of disaster
the rash actions of people and the emptiness after

People are like seasons, moods changing with time,
No one is an exemption, no matter how fine
You may plan and plot every action you make,
Still there is the sudden unplanned at stake.

Be it the past where one cannot go,
Or the future which is a danger to know
As the inevitable will happen no matter how much
One tries to prevent it will only cause such

Chaos and terror and imbalance in life,
Causing the future more fear and strife.
Developments and humans are the way to go
But hear nature cry as it progresses so slow.

Jocelyn Hu

Child This Is What I See

As I look in your eyes I see a child hurt and in pain.
And no one or nothing can make her regain,
the love the feeling of happiness she needs.
But inside she doesn't know what to do or what to see.
The people around you talk to you out of both sides of their mouth.
As I look in your eyes I see that you, child,
don't know how to believe or trust
when no one believes or trusts in you.
When I look even harder in your eyes child
I see what they say and how they make you feel.
Child look into your own eyes and analyze yourself
for that is what is needed to help you get out of this madhouse.

Ashley Chamis

Let It Flow Chemistry

Magnetism and electricity, there is a glow.
There is a connection between them. Let it flow.
Come pass my magnetic field with your body in motion.
Such an attraction. I have that notion.
Negative and positive are so opposite.
But then, if alike, there won't be an attraction.
Radioactive and full of energy.
So mystical, so deep, real dreams come alive.
When opposites attract,
"Will they collide?"
When they are together, they will repel.
But my white magic will make the spell.
Chemistry at last.
Oh boy, so fast!
The heat intense will make it glow.
So hot and charming.
Just let it flow.

Toni Triolo

I Am

I cannot be who you want me to be.
I do not want to be who you want me to be.
I do not have to be who you want me to be.

For you don't see me; know me.
Couldn't possibly conceive me.
And if I let myself.
I would start to believe
That what you think will retrieve me.

I believe in me, I live for every day.
And learn myself along the way.
Talk is just something that you say.

Words that roll off the tongue,
Lashed out to cause discouragement,
Yet your sentiment,
I won't let cause me disappointment.

I will not just be.
For who I am to you;
I am everything to me.

Mary A. Gardner

Poor Timmy Boy

At the start of my 12th school year
There was a tall, lanky, and shy guy named Timmy, poor dear.
He suddenly stopped going to school after only 126 days
His roommate seemed plain and nice, but odd in some ways.
"Where did Timmy go?" people began to quietly ask.
Rumors spread about a person who wore a black mask.
A couple of years later as the town's cop on the beat
I took a walk along the river to find a shallow grave.
The thought of poor Timmy popped up, I must be brave.
July 13, 1963 the body of Timmy was found.
July 13, 1993 a plaque, a cross and orange handle cutters
Mark this hollow ground. "Who killed this boy?"
the town's people ask, "What about the person
With the black mask? Was the orange cutter a weapon
Or just some older child's toy?
Poor Timmy boy, poor Timmy boy."

Theodore Friedman

Icicles

Icicles hanging
With silver, slender, grace
Heavy
From thin, brown, brittle branches
Catch the early morning sunlight
Casting shafts
Of shining slivers
Through the cold cold morning mist

Bill M. Clark

Prelude to Abduction

How could you not have seen beyond that goblet
more poisoned with intrigue than any foreign court
and through that fire that so mysterious sprang to life
in your unsuspecting darkened hearth
while you slept before it
your mind and napkin folded neatly back in place?

While they draped you in patriot's colors
and shot you full of infrared accusations
they ran rampant through a gentlewoman's sleeping brain
and left a thousand swirling jagged dreams to grow
then crept beneath her lowered lids
and plucked the sleeping flowers from her eyes.

Does that seem so strange to you
who had both seeds and shears
and valor of the kind
that saves the minds of me?

Amy L. Ventura

In Memory of My Brother

The angry man walks a lonely path,
For he knows not where it leads.
He shudders at his fruitless wrath,
When it drives him to his knees.

For the little girl in daddy's heart,
The only hope is time.
But now he feeds on bitterness,
And nothing seems to rhyme.

For the woman of the world, it seems,
That no one really cares.
Nobody to give her love to,
Nothing for her to share.

And the eagle looks upon his prey,
With the love for one who fills his needs.
As darkness welcomes another day,
It leaves the emptiness that it sees.

Pamela Templin

Feelings of Love

Dedicated to my mom, to whom I feel all these things
Love is an immeasurable commitment
and emotion for someone or something.
It's the reason you get up in the morning and go to bed at night.
Because you love someone, or someone loves you.
It powers the soul, clears the mind and cleanses the heart.
It's a passion for someone from head-to-toe,
it a passion that makes you never want to let go.
When you think of them day and night,
when you know, with them, that everything's all right.
It's when you feel warmth every time they're near,
when you feel empty every time they're not here.
If you get a tingling sensation every time you hear their name,
you will know it's love not a game.
Love makes what you do every day
feel so right in every way.
Love is a gift from the Heavens above,
so if you feel this things, you'll know it's Love!

Jerusalem Hailue

Through the Eyes of a Child

Through the years we all come full circle,
some of us realize that we are destined for greater things
while the majority of the world sleeps
in a deceiving dream that misleads them.
As we, the few gypsies that roam the Earth
awakening a select few who's desires and passions
break free of the chaotic normality that is the world.
As the world heads into the millennium,
everyone is occupied with nonsensical misguided plans
for the new and improved era.
Yet, we the children of the 20th century are neglected.
It has been our ideas and passions that have lead us
into the millennium, but we are forgotten.
Conformity has become a fashion statement
and individuality has become lost.
This is what I see through the eyes of a child.

Chris Torres

Thunderstorm

Screaming demons,
Riding steeds of flame across a boiling sky.
Booming,
Crashing,
With wind swept speed they soar.
Hurtling spears of hail and light they battle.
Amongst castles of cloud, black and menacing.
Rain falls to the ground like blood from their tortured wounds.
Indeed, it will be hard to sleep tonight.

Barry Mcdonald

The Universe around Me

Majestically she stood,
Silhouetted in black, purple and gold
In the glorious evening sky untold.

The feel of the gentle breeze upon my face
Embraced me within her arms to witness the dance of life.
The Earth is alive with motion in her wrinkle of time unspoken.

Time stood still in the universe that night,
As I breathed in the fragrance of the Earth around me tight.
Dark, damp, musty but fresh and clean to the beholder.

Shadows grew long and melted into one another.
A curtain of darkness silently appeared.
Only the twinkling of the stars blazed across the sky.

The energy I felt ricocheted off the stars in the universe,
And returned to Earth at a stronger force.
Felt deep within my solar plexus, the power of lightning.

I could stay here forever in my little world,
Under the stars, in this magical universe,
Embraced and loved by such a mystical force.

Nancy Sue Meyer

A Glimpse of Her

She sits by the window
In the sky seeing her dreams
Remembering the heartaches
With tears that still streams.

The moonlight catches her look,
The sadness and distress upon her face,
Knowing she's hurting and that she's wanting
Someone to fill the empty space.

She spends many nights alone
With no one to talk to—no one to hold her
Remembering all the past pains
And wonders why they ever were.

She's been used and she's been abused,
She's been taken and she's swallowed her pride
But she's never been cared for and held
And those feelings she cannot hide.

Oh, she's a beauty at one's sight, but
Those eyes hold many pains inside
Of stories untold and things that still haunt
Maybe some see it, but she's not sure, she can't decide.

Shea Stephens

Truth

Collect the shards of wisdom, make it whole
Ignite your intellect, suppress your pride
Then turn the pages of your aching soul
And read the fiery words that burn inside.

Hysteric doubts will terrorize your mind
Demonic spirits will repress your soul
But if you persevere, you'll surely find
A way to reach your everlasting goal.

You'll see the facts, for better or for worse
You'll recognize your soul's despairing cry
You'll know that fountain of the gentle force
Which issues forth the things that never die.

However much your earthly thoughts will rave
However loud your deepest passions call
You'll seek to leave the darkness of the cave
And curse the empty shadows on the wall.

Long spells of time will quickly pass you by
Your lonely candle will grow dim and fade
And when this world will wither up and die
You'll realize the truth of your crusade.

Dimitri Epstein

The Phone Call

I always hate to miss a call
When I'm in town or at the mall.
So I bought a phone machine
Said to handle everything.
It worked great until one night,
When the caller got a terrible fright.
After calling all night, only to hear,
"I'll call you back when I'm here!"
Don't worry, my dear, I've not taken off.
I just forgot to turn the darn thing off.

Robert L. Spencer

"Make Every Day Count"

I am thankful for every day I live and every
night, as I peacefully sleep.
We have been given a wonderful gift of life.
There's no written guarantee how long we will live.
We can be certain we will surely die.
We should make every day count.
There is no promise of tomorrow.
I shall not live my life in vain.
During my days of triumphs, joy, or pain,
I strive to make each day count.
I must live each day as if it were my last.
There may not be another, and seize the moment.
We can give a gift of friendship and peace.
There is no cost or pain and much to gain.
Let not life pass you by.
Why not today? If I am remembered with love
and respect by one person.
I will have made my life count.

Mary Alexander

Evaluation

Hoarded into this spherical lot,
the mass abiding malaise
Scavengers where Mammon is fraught,
whores in drunken haze

He gentle be buried by trampling toes,
she soft be lewdly viled
Betrothed cliches to heal their woes
from the breath of a molded smile

One impassioned stands up in sweeps of crowds
abraded by riotous chide
A fool alone with one voice loud
is flogged for Massa's pride

No use this song of lament now,
the tide continues on
Wipe then the blood from your brow,
and let your soul be known

Craig Summers

The Valley and the Mountain

I fell into the valley of the blues
The loss of illusions shattered
The loss of unrevealed secrets, unmet needs
The loss of fantasies that remained ever unfulfilled
I mourned that loss of the love of my lifetime
That I never even met
The loss of innocence
But the blessing of the valley of the blues
Is that just on the other side is the mountain of light
Where many secrets are revealed
Fantasies will be fulfilled
Innocence restored
And just within my view coming over the mountain
Standing tall and looking oh, so good
My prince has arrived

June Solomon

Dreaming

As I sit here I know the radio is on,
but no sound from it will I hear.
I know nothing but you, you and me in my memory.
We sit together talking, laughing, even crying.
You sing and I listen with ears opened by love.
I know you are not here but still
I can see every perfect detail.
The rain will fall, the sun will shine, but
none will effect this heart of mine.
Tears will fall, tears have fallen.
Only to wet on unknowing body.
For we are together now, if only in memory.
Soon it will be for all eternity.

Karrey Barber

Earl Grey Epiphanies

She holds the tea bag in her pudgy fingers like a rosary,
dip down deep into the confession of the cup,
release the bergamot mystery.

I met a tea-leaf reader in Dallas, years ago,
who read my destiny from the compost of a
coffee mug that said, "Ask me about Amway!"

The interior is quasi-Versailles,
an explosion of pink, puff pastry,
and trays of petit-fours, give me that Old European venue,
with the Negro in white gloves and a uniform
with epaulets, a la Admiral Halsey.

He pours the sacred Darjeeling, surrounded by high priestesses
in crisp, black taffeta. They are not allowed to look me in the eye.

The women around me have immaculate red fingernails.
The women around me sit on Queen Anne chairs.
The women around me have creamy latte complexions.
The women around me are not my mothers.

Annie White

Feelings

There is:
Joy and Sadness,
Sorrow and Cheer,
Laughter and Crying,
Pain and Happiness,
And the feelings of
Peace and Love.
But these are all just mere thoughts.
Thoughts that come and go.
Thoughts that really don't mean much at all,
When it comes to True Reality.

Vonda Johnson

A Brother's Love

A brisk morning breeze,
and the smell of a reminiscent past.
The feeling of emotion,
with each space of air that I grasp.
Wondering if at times I left him,
standing alone in this cruel world.
Was I brother enough,
to weather his strongest storm?
Or did I fall to shame at the thought,
that he would be greater than me.
Wielding our swords of words we grew.
But daily I wish that I could be
more than a statue for him to look upon.
Through the burning of the flame,
a brother's love will still remain.
Endless memories remind me,
that from forever until the dawn
Love your brother before he is gone.

Kelly Haun

Perpetual Time

The pendulum swings to and fro
Seconds pass by, where do they go?
Of every minute of every hour
The pendulum dictates its power

Of every hour of every day
It keeps on swinging come what may
Of every day of every week
No rest does it ever seek

Of every week of months to follow
We all wish sometime we could borrow
Of every month of every year
It then becomes something we hold dear

Of things that have happened good and bad
Happy and sad days we have had
Old year out, new year begins
The pendulum forever swings

'Til the end of time
Brenda Mary Quick

The Ballad of M.L. and Me

Your music knows your future.
Life was from your mother's nurture.
The g-clefts were your days left.
You must accept your friend's bereft.

The gun you hold cut to your hand's mold.
The tag says sold, and your life's too old.
You've courage my friend, 'til life's bitter end.
Your music's godsent, your valour's not pretend.

Your days were numbered, and you burned the rest.
Your trigger found the barrel that destroyed the best.
You were always here, now, you'll always be gone.
Here on we'll be thinking of you, in "another song."

Your notes have died, where's your song to go,
To help you with life's sweet rainbows?
Only God knows what afterlife holds,
Hope it has mellow, mellow, "notes". . .my friend.
G. D. Goetz Sr.

Dear Friend

For you, the sadness, the loneliness, the pain
　are now gone.
Now we're the ones left, at least we have our
　memories to hold on.
The talks, the photos, of things in the past,
　were the things we thought would forever last.

But now it's neither here nor there.
For now you're gone and in the best of care.
We were with you through the end.
For you were much more than a friend.
Treva Harris

The Sun

I wake up and look out the window.
The sky is filled with a golden-orange light.
As the sun comes up,
everything it touches is now filled with warmth and light.
The lakes are shining,
the grass is gleaming with morning dew.
The mountain tops shimmer as the sun hits their snow covered peaks.
At night, when the sun goes down,
the lakes do not shine,
the grass does not gleam,
the mountain tops do not shimmer,
but there is a brilliant light in the sky.
The same golden-orange as when the sun came up.
Jessica Leskun

My Special Gift

Every day I hoped and prayed for a special gift of my own,
as each day went by I found myself sitting all alone.
The feeling of loneliness is so much for one to bear;
it seems the world is so big that no one seems to care.
The feeling of loneliness is with you everywhere you go,
then comes a point of what to do—you don't know.
The feeling of loneliness is there in a big crowded room,
everywhere you look and you still feel all agloom.
I still look for that special gift I can call my own,
and when it comes I know I won't feel so alone.
What, you may ask, could make loneliness go far away?
Only a very special gift that can happiness to stay.
Then I realized something right out of the blue—
that my special gift I had all along and it was you.
When you have a special gift that you can call a friend,
You have a gift that will last until the very end.
Richard Reynolds

The Night's Ashes

My shipwrecked fragments wash up onto your distant shores
Which you pick up, dust off and put in your pocket
I taste the lost intoxication of your stale gin and nicotine
As I pack up the last threadbare beliefs I wore
Strewn over your floor like fig leaves ripped off
This page is your snake skin shed in a crinkled heap
I want to tear in clawed handfuls, cram into my mouth, spit out
The white wedding dress words concealing dirty underclothes
Sometimes the bullet lies too deep to even consider removing it
Lodged in the marrow of the dream's breaking spine
By he to whom you took your soul in a basket to be held
I who you once lit up greedily now a used discarded stub
Extinguished beneath your merciless twisting heel of infidelity
But now the rains come as a really unreal awakening
I watch myself happen from moment to moment
A nomad perpetually running from the certainty of uncertainty
I let the river flow from pinnacle to abyss
Hope is brought by a solitary flower floating down from quiet art
I spread my arms like a phoenix tree rising forth
From the night's cracked desert surface of ashes
Lynne Thompson

The Immigrant Song

We were friendless, love, without acclaim.
Strangers faces did not seem the same.
Now . . . the rustling leaves murmur your name
And children smile at me.

Sometimes I walk to a church nearby,
Light a candle . . . and try not to cry.
The people hurry as they go by
And children smile at me.

There were times of nursery rhymes and prayers
trains and planes and dancing circus-bears.
Small feet rushing as they climbed the stairs
would always warm our hearts.

We found freedom, Love, and hope aflame.
Strangers voices did not sound the same.
Now . . . our neighborhood respects our name
And children smile at me.
Clare Chandler Rentschler

Endless

The beach seems long and endless,
like the sound of my heart when it cries.

The dark, dark night and the cool night air
made for a nice and quiet walk along the endless beach.

For I was lost on the endless beach.
Daniel Cook

Magic

If I were magic and could will it to be
Then you would have nothing
But joy and happiness for all of eternity.
If I could right all the wrongs in your life
Then there would be no more tears and strife
Only laughter and song would make up your life.
If I could take away all your hurt and pain
Then all poetry and songs would be
Of only love, joy and peace.
If I could will these things to be, words like hurt
And pain wouldn't even be in our vocabulary.
We wouldn't even know what they mean.
Never have by our eyes been seen.
If I could will it to be, how different our lives would be
And yes, I guess we would be
Back living in the garden of Eden.

Gloria Grobe

Don't Cry for Me

Don't cry for me, for I am not alone.
I have gone home, don't you see.
Don't let my passing be your misery.
Open the gates Father, for I am home.
In Heaven where I belong.
Though I have left my friends and family,
They know I love them very deeply.
Don't cry for me, but remember me and smile
For in your heart is where I will be.
So remember these words and Don't Cry for Me.

Peter Jordan

Magic Window

Back at the magical window of my mind
Looking out, just wasting some time

With the morning light filtering through
It keeps the rain out and the cool morning dew

I look out my window staring out at my dreams
My mind's infantile thoughts and petty little schemes

Wondering what the world is all about
My mind swelling and ready to cry out

Seeing all the loves and heartaches of my life go by
All of life's toil, hardships, strife and wonder why

For my window is clear and only I can see out
Sounds can't penetrate and I can't hear even if you shout

How much more time at the magic window of my mind
How much more time at this window of mine

Anthony Mikulic

I Simply Am . . . Your Angel

There is no need to always look back
for my task is to always be there for you
There truly is no need to ever feel lonely
You never walk alone, for I am part of you

On those days when you just can't bear anymore
I will choose to carry your burdens & worries
Difficult days when you feel no one cares
I'll bring you back memories of being careless and free

When the pain gets unbearable, that tears shed no more
I will lead you to laughter and even open the door
When your faith falters and your eyes simply cannot see
I will cover you with love and you will know it is me

For I am your angel of light, your angel of love
I am the hand which extends from high up above
I am the wings of your soul when you are ready to fly
I am the one you see at birth and again when you die

I simply am . . . your angel

Martin Crespo

A Thank You Note to Jesus

First, thank you Jesus, for my life,
and for the loving parents you gave to me.

Thank you Jesus, for the Christian upbringing
my parents instilled in me.

Thank you Jesus, for the schooling
my parents were able to give me.

Thank you Jesus, for the gifts you gave to me,
and still able to use them.

Thank you Jesus, for my spouse, children,
grandchildren, great-grandchild, and for
all of my families, and for the many blessings.

Most of all, I thank you Jesus, for just who you are;
the man who died for my sins.

This thank you note, came from the heart saying:
Thanks Jesus for everything.
I love you!

Sister Carrie Holder

The First Grandson—1983

July twenty-fifth, nineteen eighty-three,
a day to recall, with joy,
when, through her pain and agony,
Donae, yelled "It's a boy."

Over eight pounds, they exclaimed,
and has all his fingers and toes,
with huge, dark eyes, and fine, fair hair,
and a button for a nose.

Three dimples frame a rose-bud mouth,
and a gaze that's straight at you,
one look, and we were lost to love;
and there's nothing we could do.

He cast us deep into his spell,
and slipped into our hearts,
and with his tiny fingers,
plucked the strings upon our harps.

The music that he adds to life,
is far beyond our brain,
so I can tell, he'll change our ways,
with sunshine and with rain.

Joanne Hearth

Child Abuse

Is something we've all experienced.
In one way shape or form.
Verbally, sexually, or physically.
It should be taken seriously.
For all the pain it brings.
Seems like it's everlasting.
Or fear is more their thing.
Sometimes you never, get over it.
The fact that you're being mistreated,
By someone who's suppose to love you.
So we withdraw ourselves, from everyone and everything.
To be alone in the darkness, to fade away out of harm's way.
Are sometimes even cry, wishing they could fly.
Like a eagle in the sky, and never descend.
But once again, that's not the way.
Come down from there, I have kind words to say.
Don't be afraid, I'll always be there.
To show you the way, trust is all I need.
From you by the way, so I'll wait as long as it takes.
Until a smile comes, across your face.

Paul Young

Strength

Life is bitter and cruel
Pain and sorrow knock you down
Somewhere from deep inside you
You have to find strength to get back up
Until you get knocked down again
This pattern repeats until the day comes
When you're strong enough not to get knocked down
This day never comes in your life
Only in death does it come

Amy Steiner

I Think It Must Be Winter

A bitter wind came pushing in
From out the Northern reaches
And choppy lines of foaming brine
Left seaweed on the beaches.

Two seagulls braved the icy waves
And didn't seem to fret
When sheets of spray would cross their way
With not one feather wet.

Dark clouds then formed a raging storm
Down through the mountain gorges
From the Island we, no more could see
Across "The Straights of Georgia."

This time of year I long to hear
Of songs the wild birds sing
So I blow my nose and warm my toes
And wait for you Sweet Spring.

Joan Wahl

Mirrored Pain

Night gnaws the insides of my gut
Feelings bite the crimson of my blood
Drowning, drowning, torrential flood
No answers to my questions, only but

Wondering with eye and mind awake
Restless, whirls the body of the lake
Physically here but spirited away
Layer by layer, my nerves began to fray

Pacing, endless streams of thought
O', cruel arrow, Narcissus without reflection
Addicted desire, drunk without the potion
Chasing circles—a heart now iron wrought

The thirst, the thirst, not deeply slaked
I would end this pain with a hungry stake
You pierce me true, through and through
End this sadness, wrapped in eternal blue

I am unlike the lonely, the Medusa
Starving, wanting yet mis-possessing
Painful to the core, deeply striking
Eternal forever, forever near, yet so far.

Surreal

Memories

We all have our memories,
memories of good times and bad times,
memories we will forget and memories that will last a lifetime.
But the memory of you will be an everlasting love.
For this memory not only exists in our mind
but in our hearts, to catch a frown and throw back a smile.
From old friends to new friends
we all have memories of the past
and memories are gifts from God,
which death cannot destroy.

Krystal Farrington

Fall . . . Is the Season

The most peaceful and thoughtful time of year for me is fall.
The green on the trees turn amber from thirst,
it comes on with a subtle slow but continuous burst.
One day it is so hot that everyone just feels lazy.
The next day it cools off and the scenery becomes hazy.
It's time to get out the sweatshirts and jackets.
Shop for gourds, mums and caramel apples at the markets.
Candles with the scent of pine, cinnamon and spice,
apple dumplings and pumpkin pies are always nice.
The smell of burnt leaves is in the air.
Children all dressed in their Halloween fare.
Beautiful color is popping out all around.
Everywhere we look there are jack-o-lanterns in town
This is my favorite time of the year,
Watching the change of season appear.
It is such a magical mystical transition.
God's palette is at work with such conviction!
What beautiful array of natural wonder
gives inspiration to paint for those who use color.
Fall is the season to fill us with emotion
to reflect on the past and look ahead with devotion.

Judith Pearl Pulaski

A Wonderful Papa

A wonderful Papa I had,
No more of my great Scottish lad.
Every time both of us were in a room,
We were always stuck together like glue.
I remember what happened that terrible day.
I remember exactly what my father did say.
Slippery and slick was the road
Airborne and across the median the car did go.
Granny's in a coma. She was hit in the head.
But he didn't make it. Papa is dead.
As I listened to this, I began to cry
I couldn't believe it, I felt a part of me had died.
I'd give anything to hear him sing a song
But now his voice is completely gone.
The bag pipe played "Amazing Grace"
To guide his soul to God's heavenly space.
So when my life has turned on a difficult angle,
I know I'll always have a guardian angel.

Erin C. Stuckey

Two Minutes

I sat in a chair on Christmas Eve,
My friend was before me, I never wanted to leave.
I wished every day that it was a trick,
Just one week before I found out he was sick.
I thought to myself, this just isn't right,
I could not see him for very long each night.
I never imagined someone could get in the way,
It was all I could think of on that dreadful day.
When I was handed the note, there was one thing I knew,
But before I could leave she said, "Let me give this to you."
I was held for five minutes, then I ran to my car.
I sped out of the parking lot, I had to go far.
I pulled up in sight of my mom at the door.
So I ran to the chair where I sat before.
I asked what had happened, I needed to know.
The doctor said, "He left just two minutes ago."
I turned to the bed, saw a smile on his face,
I knew he had gone to a better place.
I don't know for sure, maybe it was fate,
I still wonder why I had to be two minutes too late.
He was taken away, but before I started to cry,
I had one thing left to say, "Daddy, I love you. Good bye."

Kristine Bialik

Man

My mother's father would stare at the dry sky
long enough to make rain, and with a twist
and a tie mop-top ponies.
He lost a pair of fingers to the first war.
When that wasn't enough to end all,
he gained a limp in the second. Only way
was to lie twice, being once too young
and once too old. He was made of hard lines,
trenches that could cut a swath through people
and time. Age only seemed to dig in deeper,
lessening the no-man's land between
the widening fissures. His smile hung
on the toothpick half he kept slung
in one corner, the other half pocketed with
care and change, a habit come from days
when less than more was had.
And so he was, gnawed and frayed,
offering a mouthful of wet splinters.
And I, fresh from my mother's pocket,
a sharpened edge of the same grain.

William A. Johnson

The Endless Days

The rays of the sun penetrate my window
insistently
Without any regard
I am blinded until the malevolent orb
recedes into the quiet.

Since you departed—
my life has been a succession
of endless days
Purposeless
Wandering haphazardly from one thing to the next
My thoughts reminding me of how swiftly death kidnapped you
As it fled madly with clicking heels
The only sound it ever made.

I look to the moment when the endless days will cease
When everlasting night envelops me
And the twilight gently soothes the tortured chambers of my soul.

Nina Gut

Dead End

Sometimes you come to a dead end.
You don't know which way to turn,
so you call a friend.

They tell you not to worry.
"It'll be okay!"
It's really just a cop out for,
for them not knowing what to say.

Sometimes it's hard, we all know it's true.
You don't know what to say,
until it happens to you!

Shane Duckworth

God Is Our Friend

You don't have to be smart to know God
Take the Bible from the shelf and be yourself
That's how you'll know God
Just show His beauty from inside
From Him you never have to hide.
The only help you need is from the spiritual seed.
Once it is planted then your prayers will be granted.
God lives in us and is the beauty we have inside.
So don't be jealous, a braggart or full of pride
Just be proud you know the Great I Am
The Alpha, the Omega, your father, your friend.

Dorrie Fontenot

"The Story of Sam"

The story of Sam,
is very sad,
but all of it is true.
When ever I think of it,
it turns my heart blue.
But as Sam got older,
he went to Yale,
and had lots of lascivious stories to tell.
They were of girls and drinking,
his little brother Tim said he should rather be thinking.
He was in lots of debates,
and scored a bunch of telling points.
 He went home to tell of joining the war,
but almost had his head slammed in the door.
He didn't care about what his father thought,
we know that 'cause he went off and fought.
He was in lots of battles,
and accused of stealing his own cattle.
That happened when he went back to Reeding,
but almost got himself a beheading.
On February 16th of 1779,
Sam died.

Elisabeth Bochove

Silence So Loud

The pain in my eyes, the blood in my tears,
The soul in my words that nobody hears,
The wisdom I speak, the truth that I hide,
I keep my emotions bottled up inside,
The loneliness that comforts me, the forged smiles I give,
How can I be rid of this misery in which I live?
I try to scream out but no sound escapes,
And I'm shadowed with the thoughts that society rapes,
I detest those that hate me and I worship my spirit,
Death hovers above me but no one else can hear it,
I yearn for the love that I so desperately need,
There's a silence so loud it makes my ears bleed,
My tortured and mangled mind screams out in vain,
I search for a solution to end all this pain,
I walk through the valley of my demolished dreams,
All my aspirations are hopeless or so it seems,
My broken soul is in little pieces and I cannot mend it,
Evil corrupts my spirit and soon the devil will tend it,
I'm so upset by these thoughts and I'm paralyzed by my fears,
I'm sullen and I'm moody and I'm drowning in my tears,
I don't think this paranoia will end and even if it does,
I can never go back, I'll never be who I was,
Who I was before this happened, but what is this thing?
You live and learn but what lesson will this bring?

Joanna Lemoine

Alder in Winter

What grace they boast in summer's breeze;
  What ambition prompts their timberstere—
  A yard a year—
That they be tagged "the weed of trees."

But as with peers their seed may drowse
  In clinging catkins as they hold
  Through winter's cold
To habit the alder's naked boughs.

And in the slack coronal flame
  When clouds unloose their crystal-teem
  Of weathergleam
She is at once the wiggy, winter dame

Whose glitzy tresses catch the stares
  Of winter's apathetic eyes
  In keen surprise
With pendent-diamond solitaires.

Victor A. Schmidt

Brandy's Light

To my daughter Brandy
Brandy is my light. She makes it feel all right.
When my heart is dark, I just look at my Brandy.
And she makes it all feel right.
When my world looks dim and I feel so low.
My Brandy, my daughter, she will make me glow.
When I feel down, when I feel all alone.
Brandy, my daughter, you make it all gone.
When I feel pain, and I seethe cold, the rain.
I look at you, and it seems to ease the pain.
Your picture is with me always, your thoughts are too,
when your dad is down and out.
I just think about you.

Thomas Maines

On the Other Side

Mountains between us, rivers apart,
Close to each other, yet only in heart;
The mountain's so high, the river's so deep,
You come to me, darling, for but moments to keep.

To climb the mountain's an impossible dream,
To ford the rivers much harder than it seems;
To find you again will be hard enough to do,
Yet, I'd climb any mountain as long as it's with you.

Suzanne Sasser

Awareness

Open your eyes, see spectacular views,
Colors both brilliant and soft subtle hues.

Breathe in the scents of the lilacs and trees
Filling the air as they waft in the breeze.

Listen in silence and music abounds;
Noises in forests are not merely sounds.

Feel the cool wetness of dewdrops on leaves,
The rough bark, the soft earth, all the textures and weaves.

There are berries and nuts and sweet water to taste;
When you walk through a forest, do not go in haste.

Alissa Bernholc

Because

A rock with shiny little parts,
a dream turned nightmare from broken hearts.
Where is our place the fallen few?
Is it not here but their with you?
If I were you and you were me
maybe then you could see how life goes on so endlessly
and leaves behind those who laughed but really cried
and those lived but really died.

Cathy Neises

The Dark Shadow

A dark shadow touches my soul
It embraces me and makes me its own
I cannot fight it and I choose not to
I yield to the power it has over me
And I wait submissively as it consumes me
It is going to transform me, mutate me into another being
I am not afraid
I will it to grasp my being and make me one with itself
It will take my soul and leave my body to die
Yet, my soul will live on
It will thrive and become powerful
More and more so every minute
Until my soul and the shadow become one
And go on to conquer the dark land as one
One powerful and almighty being

Jessica D'Ambrosio

A Child's Mind

The soft wind blowing caresses my face.
The calm, the beauty, the peace of this place;
A place such as this, may seem hard to find.
But it is there, if we open our mind.
We become entangled in the webs of life,
Forget to relax, succumb to strife.
We don't see life as we did as a child.
When our hearts were free and our minds were wild.
For then it was no miraculous feat,
To go to the places that made our hearts skip a beat.
Our minds were open, our souls were free.
Our imaginations took us and let us be.
To the sunset beaches, with sands of gold.
To the arctic tundra, we were so bold.
We looked, we searched, we explored each place.
With a thrill in our heart and a smile on our face
So if life's mysteries are driving you wild,
Every so often just think like a child.
The soft wind blowing, caresses my face.
The calm, the beauty, how I love this place.

Gary Rich

Love's Realms

For Pamela, My Inspiration, My One
Love doth live, in realms of darkness and light,
Soaring to the mountain's peak, shining its might,
Sinking into valleys, caressing shadows of dark,
Awaiting new birth, suffering without a remark,

Oft lifting the heart, pounding out glorious song,
Or falling into abyss, wondering where it went wrong,
Nothing is as magnificent, nothing more hard,
Like rolling the dice, or flipping the card,

Yes, love is a paradox, bringing us joy,
Healing our wounds, or perhaps just a ploy,
Yet nothing can replace it, nor make us complete,
Emptiness may come, but no other's so sweet,

So raise your head high, and remember this word,
You can crawl like a worm, or soar like a bird,
To receive what you need, be willing to give,
Without the passion of love, you can't truly live!

James Hook

I Miss You

This is the story of what I was doing
After you called me at Christmas morning.
I dreamt 'bout you one night
I think it was on 26th's night.
That you called me again for the second
Unfortunately, it was just an illusion. . . .
From that moment I really wanted to call you
But I can't do anything ever.
'Cuz I don't know how to call you
You didn't give me your phone number.
Although I go to bed so late,
Like I have a natural wake-up call,
I always wake up around seven and eight
Just waiting for your next call.
This is a poem just for you
I wrote it 'cuz I really miss you
And I don't know what else I can do
I'm just letting my words run in blue.
Just let you know that all of these things are true.
Believe it or not, it's up to you. I miss you.

Budianto Suhwayudi

Dream Catcher

Caught within your gentle webbed fingers,
Tucked in between the dancing stones and graceful beads,
Lie waiting sparkling panoramas of glittering yesterdays,
Glimmers of promising tomorrows.
Are these to be my dreams tonight?
Let your powerful magic pull me inside.
Share far places and unexplored horizons trapped in soft slumber.
Carry me into wide vistas and hidden corners,
Into dreams of wisdom, visions of Nature's peace and power,
To the grace of gentle slopes and the strength of rising hills.
Let me sail to distant lands and over foreign seas,
Scale ancient mountains and fly through starry galaxies yet unnamed.
In your mystic hold, I will climb ancient trees of knowledge
And soar high across azure skies and into rainbow arches.
In your web, anything is possible;
Slip me inside your secret spell, and together we shall fly away.
Catch my dreams.

Susan Brozenec

My Worst Nightmare

I want to recover
They say I'm in recovery
It's like being awake in the middle of your worst nightmare
Whoever is with me please help me
Don't lie to me
Recovery never happens . . . Right?
Oh, but it does and you will recover
OK, so I'm in recovery
In my mind i don't have clean time
But I'm in recovery
It's like being awake in the middle of your worst nightmare
Whoever is with me just try to help me
What really happens here?
We don't really recover . . . Right?
I can't go on
Oh yes, you can and you will recover

Marian Palmer

The Beach

A cool breeze runs across ivory sands
The oceans crests and valleys seen solely by moonlight.
Two figures sit holding each others hands,
But the darkness conceals both their bodies from plain sight.

Distance and darkness; the same in effect.
Though a place such as this is shared in both our hearts.
To this place with you I should wish to defect
And stay there through the night together to never part.

'Til the time and place when our hands shall meet
This beach at night shall be a haven for feeling.
I will go there and think of you and greet
The joy and enlightenment with which I am dealing.

A cool breeze runs across ivory sands
The oceans crests and valleys seen solely by moonlight
Together as one our souls will expand
And our meeting will be much more than merely, plain sight.

Michael Richardson

Forget Me Not

As I begin to write with intentions to share my thoughts,
  Thoughts . . . that words have yet to tame.
How obvious they are, but yet hardly seen,
  The feelings I've had in this tiny time frame.

As I take the risk
  of losing touch over time,
The risk is not losing touch in our hearts,
  But yet in our minds.

Though I leave writing my last words,
  with tears I have fought,
I say this and only this,
  Forget Me Not.

Sarah Burt

Resolution for Writers

A clean new slate to fill each day,
Writing His words with all you say,
Take some time to help a new writer,
To make their day oh, so much brighter.
Remove the bitterness of rejection slips,
As their critiquing will be your tips.
Cut each month into 28, 30, or 31 parts,
Writing each day for a brand new start.
With each day add faith, trust, and hope,
Stir generously with kindness to cope.
Blend with a prayer and one good deed,
Meditating quietly just to succeed.
Season lightly with good spirits and fun,
Mixing well while enjoying the sun.
Pour out your heart on a paper of love,
Written with so much joy from above.
Garnish with a beautiful smile,
To serve the editors in a while.
Top with unselfishness and loads of cheer,
And you're bound to have a Happy New Year.

Donna Rae McCay

Love

The world is always writing about love
And the world is always talking about love . . .
But does everyone really know what love
truly is?

Because love does not come from a piece of
writing
And love does not come from a story
But, yes . . .
Love comes from the inside . . .
Love comes from the heart . . .

Love is as small as picking up a piece of
trash from the street . . .
And love is a big as refusing to fight in
a war . . .

But no matter what love is to you,
It won't do any good to simply write or
talk about it . . .
It takes something from inside . . .
Something from the heart . . .

Because that is what love is. . .
And that is what will make a difference
To you . . .
And to the world.

Paola Horevicz

Acapella in Blue

They say: "You get what you pay for,"
How come I never do?
I'm just like a chameleon,
Now a deep shade of blue.

Trials and tribulations,
I guess they'll never end,
Optimism is dangerous, but my only friend.
'Cause hopes can always go up,
But, tears can only come down,
My time here ain't forever,
And there's no place I'm bound.

They say everyone gets their 15 minutes of fame,
But, what if I gave mine away?

Sad songs bring me comfort,
Just why, I don't know,
I get high and sing along,
It's a familiar place to go.

Brian Hitchcock

The Road of Life

Living life to its fullest
Is often a difficult ride,
There are many forks in the road
And many things you must realize.
The road of life is often boring
If you always take the right path,
But when you venture off the road
You'll find a grand life that lasts.
Making mistakes is common on the road of life,
But learn from them and you will see
That living good is not a strife.
The people that don't learn from their mistakes
Often don't finish the journey,
But become old men, depressed and ashamed,
And fear they won't wake up in the morning.

Justin Green

Your Love

Your love comes to me from deep within,
The boundaries it knows none.
From morning dews to evening winds,
We become but one.
I feel it coursing through my veins
as it slowly grows,
This love is like the gentle rain,
everlasting as it goes.
As you hold me deep
within the memory of your heart,
Know that I truly do believe, for all times,
our love will never part.
And cherishing it deep within my soul,
as I truly do,
It stays with me forevermore,
because it comes from you.

Rose Sandlin

rivers of sand

yearn, yearn for the moment when i shall be one with the
ocean for i am the river without the rain. sail, sail away from
the land where i am consumed by the waters which flow
through my veins. as i dwell amongst the wreckage of
medieval bridges, and the sun has been sheltered beneath a
horizon of fear, a sky of hope . . . a smoldering burst of
altruistic satisfaction. begin, begin the lustful cries of the
devils beneath me. i gleam not for i am the sun that has risen,
but the drying waters shall soon be rivers of sand.

ben galang

Darkness

The light shone warm and bright and clear
On all in my life that I held most dear.
Beckoning, signing, leading me through
A life most beloved, tender, and true,
It increased in joy, flickered in sorrow,
Yet held a promise for tomorrow.

The light shone dim and soft, but clear
Through many a sigh and many a tear.
It helped me up and led me on
The path of maturity and wisdom, upon
Which I learned many a lesson of life:
To be happy with little, to avoid and hate strife.

The light shone low and small and unclear
For many a month and many a year.
I struggled along, head held high with pride,
Without my light as a soothing guide.
Slowly, finally, my light revived,
And because through misery I'd survived,
I couldn't resist a triumphant shout . . .
And, then, suddenly, it went out—!

Yasmine Khan

There Is Someone Who Cares

Feeling lonely and scared, one day I decided
To look for somebody that felt like I did.
Walking silently and sad, my eyes on the floor,
I felt that I wanted to die, live no more.
But all of a sudden a cry at my sight, told me,
There is someone that needs you tonight.
There goes my sadness, my wishing to die,
For there was no time to think of my life.
A box with a baby but no one to care,
I knew at that moment I needed to be there.
Soon I realized that it was not true,
My life was not sad I didn't want to die,
But someone up higher, He only knew why.
Sometimes I keep asking, why me, Lord, why me?
And I feel the answer coming inside me,
I needed you child, I needed you free.
And I understand the truth of all is, if I was not there,
Where that baby would be.

Nydia Ocasio

The Busy Bee

The season, where it all begins
Yes, it's spring time again,
The beauty is all around
Just open your eyes, it can be found,
It is that time of the year
Where you could silently shed a tear,
So, I think I will stay awhile
Sit back, relax, with a smile.

Lance Spencer

Good-Bye

Friends are like flowers in life's garden.
God really loves His garden
And He picked you to come home.
In the beauty of your smiles
You suffered hard and long.
A healing stem was not to be found
So God said, "Please come home,
A touch of understanding you always gave to others."
Now you're the music in the trees,
And the smile on sunny flowers.
Just a thought of sweet remembering
A memory sad and true.
Our friendship was a good one,
I'll always think of you.
Good-bye, dear friend.

Pamela P. Corrigan

Young Black Girl Child

Young black girl child, so young and so true
Young black girl child, you hold God's gift inside of you,
a gift to produce, a gift to reproduce,
our mothers told us so we've got to take heed—
there's a struggle going on
And you've got to face it head on,
taking no shorts, no if's, and's, or but's,
to get ahead you can never give up!
running; buggin'; forget about lovin' . . .
living in a fantasy, not wanting to face reality,
that in us we have the ability to create a nation
of kings and queens, righteous and notorious,
from that which we came, we can once regain
So let's take it back now ya'll
We were the queens of the motherland
Brought here on a boat to the promise land
All I see is a corrupted land
Trying to make it in a no black mans land!
Aids! drugs! guns! and violence!
without the black man, our race will soon be silenced

Angel Daves

The Road Not Seen

Many paths diverge in a blackened soul.
And fearing I'd find not even one,
And thus be trapped, soon crushed as coal,
I groped with hands and face for goal—
Some edge, a wall, a crack, yet none.

Then struck the darkness with my fist
Dense anger summoned to smother pain.
For hope devoured, at last no longer missed
Colored sadness frozen, dull and pissed
Beneath abandoned shadows, a soul-silent stain.

There lost to moon and sun I lay
Where ropes and chains would useless be,
And threats and slaps no longer sway.
For pulse and breath were bound away
Less life dilute forsook its journey.

Still . . . waits within a spark not lit
That crawls toward sounds and textures keen.
And stretches to touch how deep its pit.
And should that spark collide against the Ancient Wit,
Fate could again ignite my soul to travel on a road not seen.

Gwendolyn A. Pincomb

Sad Eyes

Sad eyes watching you all the time.
Whose eyes are they you ask?
Who watches you so carefully?
Is it that you don't know,
or do you not care?
Those eyes see you walk through the world,
as if everything in it was created for you.
Don't you know?
You ask whose eyes are so cruel,
to make you nervous and curious.
But you have eyes of your own.
Things are not made for you,
but things are made because of you.
Your eyes are filled with hate,
and those eyes can see it.
Whose eyes are watching you ask.
But don't you already know?
They are the eyes of one who is concerned,
who wants you to be changed.
They are my eyes.

Natalie Stratemeier

Show Your Soul

Show me your soul, I will not judge.
I only wish to know you, to feel behind your mask,
to what really lies beneath.
A place few have ever touched,
free from chains or walls.
Open the door, I will not betray your trust.
Don't be afraid, for I know it to be hard
To show dreams, fears, and your deepest thoughts,
even to be yourself.
No matter how far you run away,
or the toughness of your shield,
I see the need inside your eyes to reveal your soul.
I expect no changes from either of us;
it's not your perfection that draws me,
It's what you have deep inside.
Like a plant that needs water
it will take patience and time.
I'm willing to wait; I can see the blossoms.
Show me your soul, I wish not to judge,
only to know you beneath the mask.

Manfred Schmidt

"A Sweet Song in My Heart"

A sweet song flowing in my heart
with dear old words that will never part!
I held them then, and I hold them now
as I sing in the breeze my sweet love vow.

You're my heart, my soul, my love,
the skin on your face as white as a dove.
Your pretty, sensitive, and caring eyes
make me positive my decision was wise.

The day was approaching when we would marry
and I looked in your eyes, and said your heart I do carry.
Your gentle touch, your caressing arms,
making me laugh with all your charms.

Just to let you know, you are my life.
I am so very happy to be your wife.
As I say this now, as I did then still so true,
Always remember that I love you!

Melissa Warwick

Why a Rose

A rose soothes the mind and hardest of hearts,
    A rose is happy, yet sad;
A rose is tranquil in the nature of being.

    A rose is an endless beauty
        whose countenance you admire from afar.
A rose is a symbol of peaceful ambiance.

A rose is a spiritual aperture
    that reigns throughout the land.
A rose is a gift sent from the Almighty.

A rose makes an enchanted melody;
It creates a fragrance sweeter than perfume.
A rose can heal the wounds of mankind.

The soul of a rose is a gentle whisper,
expressing a tangible delight,
    that poignantly jaunts in the wind.

A rose like no other I long to caress,
    like those before me;
The aura of a rose is a joy to behold.

Juanita Martin

Love Fantasy

I want to kiss you all the way,
I want to love you 'til the judgement day.
I want to feel you every day and every night,
I want to taste you so I could feel all right.

I know I sound selfish, but that is only love
talking through my mouth and every part of me.
I can't stop myself from wishing to have you
everywhere and every time right here.

I lose every sense when your arm wraps around me
and when your kisses cover my body and my face.
It's like a warm rain and freezing ice at the same time,
and it's turning this world into a wonderful place.

A place where all I need is you,
a place where all I wish is you,
a place where you'll be my reality and my dream,
my hope, fear and all I shall do.

Come on, open the doors of that Heaven
where our love will be able to float in rivers and seas.
Take me there and lock the doors forever
so we can love each other and always be together.

Maja Karnik

The Excellence

The excellence unfound
Behind the sorry homeward bound

The excellence around the corner
Like the summer coming nearer

The excellence is not perfection
Like perfection is not free of the ascension

The excellence is non-existent
Like the never coming star in the distance

The excellence must not be
For now, it is obvious to me

The excellence does not know
Which way will it next go.

The excellence,
friend or foe?

Eric Campbell

'Til Today

Once upon a time, I was filled with joy.
Love was all I needed everything else I just had to avoid.
Stubborn and blinded to the fact that I'm left in the cold.
Willowing away my heart is empty, with no one to hold.
Once a girl, now a fool, for losing you.
Portraying I am happy in my own way.
'Til today who am I fooling, I'm missing you.
What should I do? What should I say?
Either way. I was happy yesterday.
Because I had you.

Deseara Watson

Crimson

A burning rage
The fire inside
A crimson inferno lighting the sky
The things she does to fuel my pain,
encourage my hate,
give me place to lay blame
So desperate to hide
Needing to run
To escape my assailant
Before she is done,
gutting my soul,
eating my pride,
breaking my spirit
and dimming my light
As hard as I try to escape, to flee
Its so hard to break away when that person is me.

Paula Kozak

Society

Many nights I spend dreaming the impossible dream
reaching for a rainbow
wanting to hold you near
yearning for your touch

stolen moments can never be enough
a brush of a hand
a glimpse
a smile
cannot replace that which I long for

our worlds keep us apart
we fight a desperate battle
to stay in touch with our feelings
can we hold on?
will we survive this test of society?
I hold you dear in my heart
and through it all
I will love you

Leanne M. Scott

A Lemon's Crush

A lemon's crush
    splits open before the world.
Its tangy bittersweet tears
    fill the cups of forgetfulness.
Its uncensored smell
    claims the lives of the damned.
Its undaunted love
    caresses the hearts of the unborn.
The lemon's crush falls through the floor
    trying to stop its unyielding cry.
It stops before
    kisses the wind
      and moves after.

Michele Critzman

My Poems

Oh poems, my poems, my desperate rhymes
Words, fit into hopeless lace
My painful confessions of terrible crimes
My wish to conquer new space

Oh poems, my poems, a powerful thread
That keeps me in this Universe
That helps me to live through the pain and defeat
Which grow not better but worse!

My quiet denial of obsolete rules
My fight for impossible goal
Oh poems, my poems, my accurate tools
The way of expressing my soul

The channel, that lets me declare my mood
As soft and as rigid, as clay
Oh poems, my poems, still not understood
I trust, you will find your way!

Anna Kozynenko

My Dolly and Me

I take my best friend where ever I go,
because my best friend I love so.
Never two closer friends will there be
then the two of us, my dolly and me.
I take her to bed with me every night.
When I feel scared I squeeze her tight.
When morning comes we start our day,
my dolly and me, we're on our way.
Where will we go? Or what shall we do?
Since I can't take my dolly to school!
I guess she will wait for me here at home.
My dolly and me will be so alone!
One day I know I will put her away.
Locked in a trunk and there she will stay.
'Til I bring her out for my girls to see,
and tell of the two of us, my dolly and me.

Carol Hall

I Surrender

I take your hand and place it upon my heart.
I knew you'd be mine forever, right from the start.
Your skin so smooth and expression so, so bright.
From the second I saw you, I knew I had to fight.
Looking at you now has made it all worthwhile.
With tears streaming down my face, I can't help but smile.
Slowly and gently I place your hand back by your side.
I sill can't believe you had to die.
But without you I have no will to live,
And for you, my love, my life I give.
I lean over to kiss your lips so tender.
I close my eyes and to you I surrender.

Eric Denette

Cobwebs

Where were you when I wept and my soul was laid bare
Were you deep inside yourself and unable to care?

There are shadows that engulf both my heart and my mind—
Forever seeking answers that seem so hard to find—

Where were you when my heart cried out for you to care?
Were you locked up in thoughts you weren't able to share?

Love is a mystery and few find the key—
That can unchain their hearts—open eyes that now see—
Yes, love is in each of us and if we allow—
it can change our lives not tomorrow, but now

Lisa Meier

What Is Love?

Love is beautiful in my eyes
It is the excitement of winning a Nobel Peace Prize

Love is the smell of a dozen of flowers
It makes your heart melt and keep you thinking for hours

Could this really be happening or just a phase
Have I really found the one I'll always crave?

What is love we often may say
Until we find ourselves in a strange place

Where we cannot escape and be by ourselves
Then we come back to reality and say I hear bells

Of the wedding day you've always dreamed of
And then we found the answer to the question
of what is love?

Melissa Hardaway

My Angel

Angels are glorious creatures that I believe exist.
I know she has possession of their essence,
For her tender touch feels like refreshing mist.
No wonder I am honored by her presence.

Her golden hair shines brighter than the sun,
Which brings every mortal soul to their knees.
A heavenly voice like hers there is none
That can bring my tensions to ease.

She's a gem that's one of a kind,
Which with time I've come to truly cherish.
"My Angel," the greatest treasure I can find
That from my heart she will never perish.

Only her beauty could give a rose shame,
For she portrays every quality of her name.

Luis Gutierrez

If I Had a Wish

If I were granted one wish today,
I'd wish I could be there to watch you play.
To hop and skip, laugh and run,
How I wish we could go and have some fun!!

There is an emptiness down deep in my heart,
That's been there since we were torn apart.
And sometimes it's hard to play their game,
But I only have myself to blame!!

If you could feel my love for you,
You'd see that part of me is missing too.
Please be happy in everything,
Embrace each joy that life may bring!!

I fear one day you'll forget about me,
But in my heart you'll always be.
And those times you feel that I don't even care,
Just look in your heart and I'll be there!!

Tina Popejoy

The Wind

Dedicated to my parents, Paul and Elizabeth Windmill
The cool wind rustles the trees. Red, yellow,
and orange leaves fly by; the color of Autumn.
Then the cold wind comes and the sky is
filled with snow. The red, yellow, and orange
leaves are covered with a big white blanket.
A few months later the hot sun comes out and
melts the big blanket. The green grass starts
to show, with patches of the blanket lying
around. In one more month all the snow is gone.
The flower buds starts to show. The warm
wind comes to shake the flower petals and
the green grass. As the breeze stops we get
ready for Autumn once again.

Betsy Windmill

As Time Goes On

Once upon a yesterday, we were children.
We played, laughed, sang songs, and even fought,
skinning a knee or two.
As we grew, we shared in each other's joy and pain,
shed a few tears and wiped them away.
We are bound together like the threads of a woven
tapestry, sharing one's mind, heart and soul.
We have taken a journey into adulthood, each
becoming our own self, expressing individuality.
The years have passed and we have grown apart,
but there is one common bond that keeps us together, Love.
Although we no longer share our yesterdays,
we have our memories to treasure not just for today,
but Forever.

Anna Logan

Forever

When I think of the wind, so softly blowing,
   I'll think of you
When I think of the soothing sunrays shining
   down on me, I'll think of you.
When I think of the stars sparkling bright as
   can be, I'll think of you.
When I think of a red rose, soft and sweet as
   nectar, I'll think of you.
When I think of Heaven, the two of us together
   happier than anything, I'll think of you
   and me together in love forever.

Jeremy Cove

Trailblazer

For my mother, who dared to blaze her own trail
how could you have known
this midnight trail would ever be
littered with cherished dreams, sown
lifetimes ago, now mistaken for debris?
and how chilling it must be for you
to find that hardship kindly graced
its shoe print upon every flower that grew,
lying flat against this trail they once laced
jasmine-kissed southern winds seem to invite
the geese earlier with each fading autumn sun
would you fly into the flickering twilight
if you had nowhere left to run?
moonlight rain floods the tide pools in eyes
that dream of lighting up the earth
but dare to shine behind stratocumulus skies
with no stars to help, what is it even worth?
then the jealous moon reprimands the betrayal
by his traitors who've been your light so far
and draws back the curtains to watch you fail
revealing instead the trailblazer you are

Misbah Faheem

Pain

Why won't the pain go away?
I forgave you to make it end.
The pain hurts more every day.
Why won't my poor heart mend?
I want this all to end for good.
No more easy outs.
I'm gonna do what you should.
You shouldn't have had any doubts.
If you don't know how I feel by now,
Then why is this worth fighting for?
If you don't love me I'll get by somehow,
Even though it makes my heart sore.
I can't and won't stop loving you.
I don't understand why there was any doubt.
There's just one thing for me to do.
I'll never stop loving you,
But I need reassurance that you still care.
Will you always love me?
Can I rely on you to always be there?
If not, then forever leave me be.

Laura Conroy

"Born to Win"

A warrior of such many don't understand.
More than a conqueror nothing less than a man.
Ten thousand soldiers ready to go to war.
I have beaten ten thousand men and I'm hungry for ten thousand more.
I stand high on a mountain alone if I must.
But I will not be defeated and I shall not lose trust.
I will fight a warrior's battle and give my very best.
And when it come my time to die I will die a warrior's death.
My faith is my shield designed with my crest,
that I wear fighting battles branded across my chest.
I never slumber for a moment my enemy is close at hand.
I must ready myself at moment's notice to fight and take a stand.
So bring all you have and fight if you desire,
but there has never lived a warrior that could quench my desire.
The bell in the beginning signals the fighters to begin,
but the last man standing is the one "Born to Win."

Buford Jones

The Girl

I see the writing on the wall and think away,
about how much I loved that girl and remember. . .

The girl who touched me in such a way,
That made my heart so warm and tender.

Her hair so elegantly blonde and curly,
So bright and smooth that day

That day she so lovingly held onto me,
While her flowing hair mimicked the yellow sun rays.

As she looked up to me from my loving arms,
Her face was so beautiful, kind, and nice

She smiled, flaunting her pearly whites like charms,
My, my they reflect like glacier ice.

As she stood to leave, exposing her luxurious body,
I was struck in awe admiring her curvaceous form

It was a struggle for her to leave me,
'Cause her body was so out of the norm.

I said good-bye, I Love you, and will miss,
She then paused and turned all the way around

She approached with the aromatic breeze and laid me a kiss,
I remember saying, "I Love that girl" as I hit the ground.

Jim Boguslawski

The Birthday Present

A birthday present
A small young child
So tiny and fragile
Being passed around for all to see

When she gets to the grandmother
The young child smiles
Everyone sings in unison
Happy birthday to you both

The child grew up
The grandmother was so proud
She lived her life to the fullest
And hopes the child does too

When the grandmother died
the child was broken
'Cause on the day she was born
She was to be her grandma's present forever

Amanda Spudich

Dreams

Have you ever heard
   that you dream hidden feelings?
Actions and desires dreamt
   identify your life's true meanings.

Your dreams show you what you want
   and what you want to be.
They point out
   what in life we can't see.

There's no one there to tell you
   what path to take.
It's only your heart and soul
   and whatever decisions they may make.

I want to be happy
   about the choices I make.
And from my heart and dreams
   should come the advice I take.

Natalie Burt

There Is a Dawn

There is a dawn that offers vision,
Yet its light may never reach our eyes
If in the night we run ever westward
More quickly than the sun may rise

For in the dawn a man stands naked,
In plain sight he bares both good and bad
So he may fight to remain in shadow
In fear of losing what he never had

There is hope in an honest moment
Wisdom grows, sharing joy and pain,
Yet when they flow we may grow to fear them
But in the fear we can't remain

There is a path that offers freedom,
But it's steep and filled with fear of pain
Yet if we keep honest with each foot step
In freedom we can remain

Matthew Groff

If Only She Knew. . . .

If only she knew I was alive,
I always know when she arrives,
My friends say I'm out of my league,
She's so beautiful I'll never get fatigue,
She has the most gorgeous face,
I feel like a mental-case,
She's white as milk,
Her skin is soft as silk,
She is the most popular of all the girls,
I'd buy her a necklace of pearls.

David Garcia

The Orchards of Lily

September 1972
When the orchards of Lily bloomed and bore
Life was so simple, 'twas all I wished for'.
My Mother was Love . . . laced with strength;
Daddy was Iron . . . veneered in down.
We collected our apples, pears, and nuts,
Gathering them home to our rampart of love.
My brothers and sisters . . . children and grown,
Shared in our pleasures, laughter, and tears.
Youth exuberant lived ALL the days,
Love was our allay . . . who could intrude?
Callow and innocent days passed unseen
And the unknown Intruder . . . I knew not his name,
Slowly appeared and with certainty came.
His name is Time, bringing Death and Change. . . .

The orchards of Lily bloom no more,
And that Strength and that Iron are laid to rest.

The cider sweet and our family tall,
And the orchards of Lily are good to recall.
Time is a circle moving ever 'round,
Nothing is lost, only more life found.
Love is forever, it does not cease,
Death cannot claim it, for love is a lease
We give away . . . and forever keep.

Patricia Alvis-Clark

Transparent

Free me of the ball and chain I thought that I let go of.
I unlocked it years ago and yet it still weighs me down
and I fear it is too late.
Love, oh, love, that glorious thing, that painful thing.
Ha ha, do not brake the rules. . . .
pressured it may be under this heavy ball and chain,
but I hold the key I thought I let go of long ago.
And now love, ah love, has taken its course of revenge.
This battlefield of love creates too many scars for me.
I fear I love too late and soon the image will clear. . . .
like crystal, I can be transparent too, but I will not
be in the eyes of the beholder, and wonder what could have been.
What a fool I would be if I went running back.
Keep your head held high
until all your problems go away in the rhythm of my fingers.
Flow with the life around you. Be with the world beside you.
As fast as the beating in your heart,
the challenge in your gut has passed you by
and you spend your life catching up
or maybe transparent can be good. . . .

Meghan Kirsic

Tree

unfairly Earth bound we stand.
firmly planted feet upon the ground,
turned deep within our dreams.
we stretch to strain the tender tenuous strand,
stolen away within ourselves.
we dare aspire to one day reach the sky,
that distant place were eagles delve.
all the while those who've tried,
at our feet long forgotten sadly lie.
locked away in some dark and cavernous place,
we stretch forth and scratch its face.
blood let loose the rain it falls.
lightning shrieks with thunderous bawls
as it rips across the sky.
the spell is cast setting us firmly in our disgrace,
sealed away inside this hell.
with depths unknown and dark as space,
screaming silently to once again be free.
you know us well you know us as . . .
    TREE

Mike Williamson

Blind Truth

I promised that I'd keep it short
I promised I would not cry,
I promised that even after you're gone
I'd still go on and try.
I promised that when you walked out that door
Everything would be okay,
I promised that I'd be happy again
I promised my life away.
I lied when you asked if I was okay
I lied when I said I was fine,
I lied when I had to hold back the tears
I lied when it came time.
I lied when I said you don't mean a thing
I lied that I'm happy you're gone,
I lied that everything is resolved
I lied that nothing is wrong.
I said I would be good
No matter what you did,
I guess I can never replace you
But without you I know not how to live.

Tara Gander

Life Is a Gift

Life is a gift
sometimes taken for granted.
Some feel they've done great.
Some wish they could re-plant it.
Others keep seeking and never find a path
while a pitiful few spend their life in wrath.
Some know what's going to happen before it begins.
Some never thought about it even after it ends.
Many treasure what they've got, many feel cheated.
Many spend most of their life waiting to be needed.
What you do with your life is not up to me,
but listen to what I've said and choose carefully.

John Barnett

Everything Has Changed

My strength is leaving me tonight
I don't know how much longer I can fight
We are slowly losing the war
I just cannot stand the pain anymore
Every day I'm surrounded by the living dead
I'm drowning in all of the lies that have been said
The only thing that I can clearly see
Is all the ignorance surrounding me
There are people killing all the time
Now it seems okay, but it used to be a crime
Yes, now it seems everything is condoned
Every day children are born and left alone
Reminders of the homeless litter the ground
Atrocity everywhere, just look around
Too concerned with the rat race and trying to win
We're destroying our world with our sin

David Haslam

Bliss

Religion is the opium for the masses—
It trashes the mind like any narcotic—
Psychotic messiahs, karmas, and dali lamas
Create hallucinations of Heaven and reincarnation
Credulous beings plague the world—
I hurl accusations, but I too emulate
Into this brainwashed state for comfort
My views distort . . .report of a higher being
What am I seeing? A paragon or propaganda?
I too am seeking the guidance of Shiva, Christ, and Buddha—
I too fall into this, in reality—
Ignorance Is bliss.

Tanu Sahota

Mom

You gave me life.
You're always uplifting others,
Especially your children and cheering us along.
A blessing to all who come into your midst.
Assure us of tomorrow when the day before wasn't so great.
Inspiring us to do our best at all times.
Gracious host to all our friends and foes.
A loving shoulder to lean on
Caring to our ills and wants with love.
Your smile warms my heart when needed.
Your laughter always lingering
when I'm far away.
You were my first teacher
Who taught me about life's journey.
Out of them all, Mom.
You're number one!
I could not, would not have another
only you, Mom.
You are truly one in a million!

Cynthia Frazier

Chains of Ignorance

What direction must a man face
To know he is pointed in the right direction
Toil in thy labor, again and again
How long must he go to realize there is no end

Pay the piper out of everything you earn
And still he comes for more
How often will the piper tell us
That paying him is all we have in store

Read the Bill and know what is right
They change the Bill so we may never know
How great is their
Might

Climb the cage, test the bars
Live your life
And don't question ours
Take the freedom they say is your right

Be smart, be wise
Raise your children, work your job
Question authority, yank that chain
And find out how really free you are

David Miller

Existence

Moving through Time with forgotten grace
as Life stays on its own fractured pace.
Coming to crossroads, again and again,
but lacking the memory to know where you've been.

Seeking a leader, a teacher, a guide—
fighting the Voice that speaks from inside.
Dreaming false truths, living true lies,
trying to see what's beneath your disguise.

Walking through fogs of pain and despair
to just catch a breath of Spiritual air.
Pushing your mind past the walls you have made,
as you force bad perceptions to seemingly fade.

Losing good wrongs and finding bad rights,
suffering from the Past's emotional bites.
Looking towards darkness, searching for light
as inverted perspectives color your Sight.

Wisdom's razor edge rips open your soul
as you finally arrive at the intended goal.
Life's lessons, they vary, and depend on your view,
for they become much easier when you're just being you.

Robert Rogers

Thank You

For all those who would listen,
This is not meant for you.

Thank you for turning your back on me,
Thank you for not caring.

Your impudence has shot down my pride,
And your ignorance has slashed my ego.

Not many would know,
And fewer would even care.

The void of my life rests in your hands,
Because you don't even know it's there.

You have molded my life more than you'll ever know,
My character will withstand your careless nescience.

I have no choice but to forget all of you,
From this agony I thank every one of you,
Thank you, my insolent friends.

Hollye Fain

Ocean of Unwanted Love

I'm lost in the sea of my own questions.
Drowning by the waves of unfulfilled promises.
Poseidon bestows no mercy for a fool,
only quakes with laughter at my folly.
He and father time gave a lesson well taught
and continue to teach with a stern hand.
This cruelty renders me powerless.
Helpless in this ocean of unwanted love.
Encompassed by an unreturned wanting
that tears the pulsating heart from my chest.
Crimson mixes with green
as my neglected vessel sinks ever further.
Falling slowly to the cold depths where failure resides.
Finally reaching the ocean floor.
Forever resting, but not in peace.

Jason Carnrike

The Picnic

'Round a long corner down a winding lane
We traveled together on the same plain
With wind in our ears and hair flowing down
Stopped at a bright clearing with brook flowing down

The blanket was outspread and the food was right there
The picnic we yearned for was now really here
We gazed and we wondered was this really true
That this picnic was just for two

Hours went by without words being spoken
Just the smiles of two people not to be broken
Without hesitation there under the sun
Two hearts embrace becoming as one

John Jacobsen

Them

You look straight at them, but you see nothing.
Look closer.
They have to be taken into existence.
It's what you may want.
To be in a mold.
A mold of you.
A mold of a double edged sword.
They do what you want and you persecute.
They do what you don't want and you drown them in you.
Thou shalt not stay.
Thou shalt not go.
For thou art bound.
Bound by your own prison of mind.
A mind of maze.
A maze of poison.
Stay your ground, but do not war for theirs.

Virginia Gallivan

The Ice Storm

Inspired by the 1998 ice storm in Montreal
I gaze at the standing tree,
shape changed, deformed,
branches hanging hopelessly
for the life they will not live
but in dream,
covered with buds of children
never to be born in a celebration of green.

With my eyes downcast, I shed a tear,
in mourning for the dying,
in suffering for the once beautiful tree.

Then I look up anew with searching eyes,
beholding the entirety of the tree.
I see branches fallen to their doom, yet!
I see branches standing green.

Life goes on, I think, life goes on . . .
. . . like the rising branches of the everlasting tree

Parissa Zohari

Recipe for Tenderness

Look into the eyes of someone you love
Only when you cannot talk to them
Think of what you would say
If it were the last day you were to be alive

Look at a picture of your best friend
Be sure it is of a time you will never forget
Remember when they moved away
And you never spoke to them again

Look at your grandfather
During his open casket viewing
Remember the two of you laughing
Then behold him motionless

Now you know Tenderness

Joseph Grigg

I Am a Girl

I am a girl with wavy brown hair
(but sometimes it's blonde streaked or blue)

I am a girl who is 5 feet 6 inches tall
(but sometimes I wear platform shoes so I look taller)

I am a girl who likes to laugh and smile
(but sometimes my smile hides my tears)

I am a girl who always has music playing in the background
(but sometimes it's just the music in my head)

I am a girl who likes to lie outside and look at the night sky
(but sometimes I'm a little afraid of the dark)

I am a girl who lives and loves and FEELS
(but sometimes I cover those feelings up to keep from getting hurt)

I am a girl who loves her life just the way it is
(but sometimes I want to be Marcia Brady, just for a day)

I am a sixteen year old girl
(but sometimes I feel more like a 30 year old woman)

I am a girl who has hurt and been hurt
(but I know it will all turn out okay)

I am a girl.

Nathalie White

Of Youth and Old Age

Music swims about our ears,
Mellow tunes of yester-blue,
And in the garden midget ferns
Flaunt their fine-leafed fronds,
Eternal evergreens.

No one listens to those tunes
Which swayed our souls like lullabies,
And now still fill our minds
With nostalgic dreams of yore.

Our youth has flown,
Is lost forevermore
Vibrant, glowing, flushed at dawn,
Burnt in a glory of its own
Now grown tranquil and withdrawn.

But youth still sings in mellow tunes,
In our dreams of yester-blue,
And the fine-leafed garden ferns
Are still eternal evergreens.

Connie Laurent

Huntington on a Thursday Night

The yellow street lamps
Beam themselves into my window
Like lightening, striking down my sins.
They wrap themselves around my body,
Hissing and spewing;
Serpents on the prowl of a broken heart.
I can still taste the residue
Of your dirty, ashtray kisses.
Your fingertips tangled themselves
In my coal hair; begging my flesh
To be their braille.

Becky Click

Roadblock to Recovery

I like myself' the way I am
There is nothing wrong I can't fix.
I like myself; the way I am
I do the best I can.
I like myself; the way I am
It's not my fault I fail so much.
I like myself; the way I am
I could do better, but no one helps.
I like myself; the way I am
Even though I am seldom understood.
I like myself; the way I am
I don't care what others say.
I like myself; the way I am.
Just accept me for who I am.
I like myself; the way I am
I only have to answer to me.
I like myself; the way I am
My shoulders stoop from all the blame.
I like myself; the way I am
I'd rather die, than change my ways.

Cathy A. Seago

God's Tears

I heard a sound last night
I thought it must be God crying
Those must have been His teardrops
Falling on my windowpane
I thought my heart would break

I stood and watched that flood
I thought it was all sorrow
And then I realized
His tears would wash away the pain
And make the way for a brighter day

Sandy Baker

Our Mothers

The four winds blew misty clouds about my head:
Whitish pale grey with silver lining.
There was a calmness within the hues.
A brighter light was approaching,
so bright it was blinding to gaze at.
A voice broke the silence; like thunder it manifested before me.

"I'm the beginning of all things. You're but clay in my hands.
I witnessed your birth; Your mother smiled lovingly
as she cuddled you in her arms.
Her whole reason for existing was your creation.
All was created for this reason.
Such a gift was promised from the beginning.
I created everything that was created.
And now I breath in the air of my own creation.
Mother I have come to save you and man of their transgressions.
Not by the flesh, but by the blood I'll shed in their place.

I've come to die in your place
so the spirit can live in all my children,
to teach man to pray once again,
build the new city from Heaven on Earth, and purify everyone's soul.
I must return to my father and open the gates of Heaven for you.
So when you witness a child's birth remember we are new;
we are angels and immortality is a reality."

Dear mother I'll be home again:
Love always your son, Jesus

> *Jeanne Laurin*

Do I Think of You

Do I think of you?
There is not a day that goes by that I don't think of you.
You bring to me a happiness that I long thought was gone.
I dream of your smile, so warm as the sun your lips so lovely as a rose.
Your eyes of blue more pleasing than any rainbow
and brighter than the night sky.
The tender whisper of your voice more appealing than any bird that might sing.
The softness of your skin that I long to touch each and every day.
I think of your compassion, caring, and loving heart
and rejoice that you're in my life.
I think of how you make me feel when I am around you
and what I feel when I am not.
You bring out the best in me because I can be myself with you without any fear.
To say that I love you could never even begin to express my feelings for you.
The closeness we share, the bond we have is only a sign of what two friends can be.
I think of you in so many ways that each and every one
I struggle to bring my tongue to say.
I find myself speechless and jittery in your presence.
Searching for the right thing to say.
You sense my nervousness and completely set me at ease.
You have a deep love and goodness that all can see
and I am thankful that I can share in it.
Yes I think of you!

> *Richard Bryant*

Mountain of Stars

There's a place in time, where my memory recalls,
The faces of angels so fearless and small.
Where a boy of four on a make-believe mountain—
Blonde hair, blue eyes—
Tells his baby sister, "I'll slay that mystical dragon,
And put the stars in your eyes."
Wanting to watch you grow, laugh, learn and play,
Yet having to live without the joyous laughter you provided each day.
So suddenly you were taken by one filled with such anger and pain,
How those of us who stand behind wish to undo that dreadful day.
Our hearts are filled with endless joy
As we hear and speak your names,
And as the years pass by so quickly, our love for you remains.
Your imaginations were without boundaries, your smiles so carefree,
That which will never be lost for you're in our hearts and memories.

> *Penny Lamon*

Class

Out of habit
In t-shirt and jeans
I grease my hands
On chicken wings
While in formal
All around well-fed
And articulate well-wiped
Blessed with immaculate
Knives and forks none
Taking note of me
At the far table end
Perhaps India
Flies at my fingers and lips

> *Barry Cutler*

Walls

It wasn't until I met you that
I realized blue meant cold:
the blue of taps and walls
and eyes,
and not the blue of skies;
the blue of your veins
pulsing under pygmalion skin,
your face a white marble statue
waiting for his gods
to let him in
because you have no say in the matter.
You waited in ice ages,
round and smooth and cold;
he was trapped within shape,
yet you waited
and grew old.

> *Christina Curtis*

Scenic Trails

Let's go ride the trails again.
Take the time to ride at 10:00.
We see a bear, a tiny wren.
A fox trots quickly to her den.

The horses always like to go.
Among tall pine trees in a row.
Where the flowers gently grow.
And there is a bounding doe.

Time to cross a gurgling stream.
Then we hear an eagle scream.
It is peaceful, it would seem.
The beauty here is like a dream.

Worry and tension fade from me.
This is therapy that's free.
We never know what we will see.
A covered bridge or buzzing bee.

Staying home is somehow wrong.
Winter really lasts too long.
Spring will call us like a song.
To the trails where we belong.

> *Pati Harris*

To Kailash

You stood up and you set out
without adding other words.
I looked at you going
slightly curved
with your nervous footstep
rolled in your desperation
lost in your thoughts.
I lighted a cigarette
I didn't want to think.

> *Federico Marsili*

Believers

Watching dew drop from the flowers seems
as if it was blood dripping from Christ's hands.
Feelings of crying out, yet knowing that I couldn't, I couldn't.
Knowing that He was strong and wise,
had the courage of ten men, was true to what he believed.
He sacrificed everything, Himself, for the good of everyone.
Clouds cover the once blue sky now, shutting the sun out, with sounds of rage.
Someone has read my mind and is telling me things can change!
Living in fear every day is something unbearable, yet it happens.
Wanting to be strong as the Savior, yet feeling the coward inside of me.
Little drops of rain began to fall, like tears shed when He died for us.
Hot on the skin, yet refreshing to the touch, giving strength.
Strength to give to others as it was given to me, to share it.
The angry black clouds are floating away and the blue sky
and the bright sun reappears.
The beauty of the day seems to say, that all is possible,
just like the dew drops and the rain, the sun will come out again.
We give and receive Love and understanding and Joy for all,
there really is hope for all of us, BELIEVE! BELIEVE!

Geraldine Stengele

To Paint You a Sunset

Tonight as the sun hangs low in the sky of purples yellows and pinks
I gaze out the window and wait for the moon to come up
Outside the colors deepen getting ready for the pure blackness
Hanging on the sun slips yellow and pink and purple slowly become black

Moments pass as the moon appears behind the oak tree in the front yard
Never has the world seemed so beautiful as I sit here and gaze outside
Releasing a sigh, I close my eyes
Deep inside you're there.

Isabelle Johansson

Soul Mate

I move to the rhythm of my fate while searching for my soul.
Now I sit here writing, the words flowing forth as the blood of my life.
A view into my heart and soul is bared for all to see,
full of love, life and passions untold.
Take to heart the words I have written for they
are the baring of my soul.
There is so much more to life and I am but a lonely light
in the darkness waiting for the one who shall set me free.
Call on me, keeper of my soul.
Let your light shine forth so that as you are I shall be.
One by one let the chains around me unwind.
I send this plea to the gods up above.
In perfect love and trust, send to me what is just.
Throughout time, through our endless lives you have always been there for me.
But in the dawn of this life I search for you still.
Call on me, keeper of my soul, call on me.
Let your light lead me from the Empires of the night.

Nantanit Smith

Passion

It's Hotter then fire!
More powerful then lightning, majestic and dynamic.
Yet it's as gentle as a newborn's touch, tender and sensitive.
It's as distant as our Milky Way, serene and boundless,
But if you listen closely you can here the thunder, mysterious . . . curious?
It can make you strong where you are weak.
It can make you dance and put the rhythm back in your feet.
It can make you shine when it rains on your face.
It can make you keep going even after you've finish the race.
It can motivate lives from young to old and from old-fashioned to new
Yes . . . Majestic, Tender and Boundless is the PASSION!
that lives inside of you . . . listen closely, can you here the thunder?

Lawrence Ferguson

A Butterfly Am I

Dedicated to L.J.—
Thank you for the push you gave me to get well!
Life is so sweet it is complete
because of love it can't be beat
It's beautiful beyond compare
with golden glitters in my hair

The butterfly it does fly free
to live it's life so pain free
A little smile does break free
from a wounded heart that was me

No longer pain to knock at my heart
as the butterfly has a new start
Flutter of wings I do take flight
to reach beyond going to new heights

A cocoon I was for a short time
I broke free and truth did I find
Oh, beautiful it is so full of grace
its beauty shines with lovely lace

Oh, butterfly stay free I say
spread those wings and fly away
Reach for the sky for you will see
A new destiny awaiting me

Linda Ann Behling-Newton

So Grand

Nigel stir the fries
He prepares a meal so grand
The luscious appealing array
Could beat the castle's banquet
Any day
The flavours of exquisite qualities
Appease and delight your
Taste senses
With a fantastic
Well done.

Nigel Pemberton

Now

Written in this backward dream
The oceans spring of innocence
And further down then it may seem
This practiced fear inheritance

Master teach of armored spells
The curtains drawn on yesterday
And after night falls into now
The wind picks up and sweeps away

Delfin Paris, III

Cradle of Rain

Falling from the stem,
calmly of the fold we descend.
On the air of our perfume,
we are the deepest red passion
in the most honorable fashion.
Off tips of thorns are feelings,
tear drops with inward revealings
of arms open wide,
bridges across the divide,
poets beneath windows
dancing love's sweet crescendo.
And we breathe of warm safe places,
casting smiles on longing faces.
Bringing candlelight slow
upon all lovers to know
'Twas to feather rain's nest,
painted a place of rest,
that God cupped our flesh.
So we transcend time a song complete
a cradle of rain ever at your feet.

James Williams

Stars Spell Out Your Name

Time goes by and it gets so hard,
You took away my heart and left my soul scared,
Your thoughts follow me throughout the day and sleep with me at night,
I find myself crying holding my pillow tight,
You found a part of me I hid so deep inside,
And brought out the me I was always trying to hide,
You took away my fears and held me oh, so tight,
You made me fall in love and everything was right,
Even though you are gone I can still hear your voice,
I can see your smiling face and feel your kiss so moist,
You are my passion for life and the joy in my pain,
You're the moon in my sky and the stars spell out your name.

Adriana Vaughn

My Brother and My Friend

(Written for Duane Temple, my brother and my friend)
When I first laid eyes upon you, my young heart was filled with joy,
On Mom's arm so gently cradled, lay a tiny baby boy;
My intent was just to hold you when I pulled you off the bed,
I felt awful when I dropped you, and you bumped your little head.
Days and years we played together while we shared each other's toys,
And I knew my younger brother was the best of little boys;
Oh, sometimes our disagreements turned into a major war,
But each time love found forgiveness in small hearts that stood ajar.
You grew tall and very handsome, games and toys were tucked away,
But the golden cord of childhood binds out hearts this very day;
Although time has quickly vanished, loved ones passed and good-byes said,
You remain my friend and brother now and through the years ahead.
Life's pathways may spread asunder, sometimes ours have been diverse,
But a fragile thread still draws us to a common universe;
When the morning breaks with brightness or the sun sets at day's end,
I'm so thankful that God blessed me with a brother and a friend.

Sharon Temple Akin

The Field

The field in which I go to every week is the most beautiful I've ever witnessed.
An old lady and I play checkers there every other week.
We lay our black and red picnic blanket down on the soft green grass
and eat cookies and drink tea.
Sometimes, if the game goes on for longer than we had anticipated,
we stay in that old field until the sun goes down or the sun comes up;
which ever comes first.
When the game is finally over and we walk home,
she always talks about her husband
and how he was a scientist and a mathematician before he died.
But, even as the old lady talks and talks,
I still think of that field sitting in the night all by itself.
Cold, alone, and without anyone to lay on its grass
or run on its vast lands.
When I get home from the field and get into my bed dress
and in the warmth of my quilt,
I make believe that the field is holding me with its warm grass
and I would have lots of leg room.

Courtney Oliveri

The Ice Snap

An ice snap in the orchard, a blackened apple cracks in half,
leaves the stem on the tree like another bare finger bone—
the mottled fox bounds away, your boot cracked the frozen red mud;
the fox had blood on her muzzle, wind licking your eyes, too sharp.
no one around—lie down; like the crow fallen as a meteor in the snow,
a halo of fleas spread like sun around his tattered pinions.
lie down; sift this stuff through your hands until your veins choke on the swallow,
your hair an ink stain blacking sugar—
Heat leaving your body escapes underground—disturbs a gopher,
who turns in his sleep root hairs dripping phosphic and ironine
into his coat: moth wing ears fold, like shy ladies, with cold.
(on your face, flakes settle as petals do in autumn)
in a gallery of heavy limbs, frozen sap, cradled in an ice snap.

Lindsey Nichols

Bittersweet Beauty

Feelings and memories
Carried away by time
Only can I remember
Your lips touching mine
Unspoken love we shared
Its underlying beauty
To which nothing compares
I am left with a memory
That I did not see
How beautiful it is
To see your love for me

Dave Fogel

Love

I am not the type to openly say it
I often do not take the time to show it
I was afraid that I would blow it
So, I took this opportunity and wrote it
I love You and always will

Michael Hudson

Untitled VI

This evening past
as the ripe and reddened sun
last gasped—and splashed
down into the open hearted
sea. It cast up in its wake
a spray of stars
to adorn the sky
which blushed in thanks.
And as the full and heavy moon
rose to take her place
among the jewels of eve

My girl, she fell into my bed
And visited her beauty on me.

Stephe Watson

The Stars

The vain notions of fame
Draw them into the game.

Into the depths of darkness
Their soul shall regress.

To the prince it will belong
All for fortune and a song.

Paying with their happiness
And love too, I would guess.
The glamour and smiles are fake
Every work rule they break.

Next time you look at a star
Remember how empty their lives are.

Kristina A. Hebert

Bad Parents

Bad parents aren't fun,
Bad parents can't run,

Bad parents that do drugs,
They have to sleep on rugs.

Bad parents that drink,
They don't try to think.

Bad parents that didn't finish school,
They aren't cool, to the golden rule.

Bad parents that don't say yes,
They are sometimes a mess.

Porsha Allen

Daddy's Little Girl

When I first saw you I knew you would be my little girl, always.
I was so proud of you!
As you grew to a young lady, I watched each stage of your life.
You were daddy's little girl.

I was always there for you, but then God called me away.
Now, when tears fill your eyes,
the son of God will drive them away for me.
And He will have the breeze kiss you for me.
He will send to you my love in the beauty of the roses,
and in the songs of the birds.

When you come to where I lay,
don't let any tear drops fall on my grave,
just wear a smile and look around you at all the beauty in the blue sky:
the birds singing their songs of love, the beauty of the flowers,
the breeze whispering in the pine and oak trees,
and the beautiful love of Jesus that is still alive.

Please don't weep for me because in peace I rest,
'til that beautiful day and then around the throne of the King,
you can share your tears of joy with me.

Until then just laugh when you think of me,
because the angels will look over me.
You are still your daddy's little girl.

Charles Harvey

The Meaning of Life

As I lie in these death ridden sheets
Putting the pieces of life's puzzle in their final resting place

Time is anything but permanent now
And the clarity of thoughts rush in as I labor life's last few breaths

So much wasted time in selfish deeds
To fulfill materialistic needs

For in the end it is not what we have obtained
But who we have become and how well we have loved. . . .

Rose Orbeck

Mother of Humility

Some human beings have no place to lay down their head,
Many others can't find work to earn their daily bread
Orphan children, adults in crisis swarm on the streets space
Beggars, sick and dying people and dragging to confess.

Mother Teresa dedicated her life to serve these people in need,
A project of hope fed by the will of doing a good deed
In her heart, everyone was a person with a divine soul,
How potentate compassion is laboring a glow life's role.

Day by day, mother of humility gained a noble reputation,
She diligently embraced the poorest of the generation,
Her best way to express God's care for all and His intentions
Thus, not to plea for rewards or a grand nomination.

Mother Teresa's example keeps to sustain a pleasant flame of love,
Her luminous aura of holiness continues to dissect the human's unresolved
People believing that Heaven rewarded her with immortality,
A spirit of the heart for such extraordinary integrity.

Aurelian Tanase

Distance

The distance between us cannot make the image of you fade from my mind.
Nor can it diminish the emotions I feel for you.
My thoughts and my desires they are always of you.
I ache and I yearn for your touch and your smile.
How I long to hear your voice without the static of the telephone line.
To once again kiss your lips,
To see the beauty within your eyes.

Graham Holiday

After You've Gone

The window glass
coated with ice
I stand by the window
hugging myself—
it's cold
Winter is here
I thought I
could hold it off
The cold wears me down
Time hurts
instead of healing
The city outside
the window—
I feel small
Ice on the window—
A cold,
effective wall

Shauna York

Love of a Rose

Drag a rose on your skin,

put life in dead men,

eyes put light in mine,

dimmed no more,

lifted from the floor like a ghost,

awoke from thoughts,

into the distance she vanished,

as if she never existed.

Jeffrey Kamphaus

Spirit

For Mom, who always knows best.
No longer care for me
For now I am gone
I have left this Earth
Now singing a sweet life's song.

I have my freedom
I spread my wings and fly
No longer asking
the harsh simple why.

My smile is wider than the sky
and my happiness is true
Just know that I'm there
always loving you.

Adrienne Strawther

Stomach Ache

i'm dying
a creatures is in my stomach
growing, evolving, tearing me apart
bubbling and growling
my stomach is being split in half
hard to eat, harder to sleep
no way to kill the enemy
it's trying to devour my insides
lurching about my intestines
clawing, scratching, ripping
i'm going to explode
i'm internally incinerating with flame
it will burst out at any time
the alien will laugh—
run around causing havoc
infest the rest of the world
painfully causing them the distress
that possesses my body

Devin Tonnochy

Come on Sun

Come on sun, you can do it, give us a big shine.
I know it's winter and very cold, quick before you change your mind.
The sky is so threatening, I suppose that means yet more rain.
That poor old weatherman tries his best, but he can't take all the blame.
Everything looks so dank and wet, the wind it cuts you in two.
Oh well, I suppose we are better off indoors, there is not a lot we can do.
It is nice to see some birds in our garden, I hope they like our food.
I spent some time making their table, so they are not pursued.
It could be so much worse; we could be knee deep in snow.
It soon covers all the ground, but with the traffic and rain it goes.
Frost and ice comes to slow us down, to rush could be all in vain.
Let us hope it all goes away quite soon, I don't even care if it rains.
There are places around we should never go at this time of year.
Driving in snow, or walking on ice, can mean only danger I fear.
Roll on the spring and new flowers in bloom, their show is so sublime.
Come on sun you can do it, give us one big shine.

Ken Mills

Dealing with Destiny

One millennium begins, another is through.
We now face a time in which old meets new.
Our generation steps up to reign over the others.
We're tired of following and running for cover.
Finally, we realize actions do speak louder than words.
We must carry out these actions,
instead of merely letting them be heard.
It's time for us to come forth and take a stand.
The world stands before us, and destiny is in our hands.
The need for guidance is pleading for you and I.
Not too long ago, we were the ones pleading . . . oh, how time flies.
Dare to be a dreamer, a person of hope and prayer.
Don't give up so easy . . . life is never really fair.
If at first you don't succeed, try again.
The key is to stick with it, and in that, there is no end.
These words of wisdom are just a start.
You are the one who decides . . . follow your heart.
Determination and worthwhile thought lie in the soul;
reach deep inside, and when you find it, don't let go.
Never regret . . . what is done is done.
How many people have gained something when feeling helpless?
The answer is none. And so it is your decision—will you take a stand?
To guide and lend a helping hand?
The choice is yours and yours alone.
The results could affect everyone's lives, not only your own.

Kristi Gatlin

Stuck in the Past

It seems like every time the world stops around me
I'm left with impressions of you on my mind
No matter how hard I try I just can't seem to
Fade memories of you with time. . . .
It's been close to a month since my world fell apart
My reconstruction inches along,
and I'm trying to piece my life back together
but without you it all seems wrong. . . .

. . . and I'm sorry that I need you, dependent on your smile
I've tried so hard to forget you, girl, but you made my life worthwhile,
If only I could change the past and make words disappear,
no price would be too high if with you I'd spend my years. . . .

Perpetually running in circles
contemplating my decisions ahead
I want to forget you and move on
but I'll never extricate from my head
the yearning I have to be with you
the desire to relive those weeks
to move on seems impossible
you're the treasure that my heart seeks

Darron Schall

Found Poem on a Fallen Leaf

Green
Yellow
Strong
and
Peaceful.
Wet
and
Withered . . . with
Dirty brown edges . . .
Strong veins
Suggest
Inner strength.
It talks to me saying:
"Let me be.
It is an honor
To be the last fallen leaf
Of the century."

Katie Scott

Will I See You in Heaven

When I die will
I see you in Heaven
and will you remember
me the way we knew
each other
Or will I just see your
soul and remember the
love we have for each
other and the fun we've
had together
Or will I just put
me away like a toy
and forget about me.

Roxi DeWolf

Screams

I scream I shout,
Yet no one hears,
I sob, I cry,
Yet no one cares,
All alone in the harsh cruel world,
Yet no one gives a damn,
They treat me like a lion,
Yet I'm a gentle as a lamb.

Michelle Dutcher

My Shangri La

I presume a winter night
I presume a bird in flight
I presume a starry sky
I presume a butterfly

I presume a sunny glow
I presume a colored snow
I presume a heated ray
I presume a lovely day

I presume an autumn leaf
Being brown brings me grief
I presume a leaf of green
Exceedingly shiny and spotless clean
I presume it does not rain
But birds are singing a sweet refrain

I presume it is quiet and tranquil
To this day I am very thankful
I presume a summer day
People are happy and making play
The sun is shining, everything is bright
No wars, no trouble, no fears, no fright
This is the end of my perfect world

Arthur H. Stevens

Depression

I would wonder for hours thinking if it was true,
but helpless to say depression is blue.

Anywhere or everywhere my tears would come through,
but my depression was still there, shining blue.

My heart seemed like it was cast out with various rays.
My life seem like it was going by, without any days.

And like I would do or say,
I could not walk without depression any day.

So day by day past and at last I finally seem to break through the glass,
my depression had fallen when I saw the summer grass.
But spite to all of thee,
my depression has not gone away as you can see.

So I can't hide behind a bush or behind a tree,
my depression is here to stay, and live with me.

Shondel Fitzpatrick

Remember the Magic

Have you ever watched a butterfly flitter around a bush?
Looking to all the world like it's being blown in every direction, not being able to grab hold.
Floating down then flapping its wings
with all its might to remain aloft. That's life struggling on.
Have you ever watch a dragon fly? It hovers for only moments,
then it streaks away, only to stop suddenly and look around,
its wings never stopping, beating so fast they are a blur.
That's time passing by. Have you looked at the morning dew
and seen the sun light glisten? The deep colors of nature
after a rain. The deep greens and browns in the earth.
The reds and oranges dotting the plants. That's beauty.
Have you ever played tag with the ocean?
Running with the waves or the ripples on a lake.
Getting your feet wet when you were trying not to, then saying "Oh well."
That's conversation.
These are the magics in our lives. These are the touches we miss.
These are simply, what we forget. I want you to remember!
Remember to look at the sunrise and say "Thank you."
Remember to look at the squirrel and smile.
Laugh at the moon and sing with the wind.
Sit down and be comfortable, close your eyes and remember.
That giggle in your stomach will rise to your lips and life will be bright again.
Remember always, the magic.

L. Philipp Neyman

My Beloved One

I watch you sleep and I watch you play.
As you give me a smile that brightens me up every day.
Your chocolate glazed eyes dazzled in the sun and the sweet taste of your lips in the long night.
My soul was lost in a city of pain 'til I met you for your love was my light home again.
I love you with every piece of my heart and as the years go by my love just multiplies.
As I close my eyes and think of you I shed a tear of love so true.
No one could ever take your place because your like the north star in the vast of space.
Now come into my arms and close your eyes and please don't leave my side.
The moon will protect you in the long night for now it's time to sleep my beloved one.

Jose Colon

MS NEEDS RESEARCH MONEY—DO YOU HEAR?

For my cousin Jean in Colorado
MS NEEDS RESEARCH MONEY—DO YOU HEAR?
MS IS: autoimmune—your body fights itself-affects central nervous system
no respecter of age—has four basic types—
is progressive—hard to diagnose—mimics
MS NEEDS RESEARCH MONEY—DO YOU HEAR?
PATIENTS HAVE; depression—fatigue tremors—spasticity—
high risk of pneumonia—wheelchair bound—some things worse
MS NEEDS RESEARCH MONEY—DO YOU HEAR?
PATIENTS NEED: love—compassion—patience—acceptance—prayer
MS NEEDS RESEARCH MONEY—DO YOU HEAR?

Sonia Aiken

Friends

I've known you for a while,
But it feels like a year.
You came into my life,
The clouds turned to clear.

We've had some good times.
Like a chain we both link,
I make you laugh,
But you make me think.

When we first hung out
You were quiet and shy,
But now you can talk,
Unafraid to reply.

I want you to know,
On this special day,
That I value our friendship
Which forever will stay.

If the world turns against you,
Just come to me.
And if it's problems I'm facing,
It's you that I'll seek.

Aasim Durrani

The Hidden Pain

I can hide my pain away
and pretend love was never there,
Yet I cannot hide the truth—
Deep down I truly cared.

The pity and the pain
is lost on a fool like me.
Lost in a sea of tears,
drowned by what was meant to be.

Yes, I can tuck it all away,
hide it deep down inside.
The pain will never show,
Yet to myself I cannot lie.

Deep down I know it's there
Waiting, hiding, cringing at the sound
of my broken heart's beating.
Waiting for love to be found.

Adam Goodall

MMMmmm . . .

Crack, hiss, fizz;
You smell so sweet,
But you are deceptive.
Corrosive acid to eat
Away at me from the
Inside out so I won't
Notice, clever. I lift
Slowly, letting your
Bubbles tickle my nose.
The burning in my throat
Does not hurt; I look
Forward to it.

Ann Martin

Goals

Set goals for yourself
For they will make or break you
When you reach for the sky
There's no limit to what you can do

Reach these goals
And learn while doing so
When you put forth your strongest effort
There's no telling how far you'll go

Jimmie Watkins

Destined to Be Famous

I've always had some thoughts of what I'd do when I grew older
If I wrote everything down it would fill up a manila folder
But here are some of the things I'd really someday like to be
Perhaps soon in the newspaper, my name you will see
The greatest thing I'd like to become is a very well-known chef
After everyone tasted my food, other chefs would have left
My spaghetti would make me famous- they'd call my Reese's pie superb
And it would all be healthy with many a goodly herb
Ideas would come to me daily, of what I'd create next
"Adam's weekly Creation" would be the gist of the paper's text
The second thing I'd like to become is a trumpeter in a great jazz band
We'd rock the world, our concerts would be in the greatest demand
And in the back is where I'd be, squealing on my horn
My fans would scream when I came on, my playing they'd adorn
And lastly I bet I'll be the greatest poet everywhere
My poetry books would be in demand, no one copying would dare
My poems would run for thousands, each word one hundred bucks or more
My word-genius would make me famous- for me people would live for
And so you see what I'd like to be in another ten years or so
The best thing about it is I'll be rolling in the dough

Adam Campbell

untitled

from the shadows you caress my soul
moving me, taking control. . . .
whispering to me of love long past
not of the future, only the past. . . .
my passion cries out for you,
my heart wants to run from you,
my body needs only the touch of your hand,
from which all of me floats away into wonderland.
be not afraid, only trust in my dreams,
together we are in paradise, so to others it seems. . . .
but i am afraid of what i feel,
for love's everlasting promise is hollow, unreal.
yet, with thy kiss, and the touch of your hand,
forever seems real, and ever after the plan. . . .
step forth from the shadows and call me by name,
do not hide from me, as if you are shamed. . . .
but not from me do you hide, so it seems,
it is all those forevers you touch in your dreams. . . .
all those promises that you can't seem to keep,
somehow get lost within the word's "to keep"
retreat back inside, where shadows can hide,
the truth of the one who is not by my side,
for you are the taker, the old dream maker,
and forever is only for the moment . . . you take her.

Connie Bennett

The Wax Museum

The wax man sits listening, lost in lovely, lonely thoughts
He thinks, but forms no real thoughts at all
His mind at ease in these pleasant surroundings
of plump, pasty persons gone rich by pilfering the proletarians
He calls it mind for lack of better words to describe the thing he knows he does not know
this Cartesian cruelty, carelessly designating our every choice
He begins to float out of the governs of reason.
He doesn't understand the self-actuating redundant, redressed,
red-dressed rescues of sanity that bind us to a reality that we can't justify
He recalls a time undaunted by outer forces, unplighted playfulness
and pondering now pounded by the demands of adult life
He postures—Are these contaminate, confounding, confused constraints,
combined in Carthage, really a contemporary way of life
He can't to save himself and all his love he clings to the world.
He knows himself and will know everything around him.
He gasps and grasps, and groans as he sees
the green, the good, the way and the means
His love, his life, his lingering lust,
his passion and portents now set in the rust
His oval, his oblong obsession with odd
His greatness, grotesqueness and fulfillment of God

Jorg Hohmann

The Beauty I See

The beauty I see
is named Laura Lee.
Without her my life
is dark and empty.
With her my life is happy.
If you could only see what I have seen
since our first date you would witness
the most beautiful person in the world
that God has created.
Her smile would win
the Miss Universe contest forever.
Her strength would win
World War 3 all by herself.
Her stamina would win
a gold medal in the Olympics.
Her heart is bigger
than the Grand Canyon.
Sometimes I wonder what keeps me going.
For it is the beauty I see
Her name is Laura Lee.

Edward Kamont

Interpretation of a Hug

A hug can mean so many things
to young and old alike
It can symbolize the love between
a husband and a wife.

A hug can be a greeting
that is given to a friend
It may accompany Good-bye
or Good-night at each day's end.

A hug can say I'm sorry
or give comfort when you're down
In fact, there's nothing like a hug
to erase a tear or frown.

A hug can be a measure of thanks
that goes deeper than sending a card;
It's the best way to say I miss you
to someone who lives afar.

You can't put a price on hugging . . .
it costs nothing to give or take
Yet it's the most rewarding gesture
in life you'll ever make.

Dianne Brazee

The Moment of Truth

You closed your eyes,
lips pursed.
I opened my mind,
and wrapped myself
around your every thought.

When your dreams
spoke truth,
silence shattered
the inner will.
Your soul's light
fed my growing mind.

I bled your truth—

To touch
what's been touched,
to feel
what's been felt,
to see
what's been seen—

Is all the blindness
of my own imperfections.

Jeffrey Nelson

So It Comes

He walks along a road the same as any street I've seen,
yet in between is stranger, somehow. . . .
in between us both, now,
is the piece we share as we approach our designated focal point:
the point where we must each decide to look away or join our eyes. . . .
a different bit of road, this, getting smaller as we close it in . . .
the universe has called it,
not A road, not The road,
Your Road.
And so it comes, slowly;
A relationship between us—in an instant born and dies. . . .
it's the last I'll see the man who thinks the thoughts behind his eyes.
So it goes.
So it's gone.

Aaron Marsh

What Matters?

Mountains of chocolate, perfectly positioned and rippled with sparks of gold
Proportioned so perfectly, I hold my breath as I think those thoughts never to be told
Is it Love? Is it Lust? Or is it a mixture of both?
Are they the same? Are there substantial differences?
Or is it the degree of each that matters?
Eyes that speak, exploring the inner thoughts of my mind
My heart stops, my blood rushes . . . are we melding, or does that come with time?
It is me? Is it you? Are we one? Are we destined? Are we in control?
Or is it the degree of each that matters?

Eleanore Hunter

Time

What's on my mind? Time.
Though you spend hours with someone
you may never have had the time to tell them how much you appreciate them.
Time is never enough. With the palm of your hand open it slips through your fingers.
Time is precious the most beautiful arrangement in life.
Time lives, Time dies; there's no in between.
Time is something you borrow but can't return.
You can't touch time or hold it;
It's out of your control. It's yours only for awhile but you can't keep it.
Time follows you around but it's not your shadow.
Time is not on your side but by it.
Time is God's allowance to you
He is the only one who gives it to you and the only one to take it away.
Now God gave time for me to be with you
to let you know I appreciate you.

Cathy Hunt

The Only

Being one of the only women in the office
The boys club continually meeting
Manager trying to fix the problems
Being one of the only women in the office
Standing on the outside looking in
Favoritism in the office runs wild
Getting no response, to the request
Manager can't remember, when request was made
Being one of the only women in the office
A secretary being paid in cash, by the manager
The manager calling potential female candidates "hookers"
if he did not like the interview, after the candidates left
Being one of the only women in the office
The manager not realizing how to take other's feelings into account, before his ego
The manager acting like a big bozo, insensitive, two-faced, loud mouth , overbearing jerk
The manager not realizing that everyone is not the same, everyone is different
Being reprimanded for speaking the truth,
The manager telling me , the secretary's wardrobe is none of my
business, when her appearance reflects on everyone in the office, and not just him
The manager attacks my character,
Being one of the only women in the office is hard to be

Nannette Morrison

The Dawning

The power of the rising sun—
To drive away the night,
The hand of God takes full control
To bring the new day forth.

As the sun moves on high,
The night time glides away:
Mother Earth wields her power
To refresh it all for you.

The sun does wane,
The night restored,
As Mother Earth yields to God
To let the night return.

Marie Hyde

Hide

When something is wrong,
I sometimes hide
Hide, so that no one can see me cry.
Then when I am crying,
I ask myself, "Why?"
"Why do you hide
your feelings inside?"
I try not to hide,
And feel brave,
But it is not easy for me
I try not to hide,
My feelings inside
Yet I guess I'm just scared, you see.
Then when I hide
I cry again
And feel the pain in me.

Carla Alo-Cabalquinto

"Love Is Hell"

Love is Hell.
War is, too.
You wish them well,
And say, "I love you."

Then they go off
To a land far away,
To fight & be lost.
"He's dead," they say.

You cry & cry
In a padded cell.
You ask God, "Why?"
He says, "Love is Hell."

K. T. K.

WITH

With my eyes, I caressed her face;

With my breath, I kissed her lips;

With my soul, I felt her warmth;

With my heart, I loved her.

Roger Williams

To Be Young Again

To be young again
How nice it would be
To live without a care
Enjoy the happy times over again
But alas young again I never will be
For now I am on a path I chose
Down this path I shall travel
To see where it takes me and beyond
But I can dream of being young again

Patricia Stephenson

A Stolen Moment

If I could have a stolen moment, where it seemed that time stood still.
I would choose a night by candle light in a rose garden on a hill.
Or I would choose an evening on a silver lake, under a harvest moon,
And I would linger until the morning hours, and that would be too soon.
Or perhaps I would choose a cabin, in a meadow by a stream.
Where in that stolen moment, love would reign supreme.
Or maybe I would choose a sandy beach,
Where the waves washed up the foam.
With a gentle breeze and the ecstacy, we would never feel alone.
Or I would choose a mountain top, underneath the starry skies.
Where there would be some shooting stars, besides those in our eyes.
If I could have a stolen moment where it was like eternity,
Here at home underneath the sweet magnolias,
Would be just fine with me.

    Joe Scherffius

!

The open vastness: it used to be so green
All these machines, men inside being mean

I stop and wonder how man kills his own!!
With the passing of each generation come louder cries: "I've grown!"

Maybe growth in wealth or size . . . just not in love
Ask Mohammad, prayers and peace be upon him, about the white dove!

    Bolbol Afandy

To Be "In Love"

Although I have gone beyond right or wrong.
I have gone to what is pure and real.
With every breath I breathe it tightens at the beauty of knowing
what it feels like to be "in love."
And although the pain of being away from you is so overwhelmingly hard to bear.
I have felt love. I have held you.
I have touched you, with a touch that can only be felt or given
with entire intensity as the touch I've given to you,
and the touch you shared with me.
A thousand feelings engross me.
Feelings that are indescribable, yet so fiercely strong and ruling to my very essence.
Should I have? I can ask myself that a million times. Should I have met you?
I thought that meeting you would free my love for you.
But it has only amplified the deepest love that comes from within me for you.
And yet with all this love I feel inside there is also a hidden sadness.
A sadness that promises no one tomorrow.
That leaves your heart open with amazing clarity of want
but closed to know if it will ever be reunited again.
So with this I must tell you that I have loved you as I have never loved another.
I have shared not just my body, but who it is I am.
And no matter where our lives take us.
You and I have been to a place that is ours forever.

    Kymi Murphy

Breaking Up

I really don't know how to tell you this, but I think that our days are through.
I'm really sorry, but I guess I just fell out of love with you.
Please don't be mad at me.
There is nothing felt anymore;
the feelings that we used to have aren't there anymore.
I am sorry for doing this; I wish I could change how I feel.
I really thought our love would last always.
I thought our love was real.
This is so hard for me to do.
I never wanted US to be over.
I still do love you, just not that way. I still want to be your friend.
I just don't want you to hate me. Please try to understand,
I've been feeling like this for a while now. I've put it off as long as I can.
I wish there was something for you that I could do or say.
But really, you'll be happier without me. It's better this way.
Just remember that I will always love you; please don't hate me.

    Melissa Cobb

here and there

here and there

night passes in gaudy silence
black scenes haunt my sight
questions unutterable
slip on a wind wept stream

you are always there
I am always here
and in that space between
the moments longed for shiver

your action hair
yawning gray dawn to light
the warmth of your body
rushing to follow as you rise

house slippers flopping the floor
rebellious robe drooping open
but most of all
the comfort born between us

as we hug the day to life

    James Hartsell

A Tribute to Mother

To a mother who had faith in God
And knew that He would help her.
Who tried to do the right things
Whenever we would err.

She worked so hard to do the things
That needed to be done.
Her gardening and baking
And taking care of everyone.

The house we lived in was quite old,
But mother tried to keep it clean.
When company was about to come
It seemed to have an extra sheen.

The cooking and the washing,
The ironing and the sewing,
The darning and the mending,
To keep her family going.

She's with her Lord in Heaven now,
He gave her strength to cope.
With all her problems on this Earth
He gave her peace and hope.

    Kathleen Boehm

Life's Destiny

One should comprehend life's dreams,
Sometimes the secret heart is a guide;
Filling the soul with creative streams,
And giving one a divine pride.

Reaching for the element of light
For virtues of noblest power,
And flourishing with eager might;
So life is serenity forever.

Life's demands are real in giving
It is a delicate and constant flow,
To all creation there is a being,
Making the battle field of life a show.

Like the destiny of breeze
Bringing a noble share,
Of soft winged touches to trees;
One must have such a daring care.

Thoughts and words are gently shed.
In a world that dawns with trust;
Dreams whisper above the dead,
Never dulling and shrinking in the dust.

    Charlotte Campbell

Elizabeth

Maiden, maiden . . . where have you hidden?
You hide yourself from me like the sun does the night.
Where have you run to, to which ocean have you sailed?
I grow weary of searching, I grow weak from the hunt,
why have you hidden from me, your one true love? Like a fly in a web
I am caught. You enter my mind, my prayers and my thoughts.
I have a rose for every year we have missed, four to be exact, and I
could not bear to collect the fifth. I wait for you at the beach were
we met, on the sand I lay and dream of your beautiful smile. Where
have you gone, and are you OK? I cannot stand this wait, I must get
away. The pain breaks my heart into thirds, every day I must
repair it, every day the pain grows worse and worse. Maiden,
Maiden . . . where have you ventured to?
When will you come back so I can say, "I love you?"
Not one more day can I wait on Earth,
for I have grown weak and tired, oh God how my heart does thirst . . .
for my maiden Elizabeth, my one and only, and first.
So I must leave this world, I cannot fight death any longer.
But even in death for you I'll hunger. I will wait for you, and deny God's call,
"Come home child, for you have pleased me well, you have done all."
Yes, I will tell the Lord I must wait, even at the gates of Hell if I must,
and even then I'll tell the demons that it is you I love. I will wait for all eternity.
Of all the glories in Heaven, you are the one I crave for, you are the one I need. It is
for you that I bleed.
My maiden . . . my Elizabeth.

Douglas Nordenstrom

Only a Woman Knows

You don't have to be a scholar, or a doctor with degree,
You don't have to be a student of high philosophy.
But of yourself you still can give and tell your story too,
To help another one in need, draw strength to make it through.
'Cause as a woman you are strong, and really understand
just how another woman feels as you reach to take her hand.
With a gentle touch and a comforting hug, encouraging words ring true,
for only you can comprehend what that woman's going through.
Terrible twos, P.M.S., teenagers on the loose,
loneliness, fatigue, and she's going to blow a fuse!
So take her hand, comfort her heart, listen to her woes.
For sister you can understand what only a woman knows.

Dawna Gay

Tranquility

Petals drip their honeysucle dew in the sweet smelling sun
As the rolling hills bellow with laughter making their bellies shake
Tranquility spreads its wings as it takes flight into the air
Songbirds sing sweet melodies that ripple through the breeze
The purest clouds cry silent tears that knock upon my door
The trees whisper tender nothingness that caressively tickles my ears
Crickets play mellow tunes and the owl says goodnight
The moon winks a small hello as the sun waves good-bye
As my silent slumber is broken with Death humming sweet lullabies

Karen Tressel

contradiction

sleepless waking,
senseless thoughts—feeling empty, full of pain
silent whispers echoing through my mind—
blinding images blaze my eyes.
cold water creeps and freezes in my bones—
all alone in darkness—longing for your arms.
crying of all lamentation—soundless to thy ears—
searching for the way out
no idea of the way in—
sitting on the cold damp floor, nothing for warmth, but my own arms—
tears fall frozen to the ground—
oh, when, oh, when will I be found?

Alta Harris

Moonbeams on My Soul

I meet your eyes
they are moonbeams
on my soul
There are echoes
in the attic
from lovemaking
that is your heart
full of sweet yearns
There are holes in my heart
which you fill
with the touch of a piano chord
and the phrase of the nightingale—
the music and tenderness of love
You bring a nestling calm
that soothes my psyche
like the aftermath of passion
lived in a dream come true
it is your arms, it is you!

Michael Williams

Aubade

Serene
is the image of the open sea
free-soaring flight
of wordspray and water
calm sighs contained in her smile

She dreams
unceasingly in the distance
of the sea waves
softly caressing the beach
She dreams

In the unending vastness
the real is etched
images never possessed
like the white laughter
of the children of the mother sea

Marie-Ange Somdah

Lear Jet Disaster

Payne Stewart in his flashy knickers
Departed Florida with his friends
To go golfing in the state of Texas
His wife Tracy tried to get in touch
Stewart's cell phone was not on
She felt helpless at this point
Not being able to talk to her husband
Any hope she felt for a miracle was gone
Due to the sorrow she was feeling
Tracy cried out in tribulation
She shed a river of a million tears

Shirley Bowerman

The Interpreter

The capital
once engulfed me,
its high stones surrounding
grey and cool.
Yet rising from its history,
your commentary,
I grew
to joy in details
finer than any
I could name
then.
Today
I met old friends,
the maps and pots and eaves
that I had viewed with you,
and words returned.

Joan M. Dahlke

The Pedestal

A shy little blue eyed girl looks up high to the man on the pedestal.
The man she placed there ever so high,
Looking for guidance and wisdom that she knows only he can give.

A young girl growing up looks at her mother
and can't believe her ears.
The man she placed there ever so high,
Walking away from the one who needs
his loving hands to grow strong.

A sad troubled teenage girl returns to the man on the pedestal.
The man she placed there ever so high,
Learning of his accomplishments and his life
with just a third grade education.

A young lady striking out on her own to find a life without him still.
The man she placed there ever so high,
Working to provide and overcome life's tribulations and afflictions

A middle aged woman looks at him
as they age through time and trials.
The man she placed there ever so high,
Loving one another as a daughter and father could only love.

Deborah Heiskell-Simmons

Caught Dry

The night worn thin,
as is the polyester moon
hanging by a thread
over my lonely shoulder—
My moonlit flesh rests wounded,
trembling
from the distant echoes of screaming angels
—trapped—
in the countless hours
depleted on dead souvenirs . . .
accumulated in oblivion
esteemed in bleeding reality—
Saturate my veins
with another brown-eyed glance
to allow what lingers
to cascade into inconsistent consistency
as raw flame and alcohol would—
A bitter vacancy soon to follow . . .
dispassionate attempts that encumber my eyes,
as my blue existence scars my sentiment.

Amy Peterson

Gift from God

As I try to think of words to comfort you, I cannot help but to think how I'd be.
If he were my child, what would I do? Would I agree?
Understanding is so far from my reach-as children are a gift from God above.
Given to us to love, take care of, and teach. You give them all of your heart's love;
Never expecting for them to be taken away.
Death of a child is not meant to happen.
They are supposed to grow more every day—
learning lessons being taught over and again.
We must try to understand His reasons, although they may hurt us inside.
God promises that His will be done, and that He'll always be there for us to confide.
Always remember that His Home is best, with even more love than we can imagine!
It's a place where the heart can truly rest and not have to deal with daily sin.
Could you give your child any more than the truth of God and His love?
For now he waits at Heaven's door, looking over you from up above.
You gave him the best gift of all; teaching him that you will never be apart.
Through those teachings was how he saw to accept Jesus into his heart.
For now he has Eternal Life in Heaven, with Jesus sitting by his side.
And knowing you will see him again should keep you strong without too much pride.
Put aside your worries and your tears,
because your son is with the best Care Giver of all.
Only in time will the pain and sorrow disappear—
just always remember, he was answering God's Call!!!

Cheryl Brazelton

The Lighthouse

High on a hill
A light house stands,
Shining its light
For all to see,
Like God's love,
Reaching out to me.
High on a hill
A lighthouse stands
Shining its light
across the land and sea.
Like God's arms
Reaching out to me.
I need not fear
For the darkest of days
For the light of my Savior
Will guide my way!

Lorraine Goodrich

Century Twenty One

At the start of the twentieth century
The flying machine had not yet flown
Wireless communication was unknown
Atomic energy then was theory.
Now satellites into outer space fly
Events all over Earth we quickly see,
One nuclear bomb can raze a city!
Progressive changes will always come,
But we, in the coming millennium,
Must utilize marvels created before
To insure peace by eliminating war.
Expanding population we must curb,
But natural life try not to disturb.
Let the enhancement of life on Earth be
Our goal in the twenty first century.

Ralph Lehman

Storm

There are dark clouds in the west
And they are getting black,
The wind is starting to howl,
The sun is getting dimmer,
And of these are signs of the storm
That will soon sweep the hills.

Lightning flashing and thunder rolling,
Across a dark midnight blue sky,
The rain comes pouring down,
The storm is here at last.

Howard A. Deaton

Baby

O', little one
the beauty of your face.
How can anyone
resist you?
The peaceful innocence
of your gaze.
How can anyone
not see you?
How sad for those
who do not accept!
For you said anyone who accepts,
one of these receives You!
And Heaven folds its Arms
around You as the Gift!
A child is the Gift of Love
from God to man.
Happy is he who accepts one
for he is enriched in Love!

Jessie M. Combs

Mother

Looking back on my life I can remeber our greatest times.
I remember lying in your arms and looking into your loving eyes.
The laughs we shared and the tears we cried.
Your hugs and kisses were a true sign
that you would always be by my side.
I remember you tucking me into bed.
Placing you gentle, warm hands upon my face
and kissing my forehead.
Sometimes I would act asleep to see
how long you would stay with me.
Sometimes seconds, some minutes,
but forever in my heart you will always be.
In the darkest times of my life you were there to turn on a light.
Watching you as I grow up insures me that my future is bright.
The wisdom you have installed into me will take me anywhere in life.
I just hope that I can find your wonderful qualities in a future wife.
To care for me when I am sick and listen to my problems.
Then to stand by my side and help me find an answer to sove them.
I want her to lift my spirts when I am feeling down.
A woman to make me smile when it seems all I do is frown.
As I would do for her as I try to do for you.
Because without you I don't know what I would do.
I could never want any other.
For I am the luckiest son to have you as my mother.

Brandon Stout

Such Joy

His left hand holds the door ajar,
while his right wheels an old man in; it's plain to see from their countenance
that these two are next of kin.
As soon as they are seated, the elder falls asleep,
and a youth emerges from the crowd to pull himself a seat.
"My God, you're like his mother!" the stranger now begins.
"It's a wonder if you make it through until this burden ends."
"I'll stop you there," the man replies. "This isn't like a chore."
"It's based on true respect and love, but also much, much more."
I remember he used to buy me things, just to show he cared.
Of course I already knew it; I could tell by his being there.
But when others chanced to ask him why he bought such toys,
he'd stop and laugh, and say quite plainly,
"It brings my son such joy."
And how we'd always play together. The times we two would spend!
I might have called him "daddy," but I know he called me "friend."
He tried so hard to be there; new ways he would employ.
And when I asked him why, he'd say: "It brings my son such joy."
So if you ask me why, young man, I care for my dad now,
that age has crept upon his face and time upon his brow;
then I'll answer, not as a man, but rather as his boy—
I'll stop, and laugh, and say quite plainly,
"It brings his son such joy."

Matthew Upton

Forgiveness

Forgive other people is to treat you well.

Don't look down on yourself
because being human has no limits possible.

For their own selves, looking excuses people,
their will never improved themself forever.

Watching other people that cannot get a correctly,
is your own self not learning good enough.

Try to be the best how much ability you have is to how clever you get.

Angry, is to get other people's mistake for punishing yourself.

A person's happiness, not because their own a lot,
is because they are hurting other people less.

Small matter not going to complete, and big thing difficult to succeed.

In this world, two things cannot wait, one is obey to love, one is donated.

Cheah Lin

Business Love

Please enter this Valentine poem
In my poetry file.
It is a love note to you
across the miles.
Of course, the reason
Is to make you smile.
One never knows
What hook to use,
That might catch a judge
on a day with the blues.
If this grease has reached
the right wheel,
make me a winner.
Have we got a deal?

Charles M. "Slow" Stanley

Deep Inside

I cry the tears of a million years
Down deep inside of me
I bottle up all the little thoughts
That could light a Christmas tree.

No one hears the screams I scream
As it's knotting up my gut.
For if they could, I know they would
Swear that I'm a nut

You see, I'm just a simpleton
Who's afraid of everything.
I left my sheltered childhood
To the life of a wedding ring.

The world outside it scares me
I never go anywhere alone.
But in my mind I travel
Knowing I'm safe and secure at home.

Cheryl Hays

Two Years Old

I don't remember life without Karen;
I only remember after,
her in the high chair
watching me
making cookies with our mother
and fumbling with the teething ring
while I mixed the batter.

Jennifer Adams

A Grandmother's Love

Nothing can compare to
A grandmother's love
Her non-failing prayers that
She showers on us all
Yes, on all her children's
Children and their children
And more a grandmother's love
Just runs forever more

Grandmothers cannot be stopped
For they know not how
This gift of love they inherit
From the almighty God

Now, even I want to shout
Exceeding with joy, to let
All the grandmothers know
That you are appreciated
For your prayers and for
Your undying love

Linda S. Collins

Reflections of Myself

I look in the mirror and I see myself,
the mere reflection of the brilliant ray of light I once was.

I rub my hands gently across my face. It is soft, but not the same.
The velvety texture is not close to the soft silky skin that was once there.

My lips pout but not with same effect they once had.
The lines near my lips hold the secret of many tales never shared
and still feel each of my lovers as if it were yesterday.

My beautiful hair has since been cut and as I toss my head back,
I close my eyes and can almost feel my hair
touching my back as it once did.

With my eyes still closed I run my hand across my body
longing to be admired as I once had been.
I stop as I feel my breasts. Long ago they lost their tender youthful look.

I open my eyes again and moan out loud . . . you're old,
and it is with a deep sigh that I add "but what a life it has been."

Julie Bruyning

The Perfect Seashell

All of my life I've been searching for the perfect one,
and finally I've found it.
The perfect seashell. Sure, I've walked along this beach,
sometimes rough, sometimes soft,
finding other shells that I thought were beautiful,
but they weren't right. Until now. Now I've found it
The most perfect, wonderful, beautiful shell.
I must keep it protected under my care with love and trust.
I don't know why, but I've let the waves come up.
They came up and caught it, tried to take it away.
But the love I give to this shell is too strong.
And so I have picked it up and carried it away from the waves.
Now that I have the perfect one, I can't imagine having any other.
There is no comparison to this shell.
It is so special in its own way. I love it.
Others may have picked it up and tossed it back. They have hurt it.
But I've found the pieces and I've put them back together. I love this shell.
Now that this shell is here in my hands, I will hold it close.
I'd give up my life to save this precious jewel.
It is so wonderful, so pure, so perfect. I love it.

Jonathan Carlson

Kicking It with God

Hey Man . . . yeah You, Lord
I know you hear me. . . .
    You hear everything.
I just want to thank You for my life, my kids,
my well being, everything!
    I know that I am difficult at times
but hey, You made me.
    I really don't have anybody that I can talk to,
who would listen like you do. Unconditionally
    I know Your love is real. Not only because
the Bible told me so, but because of all I've seen and been through . . . I'm still here!
    I feel kind of funny kicking it with You, Lord,
but I know that You don't mind
    I know that You won't turn me away, ever
    I know that You won't criticize me for my foolishness,
But You will make sure I learn from it,
even if it takes a couple of times.
    Lord. . .I ask of You, to help me be a better person
and a stronger person.
    I ask of You to stay in my family and my life.
Comfort us like You do. Forever.
    Last, but not least, I want to thank You Lord,
for letting me kick it with you.
    I love You, Amen!

Janiesha Sellers

Death

Christmas is here family is near,
Death is waiting on the wings,
Angels are calling and Heaven beckons

My time is near and all is clear
So may thee lay my body down to rest
And allow my soul to weep no more.

Lift away the tangles and burdens
as it enters Heaven's door.
Please do let my spirit go
its journey so long
its all for the best.

Do not weep do not cry
in your lullaby
As Christmas is here family is near
Heaven's waiting, angels are calling.

Katalin T. Reeves

Obsession

Fingers move
Shake your hand
Nodding down
Cold stare

Watching you
From afar
No two words
can be said

My mouth
Runs dry
At the flick
of your eye

Trying boldly
No success
I hang my head
And await what's next

Can't escape
My throbbing heart
Can't move on
Or tear apart

Jennifer Fischer

Weapons

Words like weapons,
Kill!
Dreams,
Ideas,
Piercing deep!
Shame,
Mame,
Like a thief
Steals,
Hopes
Destroying your innermost being,
Careful how you speak!
Scares cut.
Very, very,
Very, deep!
Everlasting,
Think before you speak!

Angelitta Anderson

My Nanny

I have a nanny
That wipes my fanny
One day she smacked me on the butt
So I ran away to a hut
And fell in love with a guy named Danny.

Amy Hill

My Angel from Up High

Every night when I look up at the night sky,
There always is a brightly glowing star looking
back at me.

Sometimes when I think there's just nowhere else to turn,
I look up at the sky and always see my star at burn.

When I feel like everything's over and there's nothing more to lose,
I look up at the sky and see my star aglow,
then I forget about what I've
lost and just go with the flow.

Then as I start to think,
I realize that my brightly glowing star I see in the sky at night
is just an angel watching over me from up high.

Shane Brown

The Marine Corps CREED

I am proud to be a part of what keeps our country free!
From any foreign invasion our protection I shall be!
I live the toughest life of any fighting man
and do not only the job that requires a professional but a man!
A Man who is mature and squared away to a T
who can handle any situation no matter what it may be!
Take a pack on my back and a rifle in my hand
and go out and defend our proud land!
We are made up of every color race and creed
we're a band of brothers, a very special breed
And SEMPER FIDELIS is our middle name;
it means always faithful to the corps and to each other the same.
I am so proud to be a part, of such a very unique team
so true, so proud , so honest and clean.
Yes, we are the finest fighting force the world has ever seen!
We are lean! Green! And mean! I am one of the few! the proud!
The United States Marines!
OOORRAAAHH! OOORRRAAAHH!
OOORRRAAAHHH!

James Ryan III

Buttercup Blues

Lord done been sleeping most of my life
Oh Lord, you know I was asleep in my life
You know that I was sleeping when she
came and woke me up with a kiss from the lips of my buttercup

Lord, I am begging for mercy, put some mercy in my beggar's bowl
Oh Lord, please show mercy, put that mercy in my beggar's bowl
Oh Lord, show mercy she's started a fire way down deep in the depth of my soul

Lord, don't let her leave me, it would kill me that ain't no lie
Oh Lord, please don't let her leave me
it would kill me, ain't no lie
If she were to leave me, I would go back to sleep and in my sleep I would die

Lord, give me the courage to ask her to walk by my side
Oh Lord, I need the courage to ask her to walk in my life
Lord, give me the courage to ask her to be my wife
Lord, I was sleeping most of my life, 'til she came and woke me up,
with a sweet kiss from the lips of my buttercup

John Eiselein

Imagine

I silently watch as the hawk soars through the sky
As I watch, I imagine. Just Imagine.
I imagine that I am flying
Soaring above the water, Above the land, Above the Earth.
Then I hear my name and I float back down to the ground.
Away from the freedom of the air, but back to my prison cell called reality.

Krista Balek

Stormy Seas

I know that life's a stormy sea
To which the gods have lowered me.
I know the years go floating by
As though a leaf in a windy sky.
But though the world is cruel or vile
I do not curse or hate; for while
The stormy sea of life goes on—
For me there'll be another dawn.

Brian Jaybush

Weather the Storm

A tornado chases me
The Earth quakes at my feet
The rain and the wind
Surround me
Try to drown me
I am falling to the ground
I cannot see
Nor can I breathe
Nor steady my feet
Nothing left
I've gone over the cliff
But still I live

Kelly Muma

avocado

a-vo-ca-do
rolls off my tongue.
A name that spells out
invitation.
Your brown skin,
rough and taut,
suggests unseen treasure.
Virgin green,
your colors entice me,
so I thought you'd be more attractive
when I sliced you in two.
The sunlight sparkles
on your fleshy middle,
selling me your softness.
So I touch it,
then cut to the middle
to find your mystery—
a veiny, solid mass of fertility,
guarded like a family secret.

Misty Scott

A Heart Full of Love

Here's a heart full of love,
Especially for you.
Hold it with care,
For it is fragile.

Give it love and affection,
Treat it with kindness.
And it will give in return,
For it's a heart full of love.

A. Melo

Angry Winds

I walk to work
through the woods
angry woods blown by
Angry breaths
winds of mean numbers.
Oh, I did not see the path
covered with slime
Still, I must walk
to slip, to stumble
to climb.
My duty ahead, my fears behind.

Leonard D. Schank

Losing You

This poem is dedicated to a guy, Jerry, that I used to date.
Here I stand at the bottom of a deep, dark cave
My arms outstretched, waiting for you.
But this time, your hand is not there to help me out of my cave
and, again, shield me from every harm in the world.
A shiver runs up my spine. I feel the loneliness in my heart and
Tears well up in my eyes as I realize the harsh truth.
This, was strike three, and I messed up big time.
Your hand will no longer be there for me,
This is the end, and it's all my fault.
I look around and see no one but my own shadow.
I am truly alone in this world now.
I have lost my love, my friend, and a piece of myself.
You were the one I turned to and now you're gone, forever.
I have so many problems but I'm left now, to solve them myself.
I have just come to the harsh truth that I've just lost my best friend
And I have no shoulder to cry on. The wind knocks me to my knees
And the rain pounds at my face and I bow my head.
Here I kneel, asking for your forgiveness, praying for one more chance.
You, my friend, I cannot live without because you are part of me.
I feel incomplete without you in my life.

> *Julie Marie Brady*

Untitled

Stop killing me and my children stop killing me and my children
Save us from abomination and stop shattering
the dreams we are building—God can you hear me?
Make them take the bullets out of guns and please cease this violence
Their souls are crying out Lord, sounds so loud,
yet we hear nothing but silence
Children are going to sleep at night suffering
because their little stomach hurt
while waking up daily to the damnation of Hell on Earth
So God, please reverse society's brainwash, and cleanse
their minds pure like their first day birth
Stop killing me and my children, allow our spirits to walk alongside of you
to avoid temptations and society's ills and villains
Help us see our lives' real purpose—that it is not
the materialistic aspects for which we worship,
which in themselves are truly vain and worthless
In these times of darkness guide us to the light—an eternally
burning candle be our shield in times of danger, take our hand
and surround us with angels; stop killing me and my children
Stop killing me and my children

> *Melvin Carlos Webb*

Life

Life is whatever you make of it.
It is always going to be what you want it to be, nothing more.
It is a beautiful as a snowflake, different in every way.
Each having its own unique twist or pattern.
As it slowly floats to the ground, it spins and turns, dancing magically before it hits its end.
It knows that when it hits the ground it will be gone, it will cease to exist,
yet it is still happy, dancing magically down to the Earth.

Life is also a winding path, never knowing where it will take you.
Sometimes it is crooked and cracked, at other times it is smoother than a baby's bottom.
But either way it is leading somewhere.
The end of the path is never really found, but still the path goes that way,
without looking back, and if that path sways from its destination,
someone always fixes it and makes it go the proper way.

When the snowflake and the path finally meet in solitary end, they both,
not knowing of what they meet, have seen so much that it could fill a lifetime.
With spirits high, and hearts of glory, they meet with destiny as surely
many have, and remember how they were and how they have become.
They just sit and think to themselves what a wonderful world
and remember what was theirs has been passed on.

> *Justin White*

Love

When love is born, it's like a babe
And must be treated well,
By those who feel the tenderness
Of its enchanting spell.

It must be fed with faith and hope
And clothed with deepest trust,
Without these, love will fade away
In gray clouds of disgust.

Love grows with ardor when its young
and as the years roll by,
The sparks of understanding takes
The place of flames that die.

Age only serves to mellow love
Into a treasured thing,
True love can make this life of ours
An everlasting spring.

So we should always cherish love
So that it long endures,
For peace of mind and peace of heart
Are gained when love matures . . . .

> *Charles Frost*

What Is Concealed and Revealed

Gaze no more through the evil mask
Which falsely wears a winsome smile
Its surface glows with a brazen cast
The eyes look out with wicked guile
For deep within those ancient holes
And untruthful image is conceived
Turning, churning in your soul
Causing the heart to be deceived
But by your mournful countenance
The mask must have completed its task
And turned your heart to bitterness
Gaze no more through the evil mask

> *Brandi Barnes*

Step through the Frame

In front of you stands a wall.
Beside you there is nothing.
But behind you is a door
Place your hand on the handle,
Grip it tight, it does not bite.
Twist to the left and pull it back,
Step through the frame
Into the wide open space
and do not hesitate.
Take a look around
and study all that you see.
For you, have just chosen your destiny.

> *Rebecca Glover*

Best of Both Worlds

Standing in the kitchen
facing the ocean

On the phone
with my mom

Laughing crying
Daddy dying
Being born
Giving birth
Crying laughing

Coming

Going

Knowing. . . .

> *Eugenia Calande*

The Wall

Deep within you desire has lost her drive,
and you have to look in the mirror as a reminder that you are still alive.

What a friend you could be,
If you would only look long enough to see.

You hold the hand of cynicism like a lover you're afraid to lose,
And pretend that somehow you don't have bright to chose.

What a lover you could make,
If only you would prompt the passion within to awake.

You're walking down a lonely road and have turned your back
On the lights that could lead you home.

What a mind you have to share,
If only you would look long enough to see that people care.

It's a shame when broken love has left you with such a loss,
When embracing hope hardly seems worth the cost.

What a passionate heart you have to give,
If only you would have the heart to truly live.

Sherry Isley Roberts

Through Another's Eyes

For whom the toll shall pass from here to far
from yonder I see the broken life of a tortured spirit
hanging lifeless in the muck and mire of a lie it created for itself
bound in solitude and seclusion brought on by imaginary oppression
which is drawn out in the space of a feeble-minded soul
yet as I awake things appear to be just as they were before my slumber
yet I imagined myself as someone-else
dreaming how life would be through another's eyes

James Gulyard

There's Something about South Dakota

There's something about South Dakota, sometimes it's hard to explain
It's more than the breathtaking scenery
or contrasts from hills to the plain.
Whatever it is, it's our treasure.

Is it the subtle sounds of woodwinds when the breezes brush the trees?
Or birds singing rhythmic grace notes to the fauna's melodies?
Whatever . . . its all for our pleasure.

There's something about that first fuzzy crocus
that heralds the flora parades
First yellows, then blues, next purples and pinks,
then berries and weeds of all shades.
It's a treat, beyond all measure.

It's mother natures canvas, where she creates exquisite hues.
And she has a reason, for all four seasons;
with each one, we've time to renew.
All this to enjoy, at our leisure.

Oh, yes, there's something else . . . our abundant sunshine . . .
that hasn't been mentioned yet.
It's difficult to decide which is more beautiful here
Sunrise . . . or sunset! God has blessed us, for sure.

Colleen Mahrt

My Love

Your light shines brighter than the sunlight
Creeping across my window pane,
Your voice is like a soft violin whispering sweetly,
The stride of your step is a mellow release for the strain of my eyes.
Your touch sends a soothing sensation through my inner being,
Because of you I feel like going on to higher levels
And heights unseen,
You are the one who completes my being,
Don't ever change who or what you are
I am satisfied.

Shirley Burney

Untitled

My whole life
has been spent
in hospitals

Despite my humble home
in denial,
missing
(at times) the voices,

I have made my home
with no hesitation.

And they like to poke
and probe my veins

and dispense
washing powders
and iodine

when I admit mistakes.

Danielle Rowland

I Was There

It may not seem like it,
the long hours,
the lonely nights,
but I was there.

Hoping and waiting
for something new,
not for it to show.
I was there.

To build a wall
or hide in a shell.
To block out the world.
I was there.

To lose a loved one
or maybe even a friend.
To cry for hours at a time.
I was there.

To let go and forget.
To forgive and be forgiven.
To start a new.
Yes I have been there.

Jennifer Mannix

Over Priced

Today I learned how doubly sad
the loss of what one never had;
with faith and hope one claims to own
the thought your love was mine alone;
a joyous touch of early spring
that only smiling eyes can bring
to melt the snows of winters passed
and warm a lonely heart at last;
somehow between the "then and now"
one finds that actions disavow
the promises love's dreams create;
so early spring arrives too late
to free one's heart from winter's frost,
what might have been is sadly lost.
Perhaps, perhaps one asked for more
than even Heaven had in store;
so once again one's heart must pay
for empty dreams of yesterday,
the price for this now twice as sad
to pay for love one never had.

Jack Bowen

Your Touch

You are the creator of the universe, and of every creeping thing,
But it has to be lonely, when everyone expects You to keep giving them things.
They hold their hands out for the gift, and they pay no attention to You.
I want You to know that this is not what I've come before You to do.
I want You to know I think about You everyday.
Not just for the things You have provided me with,
But because I love You in an extraordinary way.
I love the way You create a gentle breeze, blowing on a hot summer's day.
As the wind softly whispers, I pretend it's You, passionately caressing my face.
When I walk across a beach and the sand get between my toes,
I think of You playing with my feet, as I giggle for You to let them go.
When the rain falls from Heaven, I feel a subtle kiss on my cheek with every drop.
Sometimes I just stand there, and get soaking wet,
because I don't want You to stop.

So many people say they can't feel Your love in a physical kind of way,

That's because they haven't taken the time to look at You,
and gaze into Your face.

There are so many ways You share Your love with me, I needed this time to say,

I honor and acknowledge You, my love, my lover through nature's way.

Dione M. Freeman

Why Me and Who Am I Now

Why me? Why was I taken away from my brothers, my sisters,
my father, my mother, my family, my friends, why me?
Where am I going? Why am I being taken away from the motherland?
What strange land will I land on? Who will be there awaiting me when this long journey ends?
Who will I become now or what will become of me?

Who am I now? I'm African now; soon,
I'll become someone else in a strange land,
with no family, friends and surely no home. Who am I now?

Now I am African-Cuban, African-Brazilian, African-Panamanian,
African-Honduran, African-Costa-Rican, African-Spanish,
African-Bolivian, African-Dominican, African-Puerto-Rican . . .
and many more.

Who am I now? I'm a human being, who was stolen from Africa
and brought to many countries throughout South America;
now, I am African-Cuban and others. Now that I know who I am,
who are you and do you really know?

Forrest Cutler

In Memory of My Daughter (10-10-97 to 07-28-98)

I wrote this poem in the memory of my 9 1\2 month old daughter.
Nakada was the sweetest baby I had ever known,
and nothing can or ever will take her place.
I will never forget her laughs, her cries, her looks that she would make,
or her beautiful baby face.
She was and will always be my baby girl,
and I love her with every bit of my heart.
And when the Lord took her from me to have as his angel,
it tore me completely apart.
I don't understand why he took her from me,
and I will never understand that at all.
But the Lord needed a special angel,
and my little Nakada is who he decided to call.
He definitely picked out the perfect angel,
and no one could ever disagree.
Now she is my guardian angel
and will always be watching over me.
She was the best baby there could ever be,
and she sure was one of a kind.
She is my special angel, and my precious baby girl
in my heart and in my mind.

Gena Jaggers Vincent

Embarkment

Am I afraid
of what I would see
Should I look
beyond the life of me
Into the pondering pores of life
I stitch a search.
But quietly because
I shouldn't disrupt church.
If I continue believing
what is brought,
Would these new thoughts
in my head rot?
Just to reassure my
conscience,
My dreams are pure,
untouched by darkness
As for my decisions
I feel no remorse
For it was I
who chose this course.

Jennifer Everding

Runaway Train

Faster, faster spin the wheels
Where has everybody gone

Look around me
Feel the bile slowly rising
Stop this silent scream within

Stop the steaming
Stop the squealing
Of this empty soulless train

Frantic search among the aisles
Looking for my soulless self

Faster, faster, I run faster
Through the maze among my mind

Looking for an open tunnel
Realization slams against me
The wall of death is all I'll find

Teressa Mehlberg

Laughter

i hear Little childrens'
laughter All
    aroUnd me
      Getting my attention
   so Happily
    Thinking that
maybE that could
have Really just been me

Samantha Sekera

Untitled

We are the poets, mighty and few.
Our thoughts, our hearts,
our feelings, our pens,
truth our product sustains in lieu.
Our wounds, our lens
our scars, our darts,
from rankled minds truth must spew.

For we are doomed, we miserable lot.
Our illness, our strife,
our ailment, to tenfold feel
every emotion carelessly begot.
Our truth, to rightfully steal,
our knowing, our life;
doomed to die, not realizing we fought.

Richard Massa

A Soulmate's Song

It is beyond our control . . .
Two kindred spirits walking the Earth at the same time, passing and
touching only briefly, waiting another lifetime to be back together again.
When the rain kisses your face do you feel my tears?
Call out to me for I am in the wind.
Remember and feel my hair blowing against your face.
When you are in the warmth of the sun remember the warmth of my arms around you.
Put your hand on your heart and feel me there for I am part of you and you are part of me.
We are one soul, one heart, one love, sent here to Earth to find each other
and pass quietly away as two shadows on the ground.
In the next world you will know me again and there we can restore our love,
for it is not meant to be here in this time and in this place.
You know that in your heart.
Until then, keep me in that place that lets you breathe, live and love here.
For even when it stops after its tired journey, I will be there waiting,
hoping, knowing you will somehow find a way to come back to me.
But for now it is beyond our control . . .

Caryn M. Suarez

Saying Good-Bye

Awakening with a jolt, I slowly rise.
Suddenly realizing the tears flowing from my eyes,
I remember the painful reason why,
   For today is the day I must say good-bye.

My mother and father are restless but silent,
Quietly reminiscing about the time we have spent
Together as a family, all the special moments.
They still bless the day that their "baby" was sent.
My bags stand high in a tower, all packed,
Yet my heart weighs heavier than the entire pile stacked.
It feels like it has been broken, bruised, and smacked.
Cheerfulness is a feeling that this aching day lacked.

Unable to move, paralyzed on my bed, I lie.
The only parents I have ever known come in and cry.
As they hug me, we walk bravely, side by side,
To the woman and new life waiting for me outside.

I look up to find the same brown colored eyes as mine.
They search for a sign; but only yearning and sorrow is what they will
Find, for my loving family that I am forced to leave behind.
   For today is the day I must say good-bye.

Julia Bailey

Success

Success is a journey, not a destination.
It will not necessarily lead you into the next haven.
You could be caught up in greed, hatred, and booze.
And with this my friend you will always lose.
Money will be your kinship, attention will be your lust.
Before long there is no one you can really trust.
Real love will be unknown. Arrogance will be strong.
Before you know that Hell has hit you will be long gone.
Nothing will be of certain. Nothing will go unchanged.
Your heart will be the soul of empty rage.
Everything will fall short of a miracle.
You will not know the love that was once unconditional.
Those who once stood beside you now stand behind you.
They are desperate to pull you back into the life that you once came.
Try to get you out of this pick and choose game.

Bobbi Cossins

Yes, It Was My Mother

Yes, it was my mother who raised three kids and went to college at the same time.
People knew she was a strong and courageous women

She worked hard at school every day.
And everyday she would rush home to meet me a few minutes after school.

She put clothes on our back and food on the table.

Shaina Bell

Windswept

Sure as the south wind sweeps the land,
and warm spring rain revives
all that has waited through winter

So it comes to those
who've chilled, drawn aside

Allowing distance . . .
the arrival of
a new season.
A stirring,
as leaves,
blossoms,
tendrils,
shed the cloak
of dormancy,

The leap into this ballet
recognized as spring.

Leona Mason Heitsch

Grandpa

Last night,
I called your name
As I lied down to sleep
In my dream
I saw a light
And there was you,
Smiling at me
I guess what I'm trying to say,
Is that, I missed you, Grandpa!
As I held you tight
It felt so good
To be with you,
Even it was only in my dream
The power of our love,
And the knowledge you have taught me
Brings my faith, even more stronger
Thank you, Grandpa
For you have made me
What I am today

Sandra Tilton

So Beautiful a Nation's Anthem

So beautiful, a nation's anthem
Like our's oh, again will never be
Its words in blood were written
People, especially for you and me.

Listen to the sounds of freedom
The wind is whispering in the trees
Words of love, freedom, loyalty,
This it deserves, from you and me.

So beautiful, a nation's anthem
Like our's, oh, again will never be
Listen to the word's of freedom
Saying were the sons of liberty.

Listen to the sound, of freedom
The wind, it whispers to the trees
When in wait, of hope, a future
Welcome home, my son of liberty.

Luis E. Salazar

Lost in Thoughts

Lost in thought,
That I came about,
Wondering if I'd live tomorrow,
And die without sorrow.
What would it be like
Seeing for the first or last time?

Priscilla Roman

No One Noticed

A single tear slid unaware down the delicate face of the forgotten child.
In its fragile hands, a pile of rose petals, once cared for
But now shattered into a million tiny pieces.
No one noticed!
The only sound to be heard is the shattering of glass
And the outraged cries of two drunk adults. The child cringes.
No one noticed!
A window lay open.
Rain fell in the window to land mockingly on the eyeless brown teddy bear.
No one noticed!
No one noticed when the child broke in a million pieces to lay so still
And helpless in the corner of a colorless imprisonment.
And nobody even bothered to noticed the wounded brown bear
Silently crying for this broken child.
NO ONE even NOTICED.

Anna Sanford

Happy Valentine's Day

I would like to wish you a Happy Valentines Day
and to tell you I love you in a different way.
I have spent most of my life searching for that special one,
and when God blessed me with you, I knew my life had just begun.
I cannot yet describe what it is about you that I love so much;
maybe your beauty, your kisses, or perhaps your magnificent touch.
Whatever it is that keeps me coming back for more,
it is the one powerful thing I have been longing for.
You have taken an old abandoned broken heart,
and made it love again with someone it could never part.
You are everything I have always dreamed of,
and now that you are in my life, I will shower you with everlasting love.
Our love combined together, will always remain,
never faltering nor depleting, or causing grief or pain.
It is now within my heart that your love will continuously grow,
satisfying its every desire, more than I'll ever know.

I love you Margaret.

Andrew Fisher

Captured Beauty

I show horses beautiful mammals of grace and angelic movement,
when they canter through pastures of rolling green grass,
it's like a spirit being set free to collect ideas and creative thoughts,
and the grass blows in the wind like a sea in winter,
carrying the horse freely, not only is beauty captured in a rural setting,
but it is seen at a show in the horses' picturesque appearance
of a neatly-braided mane and a shiny flowing tail streaking
behind the horse like a ray of light at the end of a shooting star,
in all views, in all eyes of any living thing their beauty is seen and felt
in a calming way that surrounds and fills the air with silence.

Sara Goodman

She

She comes into my life, without permission and without warning—
Who does She think She is entering my life, trying to help me find me?
Is She the person I have asked God for?
Is She the one that is supposed to help me on my journey?
Well let me tell you about She—Let me tell you what She does to me—
She is the one who heals me—She senses my pain, and she tries to cure me—
When She Smiles, She makes me smile—She is my happiness—
She brings out the best in me—She is the missing part to my heart—
When She is not near, I miss her—When She talks to me, my ears are healed—
When She is near, I feel warmth—When She touches me, I am cured—
I Thank God for sending She—
She is my cure—She is something I need more of—
For the words are in my heart and in my head—
She is the Love I have never felt before—She is everything to me—
Words I cannot say—Words that never existed in my life—
Words that are now my true feelings—I do not care the consequences—
This heart is for you—You bring me the tears I only imagine to have—
She is always there, She is always near—I can smell her presence—
I Love her—I Love her skin, her smile, her words, her touch—
I Truly and Deeply Love You—I Love You—

Ricardo Garibay III

Visually Impaired

Can you see them hanging
motionless above your heads
finger dancing their victims
into devilish delights as they
spit out lying lines of cheating
deceptions of greed and creeds?
They're the puppet masters and
you're the marionette strung up
and controlled by their worldly ways.
They're advocates of evil whispering
undertone hisses with fearful faces
can you hear them?
Are you looking forward towards
the downfall to your spiritual
death as you cuss and fuss
and then have notions of lust
for that person next to you?

Quinn Floyd

Untitled

The clouds wrap together.
The beginnings of becoming one
A sky of dusk brings no other
But holds back none who come.

Orion and Cleo break through.
The gentle winds pick up
For we are true
As the speed takes a jump.

Thunderous howls can be heard.
Harsh winds—but yet so softly felt
Like the feathers of a bird
And the climax is soon dealt.

The sonance of escape is heard
Through the window panes that shake
When two become one; nothing obscured
And love is fully awake.

Tanya Mazur

A Love Poem

Had I the words of Shakespeare
I would have written a sonnet on
Your pure innocence,
Compared you to a summer's breeze
And your smile
To the chimes of a girl's anklets
That whisper a melody of tender joy.

But I, being poor,
Can only wrap you in dreams,
And bathe you in the velvet softness
Of my love.

I have thus toasted your angel smile
And made you all mine,
Your sweet charms have I cherished.
And thus paid homage
To a creation in God's reflection.

Ayesha Mian

LH's—Love Hallucinations

Wake up
Something's itching
Mosquito bite?
Can't find any
Tingling again
Realize it's my heart
No wonder
Dreamt of you
No use to scratch
Will always tickle
For you

Emilie Andersson

Tha City Gets No Sleep

This city that'll never sleep—illuminate mosaic,
a result of the blood sweat and tears of lost Afro centric sheep
But, the city is our cell, an industrial spored penitentiary
where the greeting at the gate reads welcome to Hell
Ya see my lost tribe of once and future kings have been persecuted,
exiled, deceived, manipulated, contaminated, exploited
and when it came to our voices avoided
The sins of the world have even affected our children—
breeding young warriors, strong, starving, cornered, and carriers of a heavy burden.
Killing each other for crumbs of bread—
enslaving one another with crack sugar cubes of tears and dread.
Never feeling complete or whole at least—
unless we have Tommy Hillfiger, Rolex's, Ice, and the Gucci fleece
We have no identity, no name, no history
just poverty and shame
We are an enigma, shadows of a pale man's crime and a soldiers rhyme
WONDERING—being bombarded with media friendly heresy
WONDERING—self destructing from within, drowning unity in shots of Hennessey
WONDERING—unable to prevent, just cry over Diallo's tragedy.

James Manuel

Friendship Knot

They say friends come and go, but when you find some, it's hard to let go.
We were brought here from different communities and formed this certain unity.
We might say we tied the knot just like when you get married.
We saw each other through the good and the bad; we even made each other laugh,
through tears and fears.
And now one of us is leaving the boat.
We tell each other that everything will be okay, we will stay afloat.
But there is a loop missing out of the knot.
How are we going to stay afloat?
Maybe if we pray hard enough, something will happen and you will come back to us.
They call us childish, even selfish.
But isn't friendship much like a toy that you play with, have fun with, even get mad
with when it doesn't work.
We get older, and are minds get stronger; we stop playing the one thing we enjoyed so much.
Some how we all feel ashamed
We let you slip away, without even knowing that it is going to hurt this much.
Do you even notice the change in us?
DEE, you changed us and we've changed you.
There always be a part of us with you, if you don't notice now but will notice it later.
But for now we will miss you. We wish you the best of luck now and later.
and DIEDRA . . . WE LOVE YOU

Shantell Stallings

The Enchanted Embrace

You breathe the cool, brisk air with gentle lips
They shine so delicate, yet smooth and strong
Satisfying deep desiring hunger of the Precious One, who's skin soaks into your dimension
Sweetness poured out and shared between them
Tangled forever together
Hearts beat, pounding with intense passion
Beats simultaneous, building a crescendo of magestical effervesence . . .
Coming is the attraction
One of potent, poignant power, greater than any ever felt
Enchanted by this enlightenment, they fall together, one with one, in each other's arms
The bond is tightly tied
A kiss capped off with a warm smile
An embrace which sends tender spirits floating into the evening twighlight
Our eyes glisten, sparkling with stars and moon's glow—a luminous vibe of peace
The night wanes, the closeness also—
Seperation comes like a knife in the night to slice them apart
Precious eyes slowly turn away, glance at the path they must continue to follow alone
Yet comfortable and safe
A good-bye to you and to me
Soon we will lie together again. . . .

Melissa Chern

A Gift

We bring them into our life,
Sometimes with apprehension,
A gift from God,
And yet no appreciation.
Beware, if they are gone from you,
Even for an instance.
Do not forget their innocence and joy,
The children are here to remind us.
Remind us of our hearts.
Gifts of materials, we adults give,
Tokens to satisfy our guilt,
Guilty of no love for others.
No Greater A Gift Can Be Had,
Than A Moment With A Child.
Cherish The Memories And
Learn From Their Love.

Holly Staggs

In God's Word

Multitudes of greatness will unfold,
In God's word great things are told.
If only you wholeheartedly believe,
His precious grace you will receive.

In God's word, wrong you can't be,
Learn by His example, be set free.
When the Holy Spirit speaks-listen,
What you hear will make eyes glisten.

Our faith in Christ will help us see,
Life is not all about me, me, me . . .
Six days it took-creation was done,
But our days of praise have just begun.

Work harder at what you should be,
Praise His name each day graciously.
We all need to be cleansed of our sins,
For that is where our new life begins.

Barbara Daywalt

Demon's Slave

Demons consume the weak
Savagely devouring as I speak
Innocence never more
Life was such a bore
Lost am I never found
My soul so tightly bound
Demons trapped me in their cage
My cries for help become enrage
The needle my soul is fed
Only hope now is when I am dead

Lisa Edgar

Dance into Eternity

I walked along a narrow path,
  which led me to a stream
And as I gazed into the waters,
  suddenly I began to dream

I visualized a maiden there,
  by far the fairest in the land
She moved like an angel,
  so I reached to touch her hand

I fell into the waters,
  but did not seem to care
We danced with one another,
  her beauty was beyond compare

For me there could be no other,
  she washed away my uncertainty
And as the stream carried us along,
  we danced our way into eternity. . . .

Curtis Thompson

My Dream

The human race is a place of integration, not segregation.
When there is discrimination in this nation we suffer from our own self determination.
The ethnic pride that we describe can only survive with nonviolence we stay alive.
My civil rights are not a light for you to switch as you please, on and off.
I'm on my knees.
Abolitionist is what you are.
My oppression near or far.
Prejudice is what you seek, unity is what I speak.
My culture lives right through me, minority is what I be.
Look at me, my brotherhood, underground railroad is where I stood.
So listen good and listen close.
I know who I am, I have spoke!

    Ivan Carrera

Did You Really Love Me?

Did you really love me when you told me all those lies?
Did you really want to be the only one in my life?
Or were all your words of love just a simple game to play
When you'd beg me to stay?
Because now I sit and cry and wonder why you left me so suddenly so fast.
And as I count the tears I shed I also count the days until I have you in my life again.
How could all you swore to me you felt deep down inside of your heart
just fall apart into a sad darkness in my heart that has left me with only
sweet memories of the tremendous love that we once shared.
But I cannot take you out of my heart, for I bear a child within me
that bears your name and lives inside me now and forever.
As our child lives and breathes, the love I feel for you lives and goes on.
And although you are no longer by my side we will be forever united.
It is hard to explain the feeling in my heart.
So many strong feelings of love, sadness, and regrets.
I gave you my heart and love in whole and in return you gave me nothing
but lies and a great happiness that has now ended with such a great sorrow.
But a great part of you lives, and grows throughout me,
and even though you have taken away your love from me
that is something that you can never take away,
for you will live within me now and for eternity.

    Berta Palucho

Forgive Me, God

God, forgive me for all what I'm doing, did and have done.
I've caused so much pain for others and mixed it with pleasure and having fun.
Forgive me God for all the mistakes that I've made,
For all the hearts that I've broke, for all the feelings that I've hurt,
And for all the wounds that I've caused.
I've caused so much pain though I knew it was wrong,
But I did it all and I'm ashamed to say that the devil in me had fun.
God forgive me and kill the demon in me,
God forgive me and release me from my misery,
God forgive me and take back my soul,
God forgive me and vanish me from this life for all.
Wounds won't be healed, tears will never dry
'Til the demon in me is sent to Hell and burns in the sky,
And that won't be 'til you take my soul from me.
So please God, release me,
And forgive me.

    Mohammad Taqi

My Favorite Place

Not a single day goes by that I don't think of my favorite place
The beauty, the serenity, the ultimate in time and space
The pleasantry sound of the roaring waves, as they crash upon the rocks
The wetness of the mist and spray, splashing me when the ocean talks
The feel of the wet and dry sand, as it squishes through my toes
As I'm running down the ocean shore, chasing those crazy sea gulls
Even the odor of the fresh seaweed entangled upon the shore
Has me breathing deeper and deeper, asking myself for more
What more could I ask for, as I watch the sun set over the plateau
The brilliant bright colors make me wish I could stay, and not have to go
The beach is my favorite place, as you now have been told
I'll continue to visit with a passion, even when I grow old

    Roland Rodriguez

Love of an Angel

Heaven sent from God above,
Put on this Earth to help and love.
A gift of kindness from the heart,
This is what I offer,
What I have given right from the start.

A single person alone I stand,
Helping anyone whenever I can.
This is the gift I give to you,
This is the greatest gift to man.

Heaven sent from God above,
Put on this Earth to honor and love.
A gift for all who can share,
A gift for all the people who care.

A single word held oh, so tight,
A gentle kiss on a lonesome night.
This I give to all who see,
This I give to those who love me.

    Debbie Thomas

On a Night like Tonight

Tonight the rain fell through
The clouds, blocking the stars.
Tonight there is no light,
Leaving me alone in the dark.

Last night the moon shone brightly,
Showing all of our fears.
Life was fine, until tonight.

Tonight the stars fell through,
Exposing all of our thoughts.
It's only on a night like tonight,
When the clouds hold back the light,
When we can hide in the shadows,
On this dark, lonely night.

Only the shadows tonight
Will protect us from the light,
The light that exposes our true selves.
Only on a night like this.

    Heather Ryan

Have You Ever

Have you ever walked upon the sky
Like sparrows in mid June
Have you ever felt deep in your heart
That love is coming soon
After many years of searching
Now I can finally say
This feeling that I speak of
To me has found its way
You feel as if you're floating
like clouds up in the sky
You do things never thought before
And not once wonder why
You could see sunset a thousand times
A thousand days could pass
And not once have such a feeling
That's why I have to ask
Have you ever felt that you could fly
Upon the skies so blue
Well that's the feeling that I get
Every time I think of you.

    John Sherbert

Daybreak

Night sky fades to dawn.
Light's slow dance on land's
      contours;
Horizons are born.

    Clarice Anne Cordoviz

At Night

Two bodies touched by the darkness,
In the night glow.
Alone with you ends with you.
Memories made with each other
Go unforgotten in our minds.
Spoken thoughts, reaching, arrive as dreamed.
Closeness felt, never distant,
Touches our lonely souls.
Shadows seen walk away,
For they know harm can never be.
Love at last, lasts forever,
While forever never ends.
Spoken words of true love gently soothe
As we listen.
The fire in our hearts
Gets its love from love's desire.
The two of us alone
Hold each other to be one, at night.

Armando Ramos

Going Home

Arriving late at night, porch light still on
sleepy kids go in to pallets on the floor, fold out sofa, bodies galore
The house smells of firewood in the stove,
hushed voices in the kitchen, exchanging their hello's.
Saturdays are always filled with fun, guys go to the lake, play cards, shoot the guns.
Girls will make a trip into town.
Maybe let the kids drive the car around, and later, if you're good, go to the creek,
If not, maybe another day this week.
Crickets come alive as night falls, June bugs and locust knocking on the front door.
The scent of horses breezes by, dogs barking, time to have another piece of pie
ahhh going home
Young families get together, laughing, playing games, children fighting over toys.
Cooking in the kitchen, dressing and wild game, everyone pitching in with the chores.
The rooster crows early in the morning, shouting,
It's time to get out of bed, biscuits and chocolate gravy or bacon and eggs instead.
Cartoons playing in the background, children glued to the TV
Girls gathered around the piano, trying to sing in harmony
gathered in the front, saying our good byes, hating to leave, hugging wiping our eyes.
Kids clinging to one another, sobbing not wanting to let go,
It will be a long time coming before we are together again they know.
ahhhh going home,
The sense of safety and comfort, familiar sounds and smells
Pinto beans and cornbread, fried potatoes, chicken,
They never taste as good as they do here.

Vonda Accurso

My Black Rose

My love is like a tall, black rose:
Her eyes weep invisible tears like the dead.
        but her crying only accents their beauty.
Her body is comparable to the curvature of the stem
        legs long and bold,
        waist defining hourglass.
Her lips are ebony tinted luscious apple red.
Yet she feels lust only for her own kind.

My love is like a tall black rose.
Her hair falls down like petals dropped from a cloud.
        yet it rolls up like the bud inside.
Her hands are similar to the beautiful splitting of the stems
        her grace gives a masterful massage.
        her fingers are like liquid glass yet firm, not brittle nor malleable.
Not even poetry can describe her beauty.
Yet she does not feel for other flowers.

My love is like a tall black rose.
Her self-esteem protects her stem like thorns,
        yet her thorns are as frail as a beam of light.
Her face is smooth like her petals
        at times her visage is as placid as a pond
        while at others her face withers from lack of knowledge.
She lives in a land of red roses.
Someday she will live with the black.

Michael Weber

Medicine Man

Medicine Man, drive away
These awful spirits
Forgotten voices of my past
Haunt me into the days to come.
Medicine Man, cure my ills
Drive away these pains that
Plague me night and day
Bring me peace.
Medicine Man, show me the way
Show me the path through darkness
Shine brightly on my life.
Medicine Man, bring me the serenity,
Serenity that only comes with death
Medicine Man, deliver me
From this pain.
Medicine Man, won't you help me?

Jason Cook

No Endorsements

Lost your pain?
Emptied vein
Stop yourself
Vital Drain
Face your day
Soul Fray
Angered God
Hero to stay
Guilt lost
Mind embossed
Heavy weight
Turned, tossed
Open pore
Closed door
Happy face
Nevermore

Scott Simmons

The Gift

Thank you for the gift,
Yes, that special one,
The one you gave to me.

The one that will last forever,
And works, only for me,
The one I will cherish,
For always, inside of me.

It can never be stolen,
It can never be broken,
It can never be hidden, or taken away.

Again thank you, for the gift,
Yes, that special one,
The one you gave to me!
Your memory.

Kansastom

I Need to Let You Go

I need to let go
I cannot stay,
And let you hurt me,
In this way.
I need to understand
She's the one love now
Someday I'll realize that,
Someway somehow.
For the time being,
I'll hold my head high,
I'll wipe away the tears,
Whenever you walk by.
So, I will smoke
And not let it show,
For I realize now,
I need to let go!

Amanda Derr

Love

I think I love him.
The very thought of him brings a smile to my face.
But what is love?
Who has the right to tell us what love is?
Is love a deep affection or strong fondness toward someone?
If so, I love him.
Or is it the unfamiliar feeling of it all?
Maybe it's the new change,
The good change in my life I love so much.
But that doesn't explain why I get so happy to be around him.
Why it cheers me up just to think about him.
Who is to say that that isn't love?
The feeling of something new, something exciting,
Something sweet, because that is the definition of this relationship.
No matter how bad I feel, the sound of his voice
Or the sound of his laughter makes me happy.
Love?
Love is the butterfly feeling you get when you're around him.
The feeling you get when you hear his name
Or the sense of his being gives you.
The longing to kiss him.
To give into his temptations because I feel that and more.
But what does a 14-year-old girl know about love?

Laura Larsen

Jesus Our Savior

He is as pure as a newborn dove.
He is guarding the gates of Heaven above.
He is full of love.
I am fortunate to have a lot of things.
I also like to think of what God may bring.
I think of the green leaves of the trees
swaying in a nice summer breeze.
I try to read the Bible every day, but it seems like I also like to play.
It seems like God molded us out of clay.
I think everything is nice, even little mice.
Life's moments can be great, plus my puppy likes it in his crate.
If you go to church and listen to the Gospel,
you will see the love of God is great.
As you know I'm talking about Jesus our Savior,
and the Bird of the Trinity can be a great favor.

Rebecca Strasburger

Whispers del Muerto

The carcass of an ocean, ever eternal,
of whirling blue whispers, echo in my heart,
thirsting for verdurous plains;
removal of my foreign state, physically, mentally,
observed by native cactus greeters
salatiously spying my internal sanctuary.

My island mind suffocating in the vast openness
of the claustrophobic-inducing canyons,
complicating my focal point, wavering my careful steps along it's edge.
Screams filter my senses suggested by murmuring winds
exalting empty oceans of ancient memories;
those who stood here before me.

Allowing these souls to take possession of me,
I fade into a red and gold canvas,
reflections of the sun's conquest.

Mary Frank

Love

Resembles a sweet, red rose,
Extraordinary beauty, passion and pain,
Once a bud, seeking the beginning of a lasting relationship,
Became an open rose, resembling the time and effort it took for your love to grow,
The bottom of your heart acts as the root of your true emotional feelings,
It takes time and love to have a beautiful rose,
But it takes your heart and soul to show someone special that you love them.

Michael Allred

Faith

It's not that He doesn't love you,
He does with ALL His heart.
It's not that He has deserted you,
Although it seams you are apart.
He promised he would never leave you,
on that you can depend.
Throughout life's trials and triumphs,
He'll walk beside you 'til the end.
Don't worry what the day may bring,
be it good or be it bad.
Your health, wealth, love, and your joy
are all part of His special plan.
As you put your faith in Him
and learn to trust Him more,
you'll discover all the many blessings
which He has in store.
"Let Not Your Heart Be Troubled" nor
feel alone or stranded.
Remember, nothing will come up today
that you and God can't handle.

Miriam Sosebee

Can You Hear the Children

Can you hear the children playing,
laughing all the time?
Can you hear the children singing,
songs full of rhyme?
Can you see the children sleeping,
all cuddled up through the night?
You don't have to buy them things,
just love them with all your might!

Cori Darwin

The Band

The curtains open,
the drums give a beat,
the flutes say a phrase,
and the piccolo repeat.

The tubas grown,
the saxes sing,
the clarinets shriek,
and the symbols ring.

The French horns whisper,
the trombones make a riot,
the trumpets laugh,
then all is quiet.

Brianna Huemmer

In Facing Grace

Blame and eyes
like ready to throw
and walls I've built will never hold.
Blame and eyes
cold and stuck
he whispers now, "You're out of luck."
Touch is stone
where shadows fall
and the ground I've known
is none at all.
Now none at all.
Look beneath (once sheltered feet)
bare and grapple now for grace
and grapple now for grace.
Word he owns and spares me not.
When all that is
is none at all
nothing to do, blame turns my way,
"Are you prepared to fall?"

Ingrid Williams

An Open Letter to My late Grandpa

A sad wake of glorious emotions, how do I handle the loss of you.
Your guidance was always present and your soul intertwined with my own.
A loss beyond expression and the fear of not having you with me as a guide, a mentor,
makes me wish not for the unknown future but for the comfortable past.
I felt safe in your wisdom that protected me
from my inexperienced stubbornness and refusal of the "correct way."
To know the only solace that I find in the absence of you
is passing that knowledge on to others in search of direction.
My legacy is your caring need to help those around you
with the lessons that taught you the facts of good and bad, right from wrong.
Day, weeks, years go by and you're always in my heart, soul, mind and heart.
I look to you for guidance in the experience of loving you and the undaunting task
of living without the greatest influence of my life.
Please feel the love now I have for you,
even though I never expressed it enough while we were together.
Respect the admiration I never showed
because it was always there even though I did the opposite.
I await the reunion we will one day have
in the place that you have since made for us all.
We can spend an eternity sharing our thoughts and wisdom's,
comparing our deeds as equals and the approach we took
in doing all that we were given to do here on Earth.

Jody Wilcox

I Lie Here Alone and Scared

I lie here alone and scared,
wondering what the future may bring.
I think out loud but no one can hear my thoughts,
No one can see my tears fall like rain,
or hear me cry as loud as thunder.
It was just a short while ago I was surrounded by friends,
but now they all flew north for the summer
while this feathered friend is stuck in the south alone and scared.
Scared of the uncertain future,
the possibility of being alone forever,
or never to touch my far away love again.
The love of my life,
the one soul who completes the emptiness in my heart.
The emptiness that is there now from the absence of her voice,
the absence of her touch,
and of those beautiful blue eyes that pierces my heart like cupid's arrow.
As I write I am still alone,
but for how long,
God only knows . . .

Kevin Costa

Sunset Rendezvous

There is a valley beyond the clouds called Sunset Rendezvous.
A very special place for anybody who's main companion was their four legged faithful friend.
Here, that very special person who may have been lonely or disabled,
sick or depressed can wait in peace and tranquility, restored to health,
for their faithful companion to be re-united with them.
Here they wait, living in harmony with nature until that special time arrives when they
are joined by their faithful companion.
Sometimes the wait is long, for more than one companion has to accompany this
special person on this final journey.
Sometimes people have departed so unexpectedly
that their companion has had to be re-homed or cared for at a rescue center.
Although they become happy and are loved again,
the love from their departed friend is never forgotten.
Sometimes a reunion will take place with a companion from Rainbow Bridge.
When the love is so great, the bond so strong,
that love will transport that pet to Sunset Rendezvous.
When, and only when all are reunited, the circle of friends complete,
they are surrounded within a cradle of love and all together they move on.
They leave Sunset Rendezvous for the last stage of the journey to their final resting place.
Free from harm, safe, and happy.
Together, never to be parted again, they make the journey where love unites them
together for ever and ever.

Sue Cooper

Autumn Nights

The silver rays steal into my Flesh,
Warmth worms through my quivering
Body,
Slowly my submissive hands reach out,
Trying to touch the evasive Heavens.
Beats intertwine under an Autumn sky,
Searching for the endless light,
The Candle that never dwindles.
Running from the Pain,
Running into the majestical mystery,
Running under an Autumn sky.

Christine Seal

Mask

Protected, unblemished ego,
The one we hide, scared to
   let go of deep emotions,
Engulfing pride worn out;
Smile to fool someone's eyes;
Beneath that smugness lies
   the truth,
It cries out HELP. . .
Somehow no matter how
   dim it might be;
Life will always make
   our minds ponder,
That our hearts yonder
In what reality has to offer;
Consoling bruises, hurt
   and anger;
Divine grace, to unmask
You and Me, once more,
   to fly and be free . . .

Elizabeth Cruz

Love

Love, what is love? Is
love a friend, or is love
someone you like? To me,
love is a very powerful
word to say to someone.
The word love means four
little meanings: There's
the l, o, v, e, and each of
those letters has a meaning.
The l means respect;
the o means kindness;
the v means truthful;
and the e stands for faithful.
If you're not able to
do those four things,
then u don't know what love is.
To me that is what love means.

Michael Portelinha

Pearl

A piece of sand
falls into soft flesh
hurts it so much so much
causes to be wrapped
by mother-of-pearl
and bring birth to
a wonderful moon and
a reflection of
wealth of world
someday brought to light
by a diver caring
to search the sea
of somebody

Michael Ehrreich

An Officer, a Husband, a Father, and a Friend

Dedicated to the memory of Cpl. Steven L. Levy
Officers came from all over to pay their final respects here;
And to mourn the loss of a fellow colleague, so dear.
Cpl. Steven L. Levy was brave enough to sacrifice his own life.
Our sympathies are extended to his 2 children & his loving wife.
We honor the department which he so faithfully served.
For 11 years, Cpl. Levy was dedicated—never becoming unnerved.
Cpl. Steven L. Levy devoted his life to ensuring safety for all.
His heart and love for others was anything but small.
There was no task given he would not attempt to conquer;
For this, Cpl. Levy was awarded the prestigious Medal Of Honor.
Cpl. Levy touched the lives of everyone he ever met.
He now joins the list of heroes we will never forget.
As Cpl. Steven L. Levy joins those in the heavens above,
May his family and friends remain blessed by God's grace and His love.
While there is no easy way to bring this tribute to an end . . .
We all agree that he will be missed as an Officer, a Husband, a Father, and a Friend.

Steve Hawk

Letting Go

Loving each other so much, and hanging on so long
you might think it might be difficult
But I think it makes us much more strong,
The friendship that we built together
Gave us memories for the past and hanging on forever
Will make the memories last, letting go will bring guilt and sorrow
And the memories we had of today are gone for tomorrow
I care for you only because I gave you my heart
And getting it back would be a start, Until I do I cannot part
You left me hurting with the worst pain of all
A broken heart and only time can heal
You made me feel you cared for me, dear, and would always want me near,
But you lied and you were wrong, you didn't know what you wanted or
To whom you wanted to belong. I feel alone and incomplete,
I barely know your name, our relationship is over,
Because it will never be the same.
Our times and special moments, that was supposedly a love thing
I am now going to call it, A High School Fling.

Daidree Heigert

sea of me

there was a time and a place where i resided alone
and all of it around me was my very own.
i stood on a piece of ground, the size was very small
only space enough for me to stand and nobody else at all.
i took years and years of crucial time to build the sea around me . . .
years and years of wasted time that could have been used to find thee.
my hopes and dreams were thrown away, with a single toss
and in frustration, i pitched my heart and it was forever lost.
to reside here in this lonely place i thought would be my fate.
but then in the distance, I opened my eyes and there i saw your face.
you walked across the sea of me and crushed the walls of time.
you took my hand and led me to a place that you were mine.

Renee Koch

She Is . . .

She is a mother grieving for her lost child.
She is the piece of glass that has cut your heart and made it bleed.
She is the bitter taste of tears as they fall like rain.
She is the perfume that brings back the painful memories.
She is the scream of pain felt from a wound so deep, it will not heal.
She is the funeral procession as it moves slowly down the road of death.
She is the look on the faces of people that have just lost a loved one.
She is black and blue.
She is a little child that has just lost her parents.
She is the heart's torment and the soul's blackness.
She is . . . SORROW

Mandi Armfield

Miracles

Miracles are like stars
that shine high above,
so hard to find at twilight
at first and second glance
but, the third time,
a single star sparkles into being
the center of the lonesome sky
and you feel both happiness and joy
for though that star is alone
it still shines ever bright
then more stars appear
so they can be like the first

Miracles are like that,
they never want to be the first
then, a brave one will come forth,
alone, but still it shines
and others follow
inspired by the first

Heather Tucker

2:34 a.m.

d
e
e
p
memory wash,
extend the
cos
mo
s,
s
l
e
e
p, a dream's
drea
m

Daniel Klass

True Love

One day I will find True Love,
Just like when a Rose begins to bud,
I will find True Love.

Mindy A. Rose

Bittersweet Love

*Dedicated To Roy Jacob Ammerman,
light of my life, I love you always.*
I Love You
You know you love me too
You said it . . .

Deep within you
somewhere in your sleep
it is me that you see
deep in the midst of your dreams
me who you wake up to
whispering sweet things . . .

I Love You
When you hold me in your embrace
and tell me I'm your everything
When you drift off to sleep,
and you wake up next to me . . .
. . . And . . .

I Love You
In your innocence
When you surrender to me
knowing that maybe, just maybe . . .
I'm right . . .

Shaunte Ann Sullivan

Climb

Although I am young I cannot believe my life has reached these heights.
Not too long ago I was just crawling at the base of this mountain, this mountain called life.
Only now as I stop to rest, to recoup, do I get a chance to look down upon my mountain.
I look over the boulders and jagged rocks I had to climb over,
then I realized that each boulder, each rock that bears my pain
had a golden area not far after.
I saw that every time I had to overcome one of these obstacles
there was a gift, a reward, if only just knowing I made it.
My mountain may not be as smooth as others,
but as I rest upon this peak I see my scars, my experiences,
which will help me through the rest of my climb.
And, I'm noticing that the mountain is getting higher and more dangerous,
the air is thinner, it's colder.
Climbing, rocks sometimes crumble beneath me to where I must hold onto other ones.
Though, no matter how many times things crumble, I must not lose my cool,
for the slightest disruption may cause an avalanche
which will pull me down beneath all of the things I've worked for,
so I would have to climb again.
So, instead I'll keep pulling myself up climbing these heights,
I'll drudge through the cold snow in pain so that someday I can reach the top.
Look down over what I've climbed, then I will proudly look above to the heavens,
smile and say "God, I've done it," I've climbed my mountain.
Then proudly plant my flag on top for all to see. I've climbed to the top!

Andrew Emanuel

Hearts in the Sand

While walking on the beach one day, and feeling rather lost . . .
I stood down by the water to try and clear my thoughts . . .
when up ahead I see a man, kneeling in the sand . . .
writing something in it with nothing but his hand. . . .
I walked a little closer, as he quickly walked away . . .
and as I came apon it, I wondered what it'd say. . . .
When I looked down and read it, I felt my heart beat true . . .
'cause in a single hand drawn heart, the words said, "I Love U. . . ."
I felt this was a message, though you didn't wanna say . . .
so I knelt down to send one back, on this very special day. . . .
In the sand, beside your heart, I drew one of my own . . .
to serve as a reminder, you will never be alone . . .
I drew my heart to interlock, to hold me close it's true . . .
and in my single hand drawn heart . . .
I wrote "I Love U 2. . . ."

Penny Cox

Scattered

A dozen of wilted Pink Roses on the shelf,
a reminder of the days of my wealth . . .
I was rich in Love and abundant in spirit, thought I had it all . . .
You left me with emptiness in the early Fall . . .
My heart scattered in pieces, not knowing how to mend.
But time is of the essence, there is no beginning, only an end . . .
I was an essential part of your life,
You say.
Then you left me on that cold rainy day.
You robbed me of my spirit, and took my soul,
I was a fool to let them go.
Remains of a broken-heart are etched in hues,
The colors of gray and black significance of the blues.
Misguided I was to truly believe,
To allow you to steal my precious possessions,
Only for you to leave.

Beverly Queen

Blessed

You're everything God intended a woman to be.
Every waking day that God gives you breath, it plays a symphony.
May I have this dance?
You my love illuminate my world and together we stand in the light.
I love the way you love me and I celebrate you in grand scale.
I love the road we have taken and I pray
that our future steps will be as blessed as the ones we have traveled thus far. . . .

Jackie Bertone

Mama

A mother loves with such sweet bliss
A mother's time sealed with a kiss
A mother knows and always cares
A mother holds the good times shared

She calls you when you need her most
She reads your thoughts across the coast
No matter where it is you roam
It's always great to be back home

She helps to make you feel worth while
She helps bring out the biggest smile
She helps you through the hardest pain
All her thoughts are so humane

Everything we say and do
I see in my daughter, too
Thanks so much for helping me
Thanks for who I've grown to be

You know all that I don't say
But I will tell you anyway
I have a lot of friends, that's true
But none who could compare to you

Kathryn Coleman

SOULMATES

Who holds you
When tears are running down your cheek
Who consuls your soul
Without even having to speak
Who do you call
When utter joy has consumed your heart
Whose touch do you miss
When you're distant and apart
Whose arms are holding you
As you lay down to sleep
Whose lips are you caressing
With such passion you could weep
Who can you tell your stories to
Knowing you won't find any judgement
Who can you listen to forever
And in their eyes still find amazement
Have you found the one?
Your heart and soul's completion
When you look into their eyes
You'll see your love's reflection.

Alina Adamian

Epoch

The sun streamed through the window
Lighting her tired face
The rain, when it came, fell silently
And nothing changed.

She begged us, "draw the curtains"
To hide the summer rain
That came and fell so silently
And nothing changed.

And in her final hour
She kissed us all good-bye
As death crept up so silently
And nothing changed.

Then she bade us leave her
With one look, a whispered smile
She drew her last breath silently
And nothing changed.

Jo Moore

Nostalgia's Twinge

How I weep for love long lost whose image shimmers through my tears,
Whose auburn curls so gaily tossed grow more radiant with the years.
Years of sadness, years of sorrows,
Of fast, false hopes and lost tomorrows.
Despair surrounds me, sadness throbs and permeates my shredded heart
That shudders and erupts in sobs like Vesuvius, torn apart.
Torn when love's sweet, soothing breath
Became the fiery kiss of death.
"You can't return," a man once said. "You can't go home again."
She may be old or even dead then all the dreams would wane.
For although in reality, love can fade away
Memories grow sweeter with every passing day.
And so, I'll keep her in my dreams where she'll be safe for evermore.
From time and toil and evil schemes, from pain of strife and threat of war.
She'll dance through meadows by the sea
And when day is done, she'll come to me.

Ray Caldwell

Thoughts of You

It is dark. I am lying down. Thinking of you. Listening to
the silence of the ocean and looking at the sky.
There are two shiny stars, they remind me of your eyes.
There's a quarter of the moon, it looks just like your smile. There's a soft
breeze outside, it reminds me of your hugs. The sand is still
warm, it reminds me of your body when you are close.
I wonder where you are. . . .
I wonder if you miss me. . . .
I just wonder . . .
I have so many questions, but no answers.
If at least you could give me a sign . . .
If at least I could feel that it is still worth hoping . . .
If at least you could tell me if I did something wrong or hurt you
somehow. . . .
I think then I would understand why you walked away.
I am not asking for too much, I just want to understand.

Natalia Fondacaro

Jimmy Giggles

It's a wonder he hasn't quit his job yet, he's worked there for four years
and he still only makes six dollars and twenty-five cents an hour.
His mom passed away some odd years ago,
when he and his brother still needed her.
His brother still cries inside, she was basically another mom to me too.
I didn't go to the funeral, it would have been too hard.
We didn't need to see each other cry,
we've always been strong and held each other up in times of need.
Who was going to be there to hold us both up.
You think you have everything, lose one aspect of you life, you're lost.
You no longer know what you're doing.
You feel like you've lost it all.
I still think about how he deals with all his sorts of pain.
I pretty much know how he thinks though,
so if I ever bring it up we'll be repeating stuff we already know.
It's a wonder he hasn't quit his job yet, he's worked there for four years
and he still only makes six dollars and twenty-five cents an hour.

Jacob Hamilton

I've Died and Gone to Heaven, but the Angels Won't Let Me In

I thought that I had been a good person throughout my life.
But not to my surprise when I realize; that my life
Was led by not me, but by footprints that had taken over me.
I don't remember living a lie. Did anyone see the tears in my eyes?
I really don't remember how I died. I cannot ask friends or family
Because I am not alive. As I float through the sky,
I'm well aware of my glorious prize. Wait a minute, what do I see?
I see the gates of Heaven that await me. I hear the sound
Of Heavenly music playing. I see the angel guarding
And blocking my way. As I started to ask why, he looks at me
With tears in his eyes. At this point I knew something was wrong.
He said to me that I could not use his shoulder to cry on.
Then I heard a voice say that whether I remember it or not
that I had sinned ,and the angels was instructed not to let me in.

Audrey Alford

Thank You, Lord

Thank you lord
For believing in me
When I was blind
You made me see
There is no better life
Then a life with you
Because you are the one
That is so true
Who forgives all of sin
You are the one
Who gives a life with no end
Thank you lord
For believing in me
In return . . .
I live a life with thee.

Destiny Siercks

On Finding Eternal Love on the Verge . . . of the End of the World

sometimes forever
   is never ever enough
so kiss me always in the meanwhile
hold me perpetually through the interim

time never ever heals
   cracked glass eyes
     short-circuited electric hearts
     and artificial ignorance

dazzling

outshining

this
  new
moon.

Thomas Hartnett

He Sees

Every time I see the sea,
I see the Lord above.
And every time that He sees me,
I pray He sends His love.

Adele M. Leach

And the Flower Wept

You held out your hand and said:
"Come, I will teach you to fly."
   I learned.

You said: "Give me your heart,
so I need not be alone"
   I gave it.

"You needed love so badly
  To show you hope," you said.
   I loved you.

I gave all freely, then realized,
You never said, "Let's share."
   I am empty.

Lynne Taylor

Bright Visions

Love alone will make us new,
Make us travel
Bright strange roads,
And think the dark
Night will never come.

Vincenzo Albanese

never done

I've never done well with ghosts.
and I don't mean those chain-wearing poltergeists people talk about in fairy tales,
I mean the sort of ghosts that play games with your mind.
I even know a few of them—Brian always liked playing games with people.
but you know—sometimes you've just got to grow up
and stop poking your brother in the back of the head.
let him focus on his driving.
but no . . . he's off, yapping incessantly about how Owen's doctor's stopped smiling,
and how it was such a shock to the world how he suddenly—ENDED.
with a crash, boom, crunch, cry,
he's ended, wrapped around a man-made redwood.
brian, I told you to stop poking your brother in the back of the neck.
I warned you to let him pay attention.
time to go to bed, honey . . . time to take the car as your sleeping place,
your home.
nowadays Brian sits on top of the dryer in my laundry room,
and whenever I'm trying to forget,
he's always there . . . poking me in the back of the neck, too.

I've never done well with ghosts.
        Jonathan Wolf

Waits and Balances

The balance lifted to meaning. The measure made.
I standing on my side of the balance, you placed the weight on yours.
I see myself quivering with fright that
The scale on my side will pop so high it will
Throw me right off the platter which holds me as I am
Ignorant of the size of the weight you've placed on your platter.

My emotions dangling and I feel the up and down of the
Question in the balance.

What can I do except remain standing on the balance plate
Waiting to see the tipping?

I feel my control gone. My senses numbed.
The trembling in my knees has gotten out of control,
And my voice is weak and dismayed.

My feet can't be still.
If I move quickly, I will fall and cause the balance to swing
to my elimination, flipping me aside.
My feet still are shaking, I hear the metal plate tremble
Against the iron circular rod which holds it. I feel the cold of the iron,
And the darkness scoffs at me of the weight from your side.

I then see myself slowly, cautiously, shaking and guarded,
Walk to the edge of the platter, sit down, dangle my feet over the edge,
And step off to the ground holding the platter with the pressure of my hands as
I lift my weight so the plate won't go flying up and hit me as I step away.

Then without a minute's time I release my hands from the platter
and it flies away—the balance ended.
        Karen Cheikhi

An Ungrateful World (From Precious to Perilous)

What is happening to our world?
I remember the anticipation of growing up and having a family.
It was nice to watch our parents go off to work, return home,
prepare a meal of hardly much and care for our needs
before retiring for the night, only to arise
with the entire next day planned from dawn to dusk.
All the neighborhood kids played together.
We shared, we loved, we protected one another.
A simple cheek kiss was the in thang, and music was about love.
Church was a must, stress was hidden, love was generously spread,
and struggling was just the way it was, but we prayed, believed, and conquered.
God's grace was sufficient.
Our wonderful world has now become ungrateful,
meaning that we have lost the ability to Love, Trust, and Live.
God's grace is allowing us time to get our lives in order.
Wouldn't it be nice that we can all finish with Peace, Harmony, Dignity,
and most of all, Love.
        Tora Davis

Understanding through Her

Ripped away
Shedding the skin
To further decay
It had to begin

Misdirected anger
Through a cold rough touch
Forever with her
But she doesn't feel much

To believe this
Eases the mind
Succumbing to bliss
But to remain blind
        Sophia Stephens

Always

No matter where I run
No matter where I hide
You're always here with me
Always by my side
When I need you the most
You'll always be here
You'll come to me
No matter how far or near
And when the times get rough
Or when the going gets too tough
I know you're every step of the way
You come and help me just enough
Even though I can't see you
I know you'll always be with me
Looking down from above
Every time that I'm in need
        Xao Thao

The Planet of Mars

On the planet of Mars
They have clothes like ours
And they have the same shoes
And same laces
And they have the same charms
And same graces
And they have the same heads
And same faces
But not in the very same places!
        Alexandria Needham

Opportunity Lost

Tomorrow I'll think about
  all that's been done
Tomorrow I'll think about
  how you were the one
To lift me up
  when I couldn't see
To soothe the ache
  that was hurting me
To hold me close
  when I was in tears
Tomorrow I'll think about
  all of our years
But today I wonder
  if I could've done more
Today I wonder
  just what's in store
I've lost your guidance
  love and friendship, too
You'll never know, Dad,
  how much I loved you
        Brandie Parker

A Promise

Never did I once believe in a person
that will bring me a happiness nor a smile
that sends a heart and soul to the ends of this Earth
and the heavens above.

You're the one that has my heart. You're the one that has turned
this stone heart into and weak and fragile organ.
Bright and shining are my days now that you have entered my life.
I wake with the thought of another day listening to your melodious voice.

When you walked into my life, you gave me the strength
and the confidence in myself to go forward in chasing my dreams.
To fight all the obstacles and overcome my fears.
A simple poem, a simple piece of parchment, will not be sufficient enough
to say that you are a glowing essence of my love and faithfulness.

For in all the rest of my living years,

I will dedicate to your happiness and to your dreams coming true.

Forever in my heart, your existence will be.

I will never be a stranger nor will I ever forsake you.

This is a vow that I make to you. This is a promise of my loyalty
and dedication to making this friendship
a ship that will never sink.

Yasmin Nieves

I Wonder while I Cry

I thought you were my true friend, but
Now I wonder why it hurts to love you.
I looked at your face and you looked
Right through me.
You took my soul and twisted it in knots.
It's not what was expected.
How does it feel to betray and belittle the one who thought you were everything?
Is that what I get for caring about our love
and wishing it could be the same as it once was?
I saw your hands as they touched mine
and now those hands are tear-stained.
They are grasped tightly together in prayer.
I do not understand how such joy
could become distorted and destroyed.
I am the survivor and that will never change.
As the tears fall upon my skin I hold my body erect
and walk into the light of another day without you!

Laverne Avant

Only Reason

She walks along the beach.
The sand is cool and moist between her toes.
The sun almost peeks over the top of the waters,
Showering the sky with peach and lavender hues.
Another gull flies high overhead, scanning the beach for a delectable meal.
She walks on.

The sand becomes soft as the water washes over her feet,
Cool like tears from the eyes of a cloud in mid-April.
She never wavers as she stares on ahead.

A breeze so warm ruffles her yellow gown.
Her sandals, size seven, sway rhythmically in her hand.
She never breaks here gaze.
Never looks to the ocean's serenity and beauty.
Why does she walk on?

For if her eyes shift to the inviting waters she would run upon them . . . not looking back.
She would hide within the salty folds from the world and its heavy weight.
She would be lost to a welcoming death.
She has dreamed of this for some time but one thing has kept her eyes focused forward.
Her four-year-old daughter, full of gaiety, is spinning in circles in the sand up ahead.
She walks on to catch up to her.

Kathlene Phillips

If Time Be Told

If time be told by beating hearts,
Until you, time surely stood still,
For joy and glee
Were never there for me
And love did I never feel.

If time be told by beating hearts,
Then with you time sure doth fly.
My heart never rests,
It heaves in my chest
With your smile, your touch, your sigh.

If time be told by beating hearts,
Then today let our clocks become one,
And measure forever
Our lives together
And never let the beating be done.

Joel Fralick

dust devil

the sky about to break
the cracked ground
howling
black birds
leaves and tumbleweeds
pushed before
someone's farm
is flying high

Michael O'Keeffe

What Could Have Been

A whisper on the skin,
     a caress that is shared.
The knowledge that we both,
     really do care.
I shed a tear
     that you cannot see.
A piece of my heart,
     you have taken from me.
Listen closely,
     and you may hear,
the sound of it breaking.
     Is this what we feared?
For what we could have had,
     we never will see.
For us, lovers and friends,
     we cannot be.
And these tears I shed,
     you will never see,
or hear the sound of my heart
     breaking within me.

Nikki Abernathy

Crying Rain

The rain falls,
softly,
as I taste the salt
of my tears at the back of my mouth.

I weep,
as the rain cleanses me
of all my hurt
and wipes away the pain
of sad loneliness.

I grieve for him
for all and for those yet to come
I feel the sorrow of a thousand deaths,
for just
One

Cullen Mackenzie

"My Inspiration"

It's been four months since you went away,
I think about you every hour, minute, second, of each and every day.
Even though we are far apart, you are always in my mind and heart.
Whenever I was down and wore a frown, you knew just what to say to bring a smile to my face.
Now you are in a very special place where I know you are being taken care of and
where you are very safe.
You changed my life in a way that is very hard to explain,
and even though I have asked myself a lot why you left me, I know now that no one is to blame.
You always knew there was something wrong and made me talk to you about it.
You always knew the right things to say to brighten up my day.
Even on rainy days, you were my light of sunshine shining
through the dark clouds and skies with a beam of rays.
You accepted me for me and who I wanted to be. You have been and still are my inspiration.
I have come to a realization that no matter what problems we face in life,
you have shown me to live life to its fullest
and to be thankful for each and every day that we are given.
Even though you are gone, you are not really because your memory is still here with me.
I love you and miss you a lot, Charlie.
You were a great friend and you touched everybody's life that knew you, especially mine.

Kristina Oakes

To Reggie, with Love

Today is the day that we say "I Do,"
All the day long I'll be thinking of you.
I feel so lucky to have you in my life,
I promise I'll do my best to be the perfect wife.
Though we may have our moments when things won't go as planned,
Stay close to my side and hold tight to my hand.
With God as our foundation we will be okay,
Whenever we feel angry, let's stop and pray.
You have already given me more than I deserve,
I hope that my mood swings haven't used up your last nerve!
The memories we've shared will be forever in my mind,
I mean it when I say you are one of a kind!
As I walk down the aisle don't be surprised
If you notice a couple of tears in my eyes.
It's not because I'm thinking "I'm making a mistake,"
It's all because I know what a wonderful husband you will make.
As we begin our life together on this our wedding day,
I can't wait to share all the love and laughter that will ever come our way.
I will love you forever until death do us part
You will always be the one who holds the key to my heart.

Jennifer Hasenbank

My Prayer

My prayer is to find someone with love and compassion, as I
find passion for love in her. The one who will take my breath
away with just a whisper of her voice that sends me into eternal bliss.
Her words I hear each day even when she is not near.
The one who I see as a white dove flying down from above
the Earth and the heavens.
If you can see what I see, if you can feel what I feel in my heart,
then, only then, you will begin to understand the true meaning
of love as it is told from above, like seeing a sunrise each day and
cherishing each moment of the sunrise.
I cannot give up hope for that is all I have in my heart; can you
even start to understand my thoughts and my mind?
Never in a million years you can see my hearts desires,
nor see clearly to understand that love is all I have to give.
But when you begin to understand, I will pour out my love to
you like wild fires that will spread though out your heart and
soul, filling up each of your desires one by one.
Until then understand my love is here waiting for you, as it
soars its wings though out the Earth and the heavens forevermore,
the love I will bring to you you'll never know
nor will I show you until you open your eyes to see
what the true meaning of love can be.

Steve Mun

Am I Crazy for Believing ?

Am I crazy for believing
That dreams really do come true?
Is it insanity that drives me
To do all that I do?
Is it such a crazy notion,
This idea of "Never Quit?"
Am I mad to take a plunge of faith
And rock the boat a little bit?
Is it totally wild and wacky
To pass on when they say stop?
Is it just a loopy obsession
To want to make it past the top?
Am I crazy for believing
There will never be an end?
To the success I can achieve
When I do all that I intend?
And if I'm crazy for believing,
If none of my dreams come true,
At least my life belongs to me,
I think, I say, I do.

Mesh Bowie

Your Love

Your love is like a clear blue sky,
It's always there when I cry,
In the blink of an eye,
For it will never be shy.
Your love could take me to the sky,
Where we could live so high,
'Til the day that I die.

David Behrens

A Winter Welcome

Withered leaves wallow
under freshly fallen snow;
Autumn says good night.

Amy Baumhardt

THOUGHTS

I thought about a world
without violence
without a war

I thought about a world
with children playing
without fear of getting shot.

I thought about a world
where only the people count,
not the races, not the color.

It was only a thought;
there is too much violence
there are too many shots.

The world forgets
to look with the soul,
and separates the people
by races and color!

Maria Garis

Untitled

For E.K.N.
Because
 Every
  Thought
 Says
  You

Anthony C. Burns

My Friend

As I stroll along this little gravel road
I come to a field as green as I have ever seen
I decide to take a rest and as I lie here watching the clouds glide through the sky
I think to myself
How these clouds remind me of our friendship
Some clouds are darker than the others
Some clouds are grayer than the others
And then there are some clouds so white that the sun shines right through them

I glance away to watch the weeping willow blow in the wind
When I glance back to watch the clouds they are gone
I realize then our friendship couldn't be like the clouds

For you don't glide in and out of my life
For your friendship and your love is in my heart and in my soul
And I thank God for putting you on this Earth
For he new that I needed you and you needed me
For our friendship is rare and I wanted you to know how much I care

Pamela Barnhart

The Lost Generation

Lost generation. Where are you now?
So many aspirations, so many dreams.
Caught in a turbulent time of Women's Liberation and war.
Decisions to make, oh what to do . . . College, job, housewife, mother?
Not quite ready to step into the world, housewife and mother is the decision.
Now 38 years later, regrets, loneliness, boredom, oh what did I do?
Now too late to do it,
too scared to go out into the big busy world, why me? Me?
Because I cared for others?
Husband, children, the needy, the animals no one wanted.
Now left at home, alone most of my waking hours,
no confidence to venture into the big world out there at my age.
Oh! What to do?
Thank God for every new day? Yes!
Too late to go back? Yes!
Too late to move forward? No!
Somewhere in this big beautiful world is a place for me and I will find it.
God will show me how and when.
The lost generation will go on and merge with the new generations.
Joy will come!

Judythe Ghosio

Alone

Standing in the sinister cool of late night he sighed.
Watching his breath disappear into darkness he felt alone.
The feeling was not the lack of company or as when guests have just left.
He felt alone.
Looking around at the trees and shadows he heard water flowing in the canal.
The moon watched him pace in his ritual fervor.
Thinking thoughts of eternity and emptiness he almost cried.
He looked up to see the stars and the moon.
Clouds crept by, adding motion to the canvas.
He smiled and stood for a short lifetime and closed his eyes.
No longer did the lights glow.
Eyes opened, he saw them still there, unchanged.
Standing in the cool of late night he sighed.

David Wallace

The Battered Old Bag

He quietly packs in the bedroom,
doing what he knows has to be done.
She stays in the kitchen,
trying to hide the tears that she cries.
The children sense something is wrong.
The battered old bag sits by the bedroom door.
She hears his footsteps in the hall,
then the door is slammed shut.
The battered old bag isn't there anymore.
It is then she knows
he is gone.
This time, forever.

Patty Birch

Fear

When I awoke this morning,
I struggled with my drink,
I could not hold the cup to mouth,
What was I to think?

I sat awhile upon my bed,
The room it seemed to spin.
My face was numb, my mouth was drawn.
'Twas quite a mess that I was in.

I could not think quite clearly,
It took a while to sink right in,
What on Earth was wrong with me?
I was really in a spin.

Last night when I was sleeping
I had a head attack, a raid!
What on Earth is wrong with me?
'Twas a stroke and I'm afraid!!

Vera Warby

THE ANGEL'S SONG

Angels came to sing that night,
Their voices loud and clear.
They said we should be filled with joy
And not be filled with fear.

We have forgotten what they sang,
Our thoughts are on The Child.
So we should read the verse again
And think a little while.

They sang a song of peace and joy
Of love sent from above.
They told us who our Father sent
To teach us how to love.

We should recall the Angel's song
And live the best we can.
Let's fill our heart and mind with love
And goodwill toward all men.

Ralph Bolick

New Friends

Every time you make a friend
  your life will bend.
Bits of them rub off on you;
  change will ensue.

Quirks of theirs, a skill or trait,
  you'll imitate.
Thoughts and views and temperament
  will leave their dent.

Both your lives will intertwine,
  and realign.
Gain some, lose some, compromise,
  become more wise.

Never will you be the same;
  it's life's strange game.
Every time you make a friend,
  your life will bend.

Marie Robinson

You Had to Go

I know you couldn't stay,
But I wanted you to.
I needed you to stay,
But you had to go.
You had to be free
Of all your pain.
I know that now,
But I miss you still.
I still love you,
And I always will.

Dalynn Schauer

A Dewy Morning's Pastel Blaze

A dawn of pale yellow, tangerine, and pretty pink,
A kindling against a backdrop of gray clouds.
A whole new world after the darkness,
I can't sleep. . . . A rooster crows an upturned face into the flowers.

And if there still were a God, then I should pray.
And if I still had a name, perhaps he'd call.
And if the world were so far simpler a place,
Then perhaps there'd be a God for me and all.

But today begins anew, just like a hundred others did,
And tomorrow promises no pretty pink.
There could be fog, or rain, or thunder. . . . even death.
So today me and the rooster merely wake—
And admire the rhododendron, flower king.

Crystal Richardson

Mother, You Are So Dear to Me

My mother you are so dear to me
For you have gave me everything, don't you see
I may not be your natural born
But I must admit you have always treated me like one of your very own
You have given me so much love right from the start
I know you're my real mother were the thoughts from my heart
You taught me what happiness means and now my heart may shine
You deserve a thank you for all of your quality time
You have made me feel special in so many ways
Because you gave me courage and kept beside me through all of those sad days
Now that I'm grown with a daughter of my own
I have realized that you are truly the best person I have ever known
You have blessed me and now I will say that these are the reasons,
    mother, why you are so dear to me

Annette Russell

I Never Thought

I never thought I'd be so happy—I never thought I'd be so lonely.
When I'm with you I'm glad—but never thought I'd be so sad.
I really wish you knew all the feelings that I have for you.
I try to tell you how much I care but I feel as if I'm not there.
I know you're listening, I wish I could try just to tell you what I feel inside.
Sometimes I think I don't belong here but where do I belong?
So many places to go—so many things to see, but what I can't see is me.
I think about how I can't face this alone.
Tell me that you love me—and that you care.
Please know that I care—I've never been this happy before.
I want you to know that I love you, I always will.
I never though my life would be like this. All I have is just one wish.
I never thought I'd be so happy.
I never thought I'd be so lonely.

Basey Martinez

A Country Beat

Look at the boots you're dancing in.
Do you fear the ground your stepping in?
Where are the her's and the grain to eat?
Where are the stars we used to see?
Hear our sound and look around.
Stomp your feet to a country beat.
She will ride around the bend.
Then we'll all be in Heaven again.
I pray to the Lord every day in my broken-down Chevrolet.
I sing to you every day. I plow the fields, I bail the hay.
I feed the kids every day in my boots, the country way.
Remember the trees they blow in the breeze.
Remember the fields we used to see.
Remember me, your free, to see in me, you're He!
Look at the boots your dancing in.
Do you fear the ground your stepping in?
Hear our sound and look around.
Stomp your feet to a country beat.

Joe Flo D.

When Doves Cry

Bound up by the chains of love,
Immortal Gods have mercy on me;
Take pity on this broken heart,
And with your power, set it free.

Destiny coincides with my fate,
Heaven above me, and Hell below;
Still I know not which way to go,
I cannot, I am trapped in sorrow.

Isolated, neglected and rejected,
Left alone to remember our end;
Its harsh cruelty washes over me,
Drowns me in contempt and revenge.

In the beginning, there was an end,
So blinded by love I could not see;
I fall to my knees cursing myself,
Why did it happen to me, why me?

My only comfort, I find in nature,
In the silent peace of the dove;
When doves cry, I know their pain
Comes from their pity on love.

Tania Musonera

For Now

Being near you
I am overcome with desire . . .
An overwhelming need
To hold you, to touch you,
To feel your lips on mine . . .
Your hands on my face . . .
Your breath on my skin.

For now, my love,
I must be content
With memories long past.
With thoughts of memories
Still to be made . . .
With stolen moments . . .
And loving embraces.

For now, that is enough . . .
For now.

Mary Alice Davis

Believe

They say to believe
To believe in the Heavens
And in the angels too
I can believe in nothing but you.
You believe and I ask why
How, when there are tears in your eye?
I used to believe in love
But the pain was too great
I used to believe in up above
But the truth is to late.
You believe and I ask why
How, when there are tears in your eye?
I had faith
It was taken away
We had each other
Now we must live for today.
Too many broken promises
Too many lies
Today is forever
Tomorrow never dies . . . .

Dawn Schumacher

Soul Mates

I dream of you through the summer's day,
of how you speak your words of language.
Yet, I feel you near me, even still, closer within my soul.
Like you should be my everlasting soul mate,
which forms me closer to the higher power than ever before.
Is there another reason why you are near me?
Are we truly souls that belong together for thine eternal youth and beauty?
I see what happens to you in my dreams.
Oh how I see your everlasting fate.
Your fate unveils its mighty pillow of strength.
Though I see in your eyes that you truly love me,
my heart still waiteth in thine crypt of fate. Do you still love me?
Did you ever truly know how I felt?
Surely if I am known to your future, you are known to mine.
Though I guess I would truly know your feelings even before you do,
like a mediocre symptom of deja vu.
I shall learn to trust you my twin of souls
and wait for you at the end of the tunnel.

Anisa Eakin

Afrolution

The revolution will not be announced. Just like a murmur it will start.
Rumble, tumble, earthquake crumble.
Run helter skelter, all you gender benders.

Hurry and give birth to young strapping sons, all you pregnant black women.
Hurry and raise them to be black and proud,
and to shout Africa out loud.

Hurry up and go home black men, stay with your women, the mothers of our children.
And raise your daughters to live like Nubian princesses.
Loving life, but leaving no room to excesses.

The revolution will be rude, awakening all who collude,
to strip the black nation of our groove.
Forget all who don't approve.

The revolution will be like torrents,
sweeping away all racial evil like water currents.
Purifying the mind,body and soul.
And that is the greater goal.

The revolution will not allow for injustice, hatred or denigration of the black soul.
And that's the reason we must all stand bold.
So that in the future the story can be told,
to all future generations of black people,
from London to Kinshasa, from Negril to Sao Paulo.
Be ready, be prepared for this revolution—of love.

Olawale Obimakinde

Untitled

Time stands alone,
having no meaning.
I try to wait the pain out,
finding only more pain awaits me.
Trying hard to deny the truth;
I can't hide the pain forever,
hoping that the truth will never come about.
I live day by day, suffering and struggling
for the suffering to stop so I may be in peace.
I don't want to be alone, only my friends understand my pain.
I can't take not
having my life go on without you. I can't face the truth,
I can't look the truth in the eyes, I can't have truth's cold, hard eyes
looking into my tear-filled eyes.
I sit in the dark and listen to my clock tick
as the seconds waste away. I feel you slipping from my grasp.
Slowly, I begin to shed a tear for everything that was unsaid.
I wish you were still here.

Danielle Whittaker

'Cause You're My Friend

When you are sad . . .
I will dry your tears
When you are scared . . .
I will comfort your fears
When you are worried . . .
I will give you hope
When you are confused . . .
I will help you cope
And when you are lost
And can't see the light of day . . .
I shall be your beacon
Shining ever so bright
This my oath
I pledge to the end . . .
Why you may ask?
Because you're my friend.

Andrew Beverly

You?

Today I felt that feeling,
Deep inside my heart,
And it was when I looked at you
Which gave me quite a start.
It's the feeling you get when
You've found the one of your dreams,
The one with whom you find
What true love means.
You had only been my friend
Us joking happily,
You helping me with homework,
I helped you a burden to free.
Somehow, today,
It all just changed,
A jigsaw puzzle,
My feelings were rearranged.
In front of my eyes
You changed somehow,
Causing my heart to jump
Wanting to be with you now.

Alexandria Hawkins

Give Me Strength

In the tranquility of silence
I can think and be myself
When I enter into society
Everyone has their chance
To try and capture my spirit
They will do with it what
they want
What happened to the times
when the spirit was always free
When we could pick and choose
our friends and our destiny
Now it seems that everyone has
some input in our lives
Whether or not we ask for it
we deal with ideas we despise
As a young girl I learned that
doing good was always best
The role models were countless
so my goal I could achieve
I knew in my heart they never
would deceive
God bless all those women who
were generous to a fault
The mothers,the sisters those
friends we can exalt

Jane Monaghan

A Simple Game?

Do you think that life is such a simple game,
That a child could play?
Just one continous party
Lived from day to day?
Do you go through life carelessly?
Hurting someone as you go
Not caring about their feelings
After all, it's their problem,you know?
But life isn't really so simple,
There's pain and loneliness everywhere.
Next time you'll be the one to get hurt.
Maybe then you'll learn to care.
But will it be too late?
Will you have ever learned
That you reap what you have sown?
You'll get paid exactly what you've earned.

Katherine Gottschalk

The Angel

And in my land so universal and free, I am an angel walking on air.
I am as free as a bird, as pretty as a butterfly, full of color and fluttering with passion.
I am pink, mauve, orange and turquoise,
I am the colors of the rainbow on the other side.
I possess beautifully tipped wings of gold and silver and I sparkle with radiance.
I dance effortlessly in the air, with form and grace,
For I am the ballerina that charms her own slippers.
I am in love with the sky, the sun and the moon,
Because they are the ingredients of my own existence.
I see the sun for energy, the moon for meditation,
And the blue sky for the power of the unknown:
I AM THE ANGEL OF THE SKY.
But I am not your normal angel, nor an angel at all.
But I can believe that I am, believe what can be, and with that,
I am the most beautiful thing you will ever see!

Rebecca Stahl

Middle School Teacher

Looking up from my end-of-the-year mess,
I see 28 young scholars hunched over their desks.
They concentrate steadily on their final exams,
And I smile to think of how lucky I am.
All of them are thinking and using common sense.
I don't know if I've ever seen them looking so intense!
Pens scribble and pencils erase.
28 pairs of eyes stare blankly into space.
They twist their mouths and scrunch their brows.
Will they remember the definition of a noun?
Sitting here now they look so calm and angelic.
It's hard to believe they made my life so hectic!
But now as the end slowly draws near,
I sit and recall the past school year.
I realize how much they've grown and I see how much they've changed.
I hope they have learned all they could in these past 180 days.
They look so much older, so mature and sublime.
They actually look serious for the first time!
And so now, as I sit back I can honestly remember
That these adorable, wide-eyed cherubs have run me ragged since September!

Jennifer Seiler

The Road of Life

Well dear, I'll tell you:
Being a teenager is like driving a car.
There are a lot of bumps along the way.
Even turning the wrong way at a busy intersection
when all the other cars go the right way.
There are always detours that get you off track
and sometimes you feel that you can't get back.
Or the time when you should have stopped but proceeded without slowing.
Every once in a while hit the brakes, look around, change lanes and turn around.
So now, dear, you know being a teenager is like driving in the fast lane.
There's no time for slowing down.

Jennifer Hagy

Carla

Like birds on a wire,
I sit waitin' for you.
Wondering why you left
Like the early morning dew.

As each other's paths,
Cross through life,
Simple words of love
Will help us through our strife.

So, is it for us to wonder
Where you went to sleep?
Or just pray to God,
To take your soul to keep.

Gary Anderson

Truth Naked

Perception,
Deception,
Silvered mirrors,
Inverted reflections.

Steven W. England

I Say I See

I say I see your heart
because I do
When you experience pain
my heart shed tears of blood

I say I see your mind
because I do
When you relate your thoughts
my mind responds in unison

I say I see your soul
because I do
When you breathe sighs of relief
my soul exhales whines of ease

I say I see your spirit
because I do
When your dreams are fulfilled
my spirit soars in jubilation

I say I see who you are
because I do
When I look at you
I see myself

Natasha Jackson

That Was Life

Once there was one
Two together made three,
One more made four,
So life went on.

One from Heaven made seven
Went on to be ten,
Seemed to be no end.
Once there wasn't any,
Now there are many.

Some began to sneeze,
Many died from disease.
In time there were only ten,
Close was the end.

More got sick, that made six;
Less one alive which made five,
Then there were two.
Gone was another, so that left one,
And then there were none.

Richard N. Hartl

I Confess

O' Lord! Heard of repay, For fair deeds we pay
On confession, You forgive they say, Hence, therefore I confess.
O' Lord! Bodily controlled my legs are, Taking me from You afar
I'm one of the creation of Your's, And forgot, You made me for.
O' Lord! Eyes behold the evil rise, Hands clap, when goodness die
Lungs breathe the air of hatred, And soul enjoy the bloodshed.
O' Lord! Not a faithful disciple, Nor thy purity resides in heart
Mind housed by evil thoughts, And hope, bad will ever last.
O' Lord! My moves are against your ways, Ear pay no heed to what you say
Lips & Tongue, together move, Never spell of peace & faith.
O' Lord! "Pool of forgiveness You are, Bless with its drop, they say
If by heart we confess, Deeds we did in the life ways."
O' Lord! I submit myself to You, With no wish of birth again
Restless I live on land of Yours, For True peace resides in You.
O' Lord! Call me and free me, From all foul feelings
For part of You I be.
O' Lord! I Confess . . . .

Rohit Chattar

Live Free

Every time I look at stars in a midnight sky
I am thinking to myself why, oh, why do people get so mad?
Oh, it always makes me sad
To watch a person kill all that's real that he could feel.

Every time I watch the clouds in a bright blue sky I wonder to myself my, oh, my, my, my.
It's all so wonderful this great miracle of life.
'Cause when all is said and done all that's sure is self-freedom.

Every time I hear the bird's flying overhead,
I whisper to myself, Birdie fly for me. It's only refusal for us to fly in life
'Cause the bird said to me, just let yourself go free.

So when I go to sleep I look at the moon
And all the chaos in my world is nothing more
Than a fading technicality of this present reality.
With all that hurts surrounding me, but all I want is harmony.

Then the sun awakes and I rise with it to face the challenge of the day
With all of Earth and all her pain to have a joyous life seems difficult to most.
When all you have to do is . . .
let your self live free!

(I am 16.)

Clare Petersen

Travelers' Dream

I want to go . . .
To a far off place
A place that's exotic
With rain forests, artics, animals
Desserts and tropical islands

I want to go . . .
Go, explore the world inside and out
Make my heart filled with content, joy
Passion and love
Going to places that are peaceful, exotic
And bizarre

I want to go . . .
Somewhere where I can find my true love
Somewhere other than here
Somewhere where I can fill my heart with content, joy, happiness, passion and excitement
Somewhere where I won't have to worry about diseases, violence, money, people or
How I look

I want to go . . .
Somewhere other than here

Arianne Babington

Precious Love

Hold me close my precious love
Caress me through the night
And never let our love be changed
Because we fight
For when we fight
It's just because
We love so very much
And cannot always find the time
To feel each others touch
Love me now, my precious love
You mean the world to me
Someday you will know
That our love was meant to be

Barbara Hostetler

From the Heart

so close
yet so far away
cannot verbally speak
what my heart wants to say

no matter where i go
no matter what i do
there's one on my mind
and that is you

can't help but think
all through the day
my thoughts became many
and can't come to say

exactly how i feel
is simple but true
but all my thinking
is only of you

Joseph Reeves

the poem that spilled

the poem spilled over into
your sonorous murmurings
into the sunlight christened sweetness
that flowed between your lips
and rendered my breath so fine
so frantic and crazed and so
grateful for the privilege of
bearing moisture and adoration
unto your bosom, within your
fragrantly spiced embraces
and long after the moon beams
have penetrated our visions
of fancy free lounging in the
park that afternoon when
the gulls were insistent upon
soaring in parade for our
party, and the daffodils
were ablossom with the pollen
of dedicated lovers enriching
each the other's beauty and expansion

Scott Weible

Me

My eyes are dark brown
And so is my hair
I love all animals including a bear
I look like my dad the most
I used to be afraid of seeing ghosts
I love basketball and cheerleading too
And I really love Winnie the Pooh
I also think I'm good in class
In every subject so far I've passed.

Dana Strang

A Loved One

A loved one I once new and loved gone forever lost to another world.
Will I see thee again? Will thee remember me? I remember you. I miss you.
Oh, dear, how, why, what, so many questions that can't be answered.
Oh, please please let this be a dream, let me awake and you be there.
Oh, come back, come back don't leave me.
Oh, I wish it wasn't you. Was it my fault, did I cause this?
Oh, don't leave me here with so many unanswered questions,
come back, oh, dear loved one, come back.
As you burry me in sorrow I know you are fine,
not enduring the pain I am feeling inside this very second,
the pain I will feel until I see thee once more.
Oh, dear loved one, what is it like to not feel pain,
to not see the hatred brought upon this world?
Oh, loved one, please come back so I can say good bye.

Holly Wooten

Until We See You Again

Is Heaven as beautiful as we've heard?
We know you are there right now.
Are you walking the streets of Gold,
With restored back and legs?

Is the countenance of His face as bright as they say?
Are you tending the flowers that bloom?
Are you seeing the unimaginable beauty of it all,
With "new eyes" that are no longer cloudy and blurred?

Are you "cooing" at your baby daughter?
Are you telling daddy we miss him too?
Are you talking with your Mamma, Papa, sisters, brother and friends?
Mamma, we know you are talking and talking with the voice God gave back to you.

We know we have to be parted from you for a while.
We know our tears are for ourselves.
We know we will see you again one day.
Jesus promised that, "If We Believe," it will be so.

Lillian Jones

The Game

Here I sit, Indian-style on my bed
The hum of the street light peeking
through my window cleverly taunts me.
Few miles are we apart, yet masses of distance separate us.

Multidimensions of thought race through my mind
Suspended in confusion, I watch you.
Surely you are aware—mindful to keep your distance and graceful to draw me in.

Faint thunder demanding to be heard in the distant night sky pretends to keep me company.
In a thousand different directions, I am pulled apart.
Entangled in your spider web of words
Frustration and intrigue circle the truth and our dance continues.

Melissa Alexander

What Is She Like?

You ask, "What is she like?"
I will tell you what she is like, paint a picture for you,
and have you see her as I see her through my eyes.
First, close your eyes and picture a woman that whose voice and beauty is so unique,
That she makes the deaf want to hear and the blind want to see.
Next, find a woman that if her mind and character are ever measured,
Her intelligence will make scholars not deserve their title
and she will make the powerful feel weak.
Now, draw a woman that if her very essence is ever seen
and understood by the soul of a person,
She can make anyone fall in love with her.
Finally, pull all of these qualities together and put them in one person.
When that is done, you will see her in your mind,
know who she is, and what she is like.

Javier Orellana

How I Feel

Depression is what fills my mind.
Loneliness is with me all the time.
I feel so unhappy and insecure
sometimes I feel like there is no more.
What can I do?
What can I say?
People in this world are so ignorant
they think only what they say
is what matters.
Why are they blind?
When will they see?
That this world is not theirs' only.
It belongs to you and me.
If you are alone and insecure
this goes out to you and others more:
Be strong, felt along.
Don't let what people do or say
get in your way.
Follow your heart and your dreams,
Fulfill your life with wonderful things.

Yomaira Molina

Misplaced Flower

A single flower
In the middle of the green
So fragile and lonely
Yet beautiful to see

It planted itself,
a misplaced seed
so peaceful and tranquil
but they call you a weed

A flower is a flower
no matter what they say
but they think you a pest
they wish you away

What have you done
to make you so hated?
a future so short
and so ill fated?

For in this universe
where there are no mistakes
we've all been misplaced flowers
who cannot be replaced

Mary E. Palminteri

Autumn

How cold the wind and chill,
So dull and dreary outside,
No lounging now at will,
With tea and cakes to hide.

The leaves have parted company
With their hosts how bare,
They stand so lonely
In the crisp, frosty air

We're mowed the lawn,
And clipped the privet hedges,
There is frost come down
Ice on the window ledge.

We're dug the tubers
To be warm and snug inside,
For flowers of the future
To hold their heads with pride.

Now we look forward to Christmas
And the festive celebration,
To the church midnight mass
And peace throughout the nations.

J. L. Ward

THE RAGING STORM

The frantic storm rages like beauty;
Beauty over the plane of a small child's face
As it aches for companionship.
 the chaotic storm rages with animosity;
Animosity over the plane of a deserted heart,
As it aches for love.
  the brutal storm rages with integrity;
Integrity over the plane of a tampered soul,
As it aches for truth.
  the intense storm rages with understanding;
Understanding over the plane of knowledge,
As it aches for maturity.
  the cruel storm rages with anger;
Anger over the plane of desolation,
As it aches for compassion.
The frantic storm rages like beauty;
Beauty over the plane of tranquillity,
  as it aches for one listener or one poet to come along
  and find . . . the calm . . . within . . . the raging storm.

Nicole Swinney

Hope

Shadows dance around screaming and shouting at me,
Trying to control my life and who I want to be.

I see little white footprints that glow on the ground,
Is this my hope to change my life around?

I fight so desperately to find that hope and dream,
But these shadows keep pushing and pulling and won't leave me.

I feel like I'm climbing a mountain and with each step it gets harder and harder,
But I know if I keep fighting I will keep going farther and farther.

Will I be the same or better when I've reached the top,
Or would have I've worn myself out so much that I give up and stop.

What keeps me going is these little white feet that seem to lead the way,
Making a path for me to follow every day.

I don't know what the outcome will be
When I reach the top of this mountain I climb,
But at least I'll have a better view of this life of mine.

I may or may not have all my questions answered
Or completed the ultimate goal I had planned,
But as long as I follow hope and my heart,
I can try to live my life the best way I can.

Wailana Johnson

Time without Her

Only a few minutes have passed,
and I am thinking that I miss her.
Only a couple of hours spent,
and I am starting to miss her.
Only one day has gone by,
and I am feeling that I am really missing her.
I do not know how many more days I can stand this waiting.
I do not know if I will be strong enough to resist all this time without her.
Even that, I have hope, that very soon I will be beside her.

Horacio Palomino

Spiritual Union

Marriage is a special bond
One hopes that's kept for life
To love and care for
One's own devote wife

To let each other live
Without fear of obsessions
To gather good thoughts
And life's little possessions
To be sincere and honest
In all of your dealings
And most of all not to
Hurt each other's feelings

To forgive each other or yourself
In times when you're hard to reach
For that long cherished goal
Of endless mental peace

To live your lives
One day at a time
No mountain too high enough
For yous to climb.

Steven Thitchener

Things Change

Things are changing,
people rearranging,
not their properties,
But, their minds,
leaving behind,
the most important thing to find,
Love? God?

Things will change,
I will die,
and I wish for you,
not to cry.

In life,
Change is only temporary,
For everything returns,
To the way it once was,
If not only in mind.

Change.

Johnny Cox

A Great Day

Today I left some dishes dirty.
The bed got made about 2:30.
The diapers soaked a little longer,
The odor got a little stronger.

The crumbs I spilled the day before
Kept staring at me from the floor.
The hand prints on the window panes
Will still be there until it rains,

"For shame, oh, Lazy One" you say,
"What did you do so great today?"

I rocked my grandchild while the slept
And held her close in case she wept.

I played a game of hide of seek.
I squeezed a toy so it would squeak.
I pushed a swing, I sang as song.
I taught a child what's right and wrong.

What did I do the whole day through?
Not much that shows, I guess it's true.

Era Turman

Valentino's Citrus Orchard: A Death Tango

The desire for simplicity is sexy and exploitable.
spinning silk is hard work
RUDOLPH VALENTINO was a friend to his enemy
the hordes of hunger.
The hunger that followed him was his
for a meal and the nation's ravenous craving for him,
but wood floors and striped suits would put him under
so as to ease the pain of his own death.
Good Christians broke tradition to adore him and,
ashamed of their longing,
had to put him somewhere where they could forever dream him young and dancing.
A black box, they decided, would do.
The funeral, a grief fantasy, an otherworldly NATASHA RAMBOVA,
collapsing for the cameras.
There is an Orange. Well bred, sweet, rich, and
satisfying in some orchard somewhere which should be called . . . VALENTINO'S
FAITH, and should be eaten with quiet gratitude and silent shame.

Gabriel Jacques

How She Feels

Once I was young and beautiful,
But now since he came
I'm just this tall thing that has no beauty
Without my green cloak I'm nothing
No one stops to see me anymore
No one plays with me anymore
Oh, how I can't wait for her to come and run him out of town
She'll restore that which was once young and full of grace
Until then I am nothing

Two days, too far, until she comes
Two hours, still too far, oh, how I long to be seen again
Yes, she's here and as she makes her way through the town, all is well
For he is slowly disappearing and I'm slowly, but surely becoming my old self
Someone stopped to say how beautiful I looked today
Oh, how I love that feeling
She always helps make me feel good
That's why I love when the sun comes

Joann Bruney

Remain

When asked if ever I should be a flower for all the world to see,
With pedals strewn, and glory named; a wonderful Prose called by you remained.

Strong with honor, bright bold; I'd shine for he has risen and glory mine.
Both bastion of fortitude He hath made; an anointed symbol, still remain.

This thorn was an enemy, but love has chosen and you descend
Into a quagmire of muck and squalor; raptured am I for there's life within.

Love for hate, thorn. Instead, beauty indeed; a life exalted we will lead!

This pedestal we sit is not so grand; life, you see, is His walking hand in hand,
Sacred, holy communion in my soul; free at last, confined to His Whole.

For the desert shows we are in want, and trouble with her stick has taught
There is a beauty in that remains to bloom—plow us under, you'll just make more room.

Prisms bright for all to see, but still an outsider I'm left to me.

Beneath the soil the dead dark remains, the imperceptible abode of the unlivable, forever profane.

Oh, Gardener, how tell us so, why beauty for us, Por, death and misery?

The answer, it seems, was spoken before. One must die to find life
Because, oh, Gardener, you'd do only more.

This is why: the foliage, vestibule, and greenery, now more than ever, are there;
The petals of eternal torment have been plucker free from her hair.

Now the seeds are rising up, proclaiming the attention of the World—
Having been pruned by her maker, the contradiction is solved.
Love your enemy as yourself, Great Gardener will do the same.

Then will fulfilled be the edicts, for in the truth—All Will Remain.

Mark D. Shoberg

Lonely

Sitting in the dark,
Waiting for a sound,
A crackling sound of rain,
A splish splash trickle of rain,
A bang against the window,
Like a beating rain stick,
Or a roaring lion dancing around
Like a Mexican clicking beetle,
The relaxing sound of rain,
Rain sounds like a friend,
When you are alone,
That's what's so perfect about rain.

Joshua Kinzler

Common Sense

Once in a while,
A grin or a smile
On your face
Will give gloom a chase.

A happy person
Is a good reason
To let you know
It will always show.

How you can tell
One can do a job well?
He is really trained
And not under restrain.

If you are able
To push back from the table
Before you eat too much
You'll really enjoy your lunch.

Edna Mae Adams

Snow Repercussions

Tramping, tramping through the snow
Catch yourself, or down you go . . .
Underneath the snowy dust,
Lies an icy, slippery crust.

Cautious drivers inch along slowly,
Reckless speedsters, splash you boldly.
Trash piles mount, but seldom go
The sanitation trucks are pushing snow.

Main arteries are quickly cleared,
But not your side street, as you feared.
Keep the kids all bundled in snowsuits,
Don't dare go out without you own boots.

And as more snow accumulates,
Our patience quickly dissipates.
We tend to think of just one thing . . .
Will it ever, ever be next spring?

Rita T. Murphy

This Guy I Work With

He's the type of man
who wears cords and sweaters
shabbily mismatched
thrown together
without consideration.
He's the type of man
who always has on tennis shoes—
blue ones with worn soles and
thick brown laces.
He's the type of man
who accessorizes with
sideburns and
a scruffy chin.
His style wears him well.

Jennifer A. Czaplewski

Let It All Out

As emotions swim around in my body,
I cry because I don't know which one will take over next.
I itch all over with anger and sadness.
The emotion, joy, seems to have disappeared.
I claw at my skin trying to let it all out.
Screaming, clawing, beating, breaking, then screaming again.
As I look at my reflection, at my blotchy, bleeding, red skin, I cry.
And the numbness takes over. I shiver and twitch from the cold.
I shake and reel from the pain. Foaming at the mouth,
I scream incoherent things into the air.
These things fall to the ground and turn to dust
Because no one is there to hear any of it.
So I breathe, then choke then gasp
For air as I go through all the emotions again.
Clawing and screaming. Beating and breaking.
Then screaming again, trying to let it all out.

     Nicole Turner

Strange World

Strange world I live in now today
Where God is being beset by man on every hand and no one seems to care
Strange world, indeed, when lowly man would set his manmade laws against
God's laws and outlaw prayer.
My heart grows cold as it looks ahead towards this desolation
Where nations rise up everywhere to scorn their own creation
Where poisoned minds and hopeless hearts and false pursuits of glory
Shut doors of churches everywhere and thus shut out the story
Of God's supremacy o'er man and man's acceptance of it
False prophets now would change that role and put God into orbit
A sleeping nation lets this be lulled by myrrh and gold
Awakening at last to see that they have lost their hold
On God and his munificence, for He won't be betrayed
And those who fail Him now must face a future without aid
Strange world I live in now today in this land blessed by God
But not so strange as tomorrow will be when we face up to the odds.
Where are all the voices that should decry this usurpation?
Why are churches silent in the midst of desecration?
Why is my voice the only voice that deplores this desolation?
Strange, strange world and stranger yet its people

     Nina B. Doughty

The Flood

Never still, never stopping, always dripping, always dropping,
Pouring down from unending highs like great waterfalls in the skies.
Making him sorrowful, making him sad, then driving him raving mad.
Beating on windows, beating hard like a mythological beast in the yard.
Lightning crashing, thunder booming, as he sat and watched ever glooming.
Plummeting to the ground, drowning small things never found.
The wind moaning and groaning and making lots of noise,
Scaring all the girls and boys.
Wetting and soaking and drenching and drowning,
As the wind ever hounding and pounding.
Water flowing like endless seas, as the wind howls through the trees.
All through the day and on into the night,
The blackness causing panic and fright.
As it rains ever more, the water begins to flood the floor.

It floods the house and all the land, covering up all the sand.
As his lungs fill with water, he thinks, "Swim! No time to totter."
But soon goes his energy and all his fight,
All that's left is the water's might.
As he sinks out of sight, his body fills with unending fright.
He dies that horrid night.

     Timothy Plunkett

Angels among Us

There are angels among us
where ever we go.
They are everywhere
only some of us know.

They are with us in good times
they are with us in bad.
They somehow just know
if you are happy or sad.

They are they when you need them,
always by your side
When ever you need then,
they will be your utmost guide.

They will never leave you,
even when you are asleep.
They are your guardian angel,
and they are yours for keeps.

Although you must know,
They are sent from above.
To help us through life,
God sent them with love.

     LoriAnne Daane

Burning Love

In the dark of night
A flame is burning.
Burning like the sun
So large and yet so bright.
It is a flame of love
Burning in my heart.
Showing me the truth
That we will never be apart.
It's a love that is so great
A love that is so pure.
A love that shows an answer
This answer I know for sure.
That we will always love each other
Because our love is true.
For true love is so powerful
This I always knew.
For my love is burning
Burning inside of you.

     Daniel Arndt

20th Century Changes

My grandma rode in a buggy
Back in 1914.
She had never seen an airplane
Nor knew what that could mean.

As a child I listened to radio,
Never dreaming of TV
The box that you could see and hear
Had not yet come to me.

I shopped in the first air-conditioned
Store in our small town.
At home we lay on linoleum
At night just to cool down.

I saw my first computer, too,
At work, and I was scared.
What was this new technology,
New knowledge to be shared?

My Daddy plowed behind a horse
Where machines now do that task.
If the 21st brings more changes great,
What is next now, I might ask.

     Retha Kay Sanders

God Bless America

This world is in such turmoil, with trouble everywhere,
While hearts are being made to bleed, with pain and such despair.
We watch while bombs are being dropped, in some far and distant
Land, we try to mend the broken hearts, and lend a helping hand.

Our soldier's fight the battles, they fly the planes of war,
They leave their homes and families here, for that far and distant shore,
they try to stop the suffering, but will it ever end?
Will lives ever be repaired? So they can try and live again.

They call it "Ethnic Cleansing," but don't they understand?
Lives are surely being lost, while fighting for their land.
For there could be a cause no greater, than for men to fight and die,
for what they believe, to be truly most sacred; so together, we must try.

America is not a perfect nation, but we hold these truths most dear.
That all men are created equal, so let us never fear.
To fight the fight for freedom, and stand for what is just.
And let us truly, always, remember that in God, we place our trust.

Nellie Oran

Guardian Angels

Last night I had the sweetest dream I was walking on streets of gold.
When I heard a sweet voice saying, "Come and see great stories never shown."
An angel stood beside me and took me by my hand.
"Come and take a walk with me as I journey through this land."
She showed me a child who looked to be four.
Her dear life was taken, her mother didn't want her anymore.
The child look so happy laughing and playing.
The angel looked at me and said, "See God hears you when you're praying."
Then she pointed to a man who had the happiest look upon his face.
I thought to myself I've seen this man some place.
The angel said to me, "Yes, you know him he lived on your street.
He lived all alone and all he did was weep."
We travelled down just a little further.
And there I saw a teenage boy talking with his brother.
He wasn't able to do that when he lived down below.
But know you can hear him singing ever where he goes.
I was thinking to myself, "Why was I shown all these things."
That's when she turned me and opened up her wings.
"Sometimes when a life is taken you don't know why.
Our dear Father doesn't like it when he hears his children cry."

Shanna Bradley

Unsung Heroes

Bravery and courage are words that make you think of heroes,
and wars, and other exciting deeds.
Powerful, bold words,8 about people fulfilling needs.
But most often, the necessary courage that it takes to face each day,
Is never talked about in any way.
The person needing a transplant who is afraid to go to sleep.
For fear it will be the last one, forever and deep.
The grieving widow with children to raise,
Who must be mother and father both, so strong, so brave.
The handicapped person who works hard to do things every day,
Against insurmountable odds, being cheerful all the way.
The big looking physically able bodied person, who has a bad heart,
And has to look like an uncaring coward,
because he can't physically take part.
The people who hurt everyday of their life,
And still participate, sing, as if there is no strife.
The facing of surgery and unknown disease it will find,
The recuperation and adjustment to its particular kind.
To face the problem, whatever it may be,
And continue down the road of life happily. These are the unsung heroes!

Mary Alice Bastian

The Shadow

A shadow on the ground,
Yet, no one is there.
Moving, ever closer,
Stopping briefly, only to stare.

I move quickly away.
My shadow, refusing to stray,
What do you seek?
There is no reply.
This shadow, very determined to pry.

Leave me be!
I bark out loud,
Silence lightened with a passing cloud.

This shadow whom I'd feared,
Passed me by,
As a cloud interrupted, the clearing sky.
Peter Davis

The Birch Tree

White birch, with your regal grace,
Reaching upward, seeking grace
Crown of emeralds, coat of white,
Shining in the summer light,
Like the scepter of a queen
Striving to command the scene.

Your pristine beauty holds the eye
Of every creature passing by
And when the birds are in the nest
You celebrate with all the rest,
With buds unfurled in leaves of jade
To give us welcome summer shade.

When winter winds begin to blow
You match your whiteness with the snow
And so life's rhythm perseveres
For you and me throughout the years
Janet S. Lundy

Fire in the Sky

Fire rains in the distance
As the horizon
Is filled
With a golden orange hue
Gray clouds converge on the Sun
While the ocean tries
To capture his rays of gold
The Sun struggles to be free
And fights through
A break in the clouds
Fire rains in the distance
As the ocean waves reach for the Sun
The Sun fights
To hold on to the day
But the clouds overpower him
The ocean reaches out
And grab the Sun with his waves
The Sun struggles to the end
But the ocean overtakes him
Fire rains in the distance
No more
Todd Uebele

LIFE

Dedication To Everybody
I wish it never happen
it came as a leaf floating in the wind
but luck is no player in this ballgame.

This ballgame is life;
you either sink or swim.
Alex Attart

We Miss You

The trees we planted together have missed you for five years
The locust, the myrtle, and the mind as weeping gentle tears each spring.
Your little farm with its creatures great and small is gone
Homer the hog, a dog named nags, Shannon your lamb, and little Henrietta,
the mouse. Your family and friends the birds and flowers, the pets of your
youth, all miss you so. Your VW Beetle, whose sound brought the joy of your
returning, remains—its brightness dimmed by your departing.
Our love and longing reach out for you the treasures memories.
Somehow your soul touches us each day your footsteps are ever in our
hearts. A desperate cry a prayer answered, when out of the dusk, clouded
with our tears appeared a mocking bird, resting where you lay sleeping.
Each time we see a mocking bird you are alive again, with it your spirit
flies into a brighter day. Your spirit lives in a better place than we
have never known. Your spirit lives within our hearts within the happiness
we shared. Your spirit lives in the hymn "Amazing Grace" sung at your last
resting place. May God bless you and may our Lord Jesus take you in his
arms for us our son, brother, and grandson.
You have gone from us, but your will always be in our hearts.

Harry C. Graham

Millennium A to Z

As	Zest
Brouhaha	Year
Clamor	X x 200
Dawns	With
Elaborate	Victoriously
Fascination	Unfurled
Gathers	Thoughts
Heralding	Scrumptious
Impassioned	Response
Joviality	Quick
Kissing	Perspicuous
Looming	Open
Millennium	Nerves

Rolf Renner

Just for You

You came into my life when I was down and low
And showed me how to love again and how this love could grow.
Your tender, kind and loving ways bring out the best in me.
They make me want you more each day showing how strong my love can be.
I love your sweet soft kisses and the way you stroke my hair.
It makes me love you that much more to know that you are there.
I didn't want to love you for fear you'd break my heart.
But my love for you is just so strong and grows stronger as we are apart
I wait to hear your voice to brighten up my day.
It brings loving thoughts to my heart in a very special way.
Without you in my life I just don't know what I would do.
My love for you grows stronger each day and this love is just for you.

Lisette A. Maute

Reflections

As I watch you lay in your bed,
All these thoughts go through my head.
A man who was once vibrant and full of life
Is now weak, thin, and full of strife.
A man who loved so many things
From taxidermy to deep-sea fishing.
You have touched so many with your thoughtful ways.
So many good memories and joy-filled days.
It breaks my heart to see you so helpless and weak
With barely enough strength to eat or even speak.
There's so much I want to tell you—so much I want to say.
But I just cannot find the words—just not today.
I remember all the good times—all the bad times, too.
How you took such good care of me and watched as I grew.
I wish I had the time to spend all the days with you.
And the time to spend all the nights to help you make it through.
You mean the world to me and you always will.
Without you, there'll be a void that no one could ever fill.
What I'm trying to say is: Grandpa, I love you and I'll miss you—me and all the rest.
But you're being taken away from us because God only takes the best.

Olivia F. Placé

Just for You

If I could touch the stars,
I'd give them all to you,
and if the moon was in my reach,
that would be yours too.
I pray to see your smile,
To warm and brighten my day.
You always seem to be in my thoughts,
you are special to me, in every way.
Like the stars in the heavens
your eyes shine down on me,
and when you close them tight,
I hope I'm what you see.
I couldn't be any happier,
especially when I'm by your side,
all the feelings I feel,
in you, I try to confide.
Sometimes the words, "I love you,"
are hard for me to say,
but my love for you is endless,
and I love you more with each new day.

Luegene Johnson

All That I Am

Understanding me
is different from understanding
your expectations
of me

If I could be
all that you thought and think
I should be

Could I be happy. . . .
Would I be free. . . .

Instead I choose to be
all that is me

Accepting people
for who they are
and not what I say
they should be

is ALL THAT I AM. . . .

Lee Booze-Battle

The Image

Yesterday I saw a man
An old friend I used to know
I always wondered if he'd prospered
If he'd ever learned to grow
And if his dreams of wealth and fame
Had come in his quest for life
And if the world did know his name
Or if it had passed him by
His face had aged his hair had grayed
His years no more than mine
The etchings on his face were clear
His love of life had died
And though he danced and rattled on
So jovial to behold
I felt a sudden chill in me
And felt my blood run cold
My feet were fixed upon the ground
I could not turn away
And then a crash the mirror broke
The image went away

D. Terneus

In Heaven

When summer is its hottest, you're even hotter.
When fall brings an amber shower of leaves,
rolling down sidewalks into vibrant piles.
Nothing even then compares to the warm brown of your eyes.
And, winter, the brightest virgin snow, won't shine, like you.
And, let's not forget spring,
full of sunshine, and flowers in bloom.
The most beautiful of any season just pales, beside you.
I mean this, from the very first time
I laid eyes on you, I knew.
I knew that you'd run inside my daydreams.
Keep me up at night.
And, cast a light on my life, like the stars bring life to the night.
But, even that's not all, my love.
I'd give you my life, to save you and still, that's not enough.
Maybe, in Heaven, I'd give you my wings.

Tangier A. Cullens

Shattered Glass

The sand so smooth on the crest of my feet
Have I found love? As each new heart beats
So soundless, yet so loud
Then it hits me, the stage of reality
Trying to let what happened pass
Yesterday keeps sticking me, like feet on broken glass

Yesterdays are gone, I tell myself
What's done is done, I kept seeing the feeling of falling in love
My life was whole, but piece by piece I fell into that fateful hole
The hole of love, so demanding, I thought I was loved, the feeling so fresh
I thought my life was filled, but there was something missing
The comfort, someone actually listening
I was drowning, in that fatal mass, the pain of the broken glass

People whom I had called my friends, one by one a relationship ends
Girls I knew, from the very start
Abandoned me with this empty heart
I wish I could have seen what I now know, there was no love, that plainly shows
Nobody was there, nobody was here, yesterday's gone, with all its tears
My lonely heart broke, and became the shattered glass

Jarrod Dean Harris

Billows from Above

A hundred shades, a thousand shapes, a godly performance before us staged.
Silver and rose, a billowy fest aloft our brow for all age.

Like crimson colored cotton gently brushed by light of our morning star.
A boon sent our way to come close from afar.

Bidding adieu, bringing a view as if Heaven sent.
Brilliantly lit in gold, or darkness in bold, fronting a frame of blue.
They're grooms to the Earth, these giant courting gents.

People around the world, different ideas in different places,
something in common a gift that we share, upon our lives it graces.

A blanket to cover our cold, an umbrella for our shade.
A nourishment to what is dry, a beauty blessed to the eye
before off to sleep we fade.

For as old as the Earth are we indebted for their marvelous
works to their credit.

Lofting about so high and free,
a gift from above shared with me.

Advancing along or seemingly still a clear blue
sky they sometimes fill.
In times of new and times old they are forever present
as if written in gold.
These splendid angels with their silver lining
gives us respect for the sun when it's shining.

Michael L. Hoggins

My Beloved

Starry nights and crisp winds blow
Cradle the words I love you so.
Awesome sunsets and radiant dawns
Let me know our love shines on.
Nature's beauty and all that lives
Tells me of the love you give.
Therefore then, I have no fear
For in heart, you're ever near.
Watching you is quite a thrill
But holding you is better still.
There is no one on Earth like you
To bathe me with a love so true.
Thus by your side I long to be
Your passion's warmth has set me free
To take me where I've never been
With you, bless God, we'll always win.

Dereck Whitesmith

Ashlyn

She's so loving
she's so sweet
she has tiny
little feet.
She cries a little
smiles a bunch
and even eats
a real good lunch.
She's getting bigger now
She's five and a half
We're real good friends
and she makes me laugh.
When she sees me coming
She comes a running.
Her mothers daughter
and a little part of me
she's all love
and as caring as can be.
My granddaughter, my bright star
Ashlyn that's who you are.

Nellie Mae Veal

Eye of the Storm

Understanding the storm
of our lives.
No one can see
when it hits.
No one can feel
the power and wrath.

Saving the souls
of those who care.
Save the hopes and love
through the battles and wars . . .

Only if the hearts
see and feel,
inside the minds
of those who are in trouble . . .

In the "Storm of Confusion."

Tomena Courtepatte

With Him

With Him to guide my walk and way
And direct my every path
I shall not fear another day
For His love doth far surpass
Any power of thought or whim
That any man could make
All my faith and trust's in Him
And my very soul is His to take

Matthew Beckman

Liquid Purgatory

Lost and forgotten, my soul was.
Surrounded by coldness and darkness, a dungeon I was in.
A prison, in which the only escape that I had known,
was that of a mind numbing liquid.
A liquid which would seem to remove the barriers of my captivity,
teasing me of freedom.

Yes, many in fact every night the liquid would give me
delusion of grandeur that I was free.
But when those moments passed, all that remained were the eyes.

The faces were shrouded in darkness, but the eyes were prevailing.
Looks of shame, disgust, and even those of mockery were what was conveyed to me.

Except for one, one image came out of the darkness, and reached for me.
These eyes were of caring and not of judgement.

The figure came closer, and its face pushed the darkness out.
An angel, she resembled, perfect in every way.
Closer, and closer she came, her touch sent shockwaves through me!
My spine wrenched as my soul came back to life!
I gasped at the heavens that I ignored for so long, and fell to my knees.

When I opened my eyes, I saw a different view,
one not skewed by the numbing liquid, and what I saw was love.

Remembered and found my soul became,
as the angel-like figure carried me out of the cold dark chamber.
The liquid was needed no more.

Michael R. Powell II

Da Blues

The blues ain't nothing but a soulful sound.
It ain't always down sometimes in low down.
And the blues ain't nothing but a shaking head
Maybe on account of something that your baby said.
No, the blues can't bring you down.
The blues ain't nothing but a soulful sound.
Some people say that the blues can make you cry,
But the blues can't make you cry.
You might be walking in the rain
when you see your best friend in his shiny ride.
And he's got your baby by his side.
The blues can make you feel but the blues can't make you cry.
I remember one time something that my daddy said.
He said, "Boy, things have a way of working themselves out."
"They ain't never as bad as they first seem."
I guess that the blues and my daddy don't share the same dream.
The blues is looking forward when up ahead just looks as bad as behind.
In time you learn that every way you turn, you burn.
Yea, the blues is looking forward.
The blues is just a state of mind.

Kevin Eblen

To Be One with the Storm

Restless, I looked out the window
Darkness and shadows rode swiftly on the breeze.
The air was heavy and my nails tap-tapped, my legs danced expectantly.
The pressure built, outside and within me.
Then the wind gained speed and my ears popped.
Brought from my daze, I turned to the glass.
Scratching and snapping; black skeletons reached out to grab me.
Smothering and suffocating; smog and gloom came and blocked out the sun.
Loud voices roared and threatened, pounding on my eardrums.
Unnatural light flashed and shades screamed, running from the glare.
I raced down the stairs and skidded out the door.
My feet splashed through angry tears and my hair lashed my face, a stinging
whip. I felt the breath of rage, heard the clamoring roar.
Up on my toes, I spread my legs and arms.
Throwing my head back I shouted and laughed.
The hands roughly grabbed me, the pain harshly gripped me, and the light
briefly blinded me. I let them do what they wished, forfeited my soul
For the chance, oh the chance, to be one with the storm.

Jessica Papia

This Is Me

Of all the things I've ever seen,
of all the things I've ever dreamed,
of all the things I've ever schemed,
of all the wonders, this is me.

William Woolery

The Powerful One

Winds blow through the blue sky
Who knows when they go by
The birds sense their presence
As the birds fly across the blue sky

The beings whom watch over the sky
As the jets fly by
The gaurdians of the blue sky
The white clouds which they ride

The mighty one above
He keeps the evil one below
And if it comes to push and shove
He will chain the evil one below

David Fekete

Little Bumble Bee

I knew a little Bumble Bee
That wanted to see what he could bee.
But all that he could Bee, Bee, Bee
was a little yellow bumble Bee.

Richard Tyler

Today

With the morning light He
Awakens me;
Light has touched my face.

All of the moments in time,
From one to the other
Have all been knit together
To make one thing—the present.
Only He knows forever.

Oh, to know the depths
And wisdom
And secrets of life.
What is truth becomes hidden
In the petty strife.

What is sure is this moment.
There is the truth.
It is only in one place.
Go to Him with a broken heart
And drink in His grace.

Corina Filler

The Paddock

Move me not into the paddock,
where the grass is lush,
and the living is easy.

Take me not to the field,
away from the race,
from the adulation of the crowd.

Give me not the expectations,
of why I can no longer race,
and how I deserve to rest.

Steal from me not,
the sweat from my back,
exchanged for a coat of warmth.

Move me not into that paddock,
where I am no longer seen,
the paddock of unfulfilled dreams.

Russell Skingsley

Say It Now!

Why wait until tomorrow to tell someone you care?
For beyond the dawn tomorrow you may not find them there.
The past now lies behind us and tomorrow may not come.
If only I have today, my missing part of me to beat upon life's drum.

Why not say, "I love you" to those that you hold so dear.
For time is such a fragile thing that death may soon appear.
Let others know you love them so there is never a doubt.
The best time is now to share these special moments
While our hearts speak so loudly within us.

If you keep your love secret it cannot multiply.
For love, when it's neglected it begins to slowly die.
Go on and let our lips speak what's in our hearts.
Just look into each other eyes.
Say it now; say it now that you care,
And that you are that missing part of me.

Paula Cooks

Flee

When I needed you.
You said you'd always be there.
Well I need you, so where are you
You said you loved me.
And said that you cared and would never leave.
So why did you leave when I told you how I felt?
If you loved me, you would have stayed.
Instead you fled and never returned.
But you told me you loved me and would never leave.
So where are you now when I need you?
When I talked to you last, you said you've been thinking about us again.
Well I thought about us too.
But, I told you I loved you for the first time in person and you fled.
And I don't think you deserve me,
Even though I love you.
I am moving on because I know it will never be again.
Until the day you figure out, you know what you want.
And what you want is me.
And when you tell me you love me for the first time in person,
I'm going to flee and let you think and wonder if we will ever be.

Alison Carter

No Matter What

There are those who will love you no matter what,
and there are those who will hate you no matter what.

There are those who will encourage you no matter what,
and there are those who will discourage you no matter what.

But there is only one to whom you must answer, no matter what;
And it is He who will love you, encourage you, and protect you, no matter what.

Odis W. Kenton, Sr

Angels among Us

Angels fly high, angel's fly low, bringing us messages to and fro,
With such beauty and bright glow, O' how they must light up as they come
and go. Standing beside us day and night protecting over us making sure
we're all right, ever so softly whispering in our ear letting us know
we've nothing to fear and always ready to wipe away a tear.
So if you stop and listen to the little whisper within
you will hear it say; "Shhh . . . All is well this day."
O' yes by the way let us ask for them when we pray
and the Lord will send them on their way.

Daniel Ray Patton

Love and Hate

Love and hate are different
Yet very much the same
Both are strong emotions
You wonder why they came.

When in love it's like a dream.
When in hate it's misery.
You must have one thing in both
And that is total bravery.

Faith is also helpful
It gets you through the tough.
But remember these are feelings
Although sometimes rough.

Enjoy the love,
But learn from the hate.
Remember these words
On your next date.

A word of the wise
I pass on to you.
Be careful with yourself
Sometimes you haven't a clue.

Shanna Harstead

I'm Lost

Without you in my world,
my love,
it was to have no meaning.
Without the sound of your sweet voice,
my love,
my heart shatters to pieces.
I will cherish you,
my love,
my one and only.
I will love you and only you,
my love,
forever more.

Mike Baker

A Deer in the Woods

At first I didn't believe it
but I had
seen
a deer.
A song
that moved like a swan
down the bank
to the brook.
By the water he stood
like a statue
Listening
Listening   Listening
For sounds not of the forest,
but for me.

Zach Williams

Autumn Thoughts

The autumn mists above us now
Looking down so gray and proud,
Gains a part of every man
To take his life, into his hands.

The autumn sun's above us now
Shining through the misty brow
Creates an illusion of life to be,
Throughout man's modern technology.

The autumn moon's above us now
Glowing deep and dark its clouds
Seeing through the leaves and trees
That life and love are forever to be.

Dennis F. Stanton

Our Father

He opened his eyes and looked into the light
beaming bright and entering his soul.
His eyes filled with tears of joy.
The sun lifting over the clouds.

Given this gift—the gift of life.
His eyes filled with tears.
No boundaries set and nothing
Will ever be broken, shattered with the guilt of lost days.
Love overpowers all.

The want, the need to be loved.
The sky most beautiful when the sun comes up.
He wonders what or who will embrace him. The longing overdue.
Break the chains, the bars that hold me.
He is given a chance.
Given this gift ,the gift of life.

Who's to say who's deserving?
He at times makes mistakes, given hardships and pain, challenges, and
obstacles to overcome.
He has a distance to achieve what is set before him.
He is a great man, given this gift—the gift of life.

Dawn M. Pelton

I Am the Rain Clouds

Temporary self-indulgence, blame it on the shadow land kids.
Where a split-second image is etched in your mind,
and fairy-tale wishes never come true.
I thought you'd never come back. I figured you were there to stay,
I know you wanted your space, I thought you had gone away.
Happier in the waste land of your dreams
where nothing but your imagination can harm you.
And I am the rain clouds. The ones which weep your pain.
Miserable implications running savage through the harbors of your soul.
The patient ticking of a death clock you know you can't control.
I am the rain clouds whispering in your ear.
I am the rain clouds you shall never fear.
Hold tight to your demolition cruisers as I take you higher and higher.
Farther away from the sadness of it all. The sadness which in life.
The life that cannot withstand the pressure
of deconstruction and the blankness of it all. Of this pathetic existence.
So be the rain cloud lords,
I cherish these sights with a sword in my hand
and the rain that falls to Earth.

Meghan Geiger

Salvation Sojourner

Child of God! Salvation Sojourner!
Jesus Christ led you from sin and death to grace and life.
The road you travel is completely paved with His shed blood
For an eternal covering of security that will not diminish, fade, or end!

Child of God! Salvation Sojourner!
Follow God's biblical road map to complete each leg of the journey.
O' Holy Spirit! O Divine Guide!
Lead your earthly emissary down this holy path as he should abide.

Child of God! Salvation Sojourner!
Living in a society that shows clearly its rebellion against God.
Plant the seeds of the gospel into the field of the world
To reap an abundance of the harvest of mankind's souls.

Child of God! Salvation Sojourner!
Be prepared for a rocky road with each mile you travel.
Your unholy enemies has many traps and pitfalls for you to fall,
But take courage righteous pilgrim in The Savior and walk tall!

Child of God! Salvation Sojourner!
This sojourn will rise up to many heights untold
And at times, will sink to depths unseen by man.
Press on child of God! Press on until your journey ends!

Perry M. Ford III

What a Day!

Woke up late
Burnt the toast
Fuel tanks empty
Skateboards broken
Missed the bus
Late for school
Detention at one
This is cruel
Pile of homework
Rained all day
Cricket's cancelled
TV's busted
Internet's busy
Dinner's late
Giblet soup. Ew Yuk!
Washing up—me again.
Stuck at home
What a night
Time to sleep
This day be gone.

Tanya Harris

Hopeful Beginnings

How different can we be
When there's still so much life to see

Hopeful beginnings
Forever loves

Too much can take place
So much to take care of

I wish everyone happiness
But smiles can fade fast

Loves are lost
In decades past.

Hold to the dreams
Still yet to come true

Look to the stars
And the hope from above

Take care to touch
Of loved ones you must

You can always find
The moments of trust.

Sheila Parish

Spell

I wrapped myself
In the red sunset.
Tomorrow will be freezing.
The sky is clear,
Deep—
As if the Great Bear
Took for a walk
Her Bear Cub.

The heart is falling
From the top
Of the highest pine tree.

When you leave
The sun will jump into the sea
To bathe in the cool waves—
To cool itself
From your blazing heat.

Come back.

Nataliya Tuchynska

Home on the Pond

We are in our new home, a home on the pond
Of which we're more than a little fond
The ducks can stay . . . they're okay
The geese not so . . . they can go.

Ducks, herons, and snowy egrets—they're like our pets
But Canada geese—that water fowl most foul—
Need more falling water, like a waterfall,
And we'd have no regrets!

Birds too: goldfinch, swallows, and woodpeckers are a sight to behold;
Hawks and crows (too many of those),
Gulls and doves all told.

We need a name for the porch where we do our viewing
All those sights . . . real delights,
And hear the sounds of tweeting, chirping, and cooing.

Flights of fancy, with a sigh,
Tend to fly away in the bye and bye

The sound we hear the most; alas, alack,
Is that of the quack, quack, quack,

And so if you all don't mind . . .
We'll just call our porch "The Duck Blind!"

Richard A. Tavolacci

While You Were Gone

Every morning a soft heartbreak without you,
Every night a lonely whisper "good night, my baby."
I am lost in these sheets where your sweet smell still cries out to me.
These walls that echo your laugh and frame a world
where you and I still dance only in my weary, torn heart.

Can I touch your hand just one more time?
Can I cup your cheek in my palm and pour myself
into your golden eyes, again?
Can I pull you to me and rest your head against my chest,
breathe you in and rock you and let loneliness fade away?
Can the days and nights of missing you end at last?

Your smile is my sunrise.
A kind word, my strength.
Your happiness, my grail.
You are the queen
who my bleeding soul seeks.
A once dark and unforgiven wanderer
calling your name in a cold wind.
Can you hear the distant cry through the empty, starry night?

Richard Ray

My Little Girl Isn't Little Anymore

I recall not long ago, I use to tuck you in at night.
You'd always give me a kiss and hug me so tight.
I remember reading stories, some were the same
night after night, and when there was a storm,
you'd run in and hide your head and cry with big tears of fright.
I'd calm your fears and dry your tears and tell you everything
would be all right, this went on for a few more years.

Then there were your bumps and bruises from trying to learn how to walk,
to ride a bike, climbing furniture like climbing mountains and trees
or those things that go bump in the night.

Then you went from soft toys and cuddly dolls to building blocks and wind—
up toys. Then to replace all those quiet times came records, radio, and all
that crazy noise, of curling hair, make up, and craziness for boys.
Oh, how I remember all those joys.

From little sleepers and diapers to bulky sweaters, tight jeans, and short
shorts, oh, so tight. In place of all those stories we now watch Dick Clark's
"American Bandstand" and of course soaps.

Now I look in on you from time to time, and kiss the cheek and get to talk
to you from time to time. Now I have those fears and tears of you'll face
in your coming years. All these years have gone by, I sit here and compare.

Marilyn A. LoGerfo

Shattered

Broken glass lies on the ground
As you speed off to her
In the puddle lies the end
I trudge back to my car

Exhaling hard a cloud of smoke
My eyes turn downward with
Useless hope to erase the scene
That's already been burned in

In sad silence I drive home
The defroster screams ice cold
Numb, stiff hands turn hard the wheel
While dead feet weight the brake

I drag myself to lonely sheets
Flop useless on my bed
Close tight my eyes to just forget
When all I did was dream

My head now aches with throbbing beats
To swallow proves a task
With anger tied to empty space
It slowly breaks in two.

Michelle Lawlor

Sanctity

Her eyes like fire,
Her hands of silken cloth,
The words she speaks are healing
She is my sanctity.

Through thick and thin she's there,
In the good times and the bad,
Her friendship heals my soul,
Her laughter is my novocaine.

She'll never know how much she means,
She wipes away my cares,
She soothes my aching heart,
Because she's always there.

She haunts my thoughts,
Emotions and prayers,
She's my safe house in this angry world,
She is my sanctity.

Katherine Smyth

1-4-3

Yeah I know I say I love you
And in numbers one-four-three
And no matter how much I tell you
Enough, there will never be
But if you take the words, "I love you"
And how much they mean to me
I couldn't explain how much I love you
But don't take my word for it, ask me
I'll do anything because I love you
I'll swim across the largest sea
I love you, I love you, I love you
Kari baby, I love you, one-four-three

Aaron Logsdon

Rain

Love can be like pain
the Earth soaked, rain
drenching the Earth with water
the birth of beauty its daughter
The seed buried beneath the Earth
like loneliness ensconced without mirth
the rain of love bittersweet
Oh, until we meet!

Gavin Marsden

Soul Reaper and the Harvester of Sorrow

My soul has alluded me, evaded and deserted me,
Giving a light for sorrow's eyes to find me.
Melancholy seeking the shadow of my sorrow,
Preying upon my remorse for pay.

Silver streams and bottomless water, you admit to have seen,
All cascade, why can't you see?
I swim above rivers, but I drown in the lake,
We all get mauled in love and hate.

My shadow lurks beyond opaque glass,
But I yearn to cleanse them and reflect my silhouette
For they will fog and blacken once again,
Then my face will fade away into guilty sin.

Satan walked the Earth, and his cape dragged across the sky,
He said that he'd shelter me from pain and sorrow, only if I would abide.
He shaded my mind with deceitful lies, and cast me into fires below,
I was left forever to grope in the dark,
With his flames to feast upon my soul.

    Brett Smith

Individual

Here we are all alone as individuals,
No one to talk to, no one to trust.

Thousand people, what do you say, what do you do?
You say nothing. You do nothing.

More and more people with more expectations.
The questions flow again, what to say, what to do.

Do nothing. Why? Because you are an individual not an expectation.

All the people gone, no one to talk to,
One person to trust. Who? You, the individual.

    Cheryl Russell

Journey

I started on this journey many years ago.
Started fast but, as time went I began to slow.
This is a journey of war between the flesh and spirit.
A journey of a soldier I became, when I was baptized in Jesus name.
The places that I go are not on land or sea, but of life's phases
That will lead me to my destiny.
I have found that the only way to travel on this journey is on your knees.
To that spiritual place no fleshly man can see.
I have climbed high mountains.
Walked through dark valleys, thought I would never see the morning light.
But, I knew if I stayed faithful and true,
Someday my journey would end in a heavenly flight.
I have learned on my journey, it is not how fast
Or slow nor how it begins but where your journey will end.

    Ruthie Jones

You Are Gone, He Is Here

I sat in stone with my name carved in stigma;
Alone with the daydream's break of your name;

You erupted with murderous rage and pierced my convictions with scandal;
Abducted by pain through a phantasm I only thought could rust with time.

Yesterday he departed with the eagle's last flight to nowhere;
Started now is a vision only angels could expose to the division

I found a destination of angelic settings united with passion;
Stations of denuded arms from the one who gave his essence to my shadow;

You no longer belong in my thoughts of fated dreams,
Forever.

    Melanie Stevens

Mother's Day

Mom, you are so special.
I love you, can't you see,
You are the best thing
That ever happened to me.

You were kind enough to accept me,
All the things that I have done.
You put my life before yours',
For that you're number one.

I could buy you flowers,
Or give you a gift from my heart.
I could write you a poem,
Or make a masterpiece of art.

All of this for you, Mom,
I love you to this day,
I wrote this poem for you, Mom,
Happy Mother's Day!

    Travis Johnson

God's Love

A mother's womb
A child's face
A father's compassion
A mother's listening ear
God is ever so near

    Mark Fairchild

Love's Dream Kingdom

Sunlight on a golden flower,
Moonlight at the midnight hour,
Sweetheart's kiss in hidden bower,
In Love's dream kingdom.

Planets in the heav'n's align,
Grapes mature upon the vine,
Around my Love my arms entwine,
In Love's dream kingdom.

Whistling winds chase clouds away,
Rustling autumn leaves make play,
I'll love you every night and day,
In Love's dream kingdom.

    William Hallworth

Me

The night was dark and stormy
the air was damp and cold
the wind it kept on blowing

The house was empty
The girl alone and cold

She tried to be happy
But the wind it told her stories
of when she was not so old

Deep down inside her
The rain began to trickle
Into all the pain untold
To some she was a princess
to her she just felt old
The thing that hurt the most
would be the reason why
The wind just keeps on moaning
while only her heart can cry

    Ang Benefield

Quenched Thirst

I was the woman at the well on that hot smothering day,
I purposely chose to go at noon in the heat of the day.

My past and my present wasn't lily white, being alone was best for me.

I journey on to the well sad, broken,
and chained to a lifestyle that left me empty and drained.

The village women shun me, they did not include me
in their circle of fellowship, they felt I didn't fit in.

The men were friendly so I turned to them, they included me in,
Little did I know at the time it would cause things to mend.

I met a man at the well who asked me for a drink,
That's how the conversation started, I didn't know what to think

He knew everything about me, inside and out.
Then He offered me a drink that I could not do without.

As I reached for the drink I felt the touch of His hand.
Immediately my thirst was quenched, I did not feel the same.

He filled my empty well that day, never to thirst again,
With living water that flows from Him, a river within.

With excitement I left my water pots and ran as fast as I could,
To share the good news in the village where I was misunderstood.

Audrey Dixon

If God Had Not Made Woman

If God had not made woman, who would be man's counterpart
Then turn around and win his heart?
Who would have his children and instantly forget the pain with a grin?
Who would be your mother? It could not be your brother.
Who would be your sister? It could not be a mister.
If God had not made woman who would you marry? Not Tom, Dick or Harry.
Who would kiss your crying tears and take away all your fears?
Who would hold you tight and make everything right?
Who would you come home to after a day's work?
And find the table set and coffee perked?
Who would do the cooking and dishes and still fulfill all your wishes?
Who would do the washing and mending and put up with your pretending?
If God had not made woman this would be a sad and lonely place
With only man in the human race.
This would be a world of no future with only a man,
If woman had not been in God's plan.

Roberta Newbern

God, Are You There?

I was hurt so bad at the age of five
I couldn't find words to tell anyone, so I kept it inside
I told myself tomorrow I will forget, but again I cried
I told myself it's over, it will never happen again, again I lied

I gathered myself and hid myself inside my soul
I thought I was safe, but hate ate away at the door
I was consumed like a graveyard, filled with woes
Is there no mercy, to keep me safe from the secrets, I hold

At the age of five, I didn't feel safe in this world
I laid awake at night licking the wounds of my bandaged soul
One day I heard, God heals broken hearts and erases all shame
If your eyes are on the sparrow, then what about me, I scold

I laid there angry at both, God and man, barely surviving my pain
Small in frame, but carrying the weight of the world on my shoulders
I was armed with enough hate, to wipe out a nation
My sould screamed out, tears of blood that could fill an ocean

God. God. . . . Hello . . . God, are you there. . . . my lord, do you care . . .
God, send the angels to come get me, and bring me there. . . .
Hello. Hello . . . God. God . . . are you there. . . . Hello God, you are there
I can feel your presence. . . . God, you were always there. . . .

Willi Ray

Unspoken

She stares at something I can't see,
and then the tears come suddenly;
I try not to stare at her in turn
yet something deep in my heart yearns
to query of her—what is wrong?
Those tears do not on your face belong
but clearly indicate to me
the troubled state of vitality
that somehow you were thrust into
by an unkind act or word; yet through
the seconds during which you cry,
the world moves on, and so do I,
for even though myself I curse,
I know if I speak, I'll make it worse.

Gerald Wexstten

Crying

Dedicated to my wife Janice
I feel like crying,
Yet I cannot.

The tears fill up my eyes,
Yet they will not drop.

My vision is blurring,
Yet still I can see.

The beauty before me,
My wife to be.

As my tears start falling,
I look up and see.

That she is crying
Along with me.

Nancy Frasier

Lost Love

The sorrow buried deep within
Burst forth as the tears begin
Broken promises fell from thine eyes
Wanting comfort as a baby cries
You opened gates to your soul
A heartache had consumed its toll
Away to sadness and bitter pain
A promise to find thy love again!

Delores Ward

What to Write?

One of the things I dislike
Is writing poems by request!
Such I would not thus write,
But it's needed for a contest!

But what shall I write then?
What inspiration will I tap?
Will it overcome common men?
Or will my muses lay a trap?

Whatever the outcome may be,
Whatever the rhymes may say,
I know that it came from me,
And they do describe my way.

Suddenly, without a warning,
I am on the fourth quatrain
So I find myself forgetting,
What motivated the complaint:

Writing quatrains in a poem
Even if I could do just one!
Yet I did manage to do them,
Just look above—it is done!

Nuno Cardoso

Ignorance

You can call me ignorant because you can only see
The differences instead of the similarities between you and me

You can tell me I don't belong here if you truly believe
That this country is not comprised of immigrants including you and me

You can criticize my standard of living as being due to my own laziness
Do you really think that I want to remain
in a place filled with so much craziness?

Imagine arriving in a country and learning a language you couldn't speak
Then to have all its people despise you
and auction you off like a piece of meat

Consider for one moment how it must feel
To be born with one strike against you and I promise you this is real

I woke up last night from a horrible dream
Someone was calling me a n*gg*r and they were shooting at me

My people have been tried and convicted
of a crime we didn't mean to commit
Being black in America is our punishment and it seems we need to repent

Often times I day dream about a beautiful place
Where there is justice and equality for the whole human race

I pray that our children will someday be able to live in harmony
    Ciara C. Anguay

Lost Cultures

Santees, Waterees, Catawbas, Cherokees: What has happened to Thee?
Your cultures we now learn about in South Carolina History.
Corn, beans, and squash you ate; Locust beer and sassafras tea you drank,
Animals and birds were signs of worship to you
And for agriculture you worshipped the sun too,
Clothes made of animal skin you wore
Tattoos of flowers, stars, and animals you bore,
Huts made of wattle-and-daub made villages you lived in with your clan,
Councils in which you met with your friends
Alliances and confederations as well
You got around by cypress canoes, and walk around without tennis shoes
Mounds that you were buried in with jewelry
and pottery to keep you company,
Clovis points and arrowheads you used as weapons,
Chunky and games like modern day football you played to have fun,
Smallpox, measles, and scarlet fever killed you
All were English diseases that you weren't immune to,
So this is your culture and what you've accomplished
To make a mark in history you have, once again I say to thee:
What has happened to the Santees, Waterees, Catawbas, and Cherokees?
    Mary Catherine Kennedy

Father Sun and Mother Moon.
Mother Moon, mysterious, calm, guiding.
Supportive and caressing, and gray with cool.
Watching over our welfare, close and approachable.
Father Sun, eruptionary and non-stop.
Bright and harsh, penetrating resourceful knowledgeable.
Dying. Lovable and rich, scarcely irritant.
Scornful and bossiness in its centralness and screaming necessity.
Protections required for life, blanket of thought, causation of vision.
Belief stemming of pandemonium.
The Earth. The child and present central result.
Chaotic battle concepts, tides of water and consciousness.
Burden of time, bleeding of Balanced process and young and old animals of oneness,
recording themselves over and over and over.
Prayer grounds, animalistic up down general prayer-mates.
Collective being conscious of system patterns consciously put there.
Infinity comes Infinity comes Infinity comes Infinity
comes Infinity—Set yin and yang.
Humans Love—Emotions are Vibrations—so intriguing and Romantic.
Our difference is ironically vast in a sea of endless difference.
Beauty abounds and with it, change.
    Jeffrey Boffo

Love

Love is the gift,
Love is the power,
Love is the sweetness in a flower,
Love is peace,
Love is joy,
Love is a baby's favorite toy,
Love is from the heart and soul,
Plant a seed and watch it grow!
    Sarah Sanchez

Dance of the Forest Floor Lights

From the blazing orb he comes
sails as though a cast-away
leaving all the sky to hum
racing on to make the day

Here he meets the shaded wood
guarding sod with armor green
plots a plan to break the hood
infiltrate the waxy sheen

Finding foe to strong on whole
searches out his tiny chinks
intrudes upon holy soul
dancing spots of many links
    Marc Riddick

HEAD

I saw him growing
Inside of you
Very inside of you
Part by part.

I saw how it took form
His vital segments
Each one of them
Until became a unit.

I had the luck
Of seeing him born to the world
Of seeing him scream to the sky
Of seeing him spin to the air.

Once it was emerged
And I perceived it on your grooves
I asked you:
And how will you name him?

And you, with a satisfied smile
By the procreated miracle
Just expressed:
It shall be called POEM.
    Ernesto Salinas

In the Spring

In the spring I sing songs
Until the long nights are gone,
And out of sight.

As I have fun,
I spin around and run,
Until I sink and think . . .

I chased a butterfly
As it swooped and looped
Across the fine meadow.

Thinking I could fly,
I jumped off a tipped tree
And by mistake,
Slipped and crushed a flea,
Or was it me?

This is my spring revere.
    Brian Antar

I Am

I am a teenager who seeks your approval.
I wonder when you'll stop putting me down.
I hear laughter,
I see smiles,
I want you to smile as you speak my name.
I am a teenager who seeks your approval.

I imagine a day when you'll laugh with me, not at me.
I feel sorrow and pain,
I touch the world, but you don't notice.
I worry that I'm not good enough.
I cry when you turn your back to me,
a look of disappointment on your face.
I am a teenager who seeks your approval.

I understand that the world isn't always fair.
I say that I can control my life.
I dream of a promising future,
in spite of the prejudices you set against me.
I try to get good grades and do what you tell me to do.
I hope that you will peel away your blinders and see me for what I really am,
I am a teenager who seeks your approval.

Jesse Rather

I Am . . .

Sometimes you act as if you don't know
who I am, but if you look within the deepest
part of yourself you will soon
see that I am always with you.

Sometimes I stand at the edge of your dreams,
waiting for you to awaken and notice me.
And still, at other times I stand beside
you as you wander about your way.

Sometimes it's as though you fear me; I can't understand the reason why.
Is it because you can't face me?
Or is there another reason,
unknown even to you?

Sometimes I am as warm as a summer breeze,
so full of love and promises of what can be.
And as time passes I may become as dark and unsure
as a black cloud rising out of nowhere.

I am as I have always been, and cannot change from who I am.
I am sorrow; I am joy; I am peace; I am war.
I am your worst enemy; I am your best friend.
Do you know me now? I am reality.

Mary Bunkley

Always You

We met just a short time ago, but I have known you all of my life
You've walked the steps beside me, and laid in my bed every night

You were the teddy bear with which I cuddled and the teammate on my side
You were my confidant and partner, and the shadow to which I cried

Although I'd never seen your face, just an image I could feel
I knew the day would come, when that image would be real

The moment that I saw you, right then I knew
I'd waited my whole life; but it was always you

We walked together for a while, hand in hand we strolled
Until that shadow I'd imagined, became something I could hold

I could always feel your closeness; that was the peace I felt inside
It was my joy and happiness, it was the foundation of my pride

I just wish I would have known, how tragedy would take you away
Because I would've given anything, if it could've made you stay

Now your shadow is still by my side and to your legacy I remain true
Because all my life I will never doubt; that it was always you

Brandie Rauber

Soulmates

A soul mate is a person
Who has a special place in your heart

She is always there
For you to share your deepest secrets
Or even your wildest dream

She laughs your tears away
And be there for your comfort

She warms you with her affection
And won't leave you alone
In the cold lonely nights

She stands right next to you
Even when the world turns upside down

She holds on to your hopes
And hangs on to your dreams

She rejoices in your joy
And tastes your pain and sorrow

A soul mate holds the key to your heart
Even if you don't realize it

She is a treasure you could cherish
Forever in your heart

Melissa Wijaya

Dreamer

Some of past,
Some of old,
Some of stories
Yet to be told.
Some of hate,
Some of fear,
Some of the one
You hold dear.
For all of time
They come and go.
They enter your mind
And make it grow.
Some go on,
Some go away,
All they are,
Are dreams anyway.

Jeramy Baldwin

The Absurdity of Romance

And Love (Oh, Love!) what folly brings
To those who dare, both fools and kings
To tame, to change, to understand
The subtleties of Love's command.

For Love cares not for our desires
Bestows itself on cheats and liars.
And those most undeserving of,
Are often times our greatest loves.

Diane Zakhary

I Miss Him

I talk to him not knowing the truth
And yet he knows too much.
He hides himself behind the walls
No one can get through such.

Society kills a beautiful face
His innocence shattered.
A fight started from stupidity
The angel's face is battered.

I knew him once a time before
The love lived is not yet dim.
His life, the way it disappeared
I can't stop the way I miss him.

Kseniya Paskar

Little Girl of Daddy's

There's a wonderful father who never let his little girl down
There's a wonderful father who when his little girl was wrong he wouldn't frown
That little girl tried so hard not to disappoint him
Because of all she did, that would be a sin
His little girl is grown now and soon she'll be on her way
Your little girl, Daddy, wishes she could always stay
Your little girl, oh, loves you so
Your little girl, Daddy, never wants to hear no
Daddy, your little girl is sorry for all she's done to you
Daddy, your little girl tries so hard just to make it through
This little girl of yours will someday really succeed
Because this little girl of yours wants you to be proud of me

Darla Ressler

Never Let Him Die Twice

A child is something rare indeed
A challenge for everyone to try to succeed
For whatever the reason the Lord has brought
him home to be with Him
In a calmer and safer place
Though our hearts and souls are an empty space
To be filled in time as we travel this long race
Knowing that crying is only a blessing
It shows how much he was loved and will be missed
Let our eyes be filled with tears
Our hearts and minds with the wonderful memories we will cherish inside
For the Lord has a place for all of us
And it might not be when we want it to be
But never let go 'cause he holds the key to the happiness we all want to see
So be grateful and happy for the time you shared
With the one you loved and held so close and dear
"May God Bless and Keep This Family"

Yolanda Glenn

The Warrior Poet

With thunderous force
nature chances the warrior poet,
as an instructor, defeat,
demands the soldier to embrace desolation,
bending are the shivering knees
confusing logic by the silent screams,
battered muscles ache in distress
beneath the barking of the mental-cemetery trees,
the red badge of courage is to be gained
by challenging the eternal sparkle of life,
although there is fear in every step taken upfront
the benefits and family strengthen the next to step to come,
as if dancing with faith every move comes to its demise
and the courage to believe dissolves in the memories of home and its bed

Jose M. Alvarez

Secrets

Have you ever had a secret?
I have.
I know you have.
What is yours about?
Shhhhh!
You don't tell me, and I won't tell you,
That's the deal . . .
But you want to, don't you?
You want to tell someone . . .
You want to drop the fragile glass that holds it with a crash so everyone will look and see it spread blatantly over the floor and they will know!
But it would be like spilling blood . . .
A shock to all
and yet all gather around to hear more . . .
Hear how . . .
Hear why . . .
So they can tell others, and you know they will . . .
Mouth shut tight and no one will ever see the smallest signal that it even exists
Except when it sneaks out and pulls your mouth into that tiny, knowing, smile only you will understand . . . .

Amanda Peters

Violence

Violence is like a fire,
raging out of control.
Growing, spreading,
and destroying everything in its path.
Rising from the hatred
of one's feelings.
As the pressure of life
continues to weaken.
With nothing more to do
than pass the blame around
from friends to family.
Starting with the only ones
who can change this hatred
and dismiss the outcome.
The parents. . . .

Heather Gerths

Unbelieving Agnostic

Dreams escape from
a far off land
And tumble into serenity and
holy nights
Whisper into my ear
about the wishes you have
conquered
And enter into my life

Heather Stillwell

Tears of Azmodan

as the world turns
the human race won't learn
giving into poor judgment
bring the rise of corruption
always leaping too fast
never looking at the past
doom of this world is coming near
as Azmodan sheds his last tear

Justin Gose

Life

So lost
In a world of hate
Led not by our minds
But by fate
Even if we want something
So bad deep down inside
Desperately fighting
Not trying to hide
Things almost never
Go our way
But we have to live life
Come what may

Dorothy Cook

Life Is What Life Was

Life is what life was
Why or what man does
We were put here for a reason
We invented spring, a season
summer comes, summer goes
Why fall comes, no one knows
With winter comes the cold
Like old stories never told
Year after year weather is strange to us
Year after year weather changes us
Out with the old, in with the new
Old ideas are so few
If you ask me, I'll say because
Life is what life was

Michael Atwood

The Walker

A black-clad walker into my eyes' view came,
My sight began to falter as the light began to wane
Above me the sky filled with dark clouds and the heavens cried out in pain,
Drowning out all other sounds then like a thousand tears, came the rain
Desperately searching for cover I had the ominous feeling of being doomed,
As the storm like a lover around the walker loomed.

The black-clad walker my direction came,
My heart began to flutter, my fear I tried to contain,
As the weight of the walker's presence on my senses preyed,
To my knees I slowly sank
The presence of the walker was almost too much to take
I turned my gaze upward and met the walker's stare,
In stunned anguish, I just knelt there.

The black-clad walker in front of me stood,
Our eyes locked in silence; I would have looked away if I could,
I knew what it was in the walker's distorted face
That set my blood boiling at such a vigorous pace,
Staring down at me was my own face,
Relating to me my horrible fate, that I finally understood
Only minutes too late.

Bree Hood

Beauty

I see beauty on the inside and a handsome man on the outside.
When I look at him, I see a man who is spoiled, charming, arrogant, gentle, and sexy.
His concern for me and my son touched my heart.
Him being the gentleman that he is moved me.
He seems to be able to sense when I'm not at my best.
He impressed me because, for a minute, it was almost as if I was his
woman and he didn't care who knew it.
He made me believe that there are some good single men left in this world.
He makes me feel so comfortable that I instinctively tell him anything that is on my mind.
Sometimes, when I look into his eyes I see my future.
The attraction and compatibility are there, but once again I have
stumbled across someone who isn't ready for what I have to offer.
I wish he could see me the way that I see him.
Not be afraid of what has been sparked between us, but embrace it;
not runaway from it, but hold on to it;
not push it away, but draw nearer to it;
not procrastinate about it, but pursue it.
I wish that for once in my life when I take the time to look deep into
someone that someone would reciprocate and take the same time to
look deep into me.
I just wish that he could see the beauty inside of me.

Shawn A. Jones

Anything Is Possible

They say that slavery doesn't exist, but I know it does.
Not in the bondage or breaking down of one's body,
But in the captivity and the breaking down of one's heart and mind.

When you lose faith in your heart and mind, you will lose
your way and your life does not seem your own.
A heavy heart and a resentful mind will keep you in these chains forever.
The key is the power within ourselves
Learn to love yourself and others and you shall feel released.

Rise up, lift yourself, lift your heart and mind and bring back
something you could never buy, steal or work a lifetime for.

Know in yourself that every day when the sun rises,
that you should be thankful for this day
and use it as if it really means something.
Because it does.

Know in yourself and in any higher power that when the sun rises,
it will always bring forth a new day and that anything is possible.

Juliana DeMasi

Fallen Angel

Once was God's chosen,
Now without her wings,
Fallen below expectation,
A sad song she sings.
Angel of God's mercy,
Filled with sinful desire
Rejected by her faith,
Banished to the fire.
Hoping to recover
This poor lost soul,
Makes a deal with the Devil,
Unknowing what she's sold.
She sold her life to darkness,
To wreak havoc at his will.
A beast of horror she now is,
Evil deeds she will fulfill.

Christopher Squires

Our House

There is a cupboard in our house
And in it lives a little mouse
Who sometimes wanders out to play
When all is quite and were away

How far he wanders we do not know
But up our stairs he surely go
for on the carpet we found there
Some scattered cheese and mouse's hair

Now in the summer when were away
The whole house is his to play
But one thing he don't know is that
Me Da! has finally got a cat . . .

Thomas Burton

You Are Not

I look at your picture,
I cry.
I feel
Tired,
Exhausted,
At the thought,
The same repetitive thought,
That you are not,
Anymore.

Alba Pergjika

Untitled #2

'Twas the faintest of scent
And whisper of rose
The softest of breeze
That hinted of love
Yet I remember not
Whence it came
And it was gone
With the wind.

Yukie Tokuda

Military Kid

I've moved from state to state
before I could close my gate
I've made a lot of friends
and seen a lot of trends
but they come and go
as I do
from state to state

Jessica Saunders

I Am the Lonely Wind

I am the lonely wind, I am the lonesome breath, breath of the prairie.
I see the coyote sob, sob like a breaking heart, sigh in the shadow.

High line is my violin, barb wire is my banjo,
My song is in the windmill, my music in the meadow.

Mourn, coyote, mourn the moon, mourn the milk-white meadow,
Mourn like a breaking heart, howl in the shadow.

I am the joyous wind, I am the giant breath, breath of Oklahoma.
Come, all you hollow men, come, all you pallid hearts, climb to the mesa.

I make the grasses hiss, I send the sage brush scent over the mesa.
I am the buzzard wind, I am the blizzard wind, I howl and bellow.

My horses are the clouds,
my spurs are lightning bolts, and my drum is thunder.
Come, all you hollow men, come, all you pallid hearts, cower and wonder.

I am the healing wind, I am the holy wind.
Come to the powwow.
I will lift up your wings, I will lift up your head,
Come all you pallid men, come to the powwow.

Bow, all you broken men, bow to the blessing wind, bow and wonder.
Run to the hiding place, run to the secret place,
To the powwow of thunder.
I am the lonely wind.

Joe Jared

WHERE WOULD I BE WITHOUT YOU ?

To the love of my life, Bobby Lynn Sisk
where would I be without you my love, oh, where would I be.
you are all I want and all that I need, everything that I long to have with me.
you have given me you and I have given you me just one week ago.
we became one love and one soul with each other.
where would we be without each other. you bring me
happiness, joy, peace and love forever true to only you.
we made our precious little baby boy of three months ago, oh, how I see him in you.
I see how much pain I caused you and I am grateful that you stayed with me because I
don't know where I would be with out your love with me.
we have came a long way with one another and I am proud to be your wife and you, my husband.
you are my precious gift from god just like are son is too,
oh baby, where would we be without one another and our sweet little boy?
I would be all alone. . . .

Donna Sisk

Delusional Ocean

My time circuits provide escape so things will not flow as they seem
A blurry realm, a better place, where logic bounds as if a dream

With paths of stone and fields of light, a paradise built with ruse and lie
A venom drip, an acid trip, as folly strewn about the sky

The endless scenes conduct themselves in bouncy flux with space and time
But I'll enjoy infinity and fester in this paradigm

Oh, fill my heart with lunacy and slow the cosmic locomotion
So I may float above the Earth and drown in a delusional ocean

Collin Samatas

Passion

Passion drowns in the depths of the raging sea within my urging soul.
It comes up for air that gives no breath of life,
but intensely suffocates without mercy.
It's a bomb that's reached its peak
and I find myself mantled over by its
immensity like a volcano whose melting lava flows on its outer walls.
An inferno that burns my flesh in agonizing desire.
It surpasses every obstacle that crosses its path without remorse.
It's a sinful lust that slowly but surely
leads me into the arms of unforgiving insanity.

Jacqueline Sanchez

My Mother's Hands

I saw you hide your hands in line
behind that lady fair
I noticed too hers, soft and white
immaculate from care.
But mom I said it's no disgrace
to have working hands like you
and had she lived the life you have
she'd have hands just like it too.

They've never touched a child
or caressed a fevered head
with hands so gently folded
all night beside his bed.

They've never worn a blister
or had calluses to show
for all they've done for others
and the kindnesses I know.

So now you see mom
yours are hands of love
and I bet the Lord will notice
when he greets you from above.

Karina Aulick

Maniac Depression

What the ****   is wrong
Inside this mixed-up head of mine?
I feel like I have lost all sense
Of feeling, humor, time.
No longer generosity
Upon my heart does pull,
But morbid curiosity.
My love fire starts to cool.
I hate because I love to hate,
And grieving I enjoy.
The pain of others pains me not.
No pity it employs.
Some people make attempts to help
With friendly compliments
That I would ordinarily love,
But that I now hate, hence
I lie in hate and pain while days
And years all pass away.
Before I know, my life is spent.
Oh God, save me I pray.

Brian Booth

The Enemy

He keeps slipping away
as each day goes on;
there is nothing I can do
but help him hang on.
He feels nothing but pain,
when he moves, when he breathes;
he keeps on praying
for just one moment of relief.
He's gotten so pale,
so fragile, so thin;
his eyes stay tired and wet,
he keeps his pain hidden within.
He doesn't want us to know
his Enemy is back;
it is slowly killing him,
he is losing contact.
When I look at him
tears weld up in my eyes;
I dread the day
I have to say good-bye.

Angela Guy

My Hun John

Just as we met at first sight
On the day we met I saw him as my light
Have he been so dear and kind to thee
Never be mean or keen to me
Rich in his ways of charm
It's a way to be alarmed
Caring to his loving self to me
Have him love and honor thee
Always happy and never down
Ready to be on top and around
Destiny is his perceptive
Daring is his elective
Eager to show his pain
I sometimes feel blamed
My heart all into him as a man
Lying thinking about him as we walk in the sand
In the end we walk as one
Never doubtful to run as one just as he calls me "hun"
Good and bad times we will love ever more as the night we met on the dance floor,
having fun.

Merenda Simmer

Purr

I have never heard anything quite as satisfying as a kitty cat's purr.
Or felt anything as playful as a puppy dog paw.
Nor have I known anything as sad as having to see one left underneath the green
growing grass.
But I find hope in the fact that when I move on, they'll be there waiting.
Purrs and Paws and all.

Jeff Meteer

Don't Forget about Me

When I move away,
This is what I will say,
"Don't forget about me."

When I move away,
I'm going to miss the days with you at Prairie Lea and all I will say is,
"Don't forget about me."

I know you hate promises,
But this is one we have to keep.
All we'll say is,
"Don't forget about one another."

I'll carry your picture near me always,
So everyone can see what a friend you are.
And all we can say is,
"Don't forget about each other."

Sarah Whittington

Pedestal

Let the crucifixion begin!
It didn't end when the blood of Christ was spilled.
As we are raised to our pedestals of persecution, rays of light fall upon out tender skin.

Restrain your ideas and live in my world amongst the roads of poverty and despair.
Seek the crossroads of delight leading to the garden of enchantment.

Drowned in the dreams of population.
The polis of Alexander turn to the society of western culture.
The change abrupt and plentiful, a bountiful harvest for few.

Forget the once but great men who showed no fear in the face of danger.
But felt in regressing yet another turn in their forsaken destiny.

Feel yourself as you lose your grip on reality and control.
You've come today to this spot where souls flee to look for something not lost

Separate the mystic and temperance as you crash into unexcavated gold mines of youth.
Laugh as the luxuries you find elevate you once again to that pedestal of loneliness.

And the blood of mortality flows all around the cup meant to catch it.

Eric Milam

A Slave Man's Word

Take away my privileges,
I'll argue my rights.
   Give me my freedom,
Or a battle I'll fight.
   Clear my name from your papers,
I'll live a free man.
   Push me out of my shelter,
I'll live on your land.
   Work me to death
With a plow in my hand,
   Laugh when I fall—
On two feet I'll stand.
   Disgrace me with words,
You pass on to your kind
   Label my body—
As a "Man With No Mind"
   Whatever you feel,
And the less that you give,
   Just makes me much stronger
And the longer I live.

Karin R. McKinney

Observation II

These must be great machines
Crafted from the hearts of
Demons or beasts with
A fury like that of a
Disastrous thunder.
There I sat, held captive
By the sound of a rash
Orchestra cracking their
Instruments in protest
Of God's peaceful nature.
Yet all this meant nothing.
I was simply observing
The sky above me as
It rebelled against the
Smooth canvas of consistency.

Lucas Schleicher

Happy to Be Alive

On a long Winter's day
'Neath a tree I did sit
Fresh air did I breath
Birds I heard sing
Lovely mountains I did see
Peace came to me
Joy I felt inside
I was happy to be alive!

Anita Havemann

Bridge of Love

Oh my beloved,
Boundless love I can see in your eyes,
Only the truth and not the lies.
Love to me is an ocean,
In my heart it's in full motion.
Depression seems far away,
Expression is here to stay.
My dear! Your love must not be in vain,
For my heart will then sink in pain.
However it seems to be,
The distance between you and me,
Is like a bridge over troubled water.
So therefore come to see,
Forget being lonely,
For sustained unity,
Brings supreme bliss to me.

Ajay Srivatsan

Salute to the Model "T"

It came in any color as long as it was black,
On the front there was a hand-crank, in the tool box was a jack.

Check the tank beneath the cushion before starting on a tour
Switch Mag to Bat, retard the spark, and block the wheels for sure

Put muscle to the hand-crank to make the engine prance
if a cylinder starts missing, whack the coil box with a wrench

neighbors looked on with envy as you drove it down the lane
And you smile and waved to show them that you really weren't vain

The roads were dirt and gravel, and very, very course
When you were stuck up to the axle, folks would tell you "Get a horse"

If you started up an incline and felt the low band slip
Just turn around, back up the hill, sit back and let'er rip

No need for air conditioning, the ventilation was first class
When running in bad weather you had curtains of Isinglass

Should the engine begin knocking, just pull over to the side
Drop the pan, refit the rod, and continue with your ride.

It would ramble down the back roads and suffer many a rut
Still friends turned out to greet you when they heard that Putt-Putt-Putt

You may talk of mighty rockets and works of that degree
But none ever changed the way we live more than the Model "T."

James M. Silver

Spring Storm

Clouds very, very dark, the Earth lonely and stark.
The sky that looks like lead, makes all the world seem dead.
Bolts of strong and vicious light flash so very very bright.
All this makes an eerie view as the world gets its just due.

The roar of rumbling explosions and thunder clapping in the heavens
Sounds like a wild battle scene and the world seems like a bad dream.
The water pours like an avalanche and on the Earth performs a wild dance.
It turns the soil to mud instead and the defeated Earth bows its head.

Oh, the clouds, the sky, the light, and the roar,
The wild rain that on the Earth does pour.
Makes me wonder frantically inside—
Has our worldly Earth in despair died?
Will the clouds turn from dark, while the earth turns bright from stark?
Will the sky change from lead, and the Earth change from dead?

Will the Son be our true light and shine out so very very bright?
Will we have a better view and will the world get its true due?
Will the roar of loud explosions cease and peace come from the heavens?
Will this terrible battle scene all go away as a bad dream?

Will the water stop its avalanche and the Earth recover from the wild dance?
Will the mud to soil instead and the defeated world raise its head?
Oh the clouds, the sky, the light, and the roar,
The wild rains that on the Earth does pour
Makes me wonder frantically inside—is our wordly Earth dead or alive?

Carmen R. Alicardi

In the Twilight

In the twilight both eve and morn,
the birds toot and sing like the sound of a horn.

The sky darkens and lightens and then lightens and darkens,
while life around listens and harkens.

The sun that heats the sky during the day,
becomes a fan that cools in the months of August, July, June and May.

The clock that chimes to signal the time becomes like a song,
until the time begin to sound like a gong.

The earth beneath us so moist and wet,
protects the plants and flowers that are not up yet.

And as for the world full of people who are still in their beds,
the silence will soon be gone with the day ahead.

Patricia Carmon

Me

I'm the one the one who loves
Who cares for others
Who helps when angry or sad and happy
I'm fun with others and love others
My mom dad and brother
Who I love like no other
Are special to me
That's me the kid
Who loves to help and be treat like I need

Juliana Uribe

Ode to a Beautiful Woman

Out of the darkness I emerged,
And behold, what did I see?
A beautiful woman, bright as the sun.
She was staring back at me.
Her majestic smile took my breath away.
I was dumbfounded as I stared in awe.
Her face was a vision of beauty.
My frozen soul she did thaw.
My life now has new meaning.
She's touched me through and through.
Her gentle touch, her soft caress,
Makes me feel brand new.
My soul has been set free,
Free to soar and glide.
And as I stumble through this life,
I want her by my side.
A humble life we would lead,
Yet a life filled with love.
No guarantees of fame or wealth,
Just me and my angel from above.

Douglas Plummer

The Stream

I am a stream
that flows through
your dreams.

I've been mistaken
for laughter,
or so it seems.

I've traveled a distance
all through your heart.

A journey of love . . .

I love playing the part.

Briane Smith

Life

Silently, as I wait to die,
I watch life swiftly pass me by.
It teases with false hope, and then,
It quickly passes by again.

Linda Morrow

It Is Time for Spring

My sweater is too tight and itchy,
My snowpants are too small.
Last week I lost my mittens,
I can't find my scarf at all!
My woolen socks have lost their soles,
My boots have lost their tread.
And I have lost the love for words,
Like skis and sled.
But . . .My fishing rod still fits,
And . . .My baseball bat still hits!
I have a kite that wants to fly,
So Winter please call it Quits!

John Paul Nohava

The Ladder

I was climbing the ladder in the forest to which I saw no end.
The struggle was constant, but I continued upward.
Each step was harder and I grew weary on my way,
But I was determined to give it all my strength.

Suddenly, I could see the end in sight,
Which inspired me to continue, on my fearless fight.
I still had a long climb ahead, but I had high hopes to make it.

I sacrificed so much, as I neared the top, laced with clouds and sunlight.
Below me, I saw how dark and far, I had forged ahead alone.
With bleeding hands I shouted, "I'm almost there!"
My lonely strong endeavor with four more rungs ahead,
I wondered what I'd find, when I finally reach my goal.

Suddenly anxiously and excited, I grabbed the second rung.
I heard a loud snap and felt my body fall, all the way to the ground
I lie there with broken spirits, bones and bleeding wounds.
I had nothing left in me, to try to climb again.
Instead, I sadly lie in the sinking hole, which I could not fight.
I'd sacrificed so much to end up in the mire, and gave up all my hope.

Carol H. Wright

The Lesson

Every day I passed a man that couldn't see, still somehow
he seemed to notice me. He would smile and wave every time
I passed by, I kind of nodded, cleared my throat and said "Hi."
One day I was out for a walk, when he called me over just to talk.
He introduced himself as Mr. Shimm, and asked why it was I was scared of him. "Even
without my eyes, I'm far from blind.
Anything is possible, just look inside yourself and you'll find,
that if you believe in the strength of your mind, anything is possible,
all you have to do is try." And for the first time a tear came to my eyes, he gave me a
hug and I started to cry. He asked why was I crying?
I said, "I've lived all of my life never trying."
He said, "Though I'm blind, I've lived my life. I have three kids
and a wife. If you go though life not trying at all, you won't get up, should ever you
fall." That was the last I saw of him
before he passed away. There's not a time in my life I don't think of
that day, he took a troubled child and showed him the way.
It's been twenty years, and I have kids of my own.
I sat them all down and taught them the path I was shown.
They all sat in silence as knowledge was fed, then we all
shed a tear at the words I said. I sent the kids off to bed, prayed to God, "Bless Mr.
Shimm, thanks for his lesson, thanks again."

Donald F. Pulley Jr.

Forgive Me

Forgive me for having brought you into this world
And have forgotten how much you needed me.
Forgive me for not holding your hand
And have helped you on your life's path with my support.
Forgive me for allowing my government to take away your school
And my authority, leaving you at their mercy.
Forgive me for not giving you my example,
real moral and religious values.
Forgive me for not listening to your calls
and not drying your tears when you cry.
Forgive me for forgetting to nurture your soul
and feeding only your physical needs,
sinking you in a journey of vice and solitude.
Forgive me for consenting that the worst of humanity
has become a daily display turning you into the most insensible
And violent person in all creation.
Forgive me for leaving you exposed to the slow human degradation
that unscrupulous minds exploit for financial benefit.
Forgive me for my lack of respect for life, because when I accepted
abortion, I simply authorized you to be judge and executioner
Forgive me for not knowing how to protect you and give you all the love you need and
above all, for not being a real parent to you.
Forgive me for failing you in every way. I beg you to forgive me, please!

Yolanda Bayuelo

I Wish It Would Rain

I wish it would rain . . .
A gentle rain.
Gentle tears flowing
So mine would blend.
No one would notice,
My utter torment and pain . . .
I could keep my front;
The mask of joy that I wear.
Nobody understands me
No one even cares . . .
The pain that I feel
Is carried by me alone.
Nobody notices when I feel this way,
Then I am questioned . . .
Why do you feel "alone?"
I cannot confide,
for I fear other people's thoughts.
So from there I cry alone . . .
I wish it would rain.

Heather Martinez

Keeper

Who is this dungeon's keeper?
He will not show his face.
Who is this dungeon's keeper?
Keeps me locked up in this place.

I have not seen or heard him.
But I am sure he's there.
I sense his presence all around.
Can feel it in the air.

This dungeon is so vast and dark.
So desolate and bleak.
How long have I been here?
An hour or a week?

Trapped in here with no way out.
And here I will remain.
By myself with all these fears.
Alone with all this pain.

And yet I fear I'm not alone.
Someone else is here.
Remaining in the shadows.
So far, but yet so near.

Who is this dungeon's keeper?
I do not know his name.
Who is this dungeon's keeper?
Why does he play this game?

Steve Moore

Recycled

Poems
numb the brain,
tickle your imagination,
softly
blow in your ear.

Poems
seductively speak to your eyes,
pull you into
their false world
of only images.
Already felt emotions,
still fighting
for more attention.

Poems,
billboards for undeserved
advertisement material.

John Huggins

The Angels among Us

I believe angels are among us.
Some people see them, some only feel them and others only hear them.
They are God's little helpers, nudging us in one direction or another,
at times protecting us from harm.

Sometimes we know they are there and we acknowledge them,
other times we ignore them.
Sometimes we just have no clue that they are there.

But the messengers of God are always there,
Loving us,
Guiding us,
Guarding us.

Yes, I believe angels are among us.

P. F. Greene

Dreams

Dreams may come in darkness or in the brightness of the day.
Dreams of love and wealth, dreams of fear or skies of gray.

But, for me they never come, these dreams.
Whether eyes are wide or drenched with sleep.
Whether the sky is bright or filled with darkness deep.
For me they never come, these dreams.

I often wonder what fills others' thoughts in waking hours,
what fills their thoughts while counting sheep.
I hope someday to know what it is to dream.
Whether awake or locked in sleep.

So tonight when darkness comes and my tired eyes give in to sleep,
and in the morning when the sun invites these eyes to open once more to weep,
I'll still be waiting for them, the dreams that never come.

Michelle Collins

OK Don't Solve My Problems

Have you any idea what distress I am in?
My bank account has but a dollar in it.
I haven't paid my rent yet.
There will be no milk in the coffee for a while now.
The tear in my dress is longer today than yesterday
The cat died last night.
My car wouldn't start this morning.
My walk in the park turned out to be a much needed shower.
I came home this evening relieved to just be able to watch "Oprah"
Only to find that I couldn't open the door.
The keys were not in my bag.
So when you see me outside the door with the tears running down my cheeks and fists banging on the walls
Don't tell me it will be OK.
'Cause OK don't solve none of my problems.

Anne Ruminjo

Progress for All Mankind

The clearing came one day, and I saw light where there had been none before
I saw the dense, red clay earth, where there
had only been nature's thick green carpet before.
I saw sky where there had only been a rich canopy of trees before.
I saw naked roots baking in an inferno
where there had only been the sun's nurturing warmth before.
I saw a large yellow bulldozer screaming out the word:
Progress!
Where mankind's true heart had stood before.
Be this progress for all mankind?
Will all the green go before the darkness stops?

Rose Kerr

In a Rhyme

The dreams we have and the hopes
Compliment like the perfect rhyme
Our two souls forming one
Stepping together in time.

Our thoughts like that of one
Our hearts in perfect stride
Connected by the love
That in our hearts resides.

Our lives in perfect tune
In rhythm with the perfect song
We're the perfect poem
Two rhymes that together belong.

Drew Dunham

"My Basic Hopes"

I hope for no more violence
On the news and on the Earth.
I hope that criminals recognize
The importance of Jesus' birth.

I hope the homeless meet their needs
For shelter, food, and clothes.
And what the homeless people go through
No one really knows.

These are hopes I wish for
In the coming year.
All you have to do is pray
And hope that God will hear.

Jarrett Severance

Gila Monster

I fly
winds at my back
threatened with the old fear
of being held in Nara's arms and
dressed for a wedding day
I never want
of the dead eagle screaming
as my mother ran to gather my
six brothers and sisters—
of the way we all cried for years
saved by Daddy's dying
and of the way I am crying now
my face hidden as I plead
"hear me, oh Lord"
because even in sleep there is
a name I can't forget was mine
long before I was old enough to know
there was no choice . . .
that I could never make
a dead eagle fly

Zillah Glory Langsjoen

stupid love poems

stupid love poems
about lovely nights
and stars shining just for them
and sweethearts so in love
so infatuated that they are
blind to the other's faults
holding on to the lie
that they are perfect
they make me sick
and arouse my pity
they don't know
how much they can be hurt
i'm satisfied to let them be
knowing how badly it will end
and that i will say
i told you so

Rachel Hedges

Verbal Portraits

If someone verbally painted your portrait,
using more than one word,
would the finished product be a masterpiece
you would be proud of or deserve?

Would the bright haloed life
you lead by day,
be replaced by a secret life you live in the shadows of the night;
that reeks of moral decay?

Would the color of your eyes be angry red or envy green?
Would the true character of your soul be hidden or would it be seen?

Would the pride you exude on canvas,
be due to the fact that God made you one of a kind,
or rather, to the fact that you are a work in progress
and in charge of your own design?

Would your portrait personify the monster
of hate that lives deep inside,
or would it qualify as a worthy human place
where the love of Christ might lodge and abide?

Would the artist's rendition of who you are,
be a work you would be happy to take home and frame?
Or would this work be such a misrepresentation of you,
that you wouldn't claim it or have it associated with your name?

It behooves us all to remember that portraits are not always painted upon

Lorraine Thomas

The Heartless Roam Free

My soul is lost in a desolate garden.
My spirit is sinking in a pool of depravity.
From wandering in the pathway of the wild,
I have had my heart stolen.
From my slumbering underneath the trees,
I have lost track of consciousness.
I no longer have the convictional wrath that orbited everything around me.
I no longer have the grace of forgiveness that judges the motives of man.
I am the old dried roots of a tree that has long ago been chopped away.
Still I am buckled to the ground and trampled into the dirt.
I run away from self-awareness.
I run into prison abeyance.
My soul is smut from gone forest fires.
My spirit is the cracked eggshell from the fallen nest.
My heart is pulsating by the way of the darkness seeping in my chest.
For my life, I am holding on tenuous chains of friends
that are as hopeless as homeless men.
The air is loneliness and I inhale it along with the hatred I drink.
The fire of life is now the fire of rage.
The staple of my heart is dead and gone.
I am proof that the heartless roam free.

Valynica D. Henderson

The Table

I looked across the table and smiled
She looked so beautiful to me
And I just wanted to thank her
For always being there for me
And for being my eyes when I could not see
For going hungry so that I could eat
And for going broke to put shoes on my feet
For giving me warmth when she shook and shivered
And for being my rock when I was scared and quivered
For giving me all her wisdom and warnings
And for making sure we always had great Christmas mornings
All the things that she wanted she put me above
And I just wanted to thank her for all her kindness and love
I looked across the table and saw an empty chair
And I longed so badly for my mother to be there
So that I could utter the words that I never really took the time to say
Thank you, mother, for giving me today

Mark Pierce

Attempts at Failure

Tell me something, sir
Was it really bad?
Didn't I try hard enough?
Your mark just leaves me mad.
What could I do better?
Maybe spend more time
Practicing and rehearsing
Each and every line?
Would that have made it better?
Or did my content stink?
What should I do next time?
Would you like some time to think?
So what was really wrong?
I don't think you know.
I don't think that anything
Could have improved my show.
But society sucked you in
And my ideas were almost true
And I'll still be damned if I'll ever
Let them tell me what to do.

Joel Hawes

Daddy

Dedicated to Angie Morta & the Morta family

Sleepless nights are all I have
Thinking about him makes me sad.
I wonder why it had to be him,
Why God had to take my daddy.

But as I grow, I'll understand
That where he is, is not bad.
So I'll stop crying
And stop being sad;
Because I realize
He is in a place
Where there's no bad.

Elissa Thompson

Untitled

Tormented is the soul
that had once known love
and lost
To have ridden on such power
only to lose the light
again
How I do long for you
my beautiful creature of heart
With eyes that pierced my soul
and visions that pierced my heart
With method
They broke
My will

Dennis Hammontree

Blinding Golden

Blinding Golden
Eliciting happy faces
With smiling, sparkling eyes
Being covered over
By a heavy grey.
Still,
You insist
As you force your way through
In rays,
  Scattered rays
And above the grey,
We see You
The Ever-Present
Still at work.

Khalid Haneef

Gray

Who knows the light better then those who live in the light;
Who knows the darkness better than those who live in it.
The light will never understand the darkness;
Nor darkness the light.

But what of the man who lives in the light and falls to the darkness,
He hates the light even more because he is not worthy.
And what of the man who lives in darkness that goes to the light
He too hates where he came from, for he now understands it.

Then a man that lives in light falls into the darkness,
And though he hates it, he learns to understand it.
After a time he returns to the light, to a place he once enjoyed.
But this is a different man; a new man; a man with understanding

This man is a rare man, a man that is a lover of the light;
A learned man of the darkness.
He prevents the darkness from growing, for gaining more followers
but does not condemn those that live in the darkness.

He is a friend of all mankind, those in both light and dark;
But the enemy of the darkness.
He is a man who as succeeded in life, though in a different way.
This is who I am, who I have become.

Rosendo Fryman

Hand in Hand

It all began with a woman and a man making a promise hand in hand.
At the time only God could see their future included me.
When I was born one warm summer night with those same hands he held me tight.
As time went by and I grew older I remember him carrying me on his shoulders.
At times I just looked up at him, always amazed at the man within.
Sometimes he'd look at me and smile; other times we'd go walk a while.
We'd talk, we'd laugh, even cry.
He'd even try to answer why,
Why at times was life so unfair.
He'd reassure me he'd always be there.
If I was scared he'd calm my fears.   When I cried he dried my tears.
But walking hand in hand with my dad even when I was feeling sad
I knew he would always say—tomorrow will be another day,
Soon another day would come and after the rain I'd see the sun.
I look back now but black all see I see.
I haven't seen the sun since he left me.
I think about his final day and wish I could have found a way.
We were hand in hand as many times before as angels welcomed him into Heaven's door.
With one last look, a final sigh, he closed his eyes and said good-bye.
And just as it started it came to an end,
hand in hand until I see him again.

Corrie Pena

Last Day

The last day I remember my true love.
Lost and left in an old town in Arkansas,
That last day makes my heart so sad it hurts so bad.
carried away in the dark with a broken heart.
The last day I shut my eyes dream of you guess you will be leaving soon.
Fading out of my head remembering you were to be mine the last day.
I still want to be the boy, you be the girl, stand under the moonlight hold
hands for the rest of our life, the rest of our days, the rest of our
nights. The last day I can't describe I don't
know why I left her all messed up inside.
She's trapped in my mind afraid of understanding what I keep inside.
The last day memories and dreams shattered
in you and me lost in your eyes you and I.
The last day I keep my feelings inside it hurt so bad I walked in my sleep.
I hear your voice, see your face, your scent is still here in my place,
soon it will be drifting away.
The last day she blames herself, she don't blame me; please blame me.
My soul is so blue live seen no other I will hold out forever.
It is now and always has been memories and dreams of that girl,
what ever happened to her on that last day.

Nathan Manning

Mystique

Screaming forgotten visions,
whisper to girls and women
like poetry.
can you smell their passion
in the rain?
The boys are chanting curses
in the shadows,
as they shine their diamonds
in the rivers of bitter-sweet honey.
Anger can be sticky,
Do you agree?
His eyes stare coolly
at the wild spring rose,
as he falls asleep with
visions of her bliss
in-which he can only long for. . . .

Heather Dahmen

the virus

sickened again
by the virus
that once destroyed
my one man army.
quarantined by the pain
that numbed my soul,
that took my last ounce of strength.
overcome by a foreign party
who invaded my territory.
i tried to make peace,
but was overcome by the trickery.
beat at my own game
by the nazis of pain.
now seeking the revenge
of a lifetime,
i try to build my allies
and challenge the virus
that took over my life.

Melissa Glen Perry Parages

Graduation

The day comes,
Where we will leave,
Never to be the same again,
Change.

Happiness.
Sadness,
They are more alike than the eye sees.

Julian Rosenberg

To Elizabeth Barrett Browning

The quiet breeze of your own words
Brings life again to tears you spent,
And felt again, the love
Of which you doubted would appear
But still, which rose upon you, unaware.

Opening this book
These things do breathe again,
As if a flower press'd
Between these leaves so long ago
Gives off it's scent anew.

It's colour still as bright
As when you plucked it from your heart
To place it not in vase, or table stand
But write it down
In Beauty's ageless hand.

And so to me, a poet
Give the hope
That love be sent
E'en when the faith in such be spent.

Joseph Bennenbroek

Time

I am honored of men, existing everywhere,
men have sought my presence on Earth and in the heavens.
All things shall yield to me.
Nothing will escape my grasp.
I am the ultimate continuum, unyielding and forever driven forward.

Men have carved monuments to me in stone and placed them in a great circle.
They have driven stakes into the earth and looked to the sun
for my shadow, and found the essence of me in a glass placed upside down.

Creative men have invented many devices
to maintain my presence in their daily lives.
The vicissitude of men may be won through me
by those who understand the virtue of my patience.
I help to heal men's wounds, to sow and reap their crops,
meet their newborns and greet them in death.

Find out what I am called I who am useful to men yet unrelenting,
holding men's destiny in my grasp.

Paul V. Willoughby

A Plea to My Love

I know that you're still in me. Somewhere deep within my soul.
When you touch my skin with your caresses our fleshes somehow know. . . .

But to my conscious mind and the heart that dwells within
Something's different about your touch that lingers upon my skin.

Can it be that you are changing? Do you long for something new?
Have you grown accustomed to the way that I've been loving you?

We're finally where we prayed that We would someday be.
Together, free to love the way We have always dreamed.
Please tell me why I feel a distance wider than the sea,
Every time I see you look away while you're loving me?

I'd never doubt your love for that will always be.
It's the changes outside in the world that you let interfere with loving me.
All I want, is what we had when our passions ran wild and free.

I don't want golden words from Someone else's lips,
Or touches that You've seen on another's fingertips.

All I want is what was there the first time that we knew
If nothing else in the world was real, the love we'd found was true!

Please lover, when you love, love only from your heart!
Allow all those things that weigh your heart to be given to the wind.
Let loving fill your heart and mind and make you mine again!

Kimberly King

A Child of Two Cultures

Too often I find myself fearing the inevitable
of having to live two opposing cultures. I feel overpowered
and torn between the two that I simply cannot choose one
over the other, nor have I been able to successfully blend the two.

At times, I question my conflicting life; could it be predestined?
Or am I carving out my own destiny?
Then I try reasoning with my state of confusion.

Other times, I dream of being very content
with only one so-called "self," for anything more harbors indecisiveness.
Life is difficult enough without the combination
of clashing traditions and values.
Only minds that are kept clutter-free and simple seem to be truly happy.

Although doubtful, I continue to share talk about the perceived gratitude
and advantages in having ownership of two cultures.
To the contrary, when looking beneath the surface of my life,
I find a complex identity hidden deep inside in lingering agony
trying to proclaim itself.

Asmahan Hooper

Together

We go through life
day by day,
we walk, we talk,
but do we get to know
the truth behind our steps,
our words?

I say, "I'm fine"
when inside I am dying.
You say, "great"
when inside you are crying.

Reach out . . . touch a hand . . .
hold someone, smile . . .
be a friend, be a savior

Help someone to live
a fuller life.
Be there
when a friend needs you.

I'll be there for you.

Julie Mayfield

Eager

Eager to kiss you,
Eager to love you,
Wanting you to love me,
Eager to hold you,
Eager to want you,
Eager for the wanting
Eager for your arms,
Eagerly waiting,
Anxiously waiting
For you to be eager for me,
I am eager,
Are you?

Kyla Phillips

Fall Passage

Beautiful golden and reddish leaves
Decorate the trees with pride,
Until the wind, the destroyer
Came to tear away the trees' joy.
The wind slashed and whipped
The trees bare,
And left them weeping in shame,
Until the day the snow came
To comfort them.

Nancy Reishus

In the World of Flowers

A flower in the mist,
So, fragile and small;
In a field of many,
With colors of all;
In the shadows of Spring,
It's feelings of Fall;
A precious flower of love,
Goes to the heavens above;
With clouds of sorrow,
The tears than follow;
To the eyes of the gardener,
It's a world of a flower.

Janie Gloria

Chi

I am the Chi
Trapped in the empirical body of he
Waiting for freedom to be
Released into infinity

Thomas Craig Angle

Trapped

What did I do to deserve this, a slap in the face when it used to be a kiss.
Being a wife and mother was included in my prayers,
now that it's happened it's become a nightmare.

I live in a world of silence, a world of violence, a world where my
opinions become my oppressions, but I dare not tell a soul. His apologies
are by giving cars, clothes and trinkets of diamonds and gold.

I even make excuses for these abuses, the suffering I bear no one knows.
Yet I continue to keep the house, prepare his meals and wash his clothes.

I gave birth to his kids but the way he treats me, you would think someone else did.
It hasn't always been this way, he loves me so he say.
But how can one love and hate in the same minute, somehow I just don't get it.

My world is a lonely world, but I'm not in this world alone. There are a
lot of women in this world of hell and they don't know what make them carry on.

I can't believe this is happening to me, but it is I'm telling the truth.
If I walk away from this life of abuse what's out there I can do.

Odis D. Booty

Sealed Secret

Everything is back again to places where they belong.
Just my feelings haven't taken the right place in my heart,
which still feels pain every time when I think of you.
I went to the place where we shared one hour together,
I hugged and kissed my only witness.
The one who knows how my heart feels for you.
But yet the only one who is older, wiser, beautiful, full of life,
and the one who will keep in secret my whispers of love.
My tree friend heard once more my cry of passion, my cry of love, and a cry of change.
As long as my tree friend still stands and time in my heart will ache for you,
I could hug her, kiss her, and tell her how I missed you,
and my secret will be sealed forever.

Carmem Pereira

God's Love Will Sustain Us

Thank you for the thorns that grow on the rose
And the turbulent bumps that cover the road

Thanks for the earthquakes that make the walls tremble
And the wind and the storms to whom all must surrender

Thank you for the mountains that stand tall and in our way
And for the desert that is dry, hot and void of rain

For the thorns protect our beauty and the bumps help slow us down
And the earthquakes that make us tremble separate the molehills from the mound

The wind, which we can't see, allows us to blow from here to there
While the mountain makes us stop and think "Will this get me anywhere?"

The desert in all her glory, that goes months without any rain
Shows that even at our lowest in God's love we will sustain

Deborah L. Vick

Winter Quiet

Snow settles on the ground, flakes drifting softly from the sky,
Slowly down they fly, turning green spring beauty into a white world of snow.

There are no birds in the sky, and no deer to rustle leaves,
Moles are burrowed, rabbits hidden,
Warm and quiet under the cold blanket of snow.

The stream lays quiet beneath the ice,
No leaping fish appear, then disappear from sight,
Now the stream is nothing more than a quiet block of ice.

"Wait!" I say, "Did something disturb the quiet?"
I look to the left, then look to the right, listening in the night.

Then I hear it faintly, calling out at dusk,
But it is nothing more than my mom, calling me home for the night.

Sarah Cappello

On the Train

On the train
I'm homeward bound
I'll jump for joy
When my doggie is found

Listening around
At all the rattling pieces
I think of peanut butter cups
Which are distributed by Reese's

In the great, grand design
What does this all mean
Could my friend really feel
Pain in his spleen

I like my ladies lean
And pretty, with a brain
I don't care much for psycho's
I like my ladies sane

On the train
I'm homeward bound
I'll jump for joy
When my soul mate is found

Nicholas Monti

One Heart

Our dreams of Heaven may come someday.
Together at last, come what may.
Two pasts join again in a dreamy haze.
Endless time nor space could keep us away.

Gregory D. Sablick

Heaven Waits

When the moonlight descends
And the stars are in place,
I'll cover your heart
With a veil of white lace.
And a soft good-bye kiss
I'll place on your face.
I'll draw back the curtains
So the stars can shine through.
You must go now my darling,
Heaven's waiting for you.

Susan M. Gosdin

The Lullaby

The song of night
Soothes the wildest soul;
Like a gently flowing river
It has a strange sort of control.

It has the strength of a bear
And the grace of a swan;
It can calm a raging lion
and comfort a young fawn.

The wind plays the strings,
The moon shines its light;
The stars are like diamonds
That glitter in the night.

It sounds very pleasant,
A sweet melody;
It carries through the meadows
And whispers in the trees.

It can calm and lull the mind
Into quiet, gentle sleep;
It can spark imagination
And give you beautiful dreams.

Christin Wilson

Love Stranded

The world was dark and man corrupt,
but the heavens opened so He picked love up.
Man with no concern except to crucify,
but they didn't know He was predestined to die.

He never said a mumbling word,
for He came back to teach the world on how to serve.
They marched Him from hall to judgment hall,
but only on the Father He would need to call.

Calvary was where they took Him
and everything was grim and to all whom watched His chances looked slim.
On a cross they nailed His hands and feet,
death took a look and had to retreat.

A crown of thorns placed on Hs head
and a borrowed tomb given for His bed.
Dripping in blood for all mankind,
love sat at His feet and watched Him shine.

Love reached up and He reached down
and the rumbling of the earthquake was the only sound.
From eternity H came and went again
and with him followed all of man's sins.

Angela D. Lattimore

Africa's Illegal Squatters of Past Decades

Africa, oh, Africa which is the Motherland, of millions of African-Americans.
Your help has come although filled with strife,
and wars by providence beyond your choice.
Africa, the heart and seat of emotions of the Earth from the dawn
of Eden's creation! To this time has been spoiled
and overrun by looters from the Cape to Cairo;
stripped by slave traders and slave masters,
filled with greed to trade human beings as if cargo and animals.

Missionary enterprise were introduced to teach savages of the land
the Gospel story of Jesus and mother Mary. But at the same time teaching
and believing that these new-found people were savages and five percent
less human. Our forefathers were made third-class citizens within their
own country and these missionaries called it the will of God, to civilize
the African continent and to take away their language and culture,
to interbreed European languages and traditions in exchange. But Africa,
your true light has come by the sovereign will of the one true God
who made man in His own image. But man-made slaves of each other,
but by His predestined plan has ordained Africa and its people to be . . .

Mintoor George de Kock

The Sin

Married for years, content with her life,
Until she met the stranger, she knew it was wrong,
But took him for granted and then there came the danger.
They found their places and snuck around,
She cheated beyond a doubt, they thought
They were slick and in control and figured
He'd never find out.
They tried to hide it, but someone saw
And told the man she deceived, she pleaded
Her case and lied about it, she thought
Her husband believed.
Angry he was at the very least, he tried
To bottle it in, but all he could think of was her nasty ways,
She committed the ultimate sin.
He had been honest and faithful and he loved her so,
He had given her all of his life, but that wasn't enough.
So he thought this is how he got back at his wife.
On a rainy night and, oh, so cold, he followed them to their place,
He watched them go in, got out of his car, and through the window he saw them embrace.

Barbara J. Rictor

Never Forget You

There's a reason and there's a need
For the sower and the seed
This seed of faith in us you've sown
Has taken root in hope and grown strong
We'll never forget you
Nor the time with us you've shared
We'll never forget you
You let us know you truly cared
Beautiful roses here today
Oh, how we wish they could stay
But the memories linger
Through the roses fade
The heart recaptures the joy they gave
We'll never forget you

Glorious J. Artis

An Ode to Landscaping

I haul the stone.
I plant the shrubbery.
I situate the flagstone.

Do neighbors know my pain?
Does sunshine help my .cause?
Does a weight belt ease the load?

They say it looks good.
They ask is it level?
All I want is a pill called Advil.

Tim Kott

Garden of Life

While riding the bus I wrote:

In the garden of life
I was refuse
left strewn
alongside the road
by someone who was unaware
I was a human being.

In the garden of life
I was left unattended
and uncared for
by someone who was not aware
that I needed those things.

Still, like an unwanted weed,
I flourished.
In spite of all attempts to ignore,
I blossomed
and acquired strength,
because in the garden of life
growth cannot be stilled.

Patricia Tyree

Billy the Kid

They call you Billy the Kid,
'Cause you say your destiny is told
In old cowboy's legend.
But only the righteous go down
In a blaze of glory.
You're the man with the pale face
On a dark horse. . .
And death is close behind
Your momma named you
William Wallace;
But that ancient hero
Would turn in his grave
If he knew how you soiled his name
And Mel would cry.
Brave of face you may be,
But a coward lives in your heart.

Michelle Keramian

A Letter to Mother

Mother,
I know you think that I've forgotten, but I still remember when . . . .
You divided the pie among the kids, leaving yourself without
We went back for seconds as you stood by, leaving yourself without
It was important to you that our clothes were new, leaving yourself without
At Christmas time you joyfully gave, leaving yourself without
You met our needs with no hesitation, leaving yourself without
You defended as a mother would, leaving yourself without

All of the above and so much more I know that you went through
I stood idly by and watched you cry 'cause I didn't know what to do
When faced with the choice you gave me life and that was the ultimate
You've done so much to prove your love, I never shall forget
Consistently felt but rarely said, I love you, I do
I often thank the heavens above for giving me to you
From,
Your Child

TK Daniels

My Worst Enemy

It has been years since I met my worst enemy,
His name is cancer—he was inside of me.
Back then my worst enemy was so sure he would win,
I thank God, family, friends, doctors,
All others who helped me keep up my chin.
No matter how many times he knocked me down,
I hoped, prayed, was loved enough to fight back
With a new strength I'd found.
He was my worst enemy, I couldn't see him, yet I knew he was always there,
An enemy that made many days for me quite hard to bear.
I decided from day one this was the worst enemy anyone could come across,
Still year after year closer I came to hearing that he had lost.
A battle between me, someone I knew who turned out
To be my worst enemy could be handed by walking away,
This battle called cancer was inside me so I couldn't leave—I had to stay.
I prayed, hoped, laughed, yelled lost faith,
Got real mad—often I'd sit and cry,
Always I found strength to try again knowing in my heart I would not die!
I kept happy thoughts, prayed was prayed for, had operations—so much more,
It's now been ten years, cancer has stopped knocking at my door.

Janet Chalke

Lucille B. Stock

She was born October 20, 1912 as her mother died at birth.
She was taken in by her aunt and grandma not knowing her soul's worth.
As a child it was hard; many challenges came her way,
So many bad things but with her great strength she forgave.
She was a light to the world, blessed from up high,
Seen so close to perfect in so many, many eyes.
Her charming smile and gentle hands made everything seem right.
Her encouraging words were so many like stars in the night.
She was a friend, a mother, and a perfect grandma,
The great influence she had on so many will never be forgot.
Her great talents and love will passed on for generations to come,
The family knot she tied in Heaven will never be undone.
As we mourn of her return to our Father up above,
Let the tears that we cry be joyful tears of love.
For she is now happy with no afflictions or pain,
Wrapped in the loving arms of her husband she will remain
Until we join them let her light be a blessing to all,
For her spirit will remain with us until we too get the call.
She is the foundation of our family, made of the finest rock,
A humble, heart warming, compassionate person, Mrs. Lucille B. Stock.

Rob Andre

How I Love Thee

With all my heart, I love thee, not from the depth or even heights
Of the Earth, but from the center of my universe.
With all my imagination and in my wildest dreams, I only see you
And me making our own way in this vast universe.
Made from the Heaven and given to the Earth, I give you all my trust.
This is how much I love thee.

Stella Pitts

Heavenly Dream

Never would I hear
Such sweet music in my ear
A blessed bird that sings
A heart filled with love
A miracle ringing clear
In this simple world of ours
A way that leads to Heaven
Through storm and desire
But I will always know
The beauty of the dream
And. in the lonely night
Loves glowing candle light
If you take my breath away
Let it be a sunlit day
Than I will want to hurry on
To see the light above the sun
To see the dream the Master dreamed
To reach the beauty yet unseen
To feel the heartbeat yet unsung.

Dorothy M. Blasims

A Love Lost

I sit in the cold
by the fire's side,
without my love,
my life and my bride.

Such a long time ago
since they took her away
with this life threatening illness
she just couldn't stay.

Jenny was her name,
and in the bed where she lay,
on that terrible night
it was her life that she paid.

We were always so happy
Jenny and me,
but it was the angels that decided
our love wasn't meant to be.

But why not give me the illness
with no cure, no pill?
Why did her death have to be
our Mighty God's will?

Brandon Thomure

Patriot

I am a patriot of the Earth,
The water-planet of my birth.
I pledge allegiance to her seas,
Her lands and sands, and forest trees.

I'll never poison her clear lakes;
Nor kill her birds, insects or snakes.
Earth's splendid rocks and layered loam,
Her diverse plant life make my home.

Enlightened by ten trillion stars,
Yet smaller than dry cousin Mars,
All creation has no other
Such nourishing, fecund mother.

No spinning planet that I know,
Save only Earth on which I toil,
Collects sunlight in which to grow
Precisely mixed with water and soil.

I question not our maker's choice,
But gratefully I lift my voice,
"Drive greed that makes pollution out;
I am a patriot, hear me shout."

Marguerite Shumway

Journey

As I left God for my earthly family, I said,
"Please God I need help."
Still in my youth, I cried, "God I need another earthly family
and God gave me yet another loving family.
And then came the time for a husband and God responded
with a good husband and then followed a wonderful son and daughter.
And I asked for more friends and they came in abundance.
And I said, "God, I'd like a grandchild and received not one,
not two but three wonderful grandchildren.
And then I cried, "God, I need yet another husband" and I received another
wonderful husband, two more families and another grandchild.
I asked, "God, please just one more friend.
I found me and I found my God again!

Marie Chartier

That's My Brother

My brother may not be much to look at to you but to me he's the best you
could have strong smart Athlete Football and wrestling he dreams of going
to the NFL doesn't matter which team he's got the muscles to make it through
but yet there's still more to this happy-go-lucky guy took second in Reign
III Wrestling now do you see there's more to this five foot ten muscle-man
than meets the eye, that's my brother.

Cynthia Plate

If I Was a Star

If I were a star, I would rest by day and shine by night.
Every morning, I will fade away,
untouched by time, only to rise again with the moon.
Every evening, I will appear in the night sky,
as if by magic, like a glittering diamond on velvet.
Every midnight I will shine my brightest for the lonely child
who looks up at me from a bedroom window.

If I were a star, I would sparkle bright among the other stars
and with our mother the moon all night.
All night I would play with the other stars happily, only to depart all
too soon when the sun comes take our place.

Then I would be a shooting star, soaring high throughout the galaxies,
seeing things no one else has seen, doing things, no one else has done.
Like seeing the Milky Way, from high above and foreign planets from down below.
Flying through Nebulas, and disappearing through black holes.

Afterwards, I'd take a rest, and grant a young child a special wish.
Finally I would be a dying star.
With a fading light, and an explosion of color, I would disappear into the galaxy, and
vanish forever.

Christina Correnti

A Dammed-Cell in the Press

Conception to birth of great attainments must not be
consenting I aborted, yielded to compromise, nor futility sown.
These deeds breed of contrary reasoning, seeds of infertility;
then the harvest becomes like dust in the wind and away gets blown.
The extraordinary's progression is immobilized
as intolerance persists in its intrusion.
Forbearance surrenders in exhaustion to
what's seemingly just a covert illusion.
Purpose will forfeit her possession to lie barren in the womb,
while mediocrity's imposed death sentence
ascribes disdain on a protesting tomb.
Lofty goals, blueprinted dreams, visionary aspiration ignite
their lamentable opposition against rejection and being denied.
Absent of time's intervention day after day, year after year,
their inevitability succumbs to tendencies of suicide.
At last, in spite of defeat's intense aggression,
hope for unforbidden fruitfulness
snatches victory from the duress of the seizer's merciless, ravaging strife.
Germinating pangs of resurrected optimism induces the
birthing transformation of a dammed-cell in the press;
hence, an experience in immensity breathes life!

Zepharra Fitz

My Dad

Who do I see?
My strong, handsome dad
Smiling at his fine family,
Two wonderful daughters,
And four fine sons he had.

Who do I see?
My strong, handsome dad
Standing in the doorway,
A kind, wide smile he had
Upon his face,
To let us know he cared.

Who do I see?
My strong, handsome dad
Running like a deer
Across the fields
Chasing many a cow or steer.

Who do I see?
My strong, handsome dad
Displaying a twinkle in his eye,
At the thought of a joke
That he silently played on another guy.
Who do I see?
My strong, handsome dad
Always working, working.
That's what my dad liked to do!

Janice Klenbaum

Crushed

Crushed by you
I will always remain
Shattered into pieces
By your words
And the memories of your touch
Tear me apart
I am speechless
As no words but yours,
Which will remain unspoken,
Could take away my pain
And the sweet whispers of sadness
Fill my heart with cruel darkness
And I fall to my knees
And lie in my blood

Ashley Nice

God's Hand

See the eagle in the sky
Drifting, floating with the clouds
The majestic Lord,
Searching for his prey.
Until upon the land below he spies
With his eaglistic eyes,
A youthful hare,
Quietly munching without a care.

Like a thunderbolt
The eagle drops,
Shooting toward the hare
Innocently munching, munching there.
But suddenly he brakes,
Stopping short, hovering.
Could the eagle care,
Floating there, just above the hare?

Dean Schultz

Loving Others

Loving yourself is knowing yourself,
Respecting each other is knowing how to respect each other,
Passing by a person and not knowing him or her and making fun
of them is not the way to respect each other,
When you see a overweight person, it's not your place to comment on them,
it is your place when you help them, instead of insulting them,
make a difference in the world, don't destroy it, cherish it,
that's including the peoples that is in the world with you.
Love one another, respect one another, oh, and one more thing,
don't judge anyone by their appearance, judge by their personality,
and people if you are being judge by anyone look the other way,
don't let no one but God be your judge.
Remember love someone and that love will be returned.

Sandra Mims

From His Eyes

In loving memory of my cousin Christopher Casillas
Today is a struggle, tomorrow is a fight.
I woke up this morning,
But will sleep eternally tonight.
Why couldn't I just go out to party,
Without being surrounded by a bunch of hype?
I was a father, friend, husband and lover.
Someone decided to play God for a minute,
and ultimately, took my life.
My one month old twin girls will now be raised by only their mother
If I could turn back the hands of time
I would have stayed home with my wife.
I just wanted to celebrate Cinco de Mayo, now my family must pay the price
As I sit here watching over my loved ones all I can do is wonder . . . .
Never again will I say "Let me introduce myself,
I'm Chris, the older brother."
I'm in a better place now, I know
My feet may never touch the Earth again,
Nor will I take another breath.
But my memory in their hearts will never go . . . .
So as I lay here in peace, my soul is able to rest.

Misti Salazar

You're Always There . . .

I'm sitting here alone in the dark,
The playground has emptied and no more screaming children hang in the balance.
The sun is going down and I watch as passing cars go by.
Headlights scream over me and move on; barely a glance,
barely a wave—I go unnoticed.
Normally, a person in this situation would feel alone,
Frightened by the dark and scared that any second, a horrible monster will
bounce out of the dark and attack. But not me, for I am not alone.
I am not bothered by the oblivious passersby and I pay no
attention to the monster as it barrels out of the dark, for I am with you.
Though you are nowhere to be seen, I see your sweet face
And how your blue eyes looked into mine as if looking for the answer to a puzzle.
And though I sit in silence, I hear your voice calling my name
and telling me how much you loved me for the first time.
Though the only thing I smell is the leaves and autumn's famous wind,
I smell you, in the shirt you let me keep.
The sweet smell of the cologne that only you wear and sweat all mixed in
to create the comforting smell that only you could claim.
Though you are gone, you are no longer audible and the smell is slowly fading,
I think of you every day and how much you loved my laugh,
and every time I did laugh you would give me that adorable grin of approval.
And I start to cry.
The hot tears feel good streaming down my face and I realize that
I have to let you go. I have to come to terms
with the fact that you are no longer here.
But in my eyes you will always be there,
Watching me, holding me, and protecting me.

Tina Swecker

The Comforter

In my hour of deepest need
Within my saddest tears
Amid a veil of loneliness
My comforter appears

He comes as just a gentle breeze
Across an empty bed
Or as a sweet, familiar voice;
A thought within my head

My pain is eased, my heart relieved
To know that he is near
This comforter of lonely hearts
My sorrow he will bear

Carole Pearce

Dream Man

The kindness of his heart.
The gentle touch of his hand.
A very sweet and loving man.
A man who will always care.
A man who is always there.
A man who will always share.
His love, and much more.
This is a man that I adore,
He's my husband you see,
And he means the world to me.
The man of my dream.

Tonya Bullock

These Tears

These tears I cry
Are meant for you.
Though I know I shouldn't,
I don't know what else to do.

The pain you brought
To my loving heart,
You swore to me
We'd never part.

But now you're gone
And I'll miss you forever,
But a hug from a friend
Proves it's all for the better.

It's hard to get over you
Even though I try.
These tears are for you,
These tears I cry.

Katie Bourdeau

What a Wonderful World

As I stand upon my house,
I look around me,
Noticing the beauty in the world.

I see butterflies fluttering happily,
Bees buzzing busily,
White fluffy clouds that look like
Beds of feathers.

When I look down,
I see people talking,
Enjoying their day off work,
But I have no day off as I work
For the Lord
And as He works in me.
And thinking of this,
I say to myself,
"What a wonderful world,
What a wonderful world."

Joelle Clearman

Carmen-Fantasie

I remember she told me springs ago
If your dreams fly in the sky,
Climb mountains, the ones black and high,
Drink the clouds and wear snow;
Your eyes will never get dry:
Your life is a voice of cry.

I remember she asked me springs ago,
Have you ever seen a lover
Who takes love for the heart of his mother
That sings when the winds blow
And dances when the phantoms play together?
I have never seen him, never, never.

I remember we met here springs ago,
She was the flute, she was the song,
The flute was short, the song was long,
I met her when she was all women,
Her perfume was soft and light,
In her eyes were the day and the night,
Today, angels said she was right,
When she told me springs ago . . . .

Ahmed Ouldbah

Panthera

Ebon velvet covers his movements,
learned in a distant place.
Strength to behold and fury to fear,
he stalks his prey with an unhurried pace.
Leopard without spots, a swarthy beast,
he is near you now; he has won his race.

Arthur Alper

My Darling

My Darling you are like no other
For your touch my soul doth aspire
If I could only be held
in your sweet embrace
If only I could kiss you any place
If we could be together
All my feelings, emotions, and desires placed in you
I'm so scared
Wondering if you still care
What I wish to say to you
Is so hard yet so true
I fell for you
But what do I do?
As you sweetly kiss my face
You kiss my lips so sweet and warm
I can't help but yearn for more
As you pull me closer into your loving arms
I fall so deeply for your charms
We are a couple lovers without a care
I shall always cherish the love we share

Rachael Silverman

Limitless Light

Your mission in life can never be found
If you remain blind to the opportunities around
When life's bright light seems dim and gone
Remember how it had once shone
If there is no limit to what you can do
Then a hopeful heart can carry you through
And renew your strength day by day
A willing mind will lead your way
Through the darkest night
Until your light returns bright
And you realize that you are no longer a shallow stream
But a vast river

Lindsay Schoures

Lunar Lament

to Allianna
It is upon her essence I cannot gaze,
But there is my spiritual destination,
Within her quintessential traits
Ultimately to usurp any preparation
(as if one could prepare for immortality)
Like vernal blossoms, so vibrant in denial
Pleasures fade quickly and perpetually
Only to nourish in contradicting revival
A much broader acclamation of glory
The effigy of corporeal strategy—Earth
Spinning near infinity in realization
Of secrets unavailable to the human story
But prolific in universal mirth
Revealing menial bio-devastation

Russell (Rusty) Taylor

The Tale of Four Sisters

A tale of four sisters who grew up apart
each in a different family, where do we start
All raised separately, the loneliness so real
no one to share with and no means to heal.
The knowledge we were sisters from some of us hid
sorrow grew for those who knew a pain they could not rid.
Each one of us had to find our own place
with no one to share each day we did face
We see how our likes have run parallel
each surviving our own private Hell.
Although by different people we were raised
our core of survival was never phased.
We cast no judgement on each others lives
for each had to do what it took to survive.
The loving heart of a sister is having a best friend
she loves you and listens no matter what's been.
This tale of four sisters who grew up apart
now has a happy beginning they share with their hearts.

Terry Smith

Life's Priorities . . . ?

Life today makes you stop and think—
    Certain areas progress, while others sink.
Too much in life is taken for granted—
    The results are ever present all over our planet.
The world is exploding with sex, drugs, and guns—
    But what happened to good ole love, hugs, and fun?
Fun isn't the same as it was way back when—
    Today it produces destruction to lives and men.
Have we somehow made a costly trade—
    Morals and values, for drugs and rage?
Many people can display patronizing concern—
    But stopping this madness is much harder to learn.
We persistently discover new cures for this or that—
    While our basic structure is falling flat.
With technology advancing increasingly fast—
    Why can't our families thrive and last?
What exactly must we do to right what's been done—
    Or is this simply the wishful thinking of one?
Yes you can certainly say, that times are changing—
    But our priorities definitely need some rearranging!

Katherine Happle

'Til the Morning Light

It's at night asleep in my bed
When the dreams of dancing filled my head.
My reality of the chair is not even there.
I dance in fields of golden wheat,
In this way my soul takes flight, 'til the morning light.
The music of my soul as my mind is free my body is not bound.
It's at night, my dreams take flight.
I dance until the morning light.

Jane Britnell

Dreams

I tilt my head up towards the sky,
And watch the stars go dancing by,
In this world my dreams come alive
There's no one here to ask me why,
There is no pain and no one can die,
If you wish hard enough you can grow wings and fly,
As I look up I see warm hazel eyes,
I rest my head back with a soft content sigh,
It hurts me to know that this world that is mine,
Will all disappear when I open my eyes,
It is so hard to stop and to realize,
This paradise to me is nothing but lies,
But I know each morning as reality hits me like a knife to my side,
I must keep my head up and learn to survive.

Christa Carter

The Face of Friendship

Safe charm describing something words half miss
shapeless laughter bestows love under scrutiny
soulless contempt
trapped
behind
loyal gasps
We blindly listen to the nothing that tells us of praise
Smirking, the voices say the insightful phrases we desire
to soften so we can overlook
the world of ourselves

Angela Carol Mitchell

A Father Is

A father is a caring man
that will miss you when you're away
He loves you always and forever,
no matter what you say.
He treats you well,
and teaches you good.
He's the only man who can do these things for you,
because no other man could.
He will take you fishing on the dock,
and tuck you into bed.
He will whisper in your ear sweet dreams,
then kiss you on your head.
He will always be the first man in my life,
because I love him so.
We will be standing side by side,
as we watch the river flow.

Barbra Boling

Forbidden Love

Entwined forms on the sand, the moon's dim caress, crashing
waves on the rocks,
the wind carrying scents—
of wine and love and desire and
blood pulsing to the rhythmic tide of the hand,touching the
body, the soul and the mind—
two forms on the sand, with the sand entwined.
That hand reaches out and beckons to
the sand and waves and the rocks and moon,
the moan of the wind kissed by pale starlight
fans the ego of Passion, her conquest, her delight.
The two forms drift and go separate ways,
Passion looks on with a triumphant gaze,
though their bands of gold are tarnished with sin,comes
another night they will again, be her conquest, her slave
controlled by her might, caught in the webbed maze of
her addictive delight.

Traci-Jean Kretzschmar

My Best Friend

Into my dark and dreary world you came,
You changed me and I will never be the same.
You gave to me a love that is pure,
Your heart, your soul and a friendship that will endure.
You found a me, I never was before,
You gave me wings and taught me how to soar.

Cheryl Shampoe

Light of Christ

I sit alone on a cold night,
something about it, seems to feel right,
the candle flickers, then goes out,
darkness fills me with uneasy doubt.

A light appears before my eyes,
As if in answer to my fearful cries,
it pierces darkness, showing a path,
to escape the grasp of Satan's wrath.

I follow the path, still unsure,
but pulled along, by a feeling of pure,
the light shines stronger, filling my soul,
with love so intense, making me whole

Michael McKenzie

Shades of Gray—the Littleton Tragedy

Blood, tears, pain.
Depression, anger, vain.
An empty life they had led,
Visions of death reeled in their heads.
Heartless, cold, inhumane.
Innocent teen brutally slain.
Revenge was what they had in mind.
They had souls of a savage kind.
Chaotic, frightening, completely insane.
So many killed, so many maimed.
Graduation was only days away.
Instead of white caps and gowns,
They wore shades of gray.
When will all this cruelty end?
Can't we push this aside and make amends?
Anguish, hurt, unreality.
All results of a heartless brutality.
So parents, hug your kids . . .
Kids, hug your friends.
Because you never know when it all will end.

Eowen Silverraven

Thoughts of Love!!!

About someone special
The passions of love burn within me
when ever I'm near you.
To feel the warmth and pleasure
of your cool sultry lips,
would be like kissing the rays of the Sun.
The touch of your hard silky body
pressed to mine would be as if I were surrounded
by a thousand Angels protecting me from
the harsh evils of the World.
As I surrender my Body and Soul
to the shelter of their Wings,
as the scent of your heavenly body
stirs my blood;
and clouds my mind and the images
of your face haunts my dreams,
with a soothing calmness in my sleep.
I can no longer stair at the blossoming beauty;
but only imagine your Shadowy shape
in my arms 'til all Eternity.

Shawn Sargent

Lyrics

Every morning that I wake up
I wake up to a gorgeous view
Every morning I wake up
I think of or I'm looking at you.
Every ounce of water I drink
is an effort to refresh me
but nothing can come close to
quenching my thirst than when you are with me.
Your beautiful black hair
flows like the Nile River
Only to be outdone by your lovely smile
that makes me quiver.
The touch of your hands
the kiss from your lips
I yearn to feel your soft back
and your smooth hips.
Many men I know dream to be like me
Not because of who I am, but who you be
My beautiful black princess. Bold and strong.
We will meet at the alter and I promise
It won't be too long.
I act sure of things, but one thing is true.
You got me baby, and . . .I Got You!

Anthony Omolewa

The Memories You Gave Me

The memories you gave me will last forever,
The times we shared I will always remember,
The memories you gave me help me remember you,
The memories you gave me, and the ones I gave you.

Jennifer Smaagaard

Deliverance

Birth:

Forced from a world of peace and silence
Pushed in fear from darkness to light
Delivered without thought into unknown hands
Solace forsaken by the severed cord

Life:

Forced to endure the hatred and violence
Lost, in fear of the darkness of night
Indifference sears the soul like a brand
Destined to join humanity's hoard

Death:

Forced by past deeds into final repentance
Fear is lost in the brilliance of the light
Delivered back into God's own hand
Life once more in the love of the Lord

Kristen Morgan

Grief

Without a backward glance
    you have slipped away
And left me in a world
    completely filled with gray.
The moments when you held me close
    and whispered words of love
Are like small puffs of smoke
    disappearing into clouds above.
My grief is inconsolable
    I feel your presence all around
For this is the day that they have
    placed you into the dark, cold ground
A place within my chest is empty
    and so very, very sore
For my heart is buried with you
    I don't need it any more.

Jacqueline Downer

Clue

Are you a good enough sleuth to solve the mystery?
It's about murder in the first degree.
If you really know the game Clue,
Then this shouldn't be hard to do.

There's a knife in the kitchen, no one used it.
Mrs. White's in the dining room with a candle lit,
A gun is locked up safe without a single bullet.
Everybody looks so guilty to me.

The library is too quiet to hang around,
But you won't get strangled if you make a sound.
I doubt if you'll get wrenched down in the lounge,
But that depends on the company you'll see.

Now, Miss Scarlet and Professor Plum were down the hall.
They were dancing, shooting pool, and having a ball.
Colonel Mustard's smoking a cigar in the study,
And Mr. Green is clean, he wouldn't hurt nobody.

All of those secret passages cause confusion,
The more clues seeks out a better conclusion.
There's one more final clue,
The answer's left out for you.

Brian McDonough

He Says

When I say, "I'm sorry," He says, "I will forgive you."
When I say, "I love you," He says, "I love you too."
When I shed a lonely tear, He dries my tear-stained eyes
When I call upon his name He answers, "Here am I."
When I say, "I'm in trouble Lord," He says, "Help is on the way."
When I say, "I'm lonely Lord," He says, "I'll come in and stay."
And when I've lost my way He says, "I'll be your guide."
And when I say, "I'm not happy Lord," He says, "In me be satisfied."
When sorrow has surrounded me I find comfort in His arms.
And when I've grown tired and weak He's the rock I lean upon
Through all the good times and the bad He's the one that I trust in.
He's my Saviour and my Master, but still my dearest friend.

Colleen Anderson

His Girl

He called me his girl,
while talking to a friend,
it felt real good knowing
that for once, I'm liked and I'm wanted.

Every time I'm with him, my heart starts racing,
I didn't know where it was running.
Until the day we were in church,
holding hands, looking in each others eyes,
with nothing else on our minds besides
the magical love we share, saying "I do."
Now both he and I know, I'll forever be his girl.

Nadia Romagnuolo

Finding Her Warmth

Chili sauce, saunas, sunny vacations
had no effect on her cold . . .

She sat across from me
dressed with the perfection of a Swiss watch.

Her eyes are ice
and black matching the bags hanging under them

Secrets of a father's desire for her, spilled from her lips
now she wishes she was dead.

Yet wants to live
wants to cut his anchor off her high heel.

Joseph Juracek

The Face of an Angel

I've seen the world in the face of my love
I've seen the Heavens in my angel from above.
Her skin more delicate
Than the most perfect rose,
So much finer than silk
At first touch, my heart froze.
Her lips are so soft
Like velvet so smooth,
But sweeter still than their taste
Is when they say, "I love you."
Her smile so sweet
So soft and so bright,
It can melt my very soul
And chase away the black of night . . .
Ah, but her eyes.
Brighter than the sun
Deeper than the oceans
Wider than the sky,
Their radiance could have only
Been stolen from Heaven so high.

Joshua Gibbs

Vicious Velociraptor

Velociraptor is one heck of a creature,
Yes, it has many deadly features

Watch out, duck down, avoid its claws,
Rips out prey's guts just like a saw,

Boy, raptors can feast on really big dinos,
Even those bigger than twelve fat rhinos,

Man, their skin is coarse and extremely tough,
Like sandpaper that's incredibly rough,

You would've found them in scorching hot places,
Now you'll find them in display cases,

Velociraptors have truncated arms,
Like a pig's trough you find at a farm,

Can you believe they're four feet tall,
Like two TV's measured against a wall,

Raptors lived to be not so old,
35 or so, but extra bold,

Swift and agile this creature was,
A lot smarter than T-Rex, it's cuz,

Now these raptors are gone; don't have a cow,
We can learn why, and most importantly how.

Edwin Yusman

Youth

To my daughter, Joylene
through my daughter's eyes, what did I see
my childhood relived from when I too was three
'round and 'round and 'round we went
surreal for me was this very moment
as if I laughed, smiled and cheered for joy
as when my mother held me as a little boy
with the music playing to fill the air
a time a parent and a child could share
as I looked at those who watched—
the seniors, the old and the young at heart—
I saw in their faces a peaceful truth
of how they too felt from their days of youth
I looked back, forward and side to side
and saw many happy faces on this carousel ride
then I looked towards my daughter's way
I shall never forget this beautiful day
new was this experience her childhood buys
for she too will remember these days
through her own daughter's eyes

Benel Aguirre

"Bleeding"

I opened my ears to see your words
How often I saw but never heard
As my hair falls in my eyes
To hide away the tears that burn
    Do you see me, God?
    I'm the one dying at your feet
    She may have washed your feet O' Lord
    But I could wash your body with all the tears I weep
Falling—Spinning
I am in constant pain
And I'm bleeding from the outside in

The words in your mouth, the stars in the sky
Wishing for love and waving good-bye
As your hair falls in my face
Do you believe that feelings lie?
    Can you kiss me then?
    To taste the truth, you just breathe in
    To live you just decide to be alive
    Once alive, you must be brave to be happy again
Falling—spinning
I am in constant pain
I am bleeding from the outside in
Will I know life again?
Or just bleeding from the outside in

Samuel Di Gangi

the bushes

snakebite and bud light
sometimes a white russian
that's how you could tell a bad day
they sat next to each other through everything
he always had a story, sometimes a lesson
she always had a sequel
if he laughed, it was rare
when she did, the entire bar knew
i knew 4 o'clock by their entrance
they hid their nickles
but knew i'd never cut them off
they lived for each other
to laugh with whoever would with them
"you work for your life" he told me
"you put your name on your work"
"people remember when you do well"
his grease stained hands held his shot glass
and she smiled at him proudly
content just to sit next to him
together 40 years

Jaymes Brooks

Those Who Stay

My life rolls by like
the credits after a movie,
the type of movie that might actually be interesting
if there weren't so much drama.
The repetitive type.
The kind that wears you out
just thinking about it.
The kind you dread, yet know that someday,
no matter how solid the plans,
will always interfere.
Yet some people actually stay,
watching each name,
each detail,
slowly scrolling by.
Noting every single one.
The people that actually pay attention
to all of life's details,
and are patient enough to
listen to all of yours.

Sarah Hautamaki

America's Valiant Veterans

They are a declining breed of folk
You see them every day
Some are invalids in nursing homes
Holding on to life's precious ways

You see others in coffee shops
Where they talk about old times
When Sergeants and Petty Officers Shouted orders down their spines

When America called they stood their ground
To save the USA
They sacrificied their precious lives
To keep America free

They answered America's calls to battlefields
Half way around the world
Hundreds of thousands gave their lives
Less than one hundred years ago

On this Memorial Day many will go to cemeteries
To honor their comrades at rest
One day they'll rise up and say
Almighty God we did our best

Melvin Bockelman

My New Perspective

From my window I can see
the flurry of activity
both natural and man-created.
The thirst for motion's never sated.

A hurried figure runs below,
racing from the wind and snow.
Was it someone that I knew?
Before I can tell they're gone from view.

The flocks of birds are growing, swelling.
Restless here, they are rebelling.
Ready to leave this blustery place,
they prepare for flight right by my face.

The view up here is quite unique.
Looking out, I find the peace I seek.
I take comfort in my height respective.
I think I like my new perspective.

Arwen Yadanza

Friends

A friend You Can believe In
And you know their always there
A friend is someone you can trust
A friend will always care
A friend knows all about you
They never let you down
They'll be there when your feeling low
They'll always be around
No Matter what the time of day
a friend will lend their hand
their standing right there next to you
Doing everything they can
A true friend understands you
they know your every thought
They'll listen and believe in you
they know your every fault
When theres times your down and lonely
just turn around and find
your friend will be beside you not very far behind
there's times when friends they often part
but their friendship never dies
you keep in touch within your hearts everyday that passes by
Yes friends are very special you can never live without
A friend will always be a friend Forever here on out

Karrie Yeoman

The Brightest Star

For every tear that falls on Earth
God places a star in the sky.
Some nights you see so many
And you find yourself asking why.

Tears are drops of Crystal Love
You feel roll down your face
They come from deep inside your heart
Where God has built a secret place.

He reaches into a bag near his throne
And pulls out a shiny new star.
He places it just right in Heaven
Where all can see it from afar.

So if you are looking to Heaven
And you see a star twinkling bright.
It may be the one that God put there
The one he placed there for you last night.

Don Croucher

Flames of Desire

My thoughts are always with you,
as the days seem to pass us by.

I know our love will grow stronger,
until the day we die.

You have given my life a since of direction,
now everything is clear.

I always want you with me,
your love to me is dear.

My life has lightened up,
your sensitivity touches me so.

I know our flame will always burn,
it will never seize to glow.

I could never hurt you,
because with each passing day.

Our Flames of Desire,
will never go astray.

This poem was meant to tell you,
Don't let me see you cry.

We'll always be together,
Like the Stars in the sky

William Nicklas

Where Were You?

Where were you when I was young and yet growing older?
Where were you when I was frightened and yet becoming bolder?
Where were you when the victory had been won, but the battle lost?
Where were you when life was free, yet I had to pay the cost?
Where were you when I was confused, not knowing how to feel?
Where were you when I was hungry, yet went without a meal?
Where were you when I really didn't want to but knew that I must?
Where were you when I was insecure yet I had to trust?
Where were you when I was humble and yet went on to boast?
Where were you when I was lonely and needed you the most?

Candal Johnson

Time

One day I return home and find
The place of my childhood diminished by time
The roof of my house which used to touch the sky
seems so low now as I pass by
I count the steps 1, 2, 3, 4
The grand staircase is no more
I thought my house would stand on a mountain still
I realize now it is just a hill

Christina M. Nelson

The Roar and the Reach

Motionless, I sit and watch
Swaggering bands,deeply merging
Pimal radra brushes, sweeping strokes
Threatening colors
Drawn from African waves,
Teased and pulled and coaxed
Nature's introspection
Looking inside the center of human fear
Offering an eye, a quiet of blue calm
Moving as I cannot
On courses tracked and plotted
By nightmares of shattered
Storefronts and dreamscapes
Howling, drunk with wet power
I hear the rage of Lear, a Jeremiad
"I come for you," you growl
In a language older than speech
And still, as you are not, I sit here
transfixed by transfiguration, I await you

Glenn Moss

The Answer

the words have always been written
and truth remains the truth
but time has possessed the man and taken
him from his youth
young questions in an older man
old answers in a younger time
a young man thinks he knows the answer
an old man knows he knows that time will
take him to the place where the answers
seek to go
all will go and never know the answer
hidden there
but time is but in one space—everywhere

Harlan Wayland

Time

When time ticks by ever so slowly
As it does when I wait to see you again
The hours seem to take days 'til they pass.

When I know I will see you again
The hours seem to take seconds 'til they pass
And the time for me to be happy arrives quickly.

Time does not stand still when you are with me
It moves as though it were on ice. . . .
Gliding effortlessly by, without a care in the world.

Derick Bodamer

Untitled

Dedicated to my husband Roy.
This feeling called love
is an angry emotion.
I cannot describe to you how I feel,
it's the blinding sun,
destroying my vision.
Although the burning light destroys my eyes,
my heart is what it feeds on,
my heart leads the way.
Salvation full and true;
saying those precious words,
I love you.
A lover's quarrel you say,
a rose bush's thorn,
I'd been slain.
The colors of the wind blow so proud and true,
there will never be another night like the ones with you.

Tiffany Jacox

Opaque Are You

Climbed in a moment
(I made sure that moment stopped).
Chain-mail linked by toxic soldier.
Impressions left, fingers in clay
Mapping the symmetry looking for Structure.
Magnified.
Mercury befriends gravity.
Crippled atoms die repeatedly
Accumulate; becomes a coral of infinite depth.
Opaque.
Subdue my warmth
Feed me insecurity
Fear water. Fear height
Cold fever ripples the putrid calm

Forgive me, standing here
Motionless, inside an invisible prison
That limits me.
Limitless spaces, crowded
By my petty prayers for lust.
I want to breath sweet ice
From the lungs of winter fruit.

I need liberty to waste it in
My bedroom.

Temi Odumosu

Baby and Mother

What a beautiful baby you are I say
for you I know it's your very first day
So tiny and innocent, sweet and true
you have my eyes, and curly hair too
I hold you and comfort you all day long
singing to you all the nursery rhyme songs
So healthy and happy you entered this world
like an angel from above, my beautiful girl
No words can describe the way that I feel
when I look at you, I just know that it's real
Forever you will hold a place in my heart
an unconditional love right from the start
For every day and moment we share
through good times and bad I will always be there
When things look to bad and you're feeling sad
remember the moments that made you feel glad
Go back to the day that we first shared together
remember our bond, baby and mother

Nicole Betker

What Is There Left to Say

I am in so much pain,
And feel as if there is nothing to gain.
I sit by myself with no one near,
Asking myself, doesn't anyone care?
No one understands
As to why I am so blue.
I feel as if no one is there,
And start to think that life isn't fair.
I think about all the things in my life,
And hope someday someone will take the sorrow away
By pulling out the knife.
For now all I do is cry,
But whenever I do,
Everyone asks why?
I try to explain,
But all they do is sigh.
I guess if they don't understand me,
I'll have to wait for the day,
When they will finally realize,
What I have to say.

Payal Tiku

Excess in Siberia

I'm crippled by my weakness that I won't let go away,
surrounded by the preasures that kill me every day.
Drown the memory of misery, wanting to forget,
ruled by all my vices this is what I get.
Unexpected isolation forms hope into hysteria,
searching for salvation like excess in Siberia.
I love it when you go away, but hate it when you leave.
I'm dangerous when I'm alone; my demon's threaten me.
Strong in thought, weak in soul, I give in one more night,
trapped in self destruction with no strength left to fight.
Unexpected isolation forms hope into hysteria,
searching for salvation like excess in Siberia.
Beyond desperation, longing to erase,
mental saturation, see the dead man's face.
I'm gone. . . .

Kevin Lidz

One Day

Like an eagle who soars through the air,
One day, I, too, will soar.
I will spread my wings and fly,
Fly away from my cocoon which has entrapped me.
Fly away like a butterfly finally released.
I'll fly away a beautiful butterfly
Ready to take the world

Like the flower that blooms,
One day, I, too, will bloom.
I will find who I am, and it will be lovely.
I will not drift in the wind
like the fluff from a dandelion;
I will know where I am going.
I'll be ready to take the world.

And, like an eagle, or butterfly, or flower,
I will have obstacles to overcome.
But I will keep on flying,
Keep on going,
Because
I'll be ready to take the world

Tennille Villeneuve

Heartfelt Images

As I sit and close my eyes
Images of you run through my mind.

You are smiling and laughing and running wild
Then you turn to me and say good-bye.

I run to you and take your hand
Then you hold me tight, right were we stand.

I pull away, but just a touch
Then say to you, "I love you so much."

You lean forward and close your eyes
And softly place your lips upon mine.

The looks you give me, make my nerves run wild
But yet sometimes I feel like a small, shy child.

I want us together, I want us to grow old.
Do you want me forever? This feeling do you hold?

In answer to this you say to me
"Baby, I love you, forever it shall be."

As you hold me close and we walk away
The image in my mind begins then to fade.

But in my heart I hope it's all true
You never know, someday, I may be old beside you.

Tyrena Peebles

Mother

No matter how grown up I get,
  Our love and friendship, I'll never forget.
I will always keep you close to my heart,
  And I promise we will never part.

Friends and boys will come and go,
  Yet you will always stay.
And this is why I love you,
  More than words could ever say.

You're my very best friend,
  One I can always trust.
You've helped me with my problems,
  That confuse me very much.

When a boy breaks my heart,
  You're there to hold my hand.
You never leave my side,
  Because you understand.

Every moment that passes,
  I thank the Lord . . .
That no one has ever,
  "cut-our-cord."

Wherever we are,
  We'll be with each other.
You are my heart, my life,
  My love, my Mother.

Jamie Stalker

Mystic Beings

This is for everyone who encouraged me to write more. Thank You.
Graceful, slender, lithe shapes darting through the trees.
Agile, quick and cunning, like the wind in the tender leaves.
Majestic is thier spirit, playful are the days.
A single horn upon the head mark their merry ways.
Silver coats with golden sheen, fiery mane and tail,
Flowing, floating, leaping, leaving a glittery trail.
Like a disappering shadow, rarely ever seen.
The Majestic unicorn's elusive as a dream.

Ashley Pattishall

Simple Things

I dedicate my poem to Bryan Parks. I love him!
Love isn't all the big gifts that you give,
It's the simple things of life and how we live,
It's how we share our secrets and our dreams,
Our fantasies and even the funny little schemes,
Love is how we reach out to our mate,
To love, honor, and communicate,
Sharing our thoughts and our fears,
Wiping away each other's despairing tears,
But the simple things are for that special one
In your life,
Like to caress, hold, kiss and someday become
Man and wife,
To make him or her feel like they are
The only one,
Playing games, dancing, just having some fun,
Knowing they are the one for you,
Making them feel special in whatever you do,
So when that special someone is
Near to your heart,
Tell one another how much you love them
And never drift apart,
This is what I call the simple things.

Carmen Sword

The Rich Man

As he stood in front of all that is his,
All that he made from his lives work.
He cried

All that he ever wanted was his
All except one thing
The single most important thing in a man's life
Something he never had because of his greed.
Love

The love of a woman
Someone to care
Someone to understand

He has everything money can buy
They say money brings happiness
But what is happiness without love

As he stairs at all that is his
He dies a lonely man
He had everything money could buy
Except the single most important thing of all
For money can't buy love

Bertram Daniels

A Feeling Never Felt Before

Have you ever heard your heart speak?
When I'm with my better half
I stop and wait to see her laugh.
Contain myself I do with force
to much ado, I seek recourse.

Constant laughter starts to cease
smile on face, oh, what a tease!
Why such blissful smile like that
helpless I'm rendered, a big smile back.

In no time our smiles do meet
Here come her lips, my heart does fleet.
Bodies of ours do make close
Here come her lips, our kiss like prose.

Oh, her lips feel good on mine
can't believe the taste so fine.
Feel so warm inside I do
we are one, no longer two.

Then I stop I think I must
inside a feeling, not just lust.
From my heart I feel implore
A Feeling Never Felt Before.

Michael Reyes

Clairvoyance

What if our outlook was bright
Bright enough to see past our differences
And bright enough to see into another's soul
Brilliant enough to dodge the color of our skin
Only to view the luster of gold that surrounds us all
Floodlights expanding our view of each other
Shooting through the universal spirit of our Earth
And beyond the apex of space
Radiate through others until we become transparent
The flow the constant the beginning and the end
Still as ice for we are everywhere
For the light will penetrate that crack to give us clairvoyance
A path of lightning to show us the way
To the heavens we fly
Not because we were dropped from the clouds
But lifted from the Earth
In search of the environment of our atmosphere
Amidst the suns rays
And God's arms

Brian LiVolsi

Inside Me

As I sit her lonely, feeling down,
I wonder, what is going on all around this small town.
The street lights flash through the cracks in the walls,
And I wonder again if there is a safe place, anyplace at all,
Anywhere else I could be.

This desolate place inside of me
Brings to my conclusion that all of my hopes and dreams
Are just allusions
And I remain with my back against this bleak wall.

Something however did make me smile
It was a mile away that I heard these words
A young couple, a small utter
Of words that meant everything and then nothing to me
They were I love you.

And I finally came to the realization that inside of me
I have no room for foolish infatuations,
All I have are my walls and cracks
Peering at me, laughing.

Denise Skalstad

How Should I Hate You?

You were always there, you were never away
You made promises, you were always the same
The places we met, the words you said
Let me keep these in me
Baby, please don't take it away
Place me in your heart, let me make you feel the pain
See me through your eyes, run my blood in veins
Love for you is all I know
Tell me please!
How should I hate you?
There was a time you made me believe
I was so hurt; still you never let me down
Words were tears when you were alone
You gave me all the love I asked for
Don't leave me alone to fight this war
Hold me in your soul, let me kill your pain
Let me feel inside you, let me not lose the lane
Love for you, is all I know
Tell me please!
How should I hate you?

Raj Kumar

Orleans Beach, August 1989

Struggling to climb that rock, perched so
delicately on the sand,
my bare-feet find no traction.
I stand in the midst of bleached shells,
while you climb effortlessly to the top.

You pull your knees to your chin
as ripples roll in from
the sinking sun. I step back
as the wind plays with your hair.

Only then do I notice that the tide
is pulling the rock away from the shore.

Steve Witherell

Interracial Adoption Deeper than Love

A face is a face, a hand is a hand, a child is a child.
The color of a child's skin is a reflection of his or her ancestry.
It's the love and acceptance that can look past the color image
and understand the identity.
It's the difference one can make to take in a child
and not focus on color alone.
It's the unity we can display for these children.
Unity based on love, respect, honor and understanding.
Not only understanding the immediate family,
but an understanding of racial harmony.

Lisette A. Cruz

Somehow

Somehow,
each day creeps into your life—
as if you were the morning dew,
dissolving
into the first beams of the sun.

Somewhere,
one thousand hummingbirds
are circling the sky—
their delicate sensibilities are tuned in,
to the sweetness inside your chest.

And somehow,
every possible beauty
has its life inside your heart.
And it follows you everywhere;
no one here is alone.

The poet is the one
who turns their cup upright,
and allows it to overflow.

Eric Leonhardt Brown

Once More, Please . . .

When you smiled it caught my eye
How could it miss when it shines brighter than the sun in the sky

And when the moon rises I look to the sky
And all them pretty stars remind me of your eyes

And when I heard you sing I thought Heaven was near
'Cause you sounded like an angel so sweet, so dear

And when I see flowers I laugh
'Cause compared to your beauty, they don't equal to half

And emeralds from mountains, pearls form the sea
You are far more precious to me

And I would cross the nine hells and sail the seven seas
If I could be with you, just once more, please. . . .

Will Sharkey

Deep inside My Heart

Deep inside my heart, though I'm not sure quite where,
There is a special place, and everyone is there.

Loved ones, friends, acquaintances, too.
They all have a place there; yes, even you.

You have a place there, somewhere deep inside,
And try as I may I just never can hide.

The way that I feel comes out every day
In the way that I act and the things that I say.

He made me this way, for what purpose I don't know yet,
But I know for sure that my future has been set.

He wants you to know from the depths of His heart
He will be with you always, He was there from the start.

So my question to you, as you go on your way:
If He saw your heart, what would He say?

Jennifer Hiett

Tie That Shoe

One day an old lady walked up to me
she said, "Sweetheart, I have a need."
I said, "Yes ma'am, what can I do for you?"
She asked, "Could you bend down and tie my shoe?"
I said, "No problem, I most certainly can.
Your wish is my command!"
She said, "You are just as sweet as you can be!"
I said, "Thank you ma'am.
What I see is that one day this could be me."

Sakeena Abdullah

A Bleeding Heart

A bleeding heart, lost never to be found;
Was this intended, when I was created from the ground?
At a place of delirium, praying to leave this state.

Everything I've done, hurt seems to be my fate.
Can love be some sort of mystery?
It's been tragic from the start, from my study of history.

Everytime I fall, I manage to put up a fight.
Through all my efforts, love just eludes my sights.
Should I try for something I know I can't achieve.
Hurt is inevitable, if love is what you believe.

A. Lloyd

Midnight Interlude

One night, as I dreamed, the skies became gray.
The heavens had been overcast throughout the day.
I woke with the sighing, and moaning of the trees,
And knew that tonight there would be no mere breeze.

With the booming of thunder, and flashing of light,
My soul stole from my body-out into the night.
It wept with the heavens, sobbed with the winds.
It forgot all its troubles, and was cleansed of its sins.

In its flight through the Earth, it outshone every star.
It soared and it swept with the waves over the bar,
It sought out the flowers, and whispered the rain
Would but caress them and ease the stark pain,

That sometime, every human heart must know.
And none dare say it is not so!
Then, with the storms subsiding, my soul crept back to me,
As the tide flows in-then-strains back again to the sea.

I have known the ecstasy of having been set free.
No longer afraid of dying, shall I ever be.
No matter if they bury me down deep beneath the sod,
For on nights like these, my soul has walked with God.

Gladyce Ford

His Gift

God has blessed you with a precious little one
But your work has only just begun
He has lent you a true gift from above
To raise and teach and nurture with love.

What an honor to be chosen by Him
To treasure and love this sweet little gem.
What awe and joy you shall feel every day
As His guiding Spirit shows you the way.

I know you with be the best you can be
And much love and miracles all will see.
As you and your little on grow with love
God and His Angels will smile from above.

Kathie Martin

Thinking of You I Just Had to Tell You

I want to tell you about something
Very special that happened today . . .

Somewhere between the early morning rush,
And calm afternoon quiet, a warm and comforting
Thought of you came to keep me company, and
Before I knew it I was smiling, thinking about
the happy times we've had, thinking about what it
means to know you and the warm feeling it brings me.
To share a moment with you in thought,
I know this won't be the only time this happens
Because I think of you so often, and because you'll
always bring a smile to me.
But somehow . . .today like everyday, thinking
of you makes my day so special . . .I just had to tell you.

Christopher Pabon

Victim Unveiled

On the prowl her strides carry confidence,
She hides behind her fan.
Taunting the petty soul of her distaste,
The dragon she wears trembles in the wind.
The power of her beauty strikes another innocent soul down,
Lustful eyes deceive her.
She takes her fan and hurls it under the dark sun of morning.

Unveiled now, she stalks another,
Dancing to a sinful tune, she purges her soul clean.
Shedding light, I am the beholder, as well as the fool,
Lost to another, the pleasures surpass me.
On the ground, the veil hides her dangers within,
Within the fire she continues her dance.
Danced with one, to be scorched by another.

William Coppage

Life Is Beautiful—La Vita E'Belle

We wake up in the morning and fall asleep at night
God bless the world, people are wrong and right
The world lives and all is created by God,
even plants, insects and the water is alive, however odd.
Life is beautiful come rain or shine
Happiness and prosperity should be yours' and mine
Live life to the fullest for it is precious
Don't regret one moment and don't be pretentious.
For life is beautiful, we love and care
We hate and cry and even sometimes scare
United we are as flora and fauna of Earth
And divided as intellectuals since the day of birth.
Life is beautiful, we all have it in common
You're not better than me—not an omen.
Life is beautiful, we thank Thee for life
Lead us to live in harmony and never strife.

Nico Willemse

Love of Mine

Your eyes are the stars and moon that brighten up my darkest night.
Your smile is the sunshine that brings the light into my life.
Your voice is the music that can soothe the savage beast.
I'll adore you for eternity, this love I feel will never cease.
When you call my name, my heart sings songs of love.
When you say you love me, angels sing from up above.
When you hold me closely, my soul feels pure emotion.
The love I've found while holding you would overflow an ocean.
Can this be my dream come true? Are you mine for real?
Do the birds sing through the night for this love I feel?
Will we be together when both of us are old and gray.
Ever since that night we met, I've loved you more each day.
I love you more than anything, my heart is yours to keep.
I'll comfort and protect you, and hold you while you sleep.
Dear love of mine, you're everything my heart has ever sought.
Think of me when you feel love, for you are in my every thought.

Matthew Endres

Acceptance

For Elliot

What are you hiding behind those eyes,
Hiding from me as I gaze into them?
Or are you hiding nothing at all. . . .
Is it as plain as the nose you playfully
Plucked from my face?

The colors in your eyes change every so
Slightly as the sun sets behind me.
I want to reach out to you,
For you to hold me tight in your arms.

Do you feel the same need to hold me close?
Are you willing to accept me?

Sierra Gentry

My Heaven on Earth

Where the wind blows
   and the mist is heavy,
Where streams ring
   like Christmas bells,
Where the birds sing happily
   and the deer leap through the forest,
That is where you will find me!

Brianna Jeffers

Twins—Age Eleven

Our twin daughters, you are now age eleven
And to us, you are truly gifts from Heaven.

It seems like yesterday you were just babies,
but today you are both beautiful little ladies.

To us you are two of the most beautiful girls on Earth,
And we are thankful every day to you we gave birth.

We could not ask for anything more than we have today,
And we want you to know that Mommy and Daddy will love you always!

Ronda Bolden

My Dear

When you say you're leaving me
Do you mean for now, or for eternity?!?!

Because if it is only for now,
Take out the garbage on your way down.

What do you mean, "I am cold and uncaring?"
Don't I let you run my errands?

Complain, complain if you like
Just think, who's sleeping on the couch tonight??!

Esan Ellis

Peace in the Snow Storm

In the middle of a blinding snow storm,
I find the ability to smile.
What were flashes of cold and fear,
Turn into a blanket of peace.

I stick out my tongue and taste the snow,
Its cold wetness in my warm mouth.
I absorb the cold air into my lungs,
I feel them push the dust out,
Letting the perfect peace of nature in.

Erynne Rice

The Spider

Dizzy spinning tangled filigree
Like the spider that reposes in my bathroom
who watches me with a thousand eyes
ravenously contemplating me
intensely glaring
he sees through me
cleaving me apart with his gaze
waiting in anticipation
for his prey
to become vulnerable at any moment
secretly, patiently
the sting of venom
luscious lethal poison,
the sweet affliction
As I lie dying, engulfed in a savorous sound
being devoured by his maimed kisses
he opens his enticing lips to speak
he murmurs, so softly, so seductively
"Come inside my mind," said the spider to the fly,
"You'll find nirvana inside here."

Carrie Winkler

One of Those People

There are people in this world that can
warm the hearts of others
Their happiness is genuine, their smiles sincere,
and their love shows in their actions
There are people in this life that light the way at midnight
They can dry tears with a smile, their ears are open,
and they always have room for one more person in their life.
At first glance they appear to be like everyone else,
but a second look reveals and extraordinary person
There are people in this world that can warm the hearts of others
You are one of those people, Tanya,
and I am blessed to have you in my life.

Terri Jerome

His Mighty Hand

He has His mighty hand in all we feel and say,
By His great example He shows us the way,
To be more like Him and to live with Him,
In our eternal home someday.

Although we may faultier and fall short of His eternal grace,
There is a way to get back to Him,
It is through faith and prayer.

Sometimes faith is hard to have,
When one never had faith before,
I wish that I had the faith to believe,
In the love that He has for me,
Then maybe I could see and know,
Of the great love He has for me,
By the touch of His mighty hand.

Terri Harb

Mon Ciel

Have you ever wondered
what was beyond
Those great, fluffy, marshmallows in the bright blue sky?
Beyond those clouds that were made by God and slowly sail by.
Have you ever thought what was beyond
Those crystals way up high? The ones thrown into the air at night
The ones that dance upon the midnight sky.
Beyond those crystals and those clouds,
You will find a place that cannot be described.
So mystical and free is this place up above
no worries, no fears, no frowns, no tears.
smiles all day, no harm comes this way.
One day this place that lives in my dream,
One day it will become a reality, c'est mon ciel
that is what it will be.

Monique N. Hill

Wondering . . .

Wondering why you let me walk away,
wondering why I left you standing astray

Wondering why you had no say,
knowing that our love could never stay.

Wondering why my love still true,
wondering why I still love you.

Wondering if our love was being laid to rest,
or if it was just being given a test.

Wondering if we should try again,
knowing we had many problems to mend
wondering if my love for you will ever end.

Wondering if we were meant for each other,
wondering if we should look for another.

Wondering why our love was torn apart,
wondering if it was even the reflection the start.

Wondering . . .

Danielle Chubbuck

Unspoken Love

Every night,
My mind and my heart get in a fight.
The breaking of my heart begins to be heard,
And it waits to be reassured.
Nothing comes and no one speaks,
And this goes on for weeks and weeks.
I drown myself in tears,
It feels like I've been waiting a hundred years.
I wait for the knock on my door,
Or the phone to ring. . . .
No one comes, nothing rings.
But still it seems like you're perfect in every way,
When you stride into school every single day.
Why won't you notice me?
How hard can it be? Don't you understand you're hurting me?
Then I feel something incredible and true,
I figure out . . . I'm in love with you.

Christina El Bayadi

War

Can't you see? People are bleeding,
Can't you see? People are hurt.
Why must we start things as ugly as war?
People are hurting, people are sore.
We say it's because they are different from us:
Religion, ideas, or just their outer crust.
And only because of this, things have to be unjust.
Stop this savageness, stop this violence, stop this blood-shed!
The children are listening, they are watching too.
Do you want us to live like this when we're grown up like you?
You think we will not understand just what is going on,
We're smarter than you think we are, this secretiveness is wrong.
Can't you see? People are dying.
Can't you see? People are dead.

Stephanie McLemore

Jesus Saves

Jesus saves . . .
Souls of despair; because he cares.
He saves the man on drugs;
He saves the woman who wants to give up.
He saves the teenage runaway;
Through his amazing grace.
Jesus saves the man standing on the corner;
Jesus saves the store owner.
Jesus saves the welfare mom;
Jesus saves the homeless person without a home.
Jesus saves the crack addicted;
The lame and the afflicted.
Jesus saves the car-jacker;
He saves the elderly attacker.
Jesus saves the robber and the thief;
Jesus can save you and me.
Jesus saves from the white house to your house;
Jesus saves without a doubt.

Cheryl Walls

Truth

God, be with me. He is, I'm sure.
He knows my every thought, my dreams, my silence.
My prayer is constant for His precious touch.
He will assure me, but for now, please,

Hear the words I say,
try to realize my sadness, the anguish, and rage.
Feel my tears, understand my pain.
I look toward truth, but there is no use.

Truth mirrors beauty; not so when declined.
Truth brings criticism, sarcasm, contempt.
To be chastised for truth is so common.
Why not just tell a lie?

Marjorie L. Allen

How Does Love Feel?

Having a party is sometimes hard,
but it just means a lot if you just send a card.
A special kiss, a gentle touch;
all these things can mean so much.
It feels like silk, and satin, and velvet.
It feels like a breeze, blowing across
the strings of a harp, it feels like a rainbow.
My feeling tells me God is love.

Glenn Donald Jackson

Losing the War

At night I cry, why don't they listen? Why don't they care?
My heart beats slower and slower.
Every time I close my eyes, tears fall one by one.
I could feel my blood circulation slow down.
My feet were getting numb and my face was turning purple.
Then I realized, I am losing the war.
I fight and struggle through the night,
Avoiding the chest pains and the headaches.
I cannot sleep, it all seems like a bad dream.
When I open my eyes the pain is still there.
When I dream, my dreams lead to one another.
The significance of the dreams, I do not understand.
But all I could feel was my heart beat in the palm of my hand.
I try hard to let go,
I try hard to survive,
I have no choice, but to let go.
I slowly close my eyes and smile . . .
I lost the war.

Alvaro D. Filardo

September

I remember it so well,
Your face crumpled and broken.
Your body limp and pathetic in
Quiet resignation.
In that moment the balance had shifted.
I was in control, should I have been jubilant and relieved?
Never, the power felt dirty in my hands.
I felt no pleasure, I could not revel in your pain.
My fear of you, and my love
Were transformed into pity.
I remember it so well,
You stood up and walked silently out;
No threats, no games.
You never pleaded, was that pride?
You said it was love, you said you loved me.
You said a lot of things,
But at that moment you were silent.
I understand you, I think I see it all now.
I see now, but the damage was already done.
I remember it so well.

Sarah Kelleher

Oh-Jay-Tee

Light rain cold enough, gray enough to bunch
tired shoulder muscles into ugly knots as tightly
drawn as the cluster of six child soldiers who hunch
together like early morning commuters
lured to the site of sudden asphalt death.
A solitary hand coldly withered and gray
lies at the stony edge of our riverbed
beckoning, or as a fleshy road sign pointing the way?
Lone scout darts from the ragged wrist
having performed a reconnaissance in depth.
Scout scurries along the gentle swell of vein,
exploring the saddle valley of twin knuckles.
A conquistador eyeing the grayness of terrain,
Meandering the slender length of peninsula,
staking claim now to the ring finger as its domain.

Michael Keleher

The Vaikuntha Man

A tribue to Srila Prabhupada (the founder of the Hare Krsna Society)
From the east he came on the Jaladuta,
His companions—Bhagavatam and Bhagavad Gita;
In his pocket barely a few paisa
But in his heart unwavering love for Krsna.
Behold the Vaikuntha Man!

The world he strode like a Colossus,
Making all and sundry Krsna-conscious.
First class mlecchas became Vaisnavas.
His limitless mercy knew no barriers.
Glorify the Vaikuntha Man!

Temples mushroomed wherever he went.
Not a single moment was misspent.
Hundreds of lost souls he reclaimed
Each and every day that he lived.
Praise the Vaikuntha Man!

We cannot repay him enough, by word or deed.
His greatest gift-the devotional seed
He beneficently planted in our hearts.
Honor him! Praise him! Offer him dandavats!
All glories to the Vaikuntha Man!

Adi Kavi Das (Motie Punai)

My True Self

My true self is like a light through
a leafy canopy.
It's limitless as water,
bright as the stars.
My true self is childlike in
every way,
My true self is something
no one can take away.
I'm a special person
deep down inside,
My personality is something I won't
try to hide
In front of fear,
I'm the face of love.
My inside's so beautiful,
It reaches beyond the
stars above.
I'm someone who's needy,
someone who cares,
someone who dreams and dares.
I'm somebody who truly will share all of my care.

Shameka Williamson

A Lost Friend

Deep in the night when I look at the sky,
I think of you and the years that gone by.
My face lights up as bright as a star,
And our days of fun don't seem so far.

I think of how your laughter was sweet,
And your sunny smile made me complete.
The look in your eyes was such a delight,
It made me smile on even this night.

I could never forget the times we had
Running and jumping in the sand.
I only wish that you were here,
To listen to my words and dry my tears.

It will never be the same without you around,
But someday we'll join and sit on a could.
Hand in hand, no one around, not a peep, nor'a sound.
The silence not broken until the day ends.
And then we'll go off just me and my friend.

Samantha Brinkey

Loma Verde

I know a young couple who live in the wood
  right at the top of the world.
Midst cathedrals of trees, and the humming of bees
  took a lonely old shack, with paint and much tact,
  with hard work and care, made a home of their own
  to love and to share.
Walking the land, axe in hand,
  eyes blue as the summer sea.
Splitting logs with one stroke, winter fires to stoke,
  a mighty Paul Bunyon is he.
Filling rooms with the rainbows she keeps in her crystals,
  sprinkling magic on pebbles and seeds.
With berries, and flowers, and blue antique glasses,
  a wise earthly lady this lass is.
Friends with the forest, friends to the beasts,
  but the greatest of friends are just he and she.
My heart warmed at their hearth, but sad to depart,
  embarked to the world far below.
An inner voice spoke "they'll never go broke,
  they're the richest people I know."

Jean La Rocca

Perfect Picturesque Performance

Practice, practice, practice
Is what they always say
But I become tired
Doing this every day

As the date draws nearer
So does our apprehension
We wonder if we're ready
For this presentation

Only one away
And we've begun to fret
For messing up would be something
That we would all regret

Our music has begun
For today is the day
We have worked hard enough
So now is the time to play

They are all congratulating us
Saying we shone like a star's ray
Telling us we looked like wonderful ballerinas
In the full length ballet

Erin Joy Muckey

A New World

As I look, moving skies before me,
As I see, blue seas shifting, making waves,
As I feel the Earth moving in different directions
New tongues speak to me in harmony

A new world evolves around a beautiful rose
ready to bloom in a strange land

As I feel the move of a child in a mother's womb
As I hear the cry of unspoken words from a child
As I touch the tears of a blessed child to
come into this world, to say the words I love
For the very first time

A new world evolves around a beautiful rose,
ready to bloom in a strange land

As I look, moving skies before me
As I see blue seas shifting, making waves
As I feel the Earth moving in different directions
New tongues speak to me in harmony

Hector M. Rivera

The Lament of August

The month of August is my name,
Such treatment extended, 'tis an awful shame.
Eleven of my "relatives" all have an event,
Alas, poor me, my patience is spent.

Starting in January and on to December
There's so many feasts, it's hard to remember,
For I, alone, am the one forsaken
Now you see why my feelings have shaken.

Maybe someday, my August days
Will enjoy the light of the festive rays,
When some honored person or historic affair
May land in the fold of my monthly lair

Gerald A. Quinn

Motives

Take me away from all that is pain,
And into my life you will bring joy.
Let's share love in one domain,
To prove no intent of a ploy.

This love I feel is frightening to me,
For I know not from whence it came.
Is it real or just a passing novelty?
Are your feelings different or are they the same?

I request of you to assure the confidence I need,
That the love you voiced is true
Show there is no intent of lust and greed,
And my heart and soul will belong to you.

To love me means all of me,
Including my flaws, many or in few.
And never question my feelings for thee,
For I love you, my darling, I do.

Eunice Walker

Seasons of Joy

Summer breezes gently blow
Forgotten is the winter snow
Next comes the April showers
They bring the beautiful May flowers
Then comes the fall when the leaves turn color
You go for evening walks with that feller
On picnics you go to the park
You stay late 'til almost dark
Then comes winter all dark and grey
A little longer the days would with you stay
Next comes the Christmas tree
And all the pretty lights to see
Summer breezes gently blow
Forgotten is the winter snow.

Dollie E. Spencer

Friends Forever

Take your sunshine where you go,
Brighten someone's day with what you know.
Always remember friends with your heart
While leaving space for new friendships to start.
Keep a smile upon your face,
Lend an ear with amazing grace.
Everything you do or say,
Show kindness every day.

Changes come, you know it's true.
Greet each with a smile, try not to be blue.
Always remember the goodness you've spread.
Then, only a few tears will have to be shed.
Revive good thoughts and feelings at night,
You'll feel better with morning's first light.
Ending old friendships can never be done,
'Cause memories keep us together each and every one.

Linda Knapp

Christmas Again

It's mid December and the days are few.
Everyone has so much to do.
Start in the morning and work into the night.
Wrapping those packages; gotta get that bow just right.

"Why do we do this?" we say year after year.
Why do we wait knowing Christmas is near?
Everything looks so pretty every color it would seem.
If only we'd spend more time on what it does mean.

The red is the blood that Jesus shed for our sin.
Think of where you're going, not where you've been.
The virgin birth is the reason for white.
Start today and get your life right.

Jesus is our comforter and comfort means blue.
When life gets tough ask him what to do.
Our God is a jealous God, and jealous is green.
Putting him above all things is what that means.

The candy cane is the shape of a staff or a J—
Stands for the Good Shepherd is why it's made that way.
There's so many little reminders as we go day to day.
So when we put away our decorations, Don't pack Jesus away.

Doris Buzan

I Would If I Could

I would if I could
But I can't so I won't
So please, oh, please forgive me
Even if I don't.

But even if I ever could
I wouldn't so I can't.
I would have if I hadn't said,
"I won't, I shouldn't, I shan't!"

But if I say, "I shouldn't,"
It really means, "I don't."
And if I say, "I couldn't,"
It means I really won't.

So, if someone says, "I would if I could,
I cannot so I won't."
And when they say, "Forgive me please."
What you should do is . . . don't!

Jon David Griffin

Universally Almost

Old West End,
political rhetoric runs rampant,
social consciousness
capped under a gilded cathedral steeple.

Dirty dark-skinned wino
sitting on the front steps,
this is not your home; this is an universal house of God!
Bums need not apply.

Revitalization?
Nothing more than a white suburbanite word
that severely lacks results.

Urban dwellers,
just board your city-provided bus
and bear your dead happy face.

You people, you Mad Dog slinging lunatics
were never meant to cross our tower's ivory truss,
to drink Jesus's blood from our golden chalice anyway.

Our wine's worth a hell of a lot more than
some panhandler's pocket change;
it's sacred for chrissake!

Kristopher Ewald

I'll Never Go Back That Way

With a sharpened pencil and clouded head,
I still do love you more than I life I led,
Because I really never go back that way!
Q. What way? You say?
A. Well I started my day with a 40 bag on my tray,
a cup of bitter coffee and I would be on my way!
A call or two to make some more hang ups,
and then I'm out the door!
And then, some time later, I'd be back
To find you waiting to see what was in store!

Then, I would say not much as I filled my pipe with some more,
As I did you would say ok, it's all right, because you were so kind,
And loved me so, you didn't mind.
And now, look at me, I'm the fool who misses you,
and finally I can see who was really cruel to you,
it was me! And that's why I'll still say:
I'll never go back that way!

Kenneth Marino

Silence

I close my eyes and visualize
Rainbows all around me.
I smell the air and the ocean out there . . .
Roses with a velvet touch.
I hear only silence, sweet and quiet.
Behind my eyes I can see . . .
Blue skies and fluffy clouds.
I touch the golden hue of Life . . .
And try to take things in stride.
Silence all around me . . .
And rainbows behind my eyes . . .
Inside of me.
I am colorful and bold
Wanting to hold
Onto what I feel.
Silence so sweet, quiet, and pure . . .
No noise or unhappiness just peace.
I close my eyes and shut out the world . . .
I breathe deeply and pray for another day.
Rainbows and roses and golden hues . . .
I see them with my eyes closed.

Sheila Shiel

My Dearest Wife

I come to you with my heart laid bare,
So you may know the love that's there,
And I want very much for you to see,
Not just what I am, but what I'd like to be

I would like to be your prince charming,
To always have a smile disarming,
Every day, ever gay, ever glad, never sad,
The best companion a wife ever had.

I would like to be your shining star,
A comfort even though clouds should mar
An occasional evening now and then,
But with the clearing, to shine again.

I would like to be your ideal,
The secret to your every appeal
No matter whatever it might be,
I wish the answer to always be me.

Darling, I want very much for you to know,
That my love for you shall forever grow,
And if I never seem to meet the test,
I wish for you my love, eternal happiness.

Charles H. Tillson

A Symbol of Love

John, a symbol of love
Who lived a life of love.
Popular by demand
From charity in voice and hand.

Trying to right the wrongs
In a world of unknown songs.
Wanting to unite
Those divided by life's strife.

Finding humor in adversity.
Smoothing the path of diversity.
Always offering a helping hand,
Sometimes not knowing the worth of the command.

A life filled with blessings,
Tendered with Christ's hand.
To know, love, and serve
Was the ideal goal of this love-filled man.

Cynthia L. Desrosiers

Butterflies in Flight

One day I awoke to see that I had wings.
Wings of glorious color that glittered and shine in the light,
I see now that I am the wings,
The color, the shining, in the bright light ahead.
For my soul now has wings and I can fly!
I am a butterfly in flight, free to be.

Natalie Smith Blakeslee

The Fear

This brother for me became a nightmare in the flesh
A living, breathing demon
You see, my fear was so real,
that it destroyed my thought process
I was afraid of him because he was what I wasn't
He was the brother the woman I loved longed to have
Not in the flesh, but in his ways.
The educated brother he frightened me
Because he already was that I wished to be.
Born on the other side of the tracks,
none of the monkeys I had on my back
He spoke to my love in ways I lacked
I search for a reason, but too no avail,
you see, when I saw him I saw where I'd failed.
The fear of that brother just should not be.
Because an educated brother could have been me.

Antonio C. Hill

Am I to Blame

Am I to blame, when you set my heart aflame
Your tender loving touch leaves me spellbound
and in your clutch.

When your eyes hold mine, love bells chime.
And my heart beats, at a quicker pace, and I long
for your sweet embrace.

When your lips crush mine, they are laced with wine.
I experience a love so strong,
I know with you, my heart and love belong.

What is this power, of love and desire,
that burns and sets my heart afire.

I know no shame, am I to blame.
Am I to blame.

Elizabeth Myra Crellin

Grandmother's Love

The love of a grandmother is strong and true.
How much she provides for me and you.
She has touched our hearts
in a way that can't be explained,
She will always be with us each and every day.
The pain and suffering she has experienced on this Earth
will go away and will no longer hurt.
When God reaches down and takes her home,
the love for our grandmother will be known.

Perry Ray Oakley II

Prison Window with a View

I used to have a window
Yes it was dirty and small
My window was in my eight by four Prison cell
People think it's a living hell
I say, oh well
Got used to the smell of rats and Lysol
Tasteless cold food and drugs
Were in every cell
No one lost sight of their loved ones at home
Because, you see, here
We are all drones
There's always someone tougher than you
So you keep your cool and try to make it through
But deep down we are lonely and lazy
Waiting for the eternal Daisy

Matthew Cvelich

A Laughing Game

Mothers talk of house and home
of all their troubles a whole day long.
Of Sue and Junior and their feverish ways,
and how to get them to run and play.
If their remedies do not work,
it's off to the office for the doctor's touch.
All though the needle gave them pain,
it also gave them a laughing game.

Quillian Gunn Sr.

Far Away

I feel far away, far away from you.
To you I am displayed as an imperfection
That holds an addiction to use you.
To you, I am an illusion, an illusion is what I am.
When in all actuality I am a formation of you.
To you, this is what you see, you see what you hear.
I know you hear me
But you understand my feelings is my biggest fear:
To you, I look dirty, dirty with lies.
The lies I have shown are able to hide my feelings far away,
Far away from you.

Patty Rose Hooser

The Fruit of Reading

Reading is but fruit for the soul.
Without it you can never be whole.
Reading like fruit ripens with age.
It livens your soul through each page.
It wheels your thoughts and imagination.
Sometimes to read on is temptation.

Reading takes us to many lands.
It shows us different colored hands.
And how those hands build a way
For everyone to read this day.
Though some are deaf or blind.
Through the people who are so kind
We made a way for people to read.
For the fruit will grow no matter the breed.

Ashley Carswell

I Am a Filipino American

I am a Filipino American
In me throbs the best of two cultures, the best of two worlds.

To this distant foreign land
My parents bravely came
With willing hands, stalwart hearts, and indomitable spirit.

In this "Land of the Free and Home of the Brave"
They've toiled and struggled
To help me gain another heritage,
My American heritage of education, success, freedom,
and the pursuit of happiness.

I am proud to be a Filipino American.
I cherish the past, yet live in the present and for the future,
With strong faith and abiding Divine Providence
The best years are yet to come!
Mabuhay! Long Live!

> *Merlie F. Guerrero*

Memories out My Window of Life

A long string of things are hanging in my mind
Forming to show emotion for everything there.
My thoughts within are demanding and the voices will not be quiet
Huge options and opinions don't matter
Only one way is direct and once there you cannot go back.
Mistakes will be made for that is life.
How boring it would be to not ever make a mistake.
Jumbling sounds and forgotten memories come back
Every now and then, but the truth is the only,
Out my window I only see massive clouds
Projecting the lonely sky. A sea of calm and humanity.
The mystery takes us to another fate.
I wonder who the sky will focus on
Thunderbolts and clouds, the good and bad combined.
It always makes me wonder.

> *Kim Millard*

Broken

In the beginning nothing mattered
In the middle things were torn apart
In the end only pieces remained
An image I cannot shake
Whether it haunts me or
Is a blessing that I have not yet found
And in the absence of conscience
I collapse in the hollow of my soul
In darkness and deceit I hide the pain
In the shallows an emptiness overcomes
In the daylight it shines too bright
In the twilight it fades away
A macabre dance of fate
A changing tide of insolence
Tempered by a sinking ship denying distress
Exonerated by an alienated idea
An age old lie of honesty and respect
An age old truth of heartache
All encompassed and covered by one thing,
   My heart and it's broken.

> *Jason McRae*

i see

i see myself in the mirror
i see a girl that looks awful
i see pain in her eyes
i see her mom and dad
i see one broken heart
i see a girl who has tried to live a hard life
i see her getting marred and not making it
i see her running and running
i see her now in heaven with god
and she is happy walking with him

> *Mallory MacDonald*

At First Impressed

A glimpse, a glance
A glimmer, a glare
What is behind the face that you wear?

When stripped away, what remains?
Feast, famine, joy, or pain?

Polished, shined, brushed, and groomed
Making a statement from across the room.

What do I see?
What do I sense?
Are you the frog?
Are you the prince?

Come a little closer
So I can look into your eye
To see inside
This mannequin guy.

Where does the plastic stop?
Where does the soul begin?
If at first you don't impress, try, try again.

> *Janel Whitney*

Mirror on the Porch

It stands atop a wooden dresser
abandoned long ago.
A blinding radiance rebounding off a shimmering surface
as an automobile glides past.

Reflections of people, birds, trees
are captured and absorbed.
Its share of snared impressions stowed away
like so many secrets never to be discovered.

Or does it stand alone as a gateway
to an unknown path
taking in those unaware counterparts
replacing them in a brilliant flash.

It captured my likeness once
as if in a snapshot. I cannot help
but wonder if it saved a part of me
or if a part of me has begun another journey.

> *Denise Asuncion*

My Wish

Whilst in the midst of Heaven and Hell
I wait alone for the ring of the bell
This bell will save me from this life;
this life of hate, hate and strife
My heart can feel it, it's just so close
I just can't grasp it, an invisible rose
Just one word, one breath or caress
will save me from hell's harness,
yet I'm stuck alone forever
This hell is dark; the cord won't sever
I cry each night, myself to sleep
Off to dream, but I wake to weep
I fear my love will never be real
I feel it inside me, but I can't feel
his arms around me holding me tight
This is my wish when the sun makes it light

> *Tish Phillips*

My Vanished Friend

In this small town I had a friend,
Who lived just up the street, around a bend.
He was diagnosed in May of '95,
With a disease which no one has survived.

In the beginning, I would stop to see him once and awhile,
No matter how hard it was, he would always put on a smile.
The days went by and weeks rushed on,
And before I knew it, another year was gone.

I knew my friend was home alone dying,
I was just so busy, busy doing nothing!!
Our lives move so incredibly fast,
I really should have stopped and reflected on my past!

Why didn't I stop in to see him as much?
Why when my friend got sick, It seemed I just lost touch,
We get so wrapped up with our lives every day,
That we forget about what's really important anyway!

Tomorrow I would say, I will stop in to see my friend
Just to show that I'm thinking of him.
But tomorrow would come and tomorrow would go, and
That distance between us would grow and grow.

Just up the street! Yet so far away,
I got this Voice Mail Message, That Steve died today.
I realize now, that it's too late in the end,
To stop by and visit my VANISHED FRIEND.

Stephen Reding

SUPERWOMAN Unleashed,
like All the Other Superheroes

She took it off—
the leash, the cape, the Spandex suit.

SUPERWOMAN is unleashed.
She wears jeans now and ratty T-shirts,
like all the other superheroes.
No more comic adventures of saving the world from evil,
she is partaking in action of the reality,
like all the other superheroes,
playing mother, father, holy Mary, and sinner,
like all the other superheroes.
She gave up her mission, her SUPERWOMAN badge,
and saved herself.

SUPERWOMAN is just known as superwoman now,
and for her that is the greatest honor of all.

Emily Cannon

Asphyxiation

Sickening sunlight shimmers on semi-sepulchral Earth,
revealing images strange of death and birth.
An old man slumps among twisted scars of rumination,
bleeding Dettol-scars and hesitation.
As I lay me down upon the ground
struggling with fears lost and found
I embraced with a metallic kiss my fear
and held her to me close and dear.
I am lost on symbolism,
filled with hate and socialism.
Standing staring alone at the barren blue
washing line like a stain in my mind,
I scattered my ashes to the wind
and overflowed with rage 'til I was blind.
And when at last I spoke,
pressed in by my skin,
my voice was old,
my soul anemic and strangely thin . . .

O tell me—where did I stop and this begin?

Ugen Vos

I AM SCI-FI POEM

I want to travel to the outer limits where another world live.
I want to see how the world will be in the year 3000.
I want to see the new age of education
and see the new computer age take over the world.
I want to see the new age of the automobile that run on energy.
I want to see the new aged of the video games.
I want to see the world come together to accept all people
and see racist views disappear into the night.
I want to see the new leaders make more programs
to assist the needy and produce higher paying jobs.
I want to travel to a time where war will not be the answer—
where killing in war will be against the law.
I want to travel to a time where these things will be possible.
I am sci-fi.

Lee Sharkey

Self-Acceptance

Awakened to reality, as if a long dream,
I opened my eyes and wanted to scream.
The scenes all around were familiar to me
Except for the happiness and pride I now see.
Who was this person? Where did she go?
I, bare as a tree after a long winter's snow,
No sight of regrets of the past,
No fear of tomorrow,
No tears shed from loneliness or sorrow;
Dreams she once had of love, wealth and fame,
Had diminished to nothing, along with the shame.
As I pondered in amazement, I looked in the mirror.
The image before me was perfectly clear.
The outward appearance was me all along;
Yet this woman before me was inwardly strong.
As I stared closely, within her, I could see.
Acceptance had won and, at last, I was free.

Cynthia Allen

True

We're falling away, closer but further
Listlessly floating, I cannot seem truer
We can shallowly hear it but not for too long
Soon it will crumble and no longer be in song
Still, though falling, it will never subside
Only stay steady dropping and eventually collide
I see the grey so clear in my path
How can this be all so heavily in my grasp
Free yet isolated I go on
Fleeing out of my conscience it's only a game
The game of regret, rejection, and other ways of shame

Heather Dowd

A Poem in a Thought

The deepest of my emotions
It pours into the open
It brings about a challenge
Of being totally free
I quench the thirst of thought
I wallow in my feelings
Will I embrace what I have created
My thoughts will come out in a poem
If I could scatter the world with the words in my thoughts
You would walk on poetry daily
The pencil is my eyes
I see only lines
But my thoughts lie within a poem

Anthony Jackson

"Love at First Sight"

I was walking through the park one day,
When a handsome man came my way,
And, suddenly, he said to me, "How do you do?"

I answered, "Fine, and you?"
And we talked for another minute or two
About things which had no meaning at the time.

His hair was dark, dark as night,
And glistened in the morning light.
His eyes, like the sea were bright and blue,
And it was at this moment that I knew
What I had been waiting for all of my life.

Now some may say, "Oh, this isn't real,"
But in my heart I know what I feel,
And whether it is wrong or right,
I do believe it was love at first sight.

Rebecca Mccorkle

Circles of Life

Everything that you do, it always comes back to you.
Everything that you see, it all returns eventually.
That's the way with the circles of life, sometimes it hurts,
sometimes it cuts like a knife.
As those circles they spin around,
everything that goes up must come down
to reality to stop and see,
that everything works so easily.
Treat others how you would treat yourself,
good karma will come and nothing else.
Put others down and you will see,
your life turn into misery.
We must understand that we are all one,
we are all one beneath the sun.
Everything in life we can't always see,
but the circles are always circling you and me.
Don't wait until the end to stop and see
that everything returns eventually,
into those circles.

Russell Hunter

(no title)

I sit
    I dream
what is it like
where you are?

do you feel pain
do you feel pleasure?

can you smell the flowers
    can you feel the breeze against your cheek
    can you see far
do you touch ground when you walk?

do you still dream?

Marian Lockett

Wedding Day Bookmark

Today marks the start of our new life together,
A day we will cherish in memory, forever.
And just as the petals of a rose must unfold,
Our future is yet a story untold.
A book yet unfinished, a new chapter to start;
In both past and present, you have written a part.
For our lives are based on the love you have shared,
The time you have given, the ways that you cared.
And so, as the rose fades and dawn becomes dusk,
And today's page in time turns for each one of us,
We pause for a moment the pen in Time's hand,
To remember our Wedding Day, ever so grand!
And we ask for God's blessing to be sent from above
To bless all Friends and Family, forever, with Love.

Kathy Hula

When the Wind Whispers through the Trees

Every day, either good or bad,
There is a time of complete silence.

The wind stops moving and everything becomes very still.

Then when you think nothing is going to happen,
The wind starts to blow.

It starts off so soft that you can hardly feel it.

Then, it grows and grows until he wind engulfs you
And you hear the whispering.

It's a peaceful whisper that says
Everything will be okay on the bad days
And that everything is great on the good days.

I know that every day I will feel the wind
And hear the whispering, on Earth and in Heaven.

So now, I always know that if I have nothing,
I have the wind whispering through the trees.

Monica Libhart

Sitting Alone

When sitting alone, I keep myself company.
Thoughts of remembrance flowing through my mind.
On the bench outside I sit, deep thinking leads me to forget.
Forget where I am, forget where I am going.

I remember that last Saturday night.
That night of laughter, that night of regret.
That night you said you loved me.
That conversation that changed my thoughts on life.
Never to forget that puzzling phrase.
"When I think of you I am speechless"
If only you knew how much I cared, but it was too late.
You fell for someone else.
Hanging up the phone with sadness, I remember what I said.
"I can't believe I let you go."

Drifting away from it all as someone speaks.
Harsh reality overcomes my innocent fantasies.
I let out a long sigh and I realize I'm back on that bench.
That bench where I always sit and relive those painful memories.
Those painful memories that I will always remember.
Those painful memories that he will soon forget.

Beth Gold

My World

Late at night when it's silent, and there's not a single sound
That's when I can hear your loving heart slowly pound
Snuggled up beside you, wanting to hold you so very tight
Oh, how I wish that sometimes, it could be forever night

Laying there beside you, thinking of all the things we share
Knowing I can always come to you with my every care
You don't have to tell me, that you're forever to me be true
I can tell it all, in the little things you do

Little things like a smile, or the simple little touch of your hand
Means more to me than a thousand wedding bands
I've just got to tell you, that you've got the cutest ever smile
I'd do anything for you, even walk a thousand miles

When things in my life are not going just quiet right
When I can't see an ending to it in sight
I know I can come to you, and you'll always be there
Ready to comfort me, and all my troubles share

I just had to let you know how I felt
And that with one look, you can make my heart melt
So remember darling, that you're the whole world to me
And I hope that you will forever be

Sadie Hector

My Life as a Cat

My life as a cat,
Is very simple in fact.
I'll tell you right know,
If you give me a snack.

The first thing I want to do,
Is lie down and sleep on you.
When you watch T.V DON'T leave the remote down,
'Cause I'll change it to the dating service for cats right know.

People think dogs are fun,
But I find them dumb.
Go to the pet store, get a cat,
If you get a dog it will break your new hat.

That's my life as a cat
See it's very simple in fact.

Ariella Nudell, age 9

Winter

Winter's so pretty, what a beautiful state,
All of the snow falling down to its fate.

Everything's gleaming looking real fine,
it must be near winter, it looks like that time.

The wind howls a song as it blows with the breeze,
Everything's happy even the trees.

The snow piles up as it falls to the ground,
Making a white wonderland without uttering a sound.

Justyn Lee

God Needed Another Angel

*In loving memory of Kimberly Ann Fountain,
May 10, 1955-Sep 14,1998*
God needed another angel,
Someone HE knew would care.
Someone who thought of others first,
And when needed, always there.

So HE watched you from Heaven, friend,
Saw your laughter and your love.
Though much appreciated here on Earth
With us, HE needed you much more above.

Never will you be forgotten, friend,
By those whose lives you have touched.
These are selfish tears we shed for you,
As we shall miss you very much.

In anger we all have asked God, "Why?"
The answer quite simple in the end,
As God needed another angel and,
HE wisely chose you, Dear Friend.

Just as you were loved, so shall you be missed.

Kate Bermond

Before

Before you, I was never lonely
I casually enjoyed the company of others
I delighted in my own.
My days were filled with the joy of song;
And each day brought an interesting bit of
    knowledge
An unexpected kindness
Poetry, Beauty, and Light.
Before you
I did not know how lonely I was.

Gina Noel D'Ambrosio

My Love for You

You're the laughter,
That comes from my lips,
The ones that can't wait for your passionate kiss.
You're the sparkle that gleams in my eye.
It appears whenever you're close by.
You're the shiver that runs up my spine.
Whenever you touch me or say you're All Mine,
Now there's no laughter, sparkle or shiver to be found.
You took them with you when you left town.
I feel dead, with all these missing parts.
There's nothing left, inside my aching heart.
Without you, there's no future I can see.
If only you'd given us a chance and trusted me.
You've got the best of me there with you,
I couldn't get it back, even if I wanted to.
And if you should say you're no longer mine.
I'd still be forever yours until the end of time.
You're stuck with me, sad but true.
My Forever love, no matter what you do.
I know you don't understand how I can,
But how could I not love such a man?
And last of all,
Please never forget,
It's been the biggest part of me since the day we met.
I am so in love with you.

Daisy Webberding

Sunshine and Coffee

You once filled my days,
with sunshine and coffee,
now, alone in the darkness
I'm flooded with memories of your laughter,
of our long walks under a timeless sky,
and sharing secrets,
that only we could smile at
Moments we made together,
never seemed to last long enough
but now I suffocate in the simplicity of
your smile, and the intensity of your eyes,
Against the will of others,
I can't seem to even begin to forget,
that only by memory,
do I trace the light of your soul,
and only by heart,
do I hear your soft voice and feel your tender kisses,
When I dream, when I sleep,when my weary eyes open,
    I wish for just one more moment,
        with your bittersweet smile.

Erin Wollinger

What Transition Sees . . .

old ways to new ways—legacy to web;
we grow and we age
or we die, oh, so slow.
once immortal, now wounded,
we strive to survive;
some fail while some fall
and some try not at all.
Yet death pales to my memories
of life and its living,
struggles and of giving.
Experience teaches hard lessons
of life as it's dying;
our climbing slows,
some fall while some fail;
as we reached for our stars,
the twinkle now gone,
we look up again to regain our way,
we see our souls—they're just farther away.

Roland Aucoin

Growing Up

When I grow up I will be glad
'Cause my brother won't be there to make me mad
Parents can sometimes wreck your dreams
But when you're a grown-up you can eat ice cream
God can help you on your challenging way
If you let Him in your heart to stay
Now it's time to go outside and play
Worry about growing up another day

Devon Laanstra

Heart

Heart, I am denying you of an unselfish love.
I wade among still waters as not to drown.
I scamper from the unknown with a gnawing fear.
I harbor the darkness for a time of self preservation.
I hold the key to the caged freedom of preservation.
Heart, pain has tolerated your total endurance.
I cannot trust you to anyone 'til I am sure.
Have patience with my denial for the present.
Time will release the moment for the extradition of the key.

E. Bran

Planet

I could hear her heartbeat when she is close to me
I could feel her warmth from a thousand miles away
When she smiles the heavens open their gates
Her voice is sweet as the sound of a mountain spring
I want to hold her, kiss her, and love her
I run to her when I am feeling down
I come to her when the morning sounds
She takes away my troubles
She eases away my fears
I simply fall to sleep
I want to hold her, kiss her, and love her
Every moment I close my eyes I can feel the pain
Every time I am with her the sun shines through the rain
Her beauty is forever a flower
Her fine sense of humor is a gentle laughter
She is beneath the velvet sky
She is always the Planet in my eyes
I want to hold her, kiss her, and love her

Earl See

Memories of a Military Childhood

My hometown was nowhere, yet it was everywhere.
Home was where the heart and family were,
station, fort, base,
with no dependence on a dwelling.

Some have wondered if I had roots, yet they were deep.
Sinking quickly and holding as a mighty oak,
adapting, stretching, forming,
letting me enrich the country landscape.

I never grew up with someone, yet matured with many.
Friendships formed in hours that lasted decades,
sergeant, captain, chief,
children sharing the universe's pathways.

Farewells came often, yet sorrow gave me strength.
With a constant hope of meeting again,
Europe, America, Pacific,
venturing half a world away.

So many changes in my life, yet such a rich heritage.
To know I was educated in the world's school,
geography, finance, politics,
teachers of all accents and nationality.
I shook the hands of brotherhood, yet remembered "old glory."
Pride of the American flag hung at every site,
reveille, alert, taps,
a love of soldiers, especially my dad.

Karen Kambestad

What Is the Purpose . . .

Have you ever laid awake at night
wondering why we are here?
What is the purpose, the meaning
or the unknown that we fear?
We see the beauty of life like majestic
mountains and steel blue seas,
but also the sadness of wars, earthquakes
and incurable disease.
Sometimes we feel like we're part of a big
game of chance
that decides who'll be happy, sad, or
be in the last dance.
All I know is that God is with us and
he must have a plan,
it could change daily like the wind or
drifting sand.
Say a prayer, love your neighbor, live
every day as your last,
and you shall be happy and these
questions will pass.

Randy Vonnahme

The Key of Peace

Sometimes when I soak my feet in the cool calm stream of memories
I feel it's beauty, its kindness.
I bathe in the shade of the tree of dreams
and hear the winds of understanding whisper,
"You are someone special, a fine man molded into a rightful owner
of The Key of Peace."
That dream always was my favorite.
It did always end the same though,
with an awakening into the real.
Into the arena of the painfully obvious to once again face
the mightiest enemy I have ever known—myself.
Created by the one before me
(whom I do resemble greatly).
Not molded—built.
Dr. Frankenstein would be impressed, to say the very least.
I am the heir to hatred and anger.
Baptized in the cathedral of emptiness.
I do have choices, they say.
I'm all grown up now and I have choices.
I CHOOSE beauty, I CHOOSE love,
I need the stream, the tree.
I need the winds of understanding.
Unfortunately "x" doesn't mark the spot I thought I was there,
I took the wrong road and my key is not here.

Dominic Hines

"In His Hands"

When I wake up to the sunshine
I can see your smile,
The beauty of the night dusk . . .
I remember for a while
When you would wake up in the morning,
And come and lay down at my feet . . .
We would talk and laugh, and start our day
Making plans we may not keep.
We would joke and chuckle about everything,
Sometimes we would even cry
Your goals and dreams where are they now?
Why did you have to say "good-bye?"
It wasn't time for you to leave . . .
What Godly reason could it be?
You were only 21 years old
Why couldn't he have taken me?
I'll be with you again someday,
I know it's in God's plans . . .
I'll say my prayers, and hold my dream,
We'll keep it in "HIS" hands.

Anna Nash

Growing Up

A little boy who runs and plays,
Full of hope and joy.
"Sit down, Shut up!" The father calls.
Mom pleads, "Be a good boy."
He calls attention to all he sees as new.
"Don't interrupt, don't chat so much!"
His father sets a rule.
"Be quiet, eat your Captain Crunch."
Then sends him off to school.
And when his grades are less then A's,
His parents both reply,
"What's wrong with you? Are you stupid?
Don't you even try?"
And as the years go by,
His face begins to change.
The smiles are replaced,
By empty looks of pain.
"He's looking like a man now!"
His father says proudly enough.
"Yes," agrees the mother, "He's all grown up."

Candi Hutchins

Bedtime Stories

It's ten p.m. and the lights are out.
It's time for my bedtime story.
I dial his number by heart, and smile.
His voice is deeply soft and soothing,
as he sweetly asks me about my day.

He listens patiently to every detail,
every funny story, every small worry.
Then it is my turn to ask him about his,
and listen to him as best friends do.

Night after night, we talked to each other.
We sang songs to each other, laughed together,
and cried together, had deep discussions,
and silly moments as all best friends do. . . .

Three years have passed now, and today
I looked up his number and dialed it,
hoping to talk to him as I often did before.
But disappointed, I left a message again,
for what seemed to be the hundredth time.

Samantha Huang

Secrets

The paint brush soars across the sky
Revealing secrets before my eyes.
The kind of secrets you need not hear
For the whispers are seen loud and clear.
Unknown treasures glisten at night.
Within all the darkness, I see the light.
I watch the stars dance with the moon
As I witness the clouds play a snappy tune.
I gaze at these three amazements
As they once more reunite.
I suppose we'll meet again,
come some other night.

Stacey Bateman

The Birdish Joy

I used to fly above the city streets
And touch the branches and the tops of trees
When golden sunrise burned ethereal fuel
And mad birds cried their hearts away, when cruel
And law-abiding citizens were making
Their peace before the Hell would break in.
Our birdish joy did not disturb their soul,
Which also did not trouble us at all.

Alexander Koudlai

life—a mystery, a story?

there is so much to say
   so much to think
but no way to express it

life's great
but yet sometimes so blank
it has so much to offer
but how much does one get?

life's a mystery, a story
all at once
but how many can solve it
how many can read it

yet this is life
so precious for the crown and glory of all creations

life

Yashmita Marwah

Wait for Me

Wait for me when your sorrow is deep,
Wait for me when your soul is asleep.
Wait for me when your heart is scorned,
Wait for me when hope seems forlorn.

Wait for me when the sun is high,
Wait for me when the weather is dry.
Wait for me when the rain starts falling,
Wait for me when the winds come calling.

Wait for me when your days grow old,
Wait for me when your nights turn cold.
Wait for me while you work through the day,
Wait for me when you have nothing to say.

Wait for me when you are red with passion,
Wait for me in medieval fashion.
Wait for me with ease and grace,
Wait for me with your beautiful face.

Wait for me when you want to flee,
For in the end, you and I will know,
Because you waited,
You saved me.

David Doerries

The Gift

He came to us as a gift sent from Heaven.
Eyes as blue as the sky,
hair the color of sun,
a smile that made your day,
a warm embrace that chased tears away.
His laughter made us smile,
his tears made us cry.
A heart made of gold.
We were blessed to have him,
even for a short while.
He was so special, Lord needed him back.
He walks with Jesus,
looking upon us with love.
Knowing our pain, feeling our loss,
Wishing us happiness and tears of joy.
"Don't cry for me," he says to us.
He is happy, for eternal life is his.
He feels no pain, he never will.
Now he is our Angel, forever more,
Guiding us until we again meet face to face.

Michaela Blaydes

To an Angel

I take your hand and you lead me
Where we are going I am unsure
I only know that I trust you
Because I love you
And I am happy
In your arms
Until with a start I awake from my sleep
Only to find that your image was not reality
It was a broken dream
Shattered when you flew away
Your wings opening in the sky
Your lips smiling as if everything was okay
But you left me behind
And everything was not okay

Lisa Finney

The Bet

Nothing more than a man,
yet so far from a god.
I see the world through eyes that have lived.
So many things I would have changed,
yet so many I would never trade.
The risks I took,
the chances I left,
nothing more then forgotton memories.
They tell me to move on,
to come out of the past.
For them, them, the ones I hate.
They are so sure of the future and know what it is.
I know not what it holds, so I fear it.
Why leave my life to fate,
when I can dwell on happier days?
The price they may pay will be great,
the reward so small.
The risk I'll never take,
the bet I'll never deal.
Tomorrow.

Michael McClure

Dew

Morning has come, the night is at end
The dew has set to dry again.
The morning has gone, the noon is in place
The hours towards evening do race.
Midday soon left, bringing evening to us here
Giving those of the night something to cheer.
Those who were early to rise are now quick to set
Those late to rise see the day has not gone yet.
The night grows young as the day grows old
The evening course my eyes behold.
There is fun to be had and stories to be heard
The night life is forever and troubled to be stirred.
But the night drags on to a close again
So the dew may set to dry again.

Brian Koenig

The Best Friend I Never Met (My Grandpa)

I might never have met you,
but I can imagine in my dreams,
what your soft touch feels like,
so wonderful it seems.
From your wonderful wisdom
to your friendship so great,
when we'd make an event
you would never be late.
When I was little I felt something wrong,
like that thing was lost for so very long.
But you are still alive in my heart,
you will always be with me
although we're apart.

Amber Russell

Dreams

Don't you hate it when your parents tuck you in to say good night
And tell you not to let the bed bugs bite?
How come they don't know what comes at night?
All the little things that make you shriek with fright.

Most kids call them bad,
And all the joy you had
Will soon disappear,
And you'll be left with fear.

Some dreams can be good;
They really, really could.
So just jump in bed
And cover up your head.

Jamie Hudacko

Peace

The Sun slowly peeks over the horizon
Awakening the Earth with a warm kiss.
The vibrant petals of flowers unfold,
The dew glistening on their emerald leaves.
The trees stretch gracefully to feel the warmth,
Rustling ever so softly in the gentle breeze.

Every dawn of every glorious day, for countless years
The sun, undauntingly, lovingly repeats this performance
Gently stirring the Earth from its peaceful slumber.
LISTEN!
Listen to the birds singing in harmony.
LISTEN!
Listen to the sounds of an awakening world.
LISTEN—PEACE—PEACE—soul-soothing peace!

Diana Kranz-Gagnon

Our Time Would Seem to Be Done

Our time would seem to be done.
The moments we shared,
The love that we dared
And all we could do to be one.

The candle was lit with a lively blaze
With its light leading the way.
But it was a love just like the day,
As it emerged but became a haze.

A love that could never be undone
Is what passionately appeared.
It was something many would have feared,
But my love for you was like the Earth's for the sun.

All that we had will never go away.
It will be there forever
As it will never dare to dissever
But be more than any could say.

And before that final adieu
We must remember the day
That our fears went astray
And I fell truly in love with you.

Ryan Rodney

Forlorn in Shadows

Deep down in the abyss of a thousand sorrows I lay.
Alone, I look back at my life past.
Never I felt warmth, never I was happy.
Maybe this is for the best . . .

I can't move no longer.
The cruel coldness of my pain has made me paralyzed.
Drowned in dreams, for none of them came true . . .

I look up, trying to catch a last glimpse of the light above.
But there is nothing. Nothing but darkness.
Tears flow from my eyes. My last drops of life, my tears.
I can hear Him coming closer, I hear His footsteps.
Soon my suffering will forever end . . .

Fredrik Larsson

Communication

Far stretch the pillars of sorrow,
rancor, regret, and remorse
Though tall wide and prodigious
still utterly shut in from the outside
Raving and raging to be set free
screaming and yelling to be heard
To love to be loved with deep understanding
To love to be known with complete depth and truth
Hateful to one, such as the same
Hateful to one, without asking the blame
Where does love flee in heavy trepidation?
To whom does the fault overthrow?
Why so tentative in expressing oneself?
Inner philosophies should not always be told
Outward opinions are hard to withhold
Far stretch the pillars of sorrow,
rancor, regret, and remorse
Until they begin to disintegrate
under this powerful force—COMMUNICATION

Anna Purdy

Mom

As I lie here alone at night,
I hope that you are all right.
I say things to you that are not nice;
everything I say is just a lie.
I only say those things when I'm mad.
I hope that you're not sad.
I hope that you forgive me
for everything I do or say.
I hate when we get in fights.
Please don't cry because I'm mad at you.
You know that all the things I say are not true.
Please forgive me.

Amanda Wyant

The Beach

The seagulls fly overhead,
And flap their silver white wings.
They pick at the clams and muck
    like angry vultures.
The sand is rough at my heels,
Tickling my soles.
The waves crash gently,
And water flows past my feet,
Numbing my toes.
I can taste the salt in the air,
And it smells so clean and fresh.
The crimson sun starts to sink,
Slowly melting below the horizon,
Cool air nipping at my skin.
The amber afterglow illuminates the ocean,
Flecking the sand with gold.
I am at last calm,
For the beach has made peace with my soul.

Stephanie Messina

Just like Me

As the tiny ant crawls across the floor
I wonder what it is thinking scared, excited,
happy, angry
Whatever it is it may be just like me:
hated, an outcast, or maybe a king or queen
Just wanting to go home or away is it right for
it to die because it's small or maybe he would do the same to me
to not be judged sent to death and not given a thought
to perish with only your guts on a boot or shoe
Maybe he was like me
we will never know or care

Derek Brunin

Adrift

A joyless room,
Sitting in her straight backed chair
On her faded lifetime,
Purple sweater backwards, hanging
Against brittle bones,
Her foot tapping, tapping on the wood floor,
Broken shoelace left untied.

For a moment, a glimmer in her eyes,
A glimpse from the past,
She weeps, tears spilling on gnarled fingers,
The light dims quickly,
Lost in her body,
Abandoned like an aging tractor
Left in the fields to rust,
Forgetting to lie down when its time to sleep.

Gloria Russell

The Encounter

I huddled within my loneliness and gazed upwards,
wishing that something magical would occur in the heavens

And suddenly, you were there

I held back tightly, never daring to believe that there were paths
for us to discover together, never able to fully believe
that you were a part of my journey.

But you were, and in you I found a light
that warmed my soul and you held courageously onto my heart,
despite my efforts to pull it all away from your grasp

I fell, my walls crumbled to dust and I allowed myself
to embrace you

Then you left, as quickly as you came.
The light has disappeared.
I shiver, numb from the cold of the experience.
In fact, I find it quite cold;
my only explanation is to believe that my heart left when you did.

My soul feels as though it is being held hostage.
There is a hollowness within me
which happens to be the exact size of my heart.
I wish it could be replaced with much more
than my acceptance that a tiny piece will remain missing forever.

Donna Ramroop

This Could Happen to You Too

But why you behaving so?
As if you better than me!
When you see me, your head rise a notch or two
As if this coulda never happened to you
A glimpse a me, sen' you runnin',
But brethren, what you running from?
'Cause you see me dutty rags
And act as if me no have no education,
You think me's a third class citizen—
Any lesser of a man.
But how you think me get this way?
Me born so? Me loss me mind? Wha you think?
Drugs and alcohol, eh? No man! That's what "them" just
Tell you to mek you feel good
I's a product of society—though "them" want to
Put the blame on something else
Don't mek them fool you,
So when you see me—a product of society—just like you,
Lend a helping hand,
For remember, this could happen to you too.

Nicole Angeline Grant

The Victim of Genesis

Slithering out after falling man,
I found a bear with his paw caught in a vine
To help him, I wriggled to him on the ground,
But what had him tangled was divine.
God had captured this innocent bear
To take revenge on me.
I would not let this take place, and I was scared.
I had to save the cub, as he was a tot.
My legs taken away, I moved up the tree
As quickly as I could.
I gnawed on that vine with my fangs so tight
that the cub was free in an hour.
As for me, I was splintered by the wood.
Those wounds have healed, though others won't.

Jeff Greenberg

The Senses

Happiness is a box of bright colors
It smells of home
And tastes like cotton candy
It sounds like a song
And feels like a hug

Acceptance is festive orange
It tastes like candy corns
And smells like pumpkin pie
It sounds like the crunch of fall leaves
And makes you feel the happiness of autumn

Peacefulness is earthy green
It smells like lilac
And tastes honeysuckle sweet
It sounds like rippling pond water
And feels like spring

Devin Schreiner

Troubles

Days pass and go
My love for you will never fade
I know everything about you there is to know
I felt as if I had it made

Then reality brushed my face
Fights and words fill the room
Love is not perfect in this case
It seems you are no more to bloom

You say you hate me
I say I hate you
The same, it will never be
Our love is no longer new

Experience makes our love stronger
In our relationship, hate is no longer
My love still will never fade
To this day, I still have it made

Joe Davis

The Innocent Victims

Oh, how they cried. Oh, how they weeped,
For they knew their mother could no longer
put them to sleep
She sang them a lullaby before they went to bed,
But now that lullaby is just in their heads

Her death was so sudden, she could hardly think,
For the man in the other car had had too much to drink.
The battered old truck hit her so fast,
It's a shame, she will not be the last

So now these children with no mom,
Have to learn to continue on
And now I show you in this rhyme,
That a loving mother and her children become,
The innocent victims of a careless crime

Brittany Alton

Why Does It Hurt So Much?

Things have changed since you've gone,
it's been three years, three years too long.
I never thought I could go on without you and Mom.
I miss you so much, the pain is always there,
I wish that I could only share.
God has helped me through those tough days,
I've cried many tears for you in many ways.
You left me with my heart broken,
I guess God needed you for His work.
I wish I could have learned more about your life.
The times we went fishing and sat on the shore,
just talking and learning a little bit more.
The memories and love you gave me cannot be taken away.
With God's help the pain will subside,
even when others leave me behind.
My heart aches every time I think of you.
You must know all that I'm going through.
Maybe it was a bad thing that I was you little girl,
you were the center of my world.
I must go on with my life, that is to be a mother and wife.
I hope you're up there watching over me,
No matter my age, your little girl I will always be.
I keep waiting for the pain to go away some,
that is why I wrote this poem.

Anna Beach

The Ladder

Ride me down my shooting star
I'm stuck upon my ladder
For fear of never going up
my heart grew so much sadder
but when I finally reached the top
no Heaven did I find
instead a hell where never could I rest my mind.

Now I've lost my sparkle
that always did show through
though no one ever noticed it
it was pure and true

Now it's time to climb back down
back to Earth to level ground
ride me down my shooting star
I'm stuck upon my ladder,
for fear of never going up my heart grew so much sadder

Laura Mcfadyen

Inspired by You

I know we are both confused right now,
I truly wish I could make it better somehow.
I feel your pain when I hear you cry,
but I've run out of ideas and things to try.

Although I am hurt, I know you are too,
and I can feel you yearning to know what to do.
I know if you could you would take it all back,
but sadly things aren't always as easy as that.

I am ignoring my hurt to try to help you,
and I know that you feel its the wrong thing to do.
But I can ignore the hurt and ignore the pain,
if it means I will see you smile again.

Emily Thompson

Darkness Is Silence . . .

Darkness is silence . . .
            deep,
                    —the unknown.
        The unknown is calling,
    whispering,
            echoing,
                    over and over . . .
        Beckoning to come closer,
    to taste its sweetness,
        to learn its secrets,
            to know all—
                Call to me—
                    as I answer,
                        to grow . . .
                            to become . . .

Lynn Pettis

Lake of Glass

Lake of glass, steam rising.
A crane calling in the distance as the sun is at first stance.
Fish dancing on the water in the morning light . . .
a flock of geese flying overhead in their days first flight.
Squirrels scampering about,
as the raccoons lay to rest.
Wrens singing merrily about the new day. . . .
as the wind wisps gently through the trees,
softly moving the leaves to and fro.
The earth's cool dampness as you walk along,
the sound from a woodpecker as he taps out his hollow song.
Wildflower's fresh scent lingering in the air,
lining paths along the river from many passing deer.
In a world as large and beautiful as ours
there is much more to explore.
Take time, clear your mind, and head outdoors!

Lynn Davis

Life

Life to me is the light you see
The spark, the flame, or glow
That shines in loving peoples eyes
So all of us will know
Heres someone for us to trust
So let our feelings show
These people will not hurt you
Their only there to give
For that's what makes their lives (for them)
So wonderful to live

Tammy Biddix

Run with the Wind

A ray of light smacks my face,
am I ready to face a brand new day?
Fear trickles inside as I reach in—
deep inside my body
I look for the strength that I need
to conquer the impending hours
The traffic light beams like a warning
My watch ticks faster and louder
Other people laugh, but I just want to scream
Wash away the sarcasm life deals us—
and run with the wind, disappear into the night

Jennifer Podolsky

Iridescent Memories

The world just kept moving when everything should've stopped
Still, silent, all things in their place
Caught in the movement of unrelieved grace
which we call life . . .
When you walked away I felt my love
stretch out like an intangible line connecting us
Your love, not yet abandoned, anchoring us through time
Feeding me from a distance
Leaving me with a yearning, subtle yet deeply
woven in the fabric of my reality
While you were not A part of me was not
Tied up in knots and Waiting, Waiting to wake to your kiss
Praying for the color to bleed black into my world . . .
You taught me about the infinitesimal gradations
of gray and the violent jazzy passion of purple
that is your presence blending into my days
Yet the world moved on—Without us.
I grew up without us
I grew outward, onward, but always looking backward
The silhouette of my heart pining for yours
As aging with wisdom and grace
new yet unknown joys came my way
Life tumbling me in its grip
And love for you mesmerizing me
in a kaleidoscope of iridescent memories . . .

Lisa Rivera

The Mom YOU Gave ME—I Am So Near—

My Friend I shared my heart and Soul.
I cried a bit and all unfolds.
I wanted to hug her, but feared rejection
Lord help me with a sense of direction.
He said, "She is my tool for now,"
and I looked up and said, "Please tell me how?"
He said, "Her love for you is from me,
and the spirit of compassion shall set you free."
So, "This, my child, is how to draw near,
A child with a bit of fear,
take her love and shed a tear
and ALWAYS KNOW THAT I AM NEAR."

Maria Gomez

Urgently Waiting

You can't make the sun rise.
        You can only wake up early
                and find a place to sit
        and wait
                        and hope the clouds part.

You can't tell the winds which way to blow.
        You can only hoist your sails
                and adjust your rudder
        and try to avoid the rocks
                as you aim for your chosen port.

You can't hasten Spring's thaw.
                You can only button your coat
        and brace yourself against the bitter wind
                and keep a fire in the hearth
                        while you dream of warmer days.

And I cannot mold her thoughts
        to fit the form of my desire.
        I can only offer her
                the greatest of who I am
        and gently make her understand
                that she is the sunrise

                        that I have been hoping for.

Kevin Smith

Pop Cans and Cigarettes

For the little girl and woman in all of us,
whoever she may be.
A red pop can
lies in the street.
Crushed in the middle,
bits of cigarette ash
seep out
hiding the words.
Pink lipstick stains
the top of the can.
The tab's been snapped off
—gone to make a chain
for some little girl
who may one day
wear lipstick
or ash in the can.

Rae Ann Rockhill

Blue Shy Eyes

Almost floats across a room
  blue shy eyes
  looking no where exactly

Too graceful to be noticed
  simply disguising the smile
  of the young clumsy child

A gaze which enlightens
  Empowered by a trueness
  Reminds of a scene once dreamt

The taste of her voice
  echoes slowly on my tongue
  smells like everything exactly

Jeff Harding

Tin·viel

When the shadows
Make the world
So cruel and heartless
And all you can do is dream,
Remember the nightingale
Who sings her song
Above for all to hear.
When the gale lets out her
Sorrow,
Remember me.
Remember I love you,
While she sings.

Jacque Revels

A Promise

Do not lose faith nor hope, my friend,
When you are in distress.
For disappointments will be yours,
The same as happiness.

This life on Earth cannot be like,
A smooth and peaceful sea.
The ups and downs are sure to come
And here on Earth shall always be.

Trust in the Lord, we pray and sing.
Angels on high with God our king.
The sky above, a blanket of love.
To warm our hearts 'til we meet above

There will be a jubilee,
Far beyond the troubled sea.
He wrote this promise to us, you know.
And signed it with a rainbow.

Do not despair, nor e'er lose sight,
Of what you hope to gain.
With faith in God and in yourself,
Your goal you will attain.

June Avery

A Keeper's Daughter

The true meaning of life can be seen,
in her deep blue eyes as they gaze
out over the water.
Beautiful colors of blue and green,
enhanced by the clear blue sky
creates dreams that may not matter.

Sea gulls, white pearls are in flight,
while the loons in the bay
sound out their haunting call
Moonbeams highlight a starlit night,
but when fog, storms and rain prevail
the foghorn warns all.

 These memories, as I grow old,
are precious to me
a God-given scene.
It's a true life adventure to be told,
a lighthouse keeper's daughter
can sit by the shore and dream.

Dorothy Richards

Children of April

Only a breath ago,
You were ripped from
Those who loved you.
Only a heartbeat ago,
With a flash and a roar
You were flung into God's cradling arms.
Years have passed
As we heal and try
To bind our torn hearts.
It only seems like yesterday
We held your hands
And watched you play.
We try to understand,
But probably never will
Maybe one day we can forgive,
But we never will forget.

Kristine Murray

Wildflower Free

Fields of flowers—
Untamed, beautiful in solitude,
No bees or butterflies
To blemish
The surrounding euphoria.
Picked a few and held them,
Taking life in my hands.
Every petal shone a different hue—
Red, white, blue, pink, black.
Love you, love you not.
Then the wind smiled
And they flew free—
Flocks of birds
Scattered in the sky,
Twirling down like snowflakes—
Kisses from the wind.
I closed my eyes,
Surprised to find out
How much they reminded me of
Tears running down my face.

Jacqueline Tsang

family

my family the pillar of my life
who built me from the ground
lifts me up when i'm low
gives me hope for tomorrow
as they put the blocks together
to make my future high above the ground
for my family is the pillar of my life

Dorothy Cheruiyot

Snowflakes

Tiny, tiny, tiny
White, cold, wet
Down, down they fell
Then, at last, they met
Small, white, cold, wet
Watch them
Marvel at them, too
Wonder just which snowflakes will one
day cover you

DanaLee Pommell

Seasons

Winter like a virgin stands
Cold, untouched by human hands
Frosty, dressed in frigid white
Shimmering in December light
. . . Yet beautiful

Spring like a gentle lover's kiss
Awakens her, the cold dismiss
The sun warms her inner soul
Blossoming love makes her whole
. . . Yet beautiful

Summer, the heat of womanhood
In full bloom, golden and good
Fulfilled by love's greatest flame
Warmed by life, she will remain
. . . Yet beautiful

Autumn, warm and filled with rest
Laying her head on her lover's breast
Leaves fall golden in waning light
Death comes swiftly in the night
. . .Yet beautiful

Judie Schwartz

Always

I've always wondered,
Is there someone for me?
And I've always pondered,
Where could he be?
I've always known
Guys were just jerks.
I've always been shown
Relationships don't work.
I've always believed
I would never love a guy.
I've always deceived
Myself with that lie.
I've always thought
That this was all true.
But that's only because
I haven't always known you.

Stephanie Slater

Loss of a Mother

My heart breaks because of you
The pain I cannot endure
Medicines do not ease the pain
For love there is no cure
Time is said to heal a wound
So patiently, I wait
But the pain constantly nags at me
By then it's far too late
Dying slowly inside
For there's nothing to live for
You burn inside of me
And will forevermore

Martin Fredrickson

Only Time Will Tell

Only time will tell,
How things will really work out.
Until that time has come,
There will always be some doubt.
Only time will tell,
What a seed will come to be.
It could be eaten by a bird.
It could become a mighty tree.
Only time will tell,
The type of man the boy will be.
He could be rotten or righteous.
He could be tense or carefree.
Only time will tell,
Exactly when you'll pass away.
You could live to be a hundred,
Or you could go today.
So, things could turn out badly,
Or they could go just swell.
But you'll have to wait and see,
'Cause only time will tell.

Robert Capell

On My Grave

On my grave, Mom
I wish that you would say
a loving daughter of you, Mom
in every little way.
As far as Daddy goes, Mom
he was never around.
So, don't worry about him Mom,
he won't be near that ground.
I wish that you would tell sis,
I love her through and through.
Even though we fought, Mom
I will always miss her, too.
I hope you will tell my friends, Mom
when they call or phone
that I will miss them all, Mom
and not to feel alone.
For I am in there hearts, Mom
and yours and sissy's, too
I will always miss you, Mom
and don't forget I love you.

Jamie Townsend

Bumble Bees

Bumble bees are neat,
They have legs instead of feet.
Bumble bees are yellow and black,
When you see them you go "smack."
Bumble bees have wings,
And enjoy collecting things.
Bumble bees like flowers,
They buzz and buzz for hours.
Bumble bees are soft and not blue,
Just don't let them sting you!

Lauryn Hahn

Thinking Back

Did you ever pass a movie theater
where hundreds of people
are standing in line?
Not one ever talks to the other.

Too bad. . . .
For the people in line
have so much more to offer
than the movie.

Lynn Lewis

softlip kisses

softlip kisses but
hard, urgent, demandingandnow
I think of
you
and i lipslockedtightinseparable
bodies much
the same(but even more desperately
trying to push against eachother
like

need pushing against want)and
so very
 very diff
erent; each its own
and wan-ting the other

waves lap at the shore
much the way we lap
ateachother here;now;always;be-

lieving (will not be
leaving soon)while outside

a city slides by.

Joaquin Terceno

Egyptian Girl

A girl with the eyes of a doe
Was sadly watching us leave.
She was not more than ten years old,
Her name was Aisha, I believe.

She was staring at us in silence,
Looking so sweet and humble,
That girl with the skin of olive,
Glittering in the sun like amber.

But in her heart the grief was arising
Of all Oriental women,
She would never see how surprising
The world around her could be.

The strand of the hills it the distance
And a small nondescript town,
She cherished that scorched, barren soil
As it was her beloved home.

She gave me a farewell token,
A colored thread-knit bracelet,
That girl with the eyes of a doe,
She was not more than ten years old.

Julia Lesnichy

How Much like Love

How much like Love is the rose
Whose bloom is soft and gentle
To the touch
Whose fragrance is rich and sweet
And calls the unwary to reach and hold
The flower by the stem
And in whose arms
There comes a pierce
For wanting to possess
The beauty of the flower there
Forgetting that the secret of the rose
Is not in possessing
But in knowing of the beauty
And the strength that lies within
How much like love is the rose
Whose bloom forever unfolds
And gives its gardener sweet recompense
For caring for
Yet never truly owning
The beauty of the rose.

Paul Ronan

storm

life's constant ocean
wearing us away
creating a new facade
covering the old
with each tiny ripple
with every tide
then there is the storm
that lay us bare
trembling
exposed
to all those that may see

Linda Dorothea Politte

Juli (Haiku)

A Praxiteles
Aphrodite, created
from charm & beauty

Aldo Cordura

With or without Himself

He is a Desperado.
Late at night.
Basking in the firelight.
The moon creates shadows.
Lonely, desperate shadows.

He is a Fugitive.
On the run.
But from what?
Himself.

He is a Rebel.
Goes against the flow.
Being his own self.
But wishing to be different.

He is a Derelict.
Why follow rules?
They were made for breaking.
He makes his own rules.

He is a Convict.
He is wanted.
But not the way he desires to be.

He is a criminal.
The law wants him.
But not to love—
To lock behind bars.

Regina Pirrie

Gone

Darkness now comes over me
As I am laid to rest.
I am none the wiser,
But I am none the less.
I begin my long earned sleep,
The first of many days.
I will never be disturbed,
Now I'm free from former ways.
I now can know no pain
Every day and every night.
My suffering has ended,
And my mind at last takes flight.
I can see more clearly now,
My eyes aren't in the way.
I now can tell no lies
For I have nothing left to say.
I will never see another sunset.
I will never see another dawn.
But since I am remembered,
I am not truly gone.

Keegan Haid

The Dreams Dreamt

In my dream I see a boy,
A young boy.
He's sitting alone.
He's in trouble.
I have to help him.
Why can't I help him?
Wait, I understand.
It's not help he needs,
It's guidance.
Guidance given not by me,
But by himself.
The boy looks familiar.
I don't know what.
Some trait, some action,
Wait a minute,
The boy is me. . . .
The boy never receives that guidance,
But stronger he grows.

Jeremy Broshear

Snow!!

As you stay in your house,
Cozy and sound,
You listen to the snow,
Fall quietly on the ground.

You take a sip,
From your hot chocolate mug,
As you snuggle your cold feet,
In the thick warm rug.

Your eyelids start drooping,
And you start to yawn,
You look outside,
And white is your lawn.

You quietly fall asleep,
Snuggled up in a fluffy white chair,
Dreaming of kittens,
And cuddly Teddy bears.

Lisa Picascia

Dance with the Light

She is light
Strong and peaceful
He is shadow
Concealed by apathy
Wants to dance
Tango with the light
Fear keeps him distant
Longing makes him stay
Dream
For dreams are power
Power to love
Vision is beauty
See it, embrace it
Give it power
Soar out of the shadowy storm
Surrender to the light
The unity is true

Shana Rosenfield

The Frosted Snow Angel

With your cheeks so pink,
and your frost-bit-nose,
Your eyes that twinkled,
and your heart that glows,
You look like an angel
that is made out of snow,
with the morning dew that
froze on you.

Emily Bajgot

Perfection

Autumn leaves blowing
A stiff north wind
Bearing down on summer's
Long-forgotten landscape
The steady ticking
Of a clock
A cat curled in the position
Of a self-indulgent slumber
The scratch of pen to paper
These things are what
Are real to me

Linda Bowlsbey

Insignificance

The sky is full of Scars
I cannot ease
The imperfectly healed-up
Hurt

Stroking the dark
Absurd
Gestures of aching so much
To restore

A balance.

To touch
This pale skin, unafraid.

But I'm alone
And I cannot replace
The Stars

Anne Lindstroem

Child's Play

Wafting on the wind in sweet descant
Trebled scales of celebration,
Hide and seek expostulation,
Incantations of jump rope chant;
Ebb and flow of rushing laughter
Break like waves unrestrained,
Tumbled children running after
O'er the lawns green counterpane;
Tourjetes and pirouettes
Entrechats, petite moppets,
Kick the can, blind man's bluff
Little boys who play too rough;
Sudden silence shouts out loud,
Curiosity queries why,
They're building castles in the clouds,
Gazing awe-struck at the sky.

Don Melcher

DNR—Do Not Resuscitate

the blue eyes that watched me as a child
looking at me now, pleading, helpless
I don't want to die
I know, I don't want you to

listening to the doctor explain
quality of life
systems shutting down
matter of time

what would you do?
blue eyes searching, frightened
if I could change places
I would sign the order

children should not take hope
from their father
to pronounce death
to seal the eyes that loved you

Jennifer Skerrett

Signs

All signs are pointing to no.
I take a look one last time,
Turn around and walk away.
Maybe you'll remember me,
Once we meet again.
Until then it's over.
I don't know how to tell you
I miss you
And I dream of when we will cross paths.
I can't find you here,
Or anywhere else.
But I'll search the sky
Through the stars.
Maybe one sign will say
Yes

Stephanie Lovell

Poetry in Motion

and as motion yawned,
inertia could only stretch
with satisfaction
in bed beside her.

Kaja Katamay

My Rose

You are
the sunshine that makes the
roses bloom
the flower that brightens
my life
the fragrance that sweetens the
air that I breathe
the softness that caresses
my nights
you are my everything
my beauty
my rose
my life

Dee Riley

Harry T. and Mona Blue

He was sailing down the streets of shame
With a girl named Mona Blue.
She showed him something borrowed—
She showed him something new.
And he was thinking of
Something old—himself . . .
When it felt like something true.

Jennie Marshall

The Bond

The bond is so strong
when you first hold them near
The meaning of life
is so suddenly clear
A soft, damp, warm little body
curled up on your lap
Bath time is over
now it's time for a nap
An impatient little tug
on the end of your shirt
A little tug on your heart
when you can't heal the hurt
A soft whisper in your ear
as if only you cared
A soft little giggle
at the secret now shared

Colleen Littlejohn

Emily

Why do I take time to do things,
when your not even around.
When you're not there to be with me,
then nothing can really be found.

Consuming is tragically pointless,
'cause I only get half of the taste.
If you're not standing beside me,
then all that I do is a waste.

The feelings I feel become worthless.
I can't see your face to compare.
My thoughts disappear before me,
all the things that I wanted to share.

The question and answer is over,
and it looks like the end has begun.
Your presence is all that's important,
just open your arms, here I come.

Josh Lind

hollow

the tears on your cheek
are more clear than diamonds
the smell of your skin
is an addictive perfume
the warmth of your tongue
is as hot as the sun
your love for me
is bigger than me

the colors are soft and mature
adult evolving danger matters
narrow the mind who can't forgive
the interruption of his blindness eyes

Michel Vander Wilden

For Matthew

They read from the good book
and buried God today
I made a new friend at the funeral
I think He would have wanted it that way

Tonya Aline Watson

Transformation

I feel the cold.
It's in my feet.
Between my toes,
It's grabbing my ankles,
I fall to the ground.
The cold is climbing up my legs,
It makes my knees tremble.
I feel it up my thighs,
And it makes my stomach flutter.
I feel it climbing up my chest,
I try to shake it off, but it's no use.
I feel it in my neck.
My mouth, my nose, my eyes, my hair
The cold has conquered me.
I feel it deep within.
I curl up into a ball,
I shiver.
Everything about me is cold—freezing.
But wait—
My soul—it is warm.
The cold slowly leaves me,
As if I have shed a layer of skin.
I am strong again.
I am warm again.

Kimmie Osborne

Oceans of Life

The ocean waves breathe
like a baby fast asleep.
A never-ending rhythm
blue as faded denim.

In my toes go,
scattering its flow.
As I look into the brightly smiling sky,
a dragonfly buzzes by.

Soon, light-hearted clouds whirl in,
the ocean's next of kin.
Renewing, reviving,
keeping the essence thriving.

Jeslyn Burger

Aching Heart

I can't control what I did
But I can control what I do
I just can't understand
Why I fell in love with you.
The sound of your voice
Keeps ringing in my ears
And I'm trying so hard
To fight off the tears.
I know it wasn't your fault
Because I caused the pain on my own
I know you're the one
But here again I'm alone.
I keep asking myself
Over & over, again & again
Why won't this pain I'm feeling
Just hurry up and end.
The hardest thing to handle
Is that of a broken heart
It's like a bullet you can't dodge
And a bullseye you can't dart.

Blair Womack

The Re-Make
of the Volkswagon Beetle

The first time I saw one
I thought they were dumb
But when I looked harder
I saw I was wrong

They are so little
Tiny, even petite
They look so darn cool
They look so darn sweet

They come in all colors
Red, blue, green, and white
They even come in the color
Of a moonless, starless night

With the new element, Turbonium
They can go super-fast
Turn on the Turbonium
Stomp on the gas

Open the sunroof
Let in some fresh air
Stick your head by the sunroof
And out flies your hair

This car beats the old one
In every department, even looks
Believe me, my friends
This car really cooks

Mike Magnifico

Adele

Her cheek
so soft against my lips,
Her hand
warm on mine.
That smile
lights my heart
and suffuses it with joy!
So short is our bonding
yet it is her whole life.
My dark eyed girl,
child of my body,
sweetest of delights.
What was my life
before her?

Bas'ka Bartsch

Mirrors

Is it me I see
When I speak to you
A mirror image
Of life done made blue

As I hear your tears
In a voice so dear
I can only wish
How I want you near

This mirror image
Of my own sad love
I can't help but think
Of angels above

When we speak of love
I hear my own life
And all my troubles
My fears and of strife

Is it you I need
When you talk to me
A mirror image
Of life meant to be

Chris Coffey

in egypt

dig, start digging
we build the house of hearts
anywhere
you shall say to strangers:
it is time

Sebastian Hoehn

The Family Sonnet

How do you acknowledge the years?
How do you remember the joy?
How do you forget the tears?
How do you optimize to enjoy?

The passing years are a pilgrimage
From generations young to old.
The family is a harbor and anchorage
As the years turn to gold.

Joys are family special events
In photos, film and an album book
Recording memories and accomplish-
ments.
The origin of a positive outlook.

Family maximizes joy; minimizes sad.
Remembering the good; diminishes the
bad.

Howard Kamin

Classical Journeys

Dedicated to my Great-Grandma JJ, my guardian angel.

Settled in front of the fireplace,
I have travelled all of the Earth.
Next to its fiery glow,
A book in my lap,
A pet by my side.
The fireplace illuminates the way.
Like on a well-worn pathway,
I do trudge along.
Through the leaves or through the snow,
Wherever I wish to go.

Sharleyne Miner

Is It Fair?

She refuses to give up this fight,
As she wants to see a certain sight.
She has the heart of a lion,
She won't give up and start cryin'
She will not lie down and die,
Like a young boy.
My mother's sister, my Aunt,
Wants to rave and rant,
At the unfairness of God!
She will not give up this fair sod!
She has given Him eight kids,
But look what He bids!

The Worst Of All Diseases!
Is It Not He, She Pleases?

Aoife Doody

The Flame

Slowly my body loses its flame
through the treacherous storm
I call Thy name

The struggle to survive
as I'm thrown about
no control of what's happening
I scream and shout

No one can see or feel what I'm feeling
My fire, my flame
is weakening and weakening

Where is the peace,
the light I must find?
The pain is too great
for my body and mind

My spirit is strong but my body is weak
I cannot communicate
I am unable to speak

The flame is now down to a little spark
I give to You, Lord, all of my heart

Now it is time for me to endeavor
My body, it dies
My spirit's forever.

Laine Tabbita

Leave Me Alone!

You have hurt my feelings
Really, really deep inside,
You have also left a scar
Deep inside my heart
Now I need someone
To come and heal the pain
So please, now I'm pleading you
To go far, far away
And let me be myself again!

Lizbeth Fuentes

precious gifts

the sun set on a summers eve
the feel of rain
the laughter from a tiny voice
the future gained
the smell of sweat from passions heat
a gentle kiss
the vision of those many dreams
where nothing's missed
the strength that lies in knowing
something more to try
the image of the man i see
reflected in your eyes

David Burns

My Love

My love for her
Is never ending.
But my heart feels
Like it's bending.
Before I met her
I never thought I'd find love
But then it happened
Like a sign from above
But I waited too long
And now it may be too late
It works in weird ways
this thing called fate
I know that if it's meant
to be it'll be
But I can't wait
I know she's for me
Why must we
Face these trials
Why must God
Mess with our dials?

Greg Schneider

Freedom

I wish someone can spare
The hurt and fear of men
To live without a care
Every man as each other's friend
No matter what his race
Or religion he may be
He can live at any place
He is in the land of the free
He should not have to think
He is less then others
He is a part of a link
That makes all men brothers. . . .

Patty Rizzo

Rejoice

Can you see the shine of her eyes,
somewhere else but in her eyes.
Can you feel the warmth of her skin,
somewhere else but on her skin.
Can you receive the joy of her smile,
somewhere else but from her smile.
Can you feel the heat of her embrace,
somewhere else but from her embrace.
Can you taste the love from her kiss,
somewhere else but from her kiss.
Her eyes shine for you.
Her skin is warm for you.
Her smile brings joy to you.
Her embrace is hot on you.
Her kiss is full of love because of you.
It is time to rejoice.

Anthony J. Ribustello

My Fallen Angel

You are my fallen angel
sent to care for me from a far.

You are my fallen angel
here to guard me.

You are my fallen angel
sent from above.

You are my fallen angel
for me to love.

You are my fallen angel
to hold me when I cry.

You are my fallen angel
to always help me try.

You are my fallen angel
to be there when I'm down.

You are my fallen angel
to always be around.

Amanda Perkins

A Weary Soul

Oh, let me go
Where the breeze blows free
Angel music
In every tree
Oh, let me go
Where the sun spills gold
On the buttercup sky
And the daisy bold
Oh, let me go
Where the brook flows clean
And the meadow grass
Is emerald green
Where the redbird sings
Its silvery cry
And the eagle glides
In the sheer blue sky
Where the wild rose blooms
And the violets peep
And the browsing deer
Gives a graceful leap

Susan Hardister

The Rock

I gave you five and a half years
only to receive a broken heart
and a lifetime of tears.

I wanted us to be equal
in everything we share.
You wanted just the opposite,
even though you knew it wasn't fair.

You picked up bad habits,
alcohol, smoking, lying and stealing
which I didn't want to see.
It caused me much pain and hurt,
even more so when you hit me!

It took a toll on me,
I became very distraught,
I had to reevaluate my life
and give it some serious thought.

So I went to "The Rock," God,
without a shadow of doubt.
Guidance, strength, belief, and faith
gave me what I needed to get out.

Denise Wallace

A Soldier's Song

Forward frail soldier I carry
Courage to mount the day
Burdens of regret and remorse
Fall like footsteps that fade away

Come country path to tread upon
Weary warman onward tread
Across that hued horizon
To that shadowed stead

And though the hour may be late
And your weary spirit earned
Each step brings a closer mile
To the victory of your return

Barbara Sue Frick

Emotional Homicide

So many kill the hearts they love;
It's so anonymously deject.
Some do it with childish anger
While others just reject.
The coward panders an unfaithful kiss
While others just ignorantly neglect.
For some love dies when they are young;
For others as they grow old
Some kill love with an act of lust:
While others use words exceedingly bold.
With indifference or lust it matters not
Loves dead soul grows equally cold.
These dead souls suffer oh, such pain;
dealing with their grief and disgrace
Sentenced to the shadows of loneliness
Where only that love can efface.
They are victims in a vacuous life
It's a terribly empty place.

Ira Mcbraeden

Pennies from Heaven

Pennies from Heaven rain on me,
Filter through my disbelief
Dance before my footsteps, in tune
Drop windswept into nearby stream beds.
Round coppers, ground down,
Rock roofed—
Emerge upstream—
Radiate—
Nourishing sky blue forget me nots.

Marjorie Aaron

I Was Born To

I was born to be a wanderer
To never settle down
To come and to go as the wind blows
To stop on my trip to nowhere only
To leave once again
And do so without leaving a trace
To never make a difference
To be a loser
To never be anything to talk about
And be forced to roll with the punches
To be eternally bored

I was born to be a quitter
And give up on my dreams
To be a grain of sand in a giant desert
To do only as the crowd dictates
To give up on my principles
And be forever miserable because of it
To wait for eternal bliss
To choke under pressure
And fail in all lives tests

Cody Hill

To My Daughters

All those years I've been there for you,
Doing what I thought was right.
Now I sit alone in wonder,
Sometimes through the lonely nights.
You've blossomed into fine young women,
No longer little girls.
Help me treat you as you should be:
Cherished, cultured pearls.
Your futures are ahead of you.
Mine still open too.
Thank you for your love and support.
Couldn't do it without you.

Patricia Petrini

Soulmates

I can feel your soul close to mine.
Within the realm of the
Universe we are apart
And yet are one
I have lived so many spheres of life
Through tears and pain untold.
Did you pass me by
Locked in your own sorrow?

Elizabeth Purdy

The Easter Show

Cathedrals . . .
brought to the last inch
of elegance
with candles and white lilies,
packed with people of
assured nicety,
resounding hosannas from
the far reaches
of basso and soprano.

Oh, gentle Lord,
forgive us this our show,
our prayers, pleas, promises
from unconfirmed confirmed
and unbelieving believer;
we may someday in an
unlighted corner quietly
commit ourselves to thee.

Frances L. Hatfield

Saying Good-Bye

The old rocking chair
Sits quietly in the big empty room
There was no noise in the air
The floors cracked
For they had not been walked

Where was this quiet place
A place we used to go
A place we use to know

The chair was rocked for years
by one and all
One generation at a time

The music was played
the laughter was shared
for we use to be there

The rocking chair sits still now
The door creaks of love
As we leave and smile
And say good-bye

Melissa Ayers

Lost without Love

Like the snows on a mountain
top where are you mother?

It's been so long since I've seen you.
How you keeping mother?
I tumble around in my bed
Hoping one morning I'll wake up dead.
Is there another to take my place?
Even wonder if he's in the race.

I built myself a bondfire to keep
Myself warm, the rains came along
and put my heart out,

Where are you, mother of my infancy,
abductor of my youth,
abortionist of my adulthood!

Turabia Jacinthia

Why

Fetus in the garbage
Newborn in the trash
Infant unattended
A child is sold for cash.

Adolescent has a latch key
A teen is free to roam
Searching for attention
Not available at home

Children killing children
What are we going to do
How could this all have happened
We haven't got a clue.

Jon Skillman

Spring

Spring is when the flowers bloom,
Spring is when the snow melts.
Spring is the season after winter,
Spring is a really great time.
Spring is when the grass grows,
It will be squishy.

Michael Schedel

Chance

Head drops down,
Eyes are shut,
The fears is overwhelming.
Face in frown,
Pain is gut,
Is life all that demanding?
Make that climb,
Take a chance,
Nothing is out of your grasp.
Out of time,
Standstill stance,
Feel time deal out its wrath.

Honie Harvey

Mother's Arms

A mother's arms are like angel wings.
They always comfort you
in your time of need.
They lead you and
guide you and hope
you do what's right.
The mother's arms
will stay strong
Even longer after
she's dead and gone.

Wanda McPherson

Oh . . . So!

In this cargo pit
I rumble with the other cases
Suit
We rumble
We stare at the clock
Oh
We feel for the other
One
But we can't help to feel sorry—
So
For packing more than we can bring
Back.

Ingrid Wendy Mikulik

The Life of One

He's on his way out
He looks young
He feels young
But yet he's on his way out
His toes look old
He has no gray hair yet
But there an oldness there
Holy pants, and torn blue jeans
Nothing left but remaining life
Even though it's short
He looks like Elvis, but yet he is not
He has no style
He has no gray hair
He has no choice but to sing his songs
And to carry on
With the attitude and spirit
Time will tell if it's good
Goodness, kindness, and enjoyment
Love fills his life
With peace on Earth

Gladys L. Houser

A Precious Part of You

Busy little fingers,
Tiny little toes.
A baby's small smile . . .
Taking away a mother's woes.

Skin so soft,
Eyes so bright.
Like a rose's petals . . .
So precious and light.

So loving and easy to hold,
So innocent and meek . . .
With cries so bold.

A life so precious,
One so new.
A life so cherished,
A life so much a part of you.

Lorraine Lenihan

Within Its Path

Listen to the wind
the rustle of the trees
pondering its origin
its cool yet gentle breeze

With it goes some article
unable to withstand.
Scenes portrayed by nature
unrestrained by man

It whispers as it goes
Its destiny well hidden
commanding as it blows
containment is forbidden.

Barbara A. White

Why Do I Do What I Do

Why do I do what I do?
3 or 4 gang bangas with their crew.
3 pregnant with no one to turn to.
Why do I do what I do?
Several kids who do not have a clue,
to some color they will be forever true.
Why do I do what I do?
"Where were you when the bullets flew?"
"Oh, I was drinking a brew."
Why do I do what I do?
Bobby wears red on his shoes.
Billy wears a shade of blue.
Why do I do what I do?
3 more busted for something they grew.
"Look what my step-dad put me through".
Why do I do what I do?
If I don't, then who?
Why do I do what I do?
I do what I do
hoping to save just one of you.

C. Scott Wessel

I Think I'll Just Lie Down and Die

Now the story's been told,
And everybody knows
The troubles that
I have been through

It seems I haven't changed,
In no one's eyes,
I think I'll just lie down and die

With no one to blame,
I'm left with the pain
Oh! To live my life, once again

But the end is so near,
I do nothing but sigh,
I think I'll just lie down and die

Oh! For a gentle voice,
And a sweet pretty smile,
I feel I could live for a while

But it seems to me now,
It was only a lie,
I think I'll just lie down and die

Robert McMullan

The Trimmings

Like going from that
short and choppy crew
To the long-haired do
that I once knew
Then buzzed again
to feel as new
It's the transitional
in between times
Where life seems a little
rough around the edges.

Nathanael Lee

Cocaine

Up the nose to the brain
Makes one feel so high
Only to be going insane
So they touch the sky
Good as gold, cocaine
Yet another mother will cry
Lost in bitter pain
As she watches her loved one die
For many will ride this train
Chasing the great lie
From the devil and his cocaine

Shelia Wilkes

Love

Love is like the skip
Of a heartbeat when
You fall in love

Love is like that stolen
Kiss from the one you love

Love is like a baby drawing
his first breath
when coming into the world

Love is like the warm feeling
You get when you give
Your life to God

Thelma Fox

Share with Me

Share with me your inner world
Reveal to me what you're thinking
Tell me when your spirits soar
And even when they are sinking

Share with me your every mood
Please permit me to explore
All your hopes and aspirations
Let me know you to the core

Share with me your true concerns
Perplexities and your fears
All your strengths and weaknesses
And don't conceal your tears

Share with me your fantasies
Your love and your obsessions
Let me understand your wants
And savor your impressions

Let me know your inner warmth
And share that special flame
Tell me all there is to know
Since I will do the same

Herb Kaack

Angels

Angels come in different forms.
They have different smiles.
All of them, definitely;
Have their own styles.

I, truly appreciate;
Those amongst us living.
They are very kind
And generously giving.

Sometimes, I wonder,
Why, they were sent;
To help someone,
While, they seem content.

I believe, God knows;
Who is in dire need,
Gratefully, sending them;
To do some pleasant deed.

Angels dwell among us,
Each and every day.
When, one comes into my life;
I want them to stay!

Peggy J. Willis

Life's Tides

Life's tides can bring joy and pain.
Soul, skill and wit all wax and wane.
At ebb you must repair and bear.
At flow new heights you can attain.

James E. Cox

Washington Crossing the Delaware

A river wide, covered by ice,
A beam of light is shown,
There! A boat to cross the river,
And soon 'tis not alone,
The light, it shines upon a man,
Standing tall and straight.
In his boat are many men,
Restless while they wait,
They go across to win a war,
Though hard as it may seem,
Their hearts and minds are set upon
Fulfilling their country's dream.

Caitlyn York

Darkness

My soul aggravated,
Aggravated by what
I don't know.

Look deep into my soul,
You'll see darkness.

My soul looking for light,
No light insight,
only darkness.

Which way to run,
So aggravated
Don't know which
way to run.
Will my soul ever find
the light?

Or will it forever remain
in complete darkness?

Jennifer Anthony

If I Could Help the Angels Sing

If I could help the angels sing
Joyful praises to our heavenly king
My goal in life will never change
To help the angels sing.

The ten commandments I will keep
Abide by the Golden Rule
As my reward may be the Lord.
Will let me help the angels sing

Let me not forget my friends
Always a helping hand extend
Help them to better understand
How they may reach the promised land.

Betty F. Mills

On My Knees

On my knees I yell.
My anger runs
Like the blood you spilled,
On my knees I plead.
My tears become a torrent,
Washing away the pain.
The stain is gone,
The emptiness remains.

On my knees, I deny.
Throw the black cloth
Over my face.
On my knees I scream.
Wear my pain,
Hear it come back.
My bugle calls.
On my knees, I know
You died.

Jenny Gosa

Closure

Sleepless nights,
Worrisome days,
If only you were here.
I wish you were near . . .
How happy we were many years ago,
How much I love you,
You couldn't know
Deep inside of me,
Is my lovely reverie,
Of our love together,
Good-bye my sweet,
I love you still

Georgie Breuers

Red

Red is like fire
Like explosions around you
I feel the third-degree burns
I see the fire circling around me
I smell the thick smoke
I taste a breath of fire

Ryan Proper

Mother Leopard

Storm tossed sea
Frightening along the coast.
Torrential rain
Running through ravines.

Glowing eyes
And gleaming teeth
Concealed in the shadows,
Wrestling with impatience.

A turn of the head.
Quiet call behind.
Wait for them to catch up,
They know not how to hunt.

Never fear,
For mother shall teach.
Just sit still, watch.
They will share the feast.

Small, scurrying creatures
Quail in terror tonight.
Mother Leopard needs to hunt.
Death will come this night.

Kristi Ann Miller

A Love Forbidden

Two lives divided, yet united;
Where will our love lead us?
Not to each other, surely,
But surely not away.

We do not have each other;
Yet, we have each other still.
Our love is there always,
But always unconsummated.

I can love you forever;
Yet, I cannot love you at all.
You are not mine,
But forever mine in my heart.

You are always there;
I have only to reach out my hand.
Yet, I must not touch you,
But hold you forever in my dreams.

Sherry Weeks

Untitled

I'm your little girl
I loved you from the start
And I know that there is nothing
That could change that in my heart.
I'm blessed to have you watch me grow
And do the things I do,
God knew what He was doing
When He blessed my life with you.

Tina Ipsen

Christmas Fun

Christmas,
is a time to sing, laugh and play.
For old Saint Nick is coming your way.
But that is not all,
for the best time of all,
is Jesus' Birthday!

Jill Ashlee Whitley

Waiting

Sunlight beaming
Wind a breezy,
Birds chirping
Chirp chirp chirping
Singing on their spring time branch.
Warmth ensuing
Coo-coo cooing
Underneath another branch.
Nature's preening, cold succeeding
Winter's frigid dance,
now becoming springtime's cunning
Visual to the mortals glance.
Swiftly calling, falling, falling
Beauty's happenstance.
Now so lightly, softly brightly
Wonders provided by natures synchronized
We mortals in her trance.
Beauty, beauty left unspoiled
Winter's breezes take control,
Lightly calming softly lies
Nature's wondrous, glorious, prize.

Ramon J. Loredo Jr.

Vietnam Why Me

I stand against the wall
My heart bowed in prayer
Wondering why he died . . .
When I was suppose to be there.
The war didn't make any sense
The deaths were too many to count
And the victories to few to remember.

So I keep against the wall
My head bowed in prayer . . .
Wondering why I was the lucky one
Why my name isn't there.

Jean Ceile

Don't Forget

Don't forget me, while my mom's away.
Don't forget to feed me,
Even though I want to play.
Don't forget to pet my head,
And please, can I sleep by your bed?
Don't forget to give me a treat
When I come and lie at your feet.
Don't forget I love you,
Even though I cannot say!

Patrice Jones

Thing I Did Today

As I sit here writing this poem
I think of all the things I did today
Broke my arm, got it X-rayed
Flown a plane
Did a little dance and made it rain
Got my face on the five cents
Became superman, now I'm Clark Kent
Went on a shuttle and went to space
Won a gold metal in an Olympic race
Went to school and tutored my teachers
Glued on a mustache now I'm a mister
What else did I do today
　　Yawn
　　　Z
　　　　Z
　　　　　Z
Fredis Mappin

Value of Life

When you live your life,
make the most of it count;
each one of us will never know,
how much time we have to go.

Don't take things for granted,
appreciate what you have,
take time to smell the roses,
try to make the right choices.

Remember all the memories
as each year passes by,
for every road that you will take
is a journey you must make.

Be thankful for all the blessings
in your life that you've been given,
cherish them all, and never forget,
who gave you life from Heaven.
Donna MacVey

Friendships

Friendships are like glass—
Very fragile.
Friendships can be powerful,
And some a little delicate.
You know which friendships are
The strong and the weak.
A fragile friendship is built with a
Little trust, not much compassion
And a few white lies.
Sturdy friendships are built of
Confidence, affection, and kindness.
We have each type of friendship
With several people.
You can tell which are the dainty,
And which are the strong.
I can see it all over.
I have come to realize that we are not
Walking on glass,
We are the glass.
Bekki Bonesteel

Change of Season

The leaves are turning golden.
The blue skies are gray.
The green grass has all withered away.
The birds have all flown south.
The squirrels have gathered their nest.
Now they will take a rest.
And for all this there is a reason.
A change of season.
Tina Marie Perkins

Meaning Found

As I search this life for meaning,
I need not look too far.
For surrounding every blessing,
my children, there you are.

Not a thing exists in this world
for which I've been more blessed.
I imagined not the joy you'd bring,
but Heaven knew me best.

My prayers are with you daily
as you search and learn and reach.
For family, surely I am meant
to love and hold and teach.

I know this precious role I play
is a gift beyond belief.
So Lord, I thank you for this time,
be it scores of years or brief.

You have blessed my life through them,
so now touch their lives through me.
And let me never wonder
what the meaning of my life might be.
Jana Johannesmeyer

To Be Born

Little infant in the womb
Let this not be your tomb
May you see the light of day
This, Oh, Lord is what I pray
May you grow as a boy or girl
And have the health to play and toil
With loving parents to teach and care
All their lives with you to share
May your choices be right and true
May you love your God as he loves you
Jack Sullivan

Love the Children

Children love everyone
For they haven't yet learned to hate
Let's show them how much they are loved
Start today don't wait.

Childhood is much to short
Take a moment with them to share
Just how special they are
To let them know how much you care.

They will look back and remember
All the time you spent
They could never forget
Everything that you meant.
Barbara G. Cavender

Smile

What could I say
That would make you smile
And what could I do
that would make it worthwhile?

If I made you laugh,
is that how to begin?
Just what would it take
for me to help you to grin?

Would it take a flower
or a smile of my own
or maybe a good joke
or should I leave you alone

I want to see you laugh and sing
I'd like to see you smile
I'd love to make you happy
even if only for awhile
Jim Burrill

Thread of Hope

The rainwater runs
Through the mountains
Like thoughts of you
Run through my mind.
The water fills the rapid rivers
As thoughts of you
Fill this heart of mine.
I'm trying to hold onto you
With just a thread of "hope"
But the tears keep falling
Because I don't hear
From you anymore.
Now my mind is closed
To any other thoughts
If you listen to your heart
Your mind will learn to follow
You may go crazy tonight
But I'll be here
For you tomorrow.
Kristopher Smith

My Bucket of Pelicans

On my walk to the moon
On the path I took
I carried along
My bucket of Pelicans

Two in total
I named each one
Fruit, the smaller
Vegetable, the taller

At a fancy cafe
Built to a constellation
The meek wallet I had
Could not meet the bill's demands.

The cafe owner
A tall man with a belly
Spit out his anger
Aboard my table

So it was all I could do
It had to be done
I exchanged my bucket
And continued my walk to the moon
Roy Skibiski

One Step Closer

One step closer
Heading toward the light
Heading up there
With all his might
Somebody came
Lead with his sight
'Cause you're getting closer
Every night
One step closer
To my Lord
One step closer
To his home on high
One step closer
To the Lord on high
Reach out your hand
To a friend close by
'Cause you are getting closer
To the Lord on high
Michelle L. Blevins

Twilight

A star far away
in the sky
is but one left behind in the dark,
with just one looking up at it,
hoping to be set free to roam
'til the night
comes again.

Amanda R. Prendergast

Bonding Love

A daughter is a treasure,
That no one can measure.
The love she shows, grows and grows.
You are friends and it shows.
You read each other like a book.
A life began and it took.
A mother's love cannot be shook.

Wilma P. Lee

Dreams

Dreams are your imagination,
What you think and what you wish,
A journey beyond the stars,
An adventure beyond belief,
Make a wish,
Maybe it will come true,
Wish a wish,
Think it too,
Dream a dream at night,
Think it in the day,
All that you can do,
Is say, say, say,
Dream a dream,
Wish a wish,
Go beyond your imagination!

Michele Petrisin

Destiny

Underneath the midnight moon
I walk alone and dream of you
The one I need so painfully
The one whose name is Destiny

When you search this heart you will see
The hopeless love that sides in me
Just you don't know or even care
My heart is uselessly impaired

I'll sit alone and feel so hurt
Wondering what my life is worth
I'd give it all just for her love
For just one day would be enough

I'm sickened by this misery
She doesn't know I'm so lonely
And you don't know how hard it is
Being alone and unnoticed

So back to night and all darkness
With the knowledge of what is
Dreaming of that girl I need
The beautiful one named destiny

James Giese

Thinking of You

To see your face
Makes me smile
To see you smile
Makes my day

Walter Nance Jr.

Stormy Seas

I stand here by the stormy sea
Awaiting for my love.
It's dark and cold and wintry.
There are no stars above.
I call to him and call to him,
But no, he isn't there.
And, oh, how I remember
When they told me to beware.
Beware of him, beware of him
He casts the devils charms.
He'll leave you in the cold dark night
With cold and empty arms.
Beware of him, beware of him
He casts the devils spell.
He'll leave you in the cold dark night
And cast your soul to Hell.
And so I turn my back upon the
Cold and angry sea
And pray the good Lord up above
You don't end up like me.

Shirley M. Keefe

There Is Still Love

God's children of the world
Don't despair
There is still love
Surrounding us everywhere

God's children of the world
Don't hang your head
There is still love
Surrounding us directly ahead

God's children of the world
Look deep inside and spread
The love we still have
To strangers passing by

God's children of the world
Yell, shout, and scream
There is still love surrounding us
Be happy not mean

God's children of the world
Please listen and hear
There is still love
Surrounding us far and near

Brenda Hyter

Where I'm From

I am from bundles of blue flowers,
Which lie by my bed.
I am from rules and love,
Which make my future so clear.
I am from James and Cindy,
Two hearts broken in despair.
I am from pop corn
With butter and salt.
I am from fields of clover
And tall brown trees with many leaves.
I am from my window,
Where the sun shines every day.
I am from a pew,
A Bible in my cold hand.
I am from pictures,
Eyes like the red of blood.
I am from old friends,
Whose memories are like water to me now.
I am from a circle,
A never-ending wheel.

Erin West

Dictating Moments

The days get longer as life progresses.
Every minute dictates the future for
Gaining the virtues of happiness
And the fulfillment one needs.
Not knowing what will happen next,
Brings me to believe life will continue
Until time is stopped.

Joshua Sandlin

The Promise

They were young as young
as young can be.

He was tall; she had grace
and a most winsome face.

They loved in their innocent way,
until the flag called him away.

Her hero never did come home;
she faced the long years all alone.

Now she's old; her hair is gray.
She remembers when he went away.

Soon she'll heed the summons sweet;
after all those years they'll meet.

How tender will that meeting be,
and they will love for eternity.

Cecelia Fenton

In the Wilderness

I was in the wilderness all alone
Then came my Savior, with Heaven adorned
Oh, how happy I was for what he had done
For God, who had brought back His Son

Jesus said, come closer my child
Then His hand was in mine
He was there all the time
So now, when I look up above

At the stars in the sky
I know somehow, he had a reason why
For saving my soul
Jesus loved me, oh, he loved me so

Mary Lorena McDowell Barbato

Candy

As I wake up in the morning
Sun gleaming down on me
Teaches me it's a new day
Daisies cover coated candy
Smiling back at me
It's the way
I express the way I feel today
So just close your
eyes and recognize
all the beauty that
surrounds you
And before you know
it the suns gleaming
down on you.

K. Morris

Invitation to Life

Come with me to the top of the hill
To look around and see what we will.
When we get there, what will we see?
All that is down here, for you and for me.

Julia Cox Wisotzkey

Pencil Breaker

Have you ever wondered
What was in a pencil?
Wood?
Lead?
Not in this one
Just tons of letters
And numbers too
123's and ABC's
All scrunched in one tiny pencil

When you write one letter
Another appears
And this goes for the numbers too

So don't break a pencil
Or all the letters and numbers
Will fall out in your lap
You pencil breaker!

Kylee Renninger

Forever Friends

You were my thought
before my sleep.
You were my conversation
within my dream.
You were my deep breath
in the morning.
You were the one
that I cried with
that I laughed with
that I held when I was scared.
And when I let go
I knew we were forever.

Amanda Downs

They

The frightened boy runs
The panting of a dry mouth
Needing direction
He doesn't know the way

They watch him
tease him
Slowly he disappears
forgotten
he wanders on
his quest not over

He hurries
They found him
They will be angry
he looks back to see
the glowing eyes of his creator
Nothingness
quiet, comforting silence
like a mothers womb

He drowsily stumbles
he knows they are close

Jakob Thomson

The Land Beyond

Somewhere over the rainbow
In a glorious land above,
Our loved ones are waiting there
Wrapped in the master's love.
There is no night, fear or pain,
No wars, storms or heavy rains;
Yes, there is a land we cannot see
Where our loved ones wait
For you and me.

Ruby Dison

Mama

It happened one early morn.
A sudden attack like a storm.
No one knows how or why.
But it sure made me cry.
We thought things were good for a while,
Up and down the hospital isle.
Seven days we hoped and prayed
That good news would come our way.

It happened one early morn.
A sudden call on the horn,
The news was good we thought at last!
The highway trip went real fast.
The Dr. & Nurses were real calm.
It hit Dad and Me like a bomb,
For hours we sat and cried.
Hoping and hoping that someone lied.

I know you're gone to a better place.
But I sure would love to see your face.
Mama you made us all feel so good.
The fun, the laughter is all understood.

Gary Spinks

Silence

He waits for me in the forest
In the early morning, dew
His arms out stretched
I run to Him
Knowing He's there to hold on to
There are things that have happened
Since I've been gone.
He waits in silence
And my heart is breaking
As I went on
When I was through,
He took my hand and with His
Soft voice He said "I love you."

You see, He forgave me
And He already knew.
On this day He still holds my hand.
Isn't it wonderful to know
God understands?

Sandy Beel

Life, the Autumn

When in the autumn of life,
I look back across the years.
In the sunset's rosy glow
The years seem washed by golden tears.
Those golden years together
When our hearts were filled with joy
I left my carefree girlhood
Behind with your laughing boy!

Elfe Roesies

Shores of Time

As I stand on the shores of time,
watching my life go by,
from the deepest darkest lows
to the soaring glowing highs.

As the sun sets in the distance,
my heart begins to cry.
I turn around to you
and you wipe the tears dry.

As I look into your eyes,
a warmth builds up inside.
I put my arms around you
and hold you from morn' 'til nigh.

Neil Hanham

Kimberly

Dedicated to the Memory of Kimberly Burgalis

The pain you suffer is not in vain
You've opened eyes worldwide
Your courage to others is a gain
Giving them hope to turn the tide

Your strength shall be a legacy
For the many who must follow
You set an example for us all
In ignorance we must not wallow

This is not a prejudice from God
It cares not how or whom it takes
Education seems to be the key
To keep us from it deadly wakes

Your footprints you leave in the sand
As you depart this world of ours
Together we take a united stand
To put AIDS in its final hours

Karen Vandevander

Stolen Love

I'm reaching out to you
But you're just not there
Where are you
Please don't go

I gave you my heart
I gave you my love
I let you in my mind
I let you in my soul

I had closed that all up
And I opened it to you
If there were a lock
You'd have the key

If you changed your mind
You don't want the responsibility
Please return the key
That belongs to me

Dorothy Burdett

Owls Odour

Out of my clothes
Owls odour fell
Guardians tip out
All my pockets
In search for feathers

And in the files
A note was made:

CAUTION
CANFLY

Anemone Achtnich

Shadowed Stranger

i am the outcasted stranger
i live in fear and danger
but i would never harm
a living, breathing soul
i seem feared by everyone
so i often hide from the sun
i can never keep warm
for everyone else is cold
i can't seem to view my face
when mirrored by disgrace
i might as well be blind
for i am the only one sees
i am just so misunderstood
this face lies as any could
the truth is held in heart and mind
certainly not in this unfound beauty.

Lauren Friedman

Into the Dark

Into the night,
the spirits take flight.
Capturing dreamers dreams,
and shining down on them purified beams.
They roam in the darkness,
calling out to the harmless.
Into the darkness they fly away,
with nothing but good to do and to say.
The love that they give,
compares nothing to the life they lived.
For they once were harmless beings,
and their praises people would sing.
So they are now wanderers flying free,
giving only to people what they have to bring.
So from now until the end of time,
when you feel a presence in your dream,
you will know what it will be.

Amber Summers

Without Title

We think all our pretty procedures
Will please everyone that meets us
We're happy and flying
But still we are dying
Not knowing the people that need us.

Stefan Halldorsson

An Imaginary World

Today begins a new day
A dawning of the sun
Forever it shall take us
Into a world of fun,
Good-bye to the real world
Hello to the new one
Where ever it shall go
That is where we'll run,
To hide from an enemy
To run from a gun
To see what will happen
Before it's even done,
Be careful what you say
Or this world will be for none
Your imagination is futile
The battle now is won,
This song we have written
This song we have now sung
So say good-bye to this world
And thanks a ton
Good-bye for now, we'll be back tomorrow
To this new world we've begun.

Lindsey Schreiner

Paint

I close my eyes
  And open my mouth
For a desired kiss with her
  But she is replaced
With you
  Painted on my eyelids

Greg Robbins

Rain

lightly refreshing
peaceful rainbows all around
quenching the fresh earth

Celesté Rodriguez

Dusk

A beautiful day
Falls into night,
But somehow, something,
Just doesn't seem right.
You are not here
So you cannot hold me,
And as darkness falls
Shadows surround me.
I imagine your arms
Holding me tight,
And I whisper a prayer
To get through the night.

Jordan Rooks

New England Eyes

An addictive gem:
An emerald moon circles.
Ella sings the highness of the moon
As my blood follows each lyrical chord,
Through a circus of clashing cymbals
Bathing on your inland sea.

How high is this green isle?
As high as the plateau will allow.
Searching the whitewater springs
And finding a short answer
There on the cusp.

Eyes close at dusk.
Eyes at the locus,
The perfumed willow capturing
A clover glade.
Standing with my microscope
For another glimpse of the Irish monarch
Wanting to cry for more.

Martin Jack

Sweet Mama's Got the Blues

It's a b**** without you, honey,
just trying to save money,
It ain't so funny, honey,
since you've been gone.

Mama's got the blues,
Not the type you wear on your exterior,
Naw, it's not that she's inferior,
It's just the interior,
Sweet Mama's got the blues.

You left her high and dry
without a place to fly.
Naw, whatchya do that for?
Sweet, Mama's got the blues.

Now that about wraps it up,
we'll mail it and glue it shut,
but don't worry she won't give up
not this old mama pup,
Sweet, lovely mama's got the blues.

Jan Lyons

Words

Words spoken in anger
Are seldom true,
Yet often hide something deeper.
An unspoken fear,
They sometimes speak
Of broken trust,
Of a heart so weak
And in need of comfort.
So when I speak, please listen,
Not to my words
But to what I'm saying.

Patricia Brown

Peace

Peace is only a starry night.
Hope is only a tiny light.
Far away but it seems so bright;
Shining on those who believe.

Love is only a mother's glow.
Joy is only the falling snow.
Faith is only what hearts can know;
Only the hearts who believe.

Christ is only a quiet birth.
Silent music that fills the Earth.
Gladly telling of all life's worth.
Sounding for all who believe;

Sounding for all to believe.

Jean Tucker

You . . .

You open me up
to life.
You are the eye of my universe,
a sparkling vein of true
color
in a grey world.
You are spring to a heart frozen by
a deep winter chill.
You are the soothing rain to a soul
parched and dry.
You are all that is fine
and wondrous.
You are the true north,
South,
East,
and west.
You are everything.
You are all.
You,
only you.

C. D. Cloyd

sifting—memory

shrinking.fading.choking.revived . . .
once i had a jesus,
        to carry me home.

n o w

prisms are smashed,
        and i am all alone.

you were my religion,
        tres simple un pret.

now there is only Fate; he
        is not answering the phone.

magenta voisens

Waiting

Though we have never met
A secret have I kept.

For some where deep in side
A friendship you cannot hide.

For a time we went our ways
To find each other again one day.

Run you may and try you might
But catch you I will one night.

Bring with me I will my Rope
Catch you I will with any hope.

Told you I was a patient man
And wait I know that I can.

David Kinsfather

The Melody of Nature

A bluebird of happiness
A cardinal of fire
A dove of love
An eagle of courage
An owl of wisdom
A robin of eternal spring
A swan of grace and beauty

Doris Porter

Month and a Half

It was a month and a half ago
Since I saw her for the first time again
Somehow I'm sure we connected
But so much has happened since then

Maybe it was only in my head
The way we seemed to get along
Could it just be my wishful thinking
I've been so d*** lonely for too long

Maybe I'll find an answer
The next time I fall asleep
Dreams are all that reassure me

And I'll get the message
The next time she looks at me
But that won't mean anything

I've been here before
I don't want it anymore
But I can't let it go on my own

Craig Hendricks

To My Lost Love

She came into my life so fast
And left the same way too

I loved her so much
If she only knew

She was so much fun
And full of delight

She made my sun shine
Ten times as bright

She left me standing
At her grave sight alone

Wondering sometimes
Of what went wrong

She brought me joy
And as much pain

But I still love her
All the same

Michael Earl Rash

You in Our Lives

The thoughts of seeing you go
Makes our heart cry so
You were our mentors
Through good and bad
It makes us so sad
To just think . . .
That you will become
The missing part of our link
You will always be a part of us
In our hearts you will stay
Even to the day we pass away
We'll always remember you
With our tender loving care

Kathleen Nancy Villano

Why

My devoted happiness must be cursed,
yet the vultures already see,
The cruel, unjustness of the world,
crawls, and feeds off me.

In my time of need I could only hope,
for someone to help me by,
Yet I stand there shivering in the cold,
asking, screaming the question, "Why?"

"Why a soul that doth not shine?"
then I turn abrupt (just to see),
That I am but in a line,
a million souls. . . then me.

Marlowe D. Gelman

Honey Wheat Bread

Practical, sensible, sweet
Always there
When I need her
The problems
I bring to her
Always important
Receive solutions

Honey wheat bread
Vulnerable
Crumbling under pressure
Burnt by life
Cries out to the
Wonder white

Honey wheat bread
With hard crust
Seemingly impenetrable
Inside
An amazing person
Waits to be realized

Susan Arevalo

Happiness at Last

Years gone by
Without a trace
A stranger in the mirror
Is all that's left
Day in and day out
Nothing familiar anymore
A new face each day
Will be a new face again
Time has no meaning
Growing tired at last
Lying down for a slumber
To finally awaken
To a wondrous place
Peace at last is found
Knowing everything again
A better state of being
No pain to be felt
No sorrow again
Heaven is home now
Happiness at last!

Tammy L. Damron

Death Becomes an Angel

Angels sent to Earth below
One day, back to Heaven will go
Since we do not understand,
We ask God to hold our hand.
It breaks our hearts and we cry
Because we know not the reason why.
Although it brings us grief and pain,
Our loss is heaven's gain

Wanda Wright

What's in a Name?

I knew a man called Mr. Dys,
All he could play was dice.

Then there was a Mr. Lys,
Was his head full of lice?

Following Lys, comes Mr. Mys,
His problem was with mice.
Next I met a man called Mr. Nys,
You guessed it. He is Mr. Nice.

Another day I met up with Mr. Rys,
With his meals he ate much rice.
And last I found a Mr. Wys,
None above could best Mr. Wise.

Oh, I almost forgot Mr. Vys,
He caught his thumb in a vice.

Dorothy G. Elliott

Listening to the Wind

I spent sometime
Listening to the wind
Its rushing sound
Music of a kind
Bringing from afar
Strong rhythm
That moves the heart
Drumbeats and melodies
Sweet songs of the birds
Roars of wild beasts
Messages of the prophets
Laughter of merry makers
The suckling and the aged
Groans of the suffering and the dying
But not a sign or whisper
That I'm in the wrong place
Just now the shrill cries
Of the insects
I could spend more time
Listening to the wind

Ras General Stano

Friendship

We were companions for a time
We stayed together over time
It was friendship that was always warm
We weathered both the sun and storm

But time has made Him torn and old
Our friendship now is growing cold
I'll just have to find one better
So it's good-bye to that good old sweater.

Frank Oppecker, Jr.

The Hangover

Woke up this morning
with a beer in my hand.
Don't know what happened.
Could I even stand?
People tell me things
that I've done and said.
I can't even remember
how I got into bed.
Tracing the evening
through the corners of my mind
I remember some things.
I must have had a good time.
Thinking back, how fun
could it have been?
Too much thought.
I need some aspirin.

Earl Fuqua

Years and Fears

We reminisce of years gone by
The good times that we shared
This happy carefree life of ours
Has just become impaired.

The aging process has begun
A fact most people fear
It's nature's way to let us know
The end is drawing near.

Our health becomes our main concern
As we live day by day
The means to ease our aches and pains
Could be light years away.

We signed up with an H.M.O.
To save a buck or two
The cost of pills and doctor bills
Had changed our point of view.

We never thought the golden years
Would treat us so unfair
If you do not agree with us
Just wait 'til you get there.

Harold A. Rensel

Water

Water running down my nose
Water dripping on my toes

Water flowing in a stream
Water rising up as steam

Water dripping with a drip, drip, drip
Cats going out to take a sip

Water is a pleasant thing
That only God can bring

Lorna McLenighan

Tailor Made

Life shares a way
that will brighten your day
you'll see it in a sign
this life of love
comes from above
it's a mystery—God's special design

No need to test
it's all for the best
why change when nothing's wrong
It was meant to be
like how life sets free
our problems in a beautiful song

Many things are like this
where the tickets already paid
even the strife
we face in life
shares a gift that's tailor made

Kelly A. Fluet

"Untitled"

Solitude is spherical
with a door for only one.
Ample enough for guests,
only one bed is done.
It asks a meager sum, just you,
then shuts you away from view,
But at departing, clicks the lock,
the seam is no more seen.

Dawn P. Barrier

Purgatory

When the light shed its evening grace,
Those among us sit straight laced.
On to see the mirror shine
Through the wall so damned divine.
Castles fall and oceans roar
For coming of Heaven before.
Only those in pain will be indulged,
For they paid the price of life in Hell,
Let me ring the final bell.

Wendy Cosgriff

Purple

Purple looks like royalty
Purple smells like freesia
Purple sounds like a stream
Purple tastes sweet
Purple feels like fleece

Rebecca Thurston

Untitled

In the velvet dark
we begin again

Walking around
face to face

Dancing before
the birth cave,

Being chased up
the sky

Left in the hot
sun to dry;

Leaning
or frowning

In four eyes
and four feet

To help us
in battle

The gift
of

Foretelling
the future

Marvin Silbersher

A Note to Dani at Sixteen

It seems as though, not long ago
We talked more than today
As life flies by, no one knows why
We often lose our way.

I look at you as my child
Forever that's what you'll be
My mind knows you'll be all a woman soon
But my heart refuses to see.

Growing up can be quite painful
Believe me, I've been there
It often seems you're all alone
No one has time to care.

The stress of life surrounds you
Like a weight it presses down;
The more you fight to get on top,
The more it feels you'll drown.

I can't keep the pain from coming
I'll help if you allow me to
Please remember no matter what happens
My love will be here for you.

Chris Harker

Eshnella

Essence sublime
Sweet silence
Captive blissful abyss
El magnificence
Supreme existence.

Geneva E. Schwichtenberg

Life

The "Son" awakens us
With the promise of a new day.

Shadows and storms come,
But don't last.

Memories are made
And old one's fade.

By nightfall, life either goes on
Or sleeps forever.

Linda Neira

Soliloquy

Light and delicate
quiet as a careless whisper
profound in silence
gentle as a rose
pure as a turtle dove
you caress me with comfort
and leave me speechless
and breathless
my soul is enticed
by your elegant way
of peace slow,
but short within distance
how can I possibly
wait on your invincible
calling to arose me
and take me to your
sweet destiny.

Stephanie Espey

Sunset

Alas, the fleeing daylight fades,
And night comes nigh in subtle shades.
The pinks, the purples, and the teals.
Long shadows cast by yonder hills.
The soul of daytime wanes its light,
And 'tis swallowed by the thirsty night.
Its light now cast upon the stars,
Like dewdrops glowing on the spars,
And mother moon with gentle glow,
Keeps watch upon my love below.

Ronald K. Coffey

A Poem like Rain

A poem falls like rain,
Whispering secrets in your ear.
Some are sad, some joyous,
All beautiful.
A poem takes you to places
Beyond the horizon, past the sky,
Singing songs you never heard,
And thoughts you never,
Ever thought to think.
Sometimes a poem shouts,
"Hey, look at me!"
Then falls silent as snow,
And you have to stop thinking
To understand.

Leah Lastovich

The Hare

There was a cute rabbit,
With a very bad habit,
Of always hopping by.

His white tail shone bright,
In my car headlights,
And I hollered, "Oh me, oh my!"

If only the hare,
Had not been there,
He'd still be with us today.

But wait, there he goes!
By the hair of his nose,
He escapes and with us he'll stay!

Jeanette L. Myers

On God

God sent his inner child to Earth
To celebrate a human birth.
To show through him and him alone
Humanity's path to God and home.
With nails in hands and feet he bled,
A crown of thorns upon his head.
With all the love that he could shed,
Showing he'd raise us from the dead.
The inner child became the son
And stated, "the Father and I are one."

M. J. Loring

Wings

If only to have wings
To fly
Away from myself

Miles high
In a cerulean sky I ascend
I fly
Looking down over the edge of a cloud
I may see
The grounded me shading my eyes
To see the other me looking down
A final good-bye from the me in the sky
And I fly
From the me
That walks the desert wastes far below

Now that we parts ways
How many days can the deserted me
Feel joy for the flying me
And how many years will the flying me
Regret the wings
That made me free

Scott Fadness

I Wanted

I wanted to believe you
When you said you cared,
When you said you were there,
When you said you meant it,
I wanted to believe you.

I needed to believe you
When you said you loved me,
When you said you didn't cheat on me,
When you said you wouldn't lie,
I needed to believe you.

I should have believed you
When I first saw your smile,
When I saw the twinkle in your eye,
When we kissed our last kiss,
I should have believed you.

Genevra MacArthur

Each Day with Kim

Thank you for the morning
This will be my way
Of telling her how special
She makes me feel each day

Thank you for the sunrise
But it does not compare
To the beauty that I witness
When I brush aside her hair

Thank you for the daylight
And all the sighs I see
Each one very special
'Cause she shares them all with me

Thank you for the evening
Of this very special day
Thank you God for sending Kim
She makes each day this way

For I can try a million times
And never find a perfect way
To tell Kim how I love her
And pray with me she'll stay

Paul Lopresti Jr.

My Angel

She said softly to him
words that touched his ears,
like butterfly wings
and warmed his throat
from deep inside him.

Moving his hands
up toward her face,
he sank beneath her gaze,
beaten down in tenderness.

Keith Ostrowski

Eternal Love

To this day I give to thee
every little part of me
My loving heart I forgive within
for every single shameful sin
When times are hard
you must believe
Don't turn your back
don't be deceived
I was sent on Earth
to die for you
with eternal love for
whatever you do
Just close your eyes
open up your heart
from you my child
I will never depart

Bernadette Pavor

Ode to the Homeless

'Tis woe and strife
A way of life.
Down and out,
It's all about.
Cold weather rain,
Life, just a pain.
Summer is hot, humid,
They learn not to be timid.
Some want better,
Some, it is no longer a matter.
Die now or later,
Perhaps, just share the tater.

Sheryl Aytes

Peace

The whisper of the wind
The rustling of the leaves
The grass in the meadow
Blowing with the breeze

The stars in the sky
The moon bright and full
Brings peace to the heart
And encouragement to the soul

The sound of the symphony
From the cricket's violin
The birds chirping in harmony
With the whisper of the wind

A moment to reflect
On true peace and tranquility

Sonja McGrew

HATE

Hated him;
wished him dead.
Had that thought
within my head.

So much hurt
at his hands;
so much pain
from this man.

Took my life,
took my heart,
took me physically
apart.

Self-defense
at my hands?
Dying, dead
I saw this man.

Now the thought
that's in my head?
My soul dying;
think it's dead.

Elaine Caudill

St. Patrick's Day

St. Patrick's Day is near
people laugh and cheer
parades, fun, and more
is what they have in store
it comes once a year
and often brings some tears
when the sun goes down
the fun stops but will come, next year

Jennifer Hablett

Sometimes and Forever

Sometimes it may
take a lot of years
just to learn
how we should love

Sometimes it may
take a lot of tears
just to understand
the different ways of

Sometimes it may
take a little courage
just so that we
will see

But the good thing about sometimes
Is that it is ours
Because forever
Is our destiny

Kenneth Martin McNeil Sr.

Fear

In time
I will cry
Because
I am afraid
Of the moon

Elizabeth Cobb

Expectation

Of him I had expected little,
And when that little came
It felt just right
For he had played my game.

Of her I had expected much,
And when her little came
I felt betrayed—
She had not played my game.

Expectation is a scrambled stew
Made by a mother up from scratch,
With luck she finds amid the shambles
Thriving adults who are her match.

Earleen Zinaman

Love Me

When I was a child
You did not care.
I had to move
With strangers to share.
Did you call?
Did you write?
No, for me you did fail
Because you were sitting in jail.

Now I don't see
Dad, mom, and sisters, too.
How do I know
What life will do?
I love my strange family,
But who is that?
The strangers who say
I love you, too.

I love my strange family,
But I cannot stay—
So do I love!

Love me if you can.

Letty Loescher

The Soul of a Sister

The soul of a sister
Is a special thing indeed
God throws in something extra
So she knows when you're in need

she has a special insight
In sensing joy or fear
When to share your hopes
Or hold a bucket for your tears

A gauged degree of knowledge
She'll impart with loving doses
A thorny vine of wisdom
That explodes in vibrant roses

The many things
Our friendship brings
Like a garden sowed with seed

Make the loving soul of My Sister
A very special thing indeed . . .

Karen Chapman Rodriguez

My Resolution . . . My Song

My resolution big, but yet small
Is to see me standing tall

Against the dreams I've stacked so high
And the things that've made me cry

Love yourself like no one will
Is what first I shall fulfill

My course in life I know must change
Although it's hard to rearrange

My past has taught me to let fate
Take me where the road is great

From you I ask for your support
If not, I'd need you to abort

No detours, no curves, I shall not wait
This mission is to take me straight

To the top where I belong
With or without you, that is my song

If you are there then we will see
And if not, it will just be me

Happy and complete, but that's not all
With or without you I'll be standing tall

Carla Burrell

Moment in Time

I am the future.
I am the past.
I am the here and now.

I am that moment in time
that never can return.
So hold me close and know
that you are blessed beyond knowing.

Margie Harbath

Great White Stallion

The mountains have been my refuge
now the valley is calling me
Ride the wind great white stallion
you are brave bold and free
When you get tired of roaming
with you I long to be
But if I cannot hold you
then I shall set you free
There are no reins to keep you
I hope that you might stay
If contented great white stallion
you will never wonder away

Jean L. Egyed

Always

It is always good for me to be nice
It always uplifts my spirit
It is always good for me to be kind
To the ones I love
Family, friends, neighbors, and others
Could be looking at each other
For the last time

It is always good for me to smile
It is like a blessing in disguise
It always makes me feel good
Without worrying about the price
So I always plan to be nice
To always be kind
To always smile, smile, and smile.

Annie R. Rogers

True Love

You are everything
I want
You are everything
I need
You are everything
I've dreamed of
You mean everything
to me

Shane M. McGarvey

Words of Wisdom

I once sought peace,
but found war.
Now, I seek courage,
and find wisdom.

I once sought love,
but found deceit.
Now, I seek truth,
and find God.

I once sought life,
but found death.
Now, I seek meaning,
and find love.

Anthony J. Shidler

Broken Hearted

As I lay upon my bed,
a tear I do not shed.

Though I have a broken heart,
a new life I must start.

As my heart flies away,
I know a new one will come and stay.

Dorease L. Lamon

The Hole

Why do things happen?
Why do things change?
Why do things last?
When are things sane?

When do you know?
When do you see?
When do you go. . . .
Where you want to be?

Why do we hurt?
When do we bleed?
Out all the hurt
In the lives that we lead.

Time tells a tale
Unbelievably true,
Into which your life fell. . . .
Into the hole which was you.

Stephanie Miller

Questioned

From A,
No promises or guilt.
Forgiveness left dry in memory banks.
Mixed emotions, the star, center stage.
Love versus money challenges
an unfair advantage.
Relying on a double standard but
standing on the wrong side.
To Z.

Kim Brown

Long Lost Love

Dedicated to my love, Onihito
We loved 22 years ago.
I lost your love to my own broken heart.
After a long, long 22 years, you entered my heart again.
This time only to stay.
Healed is my broken heart with your words
of comfort, kisses, hugs and support.
We love long, hard and sweet.
Long lost loves are we reunited again my baby and me.
I will love you always and forever

Ann Hernandez

CFIDS

It's called CFIDS:
Chronic Fatigue and Immune
Dysfunction Syndrome.
It has a list of symptoms as unwieldy as its
Name. Chronic and Dysfunction
Are the big ones.
Around and around, over and over,
Body trying to escape the talons
Of an unknown assailant.
Meanwhile, the world goes on and expects
Me to go with it.

I can't.

Marla Perkins

Cold Folded Mountains (A Villanelle)

My legs will form cold folded mountains
Out of cotton, while I wait with carved moons
For his autumn eyes to drown in.

The reflecting pools have dimmed; I found in
His absence love must mean more, but soon
My legs will form cold folded mountains.

His gossamer regard has me bound in
Fetters that keep me softly swooning,
For his autumn eyes to drown in.

Day acts as crucifix to love's demons,
I dread when night follows the blue of noon
My legs will form cold folded mountains.

In dreams, the distant mist of love's fountain
Is full, and I, for his lips slim and smooth,
For his autumn eyes to drown in.

Only in these worlds of night am I sound in
My love. Lonely I wait, under chiseled moon
My legs will form cold folded mountains,
For his autumn eyes to drown in.

Katie Cummings

Love Lost

One too many tears I have to wipe away
One too many fears become reality each day
Well don't worry, my dear,
I am not going away

Time eases pain, but doesn't fill the void
Your faith is gone, all hope is destroyed

The only thing you need your life now lacks
If I could trade, I would bring him back

No matter how you feel or what you say
Tomorrow and today
I'm by your side all the way

I'll hold you now like I held you then
I'm always here when you need a friend

Katie Turner

Summer's Ages

As lazy breezes fill the humid sky,
And oceans express their rage,
Along come the sea gulls, and the dragonfly,
That unleashes summer's cage.

The mist rises from the sapphire's heart,
And the wind exfoliates the spring,
The enchanting summer is beginning to start,
When the pelican decides to sing.

Majestic ripples crash on the beaches,
During the making of castles from sand,
The surfers head for the ocean breaches,
As sour winds sweep the dusty land.

The children sing their summer glee,
Yet the fall begins to blend,
The glaring sun on a daring sea,
Approaches the chill of winter's wind.

Christopher Fipps

Sonnet De La Luna

The moon stepped out in silver gown to rest.
Her feet were sore from running 'round the Earth.
The clouds that trail are those who love her best.
Her belly's roundness tells of the soon birth
Each month she bears herself anew for love.
So too a cleanse takes place for mortal wombs.
When moon doth toil the sky grows deep and Dove,
The white one, weaves a song on darkened loom,
While Mother Moon holds out her babe with beam.
A slice of dazzling white, She coyly smiles.
The high blue hills slide up to hide the stream.
The fresh new moon to bed will dream awhile.
So rides the night on well-smoothed wheels and hooves
We must remember life above our roofs!

Leah Harms

Make Me Smile

In a somewhat crowded and smoked-filled room,
I looked over my shoulder, and I saw you.

The spirits were high and the music flowed,
You seemed to let the music take control.

I couldn't help from taking a glance,
I took a chance, I knew we had to dance.

The rhythmic sounds filled the room,
It seemed to move, and we did too.

There was something special about you,
It was your eyes that shown right through.

Eyes, magic brown with a mystic glow,
A sense of wonder that took control—

Took control of a piece of my heart,
And I'm thankful that a friendship could start.

So thank you God for making you,
With eyes that make me smile,
And make you, you.

Robert Brunstad

future to the past

what we do today in our daily walk of life
eating, walking, education, daily fits of strife
can leave us with scars in later years
or open many doors
some may or may not see other ocean shores
remember as you walk today to notice elders lives
learn the choices you can make and make a difference in your life

Tracy McDowell

Reflections

In your daughter's eyes are
All the sky blue oceans to explore,
All the sparkling new frontiers to discover,
All the dazzling clarities of truth,
All the rainbow panoramas of possibility.

In your daughter's eyes I see
Purity of newborn thought in innocence,
Unlimited scope in the vision of imagination,
Undaunted courage of undoubted immortality,
Boundless love bursting to be shared,
Ever-seeking hope for human kindness,
Explosive joy in new accomplishments,
The quintessence of a child of God.

In your daughter's eyes I see . . . You.

Kathleen Monteleone

The Winter Breeze

The winter Breeze upon my face reminds me when
There was no problem with our race.
The world was peaceful and clean. The winter breeze was
Sometimes mean. But when the sun was bright and warm,
The winter breeze was like a song.
With rosy cheeks and bright eyes tearing, the
Winter breeze was so endearing.
So if the breeze could change direction and make the world with
Corrections,
Peace on Earth will be in place and smiles of hope upon my faces.
Our hearts are singing songs of joy for every little girl and boy,
For all the short, the weak, and the tall—strength will come
For one and all.
So bundle up and be prepared for the winter breeze is very near.

Mildred Brough

Just Ask

My eyes are sad, my heart is bent.
You know not why, but away you went.
You think again, "Oh, here she goes."
But if only you could know what it is that's on my mind,
Then instead of silence, you'd be kind.
I am not angry, but I am sad.
My heart is heavy, but I'm not mad.
In all that is said, in all that is done,
Nothing changes the fact that it is you I love.
But at times there is still pain that stalks,
Yet all we have to do is talk.
Because, I believe, "love conquers all,"
There is no need to build a wall.
For every problem, there is a cause,
None of us are without our flaws.
All we need is sheer concern,
For how others feel, we need to learn.
So why not ask; What would it hurt?
Sadness or pain you would avert.
I love you know and I loved you then,
I've always considered you my friend.
So then, instead of assuming or trying to guess,
Why not be a friend and . . . Just ask.

Robin Evans

Pamela

To my sweet, exuberant six-year-old

P is for patience, it comes and it goes.
A you're adorable from your head to your toes.
M is for mischief, mystery and motion.
E is for energy that flows like an ocean.
L is for laughing and loving and living.
A you're an angel, but you halo is slipping.

Jo Kobeck Combs

True Beauty

Look into the world full of concentration
Pierce into its soul, with deep penetration

What can I say
I love true beauty like one does ecstasy
It is our God given right
It is what we strive for
It is our destiny

So enjoy true beauty
And all that is around
For a new evolution
Is about to go down

The solution is
For the whole nation to rise above
For to know true beauty
Is to know true love!!!

So enjoy true beauty
Bask in its presence
Can you taste it
True beauty is priceless
So it is wise, not to waste it

Michael Keenan

Mandy's Poem

Some people come and some people go,
Why this happens, I don't know.
Some are true and some are fake,
Some I wish would go jump in a lake.
Up and down, all around,
But never there when I am down.

But then that special one popped in,
And never am I without a friend.
She's been there when I was nice and mean,
And even when I would cry and scream.
I'll pray that she will always stay,
And never, ever go away.

I've learned to depend
On my one true friend.
Longing for one more chance,
To hear the birds sing and dance.
Not caring to spend my last dime,
Just to talk to her one more time.

Friendships like this,
Are sort of like loves first kiss.
In a few years I'll look back and remember,
All those stars on the ceiling that shimmered.
And I won't forget to thank the one above
For giving me this gift so full of love.

Corey Rice

Through the Eyes of a Child

Jumping in puddles after a rain,
Climbing in trees with vast heights to gain,
Rolling in snow so fluffy and white,
Snowballs to make to have a big fight.

Kittens to hug with eyes of blue,
Puppies to frolic all day with you,
Butterflies to chase through fields of green
Whose wings in the sunlight glimmer and gleam.

Fish to catch on a fine summer day,
Newborn colts on bed of fresh hay,
Water in which one can splash and swim,
With a rope to swing from hung on a limb.

Not too exciting or fun it seem,
Nothing you'd think of as anyones' dreams,
These things could only be gay and wild,
When looking through the eyes of a child.

Doris Thomas

Midnight Dance

Blue wind dances with the pines at midnight
at a high pass in the mountain peaks
and leaves a sweet scent wherever she goes
her footsteps turned to deep blue rosebuds
her body in silent endless motion
singing and laughing because she is young
and will be forever.
Her fingers sweep the crimson clouds
her toes dipped in silvery waters
swirling the colors of the sky and lake
twirling with rosy mists through the forest
whirling wildly with weeping willows
bringing them joy like no one else can
singing and laughing because she is free
and will be forever.
She takes up handfuls of sparkling pebbles
and tosses them into the wondering sky
to watch them fall as shooting stars
as she leaps over the ivory moon
to land on her feet by the cool waterside
skimming the lake and the moonlit treetops
singing and laughing because she can.
The blue wind dances at midnight.

Anni Wilson

Never Forget

Our journey has ended.
It's time to start anew.
New places, new faces, a new world to see to.
Mystery, magic, all this will be there.
For starting a new life will become our new care.
But with this sudden change, frightful things may come about,
That may make us wonder and begin to doubt.
In these times of trouble, when we need to hear laughter.
It's our old friends that we will begin to seek after.
We remember the old times, the heartaches, the fun.
The parties, the dances, the days in the sun.
The memories of old, the ones we never forget,
Will be with us forever, in our minds we commit.
Old friends never fade, never seem to disappear.
Whenever you need them, they will always be near.
They were always there for you, whatever time night or day.
And always knew just the right things to do or say.
Your troubles seemed so small, your tears never came,
For with your old friends, immediate answers were named.
Life is always better when you have friends to hold.
This is what I learned and have forever been told.
Friends should never forget, never lose touch in any way.
For having your old friends will leave you with brighter days.

Tori Jacoby

Night Fears

The moon,
   shadowed by the looming clouds;
   makes more prominent the eerie silence.
Leafless limbs,
   metamorphose to skeletal, sinuous fingers,
   reminiscently beckoning.

Night has fallen . . .
   Sweet slumber,
   I pray, come to me.

Broken stillness,
   cognate to owlish screeches;
   penetrates the air with perilous warnings.
Listless dreams,
   befitting the gloomy night;
   awaken within, dark foreboding anxieties.

Night Fears . . .
   Oh, sweet slumber,
   I plead . . . please come to me.

Patricia Calorel

It's Time to Say Good-Bye

It's time to say "good-bye" although we've hardly met;
I can still hear your "hello" and I wish I could forget.
The sound of your laughter and the smile on your face,
The touch of your hand and the feel of your embrace.
The pause of silence while you try to say "good-bye,"
The tears I saw so clearly as I looked into your eyes.
Please don't say "good-bye"; just turn and walk away,
Remembering always you're in my heart to stay;
And if by chance we meet again we'll smile and say "hello,"
Never again will we be alone,
We'll be together wherever we go.

Joyce V. Officer

Empty Room

An empty room is all that remains.
The love, and joy, that we once shared
Are gone, replaced by a hollow despair
That lives in that empty room.
Grey and dusty walls, which one time were bright, and
Full of life, now adorn that empty room.
Beautiful music, we used to dance are but a long
And distant memory, that fades with time.
That old and sad empty room
Cries out for one last taste of our loving embrace.

Grisel A. Vina

Moses' Tabernacle: A Heavenly Pattern

O God, how amazing it was that in the whole of Your plan,
For fellowship with and redemption of man,
That through Moses You told of Your dwelling place there,
In veiled truths revealed Jesus with all men to share!

Of a heavenly pattern it was, and became,
The place where You met and called them by name,
Far more than a structure made with men's hands,
For You had deeper meaning within those demands.

Revelations divine of a Light yet to shine,
On sin-laden hearts, yet You said, "They are Mine,
I'm not willing to lose even one who'll believe,
I'll give them the Truth, in it's pattern I'll weave,
The plan of salvation, in force from the start,
The plan for a Savior to live in their heart!"

Only Your heavenly pattern will bring,
Peace to the soul, make the spirit take wing,
So all that is left, is hid in the cleft,
Of our Rock, Jehovah-Jireh, Lord, and King,
The One who dwells in once empty shells,
And creates within us a new song to sing.

Gloria J. Reed

Happiness Tears

My baby loves me
This I am sure of
Just as I know there are snow white doves
The sparkle in her eye and
The warmth of her smile
Pure as the love of an innocent child
She is my warmth in the winter
A cool autumn breeze
A summer night sunset
Which sets my mind at ease
A shoulder to cry on
When all is lost
A tender hug
A touch of her lips
Is enough to melt away all my fears
'Cause my baby loves me
I cry happiness tears

Karl Schoch

Dying Earth

The dying Earth is no longer green
with mighty trees that reach the sky
tall green grasses that sway in the breeze
majestic mountains that line the horizon
The air is foul with smog and smoke
the rivers flow with sludge
All God's creatures struggle to survive
in this unnatural disruption of nature
The birds no longer sing
the buffalo don't roam the plains
all the forests have been felled
the polluted ocean spits up fish
Cement cities cover the land
their pollutants fill the air
Man hunts and kills the animals
devouring the fruits of the Earth
leaving his refuse in vast piles and deep pits
Destroying the planet; land, sea and air
The Earth is dying and no one cares

Sean Hardner

Souped-Up Chevy

I pulled up to the light in my souped-up Chevy
Waitin' for a race, baby, I was ready
In the next lane came a hot-rod Ford
Tinted windows and "Sly" across the door

The light turned green and my foot hit the floor
Through the smoke I couldn't see the Ford anymore.
A smile crossed my face and I thought that I had won
Patted the dash and said, "Son of a gun."
At the next light the Ford was no where to be seen
'Cause it was waitin' up the road for me.

I decided I had to talk to this guy
And find out just where he learned to fly.
When the door opened and the driver stepped out
I forgot everything I'd been thinkin' about.

Tight black dress and legs up to there
White lace jacket and auburn hair.
Prettiest blue eyes I've ever found
And the fastest car in town.
I told my mamma I'd found my wife.
My dad pulled out an old huntin' knife
Said, "Flatten her tire if you think you're ready
'Cause you'll never catch her in that souped-up Chevy."

Cynthia Denny

My Daughter

Dear daughter, of mine, at our once again departing times.
I know our lives were not what we wanted,
We had so many ups and downer's

It felt like only yesterday,
I bought you home in my arms to keep you save,
And teach you with the rights and wrongs

But, it seemed as years went by, our time
together shorter . . . in time.

Then at last I thank the Lord,
Forgiving me back my baby girl . . . once more!

I thought this was the time for us,
To teach you all the things that you
should have already known . . .
Like cooking, baking, and sewing and Oh!
Of course, the best of all,
To dress you up on prom night,
A mother's memories, a mother's delight!

Then, at last "Graduation Day"
How proud parents stand and say . . .
She, that's my child, I raised her well!

Lenora O'Donnell

Giving In

I can smell her as she prowls up behind me
As if she was a little girl
Going to cover my eyes with her hands
I do not think she knows
I can sense her from twenty feet away

She wraps her arms around
Squeezing me
I feel trapped
My lungs are overwhelmed by her grip and smell
She says, "I love you"

I squirm
Searching for a way out
There is no escape
Her hold is too strong

I am a weak man, a man who is easily overpowered
A man who submits
I do not think I could ever break loose
"I love you too"

Corey M. Gordon

Autumn's Call

Oh, dew on autumn's chilled ground
You sparkle from the morn's sunshine;
Soon you'll melt from its warmth
Giving drink to Earth's parched ground.
Hear autumn's call.

Your radiant leaves of red, gold and orange
Bring pleasure to beholding eyes;
Gusty winds and gentle breezes
Will soon careen them to the ground.
Autumn keeps calling.

The heart of man is anticipating
The conversion from summer to fall;
He will provide protection for his gardens
With nutritional mulch leaves furnish
Autumn is fading.

Geese and ducks are flitting anxiously
Upon neighboring ponds of green and moss;
Recognizing autumn's urgent call

Instinct directs them to migrate southward.
Autumn disappears for a season.

Marie L. Barta

Time

When all the bombs and conflicts cease,
when every nation lives in peace
when poor break bread in mansions fine,
then I will toast with fruit of vine.

When women, men of every race,
perceive themselves in other's face,
when young and old walk hand in hand,
then I will dance upon this land.

When families finally live in peace,
when faith and hope and love increase,
when fathers stay to rear their sons,
then I will laugh; then I will run.

When seniors dance whenever they deem,
when young ones sleep and dream sweet dreams,
when fear is gone and love reigns high,
then I will leap and touch the sky.

When time is measured by love's embrace,
when all God's people see God's face,
in every person, big or small,
then I will be a part of all!

John J. Piantedosi

West Virginia Mountains

Misty mountain mornings of spring.
Listening to the birds as they sing,
Watching the clouds as they go by,
Looking at the beauty of the sky.

Sweet misty rain beginning to fall
Sitting on the porch trying to capture it all.
Watching the beauty of the glorious trees
As they are swaying with the breeze.

Lightening flashing across the sky,
Thunder rumbling as the storm goes by.
The sun comes flowing across the mountainside.
The morning now calm, the storm has died.

The sun is so warm and soothing to the touch.
As I sit staring at the mountains that I love so much.
Almost Heaven, West Virginia, misty mountain majesty,
Breathtaking beauty for all the world to see.

Freda R. Moore

I Thank God

I thank God that I'm black, tan
That's the color that he made me.
I am.

I thank God that I'm a woman
That's the person he made me
I am.

I thank God that I'm a Christian
That's the love and grace he has given me
I am.

I thank God that I'm me, beautiful see
That's the way it should be.

I thank God that I'm me
That's the way he created me
In his image he made me.

Belinda Hewitt

Wind

Wind, wind, what is wind?
Is it what creeps ups your back when you're cold,
Is it what cools you down when you're hot?
Is it a tornado that brings new life?
Is it a friend or not?
But really what is wind?
Guess we will never know.

Susan Mayberry

Beautiful Black Girl

Days, hours, minutes, seconds
Time to rethink confidence time to rethink
Experience you still smile, still live
Yet you're rising like the sun growing like
The flowers that are getting ready to bloom
Strong black hair with a texture that flares
The last to be feared but
The first to be dared people may think you
Don't hear but still you listen even though
You daze in a world that you think is far but
Yet so near the future calls as well as the
Walls of life might seem to not be right
Thanking the Lord for every night you saw
The stars having the time to know who you
Are opportunity is coming sooner than you
Think stay strong, hold on, and keep pressing
On you may have failed but your not a
Failure you eyes gleam in the light, God
Has made you to be loved, noticed,
And beautiful no one can tell you, who you are

Shante Robinson

Gay in the USA

Let's be politically correct today
Conveniently forgetting those who are gay
Expression is free says the KKK
As they beat and murder those who are gay
Institutions are private says the BSA
As they cheat and betray those who are gay
"It's just wrong!" So the religious say
As they turn their backs on those who are gay
It's a matter of opinion says the USA
As four of five states legally hate those who are gay
Life isn't fair, at least that is what they say
But this is how we're treated because we are gay

James J. Small

Missing Piece

In your life God sets you a goal,
that's to find the missing piece of your soul.
So in the end you're one beautiful whole.

Your missing pieces might be everywhere,
you might find one from a dare,
it might be a soul mate,
you and the person a pair.

It might be an adventure of any kind
or an impetuous find
or just when you've made up your mind.

Your missing pieces might be everywhere,
but you're the only person who has to care.

Rita Van Talenhove

We

We went down by the ocean
And sat down on the sand
Watched the water roll on the shore
And sifted with our hands

We squinted our eyes toward the horizon
Where small sail boats glided by
And colorful water skiers
Were background against the sky

We buried our feet and ankles
Constructed little hills and vales
Tossed a ball high in the air
Filled our little pails

We walked hand in hand toward the sunset
Leaving footprints along the way
Smiling, waving swim suits wet
Bronzed bodies—heads of gray

Dorothy E. Shirley

Eyes

I thought my heart had learned its lessons
I thought I had it trained
I thought that I had loved and lost and there
Was no love for me in this cold world
But when I looked into those eyes
Those eyes that spark every beat of my heart
Those eyes that are so kind and so full of love
Then I knew that I would know love
I know I will truly be happy
And when I look into those beautiful eyes
Those eyes that inspire my very soul
I pray to God that you will never stop never ever stop
Those eyes that have captured my soul
Always let those eyes those beautiful loving
Eyes look my way with tender loving care
And with a soothing glance that heals all
Know that I will always be there
Those wonderful eyes that have shone me true warm love

Kevin Terrell

Untitled

Strong enough to cry
But weak enough to laugh
Alcoholic rugburn read my mind
And left me with this empty shell
of a sunburned catatonic insomniac
while I sleep at night
I sleep more in the day
Screaming neighbors over run music
Through the walls of my clean toilet dirty carpet
Home where my shoes are left at the door
to sleep by my religious guilt

Angela Miller

The Year 2000

The inevitable is here to shear
what is near or in its atmosphere
Though we are still here it's clear to cheer
We have been blessed and everything is sincere
Tranquility surpasses and exploits the land
Though peace and harmony is at our command
Could we stand as brothers and sisters as a God once planned
Our could tyranny or bigotry prevail hand and hand
Love is something rewarded it interacted
It has to be pure, not something that's manufactured
Coming from up above, blessed and pure
I'm sure we will endure and find a cure
To be honorary and loyal discreet and uplifting
Being of sound, mind, and body
is what we are missing.

Anthony D. Sullivan

The Fight

Through blood and sweat my tears do roll,
Fighting for what's left of my soul.
Darkness and peril I must face,
To win against this demon's race.
In the light of day and the
black of night they roam.
Tearing into my dreams with their
screams and moans.
Tormenting my body and soul, 'til
I can no longer go.
No tears I will show.
For my broken armor and my will
to fight; I have no longer.
At last they have won my tortured soul.

L. Garber

A Message from Your Angel

As I look around the people that I see
Always standing there watching over me,
For friends I've known along the way
Help pave rough roads for a better day,
For thought, support, loving and caring
They gave it there all with little spearing,
I could always depend on those friends of mine
Any minute of the day, no matter the time,
There is one more thing I'd like to say
Please keep in your hearts day by day,
A gift given by the good Lord above
Blessed with a family and unconditional love,
You've given me strength more times than you know
To keep up the fight and carry the blow,
For the love you have given stored deep in my heart
Cherished thoughts of my family can't tear us apart,
For loved ones that leave us really aren't gone
They're just in another place to carry on,
If ever you need me, look towards the heavens above
Whisper the word angel, I'll send you my love.

Donna Kelly

Who I Am

I never knew who I really was
Until I saw inside myself
To find out, I had to look really hard
Into the eyes of someone else
The moment could have passed me
If I hadn't turned that way
And looked upon the hitchhiker
On the road on that cold, March day
As my car passed, I turned to glance
Looked right in the eyes of the one
The dark man with the long chestnut hair
Standing in the light of the sun
I saw myself then, in his eyes
A young girl with a bright smile
I knew he was viewing the real me
Not someone false, or vile
After that, things changed, much for the better
People (including me) were surprised
To finally see who I really was
I found out through a hitchhiker's eyes

Cassandra Van Halst

Any Day

Any day I cannot see
 The sunlight glinting off your gorgeous hair,
Any day I cannot hear
 Your appealing laughter that fills the air,
Any day I cannot smell
 The sweet aroma of you passing by,
Any day I cannot touch
 Your tender and beautiful hands with mine,
Any day I cannot taste
 The smallest morsel prepared by you,
Any day of mine
 That has no hint of you
Is Wasted.

Matthew D. Williamson

Run! Run! Run!

It's not just delusion
that's caused your confusion,
Your eyes were just seeped in loves mire.

It's not what you've seen
that's in the cracks of your dream.
Your heart set its own self on fire.

It's not when she fell clear
that's made you tremble in your fear.
Your brain read your lips—you're a liar.

It's how you can't face the sun
that your backs on the run.
Your colors won't fade beside her.

Deirdre Zemanek

Life to Me

Sinister a relative to irony.
Dwelling in the dark alleyways,
yet to strike out at the nearest object,
human or animal.
To find out such a dark force, you shall lose
one happy thing in life.
Remember, if at all possible, do not talk to
this dark stranger that is so worldly.
He may appear to be kind,
but if friendship kindles,
his talons shall grow deeper into your soul.

Melissa Kaskela

Elf-Queen

So long ago there was a day I ceased to be alone.
No longer would I watch and wait and dwindle flesh and bone.
Inside I knew that time would say if all is as it seems,
But for the while I'd have to stay apart from my Elf-Queen.

Today, today is my wedding day, Oh! how my love has grown.
I'll take the ring and then I'll say: I do to her alone.
To love and cherish our days away is all that I could deem
The best for her in every way, for the love of my Elf-Queen.

Some time from now will come a day to chill my heart as stone.
No longer will I talk and pray and sit with her at home.
In my heart I'll know her way has left me half a team;
But on I'll plod to ever say, Namarie, my dear Elf-Queen . . .

Brian Ackermann

Standing by Washington Square, a Japanese Girl Ran by Me

Sun Mie, carved of ivory,
Smoothed of crystal, polished of marble,
Luminous of luminous; in stillness you run in time.
Delecti Mie, light shifting as you pass,
The only changing on the painted vase,
Your porcelain face.
Agnes Dei, your eyes downcast,
Teach that sin is not desire;
But is in the wanting:
You leave that to others.
Ethereal and small, without really nose or mouth,
Your face is the face of a virgin
So fine that god must exist.
I see you as you are: a translucent sacred cup,
A perfection to hold a mystery I am not to know
Standing, I see you running again behind
The glass,
Realizing I am almost dead at last,
And almost don't want you,
I will hate
How you keep running in my mind.

Tibor de Cholnoky

before i go

before i go, i shall re-think
of those and theirs i loved and not
to chaste or didactic at my loss
but rather all have wept in like manner

before i go, he will be filled
of all we leave if just one moment
be cherished like sugar yet she will
know all that memory by sharing a touch
with he who knows himself likewise

yet nay, i'll stay, yet nay i must
but shall i go . . . oh sweet, sweet must i, shall i know,
as all in times sweeping arms rest with thee before i go.

andrew sarkady

people

people fear and people hate
never knowing exactly why
how much longer can peace wait?
every day we hear the lie
we are better than the rest
always born to rule
on an eternal power quest
when will they see the truth?
people are just people, basically the same
regardless of where you go
or who you try to blame.

Kendra Werden

Our Earth

Dinosaur trace fossils found
Where once dinosaurs roamed.
Birds and decaying plants lived
Millions of years ago
On moist, soggy ground.

Now horses and deer roam
With rabbits and colorful parrots,
Trees rock back and forth,
Dangling branches about to fall,
Sunlight in little rays
Comes through the branches.

Tomorrow will trees be destroyed?
Will lumberjacks annihilate the rain forest?
Will someone else care for this forest
Millions of years from now?

David Lopez

Welcome to the Rest of My Life

People say that time will heal,
but my heart tells me, that is not real.
The ache in my heart to kiss you goodnight,
is a pain I know I can never make right.
It does not matter who can see,
that losing you took a part of me.
I don't understand why I'm not there with you,
because when you left my life went to.
I relive the phone call every day,
when a few simple words took you away.
I begged and pleaded for you to stay,
although I already knew it could not be that way.
Each day I watch the fading light,
and dread the coming of the night.
When I finally give in and fall asleep,
I watch you die and I weep.
I miss you more with each passing day,
but here on this Earth I have to stay.
If I have to live this pain and grief,
I pray to God please make it brief.

Tammy Pipkin

Alone

I am alone. No one can see inside
My heart and know my dreams and joys and fears.
And in that place where heart and mind collide,
Alone is all I have to hold as dear.
But in my solitude yet there is One
Whose love does pulse within me all the while.
Though I with none to feel my heart do run,
One pulls me up and on with every mile.
And in alone I find a strength within,
Not of myself but by His greatest grace.
There's beauty in alone no one else can win.
For this is where I best can see His face.
My hidden heart only by One is known.
And thus I live the beauty of alone.

Brandon Williams

Clouded

Today brings no comfort,
tomorrow brings no solace,
yesterdays hang above me like distant clouds,
prepared for when I need to blanket myself in them to keep sane
or use them as body armor against the elements.
Sometimes when I manage to shake my imprisoning chains loose,
I chase my clouds as far as I can,
and beg them to take me back into their world
where truth was dominant and friends were forever.
But the winds of time blow them steadily onward,
leaving me as well off as an animal in a rainstorm with no shelter.

Becky Kratz

The Wild Fire

You suckle the drops within huddled clouds
You comfort the winds when thunder is loud

You drink the sun in lofty places
You embrace the world, dry empty spaces

You lift the heavens with mighty limbs
You fetter the mountains, steep canyon rims

You offer a clutch, many colored wing
You give refuge for courtship to sing

Your breath is shared by all our lands
Your death gives life to brandish the sands

Oh, ancient ones, who shadow the stones
When will your symbiotes, diviners of the loam

Seek to sanctify vast beauty in the face of dire
Vow to protect your treasures from the greed of the wild fire

Craig Chatterton

A Father's Loss

My hands were busy through the day
I didn't have much time to play
The little games you asked me too
I didn't have much time for you . . .

The guys were waiting, I had to go,
You were too young to really know . . .

But when you'd bring your picture book
And wanted me to take a look
And ask me "please" to share your fun
I'd say "A little later son"

I never tucked you in at night
To hear your prayers, turn out the light
I never tiptoed to your door
And wished I stayed a minute more

Yet you turned out to be so great
No thanks to me, I learned too late . . .

I missed so much, there's no more time
Now I know it's true, that the loss was mine . . .

For life is short, the years rush past
A little boy grows up so fast.

Joanne Sergio

It's Time

Let's start today, to change the world
For the betterment of every boy and girl
Let's give them a peaceful world to live in
Let's throw away the hate, war and the sin

Let's feed the hungry, clothe the naked
Let's uphold the laws that are sacred
Let's help the sick, and the dying
No matter what, let's keep on trying

It's time to throw away the guns, missiles and bombs
Anything else that can do the Earth or us harm
It's time for the human race to do some healing
It's time to step back and study our dealing

War has not done any of us any good
It was for God's glory, we once stood
Stop trying to take over God's green Earth
It belongs to everyone through heir or birth

Stop killing because of color, religion or creed
It's God who made us different you see
In religion let there be no compulsion or death
Unless God Himself takes away your very own breath

Jean A. Robinson

The Progressive Millennium Blues

You were a cold-hearted man,
just threw all of my feelings in a garbage can.
These days now that we're through,
I know God blessed me when I was dumped by you.
I didn't want a lover on a screen,
stuck in chat rooms, Valentino was your thing.
Sweet after awhile to everybody in cyberspace.
And you couldn't see me right in your living space.
I used to think that you were smart.
You knew all about Networking and the way to my heart.
Now I think that we were both fools.
I had to pay your provider all your past due.
You were a cold-hearted man,
moved back with your mom, just laptop in hand.
These days now that we're through,
I hope cyberspace keeps people like you.
You will never know women one on one,
pretending in chat rooms that canned response is fun.

LaDonna M. McCormick

All You Have Done

Stealing my heart was so easy for you,
True love was a fantasy
Only you could make true.
Love was transparent, like charcoal steam.
You were the one cut out of my dreams.

You were the one who woke me from sleep,
And stole my heart with a love so deep.
You opened the door to a love so dense,
You cared not for the cost and expense.

You grasped me from the darkness not a moment
Too soon, and displayed a love so pure and
Perfectly in tune.
The light in your soul was impossible to avoid:
Hate you banished, fear you destroyed.

The day I met you the loss of love
was quenched,
My soul, once so dry, was instantly drenched
By the love you give so blindly.

Heather Martin

Insomnia

Brisk is the wind that blows through your hair.
Bright are the stars that shine down upon you.
Dark is the water that holds mysteries below.
Echoes you hear from far away places,
Waves crashing, people calling, bells chiming.
Beware the train racing down the track.
The horn blowing with great intensity,
There's no turning back.
Things become calm as the hours go by,
Hearing only bells and sails of boats nearby.
The wind settles down, the stars become faint.
The obscurity of night soon to be defeated
By the radiance of day.
The birds begin to sing, as night passes by.
The world will awaken, another night aside.

Monique Lloyd

Life Is Sweet

Since I've been with you, life is too sweet,
and there's not a day that I can't beat.
Because I have you by my feet,
supporting my balance with every heart beat.
And with every breath you take, that's every move I make
to get closer to you, and say your just a dream come true;
that's fallen from thin air, and has made everything so fair.
All I hope is to keep you for an eternity, my dear.

Cathy Berrios

...yer

...k you today to keep my family
sa... ...ay. My husband, my children,
they are my life, you see, they mean so
much to me . Please! Don't let them have
a tragedy for it would devastate me.
For I know so many are taken away
without a word, a chance to say . . .
good-bye. Don't let this happen to them.
I can't bear to live without them.
I can't take care of them on my own.
Lord, I've needed you all along.
I have no control over life or death.
So Lord, that's why I'm asking you this—
don't take them from me, I pray.
Keep your hand upon them each day.
I'm depending on you, Lord, you're all
I've got when I am with them or when
I am not. I need you no matter what!
And please, don't take me from them,
for it would hurt them. For they need
me to be here and such. I hope I'm not
asking too much! No matter what we have
to face, let us always be safe.
This is what I ask today.
Keep us together forever, oh, Lord, I pray.

Margaret Kitchens

Warm

For my husband.
In the dim blue light of a Sunday morning,
You slept very still.
I lay awake turning your hand in mine.
I have always loved your hands.
I sat thinking about the places they have been,
People they have loved,
And how I have never not wanted them touching me.
Before returning back to sleep,
I placed your hand over my heart,
And wondered if the baby's hands will be like yours.
Warm.

Joelle Holdahl

What Is Freedom?

Freedom is a state of being,
Hearing and seeing
Living and breathing, loving and grieving.
Savoring the unique person you are
Going anywhere, near or far,
Helping others without thinking twice
Being naughty or being nice.
Growing old without looking back
To see what worldly possessions you lack.
Accepting your fate whatever it be
Entering the gate to eternity.

Lucy Cowan

Flowers

Flowers are for friends,
For friends who are feeling blue,
Friends who need some happiness,
For the days that are forever blue.

Flowers are filled with friendship and trust,
From the goodness of a
Friends loving heart.
For when you are given a
Flower from a friend cherish it
Forever more.

Jennifer Headley

My Elaine

I was young at the time, and I was weak and broken.
Soldiers have such times when feeling alone, sickly or near death.
I had just recovered from a bout of something
it was thought possibly the dreaded "Legionnaire's disease."

However, that day was so special to me.
It was the day my parents were coming to see me.
Weak but excited I walked down to meet them.
My daddy had never gone to war
but he knew I would soon enough.

The walk lasted some time.
Excited as I was, I guess the illness still had a slight grip on me,
but there a short distance away I saw my mother and dad,
and with them they had the one girl that I had been in love with
since our first meeting, so many years ago.

I wanted to run to her and to them but youth betrayed me
and I became shy and self-conscious.
Oh yes, she had never seen me with no hair I was so embarrassed.
But, we had a great visit and by the day's end
when they were preparing to leave my heart felt sad
I wanted her to stay forever. My Elaine.

Wars come and go and mine went,
it would be over twenty years before I could be with her again.
But now she is, and will be 'til our end, my Elaine.

David Hale

Trying to Find a Way

I need help
trying to find a way.
the path is gone,
my muscles are too weak to go
on to find the way.
I am the only one left,
trying to find a way
My friends have fallen down,
giving up their faith to go on
the way God made for us.
To walk down the dusty path
trying to find my way into happiness
and peace with my soul.
"My God, my God, why have you forsaken me?"
Give me courage, wisdom, and faith
By your mighty hand,
lead me into your glory.

A. J. Sementilli

Quad

I like to ride my father's quad,
It's fast as a little hot rod.

Riding across the desert fast,
With this quad I won't be last.

Riding the trails with all its bumps,
Making a few into really small jumps.

Taking off jumps, you could get real high,
To make you feel like a bird that can fly.

As you go up a really steep hill
You can receive a painful spill.

Riding a wheely three feet in the air,
Taking it higher, only if you dare.

When you ride you should use your head,
If you don't you could wind up dead.

Always respect the quad's mighty powers,
For when you don't you could be pushing up flowers.

Tanner Lindley

The Arkman Cometh

When the hissing, lapping thunder-gurgle
 lulls us from our placebo dreams,

and the promised blast of hot purification
fails to warm our freezer burned souls,

will we go quietly with you again?

one by one
   two by two

or
is THIS the time we jump ship?

Paul Stabin

Creases

I get the impression
that I'm creeping
on the thin line
just over the edge
of the rim of my reality
that I stretch
as I press on and realize
that I'm fallen.
My feelings ripped out when not shown
everybody's gone now, and I stand alone.

Holding tight to the edge I'm gripping.
Fight for my life but I'm slipping.
Tell me in your eyes am I fading?
My spirit dies when my soul cries
and once again I'm fallen.

I found reasons for my secrets why I never stayed.
I found creases in my feelings that gave me away.
How much longer should I wonder why it always rains?
I shouldn't bother while I'm under my silhouette of pain.

Samuel Reichman

I Love U

u make my heart fill with joy
i know i'm just a boy
but i know that i love u.
i hope that i'm with u the rest of my life
maybe you'll even be my wife.
only time will reveal
that we will love each other still.
but until then i will keep u to cherish and to hold
and keep ure heart warm when it is cold.
i love u more than life itself.

Eric Erickson

Cherish Love

Cherish love . . .
 It's God's gift from above

Falling in love is something the whole world will do

 Finding true love only happens to few.

Love is supposed to be both give and take . . .

 sometimes we just take until it's too late!

Often we forget to show that we care . . .

 Taking for granted that the one we love will always be there!

Then when their gone our heart fills with sorrow . . .

 We look to the future with empty tommorows
So cherish love with all of your heart

 because if you don't . . .

your love's sure to part!

Sheri Peace

I Think I'm in Love with You

Roses are red
Guess what I made my bed
I think I'm In Love with you
My Eyes Are Blue
It's those little things
That tug on my heart strings
So don't be shy
I'd hate to make you cry
But when your feeling blue
Smile and say . . .
I think I Love you too!
Your probably thinking I'm nuts
I'm not . . . I'm in love . . . putz!
When I think about what I have when I'm with you
I think I'm In Love With You!
When we kiss I feel so alive
I hate Abba music and the Hand Jive
I think I'm In Love With You
But if push should come before a shove
All I ask for is just a little more love
But if your feeling blue
Laugh and say . . .
I think I love you too!

Joel Itkonen

Thinking of You

This one goes out to the one I love.
When I first saw you, your beauty made me speechless
My heart . . . Skipped a beat
I thought, "when did God let an angel slip away?"
I only saw you for a little while,
But that time seemed to last forever.
If only you would be mine . . .

I can't stop thinking of you.
You are the only thing on my mind,
Weather I'm sleeping or awake, it feels . . .
Like you are right there beside me.
I can't wait until I see you again,
You're so close, yet so far away

We come from two completely different places . . .
But our hearts, our hearts are from one and the same.

Matthew Lucius

If Only

I speak but you cannot hear,
Something else holds your attention.

It was my only wish for so long
that you could see me and I you.

But you hide from me,
not wanting to get too close.

You think I cannot love you,
You think I cannot miss what I have not known.

You won't let me know you,
And you do not want to know me.

Where does that leave us?
Strangers in the house that we share.

I wish it was a home,
But you cannot call home what you
do not miss when you leave.

If only we could know each other,
If only we could understand.

Charlotte Inscho

The Coronet

I stood beside my car the day it failed to move.
'Twas out of gas.
The people passed and went their merry way.
A driver yelled, "You can't park there!"
and kept on going by.
I stood alone
amidst the crowd.
With head held high but heart deeply bowed,
I commenced to say a prayer.
"What will I do?
They'll me sure
If SOMEONE doesn't help me. . . ."
A busy afternoon it was;
I'd just returned from school just off the tracks of Kansas Avenue.
The motor coughed and died
It would not start again although I tried and tried.
I put the car in neutral
I pulled it to the side
Its rear was in the roadway—
I just broke down and cried!

Bobbie Williams

Being Apart

Being Apart is the hardest thing to do.
Having never flew, but yet I knew I could never stand
Being Apart from you,
So I got on a plane to come to you,
As I knew you felt the same way too,
And so I traveled from Kentucky to the Philippines for you,
But without your love, this I would never do.
After arriving, there was much to do,
Because I knew I wanted to marry you.
Then marrying you was a dream come true,
So we went about as new couples do,
laughing and loving, as I have never knew.
Because I love you my wife, as I will always do.
On February 9th it becomes true,
That Being Apart was going to be the hardest thing to do.

James Kinney

The Question

What if I walked up
And asked you to dance?
What if you actually said "Yes"?
What if I look into those beautiful eyes
And see my every dream come true?
What if those lips
Taste as sweet as they look?
What am I supposed to do then?
What if you are really the one
And I decide to befriend only you?
These are the questions I asked to myself
As he approached me from across the room.
As he smiled and asked me, "Can you be kept?"
I replied, "Only if I can keep you."

Jennifer Stinson

A Divine Intervention

For Gina

Time to find another place
she is gone without a trace
please forget unpleasant times
i will leave the world behind.
what i need is time away
a place, a rebirth, some kind of hideaway,
and when the truth cannot be found
a divine intervention will take me down
and she will come to save my soul
the bitterness is gone, from head to toe.

Henry Blan

Love's Promise

I fell into your presence, you took me by surprise;
I lost all recompense, when I looked into your eyes.

Close your eyes softly now, take me by the hand;
I'll show you what it feels to love, your pain I'll understand.

If crying's what you need to do, I'll kiss away your tears;
If the world seems to frighten you, I'll melt away your fears.

If hope seems to be out of reach, and all your world goes wrong;
I'll wipe away the emptiness, and hold you all night long.

If storms descend upon your world, and you're scared to travel on;
I'll find a way to rescue you, and replace what has gone wrong.

If all your friends turn their backs, and leave you all alone;
I'll take the pain away from you, and carry you back home.

Crista Carver

Seers

It may look like a haze, when you first
look at it.
Some kind of silken stuff, created to cover.
Cloudy kind of stuff
without a kindred to it.

Went on a journey there.
liked the silken stuff
hated the haze.

Rachel Mcdonald

Nora's Eyes

The depth in one's eyes
Can only be seen through one's heart.
Her eyes are mine as mine are hers.
She gave me life and for hers I would die.
Her heart is my home and my life is her meaning.
Indescribable is this:
Her meaning to me.
Though often unsaid, forever is felt.
The string that connects our hearts
Is as strong as God's Will.
He gave us each other so we could know love.
She is my light, my fear, my hope, my darkness.
She is my time, my existence, my heart, my soul.
She is my joy, my pain, my comfort, my strength.
She is my everything.
And I am her creation.

Kristina Coco

"A Man Poem"

A man is wise, but many times ignorant.
A man is respected, but never tormented.
A man leads, but never follows.
A man has, because he never desires.
A man hates, when he's not liked.
A man has needs, which can be fulfilled.
A man has eyes, but rarely sees the truth.
A man has ears, but hardly believes.
A man has honor, friends and enemies.
A man has no color, black nor white.
A man has a wish, to be loved and respected.
A man has a desire, to be loved by a woman.
A man hurts, but shows no tears.
A man runs, from what he fears.
A man cries, when he hurts.
A man laughs, when he's happy.
A man begs, when he needs.
A man seeks help, when he bleeds.
A man needs to be loved, or that man won't love back.

Carlos Borja

Forever Wonder

I could stare into your eyes 'til all the music stopped;
Forever wonder what it is I see.
The man who wants to reach into my soul and hold my heart?
Will we ever be beyond my fantasy?
I stare entranced, but doubting, turn away and take my breath,
Glance back to see you flirting with the floor.
I look down at my hands, not knowing what is going on.
For a moment all I am began to soar.
Still the music plays and time moves on around me,
As I'm stuck in moments only I can feel.
My logic tells me look beyond for others who may wait,
My heart won't let the love I'm holding heal.
When I'm alone, I think of you, of everything you are,
Imagine you are there and holding me.
And in my dreams, you come to me and though your love seems true,
I awaken to a cruel reality.
When we meet again, I find your eyes and lose myself once more.
I try so hard to see you as a friend.
As visions of our lives to come imprint upon my starving soul,
I forever wonder how to just pretend.

Jamie Porter

I Cry

Feeling utterly alone and sorry for myself.
Confining my soul and hiding like a hermit.
So scared of things to come, frightened of heartaches
and worlds of pain that I don't know how to be open.
Hopeless and very weary of predictions and
negative thoughts processed without evidence.
Delusions and feeling of rejection
occur as the rage and rebellions act out.
Afraid of attachment and dependence
on any other, I allow the anger to control me.
How is it ever possible to trust and free myself.
I lost ME a long time ago being
confined in an utter domain that
keeps me from being able to be free
of the traumatized life and pain that I felt over the aching years.
Help me break free! Teach me to understand
and entrust myself to you.
This misery has controlled my life
and I cry to mend this awful feeling
that I confine in my inner being.

Maria Slack

The King

Come quickly! See the King ride!
Hi arms, his muscles, full with pride. He slays the bad,
He helps the good,
No evil of the outside world should
Stand against the Kingdom of Ancient Brotherhood,
But nevertheless the day will come when his heart might fail,
His soul, his will, then will sail,
The Gardens of above.
And when that day comes, his son will ride,
His father's way of victorious pride,
Until they're reunited.
And from that prince the family tree will follow,
New heroes be born, their hearts never hollow.
A war will be started against the Horn of The Dark,
Their leader a demon with the blood of a shark,
The dark ones will lose, the light will rise,
Every soldier of good is strong and wise.
And so the world begins its evolution,
The lost in the future they're hidden,
From mortal who know nothing of the battle for freedom.

Mihai Iancu

Starstruck

When I touch him, stars fly in front of my eyes.
Time stops and all else is meaningless.
He lives on this Earth for me and I for him.
Nothing else exists.
When I touch him, I see beauty.
Mahogany and rustic brown swirled into one.
Long lean muscles and an admirable face combine.
They create him.
When I touch him, no one else matters.
He is God's only true beauty, only true love.
Everyone else is transparent.
Everyone else is dust.
When I feel his body, I feel man.
Masculinity and God-given power bolt through his limbs.
His hands are strong and beautiful, powerful and working.
He is a master.
When he's gone, I know it's over.
Stars, beauty, and man are lost.
People come back to my Earth and my life.
But I am satisfied.

Renee Sessions

A Fine Sunday Mourning

I swam wearily within a sea of sorrows,
Letting the soft words of the man of
Anointment settle within the dark, dank
Veil enshrouding what was left of my
Tattered mind. With a barred grin of cold
Vengeance, I battled man's greatest foe,
Yet his greatest friend. Dancing coyly
On the hands of time, coming closer, yet
Drifting so far away.
Ashes to Ashes.
Dust to Dust.
Her Love to Mine.
One flit of my eye astray and death would
Lunge with his hell emblazoned blade,
Only to have me look back and feel
All within my soul shred apart.
In that moment, in the space
Between our moments of being, I weighed
The dove of life and love to the raven
Of death and torment. Knowing the defeat to
My enemy, I stilled my heart, and lifted
Like the ancient Roman into her arms
Amongst the sweet Seraphim.

Ricky Roldan

Heavenly Reminders

My heart never so heavy
My tears fast a running
With a sudden glimpse my eyes rise
To a sky ever so stunning

Hues of lavender oh, so velvety
Clouds a marching ever so carefree
Contrasted by awe-inspiring bright light
And I am so mesmerized by what I see

My world now in slow motion
Reality left far away from me
He hears it seems my silent cries
Safe and noticed I found myself to be

Is this the god you know
One who is ever so close
This is the god I know
One who gives such beauty in a world full of woes

Sue Flemings

Together

Have you seen the old man down the road?
He'll do anything for a little change.
The man who just wants your sympathy.
He's the man just down the road,
the man who just wants a little change.

Together we can make that happen.
He's the man who needs a little love,
but he has no one to love him.
Together we can make that change.
He's that man, who'll tell you to keep your chin up,
even though his is down.
He's the man with the little cardboard sign.

We need to help him, because that could be us one day.
He's the man down the road looking for sympathy and love.

He's our man down the road and we love him enough to help him!

  K. C. Taylor

Ignition

Your vibe meets mine and our emotions ignite.

Exploding like two children falling
into a volcano of lust bubbling with erotica.

Hearts beating in sync to the musical
masterpiece, "passion," conducted by our fantasies.

Atoms within us detonate from
the intense pressure of imposing joy.

Reality is tasting sweet now,
but yet is so far away.

  Robert Whiting

Icicles

Sparkling, magnificent splendors of winter
Early morning sunlight make-up
reflects dazzling rainbows

Popsicles to small bundles of playful children
Fragile lovers of coldness

Nature's winter wind chimes
cling tightly to rooftops and branches
Even gutters provide secure homes

But they weep frozen tears
Defenseless to the coming warmth of spring

They dream of another cold season when they will sparkle once more

  Anne Marie Mohr

I Am Creative and Bright

I am creative and bright
I wonder why we are here on this Earth
I hear drums clanging away in the distance
I see trees with the sun beams shining through them
I want to make everyone smile
I am creative and bright

I pretend that I am the sun shining through the trees
I feel tired and ready for the moon to take my place
I touch nothing for in my dreams I have no hands
I worry about who will take over when I can't shine anymore
I cry about nothing for I am strong
I am creative and bright

I understand that I can't do everything
I say nothing I am quiet
I dream of great things
I try to be the best I can be
I hope that I live a great life and that I'm happy
I am creative and bright

  Melissa Downes

Soy Burgers

Open fields,
Meadows blooming clover.
Gardens in everyone's
Front or side yards.
Memories in the making.
Early mornings: the lingering smell of a skunk.
Stopping to ask if I could pick
Soybeans.
No, not for cattle, for me!
To make
Soy Burgers.
Mumbling and shaking his head, the
Farmer thought, "I was crazy."
I made soy burgers for dinner.

  Sarajane White

Today I Became a Senior Citizen

Today I became a senior citizen
straight and tall I'll stand.
Not only did I become a senior
citizen, but I became more grand.

Today I'll start taking it easy.
Go for walks when it's not too breezy.
Doing things senior citizens do,
I may even take a trip to the zoo.

I'll take a trip with a great big smile.
Visit someone I haven't seen for awhile.
Over the hills and far away
I don't know how long I'll stay.

I may sit by the pond and
look at the fishes, toss coins
in a fountain and make wishes,
whatever I decide to do
it will make me feel fresh
as the morning dew.

  Margaret Jean Dais

No Holding Back

I've got only one chance to make it, and make it right.
Green lights showing and I've got to move fast.
Can't allow myself to get caught up by the fears of the past.
Have to live every second of every day as if it were my last.

Wasted my time on so many useless things.
Let chances for love slip right through my hands.
Ran from love and my feelings due to the fear of rejection.
Lost my heart and have dealt with the pain.

I can't go back and make up for the mistakes made in the past.
Quit running and found my heart and soul once again.
When I find that girl who'll make my world whole.
I won't hold back the love for her in my soul.

  Sean Ruml

The End

What is this world coming to?
It is coming to an end.
The one last tear, I remember dear
I really could not bear.
I stood by your grave
So you could hear what I had to say,
I did not want to lose you the way I remember that day.
It really hurt when I heard the car come rolling down the street,
The paramedics stood around you,
To where I could not see,
They just don't know how much it hurt,
To stand between you and me.
It felt like someone took my heart and tore it into two.
The only thing I had left to say was "I love you, yes I do."

  Misti Morrison

A New Century

Seven, six, five, four, three, two, one,
The wait is over, and you have finally come.
Horns blasting, confetti like snowfall, cheers, laughter, what fun,
Yet, to others born so long ago, life will have nowhere to run.

We welcome you wholeheartedly with wondrous warmth.

The time has passed swiftly by and we greet a new dawn,
The end of the twentieth century, we do mourn.
The unknown terrain that lies ahead will not be feared,
The Earth is our friend, solid and strong, never to be smeared.

We welcome you wholeheartedly with wondrous warmth.

We rejoice for the newly born and people of old,
Many tales of the past century will forever be told.
We must show our respect for the heavens above,
The twenty first century feels the power of our love.

We welcome you wholeheartedly with wondrous warmth.

Jeanne Mazza

Sickness

To be healthy is one thing,
Being sick is another
You may not understand
What sickness entails,
But surely I do . . .
It's not always horrible
But for most of the time it's decciving
Under that pale,
Soft skin lies the utmost truth
Is it time to move on and let your body heal
Or did you not suffer enough
And let pain persist
Never mind, only you can decide
When enough's, enough . . .

James Stein

Sunset into Sunrise

Seasick in flashbacks and backlashes
You cast plastic lines with flashy lures and Holy treble-hook jigs
Off the bow of the Sunrise into the stern Sunset
Trolling, loosen star-drag, tighten star-drag
The backlashes, the flashbacks, waters chummed
Sea gulls follow the sunrise back to white port and lemon juice
Another cast, they're laughing: "You caught a sea gull"
Backlash / flashback, tighten the star-drag, reel in
The plastic lines, the flashy lures, the holy treble-hook jigs

Harry Epstein

Rain

Could always hear the raindrops coming
Through the cornfield and across the road,
See the drops disturb the dust;
Watch from the porch, see furrows we hoed.

As droplets became ripples, I'd cover myself,
Sneak my sister's favorite cotton skirt,
Drape it over my neck to protect all parts.
Through my sister's armor, no cold drops could hurt.

When the raindrops hit the puddles
They became boys and girls dancing for me,
Sprites jumping, flashing, and kicking their heels;
This grand ball had no entry fee.

My sisters skirt won't cover me now,
That was all a few years ago,
But to this day, from the porch I watch
The dust and the dance, covered neck to toe.

Teresa S. Wilkie

Color Blind

Our life we take for granted that's surely plain to see;
with all the hatred in this world how else could it be.
We judge each other not by our minds and souls;
instead we look to see the color that is you or me.
If all the world was blind to the color of skin,
what a wonderful world this place would be to live.
But could it truly be because of the different races
that want to be free from one another,
they scream, "You stay away from me!"
They want to be divided; want no mixing of the races.
It's easier that way so they can keep the hatred.
It's getting worse day by day,
because of what some parents say,
"Don't play with him or her, 'cause she
or he is not the same as you or me."
To teach our young to hate
has to be the saddest fate;
they can laugh and sing and play
as one United Race.

Carmen DeLeon Reyes

When I Cried

When I cried out the Lord's name,
Jesus my Savior and rescuer came.
He felt my loneliness and despair.
He let me know that He was there.

My weary soul He came to defend.
He showed me on Him I could depend.
He pulled me gently to His side,
So that with Him I could abide.

The tears in my eyes He wiped away.
He led my path so I would not stray.
My fears He relieved so I was not afraid.
I was no longer discouraged nor dismayed.

His love, strength and courage He supplied,
Because by faith on Him I relied.
I trusted Jesus to see me through,
So He gave me comfort and life anew.

Jesus my Savior I want to share,
Because as a friend none can compare.
Turn to Jesus and truly believe.
His promise of peace and you can receive.

Marie La Grange

Journal

I am a little journal that someone bought for you my dear
To write down all the things you love and all the things you fear
If you ever have a silly thought or a precious memory
Don't be afraid to grab a pen and write it down inside of me

I will protect your every thought I will give you privacy
So open your mind and fill me up with every fantasy
Tell me your ideas, your hopes, your dreams, and I won't tell a soul
For whatever you write down I will keep with me
for that is my ultimate goal

I am yours so use me well, I'll always by lying near
Tell me what is bothering you, never hold back any tear
Use me to express your feelings when you need to let them out
Think of me when you're feeling upset or if you ever have a doubt

But most of all I want to know when you're feeling happy too
I want to know when you're loving life not just when you're feeling blue
One last thing I almost forgot I really wanted to say
No matter what happens don't give up because tomorrow's another day.

Mark A. Lassoff

A Head Rub

The cranium is palpable, oval, and mountainous.
The carrier of stress, protruding elements like ears and nose,
valleys composed of dips and temples.
Hear lies a releasing area,
a massage of the temple permeates an auspicious return.
Concern wanes itself to fruition;
A bad memory turns into a good lesson.
Soon soothing words grow,
grow out of the subconscious and into vagrancy.
Emollient, the power of touch, sends you to ubiquity,
a natant on the river of "at ease"
wading then floating, even getting on your knees.
A trip delivered by those hands
pressing, playing your temple like a piano as only they can,
taking unselfish steps to please.
I appreciate the squeeze.
You care enough to adjust,
take my mind, and undo this gyros.
It must be done by someone I trust.
Now tender and warm meet
bringing an undying flame
it keeps my asking for a head rub, again and again

Benard Bennett

The Effects of Rejection on a Heart Such as This

She thinks that it was easy, I guess,
to spill the contents of my heart
like water from a tipped glass splashing,
cascading in an endless stream of love
dripping off the edge of
the plastic table cloth world
where we sat over hot dogs and Coke,
for with a swipe of her
indifferent, paper towel laden hand
she annihilated my suddenly indignant
dreams of togetherness
and left with a clear conscience of
having tidied up for the waitress,
only I was left in the aftermath
sitting in the damp remnants of my
now empty heart
feeling the pangs of disillusionment
and the silent tuggings
of regret.

Devon Milanese

Melista

As things in your life go wrong
Your strength remains bold and strong
You wake up each morning and put on a mask
Walk out the door to face each task
You're good at hiding your pain and fear
You never let anyone inside to wipe your tears
You let people think you have a perfect life
When your world is filled with hate and strife
Things are easy to forgive but hard to forget
But with your gentle soul you are still glad you met
You are the first to listen and the last to cry
You give comfort to those without even a sigh
Your loving heart was open to me
and you were there when I was in need
Sometime you wonder why life is not fair
Why you get all the pain and burdens to bear
Sometimes when you fell like running away
Think of the good things you still have today
Remember you touched more than one heart
That you took part in making their mark
You helped them greatly in changing their soul
And let them know that they, too, can be whole
When life has its ups and downs
Just remember—in Heaven you will be the one with the crown

Heather Caraway

Sonnet 3

Another night of loneliness creeps by,
The stars burning so coldly sail apace;
Who can restore my faith in God on high?
Only thee on whom He's poured His grace.
To spare myself from further tides of woe
I'd sail unto a distant, unknown shore;
When will these tears of sorrow cease their flow,
And tears of joy stream down this face once more?
But though this sojourn stretch a thousand nights,
And I a thousand miles from sweet home be,
Though I have seen a million wondrous sights,
None ever could be half as fair as thee.
  I'll turn my tiller homeward once again,
  My weary heart to thy love I commend.

Adam Schneider

We

We met but never met each other.
We knew but never knew each other.
We touched but never touched each other.
Then in an instant all that changed
and our lives haven't been
the same.

We've met and introduced ourselves
and liked who we were meeting.
We've taken time to know each other
and found we're quite intriguing.
We've touched and found enjoyment
and excitement we've never known
then in an instant all things changed
and our lives will never be the same.

WE FELL IN LOVE!

Lisa Christian

For Walter

In loving memory of Walter E. Pettie, Sr.
March has come upon us
With its strong and gusting winds.
It was then that you left us,
Carried away, up high above the clouds.

The harbinger of Spring,
Preparing our souls
With its cleansing breath;
Bringing to us the promise of Springtime,
Of gentleness and peace;

With pure joy and renewed innocence,
As beauty blooms around us;
Where, forevermore, will you remain
In our minds and hearts with love.

Tina Collison

The Lone Man

In a forest in the dark of night,
A man stands alone.
In the swamp, filled with fright,
A man stands alone.
In the battlefield full of disease,
A man stands alone.
In the plains, with a ghostly breeze,
A man stands alone.
Wait! A light, a dove, an angel!
No, the man has never stood alone!
Not in the plains with the ghostly breeze,
not in the battlefield full of disease,
not in the swamp filled with fright,
not in the forest in the dark of night.
God was with this man as He is with all of us.
No, you do not stand alone.

William Goodyear

I Often Wonder

I often wonder what runs through your mind,
  Anger, hatred, or just hurting inside.
I often wonder why you take it out on us,
  Suffering, relief, or invincible (can't be touched).
I often wonder why you use such harsh words,
  Strength, courage, or just want to be heard.
I often wonder if that you will ever change,
  Caring, laughter, will it ever be the same.
I often wonder if you regret many things,
  Life, family or is it just us kids.
I often wonder what I should feel for you,
  Sulking, sadness, but I have too much love for you.
I often wonder why you do things that you do,
  Aggravated, stressed, or is there someone else inside of you.
I often wonder if in your heart if you have guilt,
  Scarring, hurting, or is that how you were built.
I often wonder if you think what may occur,
  Disapproval, disowned, or maybe good-bye forever.
I often wonder if it will affect you in any way,
  Yes, maybe, or you only care for mom to stay.
I often wonder if there is a real man in there,
  Loving, caring, or just always being there.
I often wonder where you would be without us,
  Lonely, happy, there is no life without loved ones.

Joann Delouchrey

Light

Stare into the light,
The light of freedom,
The light to all problems,
The light that can cure all pains.

The light brightens the darkness,
The darkness that fills our life,
The light shows a path,
The true path of life,
The path of enlightenment,
The enlightenment that we need to achieve our own goals of life.

The light,
We should seek the light,
Waste no time,
As time ticks fast,
As our life fly with the time,
Seek the light,
To reach the ultimate of life.

Tsu Ang

My Mom

This woman left lonely and scorned
Sits where three children were conceived and born
A book of pictures with stories of time
Remembering such happiness that comes to mind

So many years have come and gone
It's hard to imagine days left now alone
From beginning to end she loved him and none other
Boy! how he did love my mother

He was a Christian and so was she
They loved my two brothers and they loved me
It's hard when one loses a life long mate
They were happily marred 56 years to this date

She was 14 and he was 19 when they took their vow
Wondering alone if she can make it and asking how
Night after night she sits on this bed in prayer
Wishing and hoping Dad was still there.

Sarah Higdon

Emotions

Love is as beautiful as a butterfly,
But can be taken the wrong way.
The butterfly can soon crash and die,
Just like when the sun hits the bay.
Death is as black as the deepest ocean,
But is mostly caused by a crazy devil.
Some people show it as a devotion,
And others take it to an extreme level.
Depression is as crazy as the next mad man,
Or as sad as the next drug abuser.
Soon you might be taken to another land,
Or you might consider yourself the biggest loser.
Emotions are what you feel inside,
Don't make it up and use it as a lie.

Melissa Gallo

Leaves

We are but leaves
          released from trees' safe haven at
     Autumn's beckon. Cast into unsafe winds and waters
        to journey—without dominion over velocity and
              time and destination. Aimless flurry into
                uncertainty—this is life; this is
                  what each breaking day
                  brings. Disorder from
                      order. Confusion to
                        resolution we go.
                          Set adrift , yet
                            a part of it
                              all.

James Todd

Not Words, Nor All the Roses

Dedicated to a Love Immortal
How many words do I write for thee?
Doth it truly matter how many,
For no amount of words could equal thee.
I merely write and write in hope!
O', such a hope it is to me!
A hope of we two lovers!
See how mine heart hovers!?
A thousand roses could not grow,
Not enough to equal what you have grown.
So much love, like this heart has never known.
O', seep into my chest and seize my very heart!
I tell thee no lie, it is my most worthy part.
Taste but a portion, or drown thee in me,
Either way, I shall love all that we can be.
Say what you will, and do what you may,
But I pray thee, let me in your heart forever stay.

Shawn Dusseault

Inimical Roller-Coaster

Flooding over my walk, a tidal wave of emotion.
Passing our special bench, our park-side setting.
 And then going to the dock, watching the sunset.
The boats troll by, the gulls touch down,
and glistening tears are to be found.
Space in my heart still is filled.
Even though I recognize why you had to move on.
Yet it doesn't get easier, it's as hard as ever, still.
My heart still grieves, all for that necessary lack inside of me.
To the movies, an empty seat next to me.
I drink my water, imagining where you'd be.
Far beyond my touch, and beyond my sight.
Forever, forever gone into the night.
Lost without a thought at all.
Sitting on my bed, listening to the rain pound on the wall.
And I see the heavens above.
Moving slowly, just as the healing of my loss of love.

Karl Slazinski

Guitar

"You've got to let your soul shine. . . ."
—The Allman Brothers

Sounds of
the acoustic
slide from his
worn fingertips,
untwist me
with rhythms
that string my soul,
that free my
locked down dreams.
His notes bend & stretch
release my mind
and let me calm.

Wendy Blackstone

Vex

Disturbing words crept into my ears
 my mind denied, flew into my soul
 my feelings all died

Disturbing words shot into my heart
 so nimble,
   so quick
 poisoned my cells made me so sick
     then. . . .
     dug deep into the smallest cracks of my tissues
EXPLODED, EXPLODED, EXPLODED
 bursting into pieces
 clogged up my veins I could not breathe
but only cry blood

Cynthia Talmadge

Life Is

Life is nothing but a game,
Where people try to find others to blame,
For all the stupid things they have done,
Which wouldn't of happened if they didn't have a gun.

Life is a place where people kill,
And afterwards no pain will they feel,
After getting sent to prison many times,
They still won't stop committing crimes.

Life is a place where we try to find,
A thing called love of any kind,
And I hope that my prayers are heard up above,
Because one day I hope to find true love.

Life is the place that made me realize,
That after we die, we get no prize,
And now to you I cannot lie,
If I had the choice, I'd rather die.

Cynthia Kennedy

Our Heart's Home

Running over rough ground
I stumble and fall
Full of mystery
Life's beyond comprehension.

Can one grasp the meaning of life
In a look, a touch, or the sound of a voice?
Through fullness of time, my heart and soul
Have come to care for you.

You need me and I need you
Together, we'll become complete
Our yearnings and longings fulfilled.
For in knowing you, I've become known.

At long last, our hearts have found home.

Dayna Meserve

Angel

An angel sat upon a cloud, beyond the rocky shore.
My heart flew out into her hand, to leave for nevermore.
A precious gem, a sapphire, I offered, but dismay
Besieged me dear, when with a lilt her voice responded "Nay."

Continuing my touched appraisal of her features fair
I gazed at every detail, each freckle, line, or hair
A rock as red as bathed in blood, a ruby, I deferred
The angel merely glanced at me, then sighed, then not a word.

A thousand diamonds I would give, if but to know her ways!
To bask inside her gentle laugh, to share her holidays
At length, my final gift, an emerald I gave with grace
No expression crossed her brow, no meaning left her face.

Then, as I sat on rocky shores, my eyes cast out to sea
The angel knelt close by my side and viewed the waves with me
"I love you not for gifts of sapphire, ruby, emerald,
Mere rocks crumble under time; love's not ephemeral."

And as I stooped and kissed her lips, the very Earth stood still
Time, elements, and mortal man their weaknesses reveal
For even they, with fists of iron stand humbled, mute and bowed
Beneath the love that casts its grace on sun, sea, beach and cloud.

Erik Walle

Beauty

The beauty of nature is all around,
For not just a few, but to all, if found,
Nature's imperfections impart a beauty rare,
A sort of magical quality, you didn't know was there.

So it is with people, and imperfections there,
They can give a special richness, and   impart a beauty rare,
It's not until one searches and finds this quality,
We realize beauty and perfection don't make reality.

Patricia Brierly

DEEP DECEPTION

Don't let Satan take control of your mind
Your eyes are open but still you're blind
Your perception of the situation at hand
Is far from the truth, you don't understand

He will feed you lies each and every day
Before you realize you're going the wrong way
Before too long you've fallen deep in sin
He's accomplished his goal, he wants to win

Keep following the path that he laid out
Hell will be your home without a doubt
Pain and destruction forever my friend
Tortured and tormented again and again

But if you call on Jesus before it's too late
He'll forgive your sins, he won't hesitate
Life eternal is his promise to you
If only you do what he commands you to

Audrey Hubbard

Divine

Further than imagination can take you
More than reality at its best
Greater than love's highest powers
And deeper than an ocean of enlightenment
So far into your mind that you cannot breathe
but let emptiness into your lungs
Yet what is this divine force?
And who has the power to release it?
Is it not so huge in size
That it would, surely, swallow us into our own minds.

Kristin McClain

You

Not long ago, he was just a boy.

Soon after the hurt subsided, his heart began to change.
Changes, after all, can be for better or worse.

His spirit changed in a way he cannot begin to describe.
Describing the human spirit is an infinite task.

He saw the love that she held within herself.
Like the spoiled child he was, he became selfish.

Now, the love has been tempered with pain.
The little boy is no longer innocent.

With his heart outstretched, he wishes to give her the world.
But she is young and innocent, and the world frightens her.

They are not strangers to fear, loss, and pain.
True love is the bond that keeps them together.

Now, the little boy is a man.
And as a man, he realizes his wrongdoing.
He strives to protect.
He dreams to impress.
He prays to love.
You.

Dean Kales

Hope

Cocaine
Oh, how can you take the pain?
Heroin
Covering up your tracks, never looking back.
LSD
If only you can see, what you did to our family,
what you did to me.
You hurt yourself and want to die,
but all you do is make us cry.
Sleepless nights you gave
and the memories we will save.
The worries you have given
have driven us away.
'Cause the addiction is too heavy and your mind is forever gone.
Knowing that you will never be the same,
is just a shame.
I miss the old you,
the one that we all knew.
If only you can cope
and stop with the dope,
then maybe there would be hope.

Amanda Smarsh

Father

A man with a smile worth a thousand words
But means a million to this little girl
A man with a heart of steel
An inner treasure always real
A man with the strength of any army force
Enough to carry out a family load through his life's course
A man with the knowledge of every fact
The choice is there, but never would he turn his back
A man with the guidance for every road
For every bump and crack he turned to gold
A man with the means to help and do things right
Never letting go without a good fight
A man taking on more than a reasonable share
And never complains because he cares
A man with the willingness to take any role
Even a father taking care of two souls
A man with every bit of love to offer
Through childhood and adulthood, he is my father
I Love You Dad

Jamie Cardis

Life

The most difficult test we take
is the test of life
It causes us much happiness,
but also it brings pain and strife
The paths for us to choose
loom in our minds
or them we will lose
But the pain will never go away
When we make a wrong choice,
it seems like forever it will stay
Is there a time when I can look back
and see all the things causing me hurt
were nothing but abstract?
I wish the time were here and now,
so I would know that I can get through this
Somehow

Cammie Brodbeck

What Happens to the Days?

Where is yesterday?
Did it go with the day before?
Or did I lose it behind me?
Did the past take it away?
Maybe it went with all the other yesterdays.
What happens to the todays or the next days?
Where do they all seem to go?

Michael Rodriguez

Unattainable

Your beauty like a thousand shining stars
Perfect in every detail
Your eyes twinkling and laughing
With the joy of life
I saw you only once
But now you, your image
Shines brightly in my mind's eye
But of course like the stars
Your beauty was unattainable
You seemed to slip through my fingers
At my every desperate grasp
But not long do I see thee now
Each mention of your name
My eyes become clouded
My head suddenly downcast
And I only hear the sound
Of tears splashing quietly
To the cold, hard ground
And my cries carried away
By the gentle night's wind

Richard Ryan Stevenson

Cry

Keep in mind, living is a breeze
I can laugh, I can cry, I can breathe
(Though when I'm laughing or crying, breathing can be a pain)
Sometimes people make fun of me
or call me lame.
But I just pay them no mind,
I don't act like a child.
Because, like I said, it's not living that's a pain
It's growing up that drives me insane
and tangles my mind into a web of mistakes
and yells "Yes, let's raise the stakes!"
So no matter where I turn or what I do
someone gets hurt or is feeling blue And
everything goes wrong, and I don't know what to do
And I feel as though I'm in a hole with
nowhere to run & no where to hide And suddenly I'm buried alive
And all I can do is simply . . . CRY.

Lauren Higginbotham

and there was less than nothing to the void unfilled

and there was less than nothing to the void unfilled
even less of what could be called free will
they said the judgment would be simple and swift
but in the years to come it was evident that the judgement was this
lingering in the solitude uncalled

the wrong words to use
the unordered stack that comes from that place way, way in the back
underneath the pile and waiting to be cleaned but hiding ever still
uncleaned they will stay and perhaps these words will fade away
the words that are another useless part
dirty with the insides messy and untouched but by the hot breath

lingering in the solitude uncalled
it became evident that it mattered not at all
and the caring that seemed great was just pain in caring's clothes
and the judgment filled the void and made solitude complete
simple and swift there was nothing filled and less, or no free will

so, take the words and fold them neatly in a stack
wash them up with hot water, soap and dry them with hot breath
use them and don't let them get dirty
keep them ordered in a line and don't let them change ranks
meter them out in even distribution
put your words away when there is so little left to say
but it is the quiet that is important and the telling that soils
the openness of opening lips to say the unclean, untoweled words
all the things you could tell if you were so clean

Kimberly Stephenson

Because

Care about me because I am worth caring for,
Not because you feel obligated in so many
ways to do so.

Hold me because you want to, not because
you feel you have to do so or feel it is part
of your responsibility.

Kiss me because you want to show me your
affections and feelings, not because you feel
it is the right thing to do.

Need me for all the right reasons, not for all
the things you feel I should or could do for you.
Love me unconditionally, not for what I could
be or you think I should be.

Sue Howes

Lost and Lonely

I look up into the night sky and stare.
The heavens envelop me. This feeling . . .
This feeling's incredible, like magic;
Unseen, powerful and mysterious.

A lonely star glimmers bright as ember.
As I watch in awe, I see you, feel you
Burning inside my heart with fierce passion.

My arms reach out wanting to embrace you,
But I know they can't—it is not my time.
I'll be cold and empty 'til the pyre's burnt,
For the star is a shadow of yourself.

Matthew Francis

Wander

As I wander through the valleys and the mountains capped with snow
Where ever thou shalt wander you'll be sure that I'll follow
Some day I know I'll meet you where the rivers meet the sea
Some day I know I'll meet you where ever that may be
As I sit here and wonder you get further away
Once again my hope is fading of meeting you one day

Rebecca Putnam

Today

Today I have eyes to see, and today I have ears to hear.

Today, I can feel the sun and the breeze flow through my hair.

Today I can walk a thousand miles, or climb a mountain high.
I can lift my head to Heaven and watch the birds fly in the sky.

Today, I can laugh at a joke, or flash a cunning smile.
I can stroll down the street with all my glamorous style.

Today is here right now, and I shall cherish it forever.
For tomorrow may not come, and I may see it never.

Joshah Hedrington

Spellbound

Since the dawn of time,
Men have spoken in riddle and rhyme,
None more so then Merlin,
Sorcerer, magician to the king,
Many a spell he would sing,
With eye of lizard, tongue of cat,
Legs of a spider, wing of bat,
With roots he would stew,
The potion, a deadly brew.
Whoever took a sip,
Was sure to feel a burning lip.
The more of the brew, they did take
Would twist their minds,
Their body would shake.
Stumbling to the ground,
On all fours making a hideous sound,
Coughing, choking swollen throat,
Merlin had changed them into a goat.
So never curse Merlin the man of dreams,
He may change you, something strange it seems.

Patric Russell

Decisions

There are many decisions we both have to make
Even all the promises we still couldn't break
But deep in my heart I know I care about you
And I hope that you make the same decisions too.
There are so many decisions that are tough for me
But all I really want is for us to be
Together and never apart
I could never try to break your heart.
But there's always time to feel your pain
But I hate to say time isn't enough to play this game
I don't want you to stop loving me
But I don't want you to be mad at me neither.
So always think about me and I'll think about you
And never forget you were always my boo
And try not to cry or even shed a tear
And always remember that I'll be near.

Shelina Baxter

The Next Night

Never thought I'd lose my mind,
 Love has made me crazy . . .
Now at night I get no sleep.
 My memory is quite hazy . . .
Tears flow like an uncontrollable faucet,
 Down my cheeks one after another . . .
 I will never have another lover.
Clenching my teddy in my arms . . .
 It is now trying to take your place,
The one you gave me the night before . . .
 I ask why you aren't here to wipe the tears from my face.
My door swings open and I look up with hopeful eyes,
 Nothing but a gust of wind . . .
  Tell me why'd you have to die?

Sarah Rice

Dreams

Dreams can be an amazing event
They can be an escape from reality
But they can also put fear in you
Some dreams can be a warning
While others can be a great adventure

Some people can't wait to close their eyes
While other dread going to bed
I on the other hand love to dream
Because I can't wait to see what happens next

I had dreams of tornados
I have all so had dreams of being a spy
They seem to me to be an outlet for stress
They are my release

But all and all
Dreams are dreams
And if there more
Then that's what you put into it
Because dreams are what you make of them
In our minds and in life
So Sweet Dreams
And Good-Night
Christina Ebhardt

Choices

The difficult choices we have to make
Seeking them face to face every day

I thought I had found him . . .
The true love of my life
But then that day
You came my way

I knew what I had, but I didn't know you
He was the love of my life
But you came through

So now what do I do?
Now that I'm torn
Torn between two men
Whom I can't ignore?

My heart belongs to one
And my soul the other
One is cool
The other is a go getter

So you see my choices are hard to make
But I face them each and every day
Lori Peet

Mother

What words are fitting that I can say to
the One who gave me life;
to the One who regarded the future of her
offspring over the distorted passions of
being His wife?

What can I do that will absolutely prove
all the gratitude that I feel?
All the "thank you's" and "you mean so much's"
are just plain trivial and unreal.

There are no words, no actions, no Anything
enough to convey the importance of You,
so in light of this disappointment I know
what I must do:

I will become what You've always dreamt for
me and accomplish my own impossible dreams;
I will be a success in Your eyes and I'll use
every honorable means.

And then will You see what I observe
(when I look at You with my heart)
You will see Yourself in me—a most priceless work of Art.
Maria Williams

When You Are Gone

I fear that this only exists in my head sometimes
That it's all some sort of dream
That soon I will wake
And be alone again
Alone with the void in my soul
that you have filled with your love.

I breathe in your sweet scent
Trying to etch it into my memory
So that even when you're gone
I will be able to remember it
And always have something of yours to hold to.

Just the thought of your leaving again
Fills me with such an emptiness,
I cannot even bear to breathe
Because it hurts too much without you.

I wonder why it is that I cannot seem to escape you,
You have always been, and will always be
A sort of mystery to me.
You always leave me wanting more of you

Trying to etch every tiny bit of you into my memory,
Into my soul
So that I will always have you
Even when you're gone
Ariel Benes

Angel

Shimmering, speckles of glittery dust
Dancing off flowing, graceful wings
As she glides through our lives
Unable to do much of anything,
Except comfort us in those times of
Loneliness, grief, and disappointment.
When that dust floats down and gently lands upon us,
It makes us see the sun just a little brighter,
Gaze up at the stars a little bit longer,
And throw that one starfish, which washed upon the shore,
Back into the ocean.
Simple things, that bring us a simple smile.
In those times of need.
Thank you, beautiful angel.
Gwen Ingram-Jones

6 days

the windows to my mind are covered in dew
the shades are tattered and the panes
keep falling down

no longer do i feel the gentle air blowing in
the dust has collected on the walls of my heart
and it creaks

the darkness shall last 6 more days
while the walls of this house are stubborn
they have begun to sway

your strength is the remedy to my soul
your rough exterior is the first i've found
to smooth these walls

shelter me with your rain forever . . .
Kelleigh Sanders

I Wait . . .

Like a moth to a flame, you call my name.
I wait and listen, for the whisper of my name.
Barely a caress with each spoken breath.
Thoughtful words and quiet sighs.
Give answers, hellos and good-byes.
Like a moth to a flame, you call my name.
I wait and wonder, will you always call my name?
Patricia Patterson

Angel

My feelings towards you were always discreet,
Like the silent movement of momentary feet.
My love is directed, not aimed to meet,
Like the passing of two friends in two enemy fleets.

Time is a luxury mutually we do not posses,
All these feelings are stopped processed.
A petitions soon matures to protest,
Never the affection of feeling the best.

I have loved you now for quite some time,
My feelings; like a poem, no structure, no rhyme.
With you near me love feels like a crime,
Soon I hope I'll be doing my time.

I thought that there would be a continuous fight,
But again I realized I was not really right.
I always adored you because of your might,
As I saw when you moved from the dark to the light.

Michael Sizer

Desperation

The workings of fate,
To love and not hate
there's a being stronger than we
We have given up faith, lost our innocence,
and so we look but we do not see.
Faith, the substance of things we long for
The evidence of the way things could be
can bring love and acceptance, a road to our joy,
and yet still we refuse to believe

Kate Storch

2050

Honest, I heard one this morning. It sang to me in my bed.
Could've been a Robin, or maybe it was a Lark. Beautiful music
to wake up to, I'll tell ya that. First music of that kind heard
'round here in nearly fifteen years.
Brings back memories, far away memories.

World's different now, for the better of course. No more
forests takin' up all that room. Hearing a bird sing never fed
nobody, did it? Progress in the name of humanity, that's for sure.

Well, today's the day. Trees out back are comin' down.
Something about a housing unit coming in. Only a matter of
time a guess. Well birdy, thanks for the final song. Good luck
findin' a home. Gonna be tough. Memories, far away memories.
Bye, bye birdy.

James Reichenbach

Beweisen

No reason for leaving, no reason for being,
look at me, don't know what you're seeing.
All I've had is what I miss,
to see your eyes and show you this.
Hindsight's a haze, everything's grey,
look through the window, think I should stay?
You wonder why I haven't returned,
see outside, how everything's burned?
Burned just like all that's in my mind,
burned like the future of Mankind.
The bright red flames that scald your face,
are the same that end the Human Race.
So when you see me run away,
don't ask why, just do the same.
We all have reasons for what we do,
you trust me, then I'll trust you.
And in the end, you may see why,
with the great exposure of all our lies,
what from then, will here come true,
that what I am is what's to prove.

Chadwick Whetham

Could It Be

This poem is dedicated to Kevin Rutkowski
He sounds so sweet and sincere
I think this is the one that would actually care
When we talk on the phone
I know he's the one for me, I could tell in his tone
He tells me he cares more and more
This one, I truly adore
I long to see his smiling face
And to be in his strong embrace
Whether this is love or fate, I don't know
But he says his love he will always show
I know he will stay by my side
And tell me what is wrong because he has nothing to hide
He doesn't live too far away
But what I wouldn't give to be with him every day
I think I may have found the right guy
And it all started with one simple hi

Patricia A. Zvonik

Happiness in Your Eyes

Every time I look at you, I see your love for me
Looking into your eyes is where I'll always want to be
When I look into your eyes, I see them flicker with a fire
Whether it be in anger, distress or burning with desire
The love I feel when I see the look on your smiling face
Tells me that you want me to fill that lonely, empty space
I'll do what I can . . .I'll do my best
To wipe out the memories of all the rest
Those before me have no idea what they're missing
The strength, the support, the loving and the kissing
All this and more are what I got for this, there is no doubt
I want to climb to the top of the world just to scream and shout
Just how much I love you and even more how much I care
Let someone try to take this away and I'll put in such a scare
I want you for now and I want you forever
I want the day when we can always be together
One way or another, I'll make sure we're never apart
I know this as much as I know the love for you in my heart
It grows more and more with the passing of each love-filled day
I love you now and I'll love you forever in each and every way.

Rene Seekell

A Red Rose for My Love

A single, red rose he gave her as a sign of his love
To be together forever was their dream from above,
Side by side through life
In good times and bad.
They faced it together for as long as they had,
Then the time finally came when they parted ways.
He misses her so much, these are the longest of days.
He still takes her a rose when he visits her grave,
And tells her he loves her as he bows his head and prays.
"One day, my love, we'll be together again,
I leave this rose for you until then.
I'll see you tomorrow, my love," he says as he turns to walk away,
"Soon I'll be coming home to you . . . coming home to stay."

Debbie McGranahan

Lunar

On a cold dead night
under a moon drenched sky
where a soul takes flight
and a body lie
a tale is spun with great care
amidst braids undone and crimson soaked hair
For in this night where breathe may cease
stills a life devoid of lease
for as the hour grew from early to late
her way was schewed through a barb of fate

Robert LeGrow

TURN AROUND

Turn around, my son, and you will see
My outstretched hand that's reaching for thee.
Reach out, my son, take hold of My hand.
Together, we'll see what my Father has planned.

Relax, my child, and let Me take the lead.
My Father and I know all that you need.
Relax! Take comfort in Me and you'll understand
The pathway to God and all that He's planned.

We have such a special life planned for you
If you'll just trust Me to carry you through.
Take comfort and warmth from all of the love
I give to you, as He also gives from above.

The angels are singing for you, my special one,
That goes forth to share of God's only Son.
They're dancing and singing above all the Earth,
Knowing you are spreading news of My worth!

Cheri Cornett

WE SHALL STAND

Some day we will stand
together holding each others hand
in love, Harmony, and peace,
gathering like a flock of geese.
There should not be any hate.
Remember to always love your mate.
Please, no more killing;
no more blood spilling;
no more fathers leaving home.
All they want to do is roam.
Even if he leaves his child,
he should always love them dear and mild.
People in the world today
get down on your knees—and pray.

Gloria Booker

Love So Dear

Wake with the morning sun and start your day with a kiss.
Getting ready for the day, remember to say it's him/her you'll miss.
As the day gets busy and you get into gear;
Take the time to say, "I love you, dear."
Through the day if things go wrong;
Think about your love and a pretty song.
When the day is through you'll know what to do,
Hurry home to create a quiet evening for two.
As the sun leaves, the moon will appear;
The comfort of togetherness will be so dear.
Share the love that God has sent;
It is a gift that shouldn't be broken or bent.
Before closing your eyes, one more little thing to do;
Give him/her a kiss and say, "I love you."

S. Wright

The Storm

Dedicated to Deacon John Pradia
We've made it through the storm,
The rain has finally gone.
Now its time to move on,
For brighter days are ahead.
God promised you would be blessed,
By staying at her side.
Even through all the lies,
You stood strong,
And kept praying and holding on.
Didn't He say you would be blessed?
Look around, isn't He blessing you?
You must not stray now,
For better days are ahead!
Watch God move like never before.
And the enemy will flee,
For He will not, let the enemy hinder thee.

Jacqueline Fleeks

That's Real

From the first thing in the morning
'Til at night when I'm yawning
My thoughts are of you and always you
That pretty smile and eyes
I see it as no surprise
That you are what many men pursue

I'm going to live each day and wait
And pray that it will translate
Into sweet memories and happiness for years
I want to make you smile forever
Build a bond that no one can sever
So leave behind your doubts and fears

I want to make you my wife
And LOVE you for life
Can you understand and see how I feel
With the strength from above
I will give you all my LOVE
My heart beats for you and THAT'S REAL

Carl Hatchett

Poem in the "C" #3

Beautiful hands dark and strong
say they want to touch me.
Lips that whisper words of sweetness
say they want to kiss me.
His body cries yes,
but does his heart agree?
Why me?
To carry the burden of knowing this need,
his desire . . .
his wish and fantasies . . .
I do want this,
but does he want me?
All of me,
soul and mind of me?
Or simply be a passing urge which can be
quenched . . . by anyone
willing and able?
Does he need it to be me,
Or can it be
any beauty?

Lindsay Pereira

Alyssa

Written to Alyssa from her Grandma Tina
There's great excitement as I think about you, dear.
Will you have brown, blond or dark hair?
Or will her eyes be blue, brown or green?
I only know this one thing is true!
You were woven together with love in your mother's womb
As a beautiful tapestry created by the Father's own hand,
With colors surrounding you like a beautiful rainbow in the sky.

In that moment of your arrival, Heaven will stand still,
The angels will look down as creation catches its very breath
As we all look upon your loveliness.

A sweet smile with bright ,curious eyes as you look
at the love and wonder in your mother's and father's eyes.
You're the miracle of their love, a gift long awaited.
You are coming into the arms that will love you and cherish you
with help from the Father above.

They will nurture you and always show you
the greatness of the Lord's love.
You are love.

Tina Dickinson

Scarlet Wildflower

Early last week I picked the most beautiful
wildflower anyone has ever seen before
Certainly not I
Scarlet in color with
the most fragrant aroma of
wet trees, freshly cut grass
salty wind from the beach
thin mountain-fresh air and a little gardenia
The scent fills my mind and my soul
Intoxicating . . .
Then the precious flower that was once so
glorious starts to fade and drop its petals
And pouting turns its shiny red head
down and withers
I cry for centuries
cry, cry and cry . . .
Early this morning I saw the most beautiful
wildflower anyone has ever seen before
I can still smell the aroma whenever I
walk down that path. . . .

Debby Dernberger

In Memory of Mom

You gave me life
When all of the odds were against it,
Raising me with a protective cloak,
A life of sheltered innocence.

"Are you sure you came from me?"
. . . Your constant question
As I struggled to live right,
In the shadow of someone who did
What she needed to in order to live.

Showing me always that you understood . . .
As you lived under
The protective cloak of dad.

I took that protective cloak
To shelter you
In your aging years,
As we lived together
In your final time.

Now I seek you throughout my life,
Seeking answers
In the memory of your soul.

Estelle Darrow

The Sad Poet

When I am sad, or feeling bad,
I pick up my pen and my tattered writing pad . . . .
The words flow from my very hands,
as my words become a story from my wonderland.
And as I write, my tears do flow,
for my poetry is my emotional flow,
a flood of feelings come through my words,
I'm sure that I am not alone,
when I'm writing in my lonely home . . . .
My heart cries out for you to see,
that emptiness has stolen me . . . .
It seems as if my hand won't stop,
as the words pour out like God's rain drops . . . .
For all my poems come from my heart, my hands a tool,
and they tell a lot . . . .My soul a vessel of my life,
I write each day and every night,
I am the saddest one you'd see, as I am on a voyage
to the barren sea . . . The sadness strikes all day and night,
and from my soul is where I write,
I am The Sad Poet . . .

Patricia Mendoza

The Falls

Power, rage, and strength
all within the simple shape of a horseshoe.
The trembling fear of God's wrath
weighs the cool mist to my face.
And I stand in awe.

As water thrusts itself against the rocks below,
thunder escapes to infinity.
The depth of the Lord's voice
echoes through my beating heart.
And I stand in awe.

Streams of turquoise and gray
fall to a cloud of mist.
The rush of a distant destination
runs red through these fluent veins.
And I stand in awe.

To look at something so great
brings a humble knee to dust,
And to say God does not exist?
I pity such a fool
as I stand in awe.

Jessica Aldrich

Shattered

On the outside I seem all right
As a smile slowly comes to my face
On the inside I am suffering slowly
Very slowly being beat into the ground
My pride and confidence cease to be
I am lying in pieces scattered on the dirt
Where he thinks I should be
He is happiest when he shatters me
Is this the way it should be?
My pieces scattered crumbled hurt
Thrown on to the ground
I turn to my little ones for comfort and
Strength I feel the need in their voices
They call to me I feel their need
A new strength is given to me, slowly
My pieces reconnect putting me
Whole again, I rise up to walk away
Far away with my kids to a place
Where we can smile

Neta Nitz

Passing Over

The passing was not easy.
No it was not.
When I heard the news, I felt quite queasy.
You were getting better, at least I thought.
To think that just yesterday
I held you in my arms.
But that was yesterday,
And now it is today.
I used to take our friendship for granted,
Oh, yes, I did.
I remember you well,
Even from when I was a kid.
You were always easy-going,
But always got to the point.
The words of wisdom you have shared,
Have shown me that you really cared.
Now I sit in my room and weep,
Crying into my pillow, soaked with many tears.
I think about you.
You may have passed, but I still have your memories to keep.

Mike Rottinger

PARENTS

Even though I say it, I don't think I can stress it enough
How much I love you guys, you have that special touch.
When I am down you make me feel so good.
Even when we have had our differences I knew you always would.
I am so sorry if I have hurt you in any way.
The nerve I have after you have cared for me every day.
You have always been there at troubled times.
You always gave me the money I needed,
even if they were your very last dimes.
Every time I need a friend you are there for me.
Any problems I won't tell you discover the hidden key.
You have always been the ones who had faith in me and my dreams.
I love when you are proud of me and that smile on your face beams.
Without you, I couldn't live; without you I would die.
I am sorry, Mom and Dad if I have ever made you cry.
I love you!

Jaclyn Kostukoff

A Decision

Am I nothing but a puppet,
Following the pull of my peers.
Do I have the strength to cut the ties?
To stand on my own, with beliefs strong and true.
To be different or strange, but happy and fulfilled.
This is the cry of my heart, my spirit, my being.
Do I take the plunge into the unknown?
I feel like the fool with no sense of direction.
I will let the gods guide me and show me the way.
I will follow my heart and look to within,
To find the strength and courage to be who I am.

Larissa Bukowski

A Day in the Wilderness

Dark transforms fluidly into light
The nocturnal sounds fade into the dream of day
The dynamic momentum of nature is increased
By the presence of light
Harmonious chaos everywhere
Creating, destroying, perpetuating
The light softens into an orange hue
Gray becomes darker
The veil of slumber interprets reality

Richard Kelley Jr.

WISH YOU WERE HERE

. . . and you will be!
I live in the warmth and safety of your
love for me!

I hold your picture close to my heart,
I see your smiling face,
I hear your happy laughter,
I feel your arms tighten around me,
I smell the warmth of your skin,
I feel your kisses,
I hear your heart beat!

I truly do live in the warmth
of your true love for me . . . as . . .
I know . . . you live every day in the
warmth of my true love for you!!

Angels on your pillow darling, while
we're far apart.
Though miles and miles are now between us,
I hold you close within my heart!

Barbara Brewer

A Kiss to Die For

She makes my heart stop with a single touch.
Her beauty, her wisdom, her inner self, all are too much.
Too much to pass by,
too much to give up,
too much not to live for,
but to die for seems like not enough.
I'd sacrifice my body and all else that I'd miss.
I'd give it all up for just one moment,
a moment placed in the future,
where our souls would embrace with a kiss.

Scott Nelson

Am I Right?

Am I right to love all men and creatures?
Am I right to fight for freedom on Earth?
My intention is to understand all human features
and to protect life from the moment of birth.

There are people who try to destroy these goals,
With wicked ideas and words pretending be true.
To persuade the others they play several roles
And to recognize them is only up to you. . . .

Carmen Messina

The Spotted Predator

A sleek spotted silhouette glides
silently through the grass.
Alert, agile, but vulnerable.

As the sun goes down,
Game wanders from the African bush across
The Plain,
Into the sight of the lurking cheetah.

As she springs into action her muscles sing,
She races towards the unsuspecting game,
And flings herself on to the oblivious animal.

The Cheetah's hunger is now satisfied.

Lance Gösi

People Hear My Plea

People of the world hear my plea.
Oh, please hear my plea
For our children play and laugh in harmony
without a prejudice way.
Children of the world without race gender
happily at play.
The sky is blue as the grass is green.
Stars so beautiful as if a dream?
Help the helpless that knocks on your door.
Raise the hopelessness that cries from the
children huddled on the floor.
Why do you not hear the plea!.
We are all free . . .
The world is a small speck in space.
Can you see the pain in your child's face?

Norman Walimaki

Unaware

As the wind touches my cheek,
As breeze brushes through my hair,
An unknown feeling pierces my heart.
I awake to the dark.
I cry out for my mother, but she is not there!
Just as quick I remembered my prayer.
I just have been touched by an angel unaware.

Lois Hollis

It Finds a Way

A drifting heart the stress of day
When along comes night with spirited dreaming
Where souls convene about the way
Equally they revel in playful grace
Only the daylight will extinguish their dance
For all which live lie asleep in this place
Flying freely as gleaming white doves
Just like they have wings
Yet their forms shadow human
They cradle each other
Two souls find love
A passion with substance a nearness eternal
Slowly awakened
All feelings remain
A yearning commences
To dream is a strain
Nighttime has ended
A drifting heart the stress of day
A timeless cycle
Love finds a way

Rex Sabias

So, You're the One

So, you're the one I love to hate
the one I don't need when I'm lonely
the only one I can stand when I'm angry
So, you're the one that confuses me the most
the one I doubt when I'm in need
the only one I can bear to be around
So, you're the one who can read my mind
the one who always gives in
the only one who understands me
So, you're the one who frustrates me always
the one who never seems to care
the only one I've ever really loved

Jamie Blundell

Clean Queen (For a Day)

Gazing down into an old lapidary hand held mirror
A mirror beveled by a silver spoon
 He suddenly thought with a Cheshire grin:
 "One of these days, Mary—To the Moon!"

And with a quick sniff snore
And a zip boom BANG
His onxyed heart exploded
 And a crown leaking rubies
 Hit the floor

Walter McCready

I Want You Back

I feel as if I'm dancing on clouds,
Could I be, or am I just dreaming?
You dance through my heart every day
You run through my mind every step of the way
Every time I pray, I pray to see you another day
It's as if I'm walking on clouds,
Could I be, or am I just dreaming?
Every time I see you, my heart gets loud
I really do think I am walking on clouds
You've touched me in so many ways
My love for you gets stronger every day
What is this I'm feeling
Some say it's my heart's way of healing
I feel as if I'm dancing on clouds,
Could I be, or am I just dreaming?
But deep down I know that my heart is just aglow
Because of the fact
I want you back

Leigh Chilcot

Dancing Tears

For my love
She walks in the moonlight.
It fills the field with white light.
She looks up with those big green eyes.
Two saucers staring up at the stars,
As those lights look down upon her.
Light clouds drift by the moon.
Blocking her gorgeous view of the black sky.
As she looks where the moon once was,
She feels a drop.
One little tear fell from the sky.
Soon the field is watered with a spring shower.
She feels them kiss her arms, her face.
The light water slips down her legs.
Her dark sky is now her white falls.
Her face beams with the glow of tear drops.
Once standing, staring, now dancing with the rain.
Never feeling cold as the water caresses her face.
Not feeling sad but quickly filling with glee.
As the water skips with her,
She dances with her sweet rain.

Timothy Pelletier

Unopened Mail

When the spins and reckonings of man curtail,
then comes the promise of heart's true mail;
How often we search for life's true meanings,
only to find that they are here. . . . in our
kneelings.
For what glorious moments we all can share,
when we discover truth is here, just cloaked
in despair.
For in our search for truth and peace,
comes hard times and loneliness certain in
each.
What glory we find at the end of our trail,
simply knowing life's message is
in unopened mail.
Open your eyes to life's true feelings,
you'll find little raindrops cloud our
leanings;
The footprints of time cast gloom and doubt,
But our untouched mail has miraculous clout.

Lindell Thurman

My Love

I hoped one day to meet someone like you.
To breathe your breath upon my lips
To taste the sweet desire
And savor all its delights.
Tho' apart we dream, of loves sweet song.
A kiss . . . A hug . . . A touch
So much love our hearts barely contain it.
I love you my darling and I know you love me too.
One day, babee, together we will be if
But for a moment in time.
Look into my eyes. I love you.
My friend. My lover. My love.
Take my hand and walk with me.
Together for a moment suspended in time.
Our lips touch. The fire. The passion.
The desire. Oh, my babee. My love.
A lifetime of memories to be made in a few moments.
Let me hold you. Let me touch you.
Together for now, apart tomorrow, but
Together now.

Christine Merchel

Never Say Good-Bye

This isn't good-bye to all my friends
Because we all have a friendship that will never end
We laughed cried and had lot of fun
But now, my friends, all our good times are done
You have all been my second family
By making me feel like it was the place to be
When I had a problem, you were all there
I felt so loved, so happy and aware
You never know how you made me feel
When you left your feelings with me to conceal
No matter where I'm at or what I do
I will never forget any of you
We all had our fun and it's time we moved on
All the good times are behind us, but never gone
Remember the laughs, remember the fun
You'll think about them when you tell your friends what you've done
But for now, my friends, I'm not saying good-bye
I'm saying later and I'll miss you, no lie
I never say good-bye because good-bye is forever
I always say later because we'll talk again later

Douglas Martin, Jr.

Modern Heartache, Old-Fashioned Prayer

Where is my daughter, my bright gifted one,
With light golden hair that shines in the sun.
When did she leave and where did she go?
I beg you to tell me so then I will know.

The one who replaced her is bitter like wine,
I want the one back who is so sweet and kind.
No one can reach her she's out there somewhere
With people who harm her and don't even care.

There's not much more now that I can do
It's out of my hands Lord it's up to you.
I held her and rocked her and tended her wounds
'Til she came home and said she'd be grown up soon.

"Stay out of my life, I can do it myself."
She never even knew how sad I felt.
But I had to walk on and let her go,
To experience the world,
But I hoped she would know

My love remains faithful, solid and safe
Waiting for a time to again take my place
To lead her and guide her out of harm's way
And to give thanks to you Lord for each passing day.

Can I have her back Lord, the same as before?
Without all the heartache the devil has in store?
Don't let him harm her, I beg of you
'Til such time as grace and love can bring her through.

Brenda White

My Angel

Place an angel on my shoulder to whisper gently in my ear
When I take a wrong turning or simply know fear
Someone to lift me when I fall
To be beside me when I call
To comfort me when I am all alone
To let me grumble when I want to moan
I need someone to point me in the right direction on life's road.
I need someone to help me carry a heavy load
A smile to welcome me back when I turn away
A friend to be with when I want to play
An angel to stay with me from birth until I die
To forgive me when I hurt her by telling a lie
Dear Lord, I know it's a lot to ask
To guide me through life is a mammoth task
But you know when I sit and think it through
I have an angel already, a gift from you
To dry my tears and laugh when we have fun
I've had her all my life—my angel's my mum

Margaret Smith

Soul Searching

Lilac blossoms, frozen phrases,
found alone with broken dreams,
darkness closing, sunlight fading,
far away the world does seem.

Glimpse of brilliance, heavens bleeding,
colors that do fill the sky,
stir of breezes, shadows linger,
as the clouds begin to sigh.

Windows misty, water forming,
arctic frost makes its descent,
reminiscing, still recalling,
days of youth, away they went.

Thoughts lingering, mind wandering,
echoes call found deep within,
tension breaking, spirits lifting,
sense of hope new life begins.

Ambre Witte

Just Open Your Eyes and See

Just open your eyes and see the world
With dark blue seas and people like me
The world all around us is changing
In a huge transformation.

Just open your eyes and see the spring
And all the beauty within
The birds are chirping and the leaves
Are blooming.
Now they're ready for the summer to begin.

Just open your eyes and see the fall.
The leaves are so brightly colored.
Now it is getting colder.
The butterflies have stopped their flutter.

Just open your eyes and see the stars
For they will be there for all eternity
All so beautifully burning
Twinkling in the night sky.

Nathan Tinstman

I Don't Understand

The harder I try the more hopeless it seems
You creep in my head and taint with my dreams
You're everywhere I turn in every breath I take
From the time I go to sleep to the moment I wake

You're a part of me now I have to accept that
My head won't look forward it keeps looking back
What is it that I see that I can't move on
I can't take it anymore you need to be gone

When I look in the mirror I don't like what I see
I always see you before I see me
You're making me crazy I'm going insane
You already have my heart now you're messing with my brain

With each little glance or deceiving little stare
I feel more naked more alone and more bare
Like there's really no me if there is no you
I don't understand what the hell did you do

Please let go I don't need you anymore
Take a step back I'm closing the door
To the never ending aching that dwells in my heart
Turn around and walk away it's time that I part

Tina Simmerman

Best Friend

Time is running short
as our lives have only begun.
Eventually an inseparable pair
will head down a path
the other won't follow.
They will be farther apart the ever imagined.
The sand in the hour glass
will fall steadily
Until all that is left
are memories.
Pain endured, tears wiped away,
and laughter that once shook the walls.
Each moment created an ever lasting memory,
and will leave a wound that time can never heal.
Two friends, loyal companions
will drift apart;
never to meet again,
lost in this thing called life.

Shpresa Hamzaj

Sometimes I Feel Like . . .

Sometimes I feel like a clock
Always doing the same things
My life is the same every day
Knowing exactly what I am going to do or say
And wondering what life should bring.
Sometimes I feel like a wave
Splashing onto an empty shore
Picking up thousands of grains of sand
And sometimes, just sometimes, it can become a bore
Sometimes I feel like a rock
Just sitting in the middle of nowhere
Having the sun beat down on me relentlessly
And wondering if anyone will care

Lacey Bowling

Untitled

You have lifted me when I have fallen
you showed me faith instead of doubt.
You have been there for me continually,
you were always there to help me out.
In my darkest days and nights,
I could count on you to show me light.
I haven't been easy, this I know for sure;
but you hung onto me anyway,
not knowing which way I would turn.
You gave me strength when I was the weakest.
You listened to countless cries and complaints.
When I thought my life was meaningless,
you gave me meaning.
You never hurt me by not knowing what to say;
however, you always spoke the right words.
How many times have you comforted me?
I stopped counting . . .
I would never have survived emotionally
without you in my life.
I love you.

Melissa Marano

The Forest

The river glistens in the golden sun,
yet the day has just begun.
A white tailed deer runs right by,
as the birds fly up so high.
As the flowers bloom in the spring,
tulips and roses are everywhere.
Baby robins are perched in their nest,
while their mother looks for food her best.
The salmon swim around and around,
a rabbit is what I just found.
A snake slithers right on by,
as a frog catches another fly.

Rachel M. Bronakoski

When Life Happens, or If

As a child peers through the window
The glitter and excitement inside the store
All they see is what life can give them
How if they could only have, they would be happy.

As we grow, we see life as a goal
A place to plan for
A time when we will
Or when we can

One day, we succeed, graduate
Employment, promotions
Marriage and children
Moving, building, securing our future
But still knowing someday Life will happen

Still like the child peering through the window
Dreaming of when, and if we reach that place
Having that special thing, or going to that special place.
Planning, working, crying and dreaming
Day after day. making our way
Suddenly something changes and we realize
What we had all along was life
It happened a long time ago and we didn't see it.
We were too busy waiting for If and When

Judy Ledger

Did You Have to Go?

When you left my world went away
The monster came into power
The princess became the pauper
And the queen went insane
You never forgot me way back when
But now I'm so forgotten I fear I shall   never be remembered again
I fought with you like no one else
Perhaps something more was behind my words to you
I might have loved you, I'm not sure
I guess I'll never really know
I miss you more than even God knows
But wishful thinking and a heavy heart can't raise the dead
Sometimes I think of where you are now
I wonder if you remember me, if you care enough to
I still yell at you, louder now
I guess because I want you to hear me that badly
To come back and tell me I'm being stupid
Why did you leave? Did you really have to?

Jessica Allen

Where Did the Laughter Go?

Where did the laughter go?
The touch of your hand,
Twinkle in your eye,
Warmth I felt in your arms!

When did the endless chatter cease?
Long talks into the night,
Giggles and sighs,
Teasing words to sleep by?

Was it the chase that you did seek?
Where once I was tied and now unbound.

Is the thrill gone since reality could be?
Or was I a play toy,
To see if you could pull the string?

These questions asked,
 So you can see,
How I feel inside of me.

'Tis only one more time together,
To share the time as we once had planned.
Good times to create, memories to cherish.
Is this so out of hand?

Elizabeth Lineker

A Great Day for Me

Like a robin singing in the fresh spring air
Like two children playing without a care
The first time I saw you I knew this to be
A sad day for him, but a great day for me

Your smile was breathtaking
Your eyes were earthshaking
I wondered how any man could leave you ?
I wondered how any man could forsake you ?

That day in the park when we first met
Was a day in my life I will never forget
I could sense your sorrow
I could feel your pain
Yet I new that I would love you
When you told me your name

For at that moment in my life, it was plain to see,
This would be a sad day for him, but a great day for me!

Darryl Walker

My Little Nephew

My little nephew is my buddy, I give him a bath when he is muddy.
He's fifteen months old, he's learning so fast,
when he's grown up he will be bold.
It's kind of annoying to clean up when he makes a mess,
when he was little it happened less.
My little nephew is so cute,
when he cries I make him laugh and the crying halts to a mute.
My little nephew is so sweet,
after reading this, him you will want to meet.

Nicholas Bunce

Frogiveness Overflows

Overwhelming forgiveness challenges the soul.
Special son with a rainbow robe.
Boy in a cold, dark cistern.
Brother sold to strangers, and
brought to a new place.
The tearing of clothes and a father mourns.
Man put into position to carry out a plan.
A horrible famine will fill all the land.
Realizing all the wrong that was done.
Another beloved son taken from the father.
Conditions and tricks set into motion.
A revealing and giving glory to God.
Oh, the special son and father reunited.
Embraces and tears.
Brand new place and brand new life.
God's provision fills all with joy!
Forgiveness overflows!
Would any of us be so bold?
Overwhelming forgiveness challenges the soul.

Robin Kwiatek

A New Beginning

Today we join our hearts, our souls and our minds.
Today we link our hands in love for our journey through time.

As we say our vows that show our promise of love and devotion,
We say to the world we're ready for every extreme of emotion.
On this day I ask of you one very simple thing,
That our marriage will always be more than just a ring.

Our life will be an ocean that will always ebb and flow.
No matter the change or problem our waves of love will grow.

We'll rid the tide of life as it rises to the sand.
We'll always know no matter what we'll hold each other's hand.

On this day I ask of you for you heart and your mind.
A marriage is about friendship sharing thoughts as well as time.

As we look into each other's eyes, full of passion and bliss,
We begin to gently close them and seal our vows with a kiss.

Pamela Linger

My Hobby

Before the game we get tame—
we're going to play a football game.
We get to the locker room, put on our equipment;
we could here the pastor filling our hearts with commitment.
The time has come for us to play,
we hope that we are not already late.
We get to the field that Saturday night,
we get a sudden spite from the lights.
The captains take there place on the grass,
the ref's remarks last and last.
We flip the coin, two people—both males—
one calling heads the other thinking tails.
The game starts everything, and then it is done.
It was worth it and it was fun.
So next time put on you helmet and get in the game
because you are about to experience some pain.

Kyle Daye

Private Emotion

Every endless night has a dawning day,
Every darkend sky has a shining ray.
And it shines on you, can't you see,
You're the only one who can shine for me.
It's a private emotion that fills you tonight,
As the silence falls between us as the shadows steal the light,
And wherever you may find it,
Wherever it may be, let your private emotion come to me.

Lindsay Browning

Why My Heart Cries

I'd stare at you for hours
submissive by gentle defeat
caught in your magic powers
brings men like me to your feet
I brought down the rain
to wash your silk hair
I endured the pain just to breathe your air
Is it real or just illusion
so hard to tell—too much confusion
lust or love—both deadly sins
but with every dawn—as the new day begins
my love for you grows stronger
with every warm glance
and still I wonder, do I have a chance?
to feel your magic aura
time in pure bliss
there are treasures untold in your longed-for kiss
I lose myself in the deep blue pools of your eyes
knowing I can't have you is why my heart cries
so when you are alone
don't take to fright
remember I love you
sweet dreams and good night

Jason Flynn

Old-Timers

They sit side by side holding hands
Their gray heads bowed together in quiet discussion
Her shy smile and the bright twinkle in his eyes
Makes you wonder what they speak of
So many years together
Giving and taking as needed
Living so long together
The two have become one
As one passes, so shall the other
Sharing sweet eternity as they did life

Olivia Duvall

Black-Tie Affair

My deodorant has run out again.
What shall I do but spray on cheap cologne?
So then I can pass for a gentleman.
My sleek black tuxedo I got for rent;
I slick my hair back with a fine-toothed comb,
But my deodorant's run out again.
I'm smaller in stature than other men.
I swell my chest and speak in a deep tone,
So then I can pass for a gentleman.
I'll hide my missing tooth as best I can
With pursed-lip smile I'll give to everyone,
Although my deodorant's run out again.
I practice "Good evening," like a refrain,
Practice bowing to the mirror I own;
Maybe I can pass for a gentleman.
I step out and feel cool wind on my chin.
It's a grand night for a trip into town.
My deodorant has run out again,
But I can still pass for a gentleman.

Daniel Grome

poverty

this poor life of mine full of care,
standing on the roadside with nothing to wear.
as i sit by the gutters,i watch the rich men close their shutters.
i wish luck could come my way, on such a terrible day.
How long shall i continue to wait, for a fish to eat my bait?
my life is like a stream flowing out of the river of dreams.
my mother thinks i'm a fool for dropping out of school.
i want something to call my own, something no one else owns.
i wish i could fly a plane, what else have i got to gain?
this poor life of mine full of care,
how long shall i continue to stand and stare?

wodo oji

Storyteller

The sky opens her breath to me and slips a story through
And like the sky, it's true that I am tired of being blue
Around the world she covers me and sings of crimson hues
And hovering with satin eyes born of the number two

Her gifts of light she gives before the night has taken you
And holds the sun with glory winds to brighten every few

Whispering her soft daydreams that others carry through
And don't you think the sky above is tired of being blue?

Melanie Welch

The Me I'll Never Find

These memories that flood my mind, with times I can't erase
Have haunted me with their naked truths, forcing me to see.

These memories that I have tried, but failed to leave behind
Have molded me into who I am, and the me I'll never find.

Shelley O'Brien

Father's Pride

Vision perched on father's eyes,
see separate individuals yearning their own define.
"Time will tell," is a story they are learning,
each step unshod, while on each corner lay a new pair of shoes.

Ideas right or wrong,
with some coaching makes them strong.
They fear not the world,
not the story of time,
beholding confidence as their rudder, their ship—value.

Vision blurred with tears of pride,
loving each child equal, yet separate, as they are
Reminded once more, that the reward,
is the journey behind the guide.

William G. Dahlin

My Mother, My Angel

My Mother will forever be my best friend,
A hand she is always willing to lend.
She's taught me it's important to be kind—
An example she sets time after time.
All through my life she's never stopped giving;
Life without her would have been difficult living.

My Mother has shown me it's important to be wise;
I live each day knowing I can reach for the sky.
I have always shared with her my dreams;
She accepts them and encourages me to be free.
Using her ample support and love,
I've been given the freedom and grace of a dove.

My Mother makes me feel so proud;
I can hold my head high almost up to the clouds.
There will come a day that I'll have children of my own,
I hope and pray I'll do as I've been shown.
For I have a lovely Mother that I adore;
She's warm and sweet down to the core.

Shelly Storelee

Who Knew?

One night long ago, he tapped her shoulder
She placed her hand in his
And they danced to a Glenn Miller tune.

Who knew the dance would last this long?

Lately, they talk about their "ustas"
She's taught him how to cook and make a bed
He's put up railings along the stairs.

Who knew the dance would last this long?

Now, every night at ten o'clock
Comfortable as old flannels
They reminisce, whisper g'night
Hug 'til sleep comes.

Who knew the dance would last this long?

Dolores Valeri

On Your Way—A Father's Unspoken Words to His Unborn

Dove of futility, fly west.
Sun is to setting, as end is to test.
Wings span ambitions, flight takes to hope,
Imagination covers, as snow is to slope.
Dew of sun's first warmth covered rays,
Life is to death, as age is to days.
Knowledge reaps all knowing,
Always is to learn,
Ignorance makes the fire, dreams made to burn.
Mind for the day, rest is the night,
Good makes for glory, for evil takes flight.
Will you hide, or will you stand?
Will you face the lonely band?
Head held high, the trumpets sound.
Enjoy life's unknown, prepare the down
To cradle the new must you learn from the old,
The day I am forgotten the story be told.

Eric Linnebur

October

High in a barren tree
I saw a leaf and thought of me,
hanging on in disbelief,
my youth has passed me by
and now I look for greater things that come upon
the wind—
the song of birds,
the scent of spring,
God's gift of love in everything
Betty Duffy Skinner

The Right Moment

The wind blew and the time flew, rather
the time flew and the wind blew
A moment ago. . . .

A moment ago, I was in tenth (Class X)
and now in twelfth (Class XII).
I was happy then, unhappy now.

The reasons are known,
there is no need to moan.
Still time is left and then,
It will be a moment ago.
It is better to do now, just now, just this moment
And not a moment after, otherwise
You would say, I should have. . .a moment ago!
Neeraj Soni

The Release

The pen seems to be my only release.
Emotions hidden ricochet throughout my body
Looking for a pore to escape through.
Finding none until the pen in my hand
Touches the emptiness of a page.
They rush out of the pores of my fingertips
Invading the ink of this pen
Who was once just an innocent bystander,
But is now a criminal in this devilish release.
Ink floods the ghostly white paper,
Graffiting its innocence,
Screaming words onto each passing line
Until all the tears leave the body
And the rampaged emotions subside,
Vanishing back into the pores.
Laughing the entire way at the wasted ink
And the dull, lifeless pen lying on the table.
Marisa Huck

Call upon YAH

Like a bad storm that rises
That's how trouble comes
But when we pray to YAH
He eases the pain of life's strain

When we are faced with obstacles
And jumping another hurdle, is hard to do
We can call on YAH's great name
He's the one who can pull us through

There will always be trials, tribulations
and strained relationships
We all go about like ships, being tossed on stormy seas

Call yes, call all on YAH, those who know
YAH's great name
YAH is the same today as was yesterday
YAH, he will never change

Like a bad storm that rises
That's how trouble comes
But when we pray to YAH
He eases the pain of life's strain
Pearlie Armstrong

America's Wars

Sergeants, Captains, or Privates, whomever they may be,
they fought for you and me.

Bullets were flying and finding their mark,
but spirits and souls were heavy on our heart.

People were dying around us as we were apart,
but our hearts were together from the start.

Blood and guts were out,
it just felt like you should scream and shout.

There was a lot of swearing;
love and hatred had no bearing.

I saw the sky light up from the explosive light,
then it wanted me to fight back with all my might.

There was destruction as far as we could see.
I wish it would end, but how could it all come to mend.

Medics were there to try to piece us together from the start.
But how could they when we had a hole in our heart.

Our hearts were heavy from the sights we saw,
but God Bless America for us all!
In the end it was glorious as can be,
as we did all we could for our country's liberty.
Gary A. Holman

My Freedom and My Cage

In my dreams I live out of space and time.
They are my freedom and my cage.
They free me from reality,
Or they trap me with the future.
No one can take my dreams away.
They release me from day to day.
But they tell the future—people's destiny.
Some I've tried to change,
Every time I fail.
It still happens no matter what I do.
Others tell good things
Make the unknown easier to live.
I would never give them away
For they are my freedom and my cage,
Mine and no others.
Shannon McGaffigan

A Psalm

The moon arises on the calm and quiet of the night,
    like a perpetual machine this sphere is in flight.
        For whom, for what . . . why?

Look, think, O', you who hear and have sight:
    Are we the Governors of fate,
        the Movers of orbs containing life and light?

Say: No, we depend upon the Light,
    the light that emanates from the spheres blanketing the night.

And slowly the moon descends,
    night becoming day;
        the Call is given, welcoming dawn upon its way.

Shall I offer a recitation?

Say: I seek refuge in the Lord of the dawn
        . . . from the evil of intense darkness.
Mahrad Almotahari

Love Infinity

Just to have embraced you is more than enough for me.
Just to have once kissed your lips, last me eternally.

The sweet sound of your laugh brings me joy everlasting.
The warmth of your smile is never ending.
The scent of your skin is intoxicating.

Just to have known you completes me.
Just the memory of you is love infinity.

Kenisha A. Bell

Suzette

As the light fades away another day gone in May,
No longer shall we see your face
But in our dreams
Where we can play along with Misty, Taka and Kitchie,
Whom you joined that day; we will see you on our day.
You lived with us, you earned your keep, usually nestled at our feet
In your nest you spent your day, snoring gently you slept away
And as you walk through that tunnel of light, we shall guide you
As the years pass one by one you shall not age
Nor pain shall you feel; you'll be content forever
Don't worry, we'll be there someday, cross that rainbow bridge
To take you away
But until then I bid you adieu
Smooth sailing
And peace be with you too

Brett Voss

Mom

Thoughts of me thoughts of you.
I can't put into words how much I love you.

You're always there,
Sometimes I think you're the only one who cares.

I'm never happy and I often frown.
Upon receiving a letter or hearing your voice
helps me feel better when I'm down.

I wish I could shed my skin and begin my life again.
'Cause I'll never be able to repair the damage done.

Can't change the past, but maybe I can tilt the future in my favor.
God knows, Mom, you've been a life saver.

I'm full of guilt and hurt,
And I always feel lower than dirt.

I hope I've finally reached a new stage
Which will enable me to finally turn the page.

'Cause I'm getting on in years,
And it kills me to see you shedding tears.

Robert Pollard

Inside and Outside

Years away out of memory's reach
A young woman's insides became impeached

They could no longer live in the world we know
For they would slowly burn and the ashes blow

They knew not of defense from the harshness of life
They knew only of love and peace without strife

The insides used to be one, not divided by a shell
A shell made of elusions, idiosyncrasies none could tell

Who is this woman? Oh, I know her
She is this and that, no she's not, she's

And so lives this maiden from day to day
A different face in every turn, always a role to play

For if her inside was outside
She would never be able to survive

Rosemary C. Carr

My Friend in the Mirror

When I look into the mirror, I see
a friend, who listens to every word I say.
She cries with me. She laughs with me.
She sings with me. She dances with me.
She celebrates my joys in life. She knows
all my hopes and dreams. She will never
give up on me. Never!
I look again in the mirror and there
standing behind me is a true friend.
The one that holds me when I'm down.
The one who fixes my problems.
The one who shares the dreams for life.
That friend is my dear husband.
We are as one. Partners of life.
The best of friends that two people could be.

Vicki L. Cantrell

A Brand-New Baby

When a brand new baby is on the way,
It's life's crowning joy.
Friends and kinfolk are so excited,
Be it a girl or be it a boy.

Daddy, manly, squares his shoulders,
Then takes a deep, deep breath;
Just thinking about rearing a baby,
Almost scares him to death.

In your own two hands
You're holding future lives.
Children are precious gifts of love
Between husbands and wives.

Jesus said, "Let the children come to me,"
He said, "A child shall lead them." So let it be.
Children in your care proves you're truly blessed.
With divine assistance, you can give it your best.

Juanita J. Wallis

A Time to Choose

Love has its limitations, boundaries, and borderlines.
And underneath the pleasant smile,
Inside of me, I'm crying
There is no way that I should ever have to pick or choose
Which one of them I'll keep by me,
Which one of them I'll lose,
Since I have to let somebody go,
Although I love them both.
It's obvious which one of them
I've always loved the most
The one who kept me confident
Whenever I had doubts.
One of the people in this world,
I could not live without.

Twana McCarroll

Breathe the Silent Second

To be spit out by a bold trumpet
Or let go softly and sparingly by a modest flute
Would be marvelous.
T'would be like escaping from a high-sailing aircraft
To drift and float on the breath of fulfillment the ever great!
It would please me as no one can ever imagine.
To be just one of those fortunate notes.
My method of escape would make no difference,
Just to reach those patient, appreciative ears . . . ah!
The silent second would move
And then be silent again in the next; listen,
For once I'm freed, no one can catch me.

Lynn Rulon

Tommy MacDill

I came back to this place with my dreams still intact
Over his young casket I made a great pact

In the halls of his youth. Tommy was jaded and jeered
Ye, when he was standing alone. The town loved him so dear
But behind their closed doors, his spirit they feared
And when he tried to reach high they made him pay for a year

So, Tommy his town whose love he did need
He placed them high on his shelf and made a great book
The town now so proud, they threw a parade
But quiet in the night they stalked him like prey

So they fooled him and tricked him, calling him friend
They then rumbled and tumbled him down a great hill
He struck a big rock throwing away his last thought
In the valley below lay dead Tommy MacDill

Where do I go now that Tommy is Dead
My dreams all along where there in his head
In my moment of anger, my heart in a rage
His books and his dreams I did burn in a blaze

I announce, "I am now one of You," as I lay down my pen quill
And I now have nothing left but the story of Tommy MacDill
Evan M. Grooms

A Mother's Anguish

A tragedy continues to beset us; for I bleed,
That not of my own doing, but my womb betrays me.
Thus, I am not with child; nor do I know if I ever will be again.
Angela A. Stuart

Mystic

Entering my heart your charms do bewitch
Dissolving my will with each time stitch
Wizardry, sorcery, how you beguile
Angelic your face, your skin, your smile
Relentless pulses of desire
Dawn to which has no fire
Remembering your face with all its bliss
Escaping reality to steal one kiss
I close my eyes for the day's twilight
Churning in my soul with your soft sweet light
Heaven did bless the world with you
Elven beauty with skin of dew
Edward Reiche

Wings

Butterflies are fragile things.
Butterflies have wings
A bird has notes that trill and sing; birds have wings.
My day has sunshine and blue skies,
happy thoughts, and tender sighs,
While on God my heart relies, my heart has wings.

The white dove is God's sign of peace—A dove has wings
When our "Ave's" never cease—our prayer has wings
God's promise ours and so we know
As through the trials of life we go
His hand on ours, the way He'll show
Our feet have wings.

My prayer book is my tower of strength—it has wings
My mind can cover any lengths so it has wings
Through all your suffering I'll be there
with rosary, on knees, in prayer,
Knowing that God will lead us where
Our souls have wings.
Marjorie J. Sander

A Gift of Love

If I were an angel
with wings to fly,
I'd rise above the clouds
and beyond the sky.

The gates of Heaven would open wide
I'd be welcomed there.
I'd enter to find my Lord,
as praises fill the air.

He would appear to me
aglow with light.
I'd kneel before Him,
and breathe in the sight.

Oh, Lamb of God,
my plea would be.
I fear for man on Earth,
he just won't see.

His life is full of sin and self
Instead of looking to You for help.

What gift could I give to make him realize,
The way to a better life is to look up with his eyes?
Jane C. Jordan

Heartbreak

That morning I couldn't get out of bed
I still can't believe what was said
I laid in bed and wanted to die
But my pride wouldn't let me cry
When I heard our song
It made me think of what went wrong
I thought our love was meant to be
But I guess it was just me
When will the pain go away
Or will it just be with me every day
I think of you day and night
And wish you and I will be all right
I wish I could turn back the hands of time
So you would still be mine
So I guess we'll go our separate ways
And hopefully I can heal one day
Brittany Rodriguez

Amnesty in Amsterdam

I went on a trip above the trees,
Over the ocean over the seas

I landed down in an old town
My feet never stopped once on the ground

I went to the Parliament, I went through the town
The people wanted me to stay,
The government said "No Way"

I asked, "give me amnesty," would you please?
With deep regret, we can't take that step

We cannot interfere with U.S. policy
Even though yours is such an odyssey

I left my country so you see
Because my government made a crime of me

On return to my land, should I dare take a stand
Or should I fall to my knees and beg for mercy?

Whichever I choose, I know I won't lose
The memory of a trip that was really hip

I got high on the plane, I got high on the train
I got high on the tram, seeking "Amnesty in Amsterdam"
Stan Thomas

When It's Over

What do you hold on to,
When there's nothing there,
Why should I believe anything you say,
When it's obvious you don't even care.

You got me to believe in something
To find out it was not true,
You have someone else now,
While I sit around lonely and blue.

To start over again,
Was not something I wanted to do,
I realize I have no choice now,
For there is no me and you.

I still love and care about you,
And I do not understand why,
When you turned your back on me,
I felt like I wanted to die.

Well the game is over now,
And I cried my last cry,
I guess I've finally reached the point,
Where there's nothing left to say but good-bye.

Andre Allen

My Dad

When God created this Earth
He had a definite plan in mind
To combine the finest elements
That he could possibly find.
He tried his best, and when he was through
The finest elements he placed in you.

Each individual had his share,
The little that he needed
To guide his life accordingly,
And yet so few succeeded.

There is no special formula, as we well know, now
That faith, kindness, and understanding
Have taught us the lesson how.

Now we are mature and well on our way
Through the rough roads of life—
He too will now stray.

So today we hold our heads up proudly.
Let other folks make a fuss
About a wonderful, charming husband
Who belongs to Mommy and us.

Evely Farber

A Reflection

When you look in a mirror, what do you see
What is your reflection?
Do you see War? Or peace?
Is there, an answer to your question?
Is your soul at ease?
Does something unanswerable nibble at you
Until it causes you pain like a disease?
A reflection can tell so much about a person.
It can tell whether they're kind and caring
Or if their state of mind shall worsen.
You can tell if you are daring
You have but to stare into your eyes.
Eyes keep secrets and tell truths that are untold.
Certain reflections the world denies
So that the truth shall not unfold.
Most are simply oblivious
To the depth of their soul.
Gentlemen be chivalrous
In order to keep yourself whole
In your reflection.

Carlos Y. Craig

The Dream

I settled in my favorite chair, then closed tired eyes to rest.
Of all the havens, anywhere, that has to be the best.
I closed my eyes, but not to sleep, my day was not half done,
For I had chores that wouldn't keep, but my race had been run.

A willing captive of that chair, in moments I was gone.
But then a dream slipped from its lair to carry me along;
Along through pages of the books on shelves beside my chair.
I crossed the Alps with Hannibal, and other things as rare.

I dreamed I fought at New Orleans, with Andrew Jackson's men.
Though most were killed, I only dreamed, so lived to fight again.
I attacked with Red Cloud's Sioux at the Wagon Box Corral.
I rode beside young Crazy Horse the day George Custer fell.

Then I designed the telephone, for Alexander Bell.
The same loud phone that woke me. From what? No one can tell.

Ronald G. Zumwalt

Drunks

They sit at barstools in clouds of hazy smoke
with cratered faces of stubble and dingy yellow
Scuffed boots attached to soiled pant legs
And thickened flannel jackets due to wandering
aimlessly about streets and shops
Calloused, blackened hands clasped
around the bottle or shot glass preceding them
Their only redemption
As they laugh with rotten teeth in rotten mouths
At remembrance of their own stupidity
And yet, in their sour disposition, the eyes are honest
behind the blood tree veins, beneath the yellow-stained
Iris the pain comes pulsing forth, only to be drowned out
by another hit of American brewed, European-imported liquor
As they stumble home to wifeless, childless houses
As vacant as a sparrows rest in December
Empty as the bottle that stands alone on the bar's counter

T. J. Thomas

Book on a Shelf

He was just shy of fourteen when he went away,
To go with his father, not to visit, but stay.
The days slowly passed and turned into years,
No one could do anything to wipe his mother's tears.
There were words left unsaid and words that were cold;
Looking back can't erase the memory it will hold.
In both of their hearts were pieces broken,
Only to mend if the words weren't left unspoken.
So she began to write to ease her pain,
From the emptiness that haunts her, yet hoping to gain
Maybe, someday he'll find her book on a shelf,
Only, by chance, decide to read it himself.
As the story unfolds and his eyes are drawn near,
To the dedication of my only son, so dear,
From an author who is quite well known,
Yes, it is her, my mother, author unknown.

Dianne M. VanArsdale

An Emotional Time

When the time has come to pass away
Emotional trauma throughout the day
Lonely nights and cryful tears
Remembered times and moments shared

A subject of depression; a stage of shock
Confused emotions; a psychological block
Eternal existence is never within
"For mankind is only to win"

Letting go on the grip of life
Stretching further into the light
The circle of life will surely proceed
For them in peace, they're finally free

May S. Russells

Sometimes and Other Times

Sometimes,
Love is a blanket
Warm and comforting

Other times,
Love is a dagger
Sharp and painful through your heart

Sometimes,
When someone says "I love you"
They actually mean it

Other times,
When someone says "I love you"
They just want something

Sometimes,
Life can be fulfilling
And wonderful

Other times,
Life is very unhappy
And disappointing

There is a flip side to everything
There are sometimes and there are other times.

Brandy Anderson

Dreaming

As you lie in the darkness and sleep creeps up on you,
Like shadows mocking you in the moonlight,
You look longingly out your window at the fading sunlight.
For you know one night can take you to one hundred worlds,
Some you thought only royalty could see,
And others, even in the daylight you'd be afraid to be.
Those are the ones you most fear.
A nightmare chases you until someone finally hears.
When morning finally comes and all is bright,
You feel happy and contented after surviving yet another night.

Katie Donaldson

I Stepped Outside

To all the loved ones I've left behind,
To all the friends that have been so kind,
I have a message I would like to share
To comfort your hearts and ease your despair.
My time had come, and I could no longer abide
In this old body, so I stepped outside.
I know you've been dealt a heart-breaking blow,
But when Jesus came for me, I just had to go.
I felt a body that's been scarred by its past,
But those scars don't hurt anymore for I'm free at last!
I'm rejoicing and singing and so much more,
There's indescribable beauty like I have never seen before.
When I speak of this place I beam with pride,
This haven of rest I found when I stepped outside.
This place is so special, without sorrow or tear,
And I want all my friends and loved ones to meet me here.
Jesus is the way to this glorious place,
Just trust in Him and His saving grace.
Now you'll bury this body because it gave up and died,
But remember I'm not there, for I stepped outside.

Kenneth Littleton

The American Tragedy

Rising as an entity in the dawn of the void.
Behold what I behold!
The quasi empire was epically destroyed.
Behold what I behold!
Forth is the exhorted current,
That conceives an exiled behest.
Behold what I behold!
Loyalty awakes the ancient east
And gracefully sets in the fountain of the west.
Behold what I behold!

Zaqari Pingo

To the Light of My Life

From the first day you came into my life,
My broken heart had begun to heal.
Even though I said I would never fall in love again,
It is my heart that you did steal.

You and I have had so many memorable times together,
That I greatly wish for more to come.
And though I hope we will never experience the bad times,
I will be there if ever you have some.

When you stood by my side during troubled times,
It made me love you even more.
And each time you let me know you cared,
It made my troubled heart soar.

I feel as though my life has just began,
To take a turn for the better.
This is why I am confessing to you,
In this explicit letter.

I hope you never come to the place,
Where you feel that we should part.
Because you are the light of my life,
And you have stolen my fragile heart.

Crystal Welton

Reality

Father! We come to gather in the name of love.
We are bound together by the anger deeply rooted
in the depth of our souls. Unable or unwilling
to forgive or forget past transgressions.

We wear our anger and resentment like a badge
of honor, displaying what each perceive to be
courage in the face of so much deceit.

If we allowed ourselves to face the real truth,
would we be able to stand in the midst
of face-to-face confrontations with reality?

Would we be able to accept our part in the
destruction of our lives, the path we chose
to travel, and the decisions we made on the
journey to the present?

Would it be easier to place the blame elsewhere,
because deep down not one of us is
willing or able to look reality in the face
and own up to our self-destructive behavior?

Father! We came to gather in the name of love,
bound together by the blood of Jesus.

Lillie M. Williams

Jesus, Lover of My Soul

Jesus, lover of my soul,
You alone have made me whole.
With your, love and tender care,
You, have shown me how to share.

The love that you have given me.
The things that others cannot see,
Have made me what I am today,
Including all the times I pray.

If now and then, I could save a soul,
And grasp it from the devils hold.
Then, I would say, that is my goal,
For a soul, is worth, much more than gold.

And when this world is through with me.
I'll be going home to be with, thee.
Free from all the wordly cares.
To be with, you, Lord, in the air.

Cecilia Harper

Reflecting

When I looked into your eyes, much to my surprise;
I saw love.

At no other time did I ever get so high, just can't deny;
It was love.

Embraced tightly in your arms, lost in the magic of your charm.
Confirms love.

That tell-tell tremor in your voice, leaves me no other choice;
But to hear love.

Little things you say like put off work,
Let's play, refuels the thing I call love.

With our lips combined in a kiss most divine,
like aged wine, I can taste your love.

You don't have to say it, your actions relay it;
Whatever the role, I'll play it; name the price, I'll pay it;
Just to keep your love.

Smith Randall Norris

Twilight Heart

My heart is the drapery of dreams
and softly the evening came
How beautiful the silent hour when the sun chases the stars
This twilight becomes a bridge to pass through
The night—thus becomes the day
These lovely portraits of night—twilight hears
Softly I pull the drapery of dreams
How beautiful the long twilight
Clad with silver eyes
This unites yesterday to the silent hour
Twilight gray has come for my heart to dream

Pamela Simpson King

Serenity

Follow me
To the star studded caverns of time.

To the deserts of eternal space,
Wander with me
In the beauty of the still born day,
And in the brilliance of our splendid sunset,
Tell me what you have seen

But let me tell you
About all the time that awaits
And in the darkness of the still silent night
In the dusk of the space we shared
Lose me in your eyes
That I may find you in mine

Sylvia Wharton

Bye Little Eyes

Clouds hang lazy, as jets break the sky;
Laughter calms the ride
Our peaceful sleeper
Dreams he can fly,
Counting stars and bedtime books,
Dancing on the deck, as the moon rushes by
The key that hangs is seen too late,
As they grow, our chances fade
We must look up,
Grab the key
In the eyes of the little child you see

Brenda Mayer

Cotton Candy Preamble

Dawn hit and the gray blue captives of the night melted away,
As they couldn't hold on the day.
So I don't think it will rain, but it's beautiful right now:
Sometime in the A.M. the clouds took their bow.

Embraced in the atmosphere for all time,
The tracks and marks that the sun couldn't bare.
They leave trails in time and in the air,
Gone for what seems to be good, but their memory is still there.

Morning's glory has crept up on purple mountain's majesty,
Disbanding all efforts through the duration of the night's
Now impeached promise
To commit the Earth to shadows.

The A.M. breaks through and emits a glare,
The sun I can't take, so in my mind they're still there,
As I can hold them in my heart, but not in time,
When the clouds come back the rain will be mine.

Johnny J. Reeves

Mother's Eyes

Why must I prove myself to others?
I will admit no one is perfect,
But neither am I.

I try and try to prove my love.
Yet, for some reason the love
I give will never be enough.

Sometimes when I feel
I succeeded, I still fail in mother's eyes.
I know I will never be good enough.
But still I try.

It doesn't matter how hard
I try, no matter what I will always cry,
and the tears will always be.
Because I know I failed in mother's eyes.

Michelle Lahman

Burdens

We all have burdens that we carry
Some of us try to hide them
Some wish to bury,
Some burdens are heavier than we can bear
Because they hold within frustration,
guilt, fear, and shame.
They are so powerful you see.
Capable of holding us back
from what we could be.
They hold on to us so tight.
We get lost when we try to reach the light.
Yet we are so bold
To dare judge others so cold.
We have no right because we do not
Know the burdens they also hold,
But we all hold the secret key you see.
My dear friend, the simple truth shall set you free.

Mary Mappin

Twelve Inebriated Arguments

Your private benevolence is a blundering happiness,
an aching argument—silver breath, cold and shattering.
What makes you think I'd tremble at your consequence?
Smile weak tears at your suffering attachments?
It's a system of unnecessary confusion.
My beloved mind feels your falsehood knowledge—tearing,
smearing each infant cell into obliteration, undiscovered.
I could turn away, show my unpainted wall-face to no one.

Rebecca L. Hillyer

Black Blues

I want to stretch my tears
Across the universe
And cry on the cosmos
Some kind of deep
Black blues
That Bessie never knew
And the train didn't
Go that far
I'm talking about years
Of tears
Crystallized into a
Hard, black body
Screaming for
Freedom
Freedom
Freedom
That the world never hears

Joan Wicker

Untitled

I have to tell you
I love you.
But you don't want
To hear it.
You have to hide
From your heart.
Inside a bottle
Then it seems all right.
When you woke up
I was gone.

Alex Sipos

Flood Watch

Having searched high and through many lows
having crossed most every line
I wonder now, were I to walk the Earth
if I might ever find
promise of peace and loving hearts
and endless happy dreams
but a smile I'll find today
is tomorrow not as it seems

So many tears falling now from the face of love
and here we are swept away in her sorrow flood

Man has made clear his every point
that every dollar is worth the hate
and with this point stuck the hearts
hoping for any love to save
to save a little for that day
that we might rise from this fall
and hope what little love is left
is enough to save us all

If we are not quick to dry and kiss the face of love
I am certain we are to drown in her sorrow flood

Lee Collier

To Doug

Quickly the year passed
But the day of your death erases all others.
One rare boy!
Needed, loved by many.
Crowding, needing comfort, crowding to your home to comfort.
Crowding to church in your memory the children grew.

Does God give memories
Steady and present as mountains to sustain us?

Doug, my son!
You're searching, you're loving,
You're smiling with humor fighting precocious wisdom!
We need those mountains.

Beverly Wright Yankovich

Spirit Wind

A lovely charm, your smile,
Your laughter in a June eve,
Awakened by life's spirit wind,
Echoes in love from the mountains.

The night descends in nature's bosom.
In your whisper intimacy is heard,
The inner world exposing,
Searching the depth of the soul.

Your inner beauty takes his breath away.
Good fortune smilingly heralds,
Lovers in faith and hope,
That great love is sprouting.

The flaming dawn in the East brightens.
Night toward the day is turning.
The dance of mist swings toward space,
Song birds sing out exultation.

Gustaf Erikson

Becoming a Man

Becoming a man it's more than growth,
It's not just age,
Nor a combination of both.

As we move through time,
The choices we make,
Create many paths that we may take.

As we take these paths, choosing right from wrong,
Hoping the choice will make us strong,
not strength of muscle but of spirit.

So make a choice in life, it's your right
But the choice you take you must live with, day and night.

So as you can see the point I am getting to,
Is when you become a man, it's up to you.

When did I become a man
When I chose to!

Kelly L. Bushnell

Sanctuary

A large lily pad in the middle of a cool deep quiet pond
With a gentle breeze brushing as light as a goose down feather.
A large spacious nest made up of many sticks and twigs
Anchored high up on the face of a windswept 5,000-foot mountain.

A snow-covered lodge that is snung and cozy warm inside
With an underwater entrance and tender shoots to munch on.
A huge cave with a constant temperature
And a bed of spruce or pine saplings to sleep on.

Snuggled underneath your mother and her warm feather breast
To keep out the chill of the wind or the wet of the rain.
Sleeping face to face with your sweetheart or wife
Your arms wrapped around each other and all the doors are locked.

Living in an area where there is no crime or evil activity knowing
That not only you but also your loved ones are safe and secure.
Having enough food and clothes to live from day to day
And having the income to insure that this will never end.

But the best sanctuary that anyone can have
And can know within one's heart and soul
Is knowing the King of Kings and the Lord of Lords
And praising Him every day for what He has provided you and me.

James W. Cope

One Night

A night in your arms should last forever.
My mind reeling from the sight of you,
And the smell and feel of your limbs,
Two bodies entwined in a ballet,
Twisting and sliding together,
Gently and wildly.
Your caress sends me into oblivion,
And then brings me back with a shudder,
And the realization that I am being loved,
By a vision of the gods,
An earthly representation of God.
Our tongues dance madly to and fro,
Over the endless sea of skin.
Why now, after all these years,
Do I find what I wanted from the beginning?
And now, I want to satisfy you more than I have anyone else.
For much longer than just this one night.

Jeffrey Murray

Lycanthrope

Wolves howl as the full moon rises
Night's shadows are full of surprises
skin turns inside out as I turn to the beast
hungry for the blood on which I will feast
I am the terror that stalks through the land
I am the wolf that walks like a man

My senses heighten to that of a god
I am not of this earth on which I trod
crooked horn, cloven hoof, and forked tongue
special delivery from the flames I come
waiting for the blood-crazed frenzy to engulf
I am the man that walks like a wolf

Black masses of shape-shifters abound
Lord Satan hath loosed His hound
to hunt and kill his human prey
and recede like a shadow with the coming of day
so lock and shutter your house and be in by dusk
or yours will be the blood for which I lust

Andrew Swift

Caught You

It finally caught you, didn't it?
I thought that it would someday.
I saw you were lost, almost gone
You forgot who you were day by day.
Your life was no longer for you
It was for beer bottles, crystal, and porn
Your face was no longer with youth
It was tired and hardened and worn.
You were lost about who really loved you
You thought it was haters who did
Love turned into supply and demand
And that brought you to nothing, but practically dead.

So now, it's caught you
For real this time
If only you had chosen
Heart instead of crime.
So now, it's got you good
Like a rope around your neck
And no matter how you try,
It won't let you forget.

Emily Aschbrenner

His

His breath turned on my whole body,
His whisper conquered my soul,
His lips kissed like poetry,
He seduced me, my body danced with surrender
His alluring arms held me,
His soft fingers possessed me,
Enough to where we created a passion, only imaginable.

Ariana Sanchez

Future Ambushed

No one killed that night, but all died a little more.
Choked on hell all right; any strength reserves to draw?

Breath held 'til faces blue; mosquitoes gorging rancid red.
Heavy hand of silence grew knowing all are often dead.

Touch of an angel's kiss on curved metal to kill and maim.
A shake not meant like this when we see a human slain.

Waiting with one thought; to kill with cold heart burned
with fear that is not sought. Good men to killers turned.

Relief and sadness next as day dawn's clear and dim
when from the fear comes rest until we're sent back in.

And those who live the day feel the loss of who they are;
not knowing the price they pay, but all bear the inner scar.

All died in that unreal place and will ever bear the fears.
It's just that some must face and survive more lurid years.

We each extend our hands to hold the other's heart;
to help each other stand up to the hardest part
of living with our past, loving who we are
and feeling not outcast with someone there to care.

Always faithful, Semper Fi, cried both in war and peace,
but war won't let us lie without tears upon our face.

That's as should ever be; no smiles or joy in war.
If pain we could not bear then man would be no more!

Anthony Pahl

Eternal Hell

I am wandering inside myself
Locked in I cannot escape
Lost, searching for my thoughts
Searching for my soul

Time, what is time, it is nothing
Slipping by, passing day by day
I am lost, cannot find my way
I want to leave this hell

The struggle, the fight, the search goes on
Death is creeping upon me
Gotta run, gotta hide, gotta free my mind
Gotta leave this hell

I need help, don't want help, I am all alone
Seeking death, fearing death, need to hide myself
Speaking lies, hearing lies, not knowing truth
I cannot leave this hell

I found death, death found me, it is creeping in
Cannot leave, cannot stay, cannot free myself
I am stuck, I am f*****d, I am falling
I am stuck in hell

Timothy Larson

Chilling Enrapture Part I

The footprints of this journey will forever be engraved
A symbol, when I was enslaved
To concrete tombstones of permanent winters
Freezing splinters penetrating my reminisces
With kisses of deceit
Misty whispers breezing my earlobes with climatic seduction
An introduction of undulated invitations
Into oceans of frostbit emotions
Blindfolded caution within avalanches of commotion
Onyxed chaos licking my defenses with a midnight tongue
Sweet soothing hum, of darkness tingling my flesh, arctic caress
Trapped, in a web of sleet, I'm caught
Left with goose bumps growing
The flowing of icy blood through my loin
Freezer foreplay got me going, past the point of no return
Like dry ice, sensations burn

Victor Negron

Silent in Battle

You know, when you have a nightmare and you scream, but no sound comes out;
When the silence forces its way into your mind and it screams inside your head.
That is what it is like knowing your body is slowly devouring itself;
That is what I face every day, surrounded by people yet forever alone.
No one understands the pain that I feel, forgive me
for I am unable to accurately explain it to you;
It is so hard to always attempt to put up a front of a forever positive person.
Sometimes my head is filled with so much anger and hate;
Sometimes I want to lash out and hurt whomever is near to me
so that they will know the pain I feel.
But how can you hurt someone who doesn't have the slightest hint of a glimpse,
how do you hurt someone without destroying the very fabric
that protects them from this that I feel.
Look at me, do you see outward signs of my fight?
Listen to me, do you hear?

Donna Wharran

Body and Mind

We're wrapped in a ball till the time we can crawl
This can be disastrous, so much can be hazardous
Being fed by our mother—Who else? No other.
Evident signs are showing, the body and mind are growing.

Supported by a chemical friend, it has started and just can't end.
Transported through body and mind, something new for the unborn to find.
The unborn's world is destroying its heart on the foolishness of the mother's part.
The unborn will never have a chance to give the world a lasting glance.
This addiction is not her own anymore, it has passed through veins
and seeped through pores.
Its whole world has been shattered, because nothing ever mattered.
The mother has lost control; now, can never play a parenting role.
She doesn't care if she has to lie, her main concern is to get high.

Friends and family have turned her away,
the mother and child have no place to stay.
Nowhere to run, nowhere to hide; the mother has left no sense of pride.
the unborn now can never be free—the mother couldn't hear the constant plea.

It's too late to turn back . . . this unborn child is addicted to crack.

Jenn Arsenault

A Posted Heart

I wrote it just for her and I posted it just for her,
and while I was thinking what a good deed I had done
by posting such a paper on which my heart I did outpour.
This thought has shattered not even a week later
when I find this same paper in thousands of pieces floating to the floor.

Now my soul within me grows stronger until a point where I hesitate no longer

and scream the words insignificant little b*tch.
How dare she rip up the posted paper on which My heart I did out-pour!

And to think I used to wish for days when she and I would never part.
But now I pray for a different day, the day she will die
so I can dance on her grave with the torn remains of the posted paper and of my heart.

Ashley Ledwidge

Fables of Rotten Lust

They are bargains that could crash through my window
and leave me speechless in comfort
Delicate dolls splashing in the ever-available virtue of lust
It is a delicacy to have the excellence of someone's physical possession
I will call to the floor what I have in my collection,
nothing more than Fables, Fables of rotten lust
The marksmanship of tangent positions, running amuck through my mind
I cannot afford to lay here all night
The blanket of emotion is stained,
and your pillow will not adjust to my head.
Goodnight, my sweet, rotten lust.

Paul Cannata

Clinton Limericks

There was a President named Bill
Power gave him a thrill
He won the election
Appealing to every direction
But his credibility turned out to be nil.

There was a President who didn't smoke
But he admitted to taking a toke
He didn't see any harm
In forcing his charm
And the Presidency turned into a joke.

There was a President named Bill
His main concern was a thrill
He met a big flirt
Who gave him a shirt
And helped him his semen to spill.

There was a President named Bill
Interns gave him a thrill
But he got into trouble
When a Starr burst his bubble
And the publicity bothers him still.

Billy R. Lawson

Medieval Heartbreak

Rain drops fall
For the times I've cried

The dark clouds call
For the pain I feel inside

I pray for an answer
To fill my thirst

It's growing like a cancer
And it's getting much worse

Puddles begin to form
As I drop to my knees

Lighting strikes from the storm
When I ask why and please

Blood flows from my hand
My mind spins like a tire

My heart is dipped in hot sand
And wrapped in barbwire

Then nailed to a torch
So it can be scorned

Then tied between two horses
So it can be torn

Craig Lewis

Untitled

I sometimes look up at the sky
to see the clouds so way up high.
I see the shapes and different sizes,
and reminisce about Staten Island's finest!
People think I'm from the ghetto,
they think I'm from the hood.
They think I act to black for them,
which isn't any good.
If only they can understand
that I'm a regular human being.
Maybe they'll stop callin' me niggarette,
and let me keep on dreamin'.
I have family on the island,
and I know they love me so.
I know they got my back,
and will never let me go.
There's one saying in my head,
that I finally remember,
Nothing in life is free, and I'll remember
this forever!

Ondrea Lynnett Montgomery

Slavery

I polish and I clean,
but still the white are mean,
because I'm slow and they bare my back,
to beat me cause I'm black,

I do not cry,
and I don't ask why,
but I stuff cotton in a sack,
and I work so hard because I'm black

My brother was traded today,
so tomorrow he goes away,
what family values will he lack,
Just because he's black?

My sister was killed a long time ago,
we didn't wish for her to live her life so,
today she's gone, she's not coming back,
we must pay because we're black,

I'm as proud as a peacock would be,
my colour shows no shame to me,
but I must endure the painful whack,
all because I was born black.

Lindsay Hogue

Things That Hurt

Hey little one, wake up and face the facts.
See the mean in the world.
The bastard boy that wanted, the innocent girl raped.
The daddy that said, I love you sweetie,
But never showed through.
First love, he said it was a mistake.
Mixed messages, what do they mean?
I think so, I don't know, she!! or me!!
Those words hurt.
Big tears, little tears, caused by things that hurt.
We were best friends, something went wrong, why did it end?
Accusations made by loved ones, makes you feel like s**t.
Lost love, find him or leave him, would it make a difference?
What does the future hold?
You will find out little one.
The world is full of hurt, don't make yourself exempt.
The fun and games are seldom and faded.
Put your teddy bear away, face the world, bold and strong,
Only you know what is wrong.
All the big and little things that hurt.

Shannon Olive

Devil in a Beautiful Disguise

When I look into your eyes, I see a devil in disguise;
You break the strongest hearts and then ignore a grown man's cries.
You make men fall in love until they lose all self-control;
Then after they devote themselves, you take away their souls.
Your beauty is a lure, it makes you look so sweet;
It takes a man by surprise, he never knows he beat.
To kiss your lips is truly a critical mistake;
Your lips are poisonous and you're cold-blooded like a snake.
Your smile can be deceitful, and your walk is hypnotizing;
Your voice speaks evil melodies, but still sounds mesmerizing.
Making love to you can be the deadliest of sins;
You can even satisfy a man before the sex begins.
You're greedy for the money, caring nothing for respect;
Taking gifts from gentlemen just to have something to collect.
You have no shame in stealing pride that shows a man defeat;
A man's loss of self-dignity makes your collection more complete.
Once you've gotten what you want, you leave without a trace;
Thinking of all that you have done puts a grin upon your face.
Men are foolish victims of your vast amount of lies;
But I know that you're a devil in a beautiful disguise.

Nathan Norkawski

In the dark

Don't be alone in the dark
the bushes have eyes on you.
It could be your friendly postman
or your neighbor who lives next door.
Your neighbor could be
making love to his wife,
while thinking what he wants to do to you.
It's impossible for the normal person
to fathom the thoughts they have.
How do they feel reading about themselves
and how they have terrorized the city?
"Be careful," he tells his wife,
"There's a killer loose in this town."
Little does she know
she's the safest one of all.
If only she knew all the running blood
her husband's hands had caused.
The same hands caressing her body
late at night . . .
in the dark.

Karen Redd

The House That Wasn't a Home

As I walk through this empty place!
A house that wasn't a home!
And the memories made me cry!
As I walk into each room
I have painful memories of hate and abuse!
While I cry more and more inside of me
because of the happy childhood that I never had
growing up in a house that wasn't a home!
And love was always expressed by more and more
domestic violence and hatred for reasons
that I never knew of at home, school and in my life.
While the hateful thoughts bring back
emotional plans of suicide and escape
in a house that wasn't a home!
And now many years later my scars
still bleed at night because of my screaming nightmares
from all of my years of being molested
when life was full of unspeakable atrocities!
In a house that wasn't a home!
In a house that wasn't a home!

Kenneth Bossier

Straightjacket

So you wanna take a journey into
the insanity that fills my mind
I will make this promise to you
you're gonna fear what you find
Evil images of what haunts you
shining light which makes you blind
Held back by straightjacket
residing in this cushioned cage
Don't remember when it all went to sh*t
overtaken by demon's rage
I'm so confused; I'm losing it
Can't stop screaming, consuming torment
Held back by straightjacket too scared to breathe
My life's all gone to sh*t, Death set me free
Retched insanity, extinct humanity
Losing my mind, now I am blind
Yearning the peace that I cannot find, trapped in this inescapable bind
When did it all go away?
I must be dreaming 'cause these feelings seem unreal
There's no prescription for the pain that I feel

Kevin King

Mistress

The Cloud wraps wraithlike tendrils
about the Mountain's throat and strokes its pulse.
The Mountain surges toward the sky into the soft billows of the Cloud's breast.
She settles herself further onto the Mountain
and he in return stretches into her misty swarm.
She turns and blushes, her frothy skirt rolling and swarthy.
His trees begin to tremble violently
as her cool wet stream cascades onto them,
releasing her ecstasy in torrents.
His patience is rewarded as he is drenched with pleasure.
After she has exhausted herself,
the Cloud lingers before painfully rising.
He glistens with her dew . . .
and nestles back in comfortable relaxation.
She slips away quietly and reflects the sunshine,
knowing she is the Mountains' mistress.

Sonja Johnsey

Hell on Earth

Emptiness surrounds me.
Its engulfing capacity swallows my soul.
I swim with no breath in my lungs; I am drowning.
Pain is my existence; nothing is right.

Life seems cold and dismal; why am I here?
To suffer my entire lifetime alone or to die and have my suffering known?
Meaningless and useless is my existence
But in heaven my soul will be free.

To take one's own life is never selfish,
It is the only way to escape the demons.
Happiness does not exist for me on Earth . . .
I've been searching for something I'll never find.

There is no solace within my own mind, only despair.
My life will have much more meaning
when I am gone than it did while I lived.
Death is life and a new beginning, never an end.
I want to find out what waits beyond this thing called "life."
It can't be half as bad . . .this is hell on Earth.

Margie McGonigal

Longing

I long to see your smile, for that I would walk endless miles.
I long to feel your touch, that I miss so very much.
I long to embrace you once again, to feel your lips, and soft breath like the gentle wind.
I long to kiss your sweet lips, and gently suck your finger tips.
I long to hear you scream my name,
I long for us to play the game.
I long to walk hand-in-hand in the rain,
I long for the ecstasy of love-making pain.
Most of all I long to be with you, with that in mind we'll never be through.
I long . . .

Erica Dudley

Trickle, Trickle

Trickle, trickle the life blood flows to form a pool which cannot be restored.
Such power to gain from the essence of others.
Would you like to be my lover?
A pain of ecstasy is all you'll feel and when all is done you will be no longer real.
Trickle, trickle the life blood flows to form a pool which cannot be restored.
My minions will take you into their arms and will show you the way
into the underworld that I call my own.
For you see I live forever and the darkness is my cover.
Come my love let me partake in changing you to be with me forever.
Trickle, trickle the life blood flows to form a pool which cannot be restored.

Nanette McSwiney

ammo

reminisce bliss
forget hate
learn from the thangs
we thought f***ed up fate
take it in stride
find strength in pride
here
right now
this is our rough ride
but we ridahz
survivors
wit' ambition
brotherly
family
love is our best ammunition

K Williams

Ode to Winter Bush

Release that tummy,
Let down those tits,
Winter bush
Goes great with this.

Razors rust,
Batteries die,
Lotion softens
Stubbly thighs.

New white briefs,
Weakened bras,
Comfy sweats
Greet solstice pause.

Months without
a thong in sight.
Hot love heats
Long cold nights.

Nature's gift granted
Women who agree
Life's chain can flourish
From a nest so silky.

Tara Roth

Concrete Lust

Shouting cries
Of concrete
Lust.
Misty aqua
Rains.
Pouring down
upon our souls.
Raven clouded skies.
Crimson colored cold.
Pierce the shouting
Cries.
The shouting cries
Of concrete
Lust.
Shimmering blankets
Of steaming
Flesh.
Mend the crimson cold.
Dying cries of misty lust.
Run rusted, concrete old.

Peter Scaturro

Vamp

As the candles burn down and the incense burns out,
the smell of my victim's blood fades.
Their screams are memories now as I relax in the calm of their death.
The black veil falls over my eyes as the sunsets.
Darkness and silence surround me now.
What has driven me to drain the life of others?
Have I lost my entire sanity?
Perhaps the night will bring the answers I seek.
As I sit in solitaire my beast takes over my human thoughts.
I thirst for more life force.
I must seek and kill again.
My hunger empowers me.
I cannot sit in silence for it will drive me mad!
I hunt as the killer I have now become.
I stalk the streets at night for the sun shall no longer warm my flesh.
Cold and darkness now consume my entire being.
I hide among the shadows now.
Some night you will cross my path.
Until then, fear the shadows.

Joseph R. Marsh

A Day

I woke up from a deep sleep and found the world dark.
I woke up from the death and found that you'd all gone.
I rose from my bed of glass and thought today was different.
I rose from my pleasure of pain and thought that I could do something.
I looked out the window and found your world of emptiness.
I locked out the world and found my window to all.
I went outside, I found nothing.
I stayed inside, I found me.
I listened to all of you, you told me what was wrong with me.
I listened to the voices inside my head, they told me to kill all of you.
I turned on the TV, and the people told me to be somebody else.
I turned on the radio, and heard who I was.
I locked all the doors to keep out the evil.
I smashed down the walls to get out the bad.
I laid back down in bed, the pleasure came back again.
I let the darkness surround me.
I let it all end.

Nicole Walsh

Morbid Existence

Stuck in a room as another day passes me by,
I feel the chill of death's hands pass my eye.
A rush of cold runs over my face,
I fall to the ground soon to be my resting place.
I lay on my back as death's army marches through,
Don't be surprised when it comes after you.
I remember the days when my life was before me,
Made friends all my life . . .yet became my own enemy.
Some people ask why I'm so morbid and gray,
My answer is because I have seen my final day.
I traveled through life searching for meaning,
But all I've found is what Death is revealing.
Savor your time . . .to yourself become true,
Because when you least expect it . . . .
Death's Sickle Will Run You Through!

Renan Kuri

NEWS!

So easily forgotten!
ME!
Or so I think,
another drink!
WHY?
For that is all to fill the emptiness,
to bring that easing forgetfulness!
MOMENTARILY!
Bottle it up in a jar, away behind bars,
so, so far away better of on Mars!
GONE!
But for how long?
Everyone suck my ding dong!
STRAIGHT!
So why is it even up for debate?
Did I create? NO! You create!
NEWS!
For do you believe everything that you hear?

Rudolf Martinez

A**hole

Why won't you let go from the pain that you hide.
I can see it in your eyes; why torture yourself inside
Why hold it all in and try to fight the pain
Just let it all out; you're being insane
I can't go on if you keep living this way
I'm looking out for you do you hear what I say? I love you
This isn't about that time I hit you
Oh it is? Yeah, your eye is still a little blue
But get over it and stop whining
How can I watch TV when all I hear is crying
Go make me some food I'm getting kind of hungry
But honey, you know I love you

Brian Boyd

Chasing the Sun

He waits upon the doorsteps of his heart
Lies soaking, basking in celestial light
Awaiting one who dictates beats of heart
He looks above and sees the birds take flight

Where once sang larks now crows do dance and cry
And hellish darkness now consumes the sun
Crows lurk and bide the time for soul to die
Tied down to mercy which negates freedom

A thousand moons have passed before his eyes
Like a wounded dog he lay, commenced to rot
Awaiting to emerge from death like Christ
A love profound like his in her he sought

How to make this love for her cease and part
Easier to reach the sun than her heart

Marko Gutierrez

The Party

They took their shots, they drank their beer.
They blared their music so no one could hear.
They lived for the moment, nothing else matters.
Except where to p*ss when they had full bladders.
Their rooms were trashed, along with their heads.
Passed out on floors, couches, and sometimes beds.
For those that hooked up, they went to bed with a smile.
Waking up without regrets, because it had been a while.
All this in celebration, all this because of a game.
Of course if they had lost, parties would still be the same.
Whatever happens in life, they always find a reason.
To drink for the day, the year, or even the season.

Edward Hoolehan

Space Ride

To Dad, you gave me courage to stand firm with my convictions
I'd like to take those politicians
Who think they're holy grace,
And when they cheat and lie to us,
I'd make them look in their own face.

I'd like to take those politicians
Who look as innocent as lace,
And I'd hold them to all their promises. . . .
We'd have us some court case.

I'd like to take those politicians
Who don't pick up their pace,
And when they fail to get things done,
I'd refill their jobs, or I'd replace.

I'd like to take those politicians
Who don't give a s*** about this place,
And I'd send them to some foreign land
Without water, air, or space.

I'd like to take those politicians
Who don't care for the human race,
And I'd put them on a big airship
To send them off . . . (one way) to outer space!
Pauline A. Hamwey

Limericks

There was an old ranger named Joe,
who said that he just didn't know
how, amidst this profanity,
he lost all his sanity;
now Joe thinks he'd better go slow.

There was a young dandy named Sandy;
with the Internet he was quite handy.
He met lots of women,
and he liked to go swimming;
young Sandy was handy and randy.

There was an old geezer named Tharpe,
who thought he should learn to play the harp.
A-hoppin' and a-boppin'
he went music shoppin',
but ended up catching a carp.

A salty sea captain named Conley,
who, with poems and flowers, quite fondly
pursued me and wooed me,
and he finally screwed me,
Sir Conley, so jolly and so manly.
Gina Daidone

Untitled

In memory of my loving father, George H. Doane
Isn't life a sorry lot,
Everybody smoking pot,
Sniffing coke, and blowing dope;
I wonder if there's any hope.

While most of you, sit on your a**
Drinking booze and smoking grass,

I have found the great solution
For the sins of your pollution.

Simply pray to God each day,
Tell him what you have to say,
Tell him where you've always stood,
Tell him booze and drugs are good.

Then run, find cover, hide, and stay!
'Cause God will blow your a** away.
Janet A. Doane

The Everlasting Agony

Look here now, as I weep and I struggle,
Look on with glee as I die.
Snicker and laugh since you're so much better,
See the pool of blood and pus where I lie.
My eyes have narrowed, my face become scarred,
And there's an extra dose of hate in my frown.
I can never describe the eternal pain I feel in my soul,
But it's that pain that's making me drown.
The germs are into me now, eating my flesh,
Laughing as they destroy my frail shell.
I never asked to be born, or to suffer like this,
But none hear the cries that I yell.
There are sores on my body, burning like fire,
With black bile and gore do they drip.
Silent I was born, so silent I stay,
But you should hear my screams when they rip.
No salvation, and no exit from this,
I even feel pain in my dreams.
So I'm doomed to this fate, agony is life,
Until my body bursts apart at the seams.
Keith Russo

No More, Mama, No More

To little Lisa Izquierdo—rest in peace
I remember, mama; how could I forget
That innocent child your arms once held and lovingly caressed?
"I love you, child," so many times you said,
But your crack addiction turned your love to hate.

You abused me, and so did your friends.
I was raped, burned, sodomized, and left for dead.
And when I called you "mama," you turned your head away.
Why can't I kiss you and play with your dress?
Why, mama? I don't understand.

So many times I begged,
"Mama, I'm hungry," but you laughed instead.
As you drag my bruised and frail body
And slam it against the wall,
I stay silent, mama, for you look so tall.
Why, mama? No more, mama! Please, no more, mama!

As I lie in this casket, bruised, battered, and with no name,
I forgive you, mama, for a child should never hate.
No longer will I feel pain; no longer will my eyes fill with tears.
I forgive you, mama, for all the hurt, the denial, and the hate.
No more, mama, will I ever feel your rage.
Rafael Taveras

The Songwriter

Lines of lonely that are written
And truly come from the heart
By shaky hands that feel much pain,
Just waiting for the healing to start.

Writing a song should be easy;
After all it's what I'm paid to do.
But now lines of lonely hit close to home.
Damn, my heart's been broken in two.

Up 'til now I've written other folks' pain
In many a sad country song.
Somehow these words I'm writing today
Seem so sad, and I can't sing along.

There are just no words to describe it,
All the pain and the heartache I feel.
No tune comes to mind, and I'm stumped this time.
I gotta make my heart this deal.

So heart, please will you stop hurting,
Even though it's just for a while.
Bring back sweet memories of my love gone from me
And make this old songwriter smile.
Jeannie Remillard

I Feel Your Pain

Her eyes are lost in sadness and fear;
It's as if her body is here and her mind is somewhere else
I want to comfort her,
But I don't know how
She has lost her mother;
A hug will not replace the loss she is suffering from.
Will it always be this way?
Will she ever just be the happy friend I used to know?
Does with her loss come my loss of a best friend?
Why did this have to happen to her?
She never did anything wrong
Tears are streaming down my cheeks and I don't know why
She reaches out to me and our hands are clasped together
In a way,
We are feeling each other's pain,
we are suffering deep losses together

Brianne Manton

A Phone Call

Just for a moment I felt old despair
Returning like swallows in spring, through the air.
With each breath I gasped, I could suddenly feel
Memories swarming, circling round me, so real
That I did falter and stagger and clutch and grope
For any small thing that would act as a rope.
To hang onto, 'til this dread moment be won
So as not to fall, out of reach of the sun.

I guess 'twas forever meant to be
Tests from God follow tranquility.

Maryleen Macrae

Untitled

Traces of orange, pink, and yellow
Tenderly joined; spreading gentle wings
Beauty across the morning sky

Brilliant illumination; a contrast in comparison
So full of life in the majestic rise
Yet softly embracing the eastern horizon

The hollow night, with lonely echoes
Whisked away in exuberant splendor
No artist's stroke nor teller's tongue
Could re-create the sight

Close your eyes and smell the morning air
The gentle whisper of fading voices
Ride in the currents, caressing soaring birds
This is tranquility

Jason Hinds-King

Bless Children with Trouble

I'm very, very sorry to say
That there will be no poem from me today
I've found a far, far better thing to do,
And once you know about it, you will agree too.
I watch the local newspaper for a special thing,
And when I see it, it's like catching the merry-go-round ring.
Of course it's the ring that has a bright shine.
And what I do will make living more divine.
If the article is about a child with a medical condition,
I try to make their life brighter with my rendition
With sixty-seven and a half years of woodworking skill
What I make for them gives them a thrill
It's an old fashioned rabbit in the form of a bank,
The smile I get from them is very high in rank,
I feel like an admiral, even a general, you see,
Their smile is worth a million dollars to me.

Franklin I. Ernst Jr.

My Black African Mother

My black African mother, there's nobody who has your face,
your love, and your warming embrace.
Every time I feel hopeless you say the words
that' are miraculous, to keep me focused.
You taught me the differences of wrong and right,
darkness and light, and you taught me to love instead of fight.
There's no way I can pay you back,
but without you in my life there's no way I'll be on track.
You taught me to love
my grandparents, aunties, uncles, cousins,
nieces, nephews, my father and brothers,
This love came from "my black African mother!"

Billy D. Williams

5 a.m.

At the little red barn it's morning
When the rooster crowed, the old Tom cat mewed.
Why in the world must you be so loud?
Roosters reply, as the farmer's friend I must allow.
When to arise, the time is now.
The birds all gathered in a flock
Said you are right, its five o'clock
Flapping their wings, without losing a feather.
They flew outside, to check on the weather
Clear skies not a cloud in sight.
Have a good day, see you tonight.
Off they flew to do what birds do.
At the little red barn. At the end of the lane
With the slanted roof, and black weather vane
Rooster said, good morning ladies.
Addressing the hens and the cow
Here comes farmer Charley now
I've done my duty, I'm off for the day
Flying to the loft, he went to sleep on the hay.

Mary Mills Youngblood

A Poem Has Its Reward

On bad days or good days, things can go wrong,
that's when I find a quiet place to be alone.

After I pray for guidance, I feel safe from harm,
and I find consolation and humor in writing a poem.

When I put into words whatever is on my mind,
I can often laugh at the situation and leave it behind.

Not every problem can be easily put to rest,
but remember my theory, and put it to the test.

I share these thoughts with you, to help in this regard,
if you put your thoughts into a poem; a poem has its reward.

Pauline West

Freedom Path

When I walk the path of freedom ring,
I feel the spirit of life's long dreams,
That runs as smooth as serenity spring,
Or could it be merely a dream.

I thought to myself as I walked softly away,
How I'd welcome each new day
By being thankful for the blessing I have,
Like love, peace, hope and prayers.

When I reached out to touch the life of my sisters and brothers,
And shared my knowledge and dreams with many others,
The path of freedom lives in you and I,
As we live, love and really try,
And as a reward God planted us a rainbow in the sky.

Sally Banks

Over Time

In the morning of life we crawl and move slow
To mature through time and gradually grow
And by midday we are fully grown
Out in the world and out on our own
By the time that evening rolls around
Our body is withered and grows toward the ground
When the light goes out and night appears
Do you finally face your greatest of fears
Does this greater being really exist
Or are you a person who is hardly missed
Do you believe in what's truly right
Or will you go dark like a blown out light

Todd Courtney

Love Letters

The mail runs from the highway where he rode,
into the dense forest where I walk among the trees,
clouds above me move like paper airplanes;
blowing wind like a sailboat moving
across the waters toward him;
sending my letter flying the air currents late at night;
leaving the postman behind;
to arrive on his doorstep in the early morning,
when the sun shines down with gentle kisses
upon golden fields and emerald waters.

He will awaken and smile as he smells
my perfume and sees the cat's playing
postmaster and mistress on his doorstep,
playing with my paper airplane,
one that sailed the miles to be with him on
misty mornings to fill his day with joy.

Lisa Nelson

The Shining in Your Eyes

Every time you look at me, I feel happy, safe and warm.
Like a blanket all around me, shielding me from harm.
Like the brightness of sunshine, my rainbow in the skies;
please don't ever lose the light shining in your eyes.
Every time you look at me I feel wanted and desired,
like the words of some sweet love song special and inspired.
When your hands caress my body, I can't hold back the sighs;
please don't ever lose the light shining on your eyes.
Every time you look at me I feel a heat filled up with pride,
like the only time you feel it is when I'm by your side.
I feel beautiful and loved, as my passion quickly rise;
please don't ever lose the light shining in your eyes.
Every time you look at me I feel your heart and soul,
for you are who completes me, who filled that empty hole.
I feel love and joy and truth, a life with no more lies;
please don't ever lose the light shining in your eyes.
Every time you look at me, and your fingers touch my face,
I know you've touched my heart in a very special place.
For now I see the answer, the reason your eyes shine;
for every time you look at me you see the light in mine . . . .

Shirlee A. Greco

Do We Fear Darkness?

In all my travels,
In all the shadows,
I have never seen such a deceptive terror.
It hides in the darkness.
It can take any likeness.
Most don't believe in its existence.
So temptation overcomes all resistance.
The power of darkness is very strong.
It has been around for very long.
When the light shines from the one true son,
The evil darkness trembles and is gone.
So let us stay in the light of the just and the right.
We will fear no evil under love, power and might.

Benjamin Morales

With You Again

I remember falling asleep, holding
your picture within my arms for keeps.
White clouds, bright lights
I'm seeing you again, something
I thought I'd never do.
I can hold you in my arms tight;
I feel our hearts grow with such might.
Once again I have you to call my own.
Oh, my son, how you have grown.
I have missed you these passed few years,
but I never forgot you, dear.
I always held you inside my heart
For our spirits will never part.

Vicky S. Faller

Us

When the wave of the ocean rolled over the rock
It did not crash
But continued to the top of the sand
To meet me
My feet were guided into the sea
I floated to you
We kissed gently
And it was sealed
We are in the ocean together forever now
The sky greets the water
And covers us
We never let go of each other
So we will not float away and be separated
And this is true love

Lisa Kelly

My First Thoughts of You

As I sit here in a total state of bliss,
The darkness of the day is swept away by your kiss.

You heal my wounds through and through,
There's something magic in my life—you!

It seems like just a dream when I gaze into your eyes.
I thank God I have you over all the other guys.

The moment my eyes saw yours.
I knew you were the one for me.
But I didn't ever think you would take me seriously.
Then by some miracle and a little help from a friend,
Destiny gives me what I need 'til the very end.

So if you ever give up hope and think it's all a waste of time.
Forget about it, go on with your life
And what you need is what you'll find.

Kimberly M. Young

One Kind

We are the kind who help the world.
The kind to lend a helping hand.
We are the ones no one sees, why can't they hear our cry?
We are the people that no one knows, we are but one unit.
We are all people, we are the black, white, and brown people.
We are the short, the tall, big and the small, loved one and all.
The smart and the dull, young or old, all together, all as one.
We are all of these things, all of us together, one world of love.
No matter the color, nor the race, we all live in the same place.
Fighting as one, one nation together, 'til the end of time.
We are but one family, there is only one place on earth
where we belong, of love and peace, forever.

Carreen Sylvester

Words

A blade so sharp, double-edged.
Swung with a breath and cuts with a sound.
Can profoundly damage the thickest armor.
With the ability to pierce, the hardiest heart and soul.

Comforting as a weapon.
It soothes my fears.
Defender of my peace of mind.
Eases the pain others attack with.
Oh, what a weapon this is!

Without a trained eye it can cause self-inflicted harm.
Hurt those who pose no threat.
Anger and rage loss of control.
Makes the blood redder.
As shame and guilt cries for their vengeance upon your conscience.

You only have yourself to blame.
It's up to you how you use your weapon.
It's up to you how you use your words.

Daniel Thomas Chlebowski

Different Hoods

Mr. Roger's neighborhood is beautiful to me.
They dare not show my neighborhood on national TV.

Mr. Roger's mail is hand delivered to him for free.
I hope my mail is still in my box after three.

People in Mr. Roger's neighborhood are so friendly and polite.
In my neighborhood someone is subject to die before midnight.

In his neighborhood children eat three meals a day.
In my neighborhood kids hope to eat one meal on any given day.

In Mr. Roger's neighborhood people walk around, worry free.
I worry, will I die or be arrested before I'm twenty-three?

Mr. Roger's neighborhood epitomizes the land of the free.
My neighborhood is more like the home of the brave
And we're still not free.

Polk L. Rippy Jr.

Friendly Wisdom

Seeing the old signs of a friend in trouble.
Without a spoken word.
Wanting to help and willing to share.
Having been in a few situations yourself.
Realizing the wisdom might be there.
One must not ask when the friend is deep within.
With a calm expression let them know someone is there to care.
Watch for signs which say, "I am ready to hear."
Open up to the fullest and with a helping hand.
View all possible ways to bring happiness again.

Karen Marshall Thomas

Untitled

I fear the dark possession of pain
As I lay in my bed ready to die
I hope I do not suffer a great strain
For only I will hear my helpless cry

If I enter the gates of Heaven with my mate
I wish to eat of the fruit and drink of the wine
But if I enter the pit of hell's fate
Then I know the task shall be mine

It suddenly becomes dark and I suddenly feel old
Will I enter the gates of Heaven
Or hell's tree of bark?
For I suddenly grow weary and suddenly grow cold

Margaret H. Dubinski

The Quilt

They were carefully folded within a plastic bag.
They remained a vestige of his life, molded—
the silken ties he ever wore, a tag—
a symbol of his life, enfolded.

Those fifty years, fulfilled through music, meant
for the children, friends, family, to whom he lent
his treasured gift, the devotion of his life, well spent.

There is a logo on the quilt, a fact
found one day when, with a push, and react
the needle refused to penetrate the tie. . . .
What a taste of our oft-repeated inner-family cracks!

And now, the ties are joined, as are the years—
sewn in love, each stitch a day to share.
Each stitch brings anew a memory dear—
cherished, through laughter and through tears.

It is my prayer, whoever keeps this Quilt
may find its peace, its turmoil, its triumph,
its message plainly felt
from one whose simple daily need was his tie—
now tied with his life's work into "The Quilt."

Marion A. Congdon

Quo Vadis Polonia?

A dream of many greedy shacklers,
The country with flagrant flowers, in fertile fields,
And tombs of the innocent by passers.
Her tears of amber on the time chain
Are ripping the low Baltic Sea coast
As an old pot of clay.

As a booming thunder, barred,
Just before bursting of its flushing moment,
King David's lost children's stepmother
With the wingless heart, as huge as a sun.
With burnt seals by the roads,
In temerit darkness of the night,
Bleeding helplessly, sparkled the marks.
Among her holy oaks, and sleeping heroes
From the caves of the cool peaks of Tatra,
From the mountains to the sea bays,
Prayerful voices sound: Ave Maria be full of Grace . . .
And bless the crumbs on the antique pine-wood tables
With all your might protect the land,
And give us a Prince of peace, again.

Helena Sosin

The Beauty of the Sea

The ocean's waters clear as crystal
It's breezes quiet as a whistle,
The seagull, the pigeon and the dove
Flying so gracefully up above.

The ocean's harmony, so magnificent and great
It's wonders are astounding, unable to create,
The night is cool and the winds are fair
Peace and tranquility fill the air.

The full bright moon lights up the sky.
It is most gorgeous to the eye,
The mood is still, quite and calm
Soft and gentle, as a sweet psalm.

The waters, brushing against the beach
As though aiming for something to reach,
The atmosphere is clear, with but a fine mist
Like the briliant work of an expert artist.

It seems as if the earth has ceased to exist
Like the entire world has stopped to subsist,
How beautiful is this wonderful scene
Each and every detail, so pure and clean.

Ben Brodsky

The Reality of Love

You mean so much to me,
Yet your feelings for me are a mystery.
I have told you that I like you,
With every word including love,
You are the only one I think of.
Should I keep saying you are everything to me,
And worry about what you would say?
Should I say I love you,
And see you walk the other way?
Your presence alone makes me happy,
My paranoia keeps me away.
My hope does not want rejection,
And who does I cannot say.
Should I tell you now,
And let you know how I feel,
A feeling like this is love,
And without you love is unreal.

Juan A. Munoz Jr.

Move Along

If I sit here and wait; am I not a ponderer?
I should say so.
My feet are not callused nor are they weak.
No, they are vessels to carry me along the way
I want to go.
My mind may be weary but my heart is wide open.
The seasons are changing and time will not wait.
Move along, because this Earth is receding.
Dreams are waiting and they need to be caught.
Move along, because standing says nothing.
Our lives need rebuilding and we need to be taught.
Move along, because laughter awaits us.
Our future, our destiny need to be found.
Move along, because for once in our lives our feet
need to touch real and new ground.
If I move foward and don't look back will I have succeeded,
I should say so.

Melanie Cintron

How Lucky I Am

As I walk amongst the green, yellow, orange, and red,
I think of how lucky I am
As I return home, to lay down my weary head,
I think of how lucky I am
As I wake in the morning to the bird's sweet song,
I think of how lucky I am
And as I go out once more to be where I belong,
I think of how very lucky I am!

Chelsea McGuire

Heartache Salad

Ingredients:

1 warm heart
1 cup hurt
1 cup pain
2 cups dishonesty
1 cup false hope
4 cup tears (optional)
dash of lies
dash of shattered dreams

Take warm heart filled with love, marinade in tears.
Drain slowly until empty, lifeless and has an aching appearance.
Shred coarsely.
Once completely shredded add hurt, pain, dishonesty and false hope.
Sprinkle generously with lies and shattered dreams.
Serve cold with any remaining tears.

Pamela R. Brown

That Thing That Goes Pump in the Night

We're all very glad you came through it all right.
When we heard it gave us a terrible fright.
The doctors all said you put up quite a fight.
They fixed it . . . that thing that goes pump in the night.

When it's happy it feels very full, but so light.
When in love it can soar like a white dove in flight.
When it's proud it can reach an unparalleled height.
That thing that goes pump in the night.

Now in the mending period these things I must cite.
You must watch what you drink and watch what you bite.
You can't scuba dive or go fly a kite.
Don't get too excited or get too uptight.
Follow doctor's orders, keep recovery in sight
For that thing that goes pump in the night.

We wish with all our collective might
To see you real soon back at our work site.
Smiling and happy, all sunny and bright
With an overhauled thing that goes pump in the night.

Patricia Hipsher

Raging Wrath

Now falls upon the raging wrath
Pounding away the structure,
Wiping away at our known path
The innocent soul may suffer.

Hidden somewhere was the castle I built,
Built to prevent more intrusion,
But the castle I built in the sand of dreams
With the tide was no more than illusion.

Desperate I stand as the storm comes in
I cannot hide in my castle of dreams,
The meticulous time that it took to build
Touched the storm, wasn't all that it seemed.

Cynthia Kelley Curran

What Is Marriage?

Marriage is the beginning of a new life
Between two people, husband and wife
It is about commitment, loving and caring
Sacrifice, happiness and always sharing
Two people are bound together by love
A love which comes to you from above
Today you have said yes to God's plan for you
When you professed your love by saying "I do"
So to both of you we would like to say
May you always be as happy as you are today.

Phyllis Ferrara

Forgive Me, I Didn't Mean to Die

Just another day at Columbine high
The score on your test made you want to cry
Suddenly guns were fired and bullets began to fly
Forgive me, I didn't mean to die.

I watched you as you held me in your shaking arms
You moved us out of sight and hopefully out of harm
Your tears dripped on my face and they were oh, so warm
Forgive me, I didn't mean to die.

Help finally came and people began to flee
You never left or let go of me
Your voice became distant yet sounded so clearly
Forgive me, I didn't mean to die.

My spirit surrounded you in every single way
And somehow you knew I wanted to stay
You're sorry you survived that fateful day
Forgive me, I didn't mean to die.

Sarah Gibson

World Peace

Peace is the word that is lost
within the world of war and hatred

Peace sets the scene of lost souls
finding slavery and betrayal . . .

Living in a place where everyone is free
and flowers are children waiting to be found . . .
And peace is only a whisper wish waiting to be heard . . .

In our murmured minds
Peace is blind that cannot be seen in our future

In our darkened hearts
peace is only bruised and left hushed for no one to hear

In our land, peace is forever forgotten
with falsehoods and claims of crying souls
Bleeding with tears that everyone can see . . .

Living in a place where the watchtower is hope
and truth is the state of mind that everyone keeps . . .
And peace is the laughter in everyone's hearts

Peace is the song that is shouted by sisters and brothers

Peace is the march that is marched by mothers and fathers

And peace is the way to freedom

    Joshua Clossen

Suspected Sub-Title

Distasteful dining at the feast of your life
Could easily be the sub-title of my mortal existence;
The story of an ill fated traveler
Who could not go the distance?

The tale of a pitiful dreamer
Who had lost every dream?
The yarn of a most hopeful gamer
Who is now without hope, it would seem?

Exactly how those dreams and hopes were lost matters not
Except in that they are no more
And that I have been left here believing
In the following thought and a sickening feeling
That saddens my soul to it core.

From a mysterious, mystical, magical realm
To this wonderful, wild and worrisome world
My consciousness had slipped;
But never could I ever have guessed
That mine would be such a lonely script.

    Don A. Osborne II

Stagecoach

Take a trip back in time
Have a stagecoach in your mind
Visualize the stage stop
And the early pioneers
See the stage trail up the hill
You'll capture the colors of an open land
Adventure is in your plan
Imagine the horses' reins in your hand
Crossing the plains
In the thunder of horses hooves
The stagecoach traveling on and on
Carrying travelers, luggage, mail, and gold
Exploring and broadening the scope
Of a great nation-to-be
Fathers and mothers of a new century
The stagecoach is of a bygone era now
Taking its place in history
But still we want to ride the trails of old
Being a part of an adventure bold.

    Susan Erb

I May Cry, Tho' It's Not the Done Thing

Oh, sister, my friend loved to the end,
For some time now this is birthing in my pen.

We laughed, argued, loved, cried and ate
Shared books and music, traveled and talked late.

Lived a lifetime much longer than some
We are never quite ready for our life to be done.

Margie, beautiful, regal, of elegant grace
Always, always a lady with radiant face.

I was watching my sister die
Gone it seems in the blink of an eye.

ALS moving before our eyes never lingers
A disease showing death's cruel fingers.

First robbed of arm and leg mobility
She resigned to the loss of ability.

When becoming confined to house and chair
She still maintained her humorous flair.

Next was conversation, just trying to speak
Was stolen by this ugly sneak.

Then with eyes closed and heartbeat light
Debbie saw her breath take flight.

    Midge Nelson

When You Need a Friend

If you ever fall short of a friend,
you know I'll be by your side 'til the end.
I will never let you down,
even help you change your frown.

Make you laugh and smile,
you know I can all the while.
I'll listen to you pain,
help you through the rain.

Give you a shoulder to lean on,
'cause I'll always be the one.
Advise you when you ask of me,
I'll always be your friend you'll see.

Understand your every desire,
'cause I can help put out the fire.
I'll always be there 'til the end,
when you need a friend.

    James Boyd

Life Has a Way

Some learn early, while others delay,
Of life's own teaching mode,
Which can bring an abundance of joy,
And precious memories to hold.

Life has a way of revealing,
Just how uncertain it can be,
'Cause with the utmost cherished bliss,
Comes misery, pain and agony.

No concern for status or appearance,
When you're finally figured it out,
Life has a way of flaunting
What it is really all about.

Safe smooth sailing, not a wave in sight,
Then, smack! Whom! Comes tremendous blows,
Around each corner danger lurks,
Life's reminders of its woes.

Some say, it's what you make of it,
Though time flies swiftly past,
To those you love, show it now,
Since life's way is to whirl by fast.

    Victoria Stewart

One Perfect Red Rose

For Estelle Leah Lev
One perfect red rose to place on your stone,
A piece of my heart to adorn an eternal home.

One perfect red rose to remember your grace,
And when I stare in the mirror, I stare at your face.

So many years gone, but the pain is still great.
So many long years since the closing of your fate.

Each night I lie in bed and pray for you to come.
Sometimes I hear your voice, I waken and you're gone.

One perfect red rose to celebrate your life,
A cherished mother and sister, a too giving wife.

One perfect red rose is but all I can do.
To tell you how very much I still love you.

Barbara P. Lev

In Life's Situations

Where does one turn?
When family and friends say they care.
But in your time of need no one's standing there.
When your spouse is running around.
And the love you once shared is nowhere to be found
When your children grow up and start doing their thing.
Things that tug and pull on your heart strings.
Where does one turn?
When you have a best friend that's hurting and in need of a hug.
But you can't seem to reach them 'cause they're strung out drugs.
When life throws you a curve 'cause you didn't get that job
or the recognition you deserve.
When spiritual leaders go astray.
Or Satan's riding your back 'cause you didn't take the time to pray.
Where does one turn?
When the life light seems to be growing dim.
Turn to God's Holy Word.
Your troubles will be resolved if you trust in and follow them.

Malaika T. Greene

Alaskan Autumn Whispers

In autumn we talk in whispers
And the dogs are hushed . . .
The birch leaves yellow and fall
While cranes flying south say good-bye with their call
We walk quietly through the woods
stopping, listening, looking . . .
talking in whispers.
Dogwood leaves redden,
sweet labradour tea and pungent cranberry
Waft through the cool evening air.
Suddenly the bull steps out boldly, majestically . . .
And the rifle's sharp crack
punctures the quiet . . .
In autumn we talk in whispers until the moose falls.
In winter, our table is blessed with autumn whispers.

Diane S. Ludwig

Christmas

So beautiful the stillness of the night
The North Star as it shines so bright
There is only one night on which this could be
That is the night of Christmas Eve
The night on which baby Jesus was born
As he lay cold in the eve of the morn
Then, as wise men with gold and myrrh
Came to witness this astonishing birth
God sent us his son to help rid us of our sorrows
Also to give us the promise we will be with Him tomorrows

Steven S. Mayer

Passion of the Moon

As the sunset called to the evening sky,
come let me sleep one more time with thee,
the moon rose to meet the diamonds of the night sky,
clearing the way for the warmth of the kiss
of the summer wind.

Two spirits meet in a secret place,
with the passion of the moon,
joining them with the welding of love
to each other in the many colors of the rainbow
to each looking for the valleys of thunder,
to say to each other, here is my gift,
to the passion of the moon.

David P. Soucie

The Battle of the Alamo

"Remember the Alamo!," is what they cried.
Where many brave men fought and died.
Travis, Bowie, and Crockett are some brave men we know,
Who gave their life at the Alamo.

The battle began with 150 men.
But, by March fifth there were less than ten.
Their ammunition was low.
They used their muskets as clubs to strike a blow.

The survivors were few; there where only four.
Santa Anna and the Mexican men had more.
Mrs. Dickerson, an officer's wife,
Her baby and her Mexican nurse saved their life.
A small boy named Joe, saved his life also.

In March many people knew they were dying,
But in our heart's we know they were trying.
Sam Houston's troops had to fight for their freedom again.
For their freedom they must fight and win.

The battle of the Alamo gave Sam Houston time to prepare.
All the brave men are the reason they cared.
"Remember the Alamo!" is what they cried.

Christiana Blades

Seasons

You think I've left you and gone away
But that's not true at all
For when you see those colorful leaves
I'll be with you in the fall.

As the cold, harsh winds begin to blow
And branches start to splinter
Glistening snow covers the earth
I'll be with you in the winter.

And when the grass pokes through the ground
And birds begin to sing
Beautiful flowers bloom everywhere
I'll be with you in the spring.

When the hot, blazing sun shines down on you
And you tire like a long-distance runner
See the shells on the beach that I loved to pick
I'll be with you in the summer.

So, you see I haven't gone away
No matter what rhyme or reason
I'm still alive deep within your heart
And shall stay with you for all seasons.

Linda Osmun

First Frost

She won't call her life unstable,
living on the bluffs of North Carolina.
The children shoot demands like arrows.
At night, she rests on a dusty recliner,
while poverty nestles in her backyard,
its eyes closed to the muffled southern winter
that confuses the birds further south.
If she had words to articulate
those dreams beaten sour like a dulcimer,
perhaps she could crumple into the stars.
North of Orion's belt, it would be summer again.
Sometimes she prays, with blustering gestures,
for earth to take her back like the snowdrop,
start over, dress her up in costumes—the girdle;
the nylons; tight, shiny shoes; a hoop skirt with ruffles
just a small lift over the hurdle
of missed opportunity, each vicious circle
she stumbled around, the deliberate return of spring.
Once she believed in the guarantee of seasons
and what they might bring.

    Erika L. Derany

El Caribe

Lavender, periwinkle, lemon yellow, sea foam, pigeon grey.
Cool, chalky pastels,
Pillars against the liquid azure,
Gaudy, fruit-colored petals embrace them.
Like lovers addicted to their desire,
They cling and caress the bold structures
As they bask in the baking heat of the equatorial sun.

Splendor and pride, hospitality and propriety—
Merely polite facades
That thinly veil
The raw sensuousness, the ebullient vitality,
The powerful, determined force of a people who have richly,
Soulfully harmonized nature's bountiful
Yet unpredictable providence
With man's selfish inner drives
Creating a lulling serenade causing even the coldest,
most resistant of hearts to willingly,
Gratefully succumb
To the divine mystery that is El Caribe.

    Alexandra Vozeh

Is Daddy Coming

Every now and then, my little boy will say,
"Is Daddy coming home today?"
I look at him and smile, I tell him,
"No honey, not for awhile."
I know he's never coming back!
That man was trouble and that's a fact!
But, to that child, I'll never tell,
about the pain or the hell.
To that child, his Daddy's the Best,
above all others, better than the rest!
I won't tell and spoil his vision,
I'll let him grow up and make his own decision!

    Edith Porter

Almost

Crying eyes of blood
Dying tries those in trouble
Visualizing freedom feeding on an
Empty jar of hope
Scraping spoonfuls filled with heartache
Looking through a microscope
Souls lost in the future of the universe
Voodoo, death and politics nurture those of the same curse
Bag ladies, millionaires, fast foods children
Remain in the race only to discover
They are all five minutes too late

    Paul Barrows

The Secluded Fighter

I see the way life holds you down
Trapped in the sea of fear and pain
A feeling of drowning emotions
Takes over your world of assurance

Trying to catch your breath
You slowly try to escape the burden
It is just too heavy
You sink back down

Don't give up and don't look back
Jump over obstacles holding you in the cracks
Open your wings and go into flight
Believe that your wings can take you to soaring heights

Open your heart and you will see
You can make it, just believe
Think of all that you can be

Look beyond the struggles you encounter
Hope is out there active and undeniable
Overpower all the troubles and pain
Believe in yourself the true you reigns

The tough way life holds you down

    Melissa Smith

The Military Nurse

The scars are forever, we hid them too deep to show
and we look for faces where ever we go
we hurt and cannot understand why
seeing the eyes of our dead men
we find something of dark deceit
we cannot comprehend

The ladies that went with us
the forgotten few, where are they now
they are out there now with no one to care
we need to reach out with a helping hand
with pride and understanding

They are drowning in complacency
in a land that does not understand
now they walk like ladies they have proven to be

America be counted, let them know
Just how we feel with pride
in what they did
ladies, I salute you

    Jim Coldwell

Beauty of Nature

In the morning when the sun appears,
Showing off his rays,
Wouldn't it be a little queer
If he came in gray?

One day the grass decides to cry,
As angry as can be
That he won't lay beneath the sky
Because the sky isn't green.

On the field blossomed a rose
As royal as a queen,
Thinking she shouldn't be where the lilac grows
For the lilac smells too sweet.

The sun shines more than his share
He rises far too soon.
Do you think that's really "fair"
To the silver moon?

Mice are too short, trees too tall
Nature makes no fuss.
She doesn't mind anomalies at all.
So what's wrong with us?

    Erika Jost

Words of Wisdom to My Daughter

Surely my love if we put God first
We must strive on so that we can converse.
We are not perfect, we are human beings you see,
Grains of sand passing through the hour glass of time.
You see my love, you must give and you must get.
And, when the time comes you must surely forget.
You will rumble and stumble but, you must not go asunder.
For you are sand you see,
Passing through the hour glass of time.
You see my love you will have suffering, struggles and strife
But, the great giver of life is holding your hands.
For if in him you believe and put trust
Then there will be no fuss.
For you are grains of sand you see,
Passing through the hour glass of time.

   Ella M. Pettway

Each One of Us

You love the lies you live within.
You hate the truth you hear.
You want to feel the sweetness,
but only know of bitter fear.
The way you laugh and smile
is the way that you deceive
yourself into feeling happy,
but all it is is your make-believe.
You call this world a fantasy.
You name this place a hell.
How can you contradict yourself?
How can you go and tell?
You are walking on the ropes of death
while humming tunes of life.
In one hand you're holding words of truth.
In the other a murderous, bloody knife.
How can you call out?
How can you cry?
And the truth still flows through your head
As you beg, "Oh, dear God, don't let me die."

   Talya S. Rubenstein

Man's Best Friend

Their furry faces, shiny eyes,
Look at you and soon realize

What you're thinking, how you feel,
Sense your thoughts and want to heal

The pain you go through, pain you hide,
Staying with you at your side,

Until they know that you're all right,
Protecting with all their might.

A loving friendship 'til the end
They won't desert you, they're man's best friend.

   Jennifer Dylewski

My Name Is Melanie Dawn

Who am I and what will I be?
Clouds whirl thick all around me.
Questions surround me, skies often gray.
Where is the sunlight that once fell my way?

Then through the dark comes a ray of light.
I lift up my sword to continue the fight.
No storm shall defeat me, I shall prevail.
I keep pressing onwards with a victor's yell!

My name is Melanie, the meaning is clear—
Darkness comes before the Dawn is near.
I know that my God who sees me each day
Will lift up the veil and show me the way.

   Ann Boyles

To My Parents

Here you come upon
35 years of marriage.
During that time you pushed
Four girls in a baby carriage.

As you each sit in your
Reclining chair,
Your thoughts about those
35 years are sometimes hard to bear.

Mom caring for four girls, while
Dad worked two jobs most of the time.
I often think back to the Pepsi
Bottles we turned in just to have a dime.

But there will always be a
Grandchild to love, a girl or a boy.
And now is the time of
Your life to enjoy.

With the help of God our
Family has gone through a lot,
But with lots of love and
Prayer, we cherish our family a lot.

   Debra Sherlock Belfield

I Need You

My love, you don't understand that I need you.
My life has spent every night
And day thinking and loving you.
When you walked out on me,
I felt agony and that I lost my heart with you.
You knew I would never leave you,
So why did you leave me?
Now my goal is to find the love that went off track
So that I can hold you in my arms.
One more chance is all I ask for,
But if that doesn't happen,
I will always cherish the moments spent with you
And especially I will cherish you.
My love will always be with you and no one else.
My heart no longer beats the color red but with the color black,
Like the shadow that follows you.
You just don't understand that I need you; always will.

   Michael Huffman

Racism

I know that you think of me only by the color of my skin.
Nothing's changed. You try to look deep inside,
but you can't get past it.
The brownness of my skin just stands out.
Color blindness cannot be cured unless everyone is treated.
I know that you see me,
with those devious eyes
as a thief, gangster, or thug,
waiting to attack you.
Nothing's changed.
When I walk in your store—
All eyes on me.
When I walk by your car—
You lock your doors.
How do you think I feel?
Still, nothing's changed.
I may dress a little different,
talk a little different, or walk a little different—
But I am no different within.
Underneath we are all flesh and bones.
You don't seem to understand
that we all come in several different colors
and mine just happens to be brown.
Therefore you shouldn't treat me less because of it.
I can't change the way I am, but you can change your attitude.

   Kevia Holloway

True Deceit

The brightest day, the darkest night
You hear a sound and shake with fright
You do not know, nor do you care
What makes the noise and strikes your fear
You turn your head, you hide your face
You run around from place to place
You laugh so hard it makes you cry
You're born again and then you die
You have your dreams while you're awake
You say that love is always fake
Your love for life is fading fast
You hide the future in the past
So close your eyes and go to sleep
And find your world of true deceit.

Ashley Craig

Sweet Dorothy

Dorothy is a fine lady.
She rings the bell when she's ready.
Take blood pressure or pop pills,
Sometimes she's feeling quite ill.
Be prepared to run in a blanket or teddy.

She looks like a queen in blue or red,
Sitting in lift chair or reclining in bed.
She goes back and forth between meals,
Using walker, hand rails, or she kneels.

Her daughters give her baths and use the comb.
Her beautician now comes to her home.
Permanent wave, hair color and cut,
The full treatment is a must.
Nail polish on fingers and toes,
To welcome family and friends; there's no foes.

When darkness falls outside,
A lamp makes her room still bright.
Good night, sweet Dorothy; good night.

Betty Burch

School Days

Tough multiplication math papers
Get crammed in backpacks for homework
And they get done at home so we won't sit at recess.

Lengthy Kiris tests
Help kids to see how they listen
And learn for the real world.

Super teachers teach subjects
To help kids learn different things
Get paid and have to stay at school on holidays.

Cool, smart kids
Have a blast because they are full of energy
Run and rip like a bunch of hooligans.

Crazy weird experiments
Blow up in kids' faces
Because they didn't listen.

Charlie Hust

An Angel in My Life

I heard an Angel's voice, it comforted me.
I felt an Angel's touch it soothed me.
I was lost on the road of life but an angel guided me.
When I was sick an angel healed me.
When I was hungry an angel feed me.
When I needed a friend an angel listen to me.
When my angel was called to Heaven
I knew she would not forget me.
And you, mother, will always be with me.

Stephen Scott Floyd

Wishing

Always wishing upon a star, wishing you are here.
Closing my eyes and holding you dear, wishing you were near.

Always feeling the softness of your touch across my body so warm.
Wishing you were holding me close in your loving arms.

Closing my eyes and seeing your face looking
down on me with your warm embrace,
Wishing on that shining star for our love to be
deep no matter how far apart we are.

The thought of you runs through my mind
with the words I Love You touching your lips and mine.
Wishing that some day we will be,
safe in each others arms 'til eternity.

Rhonda Vasquez

Heart Prints

So revealing, so deep.
Prints of past days,
Prints that pave the future's way.

Prints etched within,
No man can erase.
The ever present glory
Of a heart print on one's soul.

Beauty awakens the emotions so deep.
Turning the pages of life,
As a watermark on the pages of one's mind.

Not to fade, nor hide behind.
But always to see what lies beyond . . .
The ever evolving pages of life.

Linda M. Birch

Exit, for a Lost Soul

I will get lost in the shadows of the night
I will cover my pain with the blanket of the darkness
And wherever I go, inside the mist of my dreams
I will hide the failure of a life that's thrown to waste . . .

No one will miss the longings of this love
That sizzles ebullient in the depths of my soul
Waiting in vain for the angels of my guard
That would one day ring the bell of my salvation . . .

It's all in vain . . . nothing works, and nothing clicks
They look away . . . they will not care
Same as all others whom I pretend to love
And walk away without a second look . . .

I will exist for one moment . . . I will exist for another
And, in the infinity of the eternal mist
I will soon be, and then, I will not be . . .

Frank D. Luna

Only Water

I am the sea that ships sail across
from shore to shore, I will always be only water.
The rain and the wind caress me,
playing their games, for this does not bother me.
I just roll away; the moon and I dance
in its golden light and unite.
Only water.
When you leave for land my love is still there,
under the ground for this is the way of water.
Do you know me? Have you ever crossed my light?
Or rolled with my waves?
I am the sea that plays in the night.
I have watch love die on my shoulders
and blossom on my shores of water.
Muses have parted me, Jesus has walked on me.
I am a great cycle of lif—only water.

Ira L. Davis

A Mermaid's Tale

Sitting by the seaside; watching the gulls fly by.
You will soon relax, and leave the world behind.
As the strangest creatures roam about, you will never know.
Oh! How high the dolphins jump, or dive way down below.
The fiddlers begin to fiddle; the stars begin to shine.
And while all this is occurring, you shall very soon not mind.
Arising from the waters, slick as I can be.
I will soon be capturing you, and taking you away with me.
Down under we will go, beyond the surf and below;
Away to my sacred hiding place, where no one shall ever know.
Of all the treasures you will find, and the trinkets I bestow,
The tenderness and beauty will be all you'll need to know.
To see such astonishing beauty, will be an exotic sight.
For you are the only one, with whom I will share this delight.

Amanda Heatwole

In-between Days

2 days from somewhere and my
feet can't touch the ground.
I lie in a pool of sweat with a
flower growing from my eye.
The weightlessness I feel is
compounded by the sun.
Oh, how it bears down on my soul
like thunder in a storm.
I have feared this day all my life,
and yet it is surreal.
I'm not here; I'm with you and we're laughing.
Tears are falling from my face, or is it the
sprinklers above watering flowers in the sun?
I'm afraid of the dark so I'll shut my eyes
and dream of a lighted place.
Where angels sing and harps can dance
on clouds as light as air.
I'll wait for the day, patiently,
when you can meet me there.

Melanie Knudson

Enough of Beauty

exalted bird of paradise plays its harp in the Aeolian night

halts the woman with the black braids and blue eyes

she is beautiful and telling and the night fun and contagious

the spread of a stare says those pursed lips are money

but we haven't time to wait to wait to wait for our echoes

beside the hypnotic sway of the evergreens that wade

in the waves of the doting nuanced wind

Alok Sachdeva

End of Time

When I first noticed you, I couldn't believe what I saw.
My mind went blank, and my heart was up against the wall.
I'd bring you every star in the sky,
If I could be the only star in your eyes.
When you came to me and ask me out,
I knew it was fate beyond a shadow of doubt.
And when you looked in my eyes, and gave me that first kiss,
I knew another one I never wanted to miss.
And the way you held me in your arms, so tender and tight,
I knew I wanted to be with you day and night.
You promised I'd only cry those happy tears,
That's when I knew I had nothing to fear.
I want you to have, and to hold,
And give you more than diamonds or gold.
I want us to live, and to love, all of our days,
And swear we'll never part and go our separate ways
I'm very proud to say you're mine,
And I pray we'll be together 'till the end of time.

Amy Shirley

The Way It Is

As times come and go.
They are times for us to know.

Some are sad and some are grand,
All in all it's part of God's great plan,
For God feels and loves throughout all the land.

Though some are sad,
don't worry, for God will be walking
with us, holding our hand.

Carol Vinson

On the Church Steps

There is an old woman who lives in the city.
She sleeps on the church steps,
She's not looking for pity.
The parishioners who come in the morning,
Will not hear this old woman mourning.
For at the break of light, she must continue her plight,
To search for food and shelter yet for another night.

Walking around on a cold dark night, she's too tired,
Cold and old to put up a fight,
So she sleeps on the church steps hoping for a peaceful night.

The sky is her blanket, the cement her bed,
There is no pillow for her head.
Yet this old woman will go on day after day,
praying there must be a better way,
now that society has cast her away.

What would you do if this were your mother?
Would you shun her and walk away my brother?
If you are without guilt, who will cast the first stone
Onto this tired old woman's bones?
How can we just pass her by, aren't we telling ourselves lies?

Linda Cross

The Storm

The wind whistled and howled like I never heard before.
As I looked out the window I saw the
roof blow off the house next door.
Then suddenly the house itself was gone,
flying bits and pieces through the air.
In minutes quietness had returned and homes,
trees, neighbors and friends were no longer there.
Now all that is left to us who remain
is the lingering memories and the lasting
heartache and pain.

Sheldon T. Wright

Dad

Dad life was like, unto a rosebush
With branches of life, going in different directions
Some branches with many thorns of hardships
Dad tended his rosebush of life, with loving care
One day there appeared a beautiful rosebud
Alas it was not to be, for the rosebud
Withered on the vine and died
This brought dad a life time of sorrow
For this was the only son dad was to have
Through the sorrow and pain dad never gave up
As the years passed, dad's rosebush of life
Had four more rosebuds
Dad's four rosebuds grew into four full bloom roses
Alas time marches on, for dad is gone now
Dad's roses must carry on without him
To make their own rosebushes of life
But time marches on for them too
For they are withering on the vine with age
And one day soon they too will be gone

Mary Blanchard

Elvis Still Rockin'

They're singing this rock and roll and rap today
that don't make a whole lot
of sense; you got your kids on the street doing drugs,
carrying guns in the schools and got themselves in a fix
That's right, Elvis was rock and
rolling in "56,"
He sang gospel songs and rock and roll that made a lot of sense,
He had hips, lips, and fingertips,
He had style that lasted a while
When Elvis Aaron Presley died rock and roll in this world went wild,
Now it's welcome to the jungle, which is the world,
And dirty deeds you find dirt cheap, that's AIDS
Nothing shakin' but the bacon
Elvis ain't been taken'
Only by the grace of God
Ain't but two kings in this world and don't forget it
Number one is Jesus, king of our souls
Without Him you have no soul,
Number two is Elvis, he's king of rock and roll
All this rock and rap I don't know
Sorry about their luck
Got me and Elvis all shook up

Frank A. Hahn

Leaving Nothing to Chance

I've been down in the valley low
a feeling too devastating to understand
so I'm giving my life to God
leaving nothing to chance
It seems like everywhere I go
trouble is there when I arrive
and I'm left dealing with life's mysteries
wiping the tears from my eyes
But they tell me if I take Jesus with me
my burdens will be light
and somehow in my darkest hour
His strength in me will tell me everything's going to be all right
so with that kind of blessed assurance
I think I'll take the Almighty's hand and walk with He
and He with me leaving nothing to chance
This life can bring so much pain
that I can't make it on my own or by myself
I think that I can fight on and stand the rain
with a divine power's help I declare that I'm on the Lord's side
and for God I'll take a stand
I won't gamble with my life,
I'm playing it safe, leaving nothing to chance

Tiffany Stevenson

Only a Friend

Why must you be only a friend,
for my love for you is true and will never end.
There's not a day that goes by that I don't think of your face,
or the way you speak with such love and grace.
What I wouldn't give just to hold your hand,
you make me want to be a better man.
You deserve perfection as you are to me,
to be your one would be heavenly.
I want every moment with you to last for eternity.
Without you I'm only one half,
like a clock with no numbers
or a life with no path.
You make me happy, you make me glee,
what will our future hold; only God can see.
For if it's not you and me,
then what kind of life would it be?
A life without you is sorrow and pain,
a life without you is a decade of rain.
Oh, why must you be only a friend,
for my love for you is true and will never end.

William Charles Serafini

Looking at Stars from the Moon

Aching for light, the blue eye winks night.
A long shutter shot, a lasting gaze,
she subtles a sigh before she leaves,
then quietly walks away.

I know she must go.
Still, my tears shimmer under the light.

A mist forms on my glass mask and I remember
the dew on the fields of her face
spraying in the wind
and the coughing trees who bow
bending at the knees for the sweet melody
of my kite strumming her clouds.

Now, her soft line reflects warm the dawn,
and she blushes.

Alone and cold,
the sound of my breath, my only companion.

Yet, her miracle comforts me.

This strange ranger couldn't blow such glass.
Crushed blue swirled hue touched by marble fingers that reach.
The rage of sea that swells the wells of my eyes
misting my visor making it impossible to see.

I send a rocket to borrow the blue
to keep it green.

She rockets back with the light in tow
and I know she's coming.

Up here in silence, she brings me home.

Christopher Keriazis

To My Love

I did not see you coming,
You took me unaware.
I had given up on everything,
Especially love and care.

I'm sure I must have puzzled you
With my view of life,
Not knowing what to say or do
While listening to my strife.

At first I tried to push you away
Because of hurt and pride,
But I thank God you chose to stay,
For I need you by my side.

I don't know of words to tell
Just what you mean to me,
But I'm sure with much avail,
It's deeper than the sea.

You are more than I could ask for,
For your love has made me complete
And every day, as our love grows more and more,
My life becomes more sweet.

Miranda R. Benjamin

The Whispers of Autumn Thoughts

Pine trees and a mountain breeze,
Fall colors and how they please.
Leaves fall and scatter about,
Makes my heart want to shout.

Is it their color or how they glisten,
Or is it their fall and rustling about that makes us listen?

They crunch underfoot and they break apart,
is that from where we get our start?

We're a part of nature and its series of seasons.
Will peace fill our heart and become thus the reason?

Donna Kennedy

I Love You, Mommy

I know sometimes you get frustrated
Because I am so small,
And when I throw a tantrum,
You just want to set me in the hall.

I'm trying really hard, Mommy,
But I am growing, oh, so fast,
That soon these little hand prints
Will be a thing in the past.

So have patience with me, Mommy,
Teach me right from wrong.
Please give me lots of hugs and kisses,
To last a whole lifetime long.

Be a good example for me, Mommy,
For I see and hear all that you do.
You may not know it, but I want
These little footprints to fill your shoe.

I don't really know how to tell you,
How very much you mean to me.
But we both feel it,
When I give you a great big squeeze.

Betty R. Poteet

The Last Disciple

A plague called death is yearning,
Throughout my world hatred strives.
Into Hell will your soul be burning?
Sinful humans, evil rules your lives.
Conscience help us to realize.

I live and life continues.
No goals to put my mind at rest.
Self-destruction and chaos are my views!
Lord, what's the answer to this test?
New Jerusalem is my Bible's surmise.

With an uprising of the false prophets.
Religious are dying for no fear of the gods.
Evil sparks like a match is lit.
The eternal flames engulfing us and the dragon nods.
Lucifer awaits us, God says, with no surprise.

Talk with your God, he will help you realize.
Read your Bible, self-interpret and surmise.
Believe in your salvation, eternal life is the great surprise.

Isaac Hunter Ford

Life of a Champion

It started not too long ago, when his health was going bad.
That's when the doctor told him of the cancer that he had.
They knew they'd battle through it, they'd win this battle now.
He'd try as hard as possible, but didn't know quite how.
The days were getting shorter, the time was going fast.
His life was being rushed, how much longer would this last?
"I can win this cancer mom, I will fight it dad.
But this cancer isn't fair, it makes me very mad."
He'd always crack a smile, one that everyone could see.
He was learning a life lesson, that was importance of family.
The treatments grew more frequent, almost every day.
"Please don't worry mommy, I know I'll be okay."
Time was growing shorter, "It's ok son, close your eyes,"
His life was lived a champion, love and care was his prize.
"Please do not cry for me, my family and friends.
This is a new beginning, my life did not end.
Up here, this place is wonderful, do not shed a tear.
I now watch over all of you, there is nothing you must fear."
This battle that we spoke of, this battle is all done.
We can stop our crying, for this battle, he has won.

Amy Niceswanger

My Goal

It was the last minute in the second half,
The other team looked at me and started to laugh.
Sweat was in my hair,
Though I did not care.
Going for the net,
I had the ball.
The field was wet,
The goalie was tall.
I kicked the ball as hard as I could.
Go in the net,
I knew it would.
And it did.

Bassam Javed

mine and yours

you're in my dreams
and on my mind
i wish it would come true
to spend one night with you
i will take you here
also there
i don't want to let you go
'cause i'm so in love with you
your made of sugar
oh, so sweet
into my eyes you stare
you say this all the time
your eyes are so beautiful
i know that is true
i don't care who you are or where you're from
'cause i will always love you

Jessica Young

Anyone . . .

As the cars hiss by,
you cringe as I peel out of the parking lot.
Your burning anger for me is like a fire in your hands.
You have stopped hoping that someone would notice you,
anyone . . . but me.
My stupidity isn't funny anymore,
because I have invaded your mind.
Your breath is short as you realize
that good,
and strong,
are different men.
You don't have many friends,
no real ones.
No one you can talk to about the most personal things in your life.
You wish that you did,
that you had someone to talk to,
someone to trust.
Anyone . . . but me.

Kelsi Goodall

Why I Cry

Born to die in this world alone
I can cry now that they are all gone.
Feeling helpless, like I have no control
Or maybe it's that I sold my soul.
Trying to trick the world, I think I'm clever
Money comes and goes, but greed is forever.
Trying to do so much with such little time
Being the shepherd is hard when you're blind.
If I had a chance it's a distant dream
If I could sleep, I'd just awaken in a scream.
A broken heart, what a terrible loss
No one takes a moment to help me carry my cross.
Was it too much to ask for a hand?
Was my soul too hard to understand?

Ryan Bateman

Untitled (For My Mother)

Even the flattened photographs of our memories
cannot bring to life the light of you.
Nor can my fingers that trace their surfaces
searching for the sweet songs of Cat Stevens
for the beat-de-noses and butterfly kisses.

But you're certain that the moon still hangs high at night,
its pale face rising again and again to meet you
as I wonder if my arms will ever let go of you at bedtime
in that tiny pink room.

And I almost believe you
as your smile lies on the pillow next to mine
and I try and fold myself into a little girl again.

I can almost believe that time will lend me
your smile and your laugh
to wear upon my own for a little while.

Still the moon has captured and kept our past
and within you I look to find his light.

Aubrey Jacobs-Tyson

Vaya's Poem

My sweet child, with your beautiful smile
Beautiful white teeth, seen from a mile
You are with me every day of my life
Guiding me through all toils and strife
A gift from God, you were here for a while
So beautiful, so brave, courageous, and strong
We did all to keep you, you didn't stay long
You belonged to yourself from the beginning
Taught us to live life, ours also ending
Once when I thought I was sure to be gone
You said, "Get up, Ma! No! No! You are wrong!
I didn't die to take you with me
I have Grandma to keep me company
I lived my life, as you should yours
Be there for my sisters' children they bore"
I hear you, sweet darling, when I wake up
You were everyone's little buttercup
With every day, we mention your name
Vaya, my love, we miss you just the same

Valerie Horn

The Rose

Death itself is as the rose. . . .
dead & lifeless in the cold winter's bleakness
but has peace within

Tara Sweet

Thinking of You

To my best friend Sam
I'll think about you
Every day.
Hoping that you're feeling OK.
I'll pray for you
Every night.
Hoping that it works out all right.
When you're feeling sad and blue,
Just remember I'm here for you.
I'm an on call friend,
Night or day.
I'll talk you through it
And it will be OK
What you tell me
I won't repeat,
And I hope you do the same for me.
And when we get older and start to depart,
I'll remember you as a sister
And keep you in my heart.

Sarah Steinhoff

King of Hearts

He is My sunshine after the rain
His Love to us He imparts
He is the Balm that eases my pain
He is The King of Hearts

He is My rock and dwelling place
His Love comes not in parts
He's the mirror as I seek His face
He is The King of Hearts

He is the one that banishes fears
His Love transcends all smarts
He is the towel that dries my tears
He is The King of Hearts

He is the First, Last and the Most
His Love doth soothe all sorts
He's Father, Son and Holy Ghost
He is The King of Hearts

He's Strength when friends displease us
Unconditional Love to us He imparts
He is my Friend The Lowly Jesus
For He is The King of Hearts

Clarence Morris

Devil's Night

New visions, new sights.
Come take my hand on this Devil's night.
Take a look, the last you will see.
Take my hand, come dance with me.
A swirling dance with passionate heat.
Your soul so fresh, upon your body I feast.
Your soul is numb, my spirit alive.
Come take my hand, let us dance together.
The dance of power, the dance of submission.
Your fate in my hands, I throw it away.
Like you once did, when in your hands held,
My body, my soul, my fate.
Your body now gone, your soul all powerless.
I smile so grim, knowing revenge was sweet.
But as I smile and you fade, I realize.
I have sunk so deep, to the level of yours.
My spirit dirty, my soul all dark.
And I promise myself, never to do,
What you once did to me. . . .

Roberth Karman

"God"

I asked some children what "Love" "Is?"
They said "Sex" it "Is."
I said, is that "All" "It" "Is?"
What about motherly, fatherly, brotherly, sisterly "Love?"
They had no "Answer" for the "Above."
How sad that they are in ignorance of "This"
For "Love" "Is" "Bliss!"
So, don't dismiss the "Above" "Love!"
For "Love" "Is" "All" there "Is!"

Edmundo Soborski Jr.

Sometimes

Sometimes I wonder if I'm living a dream
Sometimes I wonder if it's all how it seems
Sometimes I wonder why we are here
Sometimes I wonder why there are fears
Sometimes I wonder why there are tears
Sometimes I wonder why you lie
Sometimes I wonder why I cry
Sometimes I wonder why you don't call
Sometimes I wonder if you love me at all

Mindy Tonti-Bunn

Dreaming

When the tide turns out to sea
In my heart, I yearn to be
With the rapidly receding tide
Just to go along once for the ride
I would love to feel free
With none of the everyday pressures hounding me
I would like to feel as though I don't have a care
Yet, in my heart, I know I'll never get there
My soul longs to roam
Yet, since, I have no money, my body must stay home
I would love to travel and see exotic places
To meet and get to know a few new faces
In my mind I know how foolish it seems
But in my heart and soul, I can still dream

Michelle Gorman

Mom

There are things in life in which we are thankful for,
not what is on the surface or on the floor.
Now what I'm talking about is what every person should know:
a mother who is there for you and a mom who loves you so.

I know that I put you through a lot of pain and strife,
but if you weren't here, who would be my support system in life.
We may argue and kvetch at one another
but I wouldn't want anyone else to take the place of my mother.

You have been here through the thick and the thin,
you showed your strength from without as well as from within.
The things you have shown me are worth more than money
and every time I do something stupid, I say something funny,
just to ease the situation for you and I,
because it hurts me to see my mother cry.

God, I am grateful that you have made a woman like this,
Anytime something goes wrong, she is there with a hug and kiss.
No, you can't find her on a web site or in a store,
She is one of a kind and nothing more.
Always being there for the kid who wants to sing and dance,
she says "one day, baby, you will get your chance."
I just wanted to tell her how much she means to me
and that to me she will always be the first lady.

Justin Yampolsky

Mother

Hey diddle diddle the cat and the fiddle
things a child should hear. . . .
Little Bo Peep lost her sheep,
words without worry or fear. . . .
A storybook upbringing I didn't have,
my pillow over my head is all that I had. . . .
Trying to silence the horrible words that were said,
to my mother, while I lie useless in bed. . . .
She dreamt of the day she could finally leave,
though I would lose her, I prayed for her needs. . . .
For I knew I'd survive the life I've been given,
my mother could not, to her grave she was driven.

Jim Hayes

Each New Day

Each new day is an experience if we choose to let it be,
but first we must open our hearts to enable us to see.

Each new day we make choices that can help our fellow man,
but we must be willing to listen and to follow our maker's plan.

Each new day is a beginning to enable us to grow,
but we must be willing to plant the seeds we sow.

Each new day is filled with memories from the present and the past,
but let's all give our love so our country will be united at last.

Cheryl K. Kent

Home Journey

To my family and to my friends, to all those I leave behind.
I am sorry that I had to go for it was just my time.
On the day I left you, I went to see Jesus.
He welcomed me with open arms as I entered into Heaven.
I walked with Him on streets of gold and beside the Crystal Sea.
Words cannot describe the beauty of what I feel or see.
It was then that Jesus turned to me and said, "You decide.
You may return your loved ones and to your Earthly life.
I promise you that paradise will always be here waiting.
Or you may stay right here with Me, your final destination."
I hope you understand dear ones, just why I had to stay.
Take comfort in knowledge that we'll meet again someday.

Kristine R. Siedschlag

Who Promises

Friends or lovers. It would seem, both sometimes
No promises of tomorrows, nor have any been asked for
Is it the promise you fear? Or, do you wonder if we'll be here
Tomorrow? Does fate possess wisdom?
Is it her arms that draw us together
Despite our being apart?

Unspoken thoughts, half-filled hearts
Or is it half empty hearts?
Speaking in unison when eyes meet
Between friends and lovers
Is it possible to be one without the other?
Just friend, just lover, or has fate a message?
Friends and lovers cannot be separated by tomorrow
It is fate herself who makes the promise.

Paula M. Podgorski

One Autumn

If you could only live one autumn,
and lose the leaves of pain.
Let me take away your sorrows, like a fall rain.
We could take the time, like a dormant
winter, let me build you up so strong.
The more I hold and love you, winter is not that long.
I will hold myself next to you, keep you warm
for the first spring days.
With this new life your changing, your leaves
touch the sun rays.
You would live your life so strong,
and I will be your rain.
If you would only live one autumn,
and lose the leaves of pain.

Beau Tyler Butcher

I Saw You the Other Day

I studied your photograph longer than others,
wondering what it would be
like to have you in my life.

You were standing against
a wall with a smile that overpowered
your shy eyes, so similar to mine.

I assume you were a loving person
considering the many stories I've heard.
Some say sour milk would not compare to
what I'd be if you were here.

At times I feel cheated,
not given the chance to know you.
For I was just a bud of a rose when
your smile dissolved into the light.

But I present my love to you
Though you were my mother's father
that I never knew.

Sherita T. Sparrow

Lost Love

Long ago before any of us were born,
A young girl's heart was broken and torn.

She fell in love with a man,
Who said they'd be together as long as they can

But "as long as they can" didn't last forever,
For after a war they'd never be together

The man was soon called to fight,
And one morning the girl watched his boat sail out of sight

She said to herself "He'll be back soon,"
But then she heard some terrible news the next afternoon

Her true love was dead,
Then she ran to her room and cried in her bed

What was life worth living now?
This horrid feeling she would not allow

So the next morning when the sun was still down,
She went to the beach where she purposely drown

Now she is together with her true love,
And they live, not here, but up above
Now once a year, on the 8th day in July,
Her spirit returns to the beach where she did die

Shannon E. O'Brien

Walking Slowly

I walk slowly down life's path.
I take in everything around me, waiting to see what is next.

Then out of nowhere you came. You bring more joy than you know,
all the time telling myself I've been blessed.

Blessed with the most beautiful gift in the world,
still I walk slowly, asking myself will I be that blessed again.

Knowing all along that something as special as you only comes
along once in a lifetime.

Still I walk slowly, taking everything in, not knowing that
the path of life gets harder.

More mountains to climb, more rivers to cross.

But still I walk slowly as I walk with you by my side,
I still feel blessed to have you with me.

We walk slowly together. Life's path is long, so I must be strong,
taking one day at time walking slowly.

Denise Morris

Father

Each day he rises early,
from his bed he looks so burly.
Off to work to provide us for,
through the rain, the snow, the thaw.

All day long he fixes other's problems,
he tries to make their world more solemn.

Back at night to teach us right,
he preaches about God's holy might.

Down he lay himself to sleep,
no need for him to count those sheep.

As I look back to my youth,
it appears as though he was a sleuth.

He did it all with such ease,
I thought my turn would be a breeze.

Today a father of two,
I'm so glad he was a father, too!

John R. Romano

The Giving of Yourself

When I was sad and lonely you gave me your ear
and you listened to me . . . never once judging me
When I was weak and hopeless you supported me
and believed in me and kept me plodding along the path of life
When I didn't want to go on . . . you never left my side
When I was tired you sheltered me from the storm
When I was angry and frustrated and ranting
and raving you let me yell at you and you didn't yell back
When I was frightened and shaking you hugged me
and held me close and you held my hand
When I was naive and uneducated you were patient
and you taught me and you never made fun of me
When I was crying you listened and you dried away my tears
When I was demanding and selfish, you let me be
When I had a problem and I needed to talk and to vent you offered
me your help and you gave me your advice
When I was happy you laughed along with me
When I was afraid to love you gave me your heart
and your mind and your body and your soul.
You opened my eyes and my heart and you taught me how to love again.

Jeanne McCalley

What Is Life?

Life is full of many things.
Happy things, fun things, and lots of dents and dings.
There are times I want to smile
And even go the extra mile.
Then there's times I feel alone
And can't make it on my own.
That's when I turn to God in prayer
Knowing well He's always there.
I tell Him what is on my heart
Then I'm ready for a new start.
He forgives my sins every day
And goes with me all the way.
He never gives a second thought
He's always there on the spot.
Jesus Christ will always care
He's just waiting for my solemn prayer.
Although there is a lot of strife,
Jesus Christ has given us life!

Megan Smith

He Knows

Pondering with curiosity
Between the dimensions of good and evil.
Have we mistakenly stepped out of line,
Or is this chaos what God has planned for us?
I feel as though we can come together somehow, some way.
When will that day come?
No one knows but our Father.
If He is up there He will put an end
To this disgusting behavior His children
Are unknowingly giving to the unthankful world.
Will it ever end is the question.
God knows but will we,
His children ever understand.

Paige Mayew

Dear Sometimes

On account that you happen, but not all of the time
I thought it only adequate
And absolutely necessary that I move onto always
Due to the fact that you hurt my heart,
Tie my stomach in knots,
And leave anxiety in my arms,
I am positively sure on always

Nicole Pratt

A Second Chance

Every night I kneel and pray,
Just to make it through the following day,
I made a painful mistake,
And now I must pay,
By staring through steel bars,
Watching day by day waste away.
I used to be wild, used to think I was God,
Looking back now, it feels a bit odd.
I thought I was invincible,
Telling everyone what to do,
Now I ask permission, just to do number two.
I want out real bad, not that anyone should worry,
I've gone from rumble to humbled in a great big hurry,
I'm not trying to give anyone a big song and dance,
All I ask and pray for is a second chance.

Lee Arthur Berman

I Remember

I remember seeing her shining face
as though I saw the sun.
I remember the touch of her silk soft hands
patting my back when I felt I didn't belong.
I remember the site of her big blue eyes,
they were bluer than the sea.
I remember the sound of her quivering voice
as she said a prayer with me.
We prayed to God she'd be okay
and make it through the night.
But we both knew when we looked in each
other's eyes
it's her time to pass
even though the timing is not right.
From that day on, up until now
I thank God each day
for bringing her into His world,
where I know her pain is gone.
If her pain is gone, then my pain is gone.
So this must be my home, which is where I belong.

Ashley Farrell

Us

When we part, I miss you.
When we touch, I long for you.
When our eyes meet, I enjoy your image.
When we kiss, my soul burns with passion.
When I dream, you're always with me.
When I speak, your name always seems to be in mind.
When I am sad, you always seem to put a smile on my face.
I made a wish once and it came true,
I found my endless love, I found it in you.

Liliana Kuhn

The Life of Love

The life of love is never measured,
but every moment is always treasured.

The life of love is knowing the love is true,
and nothing but love is shared between the two.

The life of love is a time that never ends,
and feeling the love as it starts and begins.

The life of love is the smile of your mate,
and the hours and seconds they're never late.

The life of love is knowing you have their mind, body, and soul,
and no secrets or regrets are left untold.

The life of love is loving each other in every way,
and awakening to their love each and every day.

The life of love is feeling their touch,
and realizing that you love each other that much.

Tamekia Shaw

Best Friend

You're gone but not forgotten my friend
What a friend you were, the best to the end.
Neither looks, nor money did matter to you
Your love was there no matter what I'd do.
You stood beside me in rain or shine
Never to complain nor leave me behind.
No words did you speak to me
Yet your affection was all I did need.
A heart of gold and coat to match
Loving brown eyes and a mouth to catch.
Long strong legs that loved to run
A great personality, always wanting to have fun.
Quick to learn, smart as a tack
So amazing to me as a matter of fact,
You'd always know just what to do
When I was down and feeling blue.
You had your own special way
No matter how bad I felt, you'd brighten my day.
You gave so much until your time ran out
You were the best friend, best dog without a doubt.

April A. Allen

Old Barns

They stand. They lean, still clad
in weathered red or grey,
with spavined roofs, some solitary
in tan fields of husks which sigh
in prairie wind. Often a nearby line
of guardian pines yet marks where home
once held a family who slept, loved, ate,
who worked outside and in from dawn
'til long past dusk.

One barn I know from watching
dust motes dance beyond its doorway
in Missouri sun. This veteran served
three generations well. Empty now
of lamb or calf, it's full of wonder
for city grandchildren scampering up
a hand-hewn ladder to the loft.

There, in fragrant stillness,
ancient straw and silver cobwebs
witness work all done with care
by many past, all done with care.

Lois Muehl

Boy

Have you ever watched the stars in his eyes
When a little boy brings you his big surprise?

It could be a toad or a bug in a box
Or a grubby little hand full of pretty round rocks.
A verse he wrote, something he made
More precious than silver and pieces of jade.
Something he has learned, you didn't know he knew!

So smile with your eyes as he wants you to do.
Give him a hug that let's him know why
You think that he is a wonderful guy.
Truly, truly yours.

Lucille Harvey

Mine . . . All Mine

Such wonderful treasure, it's all mine
Such honest, on-going passion, it's all mine
Such loving, warm arms, they are all mine
Such careful thought as not to hurt me
That's mine too
Everything I adore and love
It's all mine

Jessica Zygiel

Ever

If there was ever a time
or ever a place
where the dances at night
for we could ever embrace.
For which ever to look forward to
deep down inside
I feel it is to be better
than to run and hide
which for all the ways
you have to climb.
It feels like forever just trying to find
for the poem that's deepening forever inside
and forever to be alone!
We can never, ever decide.
Edward McClure

It Takes You

I want to make you feel better, but how can I?
How can I heat the pot of sorrow in your soul
and make it yield flavors of joy?
Right within you, you hold the key to your heart,
the power by which you decide to rejoice or mourn.
So, I can't just touch you and make everything beautiful,
though I really do wish I could.
It takes you to make you truly happy.
It takes you to tell your heart to be merry.
We choose what we look upon:
the cloud or its silver lining,
the dark tunnel or the light at the end,
the flood or the rainbow.
iIn all the evil the world presents us,
I hope you'll always choose to see some good.
I'm counting on you to do so.
Atim Nsunwara

Summer on Watermelon Beach

The summer sun gently shines
On creeping watermelon vines.

Water laps against the shore,
Sea gulls cry and waves roar.

A fisherman throws his line
With luck, on fish dinner he'll dine.

A beach towel spread out on the sand,
The sun is a warm and gentle hand.

Soothing you, soothing you to sleep,
Amid the soft, gentle roaring of the deep.
Briana Gapsis

Him

I thought that you were different,
not like other guys, but when I looked into your eyes
I saw all of the lies.
Your comforting charms graced my heart
when actually you were just confused.
But it was okay to hurt me right?
Because you were a boy who had the blues you had to choose.
You said that you loved me,
I thought it was true, but all along you were just confused.
Why did you think you could break me down,
my tears shed over you. Once again let me remind you that
when I say your name, my fingers turn to fists,
but my heart thirsts for your love again.
I know that you don't think I see you staring at me
the way you always do,
but the truth is that I don't want to look up
because I'm not over losing you.
Alyssa Scholl

When It Rains on My Parade

When I've gone as far as I can go,
God is there to lead my way.
When there's the straw to break the camel's back,
God mends it all somehow, someway.

When I'm up to here in whatever's wrong,
God comes down to make things right.
When it has rained on my parade,
Somehow, the sun shines its light.

When I am at my wit's end,
Christ is the way to carry me on.
When it seems I'm to the end of my road,
His presence assures, I'm not alone.

When I'm fed up with it all,
God satisfies my hungry soul.
When the blocks have been knocked from under me,
God makes me strong, courageous and bold.

When I am hanging by a thread,
I hold to God, by love's strong cord.
So, when I've had it with all life's care,
I find hope and victory in the Lord!
Connie L. Broach

Love of the Old

Love is a word we all use to describe
Anything from dogs to cars to pecan pie.
Love is a strong word few of us know
When it comes to other people.

There are many questions that after arise,
Like how? or when? or why?
Sometimes love finds you.
Sometimes you have to look.

Your mom wonders, who?
Your friends wonder, when?
You sit back and stare
And your love is always there.
Rachel Sherman

Guardian Angel

Looking past the sky
I was given such a shock
Because there above the clouds
Appeared an angel looking down on me
Later that night I told my grandparents
They laughed at me then told me to go get some sleep
Laying in my bed that night I realized,
The angel I had seen that day
Was just my guardian angel
Looking after me
Holly Donald

Phone

Hold on utensil of communication
Bringing news of good tidings or devastation
Just ringing for someone to "Shoot the breeze"
Or to annoy someone with gossip if you please
A loved one, an acquaintance, or someone to repent
To pass away the time in cerebral content.
Ring away phone to summon my ear . . .
To hear a friend's sorrow, or hear a friend's cheer
All plastic, metal, and wirings abound
Sitting squarely on the night table waiting to be found.
A ring here! A ring there in a monotone key . . .
A wash in sound for someone's plea . . .
Though my phone is as black as an onyx of stone.
You may seem one dimensional, but with you I'm rarely alone.
Joe Sturgis

A Dagger Called Love

With each wound she inflicted on you,
I felt your pain.
I walked next to you,
Holding your hand,
Wiping your tears,
Guiding you every step of the way.
You were lost and scared,
Unsure of what the future would hold,
I was the rock on which you leaned.
I loved you, my friend.
Despite my unyielding affection,
You thrust an unknowing dagger into my heart
With every sweet kiss you placed upon her
Crimson lips.
The anguish and pain you caused you will never know.
A scar,
The shape of love,
Has marred my innocence.
Never again can I return to the girl I once was.
My life has been changed forever.
More than you will ever know.

Elizabeth Garnett

Why

As they walk through the gates of the heavenly floor
they can see each other once more;
they know for now that they are dear,
they know for now that we are near;
they can see us smiling as they look upon.
But we are frowning as we look at dawn;.
they know when our time is done, but we just sit
back and try to have some fun.
How will we know, how will we go,
how will we do the things that are so?
And as we take a step into the day
they sit back and watch the blue jay;
why was it them, why wasn't it us,
why did they leave without the trust?
All I know and all I knew was that someday it would be you, too;
when it will happen who knows,
but what I want to tell you is how much I love you so!

Michelle McHugh

Loving You

As we grow in age, there is strife
A partner is needed for a happier life.
When God put us together in love,
All blessings are sent forth from above.
A wedding day is one to remember with great pride,
Two people joined with vows to abide.
Two lives set forth together with love and care,
In a home for laughter with no grief to bear.
The doors are open for friends to come and chat.
There is always a friendly smile and welcome mat.
Friends are special guests in life,
In times of joy or grief and strife.
Join in the happy event of the day,
And walk with us each step of the way.
Our thoughts are together in all we share,
To work together in the trials we bear.

Lola Webster

Timeless Sorrow

Silent streams of teardrops fell upon my face and pillow,
I thought of things from long ago and prayed they would be gentle.
To lose a mom and daddy too was just too much to handle,
life was cruel this was true oh, please put out the candle.
Stop the flame that starts the pain that makes my heart surrender,
to all the sad things in my life instead of all its grandeur!

Barbara Doyle

listen

yearnings, learning, trying times sliding by
like rain drops upon a foggy window pane
hiding the remaining day from them with morning eye

down, down, downwards seeking a hollow lane
each a subtle moan, a muffled groan, so alone
searching but a place to lie there in a muddied earth

patterns echoing of like unknown and known
until with shy imagination and the barest hint of mirth
the sun is joining, shining, blinding—blind

and the moment becomes and our soul sees it glisten
the whole of it at last beyond at rest combined
when for an instance we to them simply listen.

Theresa Kirk

"Hugs"

A hug is something that makes one feel special
from a friend,
relative
or lover.

Some can be great for a long lost friend
who need it the most,
hoping it won't end.

When she said she wanted one,
I wanted one too.

As she spread her arms out wide
I knew my love for her couldn't hide.

After all,
to me she's known as my lover
and I took one more step
after I decided to hug her.

Then there my hands were,
wrapped around her!

Salvatore Diglio

Today

Today was a bad day
my teacher took my gameboy away.
She made me feel like a big fool
I don't think I can ever go back to school.
Then when recess came around
I had nothing to do, everyone hated me
and there was nothing I could do.
After recess came math
my teacher made us really laugh,
but then we couldn't talk at all
a thought came in my head "Was it still fall?"
It felt like years were passing by
I wish by miracle that I would die.
Soon came lunch and everyone stared
what was wrong, am I losing my hair?
I hated this day thank God it's over
now I can go play with my new puppy Rover.

Bianca Milov

Smiling Eyes

The children so cuddly and warm in their beds,
Soft, fluffy pillows protect their sweet heads;
Drifting away as the sandman arrives,
Sprinkling sleep dust in their smiling eyes.
An angel appears with a crystal-shaped cup,
Pours love from her heart and stirs it right up;
Takes the love potion, so proudly she sighs,
And fills up the children's smiling eyes.
The moonlight is glowing so the angel sees her way,
She waves to the sandman they've had a busy day,
Together they fly through wide open skies,
Visiting children with their smiling eyes.

Ellen Spindel

The Power of You

Distant echoes, faded heartbeat barely audible in silence
Pale imitation of a former self, light dims at the height of day,
Tears shed like rain cannot hide desperation,
Trace happiness from a former life,
Memories of elation lapse
I can barely remember, I barely recall love

Smoke and mirrors, mist and haze, hollow words,
Eminent defeat reality like refracted glass goes in all directions
Never meets in one place to make its secrets known
Life never tells how to live it, instructions are nonexistent
On the fly and by teeth skins one can only improvise

Carrying on, hope springing eternal, peering through darkness,
Destroying indecision
Banging the wall of distraction loud, proud and joyful
Bold like bright blinding color
Reds, greens, yellows, blues
Pouring forth in kaleidoscopic floods

A true force of nature
That's the power of you.

Annette Green

Interior Light

I wanna catch a cloud on a sunny day
And bathe in the sun high up in the sky
I'll lean over the edge after about three hours
And observe the people as they scurry by
With a tall glass of lemonade in my right hand
And sunglasses on my eyes
The wind starts to blow nice and slow
And I sit up and sigh in surprise
The cloud unzipped his fly, took off his pants,
As he began watering the ground
Excuse me young man, this is not what I planned,
Will you please put me down
The caress of his hand, upon the ground I land,
And began dancing around
In my black and white swimsuit, with a pretty cotton hat,
To no music, not even a sound
The people are staring but I'm not even caring,
You see this makes up my interior
It's not too late, for you to redecorate,
If this makes you feel inferior

Mary L. Jackson

"The Library"

We walk the path of opportunities many time in our life. . . .
The door is always open to all who dare to step inside. . . .

Within this door you may see the world through others' eyes. . . .
Learn to speak these worlds or just be yourself. . . .

When you seem to be at life's snapping end;
the door opens. . . .
All is quite, the birds sing softly, the wind blows gently,
the flowers bloom magnificently.
And your mind drifts afar . . .
Far to somewhere you've always dreamed of. . . .

There is a flowing love,
a part of you no one knows
but everyone feels. . . .
Here your secrets are shared but never spoken.
Here you learn . . . touch . . . and love all walks of life.

Lord, thank you for this self upon a shelf.

Victoria Blackburn

Momma Matriarch

Since I was a little girl
I knew that you would be someone
The leader of our family
We all love and respect you
If you left we would be so lost
For you are the Momma Matriarch
Your love so unconditional
Your life so filled with love
You keep your faith in the MAN above
And are so glad that he sent you us
We tested your strength, we came out on top
We have learned from the life of the Momma Matriarch
Your children are all grown up and parents now themselves
They teach us with much care
All the things you taught them
When you're gone, love will keep us together
We have learned from and been loved by GOD's precious gift,
THE MOMMA MATRIARCH.

Cynthia Robinson

Memories of Dad

Walks in a park,
Talks by the pool,
Playing catch until dark,
My first day of school.
Time spent capturing the wonders of my youth,
A comforting hug as I lost my first tooth.
Movies by the fire during a winter snow,
Tennis on a sunny day as Spring colors began to show.
Smiles, hugs, and kisses on Graduation Day,
Happiness in his eyes, more than words could say.
Suddenly those blue skies changed to gray,
And Dad was unfairly taken Heaven's way.
A void that is never quite filled,
A world of warmth, so suddenly chilled.
But now I look back, and I'm happy, not sad,
For I have so many special memories of Dad.

Douglas Sass

Hidden Promises

Far stars light, cold shimmering rays
A small fire am I
Grey at night through the bare branches you reach
some soul message to teach

Exhale of steam, breath of life
mingled with the cold, light
wondering what I mean

A reflection of the day
at night you keep
as the stars in our slumber
the promise you weep

A visitation done, chilled flesh,
shivering of bone.
Your image bright, in mind,
to bed I lumber
A small fire am I,
In warmth I lie.

Timothy Motl

Bianca

Bianca's words so soft and cold,
Some of them are still untold,
And even though we wait to hear,
Knowing Bianca is very near,
We hope and pray that she sees
The glow of our voices in the midnight snow,
For we, her children see the light,
We can guide you through the night.

Ryleigh Wade

Eternity

For my children
I walked the beach at 8 A.M.
And in the wet sand
Read the hieroglyphics of the gulls prints
Punctuated by smooth and broken shells.
And for the hundredth time
I knelt to pick the treasures of the tide,
Being sure to leave enough
For the dreamers who would follow me.

Elisa Kennedy

Losing Touch

As we fell apart . . .
Indefinitely lost, translucent,
But solid in it's structure.
Stings chaotically attached among
A mass of jumbled clutter.
Has anyone set out to find me?
Have they realized I'm gone?
Say, does anyone ever see me,
Or are you the only one?
The waves undulate and break upon
My chest, with agonizing
Force. Which hurls me down into this lair,
Nothing but pain arising.
With the fading moonlight I languish,
Plaintive, alone, never found.
Wilting as I fall, I fall slowly.
Tumbling sadly to the ground.

Lena Pascale

My Precious Friend It's Time to Realize

you need love more then ever now,

More than hope, money, wisdom, drink, or drug
without it comes a slow negative death
Within the world for only love heal and the
rainbows of summer into the colors of
happiness
I understand my friend, your pain and sorrow
So reach for love and me. i will reach out
myself
   and someday it will come from within
love has away of heal the pain
it was always in our hearts, we forgot

how To Use It

Michael Bedard

Lovers for a Day

Aye, you were mine and only mine that day,
You were my joy, my happiness, my bliss,
And all my past seemed just wasted away
Without your smile and without your kiss.
I'll hide your kiss in the secret of my heart
For the rest of my empty lonely days,
Now that the night has wrenched our hands apart,
And we must keep our own separate ways.
You were my love, my only love that day.
All the beauty of the women I've loved,
All the charms of the women I've possessed,
Were all in you and you alone that day.
You were all this, you were all this and more:
The things I've never had but loved the most,
The things I know and have yet to explore,
And all the things I have destroyed and lost.
I lived a whole new life with you that day:
The triumphs and defeats, glory and regret,
The bloom of youth, the misery of decay,
The pang of parting—a foretaste of death.

Cesare Desilvestri-Camster

My Family

Dad—he's never sad
(Except when he's glad)
Mom is busy planning
My sister's junior prom
Wendy thinks she's the daughter of
The "Wendy's" founder
Melissa is and always will
Be a kiss-up
Kevin—helpful when fishing
When he's missin'
Max—still tryin' to send
That fax
Norma Jean—still thinks she's
The subject of "Candle in the Wind"
That's us
Oh, wait—me.
"Hmm . . . go away! Mom, make them stop!
. . . Won't work . . . no, Norma Jean,
You ARE NOT IN THE SONG."

Jeffrey Foshag

Brave New World

A thousand years by-gone,
An opportunity of a lifetime
They move like feeble lambs
Under the "BY2Kready" Shepherd's cruel crook

The time of reckoning now grows near,
Innocents grit their teeth in fear
One more time around the clock,
One more shot glass down the throat

"Hurrah! Alas?" the confused crowds cry,
Their promised fate not come to pass
No money spews from cash machines
No Messiah moves from the darkened clouds

Tim Gray

Who Can We Be

Masked by the cruelty of society,
we are coaxed into this charade.
Beautifying our body, our temple,
Defying our inheritance with parade.
Mocking our forefathers,
Misleading our sons and our daughters.
The progress that once was
may no longer be.
We try to find joy in young and old,
In the age where we're neither diamond nor
gold.
Where are we?
Who are we?
Who Can We Be?

Suzanne Puckett

Johnnie Lee

Mama's boy with twinkling eyes of quietness
searching life's never ending quest.
Growing into a teen
falling in love with Ada, his queen.

Boxing, Army, educating to hoot;
Oh, John, 45 years of telling the truth,
preaching, encouraging others
to God's eternal youth.

J.L. others call you now.
Sixty-three! Wisdom circled your brow.
Mama's boy now at rest
and immortalized as the family's best.

For in my heart you will always be
that young boy to me.

Lena Overstreet-Pasely

Flying on the Wind

I fly through the sky with the greatest of ease,
My powered parachute and me are one with the breeze.

We fly high and low and have such a great view,
It's Heaven on earth and I recommend it to you.

With no cockpit around me to crease my style,
It's grandeur in the heights and it leaves me with a smile.

Zipping along smoothly at such a blistering speed,
Twenty-six miles per hour is all that I need.

It's grand to be up there above the ground,
You can see forever if you look around.

The birds look on as they pass me by,
Not too close do they come to this noisy guy.

With forty-six horsepower still blazing away
I make quite some noise as I make my way.

The birds keep their distance but look on in awe,
And can't quite believe just what they saw.

Over hills and valleys, roads and crops,
We fly serenely over the tops.

From treetops to cloud base we fly through the sky,
And thank God for these moments to be alone up so high.

Robert Kessler

God Above

Anger awaits us, surely soon to be.
Shall not it destroy you, perhaps me?
Shall not our tears show hurt, times two?
Could not cease the pain, for that of love
Nor pave us not, the golden way?
Look us upward, is not help there above?
Is not God to help us today?
Did not for help, you ask, nor did I?
Is not the bed we made, not where we lie?
Cannot be saved our love, shall it die?
Has hope lost way, is for us but too late?
Can we be the passersby of hate?
Shall forgiveness not show us the way?
Will our love stand strong yet another day?
Clouds of black, cannot they be blue?
Let Sorry begin our words, and end in I love you.
When times are hard, and we're lost in love,
Remember—get your strength from God above.

Steven Humphries

Plea to Man

As I watch Sophia playing . . .
Child's simple scope . . .
mamma.
Dead, nature's law.
Evolution.
GET . . . MINE . . . MORE . . .
Blind . . . ideas in wonder . . . forgotten.
Seeds of being, planted.
Life's whisper to come.
Insane hatred of each other!!!
Petty jealousies . . . murder of love . . . cease.
Listen . . . musical light . . . voice of God,
whisper—echoes create hearing . . . memories.
Winds of joy trace the breeze . . . set your sail,
unfurl a sustenant sun . . . heal.
Embrace spirit—legacies,
free yourself.
Remember . . . close your eyes . . .
remember . . .

Mariam Haddad

Poet's Web

. . . stepping into a poet's place and
starting to read a room that opens
to other spaces with writing on walls that
open as hallways or portals that are written
with words from the natural world. . . .
. . . words wet and bright and dark and dry
and high as hills and windy 'round six at
night in late November, winter hard on
the leavings of fall. . . .
. . . getting a little lost there
until retracing the steps back
to the beginning and beginning again. . . .
and again and again beginning to
at least know the beginnings well and. . . .
. . . knowing to step slowly next time,
out of the hurry to reach journey's end,
and into each moment, each hill, each bend,
when beginning again and stepping. . . .

Steven Linehan

"Forever After"

There's problems on the street, you can feel it everywhere
The bad guys that you meet, they just don't seem to care.
Kids are killing kids, dope is everywhere
We try and solve it all with programs called DARE

If you watch enough TV, you can mastermind a plan,
To kill off your mother, and become a rich man
Well there may come a day when women are men,
Wish I didn't know now what I won't know then.

The truth is an illusion, it never ever was,
It's mangled in confusion, lost in the cause.
The truth is a dream, no one's ever slept
It's the deepest darkest secret this world's ever kept.

It's getting more primitive each and every day,
We form our little committees, but grow further away
We study nuclear science in a computerized age
And send each other e-mail to our personal web page.

If my father's father could see what I see,
I don't think he'd call this the land of opportunity.
So draw up your contracts, play games and pretend
But all your little toys, ain't gonna save you in the end.

Michael Angelo

Deuce

Holding this little brown pup in the pouring rain,
A bond was formed from which we both would gain.
You were timid and shy and didn't want to be alone,
And neither did I, if the truth be known.

You took over the house as well as the yard,
It became your turf that you would guard.
Independent and stubborn, with a big loving streak,
Only in the lap of your master would you become meek.

You dug up flowers and chewed on shoes,
Totally fearless with nothing to lose.
Playful days and sleepless nights were ours to share,
We were on top of the world without a care.

I lost sight of you briefly that Sunday afternoon,
From my mistake, our lives changed much too soon.
A dogwood tree shades your final resting place,
For you are now in a world traveling at a slower pace.

You earned the right for eternal peace,
Although the pain in my heart has yet to cease.
My prayers and thoughts are all I now have to send,
To you, Deuce—my pet, my protector, my unconditional friend.

Sheila Burney

Fashion Police

So you think you look cute in your little
tube top
Well you have another thing coming to you!
You think you're the fashion police choosing who's hot and
who's not
Walking around like you own the town
But we are not under your fashion spell
We'll choose what's cool and hip
'Cause we don't follow the fashion world's guiding tips
We're outspoken, bright colored, or dressed in black
That's what shows us who we are
We're not something cut out of magazines
We're real people not celebrities

Amanda Mayeaux

"DAYBREAK"

Thinking of the night passed and what the
daylight brings, Of how I wished the night
could last instead the truth of the light stings,

'Cause daylight is the last pursuer of
truth, the night a souls paradise while your
spirit begs to be loose,

But at Day Break or dusk the battle of
daylight and night, The two entwine each
other where one succumbs to the others might,

The sky leaves a trace of the clash between the two, one side red like fire and the
other fading to a cold blue,

The outcome sometimes uncertain, 'cause one
might mistake,

For it is not the beginning of the night
but a triumphant DAYBREAK . . .

Cynthia Martin

Never Say, "I Wish I Had"

A friend of mine, once said to me,
"What you are is what you'll be."
To cross the sky, don't go by sea.
To find a friend, just start with me.
To be someone whom you are not, or be in
some unchosen spot.
Is not a life for you nor I.
I'd rather live, than rather die.
And so my friend I say to thee.
To cross the sky, don't go by sea.
To find a friend, just start with me.
For what you are is what you'll be.

Susan Glick-Shore

Confusion

I don't know why I'm trippin' 'cause all guys are the same
You see you're not the one to blame
I always seem to fall for all the wrong guys
Falling for the temptations and all the white lies
I should know by now 'cause my heart always gets broken
I always get pulled deeper within
Deeper within the feeling of being loved
and I always pray to the gods above
I pray for all my bad luck to be over
Instead of always hiding and running for cover
Hopefully things will get better with age
So I won't have to run and hide in a cage

Molli Mcdonald

Country Boy

In a quaint little town with woods gathered 'round
lived a young boy of Irish descent
with young man's schemes and pipe cloud dreams,
but mostly of honest intent.
He liked quiet places and wide open spaces,
he liked to walk all alone.
So, oh, what a pity that he yearned for the city
for the country was always his home.
In his 18th year, giving way to his fear,
he gave two years to Uncle Sam.
And with all of his might he learned how to fight,
staying a year in Vietnam.
This military hell, with its screaming shells,
frightened him to the bone.
After the heat and the fear for nearly a year,
the country boy finally came home.
Then he sat down in thought,
but it all came to naught for he had been such a fool.
With your high IQ, some are wiser than you
for some things aren't learned in a school.

Kerry Leight

Her Destiny

She floats across the ballroom floor
Wrapped tight in the arms of a man
Her flaming tresses flow down her back
Pouting red lips are curved in a smile
But moss green eyes are restless and eager
As they anxiously scan the room
Whom she's looking for, she doesn't know
She just knows that he will come
Finally she senses his presence
And eagerly turns to face him
A startled gasp escapes her lips
For his eyes are smoldering coals
Without saying a word, he sweeps he away
Never moving his eyes from her face
He leads her silently into a secluded glen
And his lips slowly lower to touch hers
At his kiss, her heartbeat escalates
And she feels weak on her feet
Somehow she manages to whisper "Who are you?"
And the answer is "Your Destiny!"

Saajida Taalib-Din

When

When my soul is weakened so
By all I try to be
Strength is given back by one
Who loves the essence of what makes me

When my faith begins to ebb
Crushed by prejudice and lies
I turn with hope and ever find
The truth within your eyes

When my hand seeks out a place
That calms and reassures
There is no warmth until I find
A place inside of yours

When my heart lies cold and bare
Love spent on children's pain
Yours flows forth and fills the void
To let me love again

So when you ask the reason why
My loving must go on
It's your love, your strength, your heart, your truth
That stay when you are gone

Lizette Howard

Life

Along the times in my life,
I often sit and wonder, what will be in store for tomorrow?
Will I realize that there is no need for sorrow?
Some days, everything seems fine.
Then others, my heart is filled with pain.
What is the matter, am I insane?
I cannot concentrate on all the good things
that I've done, just the bad.
Then once again, I am feeling sad.
Why can't I realize, that I am whole?
What makes me so insecure?
Maybe, I am afraid of the happiness I would endure?
Sometimes I wonder, will I ever be happy?
Then I imagine my life before me,
concentrating on the positive things that I've done.
Confused! I mean what do I expect?
I'm still very young!

Carri Blackmon

Some Days Are Better Than Others

"Some days are better than others," he said if he had his drothers.
He would look at his life, get rid of the strife
and remember which side his bread's buttered.
The day's that pain long would begin with a song
as he rides to work in his car,
then reminded again when the day finally ends
when he hears it again in the bar.
When will he get over this chip on his shoulder?
His girlfriend's last present to him,
yet he wears it with pride as he brushes aside
the women that try to get in.
Maybe one day he'll be able to say
"It's time to find another"
but as of today, I'm sorry to say,
that "Some days are better than others."

John Hite

My Plea

And there you were, shining like a star
Everyone else faded away
leaving me to stare.
My heart beat quicker,
I began to shake
Is this love I feel so fast and free
Is this the way things are supposed to be?
Please come and take my hand,
pull me away from my despair.
Fill the void left open by HIM
Bring me any joy you'd like to spread.
When you come I'll ask one thing:
Don't hurt me please, just be kind
And
When the time comes and you need to let go
do it gently; don't bring back the void
Don't bring back the anger, the hurt, the pain;
just love me
Just love me
And please fill this void.

Elizabeth Lovins

Thoughts

Beauty lies deep inside nothing's long lost touching.
Lovers' hands turn to sand while the moon speaks.
I'll see you soon under stars that used to be ours.
There are people out there who share my thoughts and cares.
The clouds are not too far when you reach for the stars.
Give love to those who have none and ocean skies will turn
tie-die in the eyes of tomorrows today.
Lost thoughts pour down like an endless rain
creating a smile for one lonely child.
Peace gives what nothing is so I can finally touch
what I love so much.

Jason Herbert Kent

Peepz

I guess it can be said
that I'm mentally fed, neither muscle, mules,
nor acres can pull us out of the red.

Let's rock the covering of our head
with the locking of dreads, an emblem
that my peepz are no longer scared.
Why disguise the outer
when the inner's the light?
Hair straight and bright
should be dark and tight.
Who says, "It's foul?"   I say not right, 'cause
only my peepz in day rock night.
Amadou Diallo, may peace be in flight.

Clarence Broach

Eternally—A Prayer of Love

You walked the Earth, my darling,
and your steps made their impression upon my soul.
You wept and prayed at daybreak—
you pleaded for my love to make you whole.
You searched the cool, vast ocean
for the one true love that is your own.
Your cries were swept along the winds of the sea,
and I heard you calling me home.
The stars were beckoning you, angel,
with their brilliance and their light.
They were glowing with the promise of my flaming love
to warm your heart in the cool, dark night.
It was not meant for us to join yet;
you needed to learn how to set your spirit free.
The lessons of pain and separation
were also teaching me.
But we have traveled through
the valleys and can see the rainbow that is our sign
of the life we'll now share
together throughout the universe,
until the end of time.

Joanne Wunderle

Move Me

The music was loud and savage, the day to day beat obscene
merciless, heartless, to ravage, the breath of the unknown, unclean

The life being drawn from the sphere, of hope and despair alike
no strength to hold or draw near, from your heart hate does strike

You move right through me, to the heart of the world
like a raindrops, you wash over me
like silence, you begin to fill me
like a heartbeat, you always move me

You brought beauty with your face, laughter with your smile
You gave life such strong grace, that lasted all the while

No more broken dreams, no fear now faced alone
you brought to me all the love it seems, to call all my own

Like raindrops, you wash over me
like silence, you begin to fill me
like a heartbeat, you always move me

You move me, like the waves shift the sand
like the sun melts the snow

You move me, the way the passions flow
the way forever goes.

Just move, just move me

Karen Harbison

Walk on the Beach

Sand like velvet ribbon
Flows between my toes;
Shells—pink, gold, white, jewels;
Some pure, some marred,
Many scarred from endless lulling about
The ocean's playground, many cracked, broken.

The briny air, sticky sweet,
Caresses my arms like an anxious lover,
Sighing, restless.
The sky a blue curtain,
A print of cloud, like bunched up sheets,
Resting on the horizon bed.

Tender, cool waves lap at my legs,
Then dart away, roll out of sight.
A cool breeze holds back the sun that,
Like an anchor,
Wants to drop me to my knees.
Noon turns to dusk; the sky darkens,
I become a shadow in retreat.

Aleta Crane

Waiting

Here I sit in solitude . . .
with people all around!
Waiting my turn with him . . .
the busiest doctor in town!

Appointment time means nothing!
Just why I'll never know!
As the waiting time grows longer . . .
I have an urge to go!

I'd rather be somewhere else . . .
I've got things to do!
I don't enjoy waiting . . .
it bores me through and through!

It seems to me the clock has stopped . . .
along with movement too!
Especially beyond the doors . . .
We're waiting to pass through!

If ever the time will come . . .
when the nurse will call my name . . .
Another room she'll put me in . . .
Where waiting begins again!

Robert Duncan

Why

Why does Love always tempt me,
It leads me on, then it flees;
How can one heart completely destroy another,
Set it ablaze with passion, then walk away to let it smother?

What is it about me that's so horribly wrong,
To make happiness avoid my life and never stay to long;
What have I done to make God hate me so bad,
That he takes away every dream I've ever had?

It wouldn't be so bad, if the pain would ever end,
But love keeps torturing me, over and over again.
You think I would know by now that love will never be mine,
I'm bound to suffer through this world 'til the end of time.

Like a fool, once again I gave away my heart,
Only to have it ripped out and torn completely apart;
But this time is the last time, for I have nothing left to give,
My heart is stone, my soul is dead, there's no reason to live.

Micheal Welchel

It's a Personal Journey toward God in Heaven

Along your journey, you meet and talk to different people.
Sometimes you stay a little longer than you planned.
When you continue on your journey,
some people may follow you and others will not,
but remember,
It's a personal journey towards God in Heaven.
You may have to go right or you may have to go left,
you may have to go back because you failed that test.
Then you may get tired and rest awhile
while others continue on their journey.
But as long as you know beyond a shadow of a doubt
that there's one God and one God alone, you can't go wrong.
Even though your friends may go a different way
and other people may go another way,
let me tell you something;
God is just that Big,
big enough for all directions.
So you just continue on your journey
because all directions have one destination . . .
and that's Heaven.

Chris Roland

Understanding

I'm full of heartache.
My world is spinning.
I lost my grandpa on Tuesday.
I feel frightened and sad.
What's a girl to do?
Only to be upset and really blue.

Then God grabbed me by the hand.
And said, "Child, don't be sad."
"Your grandpa's in Heaven with me now.
I will comfort you, and help you understand."
I felt reassured He was with me.
I was no longer alone.

I don't have tears in my eyes anymore.
I see my grandpa walking in the streets of gold.
No longer in pain, because he's in God's home.
God really made the heartache go away.
I am seeing it God's way.
I will live better.
With each passing day.

Crystal Morris

A Heart for Trees

Not long ago, there once was a wood,
Where trees of age and splendor stood.
And the songs of birds were sweetly sung.
But now the curtain has been rung.

For the sound of the bulldozer rang loud and clear,
Killing the trees and wildlife so dear.
The deer and their young had no place to go,
So we shot them . . . weren't we right to do so?

The air that we breathe will someday go stale,
The glow of health will soon turn pale.
Oh, how I long for the twitter of birds in the air,
I wish I could look and still see them there.

I begged man to listen, to spare a few acres.
But deaf ears were hearing, there were no takers.
My country, my town, my Mayor, my city
Never answered my pleadings, never took pity.

So, watch for the sparrow, look for a seedling.
You may catch a glimpse, or forever be pleading
To return to the land, the beauty of spring,
But alas, it's too late . . . it's gone, there's nothing.

June R. Truax

Jesus's Promises

Jesus did not promise
the sky would always be clear
or that I would walk in flower covered pathways
all my life.

Jesus did not promise
joy with out sorrow,
peace without pain,
or rainbows without a little rain.

But Jesus did promised to me,
as he was raised upon the cross,
strength for days ahead,
rest when I became weary,
grace for the trials I may face,
his help from above,
with his unfailing sympathy,
and undying love.

Heather D. Evans

Snowflakes

The sun's rays are hidden behind velvet skies.
Skies dipped in Payne's gray,
Ready to burst open at spring's command.
But it's the snowflakes turn to play their part.
Snowflakes are God's crystals of light,
Gently sprinkling His love and faith on all.
Breathe in the fresh, cold air, the sting of winter,
And let His love warm the cold, frostbitten hearts.

Kathy Semian

The Greatest Gift

When you were born, an angel came
And said on bended knee, this is a gift, He heard your cry
Sent, with love, from God to me.
When you were born I looked to see
My gift from God above, conceived in faith and hope and joy
And unconditional love.
My eyes were thrilled, my heart was full
And as I can recall, my life was changed the day you came
Made complete by one so small.
When you were born, the angels danced
And rejoiced at your birth
'Cause when you were born, they knew He made
An angel here on earth
Now that you've grown, I'll cherish you
I'll dry your every tear
I'll love you now and always
With each day and passing year
You sparkle more than diamond rings
More priceless than a pearl, the greatest gift
I'll ever get is my precious little girl.

Katherine Gruss

This Is Just How Things Are

We are living in a world where everyone's a stranger.
Living in a world full of heartache and anger.
All that is wanted is someone to love.
Some sort of sign that there is a man above.
In this world, kindness is rare.
This is a place in which you are naive, if you care.
We walk along crowded streets.
We avoid each other; it would be erroneous to meet.
The warmest people are warm to a select few.
If you are not their type they're cold to you.
And if you decide to treat everyone as if they are the same.
Many are quick to take advantage,
seize what they can; it's like playing a game.
In a world where it is perilous to be compassionate,
and hurtful to be sordid,
It is no wonder that our minds are so distorted.

Angela Fanucchi

Grandma: I Miss You

To everyone she was a friend,
She was always there until the end.

She'd help you up when you were down,
No matter what, she was around.

Under the wing, I stayed hidden,
From any danger that seemed forbidden.

She kept me alive, she made me glow,
Without her here, I feel so low.

I kept her in mind for a start,
But now I know she belongs at heart.

Keeping memories in my heart,
No one could ever fill that part.

If she only knew how much she effected me,
Now for her I must succeed.

I must show her that I try and make her proud,
For I know she is nearby watching on her cloud.

Thinking about it I show remorse,
For her life to take such a sudden course.

For a month, inside I had to stay,
But I never forgot her, smiling up when I pray.

Darlisha Stanfield

The Gift from My Heart

Christmas is coming closer
Keep piling up the boxes
With varied colors and sizes
Under the tree with beautiful decorating at my parent's house
Since when
They are so busy in and out and come and go
Brothers and sisters and also nieces and nephews dumping the boxes
I wonder how much all that cost and which one is more expensive and
Valuable?
That big one? Or that little one?
By the way
What gifts shall I give my parents?
The best gift they always want from me
I decided to make a small box and put my heart and word in it
Mo . . . om and Da . . . ad!
I'm not going to lose my "temper"
This is the word of honor that I want to keep
forever and ever in my life.

Dr. John Han

Years

It took what seemed a lifetime,
Years and, years and, years
It only took minutes of that lifetime,
For you to touch my life and, for me to touch yours.

These years just keep on coming,
With a vengeance oh, so strong,
Again in a matter of minutes in these years,
My heart says, "I feel like I've known you,
For oh, so very long."

How say, oh years, how can it be?
A gentle someone has come along
And changed things, oh so suddenly.

In a flash of light, showing me.
How these years keep coming on strong,
I'd like to tell myself, slow down, take rest, do my best
Take note and, just keep going along.

Again, I say, oh years, how can it be?
A gentle someone has come along,
And now, these years will be different for me.

Cheryl Bularz

Spring

I hear drip drop upon the roof in spring,
when a storm bursts out of the clouds
it almost seems like fireworks
of little tiny rain drops
exploding from the heavens.
My birthday is in spring
and the presents I like most
are the beautiful weeping flowers.
The last days of spring I say
I will miss the fireworks of storms
and I will miss the flowers that bloom.
I will miss spring, but summer
is still to come.

Blair Boyd

When I Dream

When I dream of you I see us,
together, lying on an extravagantly flowery hilltop,
watching the countless white, puffy clouds.
When I am with you,
I feel as if our love could split apart the clouds
and expose the sun,
Letting it shine radiantly through.
When I am not with you,
I gaze above to the clouds
and see the sun shine luminously upon us,
As we run, together,
along the lavishly flowered hilltop.

Carly A. Meske

My Third Eye

If I had a third eye, what would I see?
Would I see hatred, or would I see Beauty?
Would all the people change,
or would everything just be rearranged?

If my third eye could see what I do
I believe that it would agree, too,
that the world is filled with many faces,
that there are so many places.

But through all this I believe it would see
The true you,
The true me.
The you and me that hides
not faces, but our true sides.

It would see that part that we don't show.
It would see the part that only we know.

Bryan G. Joyce

Life

Life is the song of a bird,
You need to be loved, you need to be heard.
Life is the giggle of a child,
You need to be free, you need to be wild.

Life is the cycle of a flower,
It needs to be cared for every hour.

Life is the page of a book,
It needs to be given a second look.

Life is the start of a romance,
You only have one very short chance.

Life is the ink of a pen,
You need strength from words of men.

Brenda J. Goodbrad

Simplicity

People rumble through existence like clouds through the sky
All taking different routes to the same piece of pie
Then the sun soaks us all with free love and not pain
And there are still those who wish to complain
Why have worries when everything is in sync
Life is what you make of it and what you choose to think
Anything can be handled and make us all stronger
When a situation is feared a problem lasts longer
Go with the flow and let the Lord's will be your guide
Live a life of courage, and enjoy an exciting ride

Michael T. McGuckin Jr.

The Tree

I sit on my front porch and watch the beautiful tree.
It is the tree of life, the branches represent a family of love,
Our family, your family, our friends, your friends.
And every new branch is a new life of joy, a symbol of love.
All the branches intertwine with so much love to give to all.
You see the leaves fall and then you see them in bloom again,
But most of all I a treasure thee,
And I love sitting on my porch to watch my tree.

Dena Petroulias

To Listen to My Father

I can't say, "I've seen the face of God,"
But I have heard His voice.
I heard it in the heart of me,
And it was wond'rous choice.

It felt as though my chest would burst,
And then returned a calm,
That filled me with a peace divine,
As sweet as any psalm.

I know that in my heart he lives,
For when my mind does stray,
His gentle voice does speak to me,
In quiet, urging way.

Reminding me to still my tongue,
From saying bitter words,
And utter not but what is sweet,
As singing of the birds.

So when the outside world seems,
To be an irksome bother,
I turn my thoughts back down inside,
"To listen to My Father."

Leo S. Coombs

Nowhere to Go

He only needed a friend to talk,
Another man to walk his walk.
He wanted to let it out, he really tried,
But instead he kept it bottled up inside.
He kept it all inside his heart,
Soon it tore his world apart.
He searched and searched for an answer,
It ate him alive like a cancer.
No matter where he went he couldn't find a way,
No one would listen to what he had to say.
He was all alone on a lonely trail,
No one took notice to what he had to tell.
If someone had listened to what he had to say,
He might still be alive today.
He did not know how he could go on,
When all he loved seemed to be gone.
It cut at his heart like a sharp knife,
It caused this man to take his own life.
Where he is now, I don't know,
But I know he had nowhere to go.

Brian Stephens

Little Eyes upon You

No matter where you go
Or what you do
Their little eyes upon you

They look to you to see
Them through their trials and tribulations ahead
Their little eyes upon you
And they'll remember what you've said

When God puts breath into your lungs
He knows that you'll be true
To yourself, the world,
And the little eyes that are upon you

So don't give up
Just keep pressing through
But, remember
Their little eyes upon you

     Angela Sumter

In His Eyes

In his eyes what did you see?
I saw the love meant for you and me.
I can't forget all that he did,
The things he taught me as a kid.
He taught me to be responsible and
to do what was right,
To be kind to others and not to fight.
The stories he told, the jokes he said,
I sit here re-hearing them in my head.
I know that where he's going is a better place,
as I take one last look at his face,
Where he's going he shall not feel pain,
But life down here won't be the same.
Now it's time to say farewell and good-byes,
But I won't forget the love in his eyes.

     Roger E. Clark

Love and Heartbreak

Have you ever loved somebody so much it
makes you want to die inside, because that
person doesn't love you back, but your heart
won't give up, because it feels that someday
that special someone will love you, too,
until the day comes that your heart decides
to let them go, then it will be that person
who is in pain and you who is not,
because they will miss you dazing at them,
and wishing that they would be yours,
and love you as much as you love them, if not more.

     Percilla Linares

My Crystals

The rain that fall from the sky
It makes me wonder why, oh why
Why does the sky cry crystal tears?
Does it take away the children's fears?
Can it make you laugh for fun
Until the show of the big orange sun?
As the crystal fall to earth
It is a new birth
The birth of a flower or grass or tree
I wonder as the rain falls on me
Does it rain crystals for everyone?
Or are the crystals only for a special person
Can you see the diamond snowflakes?
The ones my crystal raindrop makes
The cold winter wind turns a crystal to diamond
As I see the rain and snow change and
Make a wish upon a star
I wonder as I go to sleep, where, oh, where they are.

     Allyson King

Dreams

Sometimes when I dream, I see you
In my dreams you're nothing short of perfect
I reach out to you, to feel your body against mine
But in reality you're really not there

Sometimes I wish I could sleep forever
For in my dreams you never seem to fade
Without a spoken word, you know me
Everything about me surrenders to you

Sometimes after a night's dream of you
I lay in bed still hypnotized from your touch
Holding my pillows, I want you forever
Happiness with you seems never ending

Sometimes I wonder if you dream of me
Feeling the love and tenderness ever so perfect
Not wanting to wake up, longing for more
Knowing that nothing can compare to your dream

Always, there is a place for you within me
No matter if what we share is only in a dream
For if I ever need you with me
All I have to do is dream

     Amy Blum

Cherish

Handful of sweet kisses in the wind
Softest of touches that bend
Piercing stare that melts the heart
Blow of warm breath, tickles any part
Your hands laid on my face
Touch so light, unable to trace
Eyes slowly close, scent of your hair
Eyes slowly open. . . . over's glare
Fingers mesh smoothly into one
Time together, thankful just begun
Celestial embrace, caress of curves like water's feel
In my eyes you stare as our love we seal
Perfect face between my hands, kisses then ensue
Splendor of life I feel, since I have come to cherish you
Soul's windows not open but awareness of you the same
Marvel of this gift that from Heaven must have came
Twinkle in your eyes, subtle smile upon supple lips
Hand upon my neck, heart's joy as it flips
To be next to you, to simply in your midst be
Such delight as I view, this wonder I am blessed to see

     Jonathan Hunt

A Story Book

Did you ever read a storybook?
Go ahead and have a look.

When you do you will discover
worlds and adventures unlike any other.

Jungles and castles
built from your imagination,
go and make your own creation!

Just pick me up and flip the pages,
because stories are good for many ages.

They are passed down from one to to another,
keep them alive and share them with each other.

Tell scary stories around the campfire,
but be sure to watch out for the ghost and vampire!

Tales of soldiers in wartime and battle,
brave, famous generals that ride high in the saddle.

As you can see there are many things to read,
about animals and space or even poetry!

So pick up a book and excite your mind,
You'll always be surprised
at what you find.

     Alexandra Kelly

Why

Thy race is on
You see thy light
Restraint is given, failure is accepted
Shout of joy, retarded with scream of fright
If sting is felt
Motion given stages pass
Sensation of new feign
Retarding with scare still
Cleanliness but calm sweetly clean
His speed ozone changes calm is felt
Home sinks in,
Annually a repeated day is abundant
Sucker smiles are given
Changes occur accepts me why on others
Forecast for trouble at times
Habits are pickup
Practice at times safety
It goes quick sometimes strange

Marcelino A. Dominguez

Winter Arrival

The sky turns gray and motionless.
A brisk breeze turns into a crisp wind.
The bright sky quickly fades to dark.
A dead tree limb falls to the ground.
The earth turns hard and icy.
An animal scampers away in search of warmth.
The wind turns into a piercing howl.
Followed by a white drizzle.
The drizzle takes a solid form and sticks.
Everything soon becomes covered.
The momentum builds.
Mother nature, in all her fury, unleashes her powers.
The long awaited winter storm arrives.

Nancy Lee Carreiro

My Life

In this world of disappointment and sadness, I am truly lost
I seek more than mere pleasure and self gain,
But something to be valued with no cost
There is a terrible pain that has weakened my heart and soul
It is a never-ending feeling of unhappiness,
A part of my life that's untold
There's something better for me
Than life's trials that are hard to bear
It's time for me to heal
I need understanding and care
I guess I must deserve then desire,
But without love and compassion there is no hope
My search must end soon or I will expire

Stephanie Hunt

Winter to Spring

As the winter weather gives way to spring
A sense of new life it does bring

The flowers and trees do bud these days
So that we will have shade and fragrance in May

The birds return and greet us with a song
Which gives us the feeling nothing can go wrong

The snow melts and fills the streams
We watch the water flow and dream

Spring brings new life to us all
As the snow from the tree branches fall

Spring brings new life to us this way
Let us start anew on this wonderful day

Brcue R. Kent

Give Me a Sign

Sitting up one night, thinking 'bout my Lord
then I heard this voice, it told me I had to make a choice.
If I made a choice, what choices would I make?
Would I change my life, or would I stay the same?

Then there was a light that came my way,
I thought that I was dreaming,
and this is what I had to say,
Lord, please show me the way, 'cause . . .

I am so lost without you,
so give me a sign that will last my life through.
With my heart I'll pray, that with me, you will stay,
and I won't change my mind, please give me a sign.

I stood up and stared, thoughts ran 'cross my mind.
If our lives are cruel, how would Jesus Christ be so kind?
I hope that you see how much you mean to me,
how you shed your blood that day on Calvary.

So we'll take the time to pray each day.
Without you there is no other way.
Jesus, our love for you will stay.
Hold us in your loving arms, and give us a sign.

Deserea L. Byrd

Mr. Claude Cox

My new friend, Mr. Claude, a hundred years old, is quite a fellow.
He's quite unique, kind and mellow.
Has many stories to tell and does it very well.
Comes from a family of fifteen.
Started driving a school wagon at the age of sixteen
with a team of two mules named Molly and Jack.
The mules pulled a load almost more than they could take
For he had to get those children to school on time
Through the woods with plenty of pines.
Had his breakfast of biscuits, sausage, and Louisiana molasses,
He got those children to their classes.
Through snow, sleet, rain or storm,
He kept everyone safe and warm.
Roads had deep ruts in the winter and spring,
But if it was very quiet, you could hear the birds sing.
He and his wife, Lillian, liked to dance,
Went every time they got a chance.
He farmed his land of sand and red clay,
For where there's a will there's a way
Took care of his wife and son very well.

Theresa Mixon

Equality

You may see me as just a female
But I'm more than that
I am smart, strong and capable
Of doing the same work as you
So I think it is time
For you to recognize me as your equal

It is I who gave birth to you
Loved and cared for you
Stay up at nights to feed and comfort you
Provide for you from birth to adulthood
So I think it is time
For you to recognize me as your equal

I helped when you were in trouble
And listen when you needed someone to talk to
My blood is the same color as yours
And I have proven myself by always being at your side
So I think it is time
For you to recognize me as your equal

Odiah Wallace

Nations

I don't mean to start any trouble, but if I do, what the hell
There's just certain things that I simply must
Tell, I've been keeping
To myself hoping the problem would be
Solved, but instead of fading out other
Problems have evolved.

Racism, wars, crimes, and other
Complications, they've all started because
Of a lack of communication we've accepted
The wrong way of living and it's a damn
Shame, we are the same people;
Aren't we one in the same

Do you not see with your eyes and walk on
Two feet, put food in your mouth
And chew with your teeth;
Weren't you born of a woman and help conceived
By a man, mouth to talk and a brain to understand

Maybe to see the fact that the way we are
Living is wrong and we've been living this way
Too damn long in a world
Of separation, hate, greed, and manipulation

Melisa Bell

The Accession of the Undone

As a limited factor of that which is expected the
Journey of mind and matter excludes the presence
Of deunited expression made to the long lost, as far as
Alacrity concerns momentum, experience retires
Within itself, that which is surrounding to a more
Striking selfless experience concludes judgement
Without alacrity in succession brings a sum
Moving concluding in pity attires a pendulum
Of disgrace, regulating content those who are forgiven.

Russell Manchester Veach

Sweetheart

There's nothing else I would rather do
than to spend the rest of my life right here with you.
You're most delightful to be around,
always with a smile, never a frown.
Oh, I thank God for having you here with me,
sharing and caring and never disagree.
That's what all marriages really ought to be,
and I hope we set the example for all the world to see.
I love you.

Laura Baker

Missing Child

Young mother caresses small, velvet head
While new babe suckles her breast 'til it's fed.
A moment to cherish, she holds dear to her heart.
For deep inside, she feels time is short
For babies grow up, she's heard from the start.

In young mother's arms, she cradles her child,
Envisioning daydreams of how it will be . . .
First smile, first tooth, first step, and first word;
First friend, first grade, first date, and first love;
For babies grow up, she's heard from the start.

Strong, tall, and beautiful her child will be
For it is cherished, as any can see.
Wisdom and knowledge she'll try to bestow
So her child will be noble and kind at heart.
For babies grow up, she's heard from the start.

Thus young mother believes,
And she thinks that she knows.
But, shadows steps in, and doom interferes.
In less than a blink, she holds only tears,
For there is babe in her arms nevermore . . .

T. L. Hardaway

Congratulations to You

Lord, you made a beauty when you created this world.
I'm looking at a sunset that sets my mind awhirl.

I see yellow, red and orange, gray, purple and blue.
Lord, you made a beauty—congratulations to you.

I walk through a golden meadow,
I see a distant mountain high.
I hear the call of a whippoorwill beneath a clear blue sky.

I've seen oceans, rivers, lakes and streams.
Trees with every shade of green.

I love to see a rainbow, flowers fresh with morning dew
Lord, you made a beauty, congratulations to you.

There are so many wonderful things to see and do.
When the time comes for me to start anew,
I'll give credit where it's due.

Let these last words go echoing,
Thank You Lord, and Congratulations to You

Robert LaPointe

Trip, Don't Fall

Nothing like the type of rain,
But still mysterious all the same;
Liquid or a gel type form
Makes a man go insane.

On your tongue or in your eye,
Things you see are all a lie.
In a crazy man's utopia,
You can tear a hole in the sky.

With me you can't seal a thought.
It's so crazy I was brought.
To take my poison knowingly,
Strychnine always being fought.

I'll put the bubble on your spine,
Solid though, you'll feel just fine.
If my bubble decides to burst,
My gifts your nightmares, all times nine.

Take me for an alteration.
Give the normal variation.
Awaken from my almost slumber,
See it normal, God's creation.

Ken Drazen

A Jeffersonian's Melancholy Obsession

There is someone for everyone
A girl for every guy
Except for me, no girl I see
Alas, I think she died

No girlfriend or wife I have
And perhaps I never will
The girl that God had chose for me
I guess somehow got killed

I lay in bed as nighttime falls
I roll over and there I see
Lo and behold, not a single soul
No wife lying next to me.

No Valentines, no romantic dinners
No exchange of gifts and such
No snuggling, cuddling, hugging, no nothing
No smiles or kisses—no love

"We walk by faith, not by sight."
This statement is my heart's cure
For if what we see was what set us free
Then I'd be Hell bound for sure

Gary Thompson

Why Does Life Have to Be So Difficult for Me?

When I think I'm doing things right,
I always cause a fight.
I don't know what I'm doing wrong,
I've been trying for so long.

Everyday, it's something new,
Is it me or is it you?
Why can't you
Just see the good I do?
Try to take my point of view.

You treat me like a child,
then tell me to be a mother.
Which is it? One or the other?

I'm just so confused.
I thought the path that I used was the good one.
I didn't expect it to be fun,
But tell me, when do the good times come?

Stop, knocking me down, I'm trying!
But my heart is dying,
I don't know which to be . . . .
A full time mother or me . . . .

Annmarie Mill

Perfect Absolution

Fingers of golden light stream through the casement window
Bathing the room in soft shades of saffron and topaz.
Light that pulsates and vibrates, its warmth a living presence.
A man lies upon the bed, light radiating from him, transforming him.

The flesh has melted from his body but his profile
And the graceful, slender fingers of his hands testify
To the elegance of his earthly shell wasted by illness.
All that remains now is the essence of the man.

A woman kneels by the man's bedside, holding his hand.
Silently they regard each other, lips curved in gentle smiles.
Her eyes lift to the crucifix hanging above the bed
Suddenly she is overwhelmed, consumed with grief.

"Oh God," she cries, laying her head upon his pillow.
Bitter tears course down her face anointing the
Hand that rests beneath her cheek.
"Forgive me for words that wounded, for my impatience. . . ."

The words continue, a litany of pain and contrition.
The man, raising his hand, traces the sign of the cross
Upon her forehead, blessing her with her tears
He whispers, "All you ever gave me was love. . . ."

Mary A. Schifferli

Our Love

There are few people that can truly say
They fell in love in one short day.
Yet on a blind date, when we first met,
I'd of gladly placed and won that bet.
We found a love that few have known,
A love that daily has grown and grown.
With lots of respect, honesty, and trust,
We found the love no one could bust.
We'd rather be together than be far apart,
Yet when we need a little space, we give it from the heart,
And if we have a little spat and things are not quite right,
We always say we're sorry before retiring at night.
Our love is expressed in so many ways,
Hugs, kisses, and saying I love you every day.
Most people say the love we have is very, very rare
To us it seems so natural because we really care.
So as time passes and we grow old,
We pass our love for you to hold.

Shelley Russell

Wailing Woman

Mother of four, your prayers
have been heard by reason of your pain.

You feel as though you have
nothing to lose, nothing to gain
your Lord and Savior is acquainted with grief.

Mother of four it's time to release
the weights and burdens that
weigh you down;
look to Jesus, he's all around.

Nathaniel Parker

Alone

People aren't any damn good I see you're hurting,
Tell me of your pain, I'll listen, offer you hope.
What do you give me? Friendship yes,
Ignorance also,
Can't you tell how I feel,
outside I'm smiling,
inside I'm bleeding,
People passing by,
like a phantom, I go unnoticed,
can't they see,
don't they know,
How I hurt deep inside,
crying tears of blood,
I know hundreds,
but I'm alone.

Shane R. Migliavacca

Ascension

Her grace flows over their glad forms
Like lapping waters.
Where far off a mighty squall
Is blasted into sunlight and swallows
And flowers fly from her dress to the sky.
This was not a dream or some stupid "I!"
Phantoms found their way into the back, back country
And found me drunk with a stagger and a sway,
And touched me on the shoulder to bid me good day.
Everything's still as her grace wins them over,
And may I implore no one to be polite,
Except the poet who thought he saw moonlight on snow.

Alfred B. Strehli Jr.

Wind Dancer

Rituals of fantasy dance
Within the magic of the forest;
A song of mystery flows
along atmospheric winds
of a midsummer's night.

It is a song without its word,
A story unspoken.
The celestial melody floats
from the inner depths of dreams
to the earth below
as the spirit of the music is conjured.

It drifts about me
like angels in flight,
drifting, transcending into the wind dancer.
Once a wish is made under the light of the moon,
then I may dream and give it wings to fly.
The wind is the song's voice;
its spirit shall be my salvation.

Tiffany Shapiro

Memories of Sweet Corn

It is early morning.
A low lying fog is hanging over the fields,
Clinging to the rows of withering corn
That rustle about in the gentle wind.
The mystery of autumn is playing
With the once sturdy green stalks of summer;
Now only a remembrance in the mind.
Out of the magic of summer
Came the tassel-topped broad leaves
Under which lay the coveted golden ears of corn.
Emerging for my enjoyment,
My reward for patience endured.
Indulging the luscious kernels,
Butter oozing is satisfaction complete.
With memories intact,
I will wait in anticipation
For next summer's gift;
This succulent delight.

Jane West Adams

Love Connection

It's a love connection. It's a big romance.
I love sports and I love dance.
I can jump and I can slide.
I can wrestle and I can ride.
I can skate and I can dive.
There's not a wheel that I can't drive.

I can forte' and tap the buck-time step.
I can do a grapevine and an arabesque.
I can do a neck-roll and clog a cow's tail.
But my favorites are the handsprings; I can sail!
It's a love connection. It's a big romance.
I love sports and I love dance.

Samee Jo Smith

Spirit of the Dead

I have brought nothing but pain and regret
to the world around more than once or twice before.
I am fearing that it has finally caught up with me.
The guilt of killing brings me no pleasure.
There isn't a day that goes by without thinking, without craving.
Her luxurious pink lips, her cream-colored skin, and her
long chestnut hair that reminds me of silk each time I touch it.
Each time I come and sit in the tree nearby her ledge,
I tell myself over and over again, no, this isn't the time.
Who once was a man now disguises himself
as a preposterous monster with unbelievable blood thirsts.
Unbelievable powers that can cloud a man's mind!
I can take her now and have her forever, or I can have
her life running through me, filling me with the will to live.

I do not know why I am writing this down,
perhaps to just make up my mind or get the thought out of my mind.
Perhaps both.
To whomever reads this you must understand, I love her too
much to have her, I know this, and so does the monster.
Good-bye sweet rose, good-bye . . .

Jessica Stewart

Remember

Look into the heavens
And try to find what is there
Remember all that has come.
Remember and relive all that was good
And remember and learn from all that is bad.
Hold love ones tight,
And cry tears of joy for a life lived
Not for a life lost.
Remember all that was her
And cherish all memory's, left behind.

Andy Timmerberg

I'll Swim

Repeated fuzzy lines on my broken television
that I tripped over and found your band-aid,
that only covers a piece of me on paper
sent, mailed, billed, insure, assured a cure for my silent crisis
The clouds, the tick, scream—terribly, loudly. Too much
of your advice, Doc—your couch, your framed certificates, your meds
to take with food, taste my grievances, cure my mood
Kill the crow by electric shock therapy—toaster in my bath
in your mind you adjectives for sadness,
my sadness, my floods
in your world,
in your wooden ark,
I think I'll swim.

Julia Schieffer

Harmagedon Will Come

Eye better watch out,
because Harmagedon is getting closer.
He could leap upon me at anytime.
He could jump on me from anywhere.
I better look out,
because Harmagedon is getting close.
He is fast and quick to snag his prey.
He might be upon me any day.
Eye better be alert,
because at any time he might be here.
He might show up from anywhere.
Harmagedon is getting closer.
At the war of the Great Day,
God the Almighty's Day, he will play.
He would destroy plastic (Credit Cards),
the entire System that won't fear God.
I better be ready, because he is near.
At the appointed time he'll be right here.
Yes, Harmagedon will come, all in good time.
He won't be just my kitten, at play, next time.

Angel Michael Master

Poetry Inside of Me

I wake up with poetry on my mind,
In the mid of the night you'll see my light.
It will be clicking on at two o' nine,
And all of this so I may write.

I wake up with poetry in my heart,
In the morning it is ever strong.
These thoughts come whispering by like darts,
And so I write a little long.

I wake up with poetry in my brain.
My blood is carrying the words like loads.
Trickling in my head through veins,
I believe I have too much disclosed.

Jessica Dotter

Prescience

This thing, I do not actually perceive;
Rather, a disturbance
Of light and air.

Too busy for still and silent space,
Something less than knowing
Something more.

Imbued with attrition of general instinct,
Less explicit than second sight
A sure thing.

Without name, or much substance,
I cancel the cognitive process
And let it ride.

Peg Plante

Going Back

Today I am going back to before the death of my dad.
I can't remember the way he smelled.
I can't remember the way his voice sounded.
I can barely remember the way he looked.
But most of all I can't remember the way it felt to have him here.
The thought of those scares me,
because each day I am losing my memory of my dad.

I am going back to the Grand Canyon.
I will stand by the railing we stood by so many years ago,
but this time I will be standing alone.
I am going back to California.
I will walk the streets of Chinatown alone.
I will stand by the bridge in San Francisco
and look out into the water knowing
I stood her long ago with my dad.

I will also visit other places he never got to go to.
Then when it's all over and I'm back in my bed,
I will cry because my dad is not here.

Andrea Resendiz

Angels

Kindred spirits,
Fellow friends
Joyful angels
Friendly souls,
Love is a feeling only you can give,
Yet not see with eyes.
Your blissful nature in touch with me
Delightful compatriots,
Reasonable pals
Your heavenly lilts,
Compassionate laughs
Your jubilant smiles,
You elate my feelings of hope.
Your gentle caresses,
Your caring kisses
You console my fear and anguishes with your calming
Patience and warm love.
You are my angels.

Veronica Alvarez

Battered Angel

Blonde-haired, blue-eyed, bundle of joy,
A smile like the morning sunshine;
Though only two or three
One can't imagine life without her in it.
The Play-do pie for "pap"
And cookies with grandma;
This and so much more
"Smashed"
By an adult animal.
Battered, bloodied, and broken,
This little one is nursed back to health.
The outside heals in weeks,
The inside will take longer.
This little angel survived this time,
And will shine again.
Please protect the "little angels"
of the world.

James L. Miller Jr.

A True Friend

If you have a true friend
do not let them go.
Because a true friend is not bonded
by the usual things other friendships are.
It is not bonded by the usual things,
like wealth, sex, race, religion or politics.
My friend, do you know the answer?

Abraham L. Allen Jr.

Nothing Left but Memories

There she's sitting all alone, at a table she set for two
She tells herself she's crazy. There's no one home but you.
Her kids grew up and moved away, they never seem to call
All she ever sees of them, are the pictures on the wall,
Her husband gave his solemn you, 'til death do us part
The Doctors gave him weeks to live, they said that it's his heart,
She lost herself in losing him she was never quite the same
Wherever she gets frightened, she still calls out his name,
Already it's tomorrow, it's time to start again
She hears them knocking at the door, she hurries to let them in,
It's just the same old story, there's no one really there.
Now it starts to take its toll, it's more than she can bear,
Now she's hearing voices, she hears the children call
Mommy look at us, we're playing in the hall,
They say she's living in a world, that's really all her own
She's spending countless hours, just staring at the phone,
Now she really sits alone, at a home that's made for many.
She wants to have her photographs, but they didn't bring her any,
With nothing left but memories, she just waiting for the day,
When they come with open arms, to carry her away.

Darryl E. Brothers

Emotions

Emotions spinning around my head
Corner to the left I'm happy, corner to the right I'm mad
What possesses us to choose which corner?
Right always starts a fight; left is plain and simple, a smile
How can one minute a smile turn
upside down into a so disturbing frown?
Maybe perhaps you turned your head
a little too far to one side or the other
And then sometimes when you have to pick sides it causes a different
emotion called confusion
Why does everything have to be so complex?
My head is spinning along with these emotions
making sadness, happiness, madness—everything at once crowding me
Stop—give me space
Only space, sit
I sit down and write all the emotions away
Until the next day!

Jamie Forrester

My Christmas Wish, Hopes, Prayers

This Christmas ends another year
unlike any beyond the rest,
with so many things left unsaid
and so little we have done

With the new year around the bend,
let's take the time to spend
it on love, and health, and happiness,
and vacationing and rest

And for everyone out there I do not know,
I wish you peace, love, hope, and
just all the best

And with thought of so many
whom I love and have gone away
I cherish our times and thinks and thoughts.

And even though I can't have you here with me
I know you will never, ever be far away
And so, when next we meet
we will share our lives again.

Mr. Solitaire

My Husband, My Love

In September, we met;
In January, we fell in love.
In April, our wedding day we set.
In June, you were given me by God above.

In September, our first born we awaited.
In April, our lives were blessed with a son.
Our love for each other was unabated,
And we truly became one.

Our love grew even deeper with each passing day.
One winter, a second son was born.
With your own hands, you planted the fields in May.
We watched together as our sons grew tall like the corn.

Our family lived happily on our little piece of land.
Our love remained strong and true.
One January, your eyes grew misty, as you took me by the hand.
I held you tightly and prayed for God to let you live anew.

But, in May, God called you home, and you are no longer mine.
My husband you were, for years of twenty and four.
My darling, my love you will be for the rest of my time,
And when to Heaven I come, you will be my husband once more.

Linda M. Naylor

'Round and 'Round

Does it make you happy now that you said it?
Cut me straight to the bone I'll give you credit.
Gotta make you pay now, just see if I can't.
Not gonna sit here listen to you rant.

Tit for tat 'n' blow for blow, who can hurt the worst?
Gonna fix you somehow 'cause you hurt me first.
Talk about your mama and her lowdown ways.
Cuss about your friends, too. Yeah, we'll see who pays.

Screaming in the kitchen, yelling down the hall,
Kick at the furniture, throw things at the wall.
Guess we went too far now to take it all back.
I didn't mean all of that; you don't have to pack.

Said some things I don't mean, tell me you did too.
Don't want you to cry, hon, tell me what to do.
We've made it through rough times, and stormy weather,
Thing I can't believe is, We're Still Together.

Daniel C. Copeland

Alone

As the sun set slowly in the west,
Two by two birds seek their nest.
Through the trees the soft winds moan,
One lonely bird sits all alone.

The one he "loves" has spread her wings,
and flown in search of better things.
The lonely bird sits on a stone,
To watch the sunset, all alone.

The moon and stars are shining bright,
The sky will soon be full of light.
The song he sings has a lonesome tone
As he sits and watches all alone.

The dawn will break, the sun will shine,
the lonely bird asks, where is mine?
For him the sun has not yet shone,
As he watches the sunrise all alone.

Without his "love" to share each day,
The darkness will never go away.
The bright sun shines upon the stone,
Where the lonesome bird sits all alone.

Rex W. Law

Feelings

Baby you give me butterflies
That only helps me realize
How lucky I am
To be standing here hand in hand
You make me feel things I've never felt before
I love you now and forever more.
It was love right from the start
you hold the key to my heart.
I want to spend the rest of my life
with you by side.
I tell you the truth
and never no lies.
I'd never hurt your feelings
or make you want to cry.
I'll make you so happy; never sad
I'll make it so good; never bad.
It's my heart that you touch,
that makes me love you so much.

Richard Caruso

Because I Trusted

Letters and poems, words so sweet,
With such good looks, I was swept off my feet.
Foolish to think, much less to believe,
This man could ever really love me.
One day I'll be okay, the pain will be gone,
And know what I should have all along.
Crossing that line caused this awful fate,
But I will never succumb to dreaded hate.
Looking in the mirror I feel no shame,
And when tears come, I'll call out your name.
Over my head, a dark cloud does loom,
Feeding this pain 'til it is full bloom.
A long time wait, restoring my fears,
During this time, I'll shed many tears.
Why should I cry or hurt for so long,
Because I trusted, and again I was wrong!

Frances R. Oliver

The Good Soul

The good soul we have,
Yes, the one He gave us,
It's there we have to take it.
Without that soul, O yes that good soul,
it will make us and also break us!
Such a tragedy it would be,
To exempt it from daily life,
Just keep it, please keep it and never leave it.
It's not only for times of strife.
Humanity, with whom we live,
Very brittle, coarse, and mean,
also gentle, peaceful, full of life,
and beautiful like a porcelain bowl,
let's take our life in sinc,
learn from good and bad things we did yesterday and today,
because remember we have "The Good Soul"

Glossaydian Pettaway II

The Blair Witch

In slumber repose, a woodland, a Blair Witch I see.
A wrongful death, a boon, a granted death decree.
Search not, a Blair Witch cry, a warning plea.
In spirit veil, a friend, a foe neither she be.
A mortal life taken, a spirit forsaken is she.
Enter portal, a step in time, a Blair Witch see.
In one day given a test, a time allotted to flee.
A sojourn, a twenty-fifth hour, a bell tolls for thee.
The moans, a spirit cries, a Blair Witch forever see.
In times past, a spirit melds, a mortal no longer be.
A disappearance, a nightmare, a vision, a fantasy.
Not in life, but in death, the Blair Witch all will see.

Jack Keys

Hummingbird

Always in search of a scarlet flower,
Long needle-nose to drink luscious nectar,
With wings moving a million miles per hour,
The small body becomes an inspector.
A little bigger than a bumblebee,
So light it can perch on a stem of grain,
Able to dart upward quickly to flee,
He continues to stay in one domain.
At first, he flew by the pale gazebo,
Then, started toward his nested home, instead
The hummingbird appeared at the window,
While searching for a tint or shade of red.
So I observed him 'til he flew away,
And I hope he comes back another day.

Kayleen Cress

My Place

I know that we will never be together.
Even if we were I know that it wouldn't be right.
To even think about him makes me shiver all over.
When I see him with her I can't help
but think that she is taking my place,
I guess that is why I don't like her.
I feel as if she has taken my place.

Even after the way I feel about him,
I know that I truly love my husband.
I know that he is the one and only that
I am to be with. Even if I could
I wouldn't trade my husband for this other man.

Daniella Escritt

Brother's Keeper!

Am I my brother's keeper, I think I'd better be,
for if I can help another, then another may help me;

I may help by just a touch, or maybe a hug or two,
a smile may cheer a brother, who is sad and blue;

I have oft been renewed by a calm, Godly voice,
and even just a touch, gives me reason to rejoice;

A word of encouragement, may be just the thing,
that will turn a pauper into feeling like a king;

With so many small things, we help one another,
if we all would believe, we do keep our brother!

Dovie J. Lane

Spring

Inhale the beauty sense of spring
Hear the birds chirp and sing

Look at the bright flowers that have sprung
For the season of spring has begun

Red, yellow, purple, blue
These are the colors surrounding you

Outside I play all day
But night is soon on the way

I listen to the crickets chirp at night,
Look up at the stars that are so bright

Now upstairs I lie in bed
"Go to sleep," my mother said

I hear no sound, not even a peep
As the world around goes to sleep

Amanda Rose Liotine

Life

Life is like an ocean, always changing and churning,
life is like a fire, filled with hearts burning.
Life is wild, life is free.
Life is a horse's mane in the wind.
Life is a wire you should never try to break or bend.
Life is God's dream, and His creation.
You should make life your celebration!

Angela Walton

Ret

My pet's name is Ret.
Ret went in a jet.
He went up high I bet.
The vet said, "Get him down here, he's wet."
I said, "Am I going to get my pet yet?"
I got my pet.
I let him play with my barrette set.
He took off with my barrette set.
I had to catch him with a net.
After traveling all around,
Now we're going homeward bound.
Now we're home safe and sound.

Melissa Williams

Daddy's Last Words

My little Lizzie Lu,
Don't be blue.
Death cannot stop my love for you.
In life too many emotions I did hide.
In spite of sorrows I had to go through;
There were blessings so great even though they were few.
One of my greatest gifts in life, you.
Part of myself reflected in you giving me pride.
Working hard one of the only things I knew.
But my favorite thing, loving you.
My sweet little girl, I'm sorry I wasn't more true.
Even though it is my time, I will still be at your side.
Too many changes, it seems there is always something new.
This is so strange for me and you.
However you'll be fine, you've a lot of strength and
compassion to see you through.
Yet if you need me, just whisper my name I'll be there,
our hearts forever tied.
So my sweet little Lizzie Lu,
Please don't be blue.

Drea

Will You Watch over My Wings?

Will you watch over my wings as I begin to gather my things?
I'm taking a trip to a place called Earth
To experience the grandest vision of my birth.

I'm here to remind you we're more than human beings.
I'm here to remind you of many things.

We are on this journey to experience what we are not.
So listen carefully for you have forgot.

We are not killers in the night.
We are not evil spirits in this world of light.

Who we are are spiritual beings.
We are little souls from Heaven made up of many things.

We are little souls made up of pure love.
We need not hurry or push or shove.

And when my journey on Earth is done,
I will return to our home above.

And waiting there in the midst of the clouds
Will be my wings standing proud.

Jeanette L. DiPasquale

Thoughts

I have a complicated mind, I am hard to figure out;
There are things I dream up others never think about.
I hear of tragedies in other people's lives;
It breaks my heart to see their pain for I'm the one who cries.
I know that I can't live my life constantly in fear;
Yet some how it never fails I end up right in tears.
All I want is peace of mind, someone to tell me that it is okay;
So that I may have the strength to go on one more day.
My mother's life is all messed up, she hardly wants to live.
My sister-in-law feels quite the same.
They believe that there is no more either can give.
I feel their sadness although there is nothing that I can do,
But sit around and think about all that they can lose.
This world is full of people, many just like me.
It is time we learn to pull away and work on our own strategies.

Candice Kocher

My Only One True Love

Far and wide, as my heart grew strong,
To figure out why, and what was wrong.
She cast a spell, that my heart would hold,
But wanting to tell, with my heart so bold.
Those three little words, she longed to hear,
While watching the birds, as I held her near.
With her long blonde hair, and gem stone eyes,
Brought together as a pair, like two clouds in the skies,
The moment came, as my mouth opened wide,
Feeling the same, as I said the words with pride.
From deep inside I love you, I really, really love you,
These words I say are true, as she replied I love you too.
I wish you knew that dame, the girl from up above,
The one who will remain, my only one true love.

Jeffrey M. Prichard

Swimming with the Dolphins

I have dreamt of swimming with the dolphins,
but a tiger shark lurks behind.
He has followed me most of my life, not allowing me to unwind

But still I dream of that swim out in the ocean blue
If I can only shake that shark, I would have the courage to "do"

The chance to swim with these warriors comes only at a certain time
Will I be able to capture their energy and leave that shark behind?

I've mustered up the courage and my chance has finally come
To seize this opportunity . . . to swim with them as one

Patience is what I'm told, persistence is what I hear
In a race to catch the dolphins before that shark comes near

With all my might and strength I race to reach my goal
But I suddenly realize that the dolphins have control

So I stopped and grounded, seeing patience as the key
And before I realized it, the dolphins were coming to me

So I swam with the dolphins, with all the love that I could find
Soon to discover that the tiger shark was only in my mind.

Tiffany H. Nelson

Beloved Child

My beloved child, how I love you.
Through all the years and tears we have shared
It is I who feels honored.
To have loved you, taken care of you,
Then to release you and learn to let go.

To spare you of life's heartaches,
Hurts and pain would be my prayer.
But I release you to the Great Spirit,
Setting us both free,
Knowing in my heart, how high you will soar.
You are my greatest love,
But also my greatest pain.

Montella Smith

A Time for Fun

Oh, what joy, oh, what fun,
My three favorite months will now come.

October is full of treats and tricks,
candy, pumpkins, apples on sticks.

November will be a family time,
enjoying the blessings with a family that's mine

Turkey, dressing, pies and cranberry,
all dressed up and feeling merry.

December my favorite of all,
a Christmas tree big and tall,
with lots of surprises on Christmas Day,
and lots of bills for mom and dad to pay.

Bills to pay, but they don't mind,
as a better mom and dad you couldn't find.

For a child of any age, "waiting" is the hardest of all,
for you see October, November, December are the
most exciting months of all.

Jacqueline T. Jobski

A Day We Will Never Forget

The most fun we kids ever had
Is when we went fishing with dear old dad.
We stopped to pick up our great grand pop
When we got to our fishing hole, there stood a cop.

Their license he told them, he wanted to see.
They were astonished and shocked as could be.
Both reached in their pockets, but none could be found.
They knew that their butts had then hit the ground.

He gave them a ticket, nine dollars it said.
We could tell by their faces, they wished he was dead.
But they give him the money, reluctant I say.
It screwed up their fishing for the rest of the day.

All of you fisherman better take a heed.
Get you a license, it's much cheaper indeed.
If you have your license, to the cops you can yell,
Take a look at this buddy and go straight to Hell!

Alma L. Everett

A Haunted House

A haunted house upon a hill,
The rigid cliffs far below,
The gushing sea, its forceful waves,
That carry memories of those old, old days.

The misted night, its darkness pitch,
The wind blows on with all its might,
And only then can you catch sight,
Of the haunted house, with the age old plight.

The floorboards creak, the walls do groan,
The dust covered objects stand all alone,
What misery does one bestow,
Upon this pitiful sight.

Suddenly out of the quietness comes the hooting of an owl,
Who sits upon a branch so far,
In the garden of the house.
This echoed noise, its strain so high,
Adds greatly to the haunted way,
Of telling humans stay away.
Let peace linger on, do not stop this woe,
It's part of history of so long, long ago.

Colleen Frankland

The Silent Feelings

The deep side of feelings,
The absences of love,
The touches of tears upon my high cheekbones.
If there no wonder of the world,
There no polish of darkness
that live in a hollow forest.
May heartbeats of sound,
but not of love and cries
Abate the sound of love,
that spring from each lips of a man and a woman.

Treena Black

What Words Cannot Describe

When words cannot describe how I feel,
that is when I realize how much I love you.
If I were to climb the highest mountain, or swim the widest sea,
I would easily find the words to tell the tale
of the adventure I had endured, yet in loving you,
I would struggle to make you understand what words cannot describe.
If I were to see a heavenly angel before me,
I would come up with a million ways to describe how it felt.
To say how it felt when you first told me that you love me,
I would be tongue tide,
the words mean nothing when I put them up to you to define you.
Those words don't hold a torch to you and your love . . .
These are the words I say to you
when I fail to find what words cannot describe.

Ophelia Mensah Koduah

He's the Same

He created Heaven and Earth
when the whole world was dark,
divided the waters and kept them apart.
He's the one that gave us life
and loved us all the way.
He's the same Savior that we serve today.

He's the same, Yes, He's the same
as He was in days before.
He still heals the sick and provides for the poor.
He'll never forsake you. Praise His Holy name!
Just call upon Him for He's still the same.

He's the one Moses called on and had
the Red Sea part and locked the
door when Noah entered the ark.

He's the one that gave His Son,
for our sins He did pay, had His wise
men write the Bible so we wouldn't
go astray, He's the same Savior that
we serve today.

Ruby Tarlton

A Baby's Story

Ssshhh! Ssshhh! Ssshhh! My mommy says
When I start to cry,
My mommy is not a bit shy.
She holds me with lots of love,
Then I know the angels are watching above
I've been there,
I made friends, and it seems fair,
They say babies kick their moms and dads.
And half of us are lads,
Anyway, we'll always love them,
That will always be love's stem
I'm a baby full of glory.
And that will be my story.

Maggie Glide

Stream

The stream runs, runs, runs to the seashore.
Giggling, singing, laughing, gurgling.
Running always running.
Never stopping, always changing
Rushing, gushing, roaring, tearing.
Never silent, never still
Never sleeping, always running
Dashing, twisting, winding, sneaking away.
Sometimes wider sometimes narrower.
Always running, ever faster
Always going away, away, always going away.
It has come upon a friend, faster wider now.
Together frolicking, laughing, playing
River running, ever faster, ever wider
Always down, winding, twisting, twirling.
Drawing ever nearer, nearer to the seashore.
Closer now it can see the sky touch the sea
Faster now, its goal is almost met
Sprinting now and then it is there
It has gone all the way to the seashore.

Andrew Petruska

The Dalmatian Dance

The fire bells are clanging, all must get up,
With four in the air and a flip with a roll,
Clown paws sliding, this black-on-white pup,
Rounding a corner bounces off the fire pole.

She bounds for the stairs at a skidding speed,
Swishing the landing as her ears take flight,
The stairs' route is quick, missing all but three,
A bouncy ball of ears with a tail—what a sight.

No time for worry, she lands with a thump,
Whirls and scampers with all of her might,
Must catch the red engine in one mighty jump,
Chin over paws she clings, her friends in sight.

Her yelp cries "Wait!" as hands reach down,
With wagging and spinning and a wiggly prance,
She squirms in her place, watching all around
Each time the fire bell calls, the Dalmatian dance.

Edward L. Campbell

A Light in a Snowy Winter Fog

Cold as it seems and a dense amount of light.
It's there only to be seen by the naked eye.
To be drenched out in freezing rain,
And sweat just pouring off your brow.
You try so hard but the snow just keeps falling
Pushing back all those dreams that you had in the morning.
You push harder then a relief is near.
A voice calls to you come in; it's mighty cold out there.
A lantern is put on a porch to show you the light.
Fog is threatening even your light,
Putting back tools and starting back,
Getting closer then steps are near.
Going inside and getting warm makes the evening worth
More than behold from a dreadful night and a scary morn.

Rollette A. G.

The Eye of a New Day

Your lids open up to the imagination of what's to come.
Look through the window of your heart.
You will find a prism filled with brilliant colors.
Each color a symbol of life's trials and tribulations,
Each color a symbol of hope and prosperity.
As that prism radiates the power of life, it is a
Reminder that anything is possible.

William Tomasak Jr.

The War

Battles fought for land and love
fought for rights to believe
an exchange of death for life
fought for freedom's reprieve
control and power and riches
food and every other thing
freedom for every man
war does promise to bring
killing for another's welfare
makes this a just fight
taking a life for principle
seems to make this death right
but war does leave no riches
it leaves no freedom or love
it only leaves barren everything it touches
salted with men's blood
I have rarely heard stories or ever seen a battle
in which good and evil stood separate sides
I have all too often witnessed stupidity committing suicide

Matthew J. Benner

Treasured Memories

I store all my treasured memories
In the attic of my mind
I am the only one who holds the golden key
That will unlock the small carved, arched door
To all my secret and beautiful treasures
Waiting patiently for me to
Make my way up the long, steep, shadowy,
Winding, narrow staircase
Through the magical doorway
Ready to put the stars back in my eyes.

With my flickering candle
I walk slowly through the dust and cobwebs
In the ghostly light
Savoring, feeling, reliving
The love, care, comfort, warmth, blessing,
Joy, laughter, smiles, inspiration, words, music,
Hugs, kisses, sharing
Found in the eyes, arms, mouths and voices
Of the special souls who I have found
Along the winding pathways of my life

Miki Cheyene

The Teacher

Years ago I didn't know what I was going to be.
So off I went to check it out and see what I could see.
A thousand jobs both here and there—the great ones out of reach.
To show how much the minds screwed up, I decided I would teach.
School was neat, I studied hard. Did everything I could.
And after four long lost good years, a teacher proudly stood.
Got my job and settled in. My license proudly shown.
I'd do my best to teach these kids—If only I had known.
You shed your skin to make it work.
Your thoughts and heart you share.
You feel for them inside and out—and search for one who cares.
Some do, most don't. A smile as good as gold.
Bless their hearts and kick their butts,
They're young as we grow old.
I've tried for years—through joys and tears.
They've torn me through and through.
And even though we know it all, there's always something new.
And now as years go by it seems the students I have fought.
It's not the kids who've had the lesson—
It's the teacher who's been taught.

Val Walters

Bravery

On the edge of my hospital bed
All sorts of thoughts were flying through my head
Is crying for girls does it make you weak
What are you suppose to do when things look bleak

Is it brave to lie
Say everything is fine
Or is it brave to cry
And tell people why
You might help someone just like you
Isn't that what brave people do?

Life is full of tough stuff
And you might go insane
If your emotions build up
After all I've been through
I can now explain: it's okay to cry when you're blue or in pain

Bravery comes from within
It is what gives you the ability to win.
People are wrong who say don't cry
Dealing with your emotions make it easier to survive

Jonathan Ruller

War inside a Rectangle

In the world of sports
No spectacle is more exhilarating
Than two Afro-American teams
Attired in brightly colored uniforms
Whose tattooed bodies twitch
In improvisational acts of aggressive athleticism
Battling for relative superiority
In height, strength, quickness, and jumping ability
Moving non-stop back-and-forth
Inside a rectangular basketball battlefield.

Aerial and ground assaults upon a cylindrical target
A spherical missile with rotational spin
Propelled by human and gravitational forces
Moving along a trajectory over outstretched hands
Its flight ends with a flicker of a nylon net
Igniting the crowd into a frenzied roar
The unresolved conflict continues
Until time runs out
Leaving winners and losers exhausted
And the fans thirsting for more

Mark L. Taff M.D.

The Glory of Easter

Blessed is the name
Of life, Hosanna, the long awaited one.
Why, I am the dark young lady in the lovely illuminating scenes.
The stage, the stage is ever so beautiful filled
With brilliant, brilliant beautiful decor.
The crowd, the crowd, the crowd sits in amazement
As we present "The glory of Easter."
They shout what is it all about? "What is the glory of Easter?"

It is an Easter to remember,
Where the eggs are prepared and colored precisely well.
It is the best Easter that anyone can ever dream or imagine.
It is the Easter where the duck is forever fine
And where we sit at the Master's feet reminiscing the way we were.
We were lost but now we are found.
Others said, "We were blind but now can see."
Actually, we sat remembering a passerby say,
"I was blind but now I can see."
The townspeople shouted, "Who did this?"
And I stood in the midst as they shouted,
"The Master, the Master has healed the blind man."
"Come and see for the glory of Easter is finally here as you can see!"

Charlena Wells Bradley

There Is a Way

There is a way, there is a way
To open up a bright new day.

If your heart is filled with pain
Close your eyes and start again.

Don't look back to yesterday
But look ahead to this new day.

New friends to meet along the way,
New songs to sing the blues away.

New fields of flowers come into view
And song birds sing their songs for you.

The sun will shine; 'thou there is rain,
The rain will wash away the pain.

Just keep in mind new joys to find
New hope, new dreams, new peace of mind.

Happiness is yours this day
And hold this truth; there is a way.

   Merri C. Grant

Tasty Nerve Toxin

MSG, what can it be?
A toxic substance for you and me.
The FDA says, "Hey, no way!"
You can create your own
But there's an easier way . . .
A company called Glutamate
Can make us eager to clean our plate.

As it erodes our minds each passing day
Our complaints are just explained away
Help will never come our way
Because the FDA gets paid to play
With our minds and bodies that are aging fast
With the hope that we will never last
Long enough to prove our fate
Due to manufactured glutamate.
The protection of the FDA
Has continued to just keep fading away.
The delay, it seems, is to hesitate
Action against producers of Glutamate.

   Kathy Menard

Remembrance

As Christmas day dawns, we all shed a tear
For days gone by, for you're not here.
Your sparkling eyes that gave us a lift
When it was your turn to open a gift.

Fussing over your stocking with such delight
And opening each package was quite a sight!
It was such fun to buy you those silly things
Just to see your reaction to what Santa brings!

Then, on came the music and up you would get
To dance to a tune we will never forget.
Yes, we remember the days with your happy face,
And your wonderful ways so full of grace.

You enriched us and taught us and gave us your best
And now you're in Heaven enjoying your rest.
Free of all pain and worry and care
And one day we will join you there.

Yes, we miss you and love you and remember the days
When you filled our lives with your wonderful ways.

   Pam Slavik

Ode to a Dear Sister

When I am feeling lonely and blue
My thoughts, dear sister, turn to you.
I think of days that have come and gone
And of the joys and sorrows, that came along.
With laughter and some tears
Our love has lasted through the years
There is no way for you to see,
How very much you mean to me.
Although we are now, miles apart
Theres always a place within my heart
To keep those memories, I love so much
And know we can always keep in touch.
To share our hopes and dreams,
Some that did come true,
But in our hearts we know, we have done the best,
that we could do, for ourselves and loved ones, we hold dear
Our memories we will cherish, year after year.

   Maggie L. Henderson

Endless Love

Oh the joy, my beloved, the endless joy of spending time with you.
The warmth of your touch makes me understand
The depths of the love that you give to me.
Days have gone by since I've been with you,
Yet alone in a room I still feel your presence.
Although you're not here with me,
You're always here in me.
Your amazing love, oh, what endless love,
That stretches far beyond all measure.
And what peace you bring to comfort me.
I hear you in the trees, see you in the rushing river,
You are everywhere I am.
Oh, how deep my love goes for you,
This burning desire to be with you every day of my life.
But oh, how soon we will be together for eternity.
My passion for you will burn deeper every day
Until the day we may be together.
There is nothing that can satisfy this thirst for you.
My precious, my love, my beloved, you are the only one
I long for, now, forever and always.

   Stephanie Collins

Sounds of the Wild West

On a cold winter's morning, I stood in the valley
By a ranging river and listened with my soul.
The wind in the tree tops, the churning of the waters,
I stood quietly listening to the story they told.

They told of sacred mountains, of Indian tribal dances,
The honor of the red man, before the white man came.
And listening in the distance, I could hear the awful rumble,
The killing of a thousand, with no one left to blame.

The echo of a war whoop, the crack of braided rawhide,
Sounds of the wWild West, swelling in my ears.
Somehow I could sense it, the sorrow all around me,
A story of injustice, that's lasted all these years.

The death of an Indian, the burning of his home,
To prove to all the world, civilization had arrived.
There by a cottonwood, listening with my soul,
My heart began to ache, as tears filled my eyes.

On that cold winter's morning, I listened to the rumble,
I saw sacred mountains, and heard a baby cry.
The soil of this nation, soaked with American blood.
I'll never understand, why so many had to die.

   J. R. Langston

The Trip

Dogs flying over mountaintops with big black wigs
and signs that say "Jimi Hendrix for President"
while on the ground . . .
sticks with faces and voices loud as thunder
say, "Come on baby, light my fire"
while mushrooms dance by singing
"Love me tender" with little Elvis look-alikes.
The grass is doing yoga with little white towels
on their heads while rain darts at plastic wrap
trying to make it less sticky so the food will go bad.
She's lying on her back under a yellow sky with October bugs
flying around her head, but it all goes away
when one lands in her pudding.

Rebecca Fry

Sisters

We were born two different people, five years apart were we.
Through those years we grew up together.
Best friends we were at first, but then we grew apart.
In which we became enemies, with our battles and our wars.
But then we helped each other out, and became best friends again.
When our friends let us down, we were there for each other.
When we fought with our boyfriends, we stuck together.
We helped each other through the thick and thin,
and promised never to fight again.
We disagreed now and then but, still stayed together 'til the end.
We had our laughs, we had our cries.
We stayed together side by side.
And we'll stay like that 'til the day we die.
We'll never forget each other no matter what.
When we're all grown up and have new lives,
we'll still be best friends just you and I.
We say we already have best friends,
but we all know that our real best friends
are those who knew us from day one.
Now you're going off to college and leaving me alone.

Shay Wolford

To Me You Belong

Snow fell down, saw you there.
I sang for you when I hurt my foot.
Rain a-rushing in,
Wind was singin' I yelled for you,
I was there.

Whenever light turns to dark.
And all the trees sang their song.
In the darkness forever.
To me you belong.

Beside the bay, where birds were flyin',
I saw myself for you in the waves.
In sandy places when love was screaming.
I sobbed for you, I was there.

Whenever light turns to dark
And all the trees sing their song.
In the darkness forever.
To me you belong.
To me you belong.
To me you belong.

Rachel Winkles

What Do I See on Veteran's Day

Shots have fired, people are gone
Tanks shoot, while planes bomb
No where to run, no where to hide
Everyone fighting side by side
No end, no love, no peace for all
But people stay alive not ready to fall
Crying for help, some in great need
Others are safe and ready to leave.
This battle is long, but almost done
Some stay and fight, the others run.
The battlefield is covered with only a mess
Of the people who died, who can be considered the best.
People from all over give their gratitude and thanks
To who ever fought in the high or low ranks
Let's give them a moment of silence so people can pray
On this sad and lonely, but most honorable day.

Jeffrey Moynihan

Tissement

Swim in the peanut butter
flowing pumping machine
gauge your dove fangs deep
releasing pungent clustered thought
water whistles yielding dry
feelings of collapsed dreams
frizzy purple bowling balls coiled
last attempt to completely understand you
coiled frizzy purple bowling balls
hop the sky landing on grasshoppers
have you ever wondered how?
Bananas split?
Or peanut butter met jelly?

J. Dewar

Distinct Woman

Eyes greener than the grass around,
she never let a part of her body look a frown.
Hair smooth as silk and twine,
her motto was always to sip fine wine.
Clothes finer than Giorgio Armani,
she was hungry if she didn't eat salami.
Skin dark as a summer-time midnight,
it was her time to shine in the light.
More perfect than an English Princess,
time was the only thing in her access.
Nails decorated with French tips,
her favorite color was putting red on her lips.
Her thoughts were filled with treasures and tales,
the materials she wears are blue and white veils.
There was never a lie of fib that was told,
she was never afraid that she would grow old.
Never forgetting to pay the shoe repair man,
that it why she is called the distinct woman.

Arthur Chatman, III

Communizer

I'm crying from lying.
Sometimes I feel I am slowly dying.
I'm confused and abused.
From filling out applications, I am always applying.
Many times I get hired.
But for my past I am always fired.
Doing my job to the best of my ability.
Never ceasing to have humility.
Understanding my past is real.
My victims' pains will never heal.
I understand the truth is good.
But once revealed, I remain a hood.
I forgive my sinners for all they've done.
But my forgiveness is sought but never won.

Jesse Lee Washington, Jr. II

Biographies
of
Poets

AARON, MARJORIE
[a.] Encino, CA [title] "Pennies From Heaven" [pers.] Found pennies mean good luck to me. My brother was killed by a car and our grieving father hopped a freight train and left town. Mom and I needed all the good luck we could get. Searching for pennies everywhere, I stored them in mayonnaise jars; one, two, then three, and hid them under my bed. Smiling, mom said, "Marjorie, good luck is meant to be shared." Reluctantly, I shared pennies with friends. The more pennies I gave away, the more I found, and the jars were never empty! I carried the jars in a gunny sack to the florist and bought mom and bouquet of forget-me-nots.

ABDULLAH, SAKEENA
[a.] Cincinnati, OH [title] "Tie That Shoe" [pers.] Writing poems is very rewarding. It is very much a way for me to relax, and at the same time get a message out from within me. It's also a time to fully exercise my mind and "deeply" think, and that is something I thank my spiritual leader I.W.D.M for that encouragement, and I thank you for recognizing my poems, and having an interest in my work.

ACCURSO, VONDA
[a.] Belton, MO [title] "Going Home" [pers.] These memories are dedicated to Jackie Moore Brown, whose house has been made "home" to many. A lady who delighted in the company of others, welcoming their joys and sorrows as though they were her own. This poem was given to her on her 70th birthday from one who treasures many, many, more memories of "Going Home."

ADAMIAN, ALINA
[a.] Laguna Niguel, CA [title] "Soulmates" [pers.] I don't keep a journal, I write poetry. My poetry is very personal to me, since each poem reflects events in my life; heartache, hardships, tears, and joy. At the height of my happiness and in the depth of my sadness are poems expressing every moment. This poem, "Soulmates," was written for a very special man with whom I've found an unconditional friendship. One with whom I can look into their eyes and see a soul I've known before. The most precious connections are the unconditional ones. I hope everyone is lucky enough to find it once in their lives.

AGUIRRE, BENEL
[a.] San Diego, CA [title] "Youth" [pers.] Inspirations sometimes occur when least expected. This poem came to me the day my daughter and I visited the carousel at seaport village in San Diego, CA. The poem "Youth" simply describes the emotions I felt and the events that took place from the start of the ride to the end. As a reader, I hope you too can feel the same as I felt that day with my daughter when reading this poem. Thank you's go out to my entire family and encouraging and motivating me to write poetry. Joylene, my daughter, my inspiration in life, I love you.

AKIN, SHARON
[a.] Flower Mound, TX [title] "My Brother and My Friend" [pers.] This poem reflects my deep feelings of love and admiration for my brother, who has remained a faithful, lifelong friend. Miles form no barrier that can weaken the bond which we share. It is often difficult to verbalize our innermost feelings, therefore, I sincerely hope that this poem adequately expresses my joy and pride in being blessed with such a wonderful brother and friend.

ALDRICH, JESSICA
[a.] Eau Claire, MI [title] "The Falls" [pers.] There is nothing more inspirational than witnessing the true beauty of God's creation. This poem was drawn from the roaring thunder of Niagara Falls. To sit, watch, listen, and feel everything this natural wonder has to offer creates the greatest music my heart can make. The love of God is my biggest inspiration and to Him, I am truly thankful. If words cannot justify such a feeling, then all there is left to do is stand in awe.

ALICARDI, CARMEN
[a.] Victoria, TX [title] "Spring Storm"

ALLEN, ANDRE DEMON
[a.] Kansas City, KS [title] "When It's Over" [pers.] This is truly a dream come true for me. Poetry and writing has always been the way I expressed my feelings and what I was thinking. I am happy that I can finally share a part of me with the world. I dedicate this poem to everyone who has been in love and lost that someone they were in love with. I also thank my parents (Maxter and Hazel Allen), because without you none of this would be possible. And thank you for publishing my work and making my dream a reality.

ALLEN, APRIL
[a.] Macomb, IL [title] "Best Friend" [pers.] Poetry that comes from the heart can also touch the heart of others. This poem holds a very special place in my heart. It is dedicated to my Golden Retriever, Bo. Pets can have such a profound effect on our lives. They take on many roles, that of friend, companion, family member. Their unconditional love and devotion stays with us in memory long after they are gone. This poem is my way to let his spirit live on and never be forgotten.

ALLEN, MARJORIE
[a.] Norman, OK [title] "Truth" [pers.] To me, poetry is a sharing. It reflects feelings of love, happiness, sadness, warmth, and bitterness. At the time I wrote this poem, I wanted the world to know my emotional devastation. Now, happier poems flow from my heart.

ALLEN, PORSHA
[a.] Flint, MI [title] "Bad Parents" [pers.] My name is Porsha Allen and I am a fifth grade student at St. Mary's Catholic School in Mt. Morris, MI. My favorite subjects are science and math. My hobbies are swimming, basketball, running in the Crim Race, and ballet, jazz, and tap dancing. I study dance at the Terry Matlock School of Performing Arts in Grand Blanc, MI. I have lived with my grandma since I was two years old and she has sent me to private school since kindergarten. My grandma is very good to my little sister Faye and I. She keeps us in church. My family members are Faye, Carrie, Anastasia (mom), Pamela, Robert, Charmell, and Lamont.

ALLISON, ARWYN
[a.] Melbourne, FL [title] "Arthritis" [pers.] Thank you all. I have known arthritis for a long time, and I can't say that I enjoy his company, although I never have a pain when I'm sitting down. That's why I spend so much time writing. I enjoy it very much, and I am thankful for all that's happened to me and my poems. When someone asks me how I am, I always say I'm fine. That seems to be a habit of mine. I have arthritis in my knees as anyone can see getting up on my feet is the trouble with me. I can sit, and rock and sing for hours, "that's me," and I feel just as healthy as I can be. I need my stick to help me walk around, lest I should find myself sittin' on the ground. If I could find that friendly cow, it may be soon, we could take off together and jump over the moon. So why complain to others friends and kin When I feel fine for the shape I'm in?

ALLRED, MICHAEL
[a.] Vacaville, CA [title] "Love" [pers.] Years ago I dedicated this poem to your contest, to recognize those close to me, those who are inspirations to my life, my family and my friends. Now I dedicate this to the women who inspires me most, a woman I cherish and love with my "heart and soul." I love you, Nicole.

ALO-CABALQUINTO, CARLA
[a.] Clovis, NM [title] "Hide" [pers.] My name is Carla Marie Alo-Cabalquinto and I love to write poetry. It helps me understand myself better and see things clearly. This poem is one of my favorites. It describes the way I felt at that moment and how I feel at other times . . . just wanting to hide from everyone and everything, so no one can see my tears and feel embarrassed about it. I hope everyone will like my poem "Hide."

ANDERSON, ANGELITTA
[a.] Philadelphia, PA [title] "Weapons" [pers.] I believe my poetry is a gift from God Almighty, since I've had no formal training. Writing of any kind just comes to me naturally. Also I give recognition to my aunt Nana, my late mother's sister. She has given me motivation and confidence. This particular poem come about after remembering some old wounds from the sting of an adult's criticism during childhood. Those thoughtless words had left me emotionally crippled for years—unknowingly said in the heat of anger, oh, how they had melange my self-confidence. So it has been my intention for everyone to think about what's coming out from your mouth to your children or anyone else, for that matter. Because thoughtless words can leave lasting effects that could change the course of someone's whole life.

ANDERSON, BRANDY
[a.] Stockton, CA [title] "Sometimes and Other Times" [pers.] This is a great honor on my behalf because I am now a third generation published poet. It's a wonderful feeling knowing that a tradition in my family has not surpassed a generation. Thank you for giving me a chance at continuing this family tradition that will hopefully be fulfilled by many generations to come.

ANDERSON, COLLEEN
[a.] Keyser, WV [title] "He Says" [pers.] This poem was written several years ago, and tucked into a Mother's Day card that I gave to my mom. I enjoy writing lyrics to gospel songs, and Christian poetry. I have been married for 34 years to a minister whose name is Tom. I have two children. They are both married, and each have one child of their own. My son and daughter have both written song lyrics also. The reward of seeing others enjoy what you have written is wonderful; however, the honor for all I have written goes to my Lord, for He is the true lyricist, I only hold the pen.

ANG, TSU
[a.] Melbourne AL, Australia [title] "Light" [pers.] First and foremost, I would like to thank my parents for guiding and supporting me all this while. A very big thank you. I came up with this poem "Light" after being inspired by a street lamp. I was amazed by the effort of a single street lamp that tries endlessly to brighten up a park which can be pictured as our endless struggle in life. We should be like the lamp or light and try hard to achieve our enlightenment of life.

ANGELO, MICHAEL
[a.] Battle Creek, MI [title] "Forever After" [pers.] Michael Angelo is a singer/songwriter whose lyrics are poetry. "Forever After" depicts the society we live in, the problems we face, and the way in which we try to solve them. As with many of Michael's poetry/songs, they are written from the heart with the hopes of opening our eyes and seeing what is happening around us.

ANTHONY, JENNIFER
[a.] Mesa, AZ [title] "Darkness" [pers.] I wrote "Darkness" in a time of my life when I was very lost, and didn't know if I would ever see my family again. I moved 2000 miles away from my family. I've never been apart from them. I felt like every second of every day and my soul was in complete darkness. So that's where my poem "Darkness" came from. But because of my wonderful husband, my soul has found the light. So I dedicate my poem to my husband, John. Thank you, my darling husband. I love you. Because of you, my soul has found the light.

ARCHER, VALERIE
[a.] Seymour, IA [title] "Death of a Friend" [pers.]

I wrote this after the death of my grandmother. She had lived with us the last 23 years of her life. I felt the loss of not only a grandparent, but a friend. I live in a small town with my son, dog, and cat. I work as a nurse at a nearby hospital. I value family above all else and have a great love of animals. I like writing prose and poetry as well as short stories when I find the time.

ARMSTRONG, PEARLIE
[a.] Cincinnati, OH [title] "Call Upon Yah" [pers.] This poem that I wrote is first and foremost dedicated to YAH who's inspiration inspired me to write a poem that praises his holly name (YAH). Poetry allows me to express me! I live in Cincinnati, OH. I love to serve YAH. My occupation is machine operator, I just live for YAH.

ARNDT, DANIEL
[a.] Watsontown, PA [title] "Burning Love" [pers.] This poem that I wrote is my own opinion that shows the true meaning of love. I believe that true love can be found only if there is a strong feeling between two people. The love I wrote about in this poem is real, this poem was inspired by a very special person. That person I wrote about in this poem is a very wonderful lady named Samantha Walburn. If I did not have her in my life this poem would not have existed. She is a very special person to me and I wrote this poem in her honor. This is why I wrote this poem so everyone knows how I feel about the love of my life, my burning love.

ARSENAULT, JENN
[a.] Lawrence, MA [title] "Body and Mind" [pers.] I am a single mother of the most beautiful son in the world. He is absolutely the light of my life. Sometimes it is he that drives me to write. This poem came along long before he did. When I write it comes from the heart and flows right out of the pen. An idea comes and there is no holding me back whether it be fact or fiction. I sometimes write from life experiences and other times it's what I see around me in the world. "Body and Mind" was written when I was a senior in high school. I started it and had no intentions of finishing it until a friend read what I had written so far and asked me to finish it. I sat down and the words were coming so fast I couldn't keep up. This is not, however, from a personal life experience, but if one person reads this and it makes a difference in their life then it had done its job. Poetry to me is a way to say what I'm feeling, let it all out and be free.

ATTART, ALEX
[a.] Coral Gables, FL [title] "Life" [pers.] When I wrote this poem I was not only thinking about me and my life but about my mother's and father's way of life. I really think that they relate to this poem because they went through thick and thin. So when I was writing this poem I had a vision of how life was created and how we live our lives. For example, during my mother's life she went through tough times but she made it and she is now top executive in her company, Editorial Televisa. My father's life has been pretty good—he didn't go through hard times like my mother, but he also made it and has his own business right now. As you see, we're all in the saying sink or swim—we have all swam. Now it's my turn to swim.

ATWOOD, MICHAEL
[a.] Cedar Rapids, IA [title] "Life Is What Liz Was" [pers.] This poem was my first serious poem. It was conceived at a time in my life when I realized that life comes full circle, just as the four seasons. This poem continues to have special meaning for me since the passing of my father, whom I am proud to be like.

AUCOIN, ROLAND
[a.] Canton, MA [title] "What Transition Sees" [pers.] I am not prone to calm expression. Poetry to me is a struggle to excavate the needed, meaningful words from the depths of emotion while keeping

needed emotion in the words. Poetry is written emotion, heart-felt expression, the soul of a person for another's eyes. I enjoy expression, in myself and from others. Feelings are who we are: sensitive. Many more people should express themselves through poetry, but they, too, worry about reaction to their feelings. We all need to know how each other feels and be sensitive to the feelings of others.

AVANT, LAVERNE
[a.] Chesapeake, VA [title] "I Wonder While I Cry" [pers.] I work at Human Resources Office, Norfolk on the Naval Base. I want to dedicate this poem to my husband, Gregory, and my son, Jordon. I am always encouraged by them to express myself and to write from the heart. I have heard various friends speak about the pain of separation in relationships and losing faith when it comes to having love and trust. This is what has given me the true desire to write this poem. Even when things seem hopeless, always go on! May this poem inspire that hope to move on and know that things will get better and inner strength always endures.

AVECILLA, CHAMPION MOONWIND
[a.] San Jose, CA [title] "Stars at Night" [pers.] Sometimes we are too busy raising against the world that we forget to appreciate the beautiful gifts of God. At night where I am relaxing and looking up in sky, I look at the stars and the bright moon, thinking about how I spent the day, and how I will be the next day. Watching the stars as they come out calms me down. For that moment, I forget how my day had been challenging. And then the child in me takes over and that is when I start making desires, not just for myself, but for everyone else making a wish as well.

AVERY, JUNE
[a.] Naples, FL [title] "A Promise" [pers.] In the year 1997, at the age of 66, I was reborn. April of the following year I began receiving words in rhyme which I believe came from God. I have now written approximately 160 spiritual poems. Also I created a "Life of Jesus, As I See It" in pictorial form and chronological order. Both are compiled in loose-leaf binders with sleeve protectors and are copyrighted. I am as yet writing God's poetry, a gift He choose for me and I pray to continue, if it be His will. Perhaps "A Promise" will touch someone's life.

BABINGTON, ARIANNE
[a.] Coupeville, WA [title] "Traveler's Dream" [pers.] On March 15, 2000, when I was lying in bed, this poem all of a sudden hit me. I've always had the need to travel around the world since I was little. Never before had I written or liked any poem. Once I wrote "Traveler's Dream," I felt like I had the need to write more poems. Since March, I have written 20 poems and have put them on a web page. Just at 16 years old, people really do love my poems. Some people didn't even know that I could write like that, and neither did I.

BAJGOT, EMILY
[a.] Bellingham, MA [title] "The Frosted Snow Angel" [pers.] This poem's very special to me. One cold day when my class was walking in from recess I saw all of my classmates with frost-bitten noses. Their cheeks were so pink and everybody's eyes twinkled off the snow. My friend had a glowing heart so I added that to my poem. She, also, had a furry white coat on that made her look like an angel. She had her hood up so she looked like she was made out of snow. Also, her coat was kind of wet and it looked like the morning dew had frozen on her.

BAKER, LAURA
[a.] Santa Rosa, CA [title] "Sweetheart" [pers.] In writing my poems, I write for the moment, and for the thought. This gives me great joy and pleasure.

BALDWIN, JERAMY
[a.] Verbank, NY [title] "Dreamer" [pers.] Poetry

is a very important part of my life. It's one of the few ways I can truly express myself. Most of the time these thoughts and feelings come to me at the spur of the moment, then it only takes a few minutes to write. This is one that I wrote when I woke suddenly one night. I get most of my inspiration like that. As for my poems themselves, I'm a daydreamer. As you can see, it really reflects that. I'm not trying to bring out any particular emotions with my writings, I just want people to interpret my poems their own way.

BALMER, TERESA
[a.] Yuma, AZ [title] "Poetic Thoughts" [pers.] I started writing poetry 16 years ago at the age of 14. I've written poems for many different reasons; special occasions, love, death, life, friendship, seasons, etc. I have been giving them as gifts to family and friends or anyone who asked for a copy of one. I wrote "Poetic Thoughts" when I was 17, and it's the only poem I didn't give to anyone because it was meant for one person; the man who make my words a reality. Ten years later, I finally found him and he was worth the wait. We've been together since March 1998. He's been my inspiration ever since. I would like to dedicate "Poetic Thoughts" to my forever-lover, Joseph B. Davis, Jr. and say thank you for making my words a reality. I love you always.

BANKS, SALLY
[a.] Chicago, IL [title] "Freedom Path" [pers.] I live in Chicago, IL, my education is in early childhood. I am also a professional model, and fashion coordinator, a poet, and my husband James, four daughters: Cynthia, Sherry, Letricia, Tawanda, nine grandchildren, Shajuanne, Erika, Martez, Akeem, Megan, Mariah, John, Alexis, Gerard. My hobbies are poetry, craft gift baskets. Maya Angelou is my favorite poet. I love teaching young children, and molding their young minds. I love sharing my gift of poetry with other, I am currently working on a book of poems. I love to travel to new places. I would like to dedicate this poem to my grandchildren.

BARCLAY, COLIN
[a.] Bethesda, MD [title] "Man To Man" [pers.] I'm 19 years old. My goal is to shock the world. This poem is one of many to come. I wanted to be true and say what I believe. Everything I will ever do stems from man to man. Whether I say live to love, believe, and be free, or scream thug life for me. I'm the same person with the same intentions. I am a key to a bright white door. I love to write, because it lets other people look through my eyes. It's a beautiful sight.

BARRON, DENNIS
[a.] Moberly, MO [title] "God's Storm" [pers.] This poem goes back my childhood days. As a child growing up in Moberly, I loved to watch the storms come in. There was something about the awesomeness of the storms that both excited and fascinated me. The unbridled power of the storms was truly amazing, but then to think that God had it all under control was really inspiring. The rainbow after the storms always reminded me of God and all of His promises. Just to think that a God who could control these mighty storms could also love me was very humbling.

BARROWS, PAUL
[a.] Redondo Beach, CA [title] "Almost" [pers.] The only dedication, ingenuous and exhaustive in my attempt truly goes to my beloved muse, Julie Provence. Whose understanding my way of verse in its extemporary form gave me courage amid a time of besotted austerity. I can only say thanks for the love given and gave I love you.

BARTA, MARIE
[a.] New Brighton, MN [title] "Autumn's Call" [pers.] This poem is dedicated to my husband, David; children Gregory (Dale Messner, Cape Cod, MA.), Daniel, Theresa, Michael (Marcella Brunoe, Warm Springs, Oregon). Parents Victoria

Stankiewicz, Gregory O'Leary. Sister to James, Patrick, Michael, Daniel, Eileen, Elizabeth and Rita. God inspires me to express my heart through creative poetry expounding love, joy, and encouragement for all life's seasons. "Autumn's Call" last stanza: "God, the author of all life's seasons beckons us to heed His call; wanting us to embrace the forthcoming season resting in Him while brisk winds sovereignly blow. Winter approaches."

BARTMAN, ELIZABETH
[a.] Florence, OR [title] "Witness" [pers.] I wrote this poem in a very special time in my life, after my baptism. I love to write poetry and feel it's a great way to release my feelings and emotions. My dad, I believe, is who really encouraged my poetry writing from the time I was ten to now, five years later. Just being able to share my feelings about the Lord publicly gives me great pleasure, and I hope anyone who reads it takes something, hopefully good, from it.

BASTIAN, MARY ALICE
[a.] Kent, NY [title] "Unsung Heroes" [pers.] This particular poem, was born the day I faced lung surgery to see if I had the same disease my younger brother had just died of I did. I've had the reward of knowing this poem really spoke to someone else in Middleton, Idaho. Hopefully it will speak to others. I love writing poetry. I've done it all my life and share it with others. Through my teaching, I believe I've passed this love on to many others.

BATEMAN, LIDRED
[a.] W Midlands, UK [title] "No Peace for Ancient Woodlands" [pers.] Former Lady Chair, West Midlands Writers' Circle, Brierley Hill Choral Society, Officer of the Christian Church. Present R.A.S.E.N.T. Freelance journalist, playwright, poet. Work ethic. As a Republican, pacifist, humanist, I am scientifically opposed to the Law and Order of English Precedence commonly referred to as the British Constitution.

BAXTER, SHELINA
[a.] Marianna, FL [title] "Decisions" [pers.] My name is Shelina Baxter. I am the daughter of Angela and Lonnie Baxter. I live in Marianna, FL. I am "A, 13" honor roll student at Marianne High School. I also play J.V. Volleyball and J.V. Varsity basketball. I am a member of Ministries of God church located in Sneads, FL. I am a dedicated Christian and love to help people out if I can. I hope my poem "Decisions," can be helpful to many who have to make decisions.

BAYOUTH, CHRISTINA
[a.] Broken Arrow, OK [title] "I Love the Way" [pers.] This poem was written for a very special person in my life. I wrote it for him as a gift for our three-year reunion. It is a shock, and truly an honor, that my poem is being published. I only hope my words can help inspire other young people to express their feelings as well. To anyone out there, Don't Give Up! Stay focused on your goals, but don't ever stop working on your dreams until you make them come true. God bless you all, and Bryan, "I love you, too!"

BAYUELO, YOLANDA
[a.] No. Bellmore, NY [title] "Forgive Me" [pers.] I have always been a great fan of poetry; I even created an anthology of my favorite poems. The tragedy at Columbine, CO was my inspiration in creating my poem. I realized with tears in my eyes how we, as parents and community as a whole, have failed our children.

BECKMAN, MATTHEW
[a.] Bechtelsville, PA [title] "With Him" [pers.] Poetry is a hobby I greatly enjoy. I believe that my talent in poetry is a God-given gift, and I wish to share it with others. I want to dedicate this poem to my pastor, who recently surrendered to become a missionary to Africa, and I hope that others will find this poem uplifting and that it may inspire them to have a closer walk "With Him."

BEEL, SANDY
[a.] Marine, IL [title] "Silence" [pers.] This poem was inspired to me from being raised in a loving and Christian's home by wonderful parents. At a very difficult time in my life they always remembered forgive and understand to be very important words.

BELFIELD, DEBRA
[a.] Mapleton, IL [title] "To My Parents" [pers.] I wrote this poem one day after talking to my mom. Our family was going through a pretty hard time. It felt like our family was falling apart. I just wanted my Dad and Mom to know that this family could make it through anything because of all their love and hard work they showed us through the years. I come from a family of four girls. I have been married for fifteen years to a wonderful man and have two beautiful daughters. My husband and I own our own business. I like to read, write, and be with my family.

BELL, KENISHA
[a.] Jacksonville, AR [title] "Untitled" [pers.] This poem is about loving after life. It's about coping with the death of the one you love. It's a glimpse into the soul of the widow or widower. People die, but love is eternal. Life is so precious and short. If you are blessed to find true love only once, you have loved for a lifetime. I wrote this poem when I lost a very special person. I realized that you don't have to hold on to the pain to hold on to the memory. I hope readers will be inspired by my work. Keep living and loving. God bless.

BELL, MELISA
[a.] Chicago, IL [title] "Nations" [pers.] I wrote this poem when I was 18 years old, just sitting in bed with issues. I had just watched the news with some hate crime being broadcast, so mad with pen in hand I wrote this poem. I thought to myself if I could speak and be heard what would I say! As long as I can remember I've been jotting stuff on paper. I love to write sometimes. It's therapy for me. Love loving, hate hatred, envy no one, peace.

BELL, SHAINA
[a.] Hillsboro, OR [title] "Yes, It Was My Mother" [pers.] I had to do this for a school assignment on someone we looked up to. I thought about my mother because she was an alcoholic. She got clean and changed her life around for us kids. She was a single mother and still is. S he raised three kids with no help. She had no money and was on welfare and was going to college. She would be studying for a test and one of us kids would come in and say, "Mom, Eric told me to shut up" and she got really frustrated because of that. That's why I look up to my mother.

BENJAMIN, MIRANDA R.
[a.] Houston, TX [title] "To My Love" [pers.] I wrote this poem as a wedding gift for my husband. It was my way of expressing my feelings to him. It was hard for me to believe he could love me because of the many mistakes of my past, so I tried to push him away. Yet he saw through my hurt and my problems to the real me. He has loved me in a way no other person ever has, and I thank God for him. Because of his and God's love I've been able to put my past behind me and move toward better things. If you know someone like this, and I hope everyone does, please let them know.

BENNETT, BENARD
[a.] Dallas, TX [title] "A Head Rub" [pers.] I started writing poetry as a release to my logical order of thinking. Everyone laughs when they hear I write poetry (My friends, family, and even people who just meet me). I am an emotional person and I wrote "A Head Rub" because a friend of mine mocked the experience. He chastised the girl who gave me the head rubs and I wrote the poem to let her know that it was a celestial sensation. I believe that poetry fuses feelings with words, ideas with vigor, and comprehension with cilantro. The herb of life is what I'm all about.

BERMOND, SHARON KATE
[a.] Gulfport, MS [title] "God Needed Another Angel" [pers.] I wrote this poem the very same day that I lost a close friend who died of cancer. At the time it was written, September 1998, I dedicated the poem to her and gave copies to her family. Since then I've dedicated this same poem to the mother of a very good friend in London, England, who passed away unexpectedly, again to comfort the family left behind. The third and last time my poem was dedicated was in honor of father-in-law in June 1999, where it was send as part of the eulogy at his funeral. I decided to go public with this particular poem in hopes that it will help others in time of grief when they, too, lose someone they love very much. It is written not only to honor those that have passed away, but to offer comfort and strength to those of us left behind so that we can carry on with life . . . yet never forget. If my poem brings help and comfort to those that read it, then the three very special people I dedicated it to have not died in vain and their memory shall go on forever.

BERRIOS, CATHY
[a.] Ewing, NJ [title] "Life Is Sweet" [pers.] Poetry to me is a way to express the way you feel about someone or about something. What inspired me to write "Life Is Sweet" was a person that left a great impact in my life at one period of time. It's unbelievable how a person can show feelings through words. I'm change (there's) to there's change (making) to making. Happy that I can share this poem with many others that have felt the way I do about a special person in their life.

BETKER, NICOLE
[a.] Red Deer, AB [title] "Baby and Mother" [pers.] Poetry to me is an expression of the beauty which surrounds me each and every day. When I wrote this poem it was a declaration of love to my wonderful daughter, Abigail. It is her beauty that has inspired the poem, and her love which has inspired me to be the person I am today. I am so thankful for the recognition of this poem, and so blessed by the little person who made it. As she created the thoughts I have, I just simply put them on paper. S even words to live by: "You can, if you think you can."

BLACKMON, CARRI
[a.] Louisville, KY [title] "Life" [pers.] Poetry is my need for expression! I keep a red notebook filled with unfinished emotions. I selected "Life" because this is something that I can ultimately relate to. We all have times in our lives when we are confused or unsure of the decisions that are make. The answers make us who we are or who we are striving to become. Therefore, I would like to dedicate this poem to my sister and best friend. Cristi, you have succeeded in becoming every aspect of what you so eagerly desired in your life. You are my inspiration to succeed. You have drawn the path, and soon I will follow. Thank you for showing me that I am every woman.

BLAKESLEE, NATALIE
[a.] Wattsburg, PA [title] "Butterflies in Flight" [pers.] This poem inspired a booklet entitled: "Butterflies in Flight" designed to help those that are grieving and have lost a loved one. Since my near death experience I share with others "what heaven is like" through my eyes. It was through the NDE that I acquired a "gift" and share that in my talks and lectures. I reside in Wattsburg, PA, and have the love and support of my husband, Terry Blakeslee, and children: Ashley and Carrie Smith Genavie and Terry Blakeslee, Jr. I am working on a book called "Love and Light: Whispers from Heaven" with Kathie Jendrasiak.

BLAN, HENRY
[a.] Placentia, CA [title] "A Divine Intervention" [pers.] This poem was written on the spot in a matter of minutes. I have always considered myself an average poet until now. Publication means more to me than any prize or money. This poem was for a girl who broke my heart but it has mended. I'd like to thank the following: my brother Mike, my beautiful mother, my best friends, Steve and Heather whom I simply adore.

BLANCHARD, MARY
[a.] Kiln, MS [title] "Untitled" [pers.] This poem was written for my father, whom I still miss very much. I have been writing since I was nine years old. I love to write poems and short stories. I have

even started writing a book. I enjoy writing poems, but I have trouble writing short ones—most of my poems are real long. This is the first time I have send any of my writings out into the public. I have written poems for my family on special occasions. They have them in picture frames. They make a beautiful centerpiece for tables and dressers.

BLAYDES, MICHAELA
[a.] Lower Lake, CA [title] "The Gift" [pers.] This poem was written in memory of my little brother, Michael Gene Bolt, who was taken from us in an automobile accident on January 22, 1999 at the age of 18. I wanted to share his life with others and assure them that our lost loved ones do walk with Jesus and watch over us from Heaven.

BLEVINS, MICHELLE
[a.] Bel Air, MD [title] "One Step Closer" [pers.] I have been writing poetry since a very young age. It is a way for me to express my feelings and emotions. I often write during many times of my life whether they be happy or sad. I wrote this poem to express the closeness that I felt to the Lord while praying with others after a tragic event of my life. I was born and raised in Baltimore, MD. I currently live in Bel Air, MD with my three-year-old son, Sean Michael Blevins. Besides poetry I like to play sports, sing, read, and go to church.

BLUBAUGH, JOSEPH
[a.] Peachtree City, GA [title] "Maybe One Day" [pers.] I am a 17 year old junior at McIntosh High School in Peachtree City, GA. I have been writing since the sixth grade. This is my first published poem and I dedicate it to my friend, Angela, who was my inspiration.

BOCKELMAN, MELVIN
[a.] Concordia, MO [title] "American's Valiant Veterans" [pers.] I am a veteran of World War II, Chief Master Sgt., USAF, Ret. My memories often revert back to those dangerous times when our country was at risk (1941-1945). My poem reflects my emotions and remembrances to those veterans who suffered emotionally and physically as a results of the trauma of war.

BOFFO, JEFFREY
[a.] Winchester, MA [title] "Untitled" [pers.] The moment is the most precious experience. Memories, the heaviest of baggage. If you would like to live a happy life, then by all means do so. All things are alive and experiencing life within and without you, and the type of energies you expel shall construct your own life experience. Do not fear diversity, for it is this Earth's creed.

BOLING, RAYMOND
[a.] Yelm, WA [title] "A Father Is" [pers.] I wrote this very special poem for my father on Father's Day. He has been a very important man in my life and I wanted to thank him for being their for me. So as a gift I wrote this for him. Writing a poem was the most heartfelt and special thing I could think of to give my father, whom I love dearly.

BOOTH, BRIAN
[a.] Mexia, TX [title] "Maniac Depression" [pers.] First of all, let me say that I'm thoroughly delighted by the choosing of this poem to appear in your publication. Though it's not my best work, I am proud of the attention that it obviously attracted. I'd like to think Christ my Saviour and Mr. Bruce Sawyer, my English teacher. To my fellow poets, stay focused and write what you feel. Don't let logic destroy emotion, for poetry is from the heart, not the mind. Don't worry. I'm stable. "Maniac Depression" is from a time of personal depression for me.

BORENSTEIN, MARTIN
[a.] Oakland, CA [title] "Lovers" [pers.] Martin Borenstein, AIA, IDSA, architect and industrial designer, in private practice for almost 30 years, the last five devoted to affordable housing. I was, at one time, a member of the Israeli underground (Haganah), during British occupation of Palestine. I was also a lieutenant in the British Royal Navy during WW II, and a commander in the Israeli Navy

during the 1948 Israeli War of Independence. I find poetry in a functional, exciting building and in a commercial product designed for daily use. The poem you selected for publication was born of a recent painful experience.

BOSSIER, KENNETH
[a.] Castaic, CA [title] "The House That Wasn't a Home" [pers.] The poem "The House That Wasn't a Home" expresses some of my childhood when I was growing up not so long ago in America. And they say the past is always with us all in our everyday life.

BOWIE, MESH
[a.] Holland Park, Australia [title] "Am I Crazy for Believing?" [pers.] These were the questions I asked myself when things were not going my way. The last four lines of the poem illustrate my determination to be myself in a world where individuality is almost a crime. The poem answers itself with reasons why not to be underpinned by circumstance. It reinforces the choice I made to base the decisions I make for my life on principles rather than circumstances. This is a poem about claiming your right to be yourself, and to follow your own dreams beyond the stars.

BOYD, BRIAN
[a.] Cobleskill, NY [title] "Ahole" [pers.] I'm actually a Terminator. I was sent back in time from the future to murder someone, but there was a malfunction now all I can do is write poetry. Seriously, though, to me poetry is therapy. If I'm having a bad day I'll take my aggressions out on the paper. I love to write. I love my family, you guys inspire me. To all my friends—thank you for putting up with me. I love all of you, but most of all I love tacos.

BOYD, JAMES
[a.] Poneto, IN [title] "When You Need a Friend" [pers.] This poem came from my heart to someone I care for dearly. Her name is Amanda, and she's the mother of our son. No matter how things went we always tried to see through the hard times. I feel that everyone not only needs that special friend, but deserves to have one who'll be by your side 'til the end. My poetry reflects on one's life, well being, and emotions. I try to express how we struggle without feelings in the world today through my poetry. I live in Poneto, IN with my family and I'd like to thank them for supporting me.

BOYLES, ANN
[a.] Goodlettsville, TN [title] "My Name is Melanie Dawn" [pers.] I am a 68-year-old grandmother and Melanie is my middle grandchild. She is very dear to me. I wrote this because she was going through a hard time with college and looking for a part-time job. I wanted to encourage her. Her name is Melanie (which means "dark" and "dawn" which means light). Her last name is "Read."

BOZEMAN, JIM
[a.] Sanford, ME [title] "Spirit and Heart" [pers.] Before Glasnost and Peristroika, before the Berlin Wall fell, a good friend of mine was involved in a teacher exchange program with the Soviet Union. I wrote this poem and asked if she would read it (to the Russians) at an opportune moment, which she did. I wished to express that all people have the same desires.

BRAZELTON, CHERYL
[a.] Glassboro, NJ [title] "Gift from God" [pers.] This poem was written as a gift for my aunt and uncle. Their son and my cousin, Jeffrey Mosser, died of leukemia at the age of eleven. Although the pain and sorrow may never diminish, there should be comfort knowing God now takes care of these children.

BREININ, BETTY RYEN
[a.] Royal Palm Beach, FL [title] "A Breezy Summer Eve" [pers.] I grew up in Syracuse, NY, where several lakes were available for swimming, fishing, and boating. My favorite was Oneida Lake, where I spent hundreds of happy hours. Oneida Lake became a place of beauty and inspiration to me. I often sat on the beach with my Dad who taught me to swim at age four and my non-swimming Mom who was my personal lifeguard par

excellence! Many summers were spent camping across the road from the lake, a short commute for Dad. Thank you for sharing those warm memories.

BREUERS, GEORGIE
[a.] Rittman, OH [title] "Closure" [pers.] After a 12 year illness and the slow, painful death of my wonderful husband, I was inspired to put my feelings on paper. "Closure" was my way to say good-bye to him and tell him how much I loved him. This poem helps me in my grief.

BREWER, BARBARA
[a.] Lacota, MI [title] "Wish You Were Here" [pers.] I live in Michigan, U.S.A. He lived in New Zealand. I am a nurse tech. He is an open-wheel race car driver. We met on the Net and love didn't blossom and bloom, it exploded! His first call was on December. 25, 1999; we logged 43 1/2 hours. on the phone in the first nine days. He has phoned me every day, then moved here April 19, 2000. We are to be married this June. The miles between us and our love is what inspired "Wish You Were Here."

BRINKEY, SAMANTHA
[a.] Sterling Heights, MI [title] "A Lost Friends" [pers.] When I first started writing this poem I didn't know who or what it would be about, then after getting into an argument with my best friend I figured it out. My poem describes how I think it would feel to lose her and for her not to be part of my life. She's a really special person and I don't know what I'd do without her. After re-reading this poem over and over again I understand how easily you can put feelings into words. My name is Samantha Brinkey, and I'm a 13-year-old eighth grade student that gets a thrill out of writing.

BROACH, CLARENCE
[a.] Flint, MI [title] "Peepz" [pers.] Poetry has a special meaning in my life, I'm actually inspired to write through real life observation, therefore becoming a form of release. The composition "Peepz" was inspired by certain circumstances that has transpired, though I know some will view my work as a one-sided view. I'm actually very broad minded as well as open. I experience visions of peace encompassing the Earth. To these visions I have the almighty God to thank, as well as my beautiful mother Dina Broach, seed Xerious Broach, Timmoya Jones, Clyvonte Broach, Clarence Broach, Jr., Cierra Broach, and Ceon Broach. See these are my people a.k.a "Peepz."

BROACH, CONNIE
[a.] Lake City, SC [title] "When it Rains on My Parade" [pers.] The ability to write poems is something I cherish deeply because it is a way God has chosen to speak to me. As I've faced various situations in life, He inspired me with poems, each one proving to be what I needed at that particular time. As I write the words He whispered into my heart, I cannot help but feel closer to Him. With joy I receive His messages, and with added joy I write them down to share with others in hopes that they, too, will be blessed.

BRONAKOSKI, RACHEL
[a.] Summerville, SC [title] "The Forest" [pers.] This poem was written in the spur of the moment. I saw the poetry contest in the newspaper and decided to write a poem to try to help my family financially. The "Forest" and its animals are the most beautiful place I can imagine. I really like animals and beautiful things. I am ten years old, and I like to write creatively. I have been inspired by my teachers at Sangaree Elementary and Sangaree Intermediate, particularly, Ms. Batt and Ms. Boyd, who made us write creatively. I dedicate this poem to Ms. Batt who passed away last April 8, 2000.

BROTHERS, DARRYL E.
[a.] St. Louis, MO [title] "Nothing Left but Memories" [pers.] From a very young age, I learned that because I was a boy I was to hide my feelings and emotions. I was considered overly sensitive, I was often hurt deeply by harsh words spoken by my family and school mates. With the passing of my parents and having been born with creative abili-

ties, I began to use my emotions to create poems to share my feelings with others and to inspire others to do the same. "Nothing Left but Memories" reflects the lonely lives of many of the elderly, due to illness or age, living in nursing homes today.

BROUGH, MILDRED
[a.] Staten Island, NY [title] "The Winter Breeze" [pers.] I think of when I was a child walking to school with my brother Oscar, and sisters Anita Harriet, Violet, and Patty. The cold winter days we held each other's hand when crossing the big busy streets of Brooklyn, New York; we laughed, we cried, we loved, and shared all we had. Family is very important. I'm married and have four wonderful children: Kathleen, Richard, Mildred, and Maureen. I also have four grandchildren. I've been blessed with a wonderful husband. Poetry tells a story of inner feelings and makes you see things through other people's eyes. Now, in my retirement, I've always wanted to write a poem. I dedicate this poem to Mom and Dad, whom I loved so very much,

BROWN, ERIC
[a.] Yellow Springs, OH [title] "Somehow" [pers.] Eric Leonhardt Brown has published and edited several books and anthologies of poetry. He teaches creative writings and literature at the Nightingale Montessori Center in Springfield, OH and uses poetry, story telling, and drumming to work with young adults. Eric Brown lives in yellow Springs, OH.

BROWN, KIM
[a.] Bronx, NY [title] "Questioned" [pers.] I have always enjoyed writing poetry of various types and feelings. Usually, my poems are mixture of one event-by-event description. I lean toward the poetry of e. e. cummings, Gwendolyn Brooks, esp. "The Bean Eaters," and the poetry being displayed on the New York subways! My entree was an emotion dealing with "people's self made rules." I have one older sister, two brothers (older and younger), one nephew, one living parent—my mother.

BROWN, PAMELA
[a.] Hartford, CT [title] "Heartache Salad" [pers.] This poem was written while writing a grocery list. After thinking to myself what I didn't need, the words dishonesty and false hope came to mind. Thinking of previous relationships, I did not want to go through years of misery again. So, I wrote a list an turned it into a recipe in which my heart would never again be the main ingredient. This was a time in my life where I was very bitter and tired of time wasted in loveless relationships. I would like to thank God for my answered prayers and never-ending guidance. Also special thanks to my father, Donald Brown, for being there for me no matter what. I love you, dad. My son, Kevin, you are my gift from God; my best friend Paulina you've there no matter what; Lisa your words of encouragement keep me going, and finally the love of my life, Michael, you drive me crazy but I love you.

BRUNEY, JOANN
[a.] Ft. Wainwright, AK [title] "How She Feels" [pers.] This poem is written about a tree outside my window. The setting is in Alaska during the winter. The tree is portrayed as a person who has these deep feelings. I was born in Dominica, Caribbean, daughter of Shirley Bruney. Also older sister of Mario and Kernita Bruney. I think what makes me special is the fact I'm a twin. My twin brother Joel is so different from me, yet we hold that inner connection. I feel that this poem is that stepping stone to many more. Much love to St. Croix Educational Complex class of '99 and '00.

BRUNIN, DEREK
[a.] Rossville, KS [title] "Just Like Me" [pers.] When I write poetry, I write what I feel. I think everyone needs a way to express themselves. I express myself with poetry. When I wrote "Just Like Me," I thought what it would be like to be in the ant's position. Poetry has brought me a lot of happiness. I live in a small town and have a sister and four brothers. One is my twin brother. They are all very special to me. I am very fortunate to have

such good friends and family. I hope you enjoy reading my poetry as much as I enjoy writing it.

BRUNSTAD, ROBERT
[a.] Lancaster, NY [title] "Make Me Smile" [pers.] I wish I could give the gift of poetry to everyone. I seem to hear it all the time, calling me, and telling me to write it down. I hope and pray this publication will inspire me to write more and truly appreciate the gift of verse. Special thanks to the women in my life; Rose Ann, Alexandria, Haley, Helen, and Hattie. They have shown me the meaning of love, faith, compassion, and courage.

BRYANT, RICHARD
[a.] Rome, GA [title] "Do I Think of You" [pers.] I was born Richard Daniel Bryant in Rome, GA. I attended West Rome High School. In my English class is where my love of poetry started. I enjoy the romantic poems of Keats, Shelley, and the other classics. I have written over 50 poem over the years and this poem has to be my best yet. A very special person has touched my heart and this is my way of letting her know how I feel about her. I hope all that read it will be touched with love.

BUNCE, NICHOLAS
[a.] Birdsboro, PA [title] "My Little Nephew" [pers.] I am 11 years old and go to Birdsboro Elementary Center in the Daniel Boone School District in Pennsylvania, and I am in fifth grade. I got my inspiration for "My Little Nephew" from my baby nephew who is 15 months old. I love him a lot. He is just learning to walk and loves playing outside. I saw an ad for the International Library of Poetry in a newspaper and decided to write a poem. I have very good grades in writing class and love writing poems, stories, songs, and journals. I would like to write a book.

BURCH, BETTY
[a.] Wilmington, NC [title] "Sweet Dorothy" [pers.] When Hurricane Floyd headed for the coast of North Carolina, I flew to Kentucky to stay with my mother-in-law. While she was napping, I would sit on the porch and write. Taking care of her and looking at photo albums of her life was my inspiration for a long poem. The one that I submitted in the short version. Most of my writing consists of short stories about my childhood and poems about children, including my own son. I love to buy cards with interesting pictures that are blank inside, so I can write my own poem related to the picture.

BURTON, THOMAS
[a.] Cork City, Ireland [title] "Our House" [pers.] Poetry to me is a way of expressing things I see and things that happen to me in my life. I write solely for my pleasure, and if someone else feel my pleasure then I am genuinely proud at what I have accomplished. I would like to dedicate my poem to my granddaughter "Jodie."

CAMPBELL, CHARLOTTE
[a.] Fort Worth, TX [title] "Life's Destiny" [pers.] My poetry is dedicated to the memory of my beloved son, Darryl "Chino" Felan, whose love, laughter, and fun-spirited ways and values will always guide and inspire me. The poems that I have written are poems of passion of the soul and heart, hoping to restore faith in all mankind, and to lift the spirits of the human heart, the purpose being to enrich and enable lives in some small way.

CAMPBELL, ERIC
[a.] Calgary, AB [title] "The excellence" [pers.] To start, I want to say thanks to you all at poetry.com for selecting my poem. I also want to say that being 13 years old, this is my first poem published. I wrote it in the middle of the night 'cause I couldn't sleep. Thank you again, sincerely.

CANTRELL, VICKI
[a.] Palmyra, PA [title] "My Friend in the Mirror" [pers.] I wish to dedicate my poem to my darling husband "Spike." He read the first half of the poem and said that he will never give up on me, which inspired me to write the second half of the poem. We have been through a lot together, good and bad. We have

grown closer because of it. His courage and strength has and continues to get me through everyday life. I enjoy expressing my feelings through poems.

CARAWAY, HEATHER
[a.] Tishomingo, OK [title] "Melista" [pers.] I love writing poems. This poem was writing for one of my best friends on her birthday. Writing poetry is a way of expressing myself and my feelings for others. When I can't think of the words to say to someone I care about I write a poem and give it to them. I do most of my writing in my room, late at night. God has given me a talent that I truly appreciate and enjoy. God is number one in my life and he has given me a supportive family and some very special friends.

CARDIS, JAMIE
[a.] Pacifica, CA [title] "Father" [pers.] "Father" just really says it all. Without the love and support he has given me, there would have been no inspiration to write this poem. My father is this poem. This poem is my father. Thank you, dad, for making what I thought were rough times the most heart-warming learning experiences. I wouldn't be who I am today if you hadn't turned the half empty glass into a half full glass for me. I love you for dealing with my teenage attitudes, making me do well in school, coming in at curfew time, fixing my everyday car problems, being my best friend and for just being you, my father.

CARMON, PATRICIA
[a.] Troy, NY [title] "In the Twilight" [pers.] This poem was written because of my daughter. Because my daughter thought that I could express myself in poetry as well as any other poet . I never thought my poetry could be considered as good poetry or deserving of any kind of merit as being published.

CARR, ROSEMARY
[a.] Goodhue, MN [title] "Inside and Outside" [pers.] This poem describes a young girl with the softest of hearts. In order to never be hurt, she would put on a different face for anyone she met. Yes, it is an autobiography of sorts. Now, however, I am free to express my true self in my writing. Words are a type of euphoria for me. In fact, I hope to publish several of my books in the near future.

CARSWELL, ASHLEY
[a.] Morganton, NC [title] "The Fruit of Reading" [pers.] The poem means a lot to me because it is based on my family life. For example, my mom works with mentally challenged people who never have read. But, "through the people who are so kind", the people my mom works with have learned to read. These people have come along way with the help and care of others. Also, my mom and aunt are not very good readers. They take their time reading and have trouble pronouncing words. I try to help them and I think I have helped them a lot. My mom says she likes to hear me read. She says I should be a teacher. I hope to one day make that dream come true. I want to help others receive the gift of reading because there is so much you can get out of reading. Like using your imagination and learning about different countries and cultures, reading is a gift you share. That is why I wrote this poem.

CARTER, WILLIE
[a.] Sacramento, CA [title] "I Am" [pers.] My gift from God is a compilation of my life's travels as well as my all out search for the truth which is God. I'm putting my poetry from over the years in book format so you can gain some of what God has given me. My special thanks to Vera Davis-Snead. You really help me to focus on putting all of God's gift to me to work. It's working! Smile. Poems are dedicated to everyone who knows me. You are the catalysts for my experiences.

CARVER, CRISTA
[a.] Lewiston, ID [title] "Love's Promise" [pers.] Although I am only sixteen years old and have not yet experienced love, I feel that this is the way love should be. Poetry is a beautiful way of touching someone, and I want people who read this poem to feel something inside and connect with it. I believe that if you have love (not just romantic love), you

have everything. I have been writing poetry/ stories since I was thirteen. I attend Lewiston High School (Go Bengals!) and I plan on pursuing a career involving writing and working with animals.

CEILE, JEAN
[a.] Benzonia, MI [title] "Vietnam, Why Me?" [pers.] This poem means a lot to me because it tells of a time when my significant other went from a boy of seventeen to a Marine veteran in a few short months, with three Purple Hearts on his chest. I thank you, Larry Parrotte; my children, Lesa and Randy Rice; my son John Berry; and my grandchildren Remington and Alexandra Rice, because through their lives I am able to write. Thank you.

CHATMAN, ARTHUR
[a.] Chicago, IL [title] "Distinct Woman" [pers.] The poem I wrote is very special to me. It is dedicated to some important women in my life: my mother, grandmother, aunts, sisters, and cousins. My mother and grandmother's encouragement gave me the strength to write the poem. I live in Chicago, IL where I live on the south side and attends Simeon Career Academy. My hobbies are playing baseball, basketball, and football. My feelings toward poetry is that it is a way of expressing your feelings on paper instead of verbally.

CHATTAR, ROHIT
[a.] Lisle, IL [title] "I Confess" [pers.] I am from a middle class family. A family so closely knit that makes me feel that I am needed on this restless Earth. This poem is a heart-felt confession to God. Thanks to: Mom, Dad (Cryanchand and Chandrakanta Chattar), Didi and Jiaji (sis, bro-in-law and Rinni), Pammu (sis), Bindiya (wife) and my in-laws for everything they do for me. My in-laws: Mom and Dad (Hemlata and Mahendra Singtwi), Mamta, Kalpana, Menka (sis-in-law), Mummyji and Jayeshbhai Family(family and friends). Special thanks to: Yinnubhai (family friends) and family, uncle, and auntie (bro-in-law's parents), Madhuji and Rahulji (bro-in-law's sis). And finally Ranjanaji (my life's best and only friend). Thanks to all those who haven't been named.

CHATTERTON, CRAIG
[a.] Salt Lake City, UT [title] "The Wild Fire" [pers.] "Wild Fire" depicts the importance of trees in our wild lands and explains the dependency that man and animals have for them, and the beauty they add in nature. Craig Chatterton is a waterscape designer and owner of Dragonfly Water Gardens.

CHEIKHI, KAREN
[a.] Cathedral City, CA [title] "Waits and Balances" [pers.] Have you ever come to the point in your life when you let like you were put on the balance to have to either make a choice or some unknown choice was to be made which would affect your whole life? That is where I was when I wrote this poem. To be put on the balance is scary and intimidating, and doing so gives the other person such power over you. This poem is about taking control of your own destiny in love and in life. Why I wrote this poem? My fiance was being tempted to his ex-wife with one million dollars to take her back and let me go, he put me on the balance. I wrote this poem to express my feelings directly to him about being put in the position of choice. It's very unbelievably hard to complete with one million dollars. For a while he swayed between the million dollars and me. I can't imagine what he was going through as he had a million dollars tax debt at that same time and he was completely tempted to take the million dollars, but he didn't know how to do it and keep me, too. He had to choose between love and money!

CHERN, MELISSA
[a.] Newtonville, MA [title] "The Enchanted Embrace" [pers.] I believe poetry to be a genuine artistic gift of fluid expression; one that allows a heart to capture the roots of inspiration, desire, emotion, and feeling with pure language. I often utilize my gift of communicating to portray historical events and glimpses through time. "En-

chanted Embrace" reflects a precious, tangible moment in time, consisting solely of a breathtaking kiss. I must thank all friends and family for supporting my inner voice and utter desire for writing; I especially give gratitude to my dear mother, Susan, and professor, Kathy Ennis, who exposed me to many powerful poets and inspired my journaling.

CHILDERS, MICAH
[a.] Newtown, WV [title] "God is Love" [pers.] I am a fourth grade student at a school in MatGwan, WV. I love reading books. When I read, my imagination runs wild and sometimes it's hard to catch it. When I was five years old I had a poem published in the magazine "Highlights for Children." My Dad loves to tell this story. I was four years old, I was putting a puzzle together and as we were talking I said to him, "You know I'm nobody but I got to be somebody." Well, I'm on my way if I can keep up with my imagination!

CHRISTIAN, LISA
[a.] Ferndale, NY [title] "We" [pers.] I wrote this poem for my fiancee as a Christmas gift on our first year together. I put it in a frame and it hangs in our room. It tells how we were casual friends and then we got to know each other and our relationship grew and we fell in love.

CINTRON, MELANIE
[a.] White Plains, NY [title] "Move Along" [pers.] When I wrote "Move Along" I thought about people who put off their dreams until it's too late. I know of people who have goals and dreams and are afraid to pursue them. We need to stop procrastinating and just move forward. I also feel that we need to express our feelings to our loved ones and let go of grudges or hurt feelings. Tomorrow is not promised to anyone and we might not have the chance again.

CLARK, BILL
[a.] Allentown, PA [title] "Icicles" [pers.] The morning I wrote "Icicles" was a special day in my life. I had just turned forty and there had came a major ice storm the night before. Trees were heavily laden with sparkling icicles and the air was clean and crisp. A great day alive! Other works include, "My Love" and "My Soul and I."

CLARK, DOROTHY
[a.] Orlando, FL [title] "Great Granddaughter" [pers.] I just had to write and express how I felt about our great-granddaughter. She is our first. My husband and I live in Orlando, Florida. Our great-granddaughter lives in Niagara Falls, NY. We were able to go and see her on April 17, 2000. She is as beautiful as I thought she would be. Our son and family also live in Niagara Falls, NY. All the family spent Easter together.

CLOSSEN, JOSHUA
[a.] Orangeville, PA [title] "World Peace" [pers.] Writing poetry plays a very important roll in my life. All of my writings are truly my journals of how I feel and what I think of the outside world. Through the last four years, I have written over one hundred poems. "World Peace" is only one of my "truth telling" poems. I really enjoy letting others read and hopefully enjoy my writings!

COAR, STEPHEN
[a.] Mt. Laurel, NJ [title] "Universes" [pers.] I had always been interested in the precise use of words to communicate from the time I was a child in the house of seven kids. But it wasn't until I was killed and miraculously revived in an auto accident in 1993 that I became aware to the fullest extent how important each word that crosses our lips can be. During my long recovery period, my life-long love of writing both prose and poetry was given new life. Bedridden for months, I transferred my energies toward those talents and have been writing poetry and plays ever since. A book is next.

CODDINGTON, MARY
[a.] Washington, DC [title] "Rationale for Late Sleepers" [pers.] As the author of the book, *Seekers of the Healing Energy*, I've found that writing poetry is one of the most joyful and jubilant therapies of them all. Unlike prose, poetry must

be inspired, and much of mine comes to me during dreams. Many poets feel that rhyme should be reserved for satire. I don't agree, and look forward to the day when poetry grows out of its present obscurity and returns to clarity and verse that we can understand, verse that reaches our hearts without enigma and bewilderment. I'm grateful to the Library of Poetry for publishing this poem.

COLDWELL, JIM
[a.] Spring Valley, OH [title] "The Military Nurse" [pers.] This poem is the result of a lady I met in Texas who was a nurse in the VA hospital when I was there. To me, she was very special and with my thanks to all that served. I was in Vietnam for two years and I love all that served if this is in any help, use any or all I have written on behalf of all nurses who work so hard to keep people in good health around the world. As for me, I'm now retired and have lots of grandchildren to help with my time and inspire me along the golden years and with my writing.

COLLIER, LEE
[a.] Baton Rouge, LA [title] "Flood Watch" [pers.] I believe poetry to be the greatest of all art forms with which to express love. And when written with love can be greatly used in opposition towards hate and ignorance. I only hope that my poetry may help to assist a future peace. "Flood Watch" is an expression of concern as to whether there is in fact a future peace to assist. As we today may dream, we must soon think to act.

COLLINGS, TANNER
[a.] Marin City, CA [title] "11-6-98" [pers.] Music is a major influence on my writing. Primarily the Wu-Tang Clan and The Beatles. I consider what I write poetry and imaginative realism.

COLLINS, STEPHANIE
[a.] Lancaster, TX [title] "Endless Love" [pers.] This poem I wrote for my future husband at this time we are engaged and when I wrote it I didn't know we would get married. When I write, I write what is in my heart and whatever comes out on paper is what I get. I always hope it is good. My dad is an artist and in many ways I have inherited these gifts. I hope, and always have hoped, that people will look back into my poetry and see me and my personality.

COLLISON, TINA
[a.] Allentown, PA [title] "With Love from Tina" [pers.] The day Walter passed away, I stood outside for a while, and as the wind gusted and darkness began to settle in, words began to swirl in my mind. Amidst tears they were transcribed onto paper. I shared this poem with others in his family and I was honored that it was considered as my gift to him. I dedicate the publication of "For Walter" to his loving wife of 45 years, Doreene; his children, Christopher, Patrick, Nicholas Walter Sr., Theresa, Kathleen and Maria; and all of his grandchildren who knew him as pop-pop. We will always miss you. I would like to extend my gratitude to those who chose my poem for publication. It means more to me than words can express.

COMBS, JO
[a.] Ceoburn, VA [title] "Pamela" [pers.] "Pamela" describes my oldest daughter; sweet, energetic, fun—so adorable. I began writing poetry at the age of nine. My very first, entitled "What God Made" won on Alabama state poetry contest (third place). I now live in the mountains of Southwestern Virginia with my husband, Johnny. My two precious daughters, Pamela and Anita, are married and I have three wonderful grandchildren; Rebecca, age 16; Colton age one; and Makayli, born March 6, 2000. My husband and I are licensed wildlife rehabilitators and enjoy caring for injured and/or orphaned wildlife. We treat for release! We also breed and sell Catahoula puppies, and we have some great lawn mowers: Barbados sheep, also known as Black-belly sheep. We love our life in the country!

COOKS, PAULA
[a.] Mineral Wells, TX [title] "Say It Now!" [pers.] I wasn't born into the average typical family where hugs were given, sitting around the dinner table

with grace and having a wonderful meal. After supper gathering and asking how was your day? Having bedtime stories read and snuggled the night away with, "I love you." On the contrary, it was very dysfunctional with words that could scar you for life. Moreover, wondering not if day light would rise but, if you would be apart of that day break when it come over the morning sun. It's essential to hold your loved ones so close with acceptance. More importantly, give them the greatest free visible gift of all, "Love."

COOMBS, LEO
[a.] Green Valley, AZ [title] "To Listen to My Mother" [pers.] My duty is to write the words that God puts in my heart in hope that they may bring you joy, and wisdom's light impart, and for my task I only ask that I may share by giving some simple words which, when you're heard, may brighten up your living.

COOPER, PETER
[a.] MacLeod Victoria, Australia [title] "Oops" [pers.] Australian born, Peter grew up in rural South Wangaratta. As an adult he broadened his Manufacturing experience and has 17 years in management. He trained as a milliner. Until becoming a consultant in 1997 he owned a successful millinery wholesale agency and was a Committee Member for the development of a National Competency Standards draft. Peter suffered heart disease and a heart attack in 1999 resulting in surgery and a re-assessment of values and discovery. He finished his children's adventure novel (Children of the Amulet) and began another two books. Married for 21 years, Peter has two cherished children

COOPER, SUE
[a.] Kent, United Kingdom [title] "Sunset Rendezvous" [pers.] I am a volunteer worker for Cats Protection, a charitable organization devoted to the care of stray and unwanted cats and kittens. During the course of my work, I cared for Max and Topsy, two cats belonging to Mike Tickner, a Cats Protection member who was undergoing treatment for cancer. Tragically, Mike never recovered and a new home was found for his cats. Mike, Max, and Topsy were the inspiration for "Sunset Rendezvous."

COPE, JAMES
[a.] Princeton, LA [title] "Sanctuary" [pers.] As a multi-disciplined artist, I combine my tremendous love for nature and the outdoors with the God-given gifts of creating beautiful one-of-a-kind visual art, images in the disciplines of photography and drawing and painting, as well as writing about what I see, hear, feel, and do in what I call "picture poems." My poetry places you in the scene itself.

COPPAGE, WILLIAM
[a.] Monterey, TN [title] "Victim Unveiled" [pers.] In my life, many different ideas have passed before me. Whether with music, art or writing, an orchestra of information is produced in my head. With writing, especially poetry, I am able to express exactly what I see and think, but at the same time I can include a hidden theme or idea. In my poem "Victim Unveiled," there is a clear theme of a woman who does what she wants without thinking, yet she still remains unfulfilled. However, I wanted to add how this woman is loved, but she is blinded by the images her eyes cast before her.

CORDOVIC, CLARICE ANNE
[a.] Paranaque City, Philippines [title] "Daybreak" [pers.] This haiku came about at the time when I was doubting whether I could write again. Life's pressing concerns (colleges, my health, etc.) kept me away from writing for five years, and I was afraid that my "creative muscles" have atrophied. I wanted to feel the spark again, the wonderful confluence of thoughts feelings and words; but I didn't. 'Til the day I watched the sunrise from my window. Watching intently, I realized that the beauty of daybreak lay in the unhurried coming together of nature's many facets. So now, a day at a time, I'm finding back my joy.

CORNETT, CHERI
[a.] Lapine, OR [title] "Turn Around" [pers.]

Throughout my Christian life I have been God's "pencil" to use. My hands are the quills but He is the ink. Together we compose poetry to share with, encourage, and comfort others. But, as a team, our primary goal is to show all who will listen and/or read his wonderful love!

CORRIGAN, PAMELA
[a.] Edmonton, AB [title] "Good-bye" [pers.] I have always loved poetry, and have written eighty-four poems so far . My friend Ruth Bailey pass away in Feb. 2000. This poem good-bye was my way of saying good-bye to her. I have been married for forty-six years, have six children and fifteen grandchildren. I have my poems on the Internet. I find it very relaxing and comforting to put poems down on paper. I love to be able to share my innermost feelings with family, friends, and anyone interested in poetry.

COSGRIFF, WENDY
[a.] Huntsville, AL [title] "Purgatory" [pers.] Writing poetry has always been a truly enlightening experience for me, a form of self meditation. During all the years I've spent writing poetry I can't think of anything I enjoy more. "Purgatory" was written about ten years ago, during a difficult chapter of my life. I feel completely honored that you wish to publish it. I also would like to thank Penny Cosgriff personally for finding my poem, sending it in and giving it a title. I love you, Penny, you're the best!

COSSINS, BOBBI
[a.] Grand Junction, CO [title] "Success" [pers.] I feel that this poem may help me, along with many others, who should find fame not to take all they have for granted, and not to forget whom their real friends are, and most of all never to forget their family and the things that are important to them. Every day you should thank God for small favors, the talent each of us possess, and most of all your family and friends. And no matter what, never forget who really are.

COSTA, KEVIN
[a.] Buffalo, NY [title] "I Lie Here Alone and Scared" [pers.] I write poetry quite often as one of many outlets to release my emotions, whether they are happy, sad or in this care about love. This particular poem is written to the one person that has touched my soul so deeply it still hurts to not be with her. The poem is about falling in love, but not being able to realize that love. Sad to say, but I am not with the person this poem is written about anymore, but having this poem still, and having it published is like having a little piece of that love still inside me.

COURTNEY, TODD
[a.] Torrance, CA [title] "Over Time" [pers.] I wrote this poem to remind me, and anyone who reads it, that life goes by quickly and that it is important to know the truth and follow what you believe. So find what is true so you won't be forgotten or burnt out.

COWAN, LUCY
[a.] Toledo, OH [title] "What Is Freedom?" [pers.] I have loved poetry and beautiful writings all my life. At age 73 after many years of working and raising a family, I decided to "go for it!" This poem is the result of feeling free to do something I wanted to do for so many years. I have a wonderful husband, two daughters, eight step-children and thirteen grandchildren, all of whom we love dearly. I worked 31 years in the Ohio Juvenile Court System and am now retired and free to pursue my interest in any way I desire! Thank you for giving me this wonderful opportunity!

COX, JAMES
[a.] Tucson, AZ [title] "Life's Tides" [pers.] "Life's Tides" is one of one hundred and eighty plus quatrains contained in my unpublished collection of poems I entitled "It Could Be Verse." The quatrains probe a myriad of timeless and contemporary topics. Each quatrain stands alone—a concept, abrasion, disquietude or humorous observation. The collection was started when I was a student of physics in 1956 and has continued to grow through the years.

COX, JOHNNY
[a.] Jacksonville, AR [title] "Things Change" [pers.] I wrote "Things Change" when I was still in school. Now, many years later, I have found it to hold true 100 percent I invite all who enjoy my poem to view my other works at my website. My wife and I have moved Japan to teach English

COX, PENNY
[a.] Hampton, VA [title] "Hearts in the Sand" [pers.] This poem is extremely special to me, my favorite. I have the best inspiration any poet/ writer could ask for. Love my talent to God, and my father. She is also very artistic. But I owe this poem. and any possibilities it brings to one very special person, "J.M.F"—without him, this poem wouldn't have been written. "Lub, Thank You!" More of my poetry can be found online.

CRAIG, CARLOS
[a.] Detroit, MI [title] "A Reflection" [pers.] During the time I wrote this poem, I was fighting within myself. I was deciding whether or not I was living right. I feel that poetry should be from the heart. Whether long or short, poetry should be pure, open, and honest. I live in Detroit, MI and attend Renaissance High School. I love to run track, after practice one day, I really looked at myself and wrote what I saw in my eyes and what I wanted to see within those eyes and others as well.

CRANKOVICH, LINDA M.
[a.] Mansfield, TX [title] "Heart Prints" [pers.] Through the depth of knowing our inner selves, we come to recognize and appreciate the "Heart Prints" in our lives. That is, the people and experiences that bring comfort, value, understanding, and courage to us as we continue on life's journey. "Heart Prints"— a treasure box of party favors!

CROSS, LINDA
[a.] Mastic Beach, NY [title] "On the Church Steps" [pers.] I am a widow of 19 years. My children Joseph and Michael are presently married. During their childhood we were forced to move from apartment to apartment. Due to profit-seeking landlords many hardships be fell upon us, almost causing us to become homeless. It is society's obligation to protect families from living in cardboard boxes and cars. It is my hope to arouse a serious awareness concerning the problem of homelessness through my poem. Special thanks to Diane Carr for giving me the courage to believe in myself.

CRUZ, ELIZABETH
[a.] Paranaque, Philippines [title] "Mask" [pers.] I am sending my deepest and heartfelt gratitude to the members and Board of Judges of the International Library of Poetry for having chosen my work "Mask." I was greatly honored for this recognition. I felt it was of my life's greatest achievement, a chance given to a simple, unknown Filipina like me, considering there were millions of people around the world who tried their luck in this international competition. I never expected something as great as this could ever happen to me. Thus, in reverence I offer this for the glory, honor and praise to our Lord God Almighty for all his blessings and graces for making this beautiful event in my life possible.

CULLENS, TANGIER
[a.] New York, NY [title] "In Heaven" [pers.] I believe that part of what makes a person wise is their experiences in love, defeat and success. For some reason, call it irony, those elements somehow almost always travel along the same wind. What I wanted to accomplish in writing "In Heaven" was immortality for that love I felt. It surrounded me. The words I chose will always represent a moment in my life's time line. When others read it, they will understand the power and timelessness of love. They will, hopefully, think that my poem was written by a wise person, a person who believes in love in life and death.

CUMMINGS, KATIE
[a.] Asheville, NC [title] "Cold Folded Mountains (A Villanelle)" [pers.] Poetry has always been a large part of my life. It remains my most satisfying

form of expression and healing form of therapy. In the fall of 2000 I will be attending the University of the South (Sewanee) where I plan to double-major in English and Fine Arts.

D., JOE FLO
[a.] Phoenix, AZ [title] "A Country Beat"

DAHLIN, WILLIAM
[a.] Fargo, ND [title] "Father's Pride" [pers.] "Father's Pride" is a poem dedicated to my children. Regardless of the ups and downs of life, this poem illustrates their direction in life as a result of a father's guiding hand. Later, the father has to let go, allowing his children to go at life on their own which he observes how well he did his job as a father. Obviously, in this case, he is proud. I am fortunate to have two great children, Kaydee and Tanner. Children are the future, this is why I am an author of children's books as well. My recent book "The Pig and the Whale" can be found most readily on www.amazon.com.

DAIS, MARGARET
[a.] Philadelphia, PA [title] "Today I Became a Senior Citizen" [pers.] As far back as I can remember, I always loved to read and write. I love a good story or poem. After retiring I decided to try writing. Because of my love for children, I started with children's stories. From there I went to poetry. I thank the good Lord for blessing me with the ability to write.

DANIELS, BERTRAM
[a.] Haltom, TX [title] "The Rich Man"

DANIELS, TK
[a.] Sacramento, CA [title] "A Letter to Mother" [pers.] Blessed with a creative imagination and God-given talents entertaining came naturally, at an early age and determined to express my creativity, I began sharing my thoughts through song, screenplay, and poetry writing. Raised to respect God's might, I rely on his greatness as he, time after time, presents the opportunity to showcase my talents. I humbly lay the credit for this talent at the feet of my Majestic Lord. My desire is to daily renew my commitment so that I'm worthy to be known as his child. My prayer is that he continues to grant me this desire.

DARROW, ESTELLE
[a.] Atascadero, CA [title] "In Memory of Mom" [pers.] Having come full circle (birth to death) with my mother, Billy, has given me many blessings in my life. She is always with me. I am a wife to Jeff, a mom to Rebecca, Dawn, and Kristen, and a Grammie to Shemea, J.J., Roman, Akeem, and Alyheia. I am also a teacher in (middle school) at Lillian Larsen School in San Miguel, California. I love the Lord, my family, and each and every one of my students!

DAUGHERTY, RAYMOND
[a.] Mathias, WV [title] "If the Choice Were Mine" [pers.] My wife is a very talented poet, with several publications of poems and songs. I write only on special occasions. She has been bedfast for two years and sometimes my usually positive thinking weakens. I started thinking about times of departure for everyone and remembered so well the bitterly cold, windy, snowy day we laid my Dad to rest. Then, with prayer, my positive attitude returned, and I was inspired to remember and write of all the beautiful seasons, as well as letting God make our choices.

DAVES, ANGEL
[a.] Plainfield, NJ [title] "Young Black Girl Child" [pers.] Poetry to me is truly a blessed and unique gift that one is able to share with others. In my heart I know my gift to write poetry stems from the great love and respect that I have for both self and family, especially my mother and father who instilled in me, a "Young Black Girl Child" growing up, the true meaning and value of life, and I thank you. It is because of you, King and Queen, that I am who I am yesterday, today, and tomorrow.

DAVIS, IRA
[a.] Bilopie, MS [title] "Only Water" [pers.] My poem came out of my wish to become an artist and draw for a living. I am twenty-nine years old, s/m, I have an Indian-France heritage. I work hard for a living, my drawing and poems are a major part of my life.

DAVIS, KIERAN
[a.] Cleveland, NS [title] "For You" [pers.] Poetry to me is the one true art form of the soul. As a young man, I have always found it difficult to express myself in action so the only way I've ever known is the written words of a poem. To express my emotions in such a boundless form as poetry I find an inner peace and satisfaction brought on by the release of such emotional baggage as many teenagers have. In my humble opinion the art of poetry is universal and eternal and far more meaningful than any mere physical gesture.

DAVIS, LYNN
[a.] Ottawa, IL [title] "Lake of Glass" [pers.] What some people cannot see or feel living in different situations or areas they can become one with the true feelings or imagination a writer has to offer through their stories and poetry. Every day we learn from each other or our surroundings. Being able to express in words for so many is very gratifying. Therefore I am truly humble for the gift

DAYE, KYLE
[a.] Durham, NC [title] "My Hobby" [pers.] Poetry is a gift that you earn through intelligence and also mistakes. Again, no one is perfect. Don't get me wrong, intelligence comes in all shapes and sizes. You don't have to be smart or a straight A student or professional advisor to be considered intelligent. It is a gift that you achieve and maintain by yourself. As a delighted first time author, I know that it takes trial and error and mistakes to set you off on the right track. So always try your hardest

DAYWALT, BARBARA
[a.] Fayetteville, PA [title] "In God's Word" [pers.] My home is nestled in the mountains of Pennsylvania a little village called South Mountain. I have been married for 20 years to Pete and together we have one son, Joseph, 19 who serves in the U.S. Air Force. I was in the food service business for 24 years recently changing the pace, and am now a grocery store night manager. My faith in our Lord has given me the incentive and gift to pass on to others—my thoughts in poetic form. "Praise Jesus."

DE CHOLNOKY, TIBOR
[a.] Philadelphia, PA [title] "Standing by Washington Square, a Japanese Girl Ran by Me" [pers.] This poem invokes the Latinate origins of the liturgy to explore distinctions between the thought and the act in images and philosophy of Eastern mysticism.

DEATON, HOWARD
[a.] Saint Louis, MO [title] "Storm" [pers.] Howard Atlee Deaton—born in El Paso, TX on January 2, 1917. Parents are Enos Deaton and Alice Atlee. Married Shelby Janet Minor in Laredo, TX on October 5, 1943. Daughters are: Durelle Janet, born 23 October 1944 (Now Mrs. John Steffens); Son: Howard Atlee Deaton II, born 14 August 1947, married Mary Valleroy. Attended school in El Paso and San Antonio, TX. Served in CCC 18 months, Big Bend National Park, six months in New Mexico. Enlisted U.S. Army 14 June 1940, stationed at Fort Bliss, TX, Fort Sam Houston, TX; transferred to Air Force, stationed Lackland AFB, TX; Harlingen AFB, TX, Laredo AFB, TX. Served overseas two months, four days, Saipan. Honorable discharge 18 November 1945, Rank Sergeant. Worked for M.P.R.R. 33 years; retired as review analyst, St. Louis, Missouri, 1977. Poetry published in National Library Poetry, Poetry Guild, Sparrowgrass, Amherest Society, Illia Pub; many others. Member South Side Church of Christ, St. Louis, Missouri; member Trans. Comm. Workers,

formerly B.R.C. 50 years. Personal Belief: Treat others as you want them to treat you.

DELATEJA, NANCY
[a.] Miami, FL [title] "A Time to Wonder" [pers.] Poetry in my life is a reflection of the feelings and emotions experienced deep within my soul. It is through poetic expression I can reveal the meaning of life as I see it and hope to inspire others to find meaning by looking within themselves. My work with children as an elementary school teacher helps me to view life from a simple perspective and fosters me to teach through writing.

DELGADO, M.
[a.] Redwood, CA [title] "Barrio Boy" [pers.] As an educated Hispanic, I've always been caught between worlds, between barriers. This poem reflects an unidentifiable struggle to be seen and heard. I've been a novelist and a poet since the age of fourteen. "Barrio Boy" appears in my collection: *Tales of a Weeping Prince.*

DELOUCHREY, JOANN
[a.] Hyde Park, MA [title] "I Often Wonder" [pers.] I love poetry, it is an expression of oneself. For me it's a way to let me share my emotions and thoughts. "I Often Wonder," just like all of the other poems I have written, comes from my life experiences. This piece is about uncertainty and pain. It's about the hurt and confusion someone I loved very much caused me during a rough time in their life. Since that time, everything has changed for the better. Telling others how you feel can make all the difference in the world.

DENETTE, ERIC
[a.] Clarksburg, MA [title] "I Surrender" [pers.] My name is Eric Denette and I am 17 years old. My passions in life are music and poetry. My experiences in life go directly into my songs and poems. Everything comes from the heart and goes directly into my work.

DERNBERGER, DEBBY
[a.] San Mateo, CA [title] "Scarlet Wildflower" [pers.] Melancholy is the undertone of my work. Alas, it is inevitable. Years and years spent in therapy behind a ball point pen and a once stark white and ever intimidating blank piece of paper. This has ultimately saved my life. Perhaps even my soul. With a physic change the lesson of pain is the moral of my story. For instance, in "Scarlet Wildflower," I was inspired by a most beautiful lover. After picking this flower, the pedals dropped. I was very sad. If you love what is not free, it was never meant to be.

DeSILVESTRI-CAMSTER, CESARE
[a.] Rome, Italy [title] "Lovers for a Day" [pers.] Cesare A. DeSilvestri-Camster, psychiatrist and writer, is the author of scientific books and papers, of novels, short stories, and poems in English and Italian. Reared in Tuscany, Scotland, and other parts of the world, at present he is living in Rome, Italy. "Lovers for a Day" is the story of a young woman and an old ailing man who met by chance at the airport on their separate routes to different countries and lives, fell in love with each other and spent that day together. Then common sense prevailed, and they parted never to meet again. But love was there to stay.

DI GANGI, SAMUEL
[a.] Canton, OH [title] "Bleeding" [pers.] Along with all forms of art, be it music, the writing of stories or poetry, I use art as a venting ground, a way of exercising "inner demons" or conveying emotions often of sorrow, longing, regret, the hope of prayer (of which I do believe in) or just an overwhelming sense of frustration and powerlessness. I hope my work will be a piece of writing others can relate to and perhaps use to rid themselves of similar feelings and to know they are not alone in having them. I dedicate "Bleedings" printing to my family and Musewife—Daphne.

DICKINSON, TINA
[a.] San Lorenzo, CA [title] "Alyssa" [pers.] This poem was inspired by the long-awaited desire of my son Robert, and how he so wanted a child. That when the news came, that it would be a little girl I would just think of what she was going to look and be like reflecting on her mother and father. After prayer one day, I just had a sense of her presence even though she had not yet arrived. I believe the Lord just flooded my soul with these words. And now that Alyssa is here, every words is true. Alyssa is a beautiful granddaughter who is full of joy, and love always smiling. The prayers of her parents are magnified in her. And there is no end to the joy she has brought my son and daughter-in-law, Robert and Tifeny Haze. I have always enjoyed writing poems expressing how I view life from all perspectives. It is easier for me to write than to openly express myself. So word express my innermost feelings. My writing covers a broad spectrum. At the present I write to bless others. I am now engaged in writing a book just for Alyssa, so as she will know just how wonderful a gift she really is.

DIGLIO, SALVATORE
[a.] Westbury, NY [title] "Hugs" [pers.] I write poetry to speak the truth. I write about my life most of the time in a poetic way. I dedicate this poem to my family, especially my twin brother Lorenzo and my older brother, Mike, with his beautiful girlfriend, Jessica. Hey to all my friends! I wrote this poem for you, my angel, and you know who you are. Special thanks to my English teacher Mr. Megna.

DiPASQUALE, JEANETTE
[a.] San Antonio, TX [title] "Will You Watch Over My Wings?" [pers.] This poem is very powerful to me. A message from the Divine reminding us of who we really are. I dedicate this poem to my sons, Dante and Dominic, who are my teachers and I am their student. I also dedicate this poem to children all over the world to read and open their minds to a greater discovery about who they are.

DISON, RUBY
[a.] Birmingham, AL [title] "The Land Beyond" [pers.] I believe poems are expressions from the heart. It says the things we are unable to say to others. "The Land Beyond" was inspired many years ago as my dad lay dying of cancer. He went to this beautiful place, saw and talked to his mother and father, and then came back to tell us about his experience, a few days later he returned to that glorious land he described to us. I enjoy writing stories and poems because it expresses my love and feelings for others, regardless of the age race or belief.

DIXON, AUDREY
[a.] Columbus, OH [title] "Quenched Thirst" [pers.] The story behind the poem relates to the Samaritan Woman, better known as the woman at the well. After meeting Jesus she had a life changing experience. Her story is my story and the story of many other women who have experienced multiple marriages, most ending in divorce. This lifestyle has never been addressed as an addiction, but it is. There are many kinds of addictions. Multiple marriage women and men are marriage addicts. Like any other addiction, you crave it. It's a temporary fix that has to be consumed over and over again. Out of pain, this poem was birthed.

DOERRIES, DAVID
[a.] Glen Ellyn, IL [title] "Wait For Me" [pers.] This poem was written to my wife, Barbara. We have two children, Mary and Elizabeth. We live in a suburb west of Chicago, in a town called Glen Ellyn.

DONALD, HOLLY
[a.] Leavenworth, KS [title] "Guardian Angel" [pers.] I've won two poetry contests now and both of them are being published in books. It's like a just sit down to write a poem and the poetry just flows out of my fingertips. It's just awesome, I guess I wrote this poem for those who lost a friend or relatives because that's probably who their Guardian Angel is, well, sometimes. That's what angel's are for, to guard and take care of you. And that's not the only reason I wrote this poem. I wrote this poem because I like everything about angels, they're like my best friends or something. Peace and love.

DOODY, AOIFE
[a.] Co. Kildare, Ireland [title] "Is it Fair?" [pers.] I am sixteen years old. I am the youngest of three. I go to Cross and Passion College, Kilcullen, Co. Kildare. I was given the task in my English class of writing a poem about the person I most admire. It was inspired by my aunt's illness. She got breast cancer in the springtime of 1998. She is hoping for a full recovery in the near future.

DOUGHTY, NINA
[a.] Oklahoma City, OK [title] "Strange World" [pers.] Nina Doughty is the author of *Poetically Speaking*, a collection of more than two hundred poems. She is a widow and a born poet. She has been writing poetry all her life and says poetry is food for the soul. She is a member of several poetry organizations and has for years been a contributor to poet, an international magazine that is printed in India and distributed in six countries in six different languages. She was born in South Carolina, moved to Georgia and has made her home in Oklahoma with her daughter.

DOWD, HEATHER
[a.] Centervile, GA [title] "True" [pers.] I use my poetry as an emotional release. It's one sure thing that puts me at peace. I use my writing as expression of creativity. Even though some may include negativity. The main thing I strive for is for others to relate. To feel the emotion inside the poems I create. I hold poetry very close to my soul. It seems to be the only way to fill this hole.

DOYLE, BARBARA
[a.] Mountain Grove, MO [title] "Timeless Sorrow" [pers.] I thank God and the angels every day for being in my life. They picked me up when I fell the hardest. I'm happy to say my parents are still both living. They are two of the most loving and caring people I know. Because of them I found the man of my dreams, my four beautiful children, and now my little granddaughters. I would like my poetry to fill lonely hearts with a lot of hope. Remember—there's always more than meets the eye.

DRAPER, GEORGE, IV
[a.] Martinsville, VA [title] "Contemplation" [pers.] Poetry is said to be the language of imagination and emotion, but it is so much more. It speaks to everyone in a different way, but is provoked by the Creator. To truly understand what my poem means you have to not take things to literally because nothing is as it seems. A poem has multiple meanings and can be used in every situation which I have created here.

DUBINSKI, MARGARET H.
[a.] Passaic, NJ [title] "Untitled" [pers.] The poem was written as a class assignment while in my sophomore or junior year of high school. It is about death and how someone may perceive it, both by placing myself in another person's shoes and how I may perceive same. My educational background consists of grade school, middle school, high school, and business school. I recently finished courses in photography and guitar and am still seeking to continue my education through different studies of interest to me. I have always had an interest in poetry since I was young and still continue to do so today. Poetry is graceful; full of motion, with words that flow. It is like a ballerina who invokes emotions as that of a great ballerina performance.

DUCKWORTH, SHANE
[a.] Mt. Vernon, IN [title] "Dead End" [pers.] During the few months prior to writing this poem, I had seemed to have "hit the dead end." This poem express the feelings that we all seem to have sometime through life! Although this is the shortest poem that I've ever written, it means the most to me.

DUDLEY, ERICA
[a.] Oakland, CA [title] "Longing" [pers.] My writings and poetry are based on life, love, and the passions that seem to consume me. All of the writings are based on various people that I have encountered on my path. Writing gives me a chance to express how I feel, and the love that seems to always disappear, then re-invent itself into another piece of work. It is my mark on the world.

DURRANI, AASIM
[a.] Southampton, UK [title] "Friends" [pers.] This poem was written to reiterate my belief that the best relationships with members of the opposite sex are not necessarily romantic ones. I wrote this poem for Binal and Deepti, two people whom I feel very close to. I feel that poetry allows you to touch somebody's heart without being a cardiologist, to get into somebody's mind without being a psychiatrist, and to touch another soul without being omnipotent . I thank Allah for this gift which many others say I have been blessed with.

DUSSEAULT, SHAWN
[a.] Memphis, TN [title] "Not Words, Nor All the Roses" [pers.] Words are perhaps the most important thing in the world to me. Words are a way in which I can bring about profound feelings in others, bringing about change, hopefully for the better. It is a way to give others a glimpse into the peace, spirit, or turmoil of a life that is not their own, yet the reader gains an appreciation and compassion for the author, and a greater understanding of human nature. If even one person is moved by my work, out of all the people who may read this, then I have done all I could ask for and more. And somewhere out there is a person who will know this was written for her, and for her their will always be some small space.

EGYED, JEAN
[a.] Westwood, CA [title] "Great White Stallion" [pers.] I live in a small town in Westwood, CA off Highway 36. Because my eye sight is limited, I do not drive; however, I can walk anywhere I wish to go in this quiet little town. I am raising my grandniece Jessica. She is 12 years old, and going in seventh grade. Also my mother lives with me her name is Ethel Baber. I am her caregiver. She is 79. My poetry is of nature, and about people who have touched my life. I have been blessed with the ability to write many types of forms of poetry. In the past, Golden Poet's Award. Also many awards of Merit. My poems have been published in several beautiful books throughout the years. I am a song writer and a lyricist . My songs are published through Hollywood Artist, and Rainbow Records. However, I have not been recognized yet. My fondest wish is to hear one of my songs on the radio.

ELLIOTT, CRYSTAL
[a.] Salisbury, MD [title] "So Alone" [pers.] This poem was written at a time in my life when my husband and I were separated due to unforeseen circumstances, and I just put all that I was feeling on paper. Although that time is behind us, I still keep those words in my heart because without my husband I am so alone! Now that we are together again, I hope to never be apart ever again! Nack, this one's for you, my darling! I love you!

ELLIOTT, DOROTHY
[a.] Monmuth, OR [title] "What's in a Name?" [pers.] I am a high school graduate with scholarship to business college. Later I went through Evangelical Free Church Seminary and went to Belgian Congo as a missionary. After two years, I returned to U.S. with amoebic Germ and Malaria. End of that career. Learned unwritten tribal language,

"Ngbaka." This is ten in Ngbaka. I am now confined to assisted living and attached to oxygen. I do love poetry and read a great deal.

ELLIS, ESAN
[a.] St. Constant, QC [title] "My Dear" [pers.] I would like to dedicate this poem to mom, dad, Lloyd, and Taz. I would also like to thank the horsemen! Security Clerk, Arabesque, D-King, Silky, and we must not forget Rhonda! This poem is a reflection of the humour I am constantly surrounded by. I simply wanted to share it with everyone.

ENDRES, MATTHEW
[a.] Eastpointe, MI [title] "Love of Mine" [pers.] I found that I had a flare for writing poetry late in high school. Many of my poems deal with the subject of love. My inspiration for many of my poems come from feelings I had for my first true love. Every time I felt inspired, words starting pouring out of my head and to cherish them forever I started writing poetry. I have also recently written a couple of poems for my sister's wedding. I hope that you all enjoy my poem, and please share it with your love.

EPSTEIN, HARRY
[a.] Socorro, NM [title] "Sunset into Sunrise" [pers.] Percussionist, artist, glass sculptor. " Wagging tails and laughing children."

ERICKSON, ERIC
[a.] Palmdale, CA [title] "I Love You" [pers.] This is Eric Erickson and I'm 15 years old. The reason I wrote this poem was to tell my girlfriend (Elena) how much I love her. I live in Palmdale, CA and I have four brothers and two sisters and I'm in ninth grade. Some of my hobbies are video games, sports, listening to rap, going fun places, drawing, and writing poetry. I have written other poems but I really like this one because I wrote it for a special girl. That girl is my girlfriend Elena, and she really liked the poem, too.

ERIKSON, GUSTAF
[a.] Tarrytown, NY [title] "In System Spirit Wind" [pers.] Through the years I have at certain times at the spur of the moment expressed my self in rhyme. But I never had a thought about writing poetry until about nine years ago. Now that I have started to write down my thoughts and feelings in verse form, it is through inspiration that I give an emotional expression to the content of my poems. I have complied my poems in a book called *Spirit Wind*, containing thoughts, memories, and visions.

ERNST, FRANKLIN, JR.
[a.] Fleetwood, PA [title] "Bless Children With Trouble" [pers.] On May 29th, 2000 I will be an 80-year-old Pennsylvania Deutscher, we are "Not" Dutch, our forefathers did not come from Holland (that's Dutch), they came from Deutshlund, the name of Germany in the 1700's. My forefathers came in 1737.

EWALD, KRISTOPHER
[a.] Wapakoneta, OH [title] "Universally Almost" [pers.] The first half of "Universally Almost" surfaced when I was in the middle of performing landscape work at Toledo's (Ohio) Rosary Cathedral. The disparity which I observed between the wealthy of the Toledo diocese and the poverty of the overwhelmingly black neighborhood became too much of a burden to carry around in my head. So I started to commit the opening phrases to my notepad during the middle of work. The second half was written two weeks later in Wapakonetas (Ohio) waffle house. This just goes to show how truly random this crazy process can be.

FADNESS, SCOTT
[a.] Bemidji, MN [title] "Wings" [pers.] From my studio in Northern Minnesota, I express my inner visions in a variety of ways. I am a professional visual artist, although I find that writing fills the space that other visual arts cannot fully articulate. My painting and writing reflect the commonality of the struggle in the worlds of nature and human experience. It is my wish to convey a deeper understanding of these separate, yet interdependent realities through art.

FAHEEM, MISBAH
[a.] Golden Valley, MN [title] "Trailblazer" [pers.] "Trailblazer" celebrates tenacity and strength as well as hope. I wrote it for my mom, who left an abusive husband with only two small children in tow, her determination to avoid being a statistic, and her faith. My poem illustrates what I often forget to say: she is the ultimate inspiration to me. She not only made it through darkness, she left footprints that no angry wave can wash away; footprints that I can only hope myself and others will follow. I am 23 years old, soon-to-be graduate of the University of Minnesota, Twin Cities. I have been writing my stories and poems since I was very young. Some of my works have been published in the Department of French and Italian newsletter in college, as those particular works were written in French (my major) I always have to listen to Celine Dion as I write. Aside from my mother and all my friends who urge me to never stop writing, I want to thank Professor Eileen Sivert from the French Department who is always a huge fan of my work (particularly in French) and who was the first to give me the exposure I needed.

FAIRCHILD, MARK
[a.] Minneapolis, MN [title] "God's Love" [pers.] I was sitting in my chair and listening to music. I was thinking of inspiration and what keeps me focused in my life. It's God's unconditional love. God is always here. All you have to do is listen to your heart.

FARBER, EVELY
[a.] Boca Raton, FL [title] "My Dad" [pers.] I enjoy expressing my thoughts through poetry. My three sisters have this ability. I love to be able to express all of my emotions poetically. The beauty that surrounds my life with my family and friends can only be described poetically. I enjoy writing poetry for any celebration of any occasion or special commemorative day for any of my family or friends. I am not afraid to express my feelings. The world would be a better place if more people would write nice notes or poems to other people. Don't be afraid. Do it!

FARRELL, ASHLEY
[a.] Lafargeville, NY [title] "I Remember" [pers.] The purpose of my poem "I Remember" is my mom passed away when I was 12 years old. I wrote it to describe what I remember of her. I am 14 years old and live in Lafargeville, NY. The school I attended is Lafargeville Central. My sister Heather is an artist. My dad is an auto-mechanic. I have written many more poems that I would love to have viewed by poetry readers. I am interested in having my own poem book published. The title of the book I would like to have published is "Memories Forever Mine," these poems are memories of my past. Also I would like to thank my English teacher Mrs. Robinson for encouraging me to do something with my writing ability. Also I would like to thank Russel Hawkins for being there when I needed him.

FARRINGTON, ANDREW
[a.] Los Angeles, CA [title] "Heather" [pers.] Poems, for me, express moments in time. They are pictures of feelings and emotions. Unlike a photo, a poem can be personal and convey meaning to anyone and everyone. A poem does not hide behind nice clothes and fake smiles. A poem speaks the truth. As for this poem, it was written years ago in college about someone who changed my life forever. She may not a part of my life now, but in a way she'll always be there. A poem is a way of saying good-bye.

FARRINGTON, KRYSTAL
[a.] Divide, CO [title] "Memories" [pers.] This poem is in memory of my grandmother. She was very special to me and one of the most influential people in my life. I miss her every day.

FEKETE, DAVID
[a.] Gainesville, FL [title] "The Powerful One" [pers.] The reason I wrote this poem is because we all have guardian angels looking over our lives. Some people notice, some people don't, but we got to remember that when we need someone no matter

what an angel is there. So no matter what happens, look up and smile because an angel is right there looking over you making sure no harm comes your way.

FERRARA, PHYLLIS
[a.] Bloomfield, NJ [title] "What is Marriage" [pers.] Poetry is a gift from the heart, just another way of expressing feelings. The poem I wrote expresses my feelings about marriage and is very special to me because I wrote it for my daughter. It was framed, given to her and her husband on their wedding day, and now hangs in their living room. I hope you will share this with someone dear to you.

FILLER, CORINA
[a.] Irving, TX [title] "Today" [pers.] This poem as well as many others reflect a life in awe of the grace, mercy, and love of our God. It is important to me that He receive the glory for His gift of Jesus. My poetry is but a response to Him. God has filled me up beyond measure, and He satisfies my soul like nothing else. I am continually amazed by the fact that He accepts me, though I have nothing to offer Him. I pray for all people to understand God's grace in all its truth.

FINNEY, LISA
[a.] Cypress, CA [title] "To An Angel" [pers.] This poem is one of many I have written in dedication to my very dear friend, Tony, who passed away March 4, 1999. Poetry is the easiest way I've found to express my feelings and to help me get through all of my hardest times. Knowing that Tony is looking down on me and smiling is a comforting thought. I can only pray that this poem has brought comfort to even just one person who has lost a loved one and is having trouble dealing. And Tony, I love you.

FISHER, ANDREW
[a.] Flourtown, PA [title] "Happy Valentines Day" [pers.] I wrote this poem for my wonderful girlfriend, Margaret. She is a great inspiration and the words are easy to find when it comes to describing her. My ability to write poetry comes from my grandmother, who has written many wonderful poems. Due to my supportive mother and family, poetry has been extraordinary way to share my feelings. I thank God most of all for the beautiful words and inspiration along with many other things He has provided. I greatly appreciate this opportunity for my poetry to be read.

FITZ, ZEPHARRA
[a.] Greenbelt, MD [title] "A Dammed-Cell in the Press" [pers.] Prioritizing the hope of one's calling too often gets squashed under the foot of suffocating criticism and devaluation. Given to the fostering of pessimists and toxic people, it becomes a victim of sinking sand or even worse, discarded as mere scavenger portions. Not so! Hopefully, "A Dammed-Cell in the Press" will encourage those whose inner being struggles to emerge triumphant, more than conquerors-to not only dream the impossible dreams-but also fight hte unbeatable odds and be uniquely, unwavering, God-purposed Y-O-U! Your fruitfcul, renaissance spirit is not forbidden. So transform your mind from mediocrity and experience a life in immensity!

FLEEKS, JACQUELINE
[a.] Bryan, TX [title] "The Storm" [pers.] This poem was inspired by Deacon John Pradia because of his loyalty and dedication to his wife and to the church. He's an awesome man of God! May he continue to be a blessing and be blessed.

FLEMINGS, SUE
[a.] Garden Grove, CA [title] "Heavenly Reminders" [pers.] This poem is special to me for it reminds me of my creator who let me know that I was not alone at a time when I felt most alone. My poem speaks of a time when noticing the beauty of something that is often taken for granted, relieved me of my then immense feelings of hurt and despair. It is my prayer that those of you that have felt such pain of heart will remember to find comfort in nature's many beauties, and know that he who is responsible for them is close by.

FOGEL, DAVE
[a.] Dresher, PA [title] "Bittersweet Beauty" [pers.] During the summer of '99 a girl came into my life for very short period of time. During that time we connected and enjoyed a very special relationship. She is since gone from my life but in no way forgotten. On the day she left, a picture was taken that captured all of her emotions of sadness for leaving into a single photograph. This photo inspired me to write "Bittersweet Beauty" and three other poems about her. I love that she will one day read these poems, remember me and the time we shared together, and smile.

FORD, ISAAC
[a.] Newport, TN [title] "The Last Disciple" [pers.] This poem or poems have been on my mind for over ten years. It wasn't until I was saved by the word God by his son Jesus Christ in 1996, then I read the King James version of the Bible from cover to cover. Then a brief stay at a mental hospital just for a week long evaluation. That I was able to piece the line together to show what I got out of Christianity. The party isn't far away and it's invitation only. Please find your Creator!

FORD, PERRY M., III
[a.] Dallas, TX [title] "Salvation Sojourner" [pers.] My writing is an extension of my faith in my God and Savior Jesus Christ in whom has been the major influence in my life ever since my youth. Hence, "Salvation Sojourner" was based upon the Bible and the journey a Christian travels in faithfulness to God. This poem was a written reflecting on my life, primarily as this spiritual sojourn I've walked evoked so many memories that I was touched in my heart, mind, and soul to express these reflections in a creative flow. My desire is that this poem will impact all who read it for God's glory!

FRALICK, JOEL
[a.] Evansville, IN [title] "If Time Be Told" [pers.] This poem just popped into my head one night and forced me to get up and write it. It is very special to me because it was read at my wedding to my beautiful wife, Michelle. I know it is her love and the happiness she brings to my life that created these words in my mind.

FRANK, MARY
[a.] Seaford, NY [title] "Whispers del Muerto" [pers.] This piece was inspired by my reflections on the Navajo Indian reservation during my internship in Chinle, AZ. I was urged to leave my Long Island home and explore the mysteries of desert life and canyons by my supportive sister, Nancy, who found her own adventures in England with her husband-to-be, John. During my travels, I found Canyon del Muerto and Canyon de Chelly, both filled with the history of the Anasazi tribe. These places became my private sanctuaries from the stress of my work and homesickness. I would often close my eyes and listen to the wind replicating the sound of oceans I left behind in New York. Now, I find the oceans surrounding Long Island remind me of the Canyons. This is my ode to them. I am presently attending Hunter College in pursuit of a Bachelors degree in English.

FRANKLAND, COLLEEN
[a.] Middlesex, England [title] "A Haunted House" [pers.] Poetry enables me to describe the very wonders of nature. By putting my thoughts into words, I try to transform the beautiful picture or story to other people, so that they too may see the wonderment. I live in the beautiful wilderness area in the garden route of South Africa where I am amongst some of nature's richest gifts. This I am most thankful for, as it gives me great insight to express feelings.

FREEMAN, DIONE M.
[a.] Flint, MI [title] "Your Touch" [pers.] This poem was written as a love letter to God. It acknowledges his greatness and how He touches our lives through nature. Often we rush through life and miss out on the simple treasures we have been given. The daily issues of life cloud our thoughts and cause us to miss the opportunity to praise God for His beauty, love, and kindness. I use the gift of writing to encourage others to seek a personal relationship with God through Jesus Christ our Savior. I am releasing a book of poetry July 2000 called *Transformations in His Presence.*

FRIEDMAN, LAUREN
[a.] Cape Coral, FL [title] "Shadowed Stranger" [pers.] The complexities and mysteries of people's personalities fascinate me. A true believer of the expression: "Don't judge a book by its cover," I am amazed at how quickly people shrug off others based on their appearances. I also understand the pain of being one of those cast aside, for I myself have had similar experiences. This poem was one way of expressing that inner turmoil.

GAINES, PEPSI
[a.] Uniontown, PA [title] "What Is My Name" [pers.] I feel that God blessed me with the talent to express the way I feel on paper, and be able to share it with the world. I hope the people who read this poem can relate to what I am saying, and relate back to it when their feeling the way I felt. I want people to read my poem when they feel that they don't know what else to do, maybe it will open up some hearts and encourage young people to do what I do—write poetry that comes from the heart and into you

GAINEY, MELISSA
[a.] Gaston, SC [title] "Magic" [pers.] At one point, the world was too much. I was angry and disappointed, so I wrote. As time passed by, not minding me, things turned brighter. I started smiling, and I wrote. And now, in the night, while I'm dreaming, I'm searching, for when I awaken, I write.

GARDNER, MARY
[a.] Central Islip, NY [title] "I Am" [pers.] My poem is a symbol of my self-pride. It is dedicated to everyone who is tired of proving themselves to others. My college professor discouraged my writing, from her analysis I stopped writing for years until the poems that were flowing in my head wouldn't let me just give up. I wrote and submitted my poetry. I now have two Editor's Choice Awards, nominations for poet of the year, and for one of the best Poet's of the 20th century. Published in 13 anthologies, writing my life story and a book of poems. Never let anyone take you away from yourself.

GARIBAY, RICARDO, III
[a.] Taylor, MI [title] "She" [pers.] I wrote this poem for my wife Carrie. She has been the love of my life since I laid eyes on her at fourteen years of age. Carrie has been there for me from every great moment such as the success of my career, to the tragic news of being diagnosed with leukemia. This required me to have a bone marrow transplant, where she stood by my side keeping me alive. I know in my heart that Carrie is the only true love for me. Carrie is my "She" and I will love her for as long as I live.

GARIS, MARIA
[a.] Toronto, ON [title] "Thoughts" [pers.] The small accomplishment I've had with this poem has been a great honor for me. I dedicate it to my husband and children who have always supported me and appreciated my work. It is a wonderful feeling to write and have others see what you see and experience your emotions. For me, writing is a way to liberate my soul in words. I can express my feelings and emotions. I am Chilean and currently reside in Toronto, Canada.

GEIGER, MEGHAN
[a.] Lt. Suamico, WI [title] "I Am the Rain Clouds" [pers.] Poetry is important to me because it lets me express my feelings and emotions freely. Poetry is a beautiful form of art and I am glad I possess this gift. I dedicate this poem to a friend I hold close to my heart.

GIESE, JAMES
[a.] Kansas City, MO [title] "Destiny" [pers.] What is a poem? A poem is a work of art put into words. It is a palette of colors brought together in such a way that it touches those hearts and minds that read it. A poem can warm you on a cold winter day or it can show what it's like to be the one stuck in the numbing cold. Poems can even show the tiniest lit of light to you daring the darkest of all nights. So what is a poem to me—search above and you'll see. But what is a poem to you?

GILBERT, MARY
[a.] Collins, MO [title] "The Voice at the End of the Line" [pers.] When a child, the grocer would give me meat wrapping paper. I'd fold it and take it to bed and write. This poem, "The Voice at the End of the Line," was written when I lost my husband January 1987. Am moving soon to be near my sister and brother.

GLENN, YOLANDA
[a.] Humboldt, TN [title] "Never Let Him Die Twice" [pers.] Poem writing for me is a gift from God. I'm thankful for my family and the gift he has given me. This particular poem, "Never Let Him Die Twice," was written for a very special teacher. It was through the encouragement of her that I am writing today. Unfortunately, when I wrote this poem her life was beginning to change. She had just lost one of her children to a terrible car wreck. This was my way of trying to confront her. Being able to write poems to others in times of hardship and special occasion is a blessing for me. I hope my poems will always confront and touch the souls of others.

GLICK-SHORE, SUSAN
[a.] Bartlett, IL [title] "Never Say, I Wish I Had" [pers.] I, like many others, had inspiration in my life. For many years I heard my grandmother say "I wish I had done this," I wish I had done that, not knowing that her influence made me think when I die, I'm going to say maybe I shouldn't have but never I wish I had. At the age of 14 years I had a near death drowning experience. I saw the light, I heard the voice, that experience changed my whole life, I believe, for the better. The friend of mine in this poem is me.

GLOVER, REBECCA
[a.] Sydney NS, Australia [title] "Step Through The Frame" [pers.] This poem is the way I like to look at life. I believe that every challenge we are given should be tackled just as if we are walking through a door. Accept what you are given and make it what you want. I dedicate this poem to three people I hold dearly in my heart, and thank for my wonderful parents. Dedicated to my Nanna and Pop Johnson and my Granddad Glover.

GOMEZ, MARIA
[a.] Burien, WA [title] "The Mom You Gave Me— I Am So Near" [pers.] It was nine years before I learned and accepted my mother's lack of love for me. It has also taken years to heal and understand, accept and help others with these same issues. This is my purpose for going through and sharing my heart with others, even the public. I dedicate this to my dear friend with an unfailing heart, Lynn Logan. Also, my in heart adopted mom I wish was mine who has loved me through all this, Linda Halterman. Look for the moms in your life, and you, too, shall heal and experience a love we all need as children, adults, and humans. Then you, too, can help others.

GOODALL, ADAM
[a.] Joplin, MO [title] "The Hidden Pain" [pers.] I believe that from the depths of misery comes the greatest inspiration, and nothing gives more inspiration of misery and otherwise than love, or lack thereof. That's why most of my poetry, including "The Hidden Pain," deals with a lost love, a love that wasn't meant to be or the glories of love. It's a major part of everyone's life so I think that it's something everyone can relate to. Everyone's been hurt and everyone's loved, that's what makes the poetry good.

GORDON, COREY
[a.] Buffalo, NY [title] "Giving In" [pers.] My interpretation of this poem does not matter. What matters is your interpretation. I hope that everybody views my poem in a different light. Please do not let anybody force feed ideas or interpretations down your throat. Be your own as a person. Do not fear what others will think of you.

GORIN, TAMMY
[a.] Austin, TX [title] "Jeremiah" [pers.] I wrote

this poem for my son Jeremiah. It contains a special message to Jeremiah to help him along through out his life and to inspire him to never give up! Jeremiah is 16 years old now. I originally wrote part of this poem in 1984 when he was a baby, but now that he is older I feel he needs guidance in caring for himself and knowing that God is with him every minute of every day.

GOSA, JENNY
[a.] Belmont, CA [title] "On My Knees" [pers.] "On My Knees" is about the death of my wonderful aunt, Tonya, who I called Ton-Ton. She died in a car accident last year when I was fifteen. The poem is about the stages of grief I went through, from anger to sadness to denial to desolation. I knew my mom, my aunt Sandy. Uncle Monty and Paw Paw (grandpa) were feeling the some pain. I wrote this as much for them as for me. I wanted Ton-Ton to know how much she meant to us, and how her absence forever changed our lives.

GOTTSCHALK, KATHERINE
[a.] Bluffton, SC [title] "A Simple Game?" [pers.] I wrote this poem in my younger days when I was still sowing my wild oats. It pretty much sums up my philosophy on life. I write poetry to say what I can't seem to say on an everyday basis. It gives me much comfort and if it gives anyone else pleasure then I feel that I have made a contribution to life. I am an ordinary housewife and waitress as a part time. I love to play golf and write. Obviously, my poetry is better than my golf game. Maybe someday both will improve.

GRECO, SHIRLEE
[a.] Katy, TX [title] "The Shining in Your Eyes" [pers.] This poem means a lot to me because it reflects the emotion I have for a very special person, my boyfriend, Eric. When I met him I knew he was the one to make me happy. He is my one and only true love. If you could only see the light in our eyes as we look at one another. It could make the strongest man melt.

GREENBERG, JEFF
[a.] Palm City, FL [title] "The Victim of Genesis" [pers.] This poem refers to the enduring battle fought by the serpent of Genesis, even after his initial defiance of the rules. I would like to thank my father, whose endless lectures on poetry and philosophy inspired me to construct this piece of literature. Finally, I would like to take this chance to show my appreciation to the people at poetry.com and The International Library of Poetry for giving me this opportunity to showcase my poetry, as it is my first. To everyone who helped me, thank you, especially to my mother and father.

GRIFFIN, JON
[a.] Elizabeth, NJ [title] "I Would if I Could" [pers.] This poem I have written is to help people who are not self-motivated. I was one of those people before I wrote the poem. I would like to dedicate the poem to Montel Williams, as well. As a person diagnosed with MS, he continues to fight the good fight and not let his troubles take over his life. I, myself, am a person who suffers from depression. I'm doing whatever I can to keep myself from falling back into self-pessimism and this poem has done just that. I also wrote this poem to motivate people with mental illnesses as well. My hobbies are script writing, listening to music, calligraphy, and writing lyrics for music as well as writing novels.

GRIGG, JOSEPH
[a.] Sandy, UT [title] Recipe For Tenderness [pers.] I like to write, it lets me create a universe over which I have complete control. I never thought anyone would ever read it. Thank you so much.

GROOMS, EVAN
[a.] Xenia, OH [title] "Tommy MacDill" [pers.] A poem is the emotional and physical essence of a larger and grander work. A story stripped down to a poem, which like a song, can stir the spirit to great heights. My desire is the larger story, but I cannot ignore the tug to create passion and fervor through a poem. "Tommy MacDill" contains all the qualities

of a larger story but down to just a simple poem. "Tommy" is a broken love story filled with wanderlust, pride, jealousy, deception, exile, and finally realization. I dedicate this story to my Aunt Dorris.

GROOT, HARRIET
[a.] Bolton, CT [title] "The Quilt Tent" [pers.] "The Quilt Tent" is one of my many childhood memories of living on my grandmother's farm in Vermont. I have started writing these memories in poetry as it's my way for the inner child to express herself. Today I know how special my Grammie was to me. She even taught me how to make a quilt and I have made several as an adult.

GRUSS, KATHERINE
[a.] Hollsopple, PA [title] "The Greatest Gift" [pers.] This isn't just a poem to me. This is the song my heart sings every time I look at my daughter. After two years of disappointment and tears, the doctor told me I was pregnant. Then, four months into my pregnancy, I almost lost her. On my way to the hospital, I was quietly pleading with God. I promised him that if he allowed me to keep her, I would raise her to know him. Even though he knew I would fall short at times, God gave me this wonderful little girl who is the greatest blessing my life will ever know.

GUERRERO, MERLIE
[a.] Carson, CA [title] "I Am A Filipino American" [pers.] I am a retired school teacher of Los Angeles Unified School District, after 23 years of full-time teaching. My classroom students and the enthusiastic, active members of the Filipino Club, which I sponsored for 18 years at Wilmington Jr. High School, greatly inspired me to write this poem to convey to the young minds of this emerging youth, inspiring messages to uphold their aspirations, ideals, pride, and success. This poem is likewise very endearing to me. It fondly reflects my childhood upbringing, my multi-lingual, multicultural social environment, my values and caring sensitivities as a wife, a mother, teacher, community worker, and leader, and as a human being.

GUNN, QUILLIAN, SR.
[a.] Detroit, MI [title] "A Laughing Game" [pers.] "A Laughing Game" was written over thirty years ago, along with a group of short verses I called "Thoughts at Random," gathered as I road the bus to and from New York. I listened to the young mothers as they talked of their sons and daughters taking turns geting sick. After trying the folk medicine treatments offered by the older mothers, a trip to the doctors office met with results more often than not. Kahlil Gebran, Jack London, Herman Melville, the Bible, James F. Cooper, and Lanston Hughes pervaded my growing philosophy then as now. Maybe "Thoughts at Random" can come forward.

GUTIERREZ, MARKO
[a.] San Diego, CA [title] "Chasing the Sun" [pers.] This poem is special in that it reaches out to the dying heart. This to me is the true beauty in poetry. It awakens a dormant soul, awakens the spirit, and brings the heart back from the dead. Poetry gives hope to those who had abandoned it or found hope hard to come by. Most importantly, poetry can be an antibiotic, a vaccine, which cures all illness and ailments inside the human heart and soul. I hope others may draw inspiration from my poetry as I have drawn inspiration from others. My poetry is manifested from this inspiration.

GUY, ANGELA
[a.] Kingsport, TN [title] "The Enemy" [pers.] This poem is dedicated to the memory of my grandfather, Odie A. Tyler. He passed away on July 13, 1998. Cancer was his enemy. I never truly had the chance to say good-bye. Therefore, writing this poem is my way of telling him what I never had the chance to say. This poem, along with others I have written, helps to give me a sense of closure. I know right now, at this very moment, Papaw is in Heaven with a smile on his face. I love you Papaw!

HABLETT, JENNIFER
[a.] Schuykill Haven, PA [title] "St. Patrick's Day" [pers.] This poem is special to me because St. Patrick's

Day is a special holiday. I like St. Patrick's Day because it is a lucky day for many people.

HAHN, LAURYN
[a.] Livonia, FL [title] "Bumblebee's" [pers.] Lauryn Kimberly Hahn was born on November 6, 1986. Lauryn is afraid of bumblebees, that is why she wrote this poem. Lauryn dedicate this poem to the students of Riley Middle School. She especially dedicated this poem to Ms. Reed-Nordwall's six hour Language Arts Class, some of Lauryn's other poems are called "Parents," "Nature," "Antietam," and "He." Lauryn plans to be a famous poet and a model, she also wants to work with special education children.

HAID, KEEGAN
[a.] Arthur, WV [title] "Gone" [pers.] I am currently 14 years old and attend Petersburg High School in Petersburg, WV. I enjoy writing poetry very much as it helps me put my feelings and emotions into words. This poem came to me as a dream and the next day I put it into words. Besides writing poetry, I also enjoy playing basketball and soccer. Someday I plan on working with computers.

HAILEY, JOHNATHAN
[a.] Bartlesville, OK [title] "Of Golden Ghosts" [pers.] Throughout all, even common ages, certain realities represent themselves as truths. Yet with the exception of few, indeed a minor few, none seem to grasp such knowledge as gold, using it body and soul. This changes everything.

HAILUE, JERUSALEM
[a.] Wilsonville, OR [title] "Feelings of Love" [pers.] Hi! I'm Jerusalem Hailue! I'm a ten year old fifth grader. I live in Wilsonville, OR. Poetry is a way to relax and hang loose; it refreshes me! I hope to bring great joy to the families that will read my poem. I feel proved because this is my first published poem. Writing this poem has been especially fulfilling because I get to share my love for poetry with other young poets. I hope to encourage people to write poetry and to strive for their best. I believe that if you put your mind to it anything can happen!

HAMZAJ, SHPRESA
[a.] Las Vegas, NV [title] "Best Friend" [pers.] This poem was written for my best friend, and symbolizes the long road we have just begun to travel. Poetry expresses my innermost feelings and lets me escape from everyday chaos. To my family for all of the support, thank you.

HAN, DR. JOHN
[a.] Cranston, RI [title] "The Gift from My Heart" [pers.] Jimmy and his parents were my patients. Near Christmas, his mother asked me, can you treat losing temper? Who are you talking about, I asked? My son Jimmy. What? I thought he was a kind tender young man. Yes, but not to us. I wrote this poem and asked Jimmy to promise not to open this envelope until Christmas dinner and read it in front of your family. After that I heard while reading my poem, he started crying and his families tearing. Almost a year has gone by and he has not lost his temper yet.

HAPPLE, KATHERINE
[a.] Chiefland, FL [title] "Life's Priorities . . . ?" [pers.] My poem "Life's Priorities . . . ?" was written in the hopes that many people would take some time to reflect on doing their part to overcome the negative path that seems to be consuming our world and the lives of many. If more people tried harder to make a difference, then eventually we could begin to see a difference—many of life's problems will continue to multiply unless we as individuals do our part to make positive changes. The smallest effort could produce great results. So don't contribute to the problem, instead contribute all of your efforts toward working on the solution—it begins with you and I!

HARDISTER, SUSAN
[a.] Albemarle, NC [title] "A Weary Soul" [pers.] I have been a resident of Albemarle, NC since July 1985, where I attended college for medical assisting

technology. I also received a degree in veterinary case from the school of animal science in Scranton, Pennsylvania. Poetry is a gift that I received from my mother, Elsie Lou Johnson who I am dedicating "A Weary Soul" to the memory of, for without her love, commitment, and dedication to nature and its beauty, this poem wouldn't have been written.

HARPER, CECILIA
[a.] Howland, ME [title] "Jesus Lover of My Soul" [pers.] Poetry is one of my gifts from God, it's my way of saying what's in my heart. It's my way of showing what God has done for me. I'm 81 in June and five times I wasn't going to live through operations, but God brought me through. I'm thankful for his love and mercy. It's also my way of showing others what God can do for them. All they need to do is go to Him in prayer, with faith, and He'll do the rest, as you can see. By the way of thinking and expressing myself, I'm a Christian of 59 years and mother of my living children and 110 grand and great=grandchildren and great-great-grandchildren. God's blessings.

HARRIS, DEBORAH
[a.] Coldwater, MI [title] "Ode to Richard Roe" [pers.] The poem named "Ode to Richard Roe" is based on a true story of a person who was slowly introduced into what some people refer to as a vision quest teaching. It is painful, emotionally and physically, and is uncalled for. A vision quest teaching is based on the intentional use of power of suggestion, a type of hypnosis. Richard Roe is a fictitious name used in legal proceedings for a male party whose true name is not known, used especially as the second such name when two male persons are involved and real names have not been ascertained.

HARRIS, TREVA
[a.] Ashland, VA [title] "Dear Friend" [pers.] I was born May 7, 1955, in Flint, MI. My parents are Dorothy D. Bostaph and Francis A. Bostaph, husband Jimmy W. Harris married January 7, 1983. I took GED and accounting courses, Office Manager taking a writing course. From Ashland; VA. One poem published Inter-National Library of Poetry: "Last Good-byes." This poem is memory of Audrey Butler, a dear friend of my husband and me.

HARTL, RICHARD
[a.] Billings, MT [title] "That was Life" [pers.] My point of this poem is to show that life itself needs a beginning faith, a clean environment, and that it is vulnerable to extinction.

HARTNETT, THOMAS
[a.] Lindenwold, NJ [title] "On Finding Eternal Love on the Verge . . . of the End of the World" [pers.] This poem was scribbled on a napkin late at night in a dinner while waiting for some friends . . . so much for the myth of the tortured, isolated soul. It's quite a simple poem, really, and I think it speaks for itself. Take from it what you will, it means no more or less than what it makes you feel. I would like to thank my family for always supporting and encouraging me, and also Kim, for the inspiration and for convincing me to submit this piece.

HASENBANK, JENNIFER
[a.] Manhattan, KS [title] "To Reggie, with Love" [pers.] This poem was written as a gift to my husband for our wedding day. I wanted the pastor to read it at the end of the ceremony so that everyone would know how special Reggie was to me. I have found poetry to be a great way to express my love and feelings to other family members. As a future elementary school teacher, I hope to encourage my students to express their feelings through poetry, since it is such a unique way to communicate to others.

HAWK, STEVE
[a.] Lindenwold, NJ [title] "An Officer, a Husband, a Father, and a Friend" [pers.] As a volunteer with the Disaster Services branch of the American Red Cross, I am fully aware of how important it is for a community to pull together during difficult times. I was so touched by the generous support and love shown by the community in the days following a local police officer's death I felt obligated to make a contribution as well. "An Officer, a Husband, a Father, and a Friend" is not only a thank you for those who gave their lives in the line of duty, but for those who continue to do so every day!

HAYES, JIM
[a.] Port Murray, NJ [title] "Mother" [pers.] I'm not truly happy with any poem I wrote unless within the last few lines, the reader or myself will have to pause to expel a gasp or a held in breath, or to release a tear. Like a suspense thriller, I must have a clincher for me to feel a flash thought or a memory to reflect on to make that connection that I find so completely satisfying, like a smash in the face with an anvil.

HEADLEY, JENNIFER
[a.] Merced, CA [title] "Flowers" [pers.] The poem "Flowers" was written to express how I feel when I get flowers, especially when I'm down. Flowers and friends mix well, therefore this poem helps us visualize the goodness of a gift of flowers. I hope this poem can bring some light into someone's eyes or cheer them up

HEDRINGTON, JOSHAH
[a.] Washington, DC [title] "Memory of a Stranger" [pers.] It is through God that I am able to express myself through poetry, and I thank the Lord with all my heart. I would also like to thank the Oprah Winfrey show. I began to keep a gratitude journal after watching Oprah Winfrey, and miraculously discovered I had a talent for poetry. Thank you Oprah! It is my vision to someday share all my poetry with the world. I see poetry as the voice of the soul. To have that voice heard across the globe would be one of my greatest fulfillment.

HEISKELL-SIMMONS, DEBORAH
[a.] Louisburg, KS [title] "The Pedestal" [pers.] I write poetry as an expression of events, times or people that have crossed my life path. I truly believe poetry can heal a soul, mend a broken heart, enlighten wisdom or produce a smile . I dedicate this poem to my father, Woody, the only dad I've ever had. I love you, Dad!

HENDRICKS, CRAIG
[a.] Salem, OH [title] "Month and a Half" [pers.] Lovers come and go like the wind. Sometimes you find someone who touched your heart, and you fall in love, deeper than you realize. Love is a powerful force. It plays tricks on you, but if you look closely you may find that these "tricks" are your own feelings you keep hidden. That's what "Month and a Half" is all about

HERNANDEZ, ANN
[a.] Kenner, LA [title] "Long Lost Love" [pers.] I am Ann Wiggin Hernandez, 42 years old. I was born in New Orleans, LA and live in Kenner, LA. My husband, was born in Havana, Cuba and came to live in the United States when he was 11. We were happily married on, July 13, 1997. I am helping my husband, Onil Lino Hernandez Jr., raise his daughter, Katie. Onil and I met, and fell in love 22 years ago. We were engaged for 18 months and we decided to end the relationship due to conflicts in religion and our ages. We were both teenagers. After both of us marrying others and never seeing or knowing where the other was, we were reunited at the Funeral of the friend of Onil's that originally introduced us. After our divorces from our previous spouses, we were married six weeks later. I always say, "Love does have a strange way of finding you." Never give up on your long lost love. Somehow, somewhere, someway, they do surface again. Even if only in your heart and memories.

HIETT, JENNIFER
[a.] Dallas, TX [title] "Deep Inside My Heart" [pers.] This poem was inspired by a young lady who was going through some hard times. She was examining her life, and had to make some difficult decisions. I wanted her to know that she was not alone

HILL, AMY
[a.] La Crescent, MN [title] "My Nanny" [pers.] Hi my name is Amy Louise Hill, I'm from La Crescent Hokah Elementary School. I have lots of friends and relatives. I like to hang around my family, especially my cousins. I like to play soccer in the spring, I also like to play softball in the summer. I made up my poem at school when we were making books for our parents for Christmas. I was playing around and it hit me that it worked and now I'm so glad I'm a semifinalist. I've never won anything before.

HILL, ANTONIO
[a.] Detroit, MI [title] "The Fear" [pers.] My vision of poetry, is one spiritual inspiration. It was a gift from God with no formal training or writing classes. I use to write in order to express what I was feeling, in an effort to cope with the day to day stresses of my life. I started compiling a notebook of my writings Which I entitled "A Life of Poems." I would periodically share some of them with select people. However, I wrote basically for myself. Then God touched me to share my gift with the world, which is what flames my passion for writing.

HILL, MONIQUE
[a.] Huntington Sta, NY [title] "Mon Ciel" [pers.] The title of my poem, "Mon Ciel," is in French. It means my heaven. This poem is very special to me because it describes what heaven means to me.

HILLYER, REBECCA
[a.] Liberty, IN [title] "Twelve Inebriated Arguments" [pers.] Poetry is the moment beauty touched my night. It's a portal for greater thinking, for which I've always been strongly attracted to. The Midwest gave me common things, but alas, my beautiful children, Judith, Nate, and Billy are not. Nor is my beloved husband, James, whom I can thank for his never-ceasing love and belief in me. And for my friends Tony and Velvet, their fantastic life material provided the equation, making my work more than interesting. I can now know why Plath and Sexton had great talks. They made sense of the senseless; a work of art.

HINES, DOMINIC
[a.] Carneys Point, NJ [title] "The Key of Peace" [pers.] I would like to dedicate this poem to some very important people in my life: my brother Justin, for showing me the meaning of courage and perseverance. You are my hero. My wife and children, for showing me the meaning of true love and the most important characteristic a person can possess: Forgiveness. I will love you forever. My parents for making me the man I am today. The pen mirrors your soul, it will not fail you. Thank you very much for reading my poem. I hope you liked it.

HITCHCOCK, BRIAN
[a.] Atoka, TN [title] "A Capella in Blue" [pers.] My poem is about the pursuit of a very special woman resulting in failure. To me, the best poetry is with music, the best example of this is anything written by Adam F. Duritz of the Counting Crows; he is my "Robert Frost." He has inspired me to write, his lyrics have helped me so much to deal with this cynical world. I love to share my views with others in the forms of lyrics. Maybe I've thought of something no one else has, maybe my lyrics/poetry can help others as Adam's have helped me. I am 22 years old, I live in Memphis, TN. I am a self-employed mechanic.

HOGGINS, MICHAEL
[a.] Harrisburg, OR [title] "Billows from Above" [pers.] I'm reclusive by nature. My inclinations are adventures. I enjoy seeking the countless faces of beauty as my favorite pastime. When I partake in the sensation of the presence of beauty, I find a very high form of motivation that I can apply

anywhere in my life by seeking beauty. The beauty in all harmony, the beauty in irony, love, learning, the mind (both beast and human). It is this quest for beauty in which, then through me, finds expression. Such expressions may be through poetry, a good deed, an invention or idea. The poem "Billows from Above" is an acknowledgment of the beauty of the blessing of clouds. So many wonderful things we take for granted seldom are given the appreciation from which our souls can benefit. Clouds don't care, they have nothing to sell. They can only offer that which we can only accept, yet there is nothing we can take from them. The same with the wind, snow, and the essence of life. We can get snowed on, or we can open our eyes and get something out of the experience.

HOLDAHL, JOELLE
[a.] Davenport, IA [title] "Warm" [pers.] My poem is about my husband, Jason. I love to watch him when he doesn't know I'm looking. I find inspiration in my husband and my children, they are the most important things in my life. When I can express my love for them in flowing words, I feel very complete. Poetry is just my hobby. My children and my husband are my passion.

HOLDER, CARRIE
[a.] East Orange, NJ [title] "A Thank You Note to Jesus" [pers.] A mother, grandmother, and great-grandmother. She attends Bethel Baptist Church, Orange, NJ where she continues her singing to the glory of the Lord. Her family is very proud of her accomplishments in church, ministry of music, and writing. This poem is very special because it expresses her thanks to God through Jesus for His many Blessings. As it is, she hopes it will help them to thank God also, for their many Blessings!

HOLLOWAY, KEVIA
[a.] Memphis, TN [title] "Racism" [pers.] Poetry has been a part of me for a very long time. Whenever I feel the urge to write poetry, it is usually written in free verse and of a topic I have very strong feelings about. Last summer I attended Rhodes College writers and scholars camp where I signed up for the Poetry Class and wrote many poems including "Racism." The professor encouraged the class to enter our poems into poetry contest to see if they would be published. By taking his advice, my poem has been selected for publication; and I owe it all to the poetry professor at the camp.

HOLMAN, GARY
[a.] Livonia, MI [title] "America's Wars" [pers.] I was inspired to write this poem after viewing the movie "Saving Private Ryan." I was at home that same evening thinking about the movie when I started crying just like Tom Hanks did in the movie. All of a sudden the words to this poem started coming in spurts which I wrote down immediately, getting out of bed to do so. Originally I thought of another title to the poem. But, after some serious thinking I decided to select the title "America's Wars" because so many wars have been fought in the combat zone.

HOOK, JAMES
[a.] Houston, TX [title] "Love's Realms" [pers.] Poetry is existence itself, expressed in verse, and touches every facet of life as we perceive it to be. It is love, hate, fear, and joy. Poetry is the song that calms the savage beast, or the battle cry that stirs a nation to fight for its freedom. Poetry is passion, no matter what stirs such passion. And for me, poetry is an expression of the love that makes me whole, that love which I have for the three woman in my life, my mother, my daughter, and my true twin flame, Pamela.

HOOLEHAN, EDWARD
[a.] Highland, IN [title] "The Party" [pers.] In high school poetry became a second release for me, next to sports and exercising. I started writing poems because I needed to express feelings without saying them, and of course started because of a girl, Laura M., who is still one of my best friends. My best poems involve what I love, or things that are a big part of my life. "The Party" was written when I had the duty of being sober during one of my fraternity parties. Majoring in engineering doesn't give much time to write, but I'll always find time to do what I love.

HOSTETLER, HEATHER
[a.] Melbourne, FL [title] "The Orange" [pers.] I am an artist and I like to use poetry as another medium for painting pictures. I am 11 years old and I began writing and illustrating at age four. My poem has a secret message about giving and receiving. I wrote this poem to encourage people to be more caring toward others.

HOUSER, GLADYS
[a.] Columbus, OH [title] "The Life of One" [pers.] I get quiet, think long time then I write. I have a ninth grade education, and wanted to find out if I have what it takes to write poems. I was so excited my heart still is pounding from the joy of hearing from you. Thank you from the bottom of my heart. This pleases me— I feel so proud. I will let my family members see that I was right in sending the poem. Thank you.

HUBBARD, AUDREY
[a.] Bennettsville, SC [title] "Deep Deception" [pers.] I believe that my poetry is a gift from God. I was inspired not only by my seventeen year old daughter, who left home with her six-month-old daughter to live with her boyfriend and his parents, but for all who are lost in sin. My hope is that through me, God can reach those lost souls before it's too late. I thank God for this gift.

HUCK, MARISA
[a.] Columbia, MO [title] "The Release" [pers.] Poetry is my self expression. It is a gift that flows fluidly out of my pen. This poem is for everyone that believed in me and provided me with love and support, especially the one who always encourage my writing. I am originally from Ste. Genevieve, MO. I am currently attending the University of Missouri in Columbia. I am working toward my masters in Animal Nutrition. In my spare time I love to write poetry, draw, paint, hang out with friends, listen to the music, and play sports.

HUGHES, SHIRLEY
[a.] Pana, IL [title] "I Have A Dream" [pers.] I feel God has given me a unique talent to share. If my poem can motivate others to think about our children's future then my poem will have meaning, not just words written on page. I would like to dedicate this poem to my three children Melissa, Troy, and Tiffany—the most precious gifts to my life and my heart. They are my legacy of life.

HULA, KATHY
[a.] Friendswood, TX [title] "Wedding Day Bookmark" [pers.] Written for my daughter's wedding, this verse was placed on the back of a bookmark designer with the wedding flower, red roses. The bookmark was a remembrance from the bride and groom to all attendees, commemorating the importance and impact of family and friends on the lives of the married couple.

HUNT, STEPHANIE
[a.] Pompano Beach, FL [title] "My Life" [pers.] Poetry identifies with different aspects of life, and tends to display a sense of freedom of the heart and mind. Each poem I write is a personal invitation to everyone to embrace a part of me. My poem "My Life" being published is a great accomplishment, for which I am happy to share, and I hope this is one of many in regards to poetry, and life. I will always thrive in every endeavor so I can be an inspiration to my children: La Nya Monet Hunt and Asante Malik Frazier.

HUNTER, RUSSELL
[a.] Bucyrus, OH [title] "Circles of Life" [pers.] I am an artist in many aspects, but my passion belongs to music. I am currently searching for a record label to help me turn my visions and dreams into reality. This poem was inspired by the actions of the many people I've meet in today's world. I see so many people act out without any thought of consequence. So many people hurt others to cover their own insecurities and fears. I think we all need to step aside of ourselves and see what we want as a whole and as individuals. We need to realize our actions today will forever effect the reaction of our future.

HUSSAIN, MADIHA
[a.] Euless, TX [title] "A Lone Look" [pers.] Reading poetry has always compelled me to envision the world through somebody else's thoughts. My writing instincts solely come from the different people whom I have met and from whom I've got inspiration to always search you the brighter part of our lives. My poem basically deals with the faith which we have in God, that he is the one who will always straighten out the problems which we have. I believe that when something goes wrong it will take time to go right, but it will get solved and that is something in which I basically believe in.

INGRAM-JONES, GWEN
[a.] Lake Stevens, WA [title] "Angel" [pers.] It started out because I just wanted to write a poem. Then a friend was having a horrible day and I thought I'd try to cheer her up. Poetry has been a way to get my emotions and thoughts out and looked at.

ITKONEN, JOEL
[a.] Pengilly, MN [title] "I Think I'm in Love with You" [pers.] "I Think I'm in Love with You" was a poem I wrote while dating a girl whom I was very confused with at the time. I know now that I love this girl, and someday I plan on marrying her. Dedicated to Rachel Adams, because I love you.

JACINTHIA, TURABIA
[a.] Oakland, CA [title] "Lost Without Love" [pers.] This poem was written when I was 11 years old. I was very sad as a child—I tried to commit suicide. I have since earned to embrace life, and to live it to the fullest. I am now 53, thank God! A long with the Lord; I have used poetry many times, and many nights, as a refuge for tears. I have used poetry to cry for myself and others, in my time of need. Poetry makes me sad, happy, joyous, nervous, depressed. But it always made me proved to be able to feel fully.

JACKSON, MARY
[a.] Charlotte, NC [title] "Interior Light" [pers.] I am a native of Memphis, TN and have resided in North Carolina for the past six years. Poetry has always fascinated me. I love reading, and "especially" love writing it. "Interior Light" was written wholeheartedly with myself in mind. However, it applies to everyone worldwide. I feel we all have an "Interior Light." We just have different wattages. Personally, I operate at a hundred watts. As a referenced in my poem, if you don't like the way you shine, it's as simple as changing a bulb.

JACKSON, NATASHA
[a.] Rochester Hills, MI [title] "I Say I See" [pers.] Poetry has long been viewed by many as the catharsis for the soul. This I believe to be very accurate. Many times difficulty may arise in expressing our thoughts and emotions, however they seem to flow fluently in the form of poetry. They reveal the inner person that some may rarely see. Additionally, poetry serves as a uniting factor with anyone, including strangers, as we can identify with the words and most importantly the powerful meaning behind them. But best of all poetry is a valuable tool in relating to our loved ones just how we feel about them, with very little or no hesitation at all. "I Say I See" is just one example of this.

JACOBSEN, JOHN
[a.] Oshawa, ON [title] "Dream Walker" [pers.] The poem was inspired by a wonderful lady, whom I am very much in love with, Bev, it encompasses the dreams we both have and shared feelings for each other. Bev has inspired so many poems that I wrote her love and warmth brought out all of the poems written from my heart, in total I have written 18 poems she has directly inspired. I hope to one day publish these for her.

JACOBY, TORI
[a.] Cuero, TX [title] "Never Forget" [pers.] I wrote this poem as a gift for two of my close friends with whom I will be graduating with in May 2000. They are very special to me and I have had many great times with them. This poem symbolizes those memories and what they mean to me. I will never forget what we shared, and I hope they do not, either. They will remain an important part of my life, always. I hope everyone has been as fortunate as I have been having the friends that I do, and I hope everyone always remembers the memories.

JACQUES, GABRIEL
[a.] San Diego, CA [title] "Valentino's Citrus Orchard: A Death Tango" [pers.] How many people know who Mr. Valentino was? Latin Lover? Screen Idol? Exotica? He was an artist who aspired (with a degree in agriculture) to be a farmer, of oranges to be exact. He delivered truly in California, my home state. Someday I will erect a monument to him. For now, let this poem suffice. I always ask myself this question . . . what makes a man, a man?

JARED, JOE
[a.] Yukon, OK [title] "I Am the Lonely Wind" [pers.] I am profoundly grateful for two gifts that my ancestors have passed on to me: Christian faith and poetry. My great-grandmother and my grandmother wrote poems that inspired and blessed others. One day while driving in Western Oklahoma I saw windmills and mesas. Words came to me from who-knows-where, and I stopped every few miles to write them on a napkin. Finally I read the finished poem aloud and wept. Since that day many poems have come to me. Perhaps "I Am the Lonely Wind" marked by birth as a poet.

JAVED, BASSAM
[a.] Lower Sackville, NS [title] "Bassam Javed" [pers.] I started writing poetry three years ago when I was eight years old . My teacher got us to write poems and send them to the Poetry Institute of Canada. My poem was published in a book of verse titled "From a Magic Place," as well as six other students poems. The next year I sent in another poem, and so did one student from the other six. Both poems were published in a book of verse titled "A Golden Morning." The year after that (last year) I was the only person out of the seven to send in a poem. It was published in a book of verse titled "Flower from My Garden."

JOHANNESMEYER, JANA
[a.] Okeene, OK [title] "Meaning Found" [pers.] Sometimes in the quiet of the night, I just stand and watch my children sleep, being grateful for the opportunity. In times like these, I'm overwhelmed by feelings of unspoken emotion. Late at night, I felt compelled to put pen to paper and this poem was the outcome. "Meaning Found" is a personal tribute to God and the three sons He has blessed my husband and I with. I forever want Ryan, Derek, and Alec to know and remember what I did with my life was to be their mother.

JOHNSEY, SONJA
[a.] Phoenix, AZ [title] "Mistress" [pers.] We were driving through spring snow on our way back home. Having never broached the subject of nature in my poetry, and being surrounded by mist-clad mountains at that time, I was inspired to write. When I shared "Mistress" with the driver, and he had to pull off to the side of the road. I knew that the poem was complete and effective. For their encouragement, support, and love through the years, I would like to thank my mother, Sherry and my sister, Lisa.

JOHNSON, ELIZABETH
[a.] Baltimore, MD [title] "Untitled" [pers.] This poem was written at our annual church feast and reflects the love, peace, and joy we shared. I sincerely hope that other people will be inspired by our feeling of togetherness and understanding, and the love of God in each of us. I am a retired teacher. I love to read and do crossword puzzles.

JOHNSON, LUEGENE
[a.] Memphis, TN [title] "Just For You" [pers.] I wrote this poem for someone special, my girlfriend April Donald. This poem is also for Minnie, Coretta, Syntrina, Lavesa, Pamela, Quinton, Cecil, Fredrick, James, George, LaToya, Elica, Johnny, Earlie La Quita, Curtis, Carolyn, Deborrah, and especially for my mother, Doris Ann Johnson. I love poetry because it helps me express how I feel. I think that anyone can write poetry if they put their mind to it. I wrote this poem because I love my girlfriend and I wanted to let her know. My poems also help me tell people that I need a little more love. I love you all!

JONES, LILLIAN
[a.] Sims, NC [title] "Until We See You Again" [pers.] Poetry touches my innermost spirit. Since the death of my beloved mother, Estelle H. Hinnant on September 23, 1999, it has been an avenue for dealing with my grief. I needed the assurance that she is released from the body in which she was imprisoned during the latter days of her life. Writing this poem has helped this poem is also for my three brothers, two sisters-in-law, my husband, her grandchildren and great-grandchildren. They loved her as much as I do.

JONES, SHAWN
[a.] Lithonia, GA [title] "Beauty" [pers.] "Beauty" is self-explanatory. Sometimes you meet a person and see so much inside of them that you just can't help but love him. I think every woman has experienced this once in her life. I've been writing poetry since June of 1999, I primarily write about relationships. I write about personal life experiences and about the experiences of others. Writing, for me, is a way to express my feelings for those I love. I want my poetry and short stories to encourage, inspire, and uplift anyone who reads it. It is truly an honor to have my poem published. This accomplishment will help me to reach my ultimate goal of one day publishing a book of my own.

JORDAN, JANE
[a.] Hartford, NC [title] "A Gift of Love" [pers.] My faith is my strength, and this poem was a fun way to share it with others. Love is a gift from God meant to be shared with our fellow man; so grab yourself some and pass some along.

JOST, ERIKA
[a.] Grosse Pointe Park, MI [title] "Beauty of Nature" [pers.] "The only way to change a person is to change the way he thinks." One of my seventh grade teachers was telling my class that to explain how Jesus changed our world. Jesus didn't use force or violence to display His message; He used words. That is why poetry is so special to me. It can change the way a person thinks, therefore altering his actions. I had just read *Lord of the Flies* with my seventh grade literature class prior to writing this particular poem. It woke me up in the wee hours of the morning, when the world seems to be at its worst. If my poetry makes anysingle person think twice before they act, I shall have succeeded in my quest to change the world.

JURACEK, JOSEPH
[a.] New York, NY [title] "Finding Her Warmth" [pers.] I am a Franciscan priest and psychotherapist who works and ministers at St. Francis of Assisi Church in Midtown Manhattan. St. Francis has been a major influence in my work, I try to capture his simplicity in my poetry, his fervor in finding God wherever he looked, in whatever He did, and in every crevice of human life.

KAACK, HERB
[a.] Millville, NJ [title] "Share with Me" [pers.] This poem was written when I was dating my now wife, Jocelyn. She is and always will be my strength. I love her so much. She has stood by me through illness and financial difficulties. This is dedicated to my wife.

KAMBESTAD, KAREN
[a.] Elgin, IL [title] "Memories of a Military Childhood" [pers.] While working on my family genealogy, I discovered that it was difficult to put in words exactly how my childhood could be described. So, I tried writing a poem and this is the result. One of my goals is to the complete a family history with stories, poems, and pictures for generations to come.

KAMONT, EDWARD
[a.] Somerset, NJ [title] "The Beauty I See" [pers.] My one true passion is inspired by God and in my pen. I enjoy writing for others—if you ever need something nice written but can't come up with the right words . . .

KAMPHAUS, JEFFREY
[a.] Cincinnati, OH [title] "Love of a Rose" [pers.] I thank you for reaching into your own heart and touching the poem I grew in mine. The world needs to hear me. Prepare for what I can do if I'm given the opportunity.

KASKELA, MELISSA
[a.] Niceville, FL [title] "Life to Me" [pers.] "Life to Me" is about a dark time of my life. I was a teenage runaway, and I was staying in Atlanta with a friend. We were flat broke, no food and depressed. I have found that writing I can express my feelings and emotions a little better.

KATAMAY, KAJA
[a.] Los Osos, CA [title] "Poetry in Motion" [pers.] Poetry kisses me with its eyes closed; I hold its bottomless purse while every pair of jeans fits it perfectly in the dressing room. I defrost the cosmos for dinner while it smokes a hand-rolled cigar of all that is earthly and divine. I baby-sit the Muses while it's having martinis with its harem, the fire devastatingly gorgeous human senses. It may beckon me across a small ocean, but the water defies mercury and when the eyes of the waiting and the wading meet, the simple truth is understood: I have conceived her, and she has given birth to me.

KEENAN, MICHAEL
[a.] Voorhees, NJ [title] "True Beauty" [pers.] I wrote "True Beauty" to inspire everyone to seek personal fulfillment. We want the very best for everyone we know, but tend to accept less for ourselves. Settling is committing a crime against our own happiness! To fully enrich ourselves, we need a healthy mind, body, and spirit. If one suffers they all suffer. True beauty is the way of life. Fulfill your destiny and achieve greatness. Create values, never violate another person, and take nothing for granted! To complete oneself, we need to grow every day!

KELLY, DONNA
[a.] Wrentham, MA [title] "A Message from Your Angel" [pers.] I feel that my inspirational writing of poetry is a gift. Poetry wasn't always a part of my life. My first poem was written for my dad who passed away in October of 1998. I have written many poems since then. The words come to me at the speed of you reading this article with the utmost pleasure I receive in writing poetry. The admired expression the look on one's face, that I have touched their hearts is all the gratitude I'll ever need for a gift of a poem. I live on one Clark Road with my husband, Thomas.

KENNEDY, CYNTHIA
[a.] Dallas, TX [title] "Life Is" [pers.] This poem is very sad but it's reality. In this poem I described how I see and I also describe what I think of when the word "Life" is mentioned at age 13. My poem talks about the many different things that happen in life. As I re-read over my work, I am proud to say that I did it, that I made it up. I only hope that everyone who reads my poem will stop and realize exactly what life means to them. I also hope that they see just how badly we are hurting the world and ourselves. I am proud of my work and I just want everyone who reads this poem to enjoy reading it just as much as I did writing it.

KENNEDY, ELISA
[a.] Mendham, NJ [title] "Eternity" [pers.] Whether I am on the sandy beaches of New Jersey or the rocky shores of Maine, I find the sea to be a place for contemplation and renewal. Calm or stormy, early blue morning or golden evening, the sea has always inspired my creativity.

KENNEDY, MARY
[a.] Georgetown, SC [title] "Lost Cultures" [pers.] This poem was inspired by an assignment given by my South Carolina history teacher. She suggested we be creative in explaining historical events, culture, etc. decided to explain the disappearance of our Native American cultures through poetry. I am only 14, but my Grandad used to say I have an "old" soul.

KENTON, ODIS, SR.
[a.] Lorton, VA [title] "No Matter What" [pers.] Distinguished member—International Society of Poets. Published works include: "Deceive Not Thyself" (Editor's Choice Award). "What You See Is What You Get" (Editors Choice Award), "Just Because" (Editors Choice Award) and "What About You?"

KING, JASON
[a.] Hamilton, ON [title] "Elysium Dawn" [pers.] As most of us know, the hectic pace of life can become overwhelming. This poem is a place I go to find peace. All you have to do is find this place or point in your lives and you too will always have tranquility.

KING, KEVIN
[a.] Vidor, TX [title] "Straightjacket" [pers.] This poem was written during a period of major depression in my life, as most of my poetry has been. The straightjacket could have two meanings actually. It could be a physical straightjacket or a mental straightjacket. In the physical aspect, it gives you a taste of how the mentally insane may feel locked up in their cushioned cages. But the meaning I took from it was the mental aspect. In my experience, it was one-way relationship which headed down a dead-end street. The poem was actually longer than twenty lines so I wasn't able to include it all. I'm hoping to publish a book of poems in the future

KING, KIMBERLY
[a.] Bedford, PA [title] "A Plea to My Love" [pers.] Those of us who have been blessed with love have witnessed first hand the seasons of love. This poem was written during a particularly harsh winter early in my marriage. My husband is a great man who works too hard and gives too much. His work ethic is paramount and his loyalty to his work undying. Any man possessing that degree of dedication could easily forget the lesser priorities i.e. love, living, and dreaming. We're both learning about balance, which has to be one of the more intricate and fundamental lessons of life. He has been and continues to be an inspiration to me since we found each other in 1989. His name is Brandon, and I love him with my soul.

KING, SAMANTHA JEAN
[a.] Sound Beach, NY [title] "Sunset" [pers.] This poem means a lot to me. It takes me back to when I spent long summer nights watching the sunset on the beach. I dedicate this poem to my mother.

KITCHENS, MARGARET
[a.] Seminary, MS [title] "Daily Prayer" [pers.] This poem is a prayer from my heart. I would pray for my family each day, and I wondered if God heard me! So many things happen around us pretty close to home. I needed peace, so one day I wrote my prayer down in the form of a poem, and it gives me peace of mind to read it. And others can read "Daily Prayer" as well, to have peace in their heart.

KNAPP, LINDA
[a.] Windsor, NY [title] "Friends Forever" [pers.] I am 34 years old. I live in the small town of Windsor, NY located in upstate New York. I have a nine-year-old son and have been married for four years. My poetry is written from the heart, usually to boost someone's spirits. Occasionally I'm asked to write on a specific subjects. "Friends Forever" was written for a store manager who also became a friend. When she had to move on, I wrote it as proof that her happiness would stay with us. Through life's changes there are sad times, but memories keep people together no matter what the distance.

KOCH, RENEE
[a.] Naperville, IL [title] "Sea of Me" [pers.] A gift of verse comes only from the heart, and true love will never be taken for granted. This poem is for my husband, Toby. Some things are extremely personal and are hard to share. Thanks for letting me.

KOCHER, CANDICE
[a.] Wapwallopen, PA [title] "Thoughts" [pers.] I married my high school sweetheart, whom I love very much, and together we have two beautiful daughters, ages three and one. I remember telling my family as a young child that someday I will be a writer, and today I believe my dream came true. My poem "Thoughts" is about heartaches of people in and out of my life, as much as I would love to vanish their pain, I can't. By writing this poem I hope other's such as myself will realize that all though we cannot fix the lives of those around us, we can live for ourselves and still be happy. I want to thank my husband, Gene, mother, aunt, father, grandparents and all other family members and friends who believed in me.

KOENIG, BRIAN
[a.] Sidney, OH [title] "Dew" [pers.] I currently reside in Sidney, OH. My parents are Mike and Cindy, and my two brothers Mike and Ryan. I am currently studying to become an architectural, or mechanical engineer, my poetry has no inspiration but life itself.

KOSTUKOFF, JACLYN
[a.] St. Clair Shores, MI [title] "Parents" [pers.] I am thirteen years old and I wrote my poem "Parents" to show my parents that I am grateful for everything they have given me. I feel lucky to have parents that show me as much love as my parents do. I enjoy writing poems because it lets me show my feelings that I have, but may never say. Having my poem published is so exciting. I enjoy poetry and plan to make some of it into songs because I also love to sing.

KOTT, TIM
[a.] Mesa, AZ [title] "An Ode to Landscaping" [pers.] My motivation behind this poem was the fact that I moved 40 tons of stone with a wheelbarrow to landscape my desert backyard. I moved boulders, planted plants in searing desert heat—with no help from neighbors. I'm 38 years old, live in Mesa, AZ and am an insurance agent. I find poetry as a quiet outlet to release my frustrations. Instead of getting upset or mad, I translate my thoughts into soothing words.

KOUDLAI, ALEXANDER
[a.] Suffern, NY [title] "The Birdish Joy" [pers.] Can we define poetic flow? Can we command the wind to blow? Let morning dew refresh the petals. Mark pure leaves with sacred letters. What is the reason for inspiration? What is the purpose for admiration? If it is known to the poet. it's not an art but something below that. What do I mean by writing a poem? What does snow mean by snowing and snowing? What does sun mean by shining and warming? What does heart mean by losing and longing? What does eye mean by watching and blinking? What does mind mean by asking and thinking?

KUMAR, RAJ
[a.] Bangalore AL, India [title] "How Should I Hate You?" [pers.] I would like to thank Sai Baba for the talents he has blessed me with. This poem is dedicated to all the handicapped people, especially the children around the world who are in real need of love and prayers from all us. To me this would be my finest and happiest occasion to show my love and affection to a very special person. Her name is Srilakshmi (Bobby). She is and will always be my inspiration forever. My aspiration is to become one of the best songwriters of all times.

KWIATEK, ROBIN
[a.] Hillside, IL [title] "Forgiveness Overflows" [pers.] My poems come to me as I devote each and every breath I take to God. They are about everything to do with real life. They come from pain and joy. They come from ugly and beautiful. They come from being stunned sometimes by simple truths from the Bible. They sometimes come out of awe. I pray that they speak of some sort of truth.

LA GRANGE, MARIE
[a.] Jacksonville, FL [title] "When I Cried" [pers.] The words of each poem that I write are given freely to me from my Lord and Savior. I wish to dedicate this poem for my mother, Elizabeth Jones, who encouraged me to send this poem to you. Unfortunately, she passed away on May 7, 2000 at the age 71 from lung cancer. She was a very strong and courageous mother who loved all her children. She always placed our needs first. I hope and pray that my poem can bring comfort to all who read this poem. Dedicated to Elizabeth Jones, born April 28, 1929 and died May 7, 2000.

LAANSTRA, DEVON
[a.] Calgary, AB [title] "Growing Up" [pers.] My name is Devon and I am ten years old. I go to Calgary Christian School in Calgary, Alberta, Canada. I wrote this poem for my grade five Language Arts class. This poem is about the ups and downs of growing up and how God can help you not to worry about the problems of everyday life. I live with my Dad and Mom and my two brothers and one sister. I want to thank you, Mom, for entering me in this contest.

LAHMAN, MICHELLE
[a.] Kent, OH [title] "Mother's Eyes" [pers.] Acceptance was always important to me growing up, especially when it came to my mother. No matter how hard I tried I still felt like I had to prove my love. The best way I knew how was to say I love you and wait for some response back.

LANGSTON, J. R.
[a.] Fayetteville, TN [title] "Sounds of the Wild West" [pers.] Writes western novels under the pen name of "Tex Burns." I wrote this poem through the sadness of how the Indians of our country have been treated. Another poem I have written in the same vein is "Cherokee Teardrops." I inject an Indian hero into each book I write.

LARSSON, FREDRIK
[a.] Hultsfred, Sweden [title] "Forlorn in Shadows" [pers.] I am a 16-year old poet that suffers from sadness sometimes. Out of the gloomy pits of this grief comes many poems, such as this one. I really enjoy writing poems, for that is one at few things that I am good at. I mostly write poems about hearts broken by love. What more can I say? I see poetry as a gift, though I have no idea where mine came from.

LAURENT, CONNIE
[a.] Mexico, D.F. [title] "Of Youth and Old Age" [pers.] We see and we touch the world around us . . . we are part of it by virtue of our many experiences as we wind our way through life . . . it can arouse ideas which transcend reality and which may be significantly expressed only through poetry, through its visionary images. I feel a rich fulfillment when I have been able to transmit these abstractions through my poems—so I love to write poetry. As a literature teacher, I have tried to

further my students' understanding and, therefore, enjoyment of the poet's world.

LAURIN, JEANNE
[a.] Anchorage, AK [title] "Untitled" [pers.] Mothers are special all around the world no matter what language we speak; our children are a God given gift; they are every part of each of us; they grow on you and teach us new understandings about love; in reality they are our true self. I'm both a mother and grandmother. The grandchildren inspire me a lot. There has never been a greater love than Jesus in my life; God showed me how to love. My children and grandchildren continue to shape even deeper feelings of love within me. Mother Mary; Jesus' mom gave up more then most; but in the same respect, gained everything. All hearts should be as one; the family tree of Jesus Christ.

LEACH, ADELE M.
[a.] Manassas Park, VA [title] "He Sees" [pers.] As heavy, black cumulous clouds tumbled and raced across the turbulent Atlantic Ocean, I could almost feel their weight depressing my spirit. I remember thinking, "Oh, God, where are you?" The clouds were instantly scattered like a huge hand had reached down and brushed them away, and the once dark and gloomy clouds were brilliantly transformed with breathtaking light. I was so humbled that the words of "He Sees" came immediately to mind. There was a God, and that He would care enough to show such power to so small speck of humanity, was awe-inspiring as well as overwhelming.

LECRONE, M.
[a.] Helena, OK [title] "Veterans Day" [pers.] This is a poem of remembrance, inspired by acquaintances and family, current and long past. Being from rural, western Oklahoma, a sense of place in state and national heritage is part and parcel of who we are and held very dear. It is my hope, since my children are grown, they too will make time to look back remembering sacrifices made by veterans in service to their country.

LEDGER, JUDY
[a.] Seven Hills, OH [title] "When Life Happens, or If" [pers.] Life is truly a gift, one so many of us tend to ignore. In that tough moment let your heart feel and your life will be visible. Everyone has the given right to life, treasure it.

LEDWIDGE, ASHLEY
[a.] Bethinia, Australia [title] "A Posted Heart" [pers.] I enjoy poetry and being able to express your self with out being worried about what to say next, with poems you can stop and rewrite until your completely satisfied. Not many people know I write and those who get to read my pieces enjoy them. It's good to know you can cheer up someone when they've had a **** of a day.

LEE, WILMA P.
[a.] Chicago, IL [title] "Bonding Love" [pers.] I wrote this poem to my darling daughter, as I fondly call her, while I was visiting her last Mother's Day in Philadelphia, PA. She is the joy of my life, and I am thankful that I was blessed to raise a young lady such as she. My poems are generally expressions of gratitude. Poetry has offered me an outlet to express my feelings about my life experience. It has opened doors for me in public speaking that I would have otherwise not known. It has truly been a spiritual outlet.

LEGROW, ROBERT
[a.] Lynnfield, MA [title] "Lunar" [pers.] Rob Legrow resides in Lynnfield, MA. His hobbies include boxing writing, football, wiffleball, and watching "the greatest organization in all of sports," the Boston Red Sox. He is majoring in film with a minor in writing at Emerson College.

LEMOINE, JOANNA
[a.] Exeter, NH [title] "Silence So Loud" [pers.] My poem was written during a very emotional time in my life. My insecurities overpowered my ability to think clearly. Writing silence so loud was a form of therapy for me. I have used this poem and many others to cross the bridge into my soul with friends and family. Poetry has opened a new door of

understanding for me. This poem has special meaning to me because by writing it I have helped myself cope with my difficult situations. I hope others can relate to it.

LEONG, PHYABAE
[a.] Sg SG, Singapore [title] "Mirrored Pain" [pers.] After reading, one unearths huge layers of emotional angst—internally and externally. This was written about someone whom I had fallen painfully for who felt for me too but was unable to return the love. I have my beloved later father, Leong Chee Whye to thank for, as he was the one who first gently introduced and guided my literary interest with Eastern and Western poetry when I was just a child. 'Til today, my writings are still guided by my late father's loving hand allowing me to express my dark bottled-up inspirations in the form of poetry.

LESNICHY, JULIA
[a.] Charlottesville, VA [title] "Egyptian Girl" [pers.] I'm Russian and currently live in the USA. Poetry for me is a way of expressing my vision of life and memorizing some special events and people, who influenced and inspired me to write. I'm open and responsive to new impressions and constantly search for the feminine beauty in the world around me, the character of this poem, a delicate small girl in a remote Egyptian towns at the. Red Sea coast, remained in my heart, as we happened to like each other at first sight. She seemed so follow to me, and I felt sad and way about to cry when our tourist group left the town. I'm happy to be with my family how, my husband and two children. And I think we should cherish the moments, when we are together with people, whom we love.

LEV, BARBARA
[a.] Bayswater, NY [title] "One Perfect Red Rose" [pers.] This poem is dedicated to my mother who passed away 23 years ago and left behind six children, two of whom were only nine and 14. I wrote many poems over these years to try to express my feelings about this tragedy in our lives. On June 14, 1999, the eve of what would have been her 75 birthday, this poem arose from inside me and finally put on paper what has been in my heart for all these long years. The red rose was my mother's favorite flower. She was a perfect red rose.

LEWIS, CRAIG
[a.] Chesilhurst, NJ [title] "Medieval Heartbreak" [pers.] I feel that this poem shows the emotions of anyone who has had their heart broken in the most extreme way in a relationship. Through another reader's eyes it could represent hardship in the depth of a loved one. When I wrote this I was not feeling sad but as an artist I put myself in the moment and let the emotions flow through my pen. In writing this poem I hope others who read it see that although not everyone has felt this extreme sadness, no one is immune from feeling this extreme emotion.

LICHTI, LYNDA
[a.] Coatesville, PA [title] "Journey Together" [pers.] This particular poem is only the first verse in a song I have just completed and, someday, will hear on the radio! Poetry is a way for my soul to express its vision. My mother, Mary Anne Alfe, and my grandmother, Catherine Brennecke, are both extremely gifted, and I feel blessed to be able to write about anything in verse.

LIDZ, KEVIN
[a.] Thousand Oaks, CA [title] "Excess in Siberia" [pers.] I began expressing myself through poetry at the age of 14. Through the years my style has changed and progressed through many styles and formats. Here, nine years later from when I began to seriously write, I have challenged myself to use my ability in song writing as displayed in this publication. I have found this release to be the most satisfying form of expression I have yet attempted.

LINDLEY, TANNER
[a.] Glendale, AZ [title] "Quad" [pers.] I was inspired by the sand dunes to ride quads, the way mother nature shapes the dunes with her winds. Riding the dunes is like a never-ending rollercoaster

ride. The sand is so soft and silky, that landing off jumps is like landing on a Mattress. Thanks Dad, for introducing me to the joy of riding the dunes!

LINEKER, ELIZABETH
[a.] St. Marys, CA [title] "Where Did the Laughter Go?" [pers.] My poems are given to me by friends and family who entrust me with their happiness, pain, love and sorrow. I write about the feelings they awaken in me during our talks.

LINGER, PAMELA
[a.] Coraopolis, PA [title] "A New Beginning" [pers.] To me poetry is an extension of the soul. Each word is a testimony of one's thoughts, feelings, and heart. This particular poem was written for my sister for her wedding. I am 28 years old, and English major at Robert Morris College. I would like attend law school and someday retire on royalties of my novel. My hobbies are spending time with my nephew Cody, enjoying the outdoors, reading, and writing.

LITTLE, LAURA
[a.] Alvin, TX [title] "Those Eyes" [pers.] This was written when I was just an 18-year-old, single, pregnant mother-to-be and there was no significant other in my life, living at home with my parents, and with as helpful as they were I still felt utterly alone. So I wish to dedicate this poem, to my daughter Christina for whom without her I don't feel I could have ever expressed my true feelings. I love you, sweetheart.

LITTLETON, KENNETH
[a.] Chesapeake, VA [title] "I Stepped Outside" [pers.] One of the most precious gifts that God has given me is the ability to write poetry. It is the best way I know to express my feelings. This poem is dedicated to the glory of God, and to help those who are dealing with the loss of someone special. Poetry is my heart on display, and love to share my heart with others.

LLOYD, A.
[a.] Manson, NC [title] "A Bleeding Heart" [pers.] All of my thanks are to "God." My faith and trust in Him has enlightened me in every way. My experiences in life also contribute to my work. I have a very supportive family, whom I care dearly for. Lost loved ones and past relationships. This search for the perfect love has been a journey.

LOCKETT, MARIAN
[a.] Fredricksburg, VA [pers.] I wrote this poem among many others shortly after my mother passed away. Poetry writing has been a hobbies for me since I was introduced to it in my senior year in high school. Now at 29 years of age, poetry has helped me through many difficult times in my life. It helps me to really see the pain I am feeling, and I feel my poetry has been a great friend of mine. I am able to express my deepest and darkest secrets without criticism that I may receive from those around me. In many ways it has and will continue to be (as I feel) my only lifeline to my mother.

LOESCHER, LETTY
[a.] Greenleaf, WI [title] "Love Me" [pers.] I have lived in the Morrison, WI area for the past 30 years and have been a homemaker all my married life. After raising four daughters, we became foster parents. My poem is based on the experience of foster children that are terminated from their parents and going up for adoption. This is my first poem that I have ever written and I am hoping I can share some of the heartache that these children experience. If possible I would like to write more poems in the future.

LOGERFO, MARILYN
[a.] Rochester, NY [title] "My Little Girl Isn't Little Anymore" [pers.] I wrote this poem in remembrance of my daughter, Mary. She grew up, and I believe it is special to all parents to watch there children grow up. I have written a book about my life. It is called "The Two Sides of the Coin." It is in Logos Book Store, in Rochester, NY. I am in the process of writing other inspirational poem to share with other is what to do best.

LOGSDON, AARON
[a.] Tucson, AZ [title] "1-4-3" [pers.] I love to

write, my dream is to write my own music. I would like to thank poetry.com for making the release of this poem possible. And a special thanks to Kari Kaloi, you are turning point of my life and I will never forget you. Thank you! I am not done pursuing my dreams yet! I figure that if I dream hard and long enough, my dream will become a reality! And sure . . . a picture says a thousand words, poetry allows you to experience them though! Thank you everyone for your support! I love you, Mom and Dad.

LOREDO, RAMON, JR.
[a.] Los Angeles, CA [title] "Waiting" [pers.] Poetry is a way to uncover the real self inside of me. The emotions that ebb and flow are harnessed when I set pen to paper. This is truly wonderful to describe what I look like inside.

LOVELL, STEPHANIE
[a.] Indianapolis, IN [title] "Sign" [pers.] I feel that writing is a way to express one's innermost feelings of love, hate, and desperation. This poem is bared on a feeling of desperation. You know the person has left, never to return, but you have that one ounce of hope that makes you pray for them to return.

LOWMAN, RUFUS, JR.
[a.] Lexington, IN [title] "Your Angel and You" [pers.] This poem was written to my inspiration: my fiancee! The angel of my life is her because she brings courage, strength and love into my life! Most of my poetry deals with emotion and I wanted to share it with all so they to can share the love and happiness that encompasses my life!

LUCERO, SARAH L.
[a.] Des Moines, IA [title] "The Pray and Blessing" [pers.] I wrote this for a friend that was there at tough time in my life, Shannon. In 1991 I lost a younger brother and something inside came alive. Alive in the way of putting words on paper. To tell those that I love and care for how I feel. My life is now even richer with my children Jesse James and Nicole Jean. Along with their father Robert. Everything I've written is truly from my heart with love. I also have to thank my family for all their love. Thank you for this honor.

LUNA, FRANK
[a.] Los Angeles, CA [title] "For Exit a Lost Soul" [pers.] This poetry is the reflection of the constant adversity that have constantly visited my life, and that I have fought over the years. At times, I felt that I had come to the end of the rope, (fact which gave birth to this poem), but in the end, I managed to come on top of it. For that I learned that, the stronger you stand the storm, the superior you are against adversity. This also gave birth to two unpublished books, "Song for a Dead Princess," and "Jennifer the Doll," which I hope to have them published, soon, God willing.

LYONS, JAN
[a.] Kyle, TX [title] "Sweet Mama's Got the Blues" [pers.] When my children were the ages of one, three, and six, my husband was working nineteen hour days, seven days a week. Stuck in the country outside of Austin, Texas, two children with pneumonia, myself as well . . . came the birth of this poem. Sitting at the computer early one morning I simply typed one thought, Sweet Mama's Got the Blues. The rest came with ease. I write from my experience in life. Born on Long Island, New York, grew up in Miami, moved to Texas later, I feel blessed to have enjoyed so many diverse places to lived. I'd like to developed my writings skills, but even now with three teenagers I do it on the run. I enjoyed it and someday would love to write a book.

MAILLOUX, THOMAS FORD
[a.] Brigantine, NJ [title] "And Eternal" [pers.] I have a vast library and am curious about the existence of all things. As an Atheist, I accept that Existence exists, and in some manner, way, shape, or form, existence has always existed; ie. there never was an "in the beginning," but why existence?

MANNING, NATHAN
[a.] Hawallan, CA [title] "Last Day" [pers.] I wrote this poem about Anna Baldwin, who I knew a long time ago. She never knew and I never told her how much she really meant to me and there's not a day that goes by that I don't regret not telling her and I wrote this for her because I know that she went through and maybe someday she will read this and she will know how much she really meant to me, and I will always remember that last day.

MANNIX, JENNIFER
[a.] Semans, SK [title] "I Was There" [pers.] My life has been hard and this poem is something that I wrote to let my feelings out. Poetry is a bit of a wall that I hide behind. This poem is from the heart, as many others of mine. Through my poems I learn things like it is okay to cry and laugh. It's also okay to hurt but to deal with it afterwards. My poetry is part of my life. It is a gift and a very wonderful one.

MARANO, MELISSA
[a.] Param, OH [title] "You Heard My Cries"

MARSDEN, GAVIN
[a.] Cape Town, South Africa [title] "Rain" [pers.] I believe that words are holy. A picture may paint a thousand words, but it needs only one word to touch a person's heart or change a life. The beauty of words is in danger of being lost, but it is a treasure that we dare not give up on. Let us use it like rain, to access the soul, to stimulate the mind and inspire the heart. I am a social worker living in Cape Town, South Africa. My life's philosophy can be summed up by five L's: Live, Love, Learn, Laugh, and Listen.

MARSH, AARON
[a.] Vestal, NY [title] "So It Comes" [pers.] I am a graduate of the State University of New York at Binghamton. I spent my '98 spring semester abroad at the University of East Anglia, Norwich England. I wrote "So It Comes" during my studies in England. I had traveled solo through England, Ireland, France, Spain, Italy, Greece, Vienna, the Czech Republic, Germany, the Netherlands, and Belgium, and along with the many experiences I had were lessons I learned. "So it Comes" embodies one of the hardest of those lessons: that the discovery, the amazement, and the excitement can be, and often are, painfully temporary.

MARTIN, ANN
[a.] Marion, OH [title] "MMMmmm" [pers.] This poem was born from a slow night on the job. I sat and looked at the can of soda pop sitting on my desk and the inspiration came. I enjoy expressing myself through my poetry, especially when the meaning is not immediately obvious. I have a passion for the written word and creative expression. I feel my ability to write poetry is truly a gift from God.

MARTIN, CYNTHIA
[a.] Middle Island, NY [title] "Daybreak" [pers.] "Daybreak" was something I put together sitting on the poet of my old building in the S. East section of the Bronx. I wrote it in a time when there were a lot of problems going on in my life. So my only solace, happened to be studying the sky. It was peaceful and it gave me a lot of energy to write the poems the way I do. I describe my poetry as "a violin played using a razor blade." Something so sweetly written in peace, surrounded and fueled in a hectic violently atmosphere.

MARTIN, DOUGLAS
[a.] Hackensack, NJ [title] "My Little Girl Isn't Little Anymore" [pers.] I wrote this poem because I was finally leaving home to join the navy. I was going to miss my friends and family so I wrote this poem to them. I wanted them all to remember me. All my life I have never said good-bye because that means forever to me. But I say later because you never know who you'll run into over the years.

MARTIN, HEATHER
[a.] Port Orchard, WA [title] "All You Have Done" [pers.] This poem represents a first love that is still a very important part of my life. He will always be in my life as a true friend. My friends and family have had such an impact on my life, that I feel so loved and cared for. I am only seventeen years old and I feel that if I can do this, I can set my mind to do anything. My mom and dad have pushed me to become a better person in school, writing, and I will always be thankful for that. I dedicate this poem to Casey.

MASTER, ANGEL
[a.] Mount Vernon, NY [title] "Harmagedon Will Come" [pers.] Harmagedon is the name of (one of four) a kitten of kit and kat (9/13/98 to 5/03/00). Harmagedon leaps upon me to gain access to higher platforms. This past winter, he missed my eye with his claw by less than an inch. Prior to this, he cut my face about an inch away from my eye. Now, he would only leap upon me if I have a thick Jacket and a Cap on my head. My relationship with God and His love inspired me to name this kitten at birth and write this poem.

MATLAK, LAVERNE
[a.] Philadelphia, PA [title] "Midnight" [pers.] All my poetry comes from my heart. Dedicated to my family and friends who have stood by and supported me through difficult times. Timothy, Tyler and Kylie, my grandchildren, may always remember my love of reading and poetry keep it going!

MAUTE, LISETTE
[a.] Charleston, SC [title] "Just for You" [pers.] This poem has special meaning to me and my life. I am thirty-seven years old, single mother. The focus of my life has been my son and my job for many years. Then a man came into my life and changed me forever. He opened my heart to love and emotions that I had not felt for a very long time. I had never written poetry before, but the love I felt for him inspired me to write this poem as well as others. I am thankful to him for opening up a new world for me.

MAY, RUSSELL
[a.] Beavercreek, OH [title] "An Emotional Time" [pers.] Everyone goes through life deciding on which path to take. "The path of life, and the path of death." My theory: It's not the path you take. It's the choices that you make.

McCALLEY, JEANNE
[a.] Glendale, NY [title] "The Giving of Yourself" [pers.] A very special friend came back into my life after more than ten years. My personal life had experienced many trials and tragedies and many times I didn't have the strength to go on. He believed in me when I didn't believe in myself. He accepted me for who I was through the thick and thin. Thee isn't anything that we wouldn't do for each other to express the depth of our love. My special friend carried me through many fields of gray and I can never repay him for his love, sweetness, and understanding that he showed me.

McCARROLL, RICHARD
[a.] Marietta, OK [title] "Inspiration" [pers.] My poetry most often is inspired by my four children, but this one, obviously, was inspired by a woman. Writing poetry and short stories is my escape from reality. Having the opportunity to share my vision, is truly a blessing.

McCARROLL, TWANA
[a.] Cleveland, OH [title] "A Time to Choose" [pers.] I was completely overwhelmed when I discovered that the International Library of Poetry wanted to publish my poem. This is a great honor and far beyond my expectations, and I am so very grateful. Reason being because of the many people who have overlooked me and the true meanings of the things that I poetically express in verse. With the exception of my guardian Pamela Wilson, my fiancee, Marvin Crim, my best friend Joyce Oliver, and my sister Michelle McCarroll who was also born with the gift to be a poet, but didn't pursue it.

McCAY, DONNA RAE
[a.] Manchester, NH [title] "Resolutions For Writers" [pers.] This poem was one of five submitted in poetry division at the 1998 Florida Christian Writers Conference where I won the poetry award. I sure was surprised as I had never written poetry before. I dedicate this poem to Wordsmiths Christian Writers.

McCLURE, EDWARD
[a.] Ronkonkoma, NY [title] "Ever" [pers.] If you

have "Ever" awakened in the middle of the night with the thought of being with someone, for the happiness and joy found only deep down inside, but also the difficulties that it brings. My poem "Ever" is based on those feelings. So, to share my feelings with other people, somehow it makes me feel better, and I thank you.

McCLURE, MICHAEL
[a.] El Centro, CA [title] "The Bet" [pers.] Poetry to me is a passion. I feel more at ease in this world, then I do in reality. "The Bet" has a special meaning. I wrote it so I remember, know how bad things get, I'll always have my memories. This is my first work being published, but I promise there will be more one day. The difference between madmen and genius, is only success. I see life as my stepping stone, and take every day as it comes. My goal, is to share my poetry with the world. I want my voice to be heard, so I can look back, and know I made a difference. I want people to be able to read my work, and feel the same burning desire. If I get them to think, and change their own minds, I've done my job. So, would watch out, Mike's coming at you, and I'm coming full speed ahead.

McCORKLE, REBECCA
[a.] Springfield, IL [title] "Love at First Sight" [pers.] I am a senior in high school who enjoys reading, writing, playing music, and traveling. My poetry writing stemmed from an English project. Once I began to write poems, I found that it was a wonderful way to express my feelings. I encourage anyone to try and compose a poem that relates their thoughts, ideas, feelings, and aspirations. It is difficult to explain where inspiration comes from; however, I believe that it comes from deep within one's self, taking shape from a person's experiences, hopes, and dreams.

McCOY, REBECCA
[a.] Brooklyn, NY [title] "Weeping Demons" [pers.] I want everyone to know that this poem is very special to me. I want to thank my mom for guiding me, and for being understanding as I grow as a person. To my grandparents for spoiling me (you two are the best), to my brother, you'll always be my best friend. To my uncles, I love you guys. And to the rest of my family thanks for being there. Well enough said, but don't worry, you haven't heard the last of me.

McCUMBER, LARRY, JR.
[a.] Fostoria, OH [title] "Rose" [pers.] Influence and my imagination is what makes up for my poetry. Most importantly the people in my life have helped agreed deal in my naturing into a strong and open minded person. One of my biggest influences have been of music The Beatles, Bob Dylan, and John Lennon who once said "Reality leaves a lot to the imagination." That's what happened with this poem. I have yet to experience love but my imagination made it seem so very real and made it possible for me to write this poem. My feelings and emotions feel freed because of my poetry, and because of all the help along the way. I must first thank God for making this possible. I also want to thank my family Mike and Connie Ritter and my cousins, also my very good friends Andy McLaughlin, and Roger Gonzalez. And a special thanks to the girl that opened my mind to new worlds, Joanna Fallon.

McDONALD, RACHEL
[a.] Saratoga Springs, NY [title] "See'rs" [pers.] Writing is a joy to me. It allows me to express in written words what I am unable to express in spoken words

McDONOUGH, BRIAN
[a.] Nora Springs, IA [title] "Clue" [pers.] I've been writing songs/poems since I was 14 years old. Now after 15 years, my work is show to the public. This poem is from the game "Clue." There's no big story behind it. I just pieced words together and try to make a mystery out of it for the reader. And as for the answer to the poem, it happens to be the person, place and weapon not mentioned. Other than that, there's not much more I can say about it. I just hope people will enjoy reading it as much as I did writing it.

McDOWELL BARBATO, MARY LORENA
[a.] Lobi, OH [title] "In the Wilderness" [pers.] I was inspired to write, "In the Wilderness." It's about different times in my life that I felt very down and the Lord picked me up. That his love is unchanging. He is always there when I need Him. That he loves me and will never leave me. The Lord blessed me with two wonderful daughters Sallymarie and Laurajean. I am very proud of them being their mother.

McFADYEN, LAURA
[a.] Winston-Salem, NC [title] "Iris Eyes" [pers.] I am so proud of my creative daughter, "Laura Katherine McFadyen." She was born last March 5, 1986, she writes poetry, sings, paints, draws, and she's the 1st chair for three different orchestras, she plays the "cello", she is a very intense and mature 14 years old.

McGONIGAL, MARGIE
[a.] West Chester, PA [title] "Hell on Earth" [pers.] This poem express the depth of emotion experienced by someone who suffers from mental illness. I hope to convey how bleak and dismal life can be when all hope has been lost. The contemplation of suicide is apparent, death is the answer in some cases. Mental illness can lead to suicide, but it can be prevented. I wrote this poem in the hope that others will understand the severity of the disease and just how unbearable life can be for someone suffering from it.

McGREW, SONJA
[a.] Portland, OR [title] "Peace" [pers.] I have had the blessing of writing throughout my life. God has given me the ability to put my feeling down in words, with hope of allowing his love to shine through. May God bless you with his love as you read "Peace"

McHUGH, MICHELLE
[a.] Cortez, CO [title] "Why" [pers.] This poem means so much to me. I had a real good friend who had died and one night I could not sleep so I wrote this poem! I hope everyone liked it as much as I hoped they would.

McKENZIE, MICHAEL
[a.] Cumming, GA [title] "Light of Christ" [pers.] I think that poetry is a gift given to me, and to many others, and we should all use this gift. I owe my talents to God, who gave me the innate ability to write smoothly, to Mr. Rogers, who inspires me with his teachings and writings, and to all my friends who (for the most part) help me keep my spirit up, without you guys, I don't think I'd have the spirit to write, you guys are the greatest.

McKINNEY, KARIN
[a.] Hixson, TN [title] "A Slave Man's Word" [pers.] I can only imagine what it must have been for slaves, held captive not only by their "masters", in body, but also by their broken spirit within. To have a voice that is ignored, ridiculed. And silenced by the "beating of a whip." Somewhere in the whispers of his crying, the Lord heard him, and renewed his spirit, soul, and mind. And through it all, that slave man persevered. I dedicate this poem to St. James A. M. C. Church, Chattanooga, TN.

MELCHER, DON
[a.] Merrillan, WI [title] "Child's Play" [pers.] This poem expresses feelings from long ago, when we were raising our kids, friends and relatives were visiting with their kids. Lots of happy chatter and shouting as the kids played happily in the backyard. Suddenly we became concerned by an unnatural extended silence from the backyard. Upon investigation we found them innocently lying on their backs pointing skyward, conjuring imaginary cloud, pictures just being good little kids.

MELO, A.
[a.] Provo, UT [title] "Untitled" [pers.] This poem was written for and dedicated to a very special woman in my life.

MENARD, KATHY
[a.] Richmond, VA [title] "Untitled" [pers.] This poem is a result of many sleepless nights being frustrated over the FDA's refusal to protect the public against the toxic effects of the food additive monosodium glutamate. It is impossible to disclose in 100 words how this neurotoxin has affected me and my family. I am indebted to the following for their reviewing scientific data and persistence in making detrimental information available to those who will listen: National Organization Mobilized to Stop Glutamate (NOMSG) "In Bad Taste . . ." by George R. Schwartz, M.D.; wife, Kathleen. "Excitotoxins . . ." by Russell L. Blaylock, M.D. Jack/Adrienne Samuels, Ph.D.

MENDOZA, PATRICIA
[a.] Daly City, CA [title] "The Sad Poet" [pers.] I can't believe I'm finally going to see a poem of mine published! Writing poems has always been a great form of "therapy" for me, I have been writing my entire life. This particular poem, "The Sad Poet" was put in a short form for this contest. It is the story of my life. I have books filled with my poems and poems I've composed for others who've enjoyed my "words." I really believe that when you write from your heart, that it flows onto paper naturally. "The Sad Poet" was originally four pages long, and does tell my life story. I have a dream which is now a goal, and that is that someday I'll have a book of poetry published to share with everyone. I want to thank anyone and everyone who had anything to do in publishing and picking my work! God bless you all for making me feel so special.

MERCHEL, CHRISTINE
[a.] Mt. Vernon, IL [title] "My Love" [pers.] This poem was written from the inner depths of my heart and soul. This man, tho' we are apart will always hold a special place in my heart. His strength, love and gentleness are rare qualities in any person. So much love and joy he has brought to me. He gave me the courage to submit this poem. I want to thank him now for giving me so much in a short time. I will always love you don't ever forget that. God bless you. I have written many poems, and feel writing is a gift. From the depths of ones soul, he makes the pen sing.

MESERVE, DAYNA
[a.] Naples, FL [title] "Our Heart's Home" [pers.] My poem was inspired by the man I loved while I anticipated our marriage was not to be, so I give it to thee. By nature, I'm a melancholy person. I write poetry to express my feelings. Primarily, I write about faith and love. I'm an incurable romantic for I steadfastly believe that love covers a multitude of wrong. My poetry's born out of emotion's that I've experienced as a Christian (a sinner saved by grace) a daughter, a granddaughter, a sister, a friend, a student, a wife, a nurse, and a grandmother. Having faith in God has given me hope for a life filled with unconditional love, acceptance and approval with those I love.

MESSINA, STEPHANIE
[a.] Long Beach, NY [title] "The Beach" [pers.] This poem started out as extra credit for English class, but has given me more than I could ever have anticipated. I submitted it to several school contests, and one gave me instant publication. To take it further, I gave poetry.com a shot. I jumped for joy after receiving a notice in the mail. This simple piece of poetry was inspired by my two, right on "The Beach." I hope that people cannot only enjoy it, but feel as if they, too, are at the beach. Thank you to my family and friends, but especially to my English teachers who have re-awakened the poet within me.

MIKULIC, ANTHONY
[a.] Lockport, IL [title] "Magic Window" [pen.] Ynot [pers.] I was born January 17, 1942 at Oregon, IL. My parents are Michael E. Mikulic and Marie R. Mikulic. My children are Ann Raulene, Jan Gerette, Michaeljon Anthony. My grandchildren is Laura. Disabled American Veterans, Paralyzed Veterans of America, American Legion, Distinguished member of the International Society of Poets. 1999 International Poet of Merit Award, Numerous Editors Choice Awards, Builder and Crew Member of Guinness book of record Holder "The Blue Flame" fastest rocket

engine vehicle, October 23, 1970. Dedicated to my Neurologist, Michael R. Schwatz MD, who's expert medical care has enabled me to continue to live a quality and productive life fulfilling my dreams and poetic quest.

MILL, ANNAMARIE
[a.] Schwenksville, PA [title] "Why Does Life Have to Be, So Difficult for Me?" [pers.] I wrote this poem to my parents when I was seventeen years old. I got pregnant when I was fifteen and had a baby girl when I was sixteen. I entered this poem hoping it could give teenagers some sense of how emotionally confused you become. It's not only the night awake, the diapers, and being home while your friends are out having fun. It's how you feel inside—who am I? You now have to put your needs aside and devote yourself one hundred percent to this baby that will depend on you for the rest of your lives.

MILLARD, KIM
[a.] Savage, MN [title] "Memories Out My Window of Life" [pers.] "Memories Out My Window of Life" is about not having regrets of past situations. It's about moving on and looking forward to the mysteries of the future. I've been lucky enough to inherit a creative streak from my mother. Poetry is a great release for me. It's a hidden talent many didn't know about until now.

MILLIAN, JANET
[a.] Weston, MA [title] "Awaking of Spring" [pers.] I love writing poems. The love of writing poems is like the love I have for my family. And remembering the birth of my children seeing their little faces so innocent like the waking of spring.

MILOY, BIANCA
[a.] Livingston, NJ [title] "Today" [pers.] I got my idea for this poem based on some of my friend's lives. They sometimes say they don't like themselves so I thought I could write about it. To me poetry means life in words. It's hard to explain life that is, and when people put it in a poem it is amazing.

MOHR, ANNE
[a.] North Riverside, IL [title] "Icicles" [pers.] Anyone who grew up in or near Chicago knows the agonies that winter brings, the traffic, the plowing (or lack of), the bitter cold wind . . . but nature provides simple yet simple beauty all around us to warm our spirits. Even if it's as simple as around us to warm our spirits. Even if it's as simple as an icicle. That's why I enjoy writing poems. Hopefully, they help to create a tiny escape from a world of relentless responsibilities, an overwhelming garden of technology, or a bone chilling cold day. Special thanks to my wonderful husband, Ron, my late mother and father, mom, Pudgy, and, my dear friends for always keeping my spirit warm and my heart filled with love.

MONTELEONE, KATHLEEN
[a.] Belmont, MA [title] "Reflections" [pers.] My daughter was almost lost to me at birth by a terrible illness. When the crisis passed, she opened her vibrant blue eyes for the first time and I glimpsed the heroic spirit within. It was then that all my faith in life and destiny returned to me. I was swept away by the miracle that she was and the force of will in this tiny body to fight for life and win. No matter what challenges the years bring me, nothing will ever surpass the strength and beauty I witnessed at that moment in her eyes.

MONTGOMERY, DONNA
[a.] Silver Spring, MD [title] "The Encounter" [pers.] Writing has always been a form of therapy for me; it provides me a certain freedom. I believe there is a reason for every person that comes into my life; learning the lesson is what helps us to grow. After a long absence, I heard from the man I wrote about in "The Encounter." Talking with him brought back the memory of how I felt during the relationship. We are now on good terms, he made his amends to me, and I acknowledged my mistakes as well. Afterwards, I took about five minutes and wrote "The Encounter." It gave me peace.

MONTGOMERY, ONDREA LYNNETT
[a.] Staten Island, NY [title] "Untitled" [pers.] I live with my parents and my brother, Bacari (who is also my best friend), in Staten Island, New York. I'm fourteen years old and attend Susan E. Wagner High School. I enjoy working with children, playing basketball, singing, dancing, and surfing the Internet. "Untitled" was written because when I started high school, my classmates just automatically assumed I was straight from the ghetto. So, one day I came home, turned on some music, picked up a pen and just started writing. When I was finished, all the words I had just written turned out to be a beautiful, "Untitled" poem.

MOORE, FREDA
[a.] New Carlisle, OH [title] "West Virginia Mountains" [pers.] This poem is special to me I was born in West Virginia, Dec. 22, 1951. The mountains will always be home at me, no matter where I live. I feel that my inspiration came from God. I give him my thanks and praise. Without him, I would be nothing. He gave me life, sight, hearing, smell, and feeling. Without that I couldn't have written this poem. I also owe my Dad, Mon, Brothers, Sisters, Husband, Children, Grandchildren, and our Aunt Nellie who told me I could do anything I put my mind too.

MORRIS, CLARENCE
[a.] Cincinnati, OH [title] "King of Hearts" [pers.] As a young boy growing up in Paris, KY., my mother encouraged me more to recite rather than write poetry, so other than "Roses are Red" . . . when in grade school, I wrote no poems of my own until 1986. After dedicating my life to Jesus, I was attending a special class at Greater Emanuel Apostolic Church, Cincinnati, Ohio, when I recited a poem written, of course, by someone else. After this members of the church began to ask me to write poems for special occasions and the words always just seemed to flow. My inspiration, Jesus.

MORRIS, CRYSTAL
[a.] Porterville, CA [title] "Understanding" [pers.] This poem is dedicated to my grandpa Arlin Morris, who passed away on February 1, 2000. He was one of the greatest people in my life, and I will always treasure the memories we have had. I felt that my Grandpa Arlin was my inspiration when I wrote understanding, and because of his strength and courage he will never be forgotten. I feel this poem reflects how I felt on that very sad day, when I thought the pain in my heart and tears in my eyes would never go away.

MORRISON, MISTI
[a.] Edwardsville, IL [title] "The End" [pers.] I think that poetry is a gift as well as a reward. Everyone can write poetry as long as they believe in themself. I love writing poems whenever I am excited, sad, etc. Just to express what I am feeling. Poems are great gifts for anyone. Now, a little about myself: I am a sixteen years old caring person. I live with my mom, stepfather, my two sisters and my brother. They inspire me very much. I hope that this poem and my upcoming poems are shared with everyone.

MORROW, LINDA
[a.] Hampstead, MD [title] "Life" [pers.] Poetry provides me with a means to deal with my feelings, whether they be happy, sad, beautiful or ugly points in my life. My shyness is set aside, and I can easily convey my innermost thoughts. There is always a life experience behind my words. The artist in me loves the lyrical flow of putting words into poetry to celebrate all of the special moments of my life. I can tuck these words into my own unique verse and treasure them for generations to come.

MUEHL, LOIS
[a.] Iowa City, IA [title] "Old Barns" [pers.] "Old Barns" comes from three interwoven pleasures in my adult life. Traveling back roads with leisure to observe their revealing scenes; sensing more and more unspoken connections between generations past, present, and future; starting with a phrase or an idea, and discovering what kind of poem may grow around it. For me, the joy in writing poetry is to try and try again, to distill dailiness always into truth and sometimes delight.

MUMA, KELLY
[a.] San Jose, CA [title] "Weather The Storm" [pers.] "All I have is yours, and all you have is mine. And my glory is shown through them." John 17:10

MUN, STEVE
[a.] Los Angeles, CA [title] "My Prayer" [pers.] My greatest influence in my life is my grandmother, my mother, and my sister, who raised me since I was young. They taught me how to give unconditionally and to love others. I thank God that they were in my life every day. To this day I always go to them for advice. The poem reflects on my struggles to find that special someone. If you really open your eyes you will begin to understand the true meaning of love. Never give up hope for that is all we have in life.

MUNOZ, JUAN A., JR.
[a.] Pharr, TX [title] "The Reality of Love" [pers.] Why would someone indulge themselves into poetry? Sometimes words are all you have to make a point and sometimes that is all you need.

MURRAY, KRISTINE
[a.] Bethany, OK [title] "Children of April" [pers.] "Children of April" was written in remembrance of the children who died in the Oklahoma City bombing. As we approached the fifth anniversary of that tragedy, and the memorial was completed and dedicated, it was a time of reflection for me. I felt strongly compelled to choose this poem over others I might have selected for entry because I felt its message needed to be shared. I hope we never forget what hate did, but at the same time, I want all to remember how love overcome hate in Oklahoma.

NABORS, ERIN
[a.] Madison, MS [title] "Sifting Memory" [pers.] "Sifting Memory" is that one poem of mine which has been permanently etched inside my mind. You see, I just don't believe she really wants to allow me to forget that overwhelmingly hurtful period in my life. For that I am grateful. She serves as a blatant reminder of a place I will never find myself in again. luv.charmz.luv.+ may the fairies be with you.

NASH, ANNA
[a.] Paw Paw, IL [title] "In His Hands" [pers.] My inspiration comes from my 21 years old son. In 1993 I was a passenger in a near fatal auto accident, that left me paralyzed. My son Michael was my angel then, as well as now! He gave up and built his life around me and my care. In March of 1996 he was a passenger in a fatal accident. My son was taken only nine days after he had a son of his own. His loss is great . . . His son is turning four, this is what my heart said as I remembered and missed him.

NEGRON, VICTOR
[a.] Brooklyn, NY [title] "Chilling Enrapture Part I" [pers.] Unspoken words of my soul are a white canvas. Adagio artistry, empty of shades and expressions. Unshadowed revelations of this confined voice will unveil clouds of complexities, poetically surfacing through torments turbulence. In search of vengeful verse it's scripted redemption in form of scared dialect. Ink teardrops now tainting the canvas with intellect. The truth of "me" becomes revealed, yet too many I'm further concealed within the abstract armor of my metaphors!

NEISES, CATHY
[a.] Valparaiso, IN [title] "Because" [pers.] This was a dark time in my life and I hope that this poem will help others to believe just because.

NELSON, JEFFREY
[a.] Phoenix, AZ [title] "The Moment of Truth" [pers.] "The Moment of Truth" is one of my more unique poems. It is about that exact moment, that one split second in which you realize you were wrong. More than that though, it is that same moment when you step outside yourself and realize why. This poem is different because it is actually a combination of two separate poems written at different times. Each was lacking in one way or another and after reading them side by side, I saw one perfect poem. I actually used the beginning of each poem to create the one you now see.

NEWBERN, ROBERTA
[a.] Buffalo, NY [title] "If God Had Not Made Woman" [pers.] I believe in God and I believe God made woman for a purpose. This world would be a sad lonely place without a woman. I wrote this poem for my mother and the women in my African American family.

NICESWANGER, AMY
[a.] Carroll, IA [title] "Life of a Champion" [pers.] I feel that poetry is a way to express one's feelings without speaking the words. My poem, "Life of a Champion," is written for a nine year old boy, who recently passed away due to cancer. Writing this, was my way of saying something for the family. Poetry is a way one can share personal feelings with each other. As a sophomore in high school, I feel that poetry is a source of understanding of hope, death and love, as well as all emotion and can be used in all pathways of life.

NICHOLS, SHANNON
[a.] Aurora, IL [title] "Moon Lighting" [pers.] I see pretty as opportunity to learn about yourself. Whether you write it or appreciate someone else's, you become so aware of who you are as a person. You are forced to face your wants, your fears and your dream. Such knowledge of one's self is power. Once you know yourself you are free to give yourself, to other people. It's something everyone has the power to do. "Moon Lighting" is a sensuous poem about the wonders of life taking notice of the life around us. Even in the darkest of times, there awaits a new beginning. Life is a gift, and the greatest inspiration.

NOHAVA, JOHN
[a.] Springfield, MO [title] "It is Time for Spring" [pers.] I got my love for reading and writing short stories and poems from my second grade teacher Ms. Young. She made a big difference in my life. I like to skateboard and snowboard. Anything that has to do with the outdoors. I also like to watch the X games on T.V. This poem is for the love of the outdoors, and the kid in all of us.

NORDENSTROM, DOUGLAS
[a.] Las Vegas, NV [title] "Elizebeth" [pers.] I wrote this poem not with my hand but with my heart. "Elizebeth" is about a love I lost in the years past, and how the fire inside still burns for her. If it were not for poetry, then my emotions would build up inside of me and never get set free, and that would drive me to insanity. So I thank God for poetry, and I wish well to all the other poets in the world.

NORRIS, SMITH
[a.] Gallatin, TN [title] "Reflecting" [pers.] My poem "Reflecting" was inspired from remembering my emotions when first meeting the love of my life. My senses instantly recognized an ancient soul-mate and prompted my commitment to share this life with her at any price. Many years have passed now and our love has deepened beyond my expectations. The only price I've paid has been giving love in return. The best investment I've ever made.

NUDEL, ARIELLA
[a.] Montreal, QC [title] "My Life as a Cat" [pers.] My name is Ariella Nudell. I was born on April 30th, 1990 at the MJGH (Montreal Jewish General Hospital). Now its four days until my birthday. This is the best birthday present I've ever received from anyone. It all started when I was on the internet, I pressed a button and it just went to another site! It said poetry come. I gave it a try for the fun of it, the funny part about it, I didn't even do my poem more than once. I had fun writing it. After I showed my mom, she didn't think much of my poem, but I figured I'll enter it any ways. When I got your letter, I was sure it would say, "Sorry, you did not win—but please try again later." When I opened the envelope I was so excited! I never thought I had such a talent in poetry. You don't know how happy you made me feel of making my poem important. And all I wanted to tell you is, thank you very much!

OAKES, KRISTINA
[a.] Franklinville, NY [title] "My Inspiration" [pers.] I like to write poems to express my feelings because sometimes saying it with words is too hard to do. This poem is of great meaning to me because it is about a great friend who I believe was put on this earth to show everybody that no matter what you are faced within your life, to never let it get you down. He really, truly touched everybody's life that knew him! So, I wrote this poem because I wanted everybody to believe that there really are angels in this world and I really believe that he was mine.

OAKLEY, PERRY, II
[a.] Henderson, KY [title] "Grandmother's Love" [pers.] Dedicated to Tennie Love and Mauder Oakley. Two women that were wonderful and loving. Both touched my heart and life in so many ways. These women were my grandmothers.

OCASIO, NYDIA
[a.] Belpre, OH [title] "There Is Someone Who Cares" [pers.] This poem is very special to me, because it was an inspiration I received from God above. While I was sitting in front of he computer and at the Poetry's Site, thinking on what to write. Please share my poem with others, that it might help anyone or their loved ones.

ODUMOSU, TEMI
[a.] London, UK [title] "Opaque Are You" [pers.] Sometimes we create imaginary obstacles on the way to our goals. Boundaries which make us feel secure when we are defeated. These are moments which we, however, can all overcome. I dedicate this to my grandfather. I thank you, Sarah.

OFFICER, JOYCE
[a.] Greer, SC [title] "It's Time to Say Good-bye" [pers.] Rarely do we meet someone who becomes both our muse; our inspiration and our best friend. Inspired by and dedicated to Stuart Arrow.

OGUNBITAN, FESTUS
[a.] Canyon Country, CA [title] "From Drug Relief to General Relief" [pers.] I thank God for giving me the talent of writing. I have written this poem from looking at the turn around is some people's life. I feel that I could appeal to their weary soul, through the lyrics of my poem, and bring them out of the shadow of the valley of destruction in drug addiction. I dedicate this poem to the memory of my parents, Mr. Samuel Oguniyi Ogunbitan and Mrs. Matilda Ajibola Ogunbitan of Christ Apostolic Church Olugbode Ibadan, Nigeria West Africa.

OMOLEWA, ANTHONY
[a.] Newark, DE [title] "Lyrics" [pers.] This poem was written as a Valentine's gift to my soulmate, Nical Edwards. I mean every word I wrote. I plan to spend the rest of my life with her and love her very much.

OPPECKER, FRANK, JR.
[a.] Athens, GA [title] "Friendship" [pers.] I wrote the "Friendship" poem when I was fourteen years old. (I'm seventy-six). It is one of my favorites. I also like to write limericks, and won the Limerick contest sponsored by the Athens Library in 1993. As an instrumental music teacher I retired from the New Jersey Public Schools in 1983, and moved to Athens, Georgia in 1986.

ORAN, NELLIE
[a.] Crossville, TN [title] "God Bless America" [pers.] I would like to thank God for allowing me to be born in the greatest nation in the world, the "United States of America." To see Old Glory waving proud. To our forefathers, our soldiers, our heroes, who have fought and died in order that we might have our cherished freedom. To my husband Tulis who served our country honorably. To his children Mike, Gwen, Judy, James, Doran, and Ginger. To my mother Margie Simpson Powers, who was my inspiration, along with my four children, Terry, Deidra, Brian and Tammy, I thank God for this opportunity.

OSBORN, DON, II
[a.] Dallas, TX [title] "Suspected Sub-Title" [pers.] Some view my poetry as fluff: A sellout for the easy themes and sure to be rhymes. While theirs is true art, because their poetry speaks the brutal truth of life on the streets. And using every four-letter word ever thought, spoke or heard, they verbally paint the picture they see. Yet, all those four-letter words are just f***ing ugly: A phrase I would have termed fugly, but where's the art in that? Poetry is the art of perceptions expression: Rather than proclaim ugliness, I write of the hope for the boundaries possibility of the beauty of life in love and laughter.

OSMUN, LINDA
[a.] Bloomfield, NJ [title] "Seasons" [pers.] I feel the greatest gift I could give someone is to honor them, or their memory, in a poem. At times, I do not outwardly express what I think or feel, so my poems do the speaking for me. "Seasons" was written after a tragic death of a family member. Even though loved ones pass on, it gives me great peace to know that in some way they are still with us.

OSTROWSKI, KEITH
[a.] Murrells Inlet, SC [title] "My Angel" [pers.] There are times in our lives when we find ourselves seeped in darkness; where our spirits cry in the midst of despair, forever searching for the love that has seemed to abandon us. Then unexpectedly we meet another, who fills us with light, awakening a memory of a union in heaven now realized on earth. So thank you Mary, my wife and my angel for your undeniable love.

PABON, CHRISTOPHER
[a.] Bronx, NY [title] "Untitled" [pers.] I was inspired to write this poem because I missed my girlfriend (actually she was my first love). I was stationed in the army on school field Barracks Oahu, Hawaii many miles away from home in New York City where she was. The love I felt for her was the deepest and purest and honorable love a young man could feel for a young woman, I truly loved this young woman with all my heart and soul. This is why I dedicated this poem to my very first love of my life, Blanca Rosa Bracero. Thank you for your love, Chris P.

PALMER, MARIAN
[a.] Pittsburgh, PA [title] "My Worst Nightmare" [pers.] This poem reflects just some of the desperation that addicts experience twenty-four hours a day, seven days a week. These words surfaced during a moment in recovery when I didn't feel as though I was recovering or ever would. I have one year clean and sober out of twenty-five years addicted, and today there is hope in the midst of my desperation. Someone that loves me very much told me "don't pick up the first one and God will do the rest." Today God answers my questions. I wrote fourteen lines of this poem, God wrote to other two.

PALMINTERI, MARY
[a.] N. Babylon, NY [title] "Misplaced Flowers" [pers.] I've been waiting poetry and ideas down since I was a child. Usually in the middle of the night when I could not sleep. When I saw then ad for this poetry contest I pulled "Misplaced Flowers" from my personal archives. I chose it because I felt that most people could relate to it. After all we've all felt like "Misplaced Flowers" at times haven't we?

PALUCHO, BERTA E.
[a.] Falls Church, VA [title] "Did You Really Love Me?" [pers.] My name is Berta E. Palucho and I am 18 years of age. I live in Falls Church, VA. I wrote this poem for my boyfriend who is no longer by my side and who was also the one true love in my life. I was in an accident in which I was left unable to walk and sometimes I sit and wonder if that is why he said good-bye. This poem was written because of a great sorrow that has overcome my life. I find a type of freedom by writing poems of my life and how hard it has been for me and others, and I hope that my poems can inspire people to move one and live happy no matter what happens.

PATTON, DANIEL
[a.] Freedom, IN [title] "Angel's Among Us" [pers.] This poem is a simple reminder of just how

the Lord God intervene's and protect's His children. It also reflects on just one more way He communicates with us. The poem is very special to me as with all my writings, for I feel the Lord inspired me to write and in my poetry He enables me to express my most deepest heart felt emotions and then share them with others. I hope and pray that all who read this and others find some security, hope or some comfort in time of crisis or just for simple inspiration. More importantly may they know the Lord is always with them. (The light has always been on) love and thanks to my mother for her guidance. May God Bless All.

PEAK, BENJAMIN
[a.] Stuarts Draft, VA [title] "Blue Clarity" [pers.] Autumn is a time of change that I felt was congruent with the changes in my own life. I believe poetry captures emotional and spiritual experiences better than any other medium. In this poem, I explored our minuscule existence that is so important when connected to our created universe.

PEET, LORI
[a.] Niceville, FL [title] "Choices" [pers.] Poetry to me is a way of expressing your inner most thoughts and dreams. In this poem it showed the love that I had for two different people and the passion that I had with them. So thank you to the men (Brandon and Micheal) for making this possible. I'll leave you with this thought; beauty is from within no matter how you express it.

PELTON, DAWN
[a.] Roselle Park, NJ [title] "Our Father" [pers.] "Our Father" has a very special meaning to me. It was written with my family and friends in mind. We all have obstacles to overcome. Our greatest achievements were finding each other and our true selves in the journey of life. My nephews are wonderful gifts of life!

PEREIRA, LINDSAY
[a.] Montreal, QC [title] "Poem in the "C" #3" [pers.] Poem in the "C" #3" is an autobiographical piece encompassing confusion between desire and the need for a soulful bond. Realization of perhaps the wrong love at the right time, yet the clinging hope of an unrealistic reality. This piece reveals the romantic naivete of a young woman falling, trying desperately to hold on, but ultimately losing the struggle inside her. The moral: the fantasy of what you want to see blurs the reality of what is. Lindsay Pereira, just a small town girl living in Montreal, currently studying English Specialization and Art History at Concordia University, and loving it.

PERGJIKA, ALBA
[a.] Champaign, IL [title] "You Are Not" [pers.] "You Are Not" represents the final stage of the pain. I felt over the loss of one of my loved ones. This poem describes my readiness to put the sadness away and accept the reality of the loss. I hope that by reading "You Are Not", the ones who have been under the same circumstances will, like me, find the courage to fight the pain and hug life again.

PERKINS, MARLA
[pers.] For better or worse, most of the people who see CFIDS patients are doctors and view such patients from a clinical perspective. That perspective misses the essence of trying to live with a disease that doesn't go away. This poem is an effort to help communicate that essence from the perspective of someone who lives with the disease every day. I am delighted to see it in print. I live in Ithaca, New York, with a codependent cat and a turtle who spends most of his time under the couch.

PERKINS, TINA
[a.] Abernathy, TX [title] "Change of Season" [pers] My poem, "Change of Season" was inspired by the woods in my backyard in Belleville, IL. I was sitting at my kitchen table drinking coffee, staring out the window. It was early fall, and it just sort of popped

in my mind. I love to write, and I know poetry was a gift given to me from my God in heaven, and it is truly one of the greatest pleasures of my life. And I am very thankful that I get to share it with you.

PERRY, MELISSA
[a.] Harwood Heights, IL [title] "The Virus" [pers.] Being published is a wonderful accomplishment! I am totally overwhelmed with joy. My poetry is my lifeline. It is my story, my soul on paper, my happiness and pain. It keeps me going, it keeps me sane. Thank you.

PETERS, AMANDA
[a.] Amherst, NH [title] "Secrets" [pers.] The poem "Secrets" is special to me because it is my way of thanking my Friends for the trust they have had in me over the years. Secrets are hard to keep to yourself, but it is harder to know who to trust with them. I thank Laura, Elisabeth, Sari, Karissa, and all the rest of my friends and family for being my inspiration.

PETERSON, AMY
[a.] Bridgeton, NJ [title] "Caught Dry" [pers.] My work signifies through heartbreak and the need to grasp what little hope remains for another glance of desire from the one I found to be so perfectly fitting in my humble perspective. "Caught Dry" is a reflection of my loneliness and the lack of will to sustain a stable course of love. I find this poem to be a great means to express my truest of emotions towards a faint memory I hold so tightly, yet the distance in his eyes prove to fall short of that which I long for.

PETRINI, PATRICIA
[a.] Hamden, CT [title] "To My Daughters" [pers.] Poetry soothes the soul and takes the stress away from busy days. My daughters and husband are my life and I couldn't have accomplished anything without them. I hope my poem touches many people who feel the same way.

PHILLIPS, TISH
[a.] Virginia Beach, VA [title] "Untitled" [pers.] If you have ever had someone you love kept at a distance then you should understand this poem. The lonely feeling as you lie alone at night, thinking of them. I dedicate this poem to someone very close to my heart and that has become a part of my soul. You know who you are, and that I miss you and will always love you.

PIANTEDOSI, JOHN
[a.] Lynn, MA [title] "Time" [pers.] I am very happy to share my poem, time, with you in in-between days! I have been involved in the area of education for nineteen years. One of the things that I learned is the arts, music, poetry, dance, sculpture, etc, express that which lecture and text fall short—truth in its essence. I hope that I shared in this poem truth, the truth of a beautiful, yet broken world. It is much easier to share truth than to be a vehicle of truth by daily example. Maybe the "when" can be now! Peace! Maybe the "I" can be "we!" (It already is!)

PICASCIA, LISA
[a.] Holmdel, NJ [title] "Snow" [pers.] To me, poetry is something we should all share. It should not be kept a secret. I get my ideas for poems from my family, friends, and especially from landscapes. I love to write about seasons and what they mean to me. Since I have four sisters. I always have something to write about. In addition to writing poetry, I enjoy playing, piano, playing soccer, and drawing.

PINGO, ZAQARI
[a.] Oregon City, OR [title] "The American Tragedy" [pers.] From the poetic, the creator created. At dawn verse was the language unifide the prism of prophetic integrity. Our perceptions toward the conclusion are entrapped among beauty and "The American Tragedy." On behalf of the Infinite Decision shalt be final. On behalf of the Infinite Inquiry shalt nurture the curious. Kneeling, in the imperial valley possessing the mountain top. The

morning stars hold in custody the outshined sun. The horizon seeks asylum, waiting vengeance. To mine readers: May the halo of eternity sing in the chorus of thy will! May the life of love compel as the love of life!

PIPKIN, TAMMY
[a.] Flint, MI [title] "Welcome to the Rest of My Life" [pers.] This is the only poem I have ever written, to me it is an outlet for the feelings and emotions I could not express verbally. This poem was written shortly after the accidental death of my 11 year old son Robert, who was my life, my joy and my heart. Until we meet again, son, I love you and I miss you.

PLACE, OLIVIA
[a.] Monrovia, CA [title] "Reflections" [pers.] This poem was written a couple of days before my grandfather passed away. It was the last time I got to spend alone with him in reflection of the way I remembered him. As the poem states, these were all the thoughts that ran through my head as I watched him sleep. All these thought, feelings and memories were from the heart. I was honored to share this poem with my family and friends at his funeral. This is dedicated in loving memory to my grandfather, Park (Bill) Chow. He'll always be in my thought and in my heart.

PLUNKETT, TIMOTHY
[a.] Minden, LA [title] "The Flood" [pers.] The idea came from a spring thunder storm to my mind, to the paper. The flood was born, I was sitting at my desk late one night listening to the thunder and the water hitting the window. I started writing about what I heard mixed with a little fear and a tortured soul. The flood is one of my best works of art. I hope you enjoy it as much as I have.

PODGORSKI, PAULA
[a.] Wallkill, NY [title] "Who Promises" [pers.] My poetry is birthed through life experienced. Due to it's personal nature until now I've hesitated to share it. It's spirit as I feel it, taste it. Raw, unclothed. Pure truth as I perceive it to be. This poem was inspired by one whose impact for a brief moment in time gave me the most incredible joy I've even known. Followed by the most intense sorrow I've had the misfortune to endure. I dedicate this poem for all the Paul and Paula's who read it. Fate and wisdom are partners. I wish you listening hearts as friends and lovers. Blessings.

POLLARD, ROBERT
[a.] Sterling Heights, MI [title] "Mom" [pers.] I have found that writing is a way for me to express my innermost thoughts and feelings. I have many regrets regarding decisions I have made and I'm looking forward to the opportunity to turn the page to a new chapter in my life. My poem being accepted for publication has given me back some self-confidence for sure.

POPE, ROB
[a.] Surrey, BC [title] "Angel" [pers.] Poetry is the written reflection of thought. This poem was written on the morning of a funeral for a dear friend. His life was short but he truly touched everyone's lives that had the good fortune of meeting him. I often write when I am inspired by either trying to make someone smile, or get a good laugh. I wrote this time because my life was truly changed by unquestioned friendship, which I remember with both a tear and a smile.

PORTER, DORIS
[a.] Hollywood, MD [title] "The Melody of Nature" [pers.] This birthday poem was a special tribute, to my dear aunt, on her 70th birthday. She loved her fine feathered friends. She is to me, a reflection of these special friends in life. The poem was presented on an engraved plaque.

PORTER, EDITH
[a.] Des Moines, IA [title] "Is Daddy Coming"

[pers.] I'm 36, a grandmother, mother of two grown children, and a four year old! I'm single, black and strong! Most of my life I've done things wrong! But I'm learning good from evil. I'm disearning! Many roads I've traveled, some paved most graveled! But I'm better and wiser for every mistake I've made. Not all was my fault, sometimes I just got played! Learning to overcome and forgive myself! Learning when, to put pride on a shelf. From my heart, I'll continue to write poetry, my goal? To meet Miss Oprah Winfrey! Peace, Queen E. Lady of Rhyme and poetry!

POWELL, PATTI
[a.] Terra Alta, WV [title] "The Day of Wonder" [pers.] I feel that I have a gift for writing poetry the words just seem to come in my mind. Sometimes what I am feeling and other times what I think other people need to hear. I hope this poem inspires a reader in some way.

PUCKETT, SUZZANE
[a.] Lisbon, OH [title] "Who Can We Be" [pers.] First I'd like to dedicate this poem to my husband. Who inspired me to make the step of making my poetry public. This poem was a reflection of a rough time of acceptance from society. As every other trying to succeed in the perfect physical, mental and emotional lifestyle of the "good" society. Thank you for the opportunity to say my opinion in verse. My view has finally became; society is not always the perfect role model.

PULASKI, JUDITH
[a.] Beloit, WI [title] "Fall . . . Is the Season" [pers.] Being a painter all of my life . . . when I write poetry, I like to paint a picture with words as well. Fall is a beautiful time of the year and inspire me in every way artistically. Poetry is a way to unleash the inner feeling and calm the soul.

PULASKI, JUDITH
[a.] Beloit, WI [title] "Cracks on the Ceiling . . ." [pers.] Poetry has been a way for me to tell the stories of my life that have been so precious to me. My time on the farm in the Kickapoo Valley of Wisconsin were the best times of my life with my beautiful Gram. The scenery in the valley is just breath taking and brings out the best poetry and paintings in me as an artist.

QUEEN, BEVERLY
[a.] Orwell, OH [title] "Scattered" [pers.] This poem is about a friend, I met briefly. He entered my life as a kindred spirit and left me suddenly, leaving only words to express our love and friendship. I feel poetry is a special talent that was bestowed upon me. I express my feelings through my poems, the words just float onto the paper. The inspiration comes from deep within. The encouragement to share my words comes from a dear friend whom I consider as my "daughter." I hope that others who have this special gift will release their expressiveness and let many be inspired by their words.

QUINN, GERALD
[a.] Boston, MA [title] "The Lament of August" [pers.] I've written a few poems in my times. I always believe in rhythm. The first and third line should rhythm, or first and second line should have rhythm. The poem should tell a story. My wife has just returned from shopping. My writing is atrocious, as I pen this. Oh well, back to penmanship! I just can't swallow the idea of poetry being written without rhyming. If one desires telling a story, tell it. If one wants to poeticize, then let's leave rhyming!

RAMOS, ARMANDO
[a.] Brownsville, TX [title] "At Night" [pers.] Writing plays a very important part in my life. It is through poetry that I am able to fully express myself. It is from life's experiences that inspire me to write. This poem, written in 1993, comes from the greatest inspiration, love. And as life goes on so does my poetry.

RAMSAY, LAURA
[a.] Arlington, MA [title] "Rings of Silence" [pers.] Though I have been writing poetry since grammar school and have been writing ever since, I have discovered poetry is a wonderful medium to express not only love and joy, but difficult emotions as well. I find it therapeutic and allows release and clarification of feelings. I am not always aware of poetry is profound, thought provoking, beautiful and a genuine expression of creativity and hope. Fellow poets, I am honored to be in your rank

RASH, MICHAEL EARL
[a.] Cincinnati, OH [title] "To My Lost Love" [pers.] "To My Lost Love" was my outlet when my girlfriend, Amy, was killed in a car accident at age 16. I would like to thank my mother Wanda Sims for always being there for me. To Jean and Fred Wyatt, with their encouragement this poem has finally seen daylight after eleven years. To their son David for being my backbone in life. I would like to acknowledged my father Timothy, my brother Scott and sister Elizabeth Rash, I love you. For those who have had painful losses remember this, "All great storms must pass to let the sunshine through."

RASNICK, KAREN
[a.] Brockton, MA [title] "Love is Hell" [pers.] Most people who read my poetry ask me where it comes from. I think they expect to hear some big story from my life which inspired it. Ninety percent of the time, there is no such story. The words just come to me and I write them down in a way that feels right. Although poetry is a form of expression for me, what you read isn't necessarily what I needed to express at the time that I wrote it. The poem was simply my release mechanism. It feels good knowing other people can enjoy it, too.

RATHER, JESSE
[a.] Camarillo, CA [title] "I Am" [pers.] I Am is in memory of all who have suffered because of an undeserved reputation. From my family, I have always experienced love. However, in public, I am not given respect, because I am thirteen. I don't have the talent of song or story, so the only way that the world will truly understand my feelings, is poetry. This poem was encouraged by my dog, and supported by my mom, dad, and teachers, Mrs. Fairchild, and Mrs. Dallape. I hope it'll allow the world to take a second look, and give a second chance to the people who seem most alienated.

RAY, RICHARD
[a.] Columbia, SC [title] "While You Were Gone" [pers.] I generally write short fiction and novels. However, since I met Penny, I've written tons of poems. I never knew I had it in me. She found the poet hiding in my heart. Who knew?

REAGAN, ROBIN
[a.] Lafayette, IN [title] "The Infidel" [pers.] I am an Indiana native who resided in Montreal, QC for twelve years. Where I have done much of my writing, including a novel yet to be published. My first short story was published at eight years old. The bulk of my poems were originally written as lyrics. Difficulty finding musicians with a similar musical vision has prompted me to publish them as poetry. I studied opera for seven years but enjoy being involved in a wide variety of music styles. An animal lover and activist, I hope to be taken on at the Veterinary Medical School of Purdue University.

REDD, KAREN
[a.] N. Little Rock, AR [title] "In The Dark" [pers.] Poetry is new to me. My friend is the one that got me interested in it, only mine were a little different. Mine range from things that go bump in the night, to writing about the Arkansas Razor Backs that I am so very proud of my dad was a very good writer of short stories. But he were about normal people not the kind he and my mother taught me to be afraid of, like mine are. Thank you

dad, thank you mother, and thank you Linda for being the one who inspired me to give it a try.

REED, GLORIA J.
[a.] Edmond, OK [title] "Moses' Tabernacle: A Heavenly Pattern" [pers.] This poem was an outpouring of my heart after attending a bible study of the Old Testament Tabernacle, written by Beth Moore. Prior to that, I had gone through a very difficult personal struggle, surrendering life-long issues to my Lord and Saviour, Jesus Christ. Since childhood, writing poetry has been my way of expressing thoughts and emotions that have had a deep impact in my life. It is my hope and prayer that other smight be blessed and challenged to discover the awesome truths revealed in Moses' Tabernacle.

REEVES, JOHNNY
[a.] Tucson, AZ [title] "Cotton Candy Preamble" [pers.] Verse and Phrases have been a part of me, all my life. I used to scribble them down on anything that was handy. Someone encouraged me to keep a notebook with me. Never did I think of publishing the stuff going around in my head. I wouldn't even let anyone read it. It was just my private thoughts. When I finally let someone read it, she said "these need to be shared." Thanks Mom, for giving me the courage to share my poem.

REEVES, JOSEPH
[a.] Tempe, AZ [title] "From the Heart" [pers.] This poem was written about a very special person in my life and shall remain special until the end of time. This person inspired the thoughts and feelings in this poem many years ago and I will always remember her.

REICHENBACH, JAMES
[a.] Lancaster, PA [title] "2050" [pers.] In the past few years, I have become increasingly fearful as to the viability of this planet of ours to sustain future generations. Basic logic holds that infinite growth cannot continue within a finite area. Unfortunately, the simplicity of this concept may have led many of us to overlook it's importance. My commitment to speaking out on issues of importance to me has been consistently supported by my family. My beautiful children Madison and Isaiah, my nieces Sharon and Teyairra, the love of my life Myrna, my mother Anne and my sister Chris. Thank you all.

REICHMAN, SAM
[a.] Port Washington, OH [title] "Creases" [pers.] You gotta let it go and twist the profile. Break their mold and find you own style. They tried to make me. So I couldn't break free. When I tried this world humbled me. Now I'm trying to break through and get a grip. Of the core truth in the element. Of the life there is when we fall behind. No time to forgive . . . just survive.

REINAUER, PHYLLIS
[a.] Mahwah, NJ [title] "Reflections" [pers.] Since the age of five, I have been writing poetry. I attribute this to the fact that my parents read to me at a very early age, were writers and public speakers themselves, and encouraged me to express myself through the written word as I grew. During my career in publishing and advertising, I have written everything from abstract to TV scripts, feature stories and novel; however, poetry has been, and always will be, my favorite means of expression.

RIBUSTELLO, ANTHONY
[a.] Bronx, NY [title] "Rejoice" [pers.] Poetry is what keeps me grounded in life. I know the importance of stopping to smell the roses. The little things in life are paramount, otherwise we are simply marking time as if we where imprisoned. Being raised in New York City, I live hard and play hard, writing poetry gives me balance.

RICE, COREY
[a.] Moraine, OH [title] "Mandy's Poem" [pers.] I wrote this poem in the summer of '97 for my best

friend Amanda Garrett. I would have never thought we could have come as far as we have, but she is still one of my favorite people. It's amazing how words will come back to haunt you; but now, more than ever, I pray that she will always stay, and never, ever go away. Mandy now has cancer and is fighting the battle of her life. I don't know what tomorrow holds, but I am thankful for every moment I've had with her.

RICHARDS, CHARLES
[a.] Crawfordville, FL [title] "The Creator" [pers.] This poem describes my wish to create a world for the people I care about. Poetry is important to me as a song writer and of poems like this. There is not much to do in Wakulla where I live, except her music and the arts. My hobbies are poetry, guitar, fire fighting I enjoy doing things that no one expects, like wearing a zoot suit to my senior prom. I don't like being like everyone else. Being unique and poetic is a gift from God.

RICHARDS, DOROTHY
[a.] Grand Rapids, MI [title] "A Keeper's Daughter" [pers.] My thoughts on lighthouse living are memories. Stemming from a heritage of lighthouse keepers-great-grandfather, Grandfather and father. I was born in a pictures love lighthouse, on the shore of Lake Superior in Keeweenaw County, Michigan. Being so close to nature in this unique life, inspires my poetry and plans for an autobiography.

RICHARDSON, CRYSTAL
[a.] McKinleyville, CA [title] "A Dewy Morning's Pastel Blaze" [pers.] I am just a girl whose life has found it's way reading across a long and jagged road, but to know pain is to cherish beauty, and twisted paths make way for the loveliest stories. So, to those who have harmed me, I forgive you. To those who have left me behind, I still hold on to the initial truth of all existence, love. And thank you to all my teachers, (educated and uneducated), with a special thanks to my standard of perfection I will never forget.

RICTOR, BARBARA
[a.] Willoughby, OH [title] "The Sin" [pers.] This poem was written because so many people cheat on spouses and take for granted they will never get caught. Even if your spouse never catches you, don't forget you're still being watched.

RILEY, DEE
[a.] Ashtabula, OH [title] "My Rose" [pers.] "My Rose" was originally created as an overlay for a photograph of mine with the thought of perhaps becoming a greeting card. My Aunt Rose loved the verse, and of course, sharing the name, it has special meaning to her. This is my first attempt at poetry. Through the ages, the rose has been a symbol of eternal love, thus the poem was designed to convey that thought.

RIPPY, POLK, JR.
[a.] Bronx, NY [title] "Different Hoods" [pers.] First I would like to give "all praises and glory to God." I am thankful to have strong family ties and a few true friends. Writing poems is a genuine way to express personal feelings. I enjoy writing poetry that a reader can personally relate to.

RIVERA, LISA
[a.] Bronx, NY [title] "Iridescent Memories" [pers.] I am honored to have my first published poem grace such a prestigious collection. Iridescent memories is dedicated to all my past loves. This poem embodies the nature of life, passionate love and the growth of the spirit. It is a reflection of the emotional complexity that fuels poetic expression. Throughout my life, I have loved poetry for its condensation and distillation of emotions that defy common description. As with all artistic forms, its beauty springs from the creative process that is an integral part of the human spirit.

RIZZO, PATTY
[a.] Woodmere, NY [title] "Freedom" [pers.] Poetry is an art. An artists tools are brush paint

and canvas. A poets tools are pen and paper both express their feeling through these tools . . . my poem "Freedom" was written with love and understanding for my fellow man.

ROBINSON, JEAN
[a.] New York, NY [title] "It's Time" [pers.] Poems are one of the ways I express myself. I am the third middle child of four siblings. Three girls, one boy. I have always seen things differently and found it easier to write it down, than to verbally express it. Growing up, I've seen a lot of injustice in this world. I have always wanted to assist in healing the wounded and strengthen the weak. I want to know before I leave his world, that I have done my part in making this world a better place to live in. Not only for us but for the many generations to come. It's time.

RODGERS, LAGUAN
[a.] Buffalo, NY [title] "Ah Friend" [pers.] A lot of times, people get caught up in making poems into these wordy, philosophical messages. As a writer and avid reader of poetry I look into myself to see what is complex but yet grasp those things with simplicity and emotional accuracy. These raw, honest feelings are my poetry. The poems are always there inside. We are just trail stations where the experiences pass through on an ongoing journey. "Ah Friend" is just my attempt to explain my feelings about true friendship, hoping that someone else can relate.

RODNEY, RYAN
[a.] Silverdale, WA [title] "Our Time Would Seem to be Done" [pers.] Poetry is an emotional outlet for me and provides serenity for my thoughts. My poem feeds off that desire as it is one that captures my real life yearning and places it in the confines of a structured rhyme. The goal of any poem is to present feelings to a reader in the hope that those feelings can be brought out within that reader, as is the goal of this poem. That is what the success of any poem should be based on and that is what I would base the successfulness of my poetry career.

RODRIGUEZ, CELESTE
[a.] Tecumseh, MI [title] "Rain" [pers.] This poem symbolizes that with new rain comes some sort of a calming peacefulness all over the world. Rainbows always make me a more calmer individual. We always seen to get rainbows around this part of Michigan, since we live near Lake Erie.

RODRIGUEZ, KAREN
[a.] Odessa, FL [title] "The Soul of a Sister" [pers.] I live in Tampa, FL with my husband Dennis. He has given me the inspiration to start writing again. My wonderful family have all inspired me to put my feelings into words. It has always been one of my dreams to have something published, and now, that has come true. I feel honored and hope that one day I may publish a book. I hope others can find something or someone to relate to in my writing. Dennis, I could not have done it without you! This poem, of course, is for my sister, Sandi.

RODRIGUEZ, MICHAEL
[a.] Corpus Christi, TX [title] "What Happens to the Days?" [pers.] I wrote "What Happens to the Days" because I had to write a poem for English and because days seem to fly by like minutes. I then thought that it was a good poem and wanted other people to see. So then I saw poetry.com and entered the contest.

ROLAND, CHRIS
[a.] Cumberland, RI [title] "It's a Personal Journey Towards God in Heaven" [pers.] To God, be the glory, I'm a person that love's God through Jesus Christ my Lord and savior. I love my family and friends. If I can, I try to help those who are in need. The spirit of God and my desire to help people inspired me to write this. To let people know that everybody's journey in life is different and the choice is their as to which direction they should travel. For more God inspired writings please contact the Inspirational Messenger.

RULON, LYNN
[a.] Mt. Ranch, CA [title] "Breathe the Silent

Second" [pers.] Poetry, story and song have been bright threads through my world as long as I can remember. I wrote this poem 32 years ago as a teenager and it's turned out to be quite a patient treasure looking back I'd have to say that this poem captures the spirit of my mother, June. In so many ways her life touched mine as one of those wonderful, fleeting notes. This well of inspiration is sweeter now that the desire to share is fulfilled.

RUML, SEAN
[a.] Clinton Township, MI [title] "No Holding Back" [pers.] This poem represents me finally getting over my fear of falling in love. Finding that special person to share the rest of your life with is at times very difficult. Someday I will find the girl who will be the love of my life. I hope that the people who read my poem will walk away after reading it inspired to fall in love again or find love for the very first time.

RUSSELL, AMBER
[a.] Collingwood, ON [title] "The Best I Never Met (My Grandpa)" [pers.] Hello, my name is Amber Russell and I'm 12, going on to 13 and I live in a wonderful town called Collingwood, ON. I attend as a grade seven student at really cool school called Admiral Collingwood.

RUSSELL, ANNETTE
[a.] Malvern, AR [title] "Mother You Are So Dear To Me" [pers.] Russell, Annette Malvern, Arkansas. This is my first poem, which I hold so very close to my heart. I dedicate my poetry to my dearest mother as a gift of love and to thank her for inspiring my life.

RUSSELL, GLORIA
[a.] Belfair, WA [title] "Adrift" [pers.] I wrote "A Drift" feelings there are too many people in nursing homes, that have been forgotten. Please take time to visit them, they need us. I also want to thank my youngest daughter, Kelli. Russell Agodon, an accomplished writer for inspiring me to write at age sixty five. I have had many happy moments writing and sharing my poetry.

RUSSELL, SHELLEY
[a.] Longview, WA [title] "Our Love" [pers.] I enjoy writing poetry. It helps me to express my love for my family and friends. I am inspired by my husband, children, and grandchildren. This poem shares the love that I have with my husband, Jim. We have been married almost thirty years by having my poem published, it will show him how much I love him. It puts our love down in history so, I dedicate my first published poem to my husband, Jim with love for all his love and support.

RYAN, HEATHER
[a.] Hendricks, MN [title] "On A Night Like Tonight" [pers.] I have lived most of my life pretending to be someone else. This poem expresses my need, but fear, to open up and show my true self. I knew that I would always be different. I was often told I would not be successful. While other friends worried about make-up, I was busy writing. It is an honor to have my poem selected, and I am very enthusiastic about my achievement. Thank you from an eleven-year-old poet.

RYAN, JAMES, III
[a.] Egg Harbor City, NJ [title] "The Marine Corps Creed" [pers.] Being one of America's front line defenders takes on a special meaning, it feels like it's you against the world. And being part of America's finest fighting force, when the mission is on for a marine; there's no turning back, we don't retreat. As then to keep highly motivated we profess the creed over and over, in our minds, hearts, and souls; and then the movements of combat happen like clockwork. And any mission we set out on is fulfilled completely 100%; for God, country and corps.

SABIAS, REX
[a.] Bay City, MI [title] "It Finds a Way" [pers.] It is my conclusion that life with all of its uncertainty and variety are unwritten poems waiting for an emotion to trigger their creation. My poem "It Finds a Way" was one of those emotions. The ability to express my dreams and feelings in verse, released

my negativity and allowed me to move to a richer state of being. This poem is dedicated to my wife Janet who is the cause of my inspiration and happiness.

SALINAS, ERNESTO
[a.] Mexico City, Mexico [title] "Head" [pers.] I don't write very much, but I enjoy writing poetry enormously, it represents my thoughts and several moments of my life. I owe this to Charles Bukowski, the writer. To be an unknown writer in my country and this being my first public recognition makes me feel extremely proud. Short science fiction, fiction, and erotic stories are in my writings, but poetry is what I prefer to write. One day, the poem "Head" grew into my brain and I like it very much.

SAMATAS, COLLIN
[a.] Oak Brook, IL [title] "Delusional Ocean" [pers.] This poem was written during my adolescence, one of the darker times of my life. I daydreamed a great deal, escaping my depressing beauty by entering fantasy worlds in my mind. Unfortunately, my dissociation took control and concentrating on anything in the real world became extremely difficult. "Delusional Ocean" attempts to capture the conflict between my yearning to escape reality and my desire to control the spontaneous daydreaming.

SANCHEZ, ARIANA
[a.] Menlo Park, CA [title] "His" [pers.] Poetry is words with so much emotion, from the depths of the unconscious.

SANCHEZ, JACQUELINE
[a.] Stony Point, NY [title] "Passion" [pers.] I am inspired by experiences I've lived that make me the person that I am. Writing is my way of easing pain shaking happiness, or simply showing others my love for them. I wrote this for someone who I loved very much, and who I deeply admire. This is for you Boo. Thanks for loving me now and forever. I will never forget you. If anyone loved someone the way you loved me, the world would be a much wonderful place than it already is. I was very lucky to have met you.

SANDER, MARJORIE
[a.] Springfield, MO [title] "Wings" [pers.] This poem was written for a dear friend of mine. I have always a written poems (my mother did, too). I am enclosing another poem that explains my philosophy of life. I am very much family oriented and make friends easily. I also sing and love music of all kinds. The most beautiful in this world are the little children, I believe we are all brothers and sisters and born into this world to help each other. Poetry is a kind of intimacy that meets the needs of each individual. I would like to buy more copies of this book. Perhaps one day they will be available.

SANDLIN, ROSE
[a.] Germantown, OH [title] "Your Love" [pers.] I have written poetry since I was very young. To me poetry is the ultimate expression of our innermost feelings. This is a special gift that I have been given. This poem reflects "young love" whether it be newly weds or oldly weds. Love is always young.

SANGILLO, KATHLEEN
[a.] Saco, ME [title] "Trust Leteral Twinmates" [pers.] I started writing poetry as a very young girl. To me, it was a way of putting my very inner most feelings on paper and letting my soul be my guide. This poem is most special, because, if two people have complete trust, they will be lifelong soulmates. I live in Saco, Maine and have all my life. I am 41 years old and have five beautiful daughters and four gorgeous grandchildren. My hobbies are of course, writing, weight training, swimming and horseback riding. This poem is dedicated to my twinmate, to whom I have not yet met, but my heart knows I will.

SARGENT, SHAWN
[a.] Jersey City, NJ [title] "Thoughts of Love!" [pers.] I have always considered poetry an outlet of escape and a way for me to express myself, and show how I'm feeling. My sister Marie has always told me to express what I am feeling, but this particular poem is dedicated to a special young lady

who has meant more to me than words could ever say. You are my world "Susan." And to my family members, what can I say but no amount of words will ever repay you for what you have done for me and what you had to give up over the years to insure my education and personal growth. Thank you: Marie, James, Arnold, Michael, Tiny, Christopher, Yolanda, Lamont, and most my mother, Lottie, for without her I would not be here.

SARKADY, ANDREW
[a.] McHenry, IL [title] "Before I Go" [pers.] Andrew Sarkady, business executive, father of four and grandfather of two, continues to pursue his dream and avocation of being an artist, painter, poet and creator of new art forms. He completed a strong academic foundation in the cultures and religions of man and after forty years is still evolving his art appreciation, even to include appearing on the 'silver screen' many times in the movie "Ground Hog Day." Andrew's home in McHenry, IL. proves to be the right setting for more poetic abstracts lake "Before I Go."

SCATURRO, PETER
[a.] Las Vegas, NV [title] "Concrete Lust" [pers.] This poem basically exhibits a deep expression of passion and lust, and the power it can impose when two special souls connect. I enjoy expressing myself through different creative aspects such as poetry, painting and sculpture, being a chef by trade I have many opportunities to let the creative juices flow.

SCHANK, LEONARD
[a.] Liverpool, NY [title] "Angry Winds" [pers.] My teachers in school led a young, inner city kid to appreciate poetry. The military allowed me to mature and graduate college because of the GI Bill. I enjoyed my graduate work and my teacher/counselor career. Now, a retired teacher, I would like to inspire others to enjoy the beauty of poetry. The supreme challenge for all is to put words on paper and bring about personal appreciation of people, nature, wonder and love.

SCHEDEL, MICHAEL
[a.] Aurora, CO [title] "Spring" [pers.] This poem can really make you think of spring and you can visualize the squishy grass, I mean like feeling it! The feeling can get you up, up and happy.

SCHERFFIUS, JOE
[a.] Citrus Heights, CA [title] "A Stolen Moment" [pers.] I was inspired to write this poem when my inner being was in its most selfless state, offering a small glimmer of true spiritual love, and offering my vulnerability as a true sacrifice. I am pleased to share this inspiration of love with the world.

SCHLEICHER, LUCAS
[a.] Collinsville, IL [title] "Observation II" [pers.] My poetry tends to observe conflicts between the simple and the complex, between peace and chaos. This wasn't planned but rather discovered after writing many poems. My writing help me to understand my conflicts and myself so that I might understand others and their conflicts as well. It is my hope that in time these observations will lead me to a better understanding of all those around me and that I might arrive at a peace

SCHNEIDER, ADAM
[a.] Columbus, OH [title] "Sonnet 3" [pers.] A poem is a glimpse into the soul of the poet. This poem is dedicated, along with my heart, to Maria Teresa Schiappa, a woman whom I love very much. Love is the most wonderful thing on this earth, but sometimes it can be very hard to deal with, especially when it's unrequited. We seek remedies to the pain in all sorts of places, but, in the end, the only true cure lies in our own souls, and those of the ones we love. My poem tries to express this; come what may, solace lies in your true love's heart.

SCHOCH, KARL
[a.] Whitehall, PA [title] "Happiness Tears" [pers.] I write mostly what I feel and about everyday things which happen in everyone's life. "Happiness Tears" was inspired by my true love and soulmate

Donna Hall, three weeks after we met. Her love and positivity in my life is very strong. I hope that it will bring the same happiness to your life. I never thought any of my poetry was good enough to be published. If you're a poet and feel the same, take a chance and share your thoughts. It may achieve world peace and love. A true utopia, for all to experience.

SCHOLL, ALYSSA
[a.] Westerville, OH [title] "Him" [pers.] This poem is very dear to my heart because it is about a breakup that I had with my ex-boyfriend. It tells the whole story word for word.

SCHOURES, LINDSAY
[a.] St. Catharines, ON [title] "Limitless Light" [pers.] I feel poetry does not have to rhyme or follow a specific pattern in order to convey a message properly. However, some degree of emotion and knowledge must be incorporated in order to personalize it. I am sixteen years old, and attend Governor Simcoe secondary school in St. Catharines, Ontario Canada. I would like to thank all my wonderfully unique teachers for providing me with that knowledge. Also my family, including, Kim and Danny and my best friend Shari Moore as well as her parents Brian and Linda as they have all played major roles in my life.

SCHREINER, DEVIN
[a.] Blue Springs, MO [title] "The Senses" [pers.] My poem was written as an in school assignment. I am a 13 year old 7th grade student at Hall McCarter Middle School in Blue Springs, Missouri. I have wanted to be a writer and have dreamed of someday being published. I never thought it would come so soon. I am very excited, proud and honored to be part of this publication. This has given me encouragement to persue my dream. I would like to say "Thank you" to those who chose me to be part of this.

SCHUMACHER, DAWN
[a.] Lombard, IL [title] "Missing You"

SCHWICHTENBERG, GENEVA
[a.] Richland Center, WI [title] "Eshnella" [pers.] This poem commemorate my experience of fellowship with the someone who is utmost in my life—the Lord Jesus Christ! It expresses the awesome depth of feeling and peacefulness attained as I commune with Him. Having this timely opportunity to share this blissful experience via this poem is tremendous. I pray that all who read this poem will be drawn to desire the same beautiful communication experience with their Creator, God Almighty. I pray their lives may reach the sublime—taking and sharing with God. Supreme essence—a beautiful relationship with God. To have a personal relationship with Jesus Christ is truly awesome!

SCOTT, KATIE
[a.] Fresno, CA [title.] "Found Poem on a Fallen Leaf" [pers.] My name is Katie Scott, I am 12 years old. I attend Tenaya Middle School in Fresno, California and I am in the 7th grade.

SCOTT, LEANNE
[a.] Browns Plains [title] "Society" [pers.] My poems reflect my thoughts and ideas at given moments in my life. I enjoy putting my thoughts into words to express emotions not freely given. I'm an average person with an average life I enjoy simple pleasures and my dream is to lead a stress free, comfortable existence.

SEE, EARL
[a.] Ontario, CA [title] "Planet" [pers.] I dedicate this poem to the most beautiful woman on this planet. This poem best expresses my feelings for this very special woman that God has placed in my life.

SEEKELL, RENE
[a.] Catasauqua, PA [title] "Happiness in Your Eyes" [pers.] I have always been able to express my strongest feelings through poetry when I can't seem to find a way to express them vocally. This poem means a great deal to me because it was

written to my true love. It took me 27 years, but I finally found my Mr. Right and this is how I was aptly able to tell him exactly how much he means to me. Hopefully through my poem, it will help someone else to show someone they love just how they feel when they don't have the words to say it themselves.

SEILER, JENNIFER
[a.] North Wales, PA [title] "Middle School Teacher" [pers.] Thank you to the 1999–2000 PiTeam at Pennbrook Middle School in North Wales, PA! I could not have written this poem without the inspiration of my 125 seventh grade English students. I truly love my job. Being a teacher is challenging, difficult, hectic and fun, but interacting with my students everybody and building relationships with them as they learn is the Ultimate reward that makes everything worthwhile. I thank God daily for my job and for leading me to Pennbrook Middle School. Me desire is for my students to develop a love for writing as I have.

SELINGER, JOSEPH
[a.] Delta, BC Canada [title] "Old England's Lost in Time" [pers.] This poem represents a time in history that was magical. In old England, romance and chivalry we're alive and prospering. Mythical dragons were born out of men's fears and fantasies. Mother earth was the stage and her fruits, the ingredients that supplied the magician his potions, the knight his battle grounds and the romantic a setting to play out his fantasies. I dedicate this poem to my wife Linda and my sons Brett, Andy and Colin, in hope that through the eyes of a poet Old England and all that she represents will never be lost in time.

SEMENTILLI, A.
[a.] Erie, PA [title] "Trying to Find a Way" [pers.] First and foremost I would like to thank God. He is my inspiration and my savior. I thank my teachers, friends, and companions who helped me with my poetry. I would also like to thank my three best friends Anthony, Jamila, and Abbey for just being there. Finally I would like to thank my friend Christa. She showed me the bright inspiration of Christ. That's the best inspiration a person can get!

SEMIAN, KATHY
[a.] Conneaut Lake, PA title] "Snowflakes" [pers.] On a cold, snowy Saturday in February, the desire to draw something creative at my drafting table was overcome by the urge to write something creative. As I watched the snowflakes fall, I thought about their beautiful, intricate designs. I also thought about faith and hope; even a little can brighten the lives of so many people. I received a Bachelor's degree in Art with departmental honors from Thiel College in Greenville, Pennyslvania in 1996. I went on to Edinboro University in Edinboro, PA and studied drawing and painting at the graduate level.

SEVERANCE, JARRETT
[a.] Toronto, OH [title] "My Basic Hopes" [pers.] I wrote my poem as a homework assignment for my 6th grade literature class at St. Francis Central School, Toronto, Ohio. We were asked to write about the year 2000. My poem is one of hope for the millennium.

SHARKEY, LEE
[a.] Milwaukee, WI [title] "I Am Sci-Fi Poem" [pers.] My poetry talent is a gift from God. I see and live some of the poems. I write poetry that comes from God that moves people's hearts and mind.

SHARP, RICHARD
[a.] Ajax, ON [title] "The Problems of the City" [pers.] The inspiration for this poem, came to me shortly after moving from a small northern Ontario City to a big metropolis in Ontario. I could not believe the amount of garbage I had seen strewn in the streets after a walk home from work. This poem is the result of what I saw on that fateful walk.

SHAW, TAMEKIA
[a.] Taylor, MS [title] "The Life of Love" [pers.]

I feel that poetry is a special expression of feelings mended with thoughts on the different emotions of life. Poetry is a special gift that free my mind to write verses of things that are important to me. This poem expresses my feelings of what the life of love means to me. I feel that love should be treasured, and share between only two. I feel that every relationship should have these qualification in order to have a successful and healthy love. Once a person have experience this type of love, my understanding should delight the presents of your soulmate.

SHELTON, PATRICE
[a.] Baltimore, MD [title] "The Garden of Eden" [pers.] I love getting creative with a combination of my imagination and my perspective of life. For example, in "Friday the Thirteenth", many of those bad things happened to me but not in one day. They all happened in a period of about three months. If I ended up as a popular poet when I'm all grown up, my goal would be to do a mixture of poems. Some for and light-hearted like "Friday the Thirteenth," some inspirational like "The Garden of Eden" and many more styles to write. I love to write and I want to keep on.

SHIRLEY, AMY
[a.] Paw Paw, WV [title] "End of Time" [pers.] Poetry is truly a God given talent. I write poetry based on how I feel. Some sad, some happy, but I give all the glory unto God, because without him, I wouldn't have this talent. I want to thank God first of all, because without Him we are nothing, and second I want to thank my family and friends for inspiring me and believing in me. God bless you guys (you know who you are). Peace and love.

SHIRLEY, DOROTHY
[a.] Indianapolis, IN [title] "We" [pers.] "We" is intended to encourage senior citizens to always enjoy life. Whenever I visit my daughters in California, I head for the beach to view the ocean and walk barefoot in the sand. Writing poetry allows me to express my imagination and memories. Having had ten children, my family now covers four generations. I live inner city in the Mid-west. I graduated from college in 1996, Magna Cum Laude. I'm a job developer for persons 55 and older. My hobby is sewing. My philosophy is, "Just keep getting up in the morning." I thank God, "My cup runneth over."

SHOBERG, MARK
[a.] Clifton, CO [title] "Remain" [pers.] Sometimes, when we are asked to describe ourselves with one word, that one word usually carries meanings, stigmas, or any number of preconceived ideas, that many times are tainted as beyond recovery. It is therefore with some reluctance that I call myself a Christian: for I am not religious, yet I follow the lamb wheresoever He goeth. This poem is about love and acceptance. God is love, and I believe that one day, all mankind will partake of that love, but every man in his own time. The Garden in the poem is all the souls that have ever breathed and lived; the reason the Garden is so green to the few that see it, is because the doctrine is eternal torment and everlasting hell, are being pruned back, and the true image of God is being broadcast throughout all the earth. If God loves one, God loves all, and if He reconciled myself back to Him, He will only do the same for all He creation: All Will Remain!

SILBERSHER, MARVIN
[a.] Lake Hopatcong, NJ [title] "Untitled" [pers.] Poetry was my father's way of commemorating special occasions. He wrote love poems to my mother and verses for our growing up. The Torah, the book on the desk, was a poem. Of all human creations, I feel that poetry is the most remarkable. One is allowed to say things that might never be expressed or revealed. It's as if a door the heart and soul is always there. Celebration and worship have been the poems that people have prayed with.

I write every day in the same way that prayer inspired us. It is my form of worship.

SILVERA, TRICIA
[a.] Uniondale, NY [title] "Storm" [pers.] I have written poetry for as long as I can remember, but I wrote this once specifically for inspiration as I was at a crossroads in my life. Going through marital problems doesn't mean life ends, it helped me realize that I had closed too many doors with regard to self expression. Also having a five year old daughter who views every experience with innocence and wisdom of truth only a child could have, has encouraged my optimism and that coupled with my belief that there is a power greater than us has released my creativity once again. I have also gone back to college for my B.S. in Elementary Education.

SILVERMAN, RACHAEL
[a.] Boca Raton, FL [title] "My Darling" [pers.] "My Darling" is written for a lost love. The poem symbolizes my desires, aspirations and feelings I have deep within for a love I once had. Having such emotions at fourteen, it's not easy. Since I could never say I love you to my darling, I decided to write about it. It is my sincere way of expressing my love. I miss him and hope he still cares. I hope you enjoy reading my poem as much as I loved writing "My Darling."

SIMMER, MERENDA
[a.] Erie, PA [title] "My Hun John" [pers.] I feel that poetry is a unique gift from God which betrays the inner beauty of the heart. My poem "My Hun John," talks about the story of our dramatic life portrayed within the last one year and a half, I am very proud to say I am special not only for what I create in poetry but which poetry is a fond art of mine. Perhaps, I hope poetry touches your heart as it did mine when I wrote this poem this dedicated to this man I really truly deeply love.

SIMMONS, SCOTT
[a.] Crofton, MD [title] "No Endorsements" [pers.] "No Endorsements" Warning: Reading this poem with 3-D glasses will not aid you in the understanding of its meaning, nor will you gain any special optical advantages over similar readers lacking 3-D glasses.

SIMS, EDYTHE
[a.] Chicago, IL [title] "Beautiful Hours Are Here" [pers.] Poetry has a great meaning in my life. In writing I seek to touch the spark of divinity that dwells in all mankind telling the beauty of life and the importance of time. I am a teacher and minister. I came from a large family. Three sisters, five brothers. I am the only writers. I live on the south side of a large city, Chicago, IL. I like reading and traveling. I have been in seven different countries meeting many people and cultures, and when I write I write from my visions.

SISK, DONNA
[a.] Texarkana, TX [title] "Where Would I Be Without You?" [pers.] First of all I would like to thank the Lord above for giving me my talent for poetry. And for allowing me to have my son, and for giving me my wonderful caring and loving husband.

SKERRETT, JENNIFER
[a.] Nashville, TN [title] "DNR—Do Not Resuscitate" [pers.] I reside in Nashville, TN and perform stand-up comedy as a hobby. I graduated from Cochise College in AZ and have traveled extensively. I discovered poetry to be the purest form of expression and this poem reflects the experience of my father's death—who I miss terribly.

SKINNER, BETTY
[a.] Port Jervis, NY [title] "October" [pers.] Thank you for using my poem. It is dedicated to the memory of my husband of 40 years, who passed away so suddenly on a beautiful October day. It reflects to me; the cycle of life itself.

SLATER, STEPHANIE
[a.] Lawrenceburg, TN [title] "Always" [pers.] As a young writer who received poetic talent from my mother, I would like to thank the one person who inspired me to write this poem, my wonderful boyfriend, Anthony Cox. I am 14 years old and hope to major in journalism because I want writing to be the main part of my lifelong career. Writing is a way to express my innermost thoughts, feelings, fears, and desires. I consider this a gift that is the place able.

SLAVIK, PAM
[a.] Stanhope, NJ [title] "Remembrance" [pers.] This poem was written by me and read on the first Christmas after my mother's passing from cancer. She was such an integral part of our Christmas celebration and of our lives and is greatly missed. This poem expressed my "remembrance" of my mom as we began a new and different celebration of the Christmas season without her presence. Writing has always been a way of expressing my heartfelt feelings.

SLAZINSKI, KARL
[a.] Sarasota, FL [title] "Inimical Rollercoaster" [pers.] When I exalt or hurt, when I am in pain or am happy to be alive, all is poured into my prose. Communication is the ultimate gift: the passage of ideas from one to another ensures the continuation of the feelings, and the sharing of one's very soul. Through my poetry, I learn about myself. I wish to try to share this glimpse of my essence with everyone reading *The Fountain of Peace*. To the readers: I thank you for your support. To my parents: I love you; you make it all possible.

SMAAGAARD, JENNIFER
[a.] Forest Park, GA [title] "The Memories You Gave Me" [pers.] Writing poems, short stories, or non-fiction is something that runs in the family. My mother, also is currently writing. This poem is actually very old, I wrote it 13 years ago at the age of seven about a best friend I lost to moving around. It now has more meaning to me because of a man I fell in love with, that brought this poem back to life.

SMALL, JAMES J.
[a.] Denver, CO [title] "Gay in the USA" [pers.] Poetry is the language of the soul and I am honored to beatle to shake my soul thoughts with you.

SMARSH, AMANDA
[a.] Hummelstown, PA [title] "Hope" [pers.] I remember writing this poem, the day my sister Natalie decided to choose a life of drugs over her three month old son. She left him to be raised by my family. I remember being angry, and for some reason these words just came to me, so I wrote them down. That was six years ago, but this poem never left my mind. Hope represents our everyday struggle to understand her addiction. We pray that someday Natalie will see just how precious life is, and I feel that while Natalie is alive, there will always be hope.

SMITH, BRIANE
[a.] Simi Valley, CA [title] "The Stream" [pers.] "The Stream" tells a short story of who I am and where my distance in life has taken me so far. At age seventeen I've flowed through many dreams already I was little Miss Hollywood, went on to do volunteer work with the West Valley Police Department, played the violin at age eight, received an certificate of Accomodation from the city of L.A. at age ten, became a L.A.P.D. Explorer, was Indian Student of the Year, also awarded the Dare Essay Award and the Principals Award. Currently as Sophomore President at Simi Valley High School, past Freshman President, Junior Elect President, Cheerleader, Hoby Participate, cheered in the Pro-Bowl in Hawaii, and still carrying a 3.8 grade average. This summer. I'm training to be a personal trainer and aerobic instruction, quite a stream, with dreams and a journey that's just begun.

SMITH, KEVIN
[a.] Boulder, CO [title] "Urgently Waiting" [pers.] I have yet to plan to write a poem. Anything I write is merely a spontaneous expression of my thoughts or my mood, inspired by sight or memory or emotion. Thus I find myself writing about the things that affect me the most, positive or otherwise. I write because it helps me understand what is most important to me. I really only write for myself, but if someone else gets something from reading my ideas, I guess that's a bonus.

SMITH, KRISTOPHER
[a.] Overland Park, KS [title] "Thread of Hope" [pers.] This piece of art is only possible due to the fact that I have recently found one of the reasons God put me on this earth and that is to share every experience in my life rather it is positive or negative and to do that in my poems and short stories. I complete for you to read and live through the words I print on paper in your own way. I also enjoy writing song lyrics to express my thoughts and feelings. Thank you for your time and interest! Follow your dreams they can come true.

SMITH, MONTELLA
[a.] Wichita, KS [title] "Beloved Child" [pers.] Writing poetry has been my saving grace. Part of my her. Tage is Native American, so of course that comes through. My poetry is written from my spiritual center from which the words flow. This is God given gift, which I need to share with the world to help heal the pain we all carry.

SMITH, NICKI
[a.] Oklahoma City, OK [title] "I Must Walk Again the Wooded Path" [pers.] My poems come like a gentle rain and lay down upon my heart. I am native American and Irish. I love nature and family. I've written poetry since childhood. My occupation is care provider and lover of life. I'm sixty-seven years of age. I'm happy, joyous and feel free to be me. For this I am grateful. Dedicated to great great grandparents Sarah Elizabeth Snow and Jessie Clinton Casey.

SOSIN, HELENA
[a.] North Miami, FL [title] "Quo Vadis Polonia?" [pers.] Historic connections of Poland and Jews are just as the mystery of wine drinker is. Lehistan . . . A Keg of global gourmet grandchildren reaching out to imaginary beyonds for consolation and solutions, dreaming extraordinary visions, and blurring them by veils of denial, bypassing redblooded facts— obstructing own way of brotherly progress. Such is the country where I drank the music of poetry from my mother's breasts. And where my Jewish friend Sally Nuta perished due baton-buts of war.

SOUCIE, DAVID
[a.] Henderson, NV [title] "Passion of the Moon" [pers.] David Soucie, born and raised in Kankakee, IL. Been writing poetry since I've been ten years old. Like to read poetry of Elizabeth Browning when I was ten years old. All poetry has a meaning to those who read it with the eyes from the heart and soul or as the wise say with the mind's eye this is where love, tears of joy and laughter come from also the many colors of life dwells.

SPARROW, SHERITA
[a.] New Castle, DE [title] "I Saw You the Other Day" [pers.] This poem was written in the form of a letter to my grandfather who passed away when I was born. This poem served as a cleansing of enclosed feelings that I never expressed to anyone. So if I was given a chance to write to my grandfather, this poem is what I would send.

SPEEGLE, CHASE
[a.] Streetsboro, OH [title] "One Chance" [pers.] For Melissa Durham. I love you. One chance.

SPINDEL, ELLEN
[a.] Los Angeles, CA [title] "Smiling Eyes" [pers.] I was inspired to write "Smiling Eyes" after a meditation I had one day. Originally, I wrote this as a song, and the words just flowed through me. It was as though my pen glided across the paper effortlessly. I have been writing children's poetry, songs and stories for many years. I am currently Director of the Young Performer's Program at Lee Strasberg Acting Studio in Los Angeles, California. Children melt my heart and fill me with their love. I dedicate this poem to all the children in my life, they do have smiling eyes.

STANO, RAS
[a.] Hartford, CT [title] "Listening to the Wind" [pers.] I should have submitted my poem "Time" I said to myself when I saw the title of this collection. Writing is one of the most natural things about me and I draw inspiration from everything imaginable. Now I remember sitting alone at the Labadi Beach that breezy evening gazing blankly across the roaring sea imagining so much information carried in the rushing wind. I could swear I heard them. I realized I was listening to the wind. I am a musician, singer, songwriter, story writer, poet and playwright. Through these I express my experience, emotions, desires, imagination and belief.

STANTON, DENNIS
[a.] Woonsocket, RI [title] "Autumn Thoughts" [pers.] I began writing poetry years ago while I was attending school. Wondering through the Catskill Mountains, I came upon a cemetery. It told a story of the rich, the young and the slaves . . . I walked around; read and photographed the cemetery, including those stone inside and outside. One truly caught my eye, as it listed a poem upon it. I remember it as well today, as if I were still kneeling down reading it off 13 years ago. It has brought me to show what my writing style is. I write about what I can see, hear and whatever I can feel.

STEVENS, ARTHUR
[a.] South Oxhey, Watford [title] "My Shangria La" [pers.] Adapted to the film of Shangri La born London 1920. Five years Raf Liason Officer to American 8th Air Force Bomber Command, Brampton Huntington. Took up poetry five years ago whilst holdaying in Malta. I have a flare for it. Two daughters, retired collector. Peace with negotiation not wars. Terribly pleased I am your choice if it goes further I will rejoice maybe reach the summit of the poetic peak it will be the achievement from which I seek.

STEVENS, MELANIE
[a.] Mentor, OH [title] "You Are Gone, He Is Here" [pers.] Everyone has inner thoughts as well as hidden emotion. Poetry to me us a book of medicine that helps heal yourself and cleansed the soul. It's a release of all repressed feelings put on paper, so you may know yourself as a person and how you can express yourself truly. In this particular piece, it is about my first true love who I was with for a number of years, ending the relationship forever and finally putting a closure to the past. I had finally met someone else who loved me for who I was and provided me that strength and confidence I never had. A broken heart is one of the most painful situations to go through, so this piece helps guide me to my happiness and hopefully those who can relate and read this can help them understand life is a beautiful thing and is a way too short to settle for less than what you believe in.

STINSON, JENNIFER
[a.] Jackson, MS [title] "The Question" [pers.] This poem is dedicated to my best friend, Terry, who taught me to release the past, grasp the present and reach out to the future. He taught me how to live and love, once again. This poem commemorates the night my life was changed. I hope the passion with which it was composed will be shared by many.

STOUT, BRANDON
[a.] Ellensburg, WA [title] "Mother" [pers.] When I write my poems, I make sure that most everyone can relate. I don't have to use big words and confusing phrases to get my point across. My poem "Mother" is obviously about the love and respect my mother and I have for each another. I am sure that there are many other sons that have the same feelings for their mother as well. She has made me what I am today. Therefore, I want to dedicate this book (that I am fortunate to have one of my poems into her. I love you Mom. Your son, Brandon

STRASBURGER, REBECCA
[a.] Yorktown, VA [title] "Jesus, Our Saviour" [pers.] I'm 12 years old. I live in Virginia and attend Our Lady of Mount Carmel School. My younger brother is Greg and my younger sister is Brooke. Boomer is my Labrador Retriever. As said in my poem, I believe we are fortunate because we're blessed with the gift of life. Some people take life for granted, and that's wrong. As a Christian, God is my focus, and my goal is to be with Him in heaven. I want to thank Sister Martha Ann Titus because she teaches me about God and shows me God's love every day.

STRATEMEIER, NATALIE
[a.] Oklahoma City, OK [title] "Sad Eyes" [pers.] I enjoy watching people. I just thought of the poem as I was online. To me it means that when I see someone who is doing something they're not supposed to do, I grow sad. This is my way of conveying those feelings.

STRAWTHER, ADRIENNE
[a.] Anchorage, AK [title] "Spirit" [pers.] I'm 14 years old. Though my age is young, I feel as if I'm not. In the difficult experiences I've been through my writing has been a gift. In the poem "Spirit" I wrote about my mother. She has been diagnosed with cancer three times and time can only tell when she will rest again. "Spirit" explains that after a loved one dies they are still there with you. I thank the stars and my Jesse who both have given me a gift. I could never ask for more.

STREHLI, ALFRED, JR.
[a.] Twin Lakes, CO [title] "Ascension" [pers.] As a child living in the Llang Estacato, "The Staked Plains" of Texas, I came to see the arid canyons and mysterious vistas from the breaks of the caprock as revelations. Later, in the Boy Scouts, I began to understand nature as do the Commanches and the Kiowas: Something one participated in gratefully. I spent many a happy hour growing towards maturity wandering in a complete solitude about Texas, New Mexico, and Colorado. The Western Tradition from Rimbaud through Rilke and Frost is important to me, and I relish whatever journal of poetry and painting that I come across.

STUART, ANGELA A.
[a.] Franklinton, NC [title] "A Mother's Anguish" [pers.] Poetry has been my passion for many years; a way to express myself in the truest form I know, through the penning of desires, hopes, and dreams. I am honored to have my poem chosen for publication. In 1997, my husband and I, lost our baby girl, "Audrey Celeste", who was born prematurely. Thus, faced with an intense loss, the emptiness inside. However, we still cherish her in our hearts; while struggling to be blessed with another child. I am sure there are others who share this pain. Hopefully, "A Mother's Anguish", will remind them: They are not alone!

STUCKEY, ERIN
[a.] Pine Lake, GA [title] "A Wonderful Papa" [pers.] I wrote this poem for a class assignment at school. The assignment was to write a poem about someone or something, of great importance to us, which we had lost. The first thing that come to my mind was the unexpected death of my grandfather. He was loved by everyone who came in contact with him. I had not only lost a grandfather, but also a kindred spirit. This poem has helped me express just how important he was and still is to me. I was 16 when

this was written. I enjoy playing guitar and piano. I am in the top 5% of my class with a 3.83 GPA.

STURGIS, JOE
[a.] New York, NY [title] "Phone" [pers.] I wrote this poem at a time I felt most vulnerable and alone I was going through a mixed bog of emotions I needed to release my "realness" my phone ring and a long lost friend called. I devoted this poem to him.

SULLIVAN, ANTHONY
[a.] Wellford, SC [title] "The Year 2000" [pers.] This poem is a example of everyday life in our industry and corporate America. We are God's children and should convey to each other brothers and sisters. If everyone had my vision you would be so spiritual and graceful. I love people and writing poetry to send out a true message makes me fill proficient. It is a great honor and a privilege for me that someone has acknowledge my poetry. I wish that this could be a full time profession for me. I'm also a song writer. I'm very versatile. You give me a subject or object or anything I could make it a song or make it a poem. It's been my all time wish to be a writer of some sort. Of course in some perspective I would need to be fine tuned. But the gift is there and whether I become famous or not I'm glad God blessed me with this gift. Thank you for this most momentous occasion in my life.

SULLIVAN, HELEN
[a.] Weymouth, MA [title] "The Wonder of it All" [pers.] Writing has been my favorite pass time for years. I started writing for children very early. I have written games and plays and short stories. This poem was inspired in me by an experienced that has stayed with me for many years. It happened while walking in the breathtaking "Big Blue Hills" in Canton, MA. It was a most wonderful moment in my life! I am most grateful to you for selecting my poem for your book! I hope to publish all my works someday.

SULLIVAN, SHAUNTE
[a.] Blythe, CA [title] "Bitter Sweet Love" [pers.] I've been told that my Great Grandma Birdsong, loved to write, my grandpa once said, "She's got that Birdsong talent." But I owe this achievement to God for blessing me with this talent. This poem will always be very special to me, my best friend, Roy Jacob Ammerman is owed the credit for the inspiration of this piece. He is a blessing from God, into my life and I will always love him, nothing could ever come close, or replace the special friendship and love we have for one another. Thanks for reading, and God bless.

SUMTER, ANGELA
[a.] Columbia, SC [title] "Little Eyes Upon You" [pers.] This poem is dedicated to my son. Lorenzo and all parents. "Little Eyes Upon You" is a message saying to parents be careful what you say and do around your children. In our children' eyes we (parents) do no wrong. We are our children's first role model. When they see you do something, they feel it's okay for them to do the same thing. Believe it or not we set the path for which our children follows. When you least expect it and when you think they're not paying attention, surprise, their little eye's upon you.

SWEET, TARA
[a.] Indianapolis, IN [title] "The Rose" [pers.] To me poetry is art, and art is a reflection of life's beauty. I was inspired to write this poem not even a month after my mother died at age fifteen. Everything in life I believe, happens for a reason. Even an untimely death.

TAALIB-DIN, SAAJIDA
[a.] Pembroke, Bermuda [title] "Her Destiny" [pers.] I discovered o passion for writing poetry as a high school senior. "Her Destiny" remains my all-time favorite. As a lover of historical romance novels, I was attempting to capture the mystery of falling in love. I am a great believer in love of first sight. "Her Destiny" is a poem about my own hopes of love.

TABBITA, LAINE
[a.] Tampa, FL [title] "The Flame" [pers.] This poem was written as a comfort to friend whose mother had just died of breast cancer although her death was expected, losing a loved one is never easy. I wanted my friend to know that even though her mother had left this world, she still lives on in another. For me, poetry is a great form of self-expression and stress release. It helps put life's struggles in perspective and gets me through tough situations. Thanks to my mom who always encouraged me to use my talents and express my feelings.

TANASE, AURELIAN
[a.] Warren, OH [title] "Mother of Humility" [pers.] My wife Joyce and I are both orphans. I work for the Tribune Chronicle and my wife works for Trumboil Hospital. We love people, nature, art, wildlife and music. I believe writing brings a state of good health, nobility and achievement. Faithfully, I wrote this poem to cherish the wonderful memories of Mother Teresa's humble living. She illuminated God's love for us and she is an example of the holiness. Poetry to me is a river of life, composed from true words, feelings and morals which like a cascade, penetrates into someone's soul, heart and mind to restore them with vitality.

TAQI, MOHAMMAD
[a.] Chico, CA [title] "Forgive Me God" [pers.] Poetry is a gift that I should thank God for giving it to me. Also, I should thank my mother because she once told me that "No matter how evil a person can be, there is always a part in him/her that feels the guilt and asks for forgiveness." That's the story of my poem.

TAVOLACCI, RICHARD
[a.] Farmington Hills, MI [title] "Home on the Pond" [pers.] My poem was written to give my four grand nieces a chance to see the pond and its wildlife through their imaginations. Then they could add some giggling, snickering and chuckling to ". . . the sounds of tweeting, chirping and cooing." My grandnieces have their own kind of Wild Life. You see, they are Water Sprites! Marissa leaps out of her Brook. Hanna paddles up the Creek. Claire Amelia floats Downstream. Olivia glides across the Pond. "Our Water Sprites have exciting days and dreamy nights travelling on scenic waterways, tasting sweet delights." (. . . but that's another story!)

TAYLOR, K. C.
[a.] Wylie, TX [title] "Together" [pers.] This poem is based on one homeless man. On a field trip in third grade we passed a few homeless men, one of them had no sign and didn't ask for anything. I am the writer. I am ten years old and in 4th grade. I live in Wylie, TX. I started writing in 2nd grade. My friends say I'm going to be a famous poet. Thank you, Wylie, for the inspiration.

TAYLOR, LYNNE
[a.] Zebulon, NC [title] "And the Flower Wept" [pers.] My love of poetry comes from my mother, who enjoyed all things beautiful, and who taught me that, with faith, all things are possible. My father gave me the gift of encouragement and support through all my crazy endeavors.

TERCENO, JOAQUIN
[a.] Stratford, CT [title] "Softlip Kisses" [pers.] Jack Terceno wrote "Softlip Kisses" in the style of E. E. Cummings, after being inspired by a special night in Manhattan. Terceno is a novelist, playwright, poet and journalist living in Stratford, CT. His play "Death Wears White" was first produced in Stratsford in 1998, and he is currently seeking a publisher for his novels and short stories.

TERWILLIGER, JEAN STEWART
[a.] Akron, OH [title] "America The Great" [pers.] I was born in London England, then came to the USA raised two Sons alone, working I have always been able to put my feelings on paper in the form of poetry, it has been a sense of peace for me, the

words just flow. This poem was inspired because of so much violence, so much anger, in America now, if only people would band together and be thankful for "what they have," instead of "what they have not" and take a hard look a the rest of the world.

THAO, XAO
[a.] Charlotte, NC [title] "Always" [pers.] "Always" is not about family, friends, or the everyday world all around you. All these things are very important but "Always" is about more than that. It's about faith and guardian angels. It's about the world that we cannot see. I know that each and every person is special, even if they do not believe it. I have personally seen my guardian angel so I know that it exist, yet, even if you do not believe, know and realize that you are being watched very carefully. Know in your heart that you are loved and cared for. Treasure it always.

THITCHENER, STEVEN
[a.] Staatsburg, NY [title] "Spiritual Union" [pers.] This poem was derived from a special relationship with a young lady named Melissa who was a wonderful part of my life for a while. Subsequently the bond didn't hold as I had hoped, but my search for that special blend of the heart and soul will eventually lead me to a "Spiritual Union." I hope it inspires all readers who haven't found that special someone yet, and to all who have, you have located the most elusive piece of the puzzle of life.

THOMAS, DEBBIE
[a.] Scranton, PA [title] "Love of an Angel" [pers.] I have always been taught, it is more rewarding to give, than to receive. And it is through my poems, that I see how many people are truly inspired and touched by the words I've written. And how sometimes, my poems express their own feelings and emotions words which they have trouble writing or find hard to say themselves. A simple poem to share with others, one to brighten their day, put a smile on their face or say I love you in a special way. This to me is the most valuable achievement any writer could ask for.

THOMAS, STAN
[a.] Abilene, KS [title] "Amnesty in Amsterdam" [pers.] "Amnesty in Amsterdam" is a true life experience. Setup on drug charges, I felt that the U.S. Justice System had betrayed me for monetary value. During the court trials I defected to the Netherlands, with a one-way ticket I left for Amsterdam in June 1995. Unable to obtain amnesty I voluntarily returned to the U.S. I am now through with the courts and have taken a stand against this "Arbitrary Drug War" that plaques this country. Someday soon I wish to return to the Netherlands, this time with my loving wife Melinda and my two children, Chase and Chasity.

THOMPSON, ELISSA
[a.] Philadelphia, PA [title] "Daddy" [pers.] I wrote this poem for my friend, because her father passed away. I promise her that if I got this poem published I would write a dedication for her; so I did. This poem came from my heart, to angel's heart's. I hope she is glad I kept my promise, I am.

THORP, CHRIS
[a.] Muskegon, MI [title] "Lunatic" [pers.] My story is that my friend called me a lunatic over something silly, and being a far of Poe and Shakespeare, I began to write, poetry give me the chance to express my hobbies of war games and RPG's, I am 14 now and I write poems, and I'm writing, a book presently untitled. I have written poem for quite awhile and hope to upgrade into books and become a very famous novelist aside from being a lawyer, or an astronomer.

TILLSON, CHARLES
[a.] Medina, OH [title] "My Dearest Wife" [pers.] I wrote this poem to my wife in 1947. I was out of the Air Corp and working full time, going to college at night, seeing very little of her. We lived close to her parents. She was still in shock from giving birth to twin sons, but both had died just days after birth. Her mom rather than me was her

solace. I knew I was playing "Second Fiddle" and I wanted to be "First Fiddle." I loved her. The poem worked, and perhaps saved our marriage, which lasted until her death 39 years later.

TONTI-BUNN, MINDY
[a.] Bainbridge Island, WA [title] "Sometimes" [pers.] Friendships are the foundation of life. I would like to send my love and thanks to all my friends and my sister. I wrote this poem about a close friend of mine. Poetry is very important in my life, I devote lots of time towards it. I have a big family who support me in my writing, thank you. Thanks to my dad and step-dad for helping with my L.A. classes and encouraging my poetry. I live on an island and direct all into soccer, snowboarding, and of course my friends. I owe this to Trisha, thank you.

TORRES, CHRIS
[a.] Newport Richey, FL [title] "Through the Eyes of a Child" [pers.] In my writings; my views of the world, life, family, and the ever escaping love of my heart are brought to life. Although my body is only 25 years of age, my mind is immortal. Knowledge is not only a gift to be cherished but also should be shared. I find that writing allows me to express my views and seek out my answers to the ever eluding questions that perplex our daily lives. I hope that you enjoy my gift. For there are many more to come.

TOWNSEND, JAMIE
[a.] St. Louis, MO [title] "On My Grave" [pers.] This poem marks a very special time in my life. A time when my world was turning upside down, and changes were taking place. But in the midst of this, I was writing poetry and truly expressing what I was feeling. I feel that poetry is release in good and bad times. My only hope is that someday my poetry will touch another soul as many poems have touched mine.

TRACY, JOYCE
[a.] Pensacola, FL [title] "Psalm for the Divorced" [pers.] During a very low point in my life, one night I was inspired to write. What; I did not know. With pen and paper I begin to write and this little poem is the outcome. It was used to begin a healing within me. As I read it many times, over and over, it always seemed to speak to my very soul: as if God Himself was right there with me. For it was not I the words came from, but the One up above. (I was only His instrument). I pray that it will do, for others just a simulance of what it has done for me.

TRESSEL, KAREN
[a.] Sheffield Lake, OH [title] "Untitled" [pers.] I have always enjoyed trying to give life to inanimate objects. Most of my works, this included, I wrote when I was a teenager. It was a very significant time in my life where my eyes were always shut and my mind always wide open. We are here for only an eyeblink, it would be such a shame to miss the never-ending beauty around us because we are too busy looking straight ahead in black and white instead of looking at the magnificently colorful kaleidoscope of life. And when we finally stop to look, it's too late.

TSYGAN, LEONID
[a.] Brooklyn, NY [title] "A Spider and a Fly" [pers.] "A Spider and a fly" I was born December 22, 1938 in Kiev, Ukraina. In November 1979 I came to New York, Brooklyn. My wife Zhanna Polonskaya, his daughter Svetlana, my son Russell and his girlfriend Aly and father-in-law Iosef support me in my poetry life. "A Spider and a Fly" is reading-tale to "Mukha Tsokbiukha," by Russian children classic writer Kornei Ivanovich Chukovsky (1882–1969). But I give new view; what happen when spider fall in love with fly.

TUBENS, DAVID
[a.] Nashville, TN [title] "Untitled" [pers.] For as long as people are willing to read, I will be willing to write. I enjoy writing poems that are positive, inspiring and full of hope. Sometimes we need to slow down and enjoy this thing we call life. Should bad things happen in your life; just know that God is there for you. He always was. And even though you might not know Him. He knows you! To my daughters,

Megan and Jennifer, Daddy loves you! I thank God every day for blessing me with you two. You guys are the best thing that has happened in my life

TURNER, KATIE
[a.] Clio, MI [title] "Love Lost" [pers.] My poem is dedicated to the memory of Paul Lahar. Four years ago he lost his life in a car accident. I wrote "Love Lost" for Tim, his brother. I have never been good at explaining how I feel, but I could always write my thoughts on paper. Tim is the one I do and will always love. I felt that I needed to explain my love for him, so I did it in the poem. I feel that I got the point across. I hope that others can find peace from my words.

TURNER, NICOLE
[a.] Dominguez Hills, CA [title] "Let it All Out" [pers.] I don't consider myself a poet. I am an artist and poetry is just another form of expression. My poem, "Let it All Out", was inspired by (Academy award winner) Angelina Jolie's performance in a movie called "GIA." She's a brilliant actress and the feelings she projected in one scene of the movie stood out in my mind as I was writing this poem, only because I could relate to the feelings Angelina expressed so well in her character. Angelina Jolie is a big inspiration to me and my poetry. She's amazing. My family also inspire me to write. Poetry is a good outlet for all of my emotions. It's a constructive way to express feelings or to say things on paper that one might not be able to say out loud. I'm very grateful that I have this gift.

VAAGEN, DEBBIE
[a.] Harwood, ND [title] "Petals of Love" [a.] Poetry is sometimes an easier way to explain how you feel without having to say it. I was adopted by my stepfather, whom I never called Dad. Our relationship was very difficult. It wasn't until I became a parent myself that I understood the great gift that he gave me, and how much I loved him. I wrote this poem and gave it to him on Father's Day. I do not write a lot of poetry. I feel that poetry is inspiration, and come from within. In this case a promise of forgiveness, love, and accepting.

VAN HALST, CASSANDRA
[a.] St. Albert, AB [title] "Who I Am" [pers.] Poetry is a very important part of my life, and I am glad to be able to share Who I am with everyone who wishes to read it. I have been influenced greatly by my great-grandmother, who showed me the beauty of written words. As a fourteen-year-old girl, I am very happy to see my poetry respected in the adult world. I encourage others to write what they dream, as I do.

VAN WAVEREN, KAILI
[a.] Charlottesville, VA [title] "Guilt" [pers.] This poem describes my feelings and the workings of my mind when I was an active cocaine addict. I tried to depict the misery I constantly felt. I am currently a sixteen-year-old college student and no longer feel the despair expressed in my poem.

VANARSDALE, DIANNE M.
[a.] Mt. Pleasant, PA [title] "Book on a Shelf" [pers.] I began writing poems as a way to express my feelings. I have found writing to be a therapeutic and stimulating way to express those feelings. I dedicate my poem, "Book on a Shelf" to a young man who's love and life I cherish from the bottom of my heart and soul. I hope my poem's inspiration can touch the lives between mothers and their sons in all the world. "I love you, Jonathan!"

VAUGHN, ADRIANA
[a.] Norco, CA [title] "Stars Spell Out Your Name" [pers.] I am seventeen-year old junior at Norco High School in Norco California. I've been writing poetry for as long as I can remember, and I know it's at least the one thing I'm really good at. I feel that this is a gift. No matter how frustrated, miserable, or happy I am, I can vent through writing. Every poem I write has to do with some kind of impact my life has had on me, or another uncertain road taken. That's what makes it real to me. I was going through that. So who, more than

me, knows exactly how it felt? That's what my poetry is about: real life.

VEACH, RUSSELL
[a.] Los Angeles, CA [title] "The Accession of the Undone" [pers.] My poem "The Accession of the Undone" gives the reader experience in the matter of accepting the idea of friendship and at calamity thus fringing profoundness of intrigue expressed disseminating a great idea of acceptance of thought in society. Ranging from friendship to advanced particularity in thought, and reason, activity is wasted in control of position in loveliness, particularity competes with carelessness, giving a flighting effect disposing of critical measure. In corpulence of the acetic genre a particular mode in superstructure or meaning, seems to give a nonchalance in new belief.

VILLENEUVE, TENNILLE
[a.] St. Walburg, SK [title] "One Day" [pers.] "One Day" is a poem about growth and achievement. As a teenager, I have many dreams that I hope to achieve. Writing this poem was my way of expressing my frustrations about being young and to convince myself that life will improve. I am only at a stage in my life, just as a budding flower is. This stage shall pass, and I will grow; I will become sure of myself and where I am going. I will achieve my goals, one day.

VINA, GRISEL
[a.] Union City, NJ [title] "Empty Room" [pers.] For me poetry is an extension of one's soul. It's everyday life, joy, and heartache put into beautifully-intricate words that always will be cherished. I would like to give special thanks to my mother who has encouraged me to reach for the goal no matter the adversity life gives you, and to my aunt who always has supported my every step to achieve my dreams. That's why all that I am, and will be, in life I owe to them.

VINSON, CAROL
[a.] Lansing, OH [title] "The Way It Is" [pers.] With God all things are possible. Please keep God with you. For He has never left you. Love to all God's children.

VOS, UGEN
[a.] Krugersdorp, South Africa [title] "Asphyxiation" [pers.] Certain experiences in life, I suppose, stay with you. Even though you may not be aware of them, they're always there on a subconscious level. Like moths fluttering around a streetlight, their urgency seems to multiply, growing more insistent with time. More than anything I suppose this poem is an expression of the way I perceive the world, my thoughts, my feelings . . . the stuff you don't just tell anybody. Ten years from now I'll still be able to look at it and remember the way I felt today. Will I even recognize the young boy hurriedly scribbling this late at night?

VOSS, BRETT
[a.] Colorado Springs, CO [title] "Suzette" [pers.] I first started writing poetry when I was 13. That was last year. At first I never really cared about poetry, until we were assigned to write a poem about nature and the outdoors. But now I love writing poetry. It's a great way for me to unwind, and I hope to someday have my very own poetry book published.

WADE, RYLEIGH
[a.] Hamilton, VA [title] "Bianca" [pers.] I wrote this poem for a class assignment two years ago. My inspiration was a character in a story. This poem was also entered into an art show in Leesburg, VA. Poetry is very special to me and I enjoy writing it.

WALIMAKI, NORMAN
[a.] Selah, WA [title] "People, Hear My Plea" [pers.] My poem is for the world so they can learn to get along as a family. Children are our future. The world is our future. If the world dies? God save us all.

WALKER, DARRYL
[a.] Chicago, IL [title] "A Great Day for Me" [pers.] As we just start off in this "New Millennium," it is still sad to see some of the effects of the "Old Millennium" still with us; primarily I speak of "lost loves!" Thus I dedicate this poem to the many who have had that special someone and

then unexpectedly lost them to another. Ask yourselves! Did I really try to make it work? Can I accept the fact that just maybe I let a "Diamond" get away? Well, if so, always remember, "one man's loss is another' man's gain!" And what you think may not be valuable today could be irreplaceable tomorrow!

WALLACE, DENISE
[a.] Rincon, GA [title] "The Rock" [pers.] I graduated from Effingham County High School in June '93 with a Hope Grant and college and vocational seal on my diploma. I graduated from Savannah Technical Institute in April '96 with an A.A. in Secretarial Science. I am presently employed at Effingham Hospital as a Medical Records Clerk. I am currently taking a continuing education class, Medical Terminology, at Savannah Technical Institute so I can become a part-time Medical Transcription at Effingham Hospital. My hobby is poetry writing. I write poetry as a way of expressing myself to deal with the issues of my life.

WALLE, ERIK
[a.] Toronto, ON [title] "Angel" [pers.] This idealistic load of tripe was brought to you by yet another cynical, depressed atheist, because the world can always use a few more. Remember, little people: I truly and deeply love each and every one of you, right up to the point when I decide not to anymore.

WALLIS, JUANITA
[a.] Quay, NM [title] "A Brand-New Baby" [pers.] My mother (belated) had a saying which I truly believe. She said, "Children are our Deposits in our future; Grandchildren are our dividends, great grandchildren are our compounded interest!" I began drafting "A Brand-New Baby" when two of my granddaughters and their husbands proudly announced they were expecting their new babies in the year 2000. The poem "A Brand-New Baby" expresses how important children are and the love we share in caring for them. We're looking forward for the new arrivals' birth dates and given names to add to our family trees.

WARWICK, MELISSA
[a.] Simsboro, LA [title] "A Sweet Song in My Heart" [pers.] This poem was written for someone that holds a special place in my heart, my husband. I want him to know I love him very much. I am a 20-year-old mother of one, happily married, and from Arcadia, LA. I hope to pursue my nursing degree and continue writing on the side. I am originally from Greensboro, NC. I would like to tell all of my family and friends who may see this I love them. Also, a special thanks to my mom's friend, A. Rawleigh. (Thanks for inspiring me to write.) I love you!

WASHINGTON, JESSE, JR., II
[a.] Buffalo, NY [title] "Untitled" [pers.] I was inspired to write this poem from my own lifestyle. I was trying to hide my military past. Today I no longer hide the truth. Therefore, "God has blessed me." God is the truth and the light; I now see nothing is impossible for God. I teach, preach, and volunteer. I am the communizer.

WATSON, TONYA ALINE
[a.] Redding, CA [title] "For Matthew" [pers.] "For Matthew" was a gift to Matthew Alper, author of *The "God" Part of the Brain: A Scientific Interpretation of Human Spirituality and God* His good book, having personal and social relevance too, inspired me. The poem is a humorous yet poignant response to the tongue-in-cheek dedication of his fourth edition. It is word play on the eupheminism of a popular religious text, the anthropomorphic image of a western civilization God and common grave side commentary. And finally, it is personal sentiment.

WATT, TOM
[a.] Bethlehem, GA [title] "The Gift" [pers.] This poem is for all the people that have passed through my life, good or bad, living or dead, which have touched me in some way. With love to all.

WEBB, BENNIE
[a.] Jeffersonville, IN [title] "Ballet" [pers.] I was

blessed with a gift that I never took notice of. If it wasn't for a good friend that took notice and pushed me, I would of never realized my potential. We all have inspirational "Fairies" helping us and if we listen, doors of ourselves will unlocked, open new worlds to us more, and thank you, Fairy!

WEBB, MELVIN CARLOS
[a.] Highland Springs, WA [title] "Untitled" [pers.] My poetry, I feel, is my Lord's way of allowing me to be able to express myself, my views, and my perspectives on life. My poem "Untitled" is one of my ways of expressing both my hurt and anger on the topic of society and its uncaring state of mind. I hope this poem and its message will be able to possibly influence some person into making a change to better themselves and the world we live in. Melvin C. Webb II is the son of Melvin and Nancy Webb. He has one sibling, a brother, Jamie Webb. He has a loving and supporting wife, Beverly J. Webb, and daughter, Armauni M. Webb, who is the light of his life and who provided his inspiration for this poem.

WEBER, MICHAEL
[a.] Sunnyvale, CA [title] "My Black Rose" [pers.] "My Black Rose" conveys love and affection beneath words of sorrow and dull reality. Hayley Jackson inspired and motivated me to write, and with love, I dedicate this poem to her.

WEEKS, SHERRY
[a.] Elkmont, AL [title] "A Love Forbidden" [pers.] Haven't we all at some point in our lives experienced that "Love Forbidden?" From that first teenage crush on a favorite teacher, through the first puppy love romance, into adulthood, when circumstances prevent our relationship from working out, we have all faced the pain and loneliness of a broken heart. This poem is for those who have been or are now in this situation. Please know you are not alone. I understand.

WELCH, MELANIE
[a.] Pensacola, FL [title] "Storyteller" [pers.] What a wonderful escape in a world that sometimes isn't so wonderful. Poetry means something different to everyone, and that is what it is to me, an escape. My own personal door leading to the abstract that I can create myself. It can also be a means of communicating thoughts or feelings that are otherwise difficult to express. The beautiful thing is, in this branch of creativity and art, everyone has a voice. Poetry is something that doesn't have to be learned, just felt.

WENSEL, PAULINE
[a.] Durham, NC [title] "This Day" [pers.] I was inspired to write this poem, because of people I come in contact with at work. I'm motivated to write by happenings in everyday life.

WEST, ERIN
[a.] West Port, KY [title] "Where I'm From" [pers.] Writing has been a gift to me. When I was younger, I decided that I wanted to grow up and be a writer. So, I wrote poems to express the way I look at life and all the joyous outcomes that come along with it. I wrote this one specific poem with the perspective of my life. This poem is about my life and everything that is greatly important to me. I owe this poem to my family and my boyfriend. Everyone has been behind me through the most important dream of my life, writing.

WHARTON, SYLVIA
[a.] Oakland, CA [title] "Serenity" [pers.] "Serenity" was written during a time when I was very much in love. It is dedicated to the beauty and splendor of young love. I have been blessed with the ability to express my thoughts and feelings and have often been called upon to express those of others. I am eternally grateful for this gift and look forward to publishing a book of poetry.

WHITE, BARBARA
[a.] Bakersfield, CA [title] "Within Its Path" [pers.] Writing has become a pleasurable means by which I express appreciation for elements that link

us to life yet are sometimes misunderstand or unappreciated in their uncontemplated state. Poetry lends itself to the simplest things, enabling us to fathom life's exchanges, deeming them worthy of elaborating. My poem "Within Its Path" demonstrates this truth. I feel so very fortunate to be able to seek and find that which is beautiful in most things and feel warm at heart by my findings.

WHITE, BRENDA
[a.] Duluth, GA [title] "Modern Heartache, Old Fashion Prayer" [pers.] I have always enjoyed writing poetry, putting my feeling and thoughts in verse. This poem was inspired by a personal experience when I, like so many parents today, realized my child was being influenced by peer pressure, drugs like crack cocaine, and a society that is rapidly loosing its morals, direction, and purpose. This poem came from my heart, and I hope it may bring comfort to other parents on the same journey, as we remember that we cannot always protect our children, but through faith we can still have hope for a better tomorrow for them, and for us.

WHITE, JUSTIN
[a.] Brampton, ON [title] "Life"

WHITE, MARY
[a.] Santa Claus, IN [title] "My Little Girl" [pers.] After holding my daughter for the first time, many thoughts went through my mind. While in the hospital, these words were written to her. This was forty years ago, and I must say I am proud of her for who and what she is today. Diane has an older brother, Wade, and a younger brother, Wayne. A poem was written to each of them many years ago also. Speaking from a mother's heart, I love them all very much, and my life has been very rewarding. They were worth it!

WHITE, NATHALIE
[a.] Schooleys Mountain, NJ [title] "I Am a Girl" [pers.] This poem is very meaningful to me. A year ago, during the summer when I was sixteen, I was going through the typical depression and confusion that comes with the age. One day I decided to write about my quirks and mannerisms, my emotions, what defined Me. "I Am a Girl" was the fruit of my labors. It was very therapeutic to write, and to this day it is my favorite of all the poems I've written. I'd like to send my love to my best friend Dave, because if it wasn't for him I'd never have gotten myself in gear and sent in my profile. My love also to all my friends and family.

WHITE, PEARL
[a.] Indianapolis, IN [title] "My Lord and I" [pers.] Having been truly blessed, above all odds, to be 82, a 34-year widow with four healthy, successful children, ten grandchildren, and nine great grands, how can I not say, "To God Be the Glory," for the things He has done in all our lives. He is worthy to be Praised! He rules and super-rules! He is God all by himself! He knows what is best for His loved ones and He will take care. He only asks us to Believe, Trust, and Obey Him, and then Love one another as He loves us.

WHITE, SARAJANE
[a.] Laguna Beach, CA [title] "Soy? Burgers" [pers.] It had never before occurred to me that poetry actually came from one's experiences, for one instant. This is one instant. I was heading home from work and saw a field of soybeans, and I did stop. I thought the farmer was silly, because he thought I was crazy. Dinner was good? It just occurred to me that I should've taken the farmer a "Soy-Burger."

WHITING, ROBERT
[a.] Satellite Beach, FL [title] "Ignition" [pers.] I love poetry because it fills the always looming void of boredom that likes to visit from time to time. I prefer to create poems that, for the most part, can be understood somewhat by my fellow man. I don't believe in writing poems that just "sound" good and make sense only to the poet. A lot of poets write for themselves, but I write, not for myself, but for those hungry for a mind expansion.

WHITLEY, JILL
[a.] Smithfield, NC [title] "Christmas Fun" [pers.]

My name is Jill Whitley, and I live at Brogden, NC, near film star Ava Gardner's birthplace. I attended Princeton K-12 and have attended Johnson Christian/Smithfield. I would like to thank all my teachers, especially Mrs. Janet Bone and my third grade teachers Mrs. Patricia Cockrell and Mrs. Melba Woodall. I enjoy softball, swimming, and thinking up and writing poems and songs. I wrote "Christmas Fun" in Dec. 1999 at the age of 8. I am honored and thrilled to have it chosen for your book. I would like to dedicate it to my parents, Jay and Jan, sister Jena, grandmother's Helen McLamb and Edith Whitley, and my Papas in Heaven, Buck McLamb and HJ Whitley. My love and prayers always to my family, friends, and the Lord.

WHITNEY, WILLIAM
[a.] Maitland, FL [title] "Perpetual Motion" [pers.] I have summered on a lake on Cape Cod all my life, as did my family before me. Now that I am retired—I was an architect—I am writing brief recollections of my life and of that place: some prose, some poetry. They are intended to admit nostalgia and show continuing love.

WHITTAKER, DANIELLE
[a.] Pitman, NJ [title] "Unsaid" [pers.] I wrote this poem for a friend of mine. His grandfather was placed in the hospital and was not doing good. He had a hard time saying good-bye to his grandfather. I wrote this poem to help him. I am 16 years old and I live in Glassboro, NJ. I love to listen to music; it helps me to write. My parents always support me in my writing. I love them very much. I also want to thank my best friends: Susan, Steve, Denise, and Marc. I love you all.

WIGGINS, ELEANORA
[a.] Queens Village, NY [title] "Over Come" [pers.] I have always loved the written word and the magic of putting them together. I could do nothing else but lay pen to paper. This poem is very special to me because there have been numerous people who encouraged and upheld me during many trials, joys, and sorrows. I praise our Lord for my gift of communicating His love. I thank my husband, children, sisters, brothers, brother-in-law, uncle, father, etc. All have stood before the Lord on my behalf, interceding for my strength and success. The prayers of the righteous avail much. I love you all

WIJAYA, MELISSA
[a.] Jakarta Selatan, Indonesia [title] "Soulmates" [pers.] I was thrilled when I found out that my poem was to be published. Poetry is a gift that God has given me, and one I will cherish forever. My inspiration for this poem came from the many people who have encouraged me through thick and thin. Through this poem, I would like to thank my Mam, Pap, and my sister Marcella, for their enduring love and support. My great appreciation goes to my teachers, Mr. Geoff Mariott and Ms. Abi Hull, who discovered and mentored my talents and are responsible for my passion in language arts ever since. This poem is dedicated to my real-life "soulmates," Lisa and Sahil.

WILCOX, JODY
[a.] Colorado Springs, CO [title] "An Open Letter to My Grandpa" [pers.] Born and raised in Iowa, I currently live in Colorado Spring, Colorado with my wife Angie. While attending the University of Iowa and majoring in English, I realized writing would always be a major part in my life. Words that flow from one's soul to the paper is greatest gift you can share with people. This poem was written for my Grandfather who passed away in 1999.

WILKES, SHELIA
[a.] Fayetteville, NC [title] "Cocaine" [pers.] I am retired military. I enjoy writing poems; I have support from my daughter, Teshia Morgan, and my grandchildren

WILKIE, TERESA
[a.] San Antonio, TX [title] "Rain" [pers.] Emotions too abstract to describe are what I want to capture the joy of carefree days and the sadness of lonely days. We all have these feelings but hesitate

to appear too gleeful or blue, or exceedingly vulnerable. The basic instinct is to hold back. My writing began and continues as an outlet for hopes and fears I don't express to anyone. It is a paradox that I also believe that no one can love me unless they know me. Go figure! Come with me on a highway, that intersects happy and sad, and we'll make subtle stops in-between.

WILLIAMS, AARON
[a.] Alamoso, CO [title] "Halfway Free" [pers.] Growing up on Disney and Pop Tarts, my world was bright. After the Pop Tarts, I began to read and write. I skipped my 10th grade year, only to be kicked out of school my 11th grade year. Being kicked out worked to my benefit because in Fall 2000, I will be attending U.U.S.C. (Utah Valley State College) in Orem Utah, at the age of 17.

WILLIAMS, BILLY
[a.] Cincinnati, OH [title] "My Black African Mother" [pers.] This poem is special to me because you have only one mother, and why wait until Mother's Day to celebrate your mother, when you're supposed to be grateful to have her every day. This poem symbolizes all black mothers across the world who suffered from pain, struggling, crying, dying, or making a change, so their family, friends, and / or children can have that free spirit with them. We shouldn't cry.

WILLIAMS, BRANDON
[a.] Des Moines, IA [title] "Untitled" [pers.] We all go through times of being alone in life. Those times in my own life have been fairly frequent; and yet there is one thing that I have learned. That is that no matter how alone I may be in this world, my Lord Jesus Christ is always with me. As long as I remember that, being alone with Him is beautiful.

WILLIAMS, CHARLEY
[a.] Zephryhills, FL [title] "The Waves" [pers.] I wrote this piece looking through the eyes of an old man who has outlived his beloved wife. Every day he goes to the beach and lives his life thinking about his past. With patience he lovingly watches and waits for life's end so he can greet his wife again. I have been writing poems, books, short stories, and songs all my life. It is my way of personal pressure release from life's stress. I just shared my view with anyone until now.

WILLIAMS, JAMES
[a.] Boise, ID [title] "Cradle of Rain" [pers.] Where is my station among poets? Not the brilliant, but the many. I conclude it matters not, for I love to pour my feelings into the bowl of poetry stirring and painting. It exposes my heart like no other thing I know. That, for me, is like free falling from the clouds while never being sure the parachute will open.

WILLIAMS, K.
[a.] St. Petersburg, FL [title] "Ammo" [pers.] Poetry has been an outlet of every emotional event in my 25 years of life, especially for pain. "Ammo" was written after my brother attempted suicide. My brothers and I have always been more like best friends. All of us had gone our separate ways in 1998, and no longer had that support, that by this time, we realized we needed so much of the many poems I've written this one touches my heart more than any. "Ammo" truly declares that love conquers all.

WILLIAMS, LOUIS
[a.] Prichard, AL [title] "Untitled" [pers.] To me poetry is like a beautiful array of freshly-cut flowers. Their beauty makes your eyes glow, their fragrance saturates you completely, and the gesture of giving them brightens a dreary day. The assassinations of President Kennedy and Dr. King were instrumental in my endeavor to write poetry, and so were poems by Helen S. Rice.

WILLIAMS, MARIA
[a.] Green Creek, NJ [title] "Mother" [pers.] Poetry is a precious gift that I have inherited from my mother. I wrote this poem to not only thank her for all she's done for me, but also to let her see

all the beautiful aspects of herself mirrored in me. I love you, Mom. Thank you.

WILLIAMS, ROGER
[a.] Willinboro, NJ [title] "With" [pers.] I wrote this poem in August 1971. I just liked to write what was on my mind at the time, no particular reason. On December 21, 1999, my true soulmate, "My," was injured in an automobile accident, and I nearly lost her. It was then I found out just how much I truly loved her. I also thought of my parents, Lee and Bobbye, who are true soulmates and that gave me strength for the way I felt. The poem fit so well with how I felt, so I wanted to share it with others. Everyone has a soulmate, and love is forever.

WILLIAMS, ZACH
[a.] Saratoga Springs, NY [title] "A Deer in the Woods" [pers.] I am 13, and I am in 7th grade. One day, Mr. Madison, my Language Arts teacher, assigned the class to write an outline of a story from a picture we drew. Later that semester, he gave us an extra credit project to make a free verse poem out of our story picture. This was one of my first poems I have ever written. I decided to write my poem about a deer in the woods because I live near the Adirondack Mountains where deer are a fairly common sight, and I was inspired to write about them. I go to wilderness camps during the summer and often see deer there and at my grandparent's house. One of my favorite things to do is to be a silent observer of nature.

WILLIS, PEGGY
[a.] Idaho Falls, ID [title] "Angels" [pers.] Last August, I went out to the patio with my writing material in hand and sat down by the table to write. The poem of "Angels" came to me, and I wrote it down very promptly. I grew up on a farm in St. Leon near our town. I am the seventh of fourteen children and the proud mother of seven. At a very young age, I developed a love for poetry. I've written it since age thirteen. My education consisted of finishing the ninth grade. Thank you kindly for publishing my poem.

WILTSHIRE, M.
[a.] Wellington, New Zealand [title] "The Moon" [pers.] I am a fifteen-year-old high school student. My first poems came from school projects, and my interest grew from there. According to Celtic legend, there are three goddesses: Maiden, Mother, and Crone, respectively represented by the moon cycles; waxing, full, and waning. I wrote "The Moon" on the February 2000 full moon, when I found the night particularly inspiring. I hope that people will read my poem and feel the magic and myth created by the moon in so many different cultures.

WINDMILL, BETSY
[a.] Vernon, BC [title] "The Wind" [pers.] This poem, "The Wind," is a very BIG part of my life, because my last name is Windmill. Also, the wind seems to bring in four seasons where we live in Vernon, B.C., Canada. I have three sisters: Abigail, Evangeline, and Celeste. I live in a three-story log house, on three and 1/2 acres. I home school online with Anchor Academy, and that's how I found out about poetry.com. I was eleven when I wrote "The Wind," and it is dedicated to my parents, Paul and Elizabeth Windmill.

WISOTZKEY, JULIA COX
[a.] Pompano Beach, FL [title] "Invitation to Life" [pers.] This poem was written by me while attending an early childhood education course at Columbia University. While it was meant to be read by children, there is that child in each of us that reaches out for new perspectives, new ways of looking at life with all its wonders and in all its simplicities. Poetry has always been that little "hill" to me from which, in reading and writing it, I have enjoyed the new vistas it has painted upon my mind.

WITTE, AMBRE
[a.] Denver, PA [title] "Soul Searching" [pers.] Drowning in a world consumed by regret, we learn to swallow our sorrow. With each tear we shed, despair embeds itself deeper within our soul. Optimism may fade and dreams may shatter, however,

even in our darkest hour, hope has not perished. Individuals come into our lives, forever embracing us with their presence. Thank you for being there for me when I needed you. You know who you are, and I love you. We live in a broken world. It's our choice if we wish to pick up the pieces and begin to live.

WOLF, JONATHAN
[a.] Worcester, MA [title] "Never Done" [pers.] The poetry I write generally is a reflection of the experiences and moods that I have encountered. "Never Done" is about two friends of mine who have died in recent years and helped me to think the way I do now. The big thing I learned was: "Water cleans the body, weeping the wind, but laughter cleans the soul." Blessed be!

WRIGHT, S.
[a.] Kenner, LA [title] "Love So Dear" [pers.] My name is Sandra, and I enjoy writing. "Love so Dear" was written on February 17, 1998. I enjoy reading and would like for everyone to read to children. I am married. I have a son and daughter-in-law, and I have a daughter and son-in-law. I have two grandchildren. I would like to remind everyone to make each day special. Sharing a publication with my family is special. It is for them. I love you, Mom!

WRIGHT, WANDA
[a.] Saraland, AL [title] "Death Becomes an Angel" [pers.] Poetry is away of expressing feelings that are otherwise hidden. This poem was written in memory of Alan Holloway, who was a very dear friend. He is loved and missed by all who knew him.

WYANT, AMANDA
[a.] Anaconda, MT [title] "Mom" [pers.] This poem is very special to me, as my mom and I had an argument a couple years ago. I wrote this poem for my mom to express my feelings towards her and how I felt about our relationship. Poetry is a great way to express your feelings to someone. I want to thank my parents, Dan and Debbie, my Grandma Clara, my best friend Mellisa and all of my other friends, my boyfriend, Phil for everything. I especially want to thank Suzane for telling me to enter my poem to poetry.com.

YEOMAN, KARRIE
[a.] Bellingham, WA [title] "Friends" [pers.] This poem was written a few years back in my life and has always been a family favorite. It is dedicated to many close friends, come and gone, who have always been there for me, and also dedicated to my four wonderful children, who always believed their mom's talents. They are: Brandon, Ryan, Josh, and Matthew. I love you guys. Also, this is to a very special friend who is in Heaven now, and her memory will always be with me. Vesta Henson, thank you for your special gift you have given me—your friendship! Also, I want to give special thanks to my husband, Scott Yeoman, who has given me a chance to start over, and, most of all, to God. He is the reason I am.

YOUNG, KIMBERLY
[a.] Corpus Christi, TX [title] "My First Thoughts of You" [pers.] I believe circumstances in life don't just happen by chance, they happen for a reason like when someone so extraordinary comes into your life at just the right time and everything seems to happen so magically. I look at this as a gift. God knows what your heart wants. With patience, faith, and kindness, He will give you what your heart needs. I believe that words of wisdom feed the heart, mind, and soul and can heal a spirit that has been broken. With wisdom brings knowledge which is the key to peace and happiness.

YUSMAN, EDWIN
[a.] Fairfax, VA [title] "Vicious Velociraptor" [pers.] This poem started off as a part of my school project. I chose to do my project on Velociraptors because often watching movies such as Jurassic Park, they interest me and I wanted to know more about the fierce creatures. I feel that my poem describes raptors as a very not-well-known creature, but it isn't. Many people have researched the dinosaur, and know a lot

about it. I am proud to be one of those people, and wish more people can learn, too.

ZINAMAN, EARLEEN
[a.] San Antonio, TX [title] "Expectation" [pers.] I am a seventy-eight-year-old, retired elementary teacher, A WAC in WW II, I met and married a Jewish kid from Brooklyn, now deceased. I have a son, two daughters, and an almost daughter-in-law. Since early seventies membership in a consciousness raising group, I am a highly vocal advocate of women's rights. About five years ago I became furious with my younger daughter when she refused to comply with my wishes in a matter that also involved my son. I wrote this poem as I came face to face with my contradictory self.

ZLOTA, DRAGOS
[a.] Chicago, IL [title] "Snow" [pers.] I was born in Romania, a place where the verse rises in the Carpathians Mountain's shadow, the metaphor dances ancestrally in the people's souls, God knows he is loved fearful and merciful, yet the points of the compass, sometimes propitious, sometimes not, gathering with us, building history. As for my poetry, I hope that it is the map of the soul and vision of the universal unanswered. Nevertheless, I would like to thank God for the ray of light he implanted in our souls: for the smile of a child or his crying, for the sunrise, for today's day but most of all tomorrow's day because poetry will never die until the last man dies.

ZOHARI, PARISSA
[a.] Montreal, QC [title] "The Ice Storm" [pers.] I call myself a "naturalized poet," turned into one by hardships! 1998 depicts the harshest emotional journey of my life. Two years after separating from a 12-year companion, I was already experiencing difficulties with my new mate who was, is, and always will be the love of my life. During the aftermath of the ice-storm, I was walking the streets seeking a way to breathe and a reason to live. My path took me to the trees ruined so ruthlessly by the very nature that created them. I understood their solemn pain; I was one with those broken trees.

ZUMWALT, RONALD
[a.] Molalla, OR [title] "The Dream" [pers.] I have written poetry since high school. This poem, ("The Dream"), was written as I dreamed it. I have always studied history, and as I am a Native American, I have especially studied history from our standpoint. I am 64 years old and still write poetry for family and friends.

Index
of
Poets

Index

A

Aaron, Marjorie 153
Abdullah, Sakeena 127
Abel, Daniel 5
Abernathy, Nikki 82
Accurso, Vonda 71
Achtnich, Anemone 158
Ackermann, Brian 170
Adamian, Alina 77
Adams, Edna Mae 91
Adams, Jennifer 59
Afandy, Bolbol 56
Aguirre, Benel 122
Aiken, Sonia 53
Akin, Sharon Temple 48
Albanese, Vincenzo 78
Aldrich, Jessica 186
Alexander, Mary 29
Alexander, Melissa 89
Alford, Audrey 78
Alicardi, Carmen R. 108
Allen, Abraham L., Jr. 245
Allen, Andre 198
Allen, April A. 227
Allen, Cynthia 135
Allen, Jessica 192
Allen, Marjorie L. 129
Allen, Porsha 48
Allison, Arwyn S. 33
Allred, Michael 74
Almotahari, Mahrad 195
Alo-Cabalquinto, Carla 55
Alper, Arthur 119
Alton, Brittany 144
Alvarez, Jose M. 104
Alvarez, Veronica 245
Alvis-Clark, Patricia 43
Ament, Elizabeth 15
Anderson, Angelitta 60
Anderson, Brandy 199
Anderson, Colleen 121
Anderson, Gary 87
Anderson, Uriah 12
Andersson, Emilie 68
Andre, Rob 116
Ang, Tsu 179
Angel, Angie 12
Angelo, Michael 232
Angle, Thomas Craig 113
Anguay, Ciara C. 102
Antar, Brian 102
Anthony, Jennifer 155
Archer, Valerie 146
Arevalo, Susan 160
Armfield, Mandi 76
Armstrong, Pearlie 195
Arndt, Daniel 92
Arsenault, Jenn 205
Artis, Glorious J. 115
Aschbrenner, Emily 204
Asuncion, Denise 134
Atkins, Bonny 19
Attart, Alex 93
Atwood, Michael 104
Aucoin, Roland 139

Aulick, Karina 106
Avant, Laverne 82
Avecilla, Champion Moonwind 19
Avery, June 148
Ayers, Melissa 153
Aytes, Sheryl 162

B

Babington, Arianne 88
Bailey, Julia 67
Bair, Christina 64
Bajgot, Emily 150
Baker, Laura 242
Baker, Mike 97
Baker, Sandy 45
Balash, Anna T. 13
Baldwin, Jeramy 103
Balek, Krista 61
Banks, Sally 210
Barber, Karrey 29
Barnes, Brandi 62
Barnett, John 43
Barnhart, Pamela 84
Barrier, Dawn P. 161
Barron, Dennis W. 189
Barrows, Paul 218
Barta, Marie L. 167
Bartlett, Echo 5
Bartman, Elizabeth 81
Bartsch, Bas'ka 151
Bastian, Mary Alice 93
Bateman, Mildred 24
Bateman, Ryan 223
Bateman, Stacey 141
Bates, David 5
Batten, Lisa 73
Baumhardt, Amy 83
Baxter, Shelina 182
Bayouth, Christina 146
Bayuelo, Yolanda 109
Bazzell, Barry 19
Beach, Anna 144
Beasley, Marianne 9
Beckman, Matthew 95
Bedard, Michael 231
Beel, Sandy 158
Behling-Newton, Linda Ann 47
Behrens, David 83
Belfield, Debra Sherlock 219
Bell, Kenisha A. 196
Bell, Melisa 242
Bell, Shaina 67
Benefield, Ang 100
Benes, Ariel 183
Benjamin, Miranda R. 222
Bennenbroek, Joseph 112
Benner, Matthew J. 250
Bennett, Benard 178
Bennett, Connie 54
Berman, Lee Arthur 227
Bermond, Kate 139
Bernholc, Alissa 36
Berrios, Cathy 171
Bertone, Jackie 77
Betker, Nicole 124
Beverly, Andrew 86
Bialik, Kristine 34
Biddix, Tammy 145
Birch, Linda M. 220
Birch, Patty 84
Black, Treena 249
Blackburn, Victoria 230

Blackmon, Carri 234
Blackstone, Wendy 180
Blades, Christiana 217
Blan, Henry 174
Blanchard, Mary 221
Blasims, Dorothy M. 116
Blaydes, Michaela 141
Blevins, Michelle L. 156
Blubaugh, Joseph 188
Blum, Amy 238
Blundell, Jamie 190
Bochove, Elisabeth 35
Bockelman, Melvin 123
Bodamer, Derick 124
Boehm, Kathleen 56
Boen, Gladys Den 18
Boffo, Jeffrey 102
Boguslawski, Jim 42
Bolden, Ronda 128
Bolick, Ralph 84
Boling, Barbra 120
Bondi, Salvatore 17
Bonesteel, Bekki 156
Booker, Gloria 185
Booth, Brian 106
Booty, Odis D. 114
Booze-Battle, Lee 94
Borenstein, Martin 26
Borja, Carlos 174
Bossier, Kenneth 206
Bourdeau, Katie 118
Bowen, Jack 63
Bowerman, Shirley 57
Bowie, Mesh 83
Bowling, Lacey 192
Bowlsbey, Linda 150
Boyd, Blair 237
Boyd, Brian 208
Boyd, James 216
Boyles, Ann 219
Bozeman, Jim 136
Bradley, Shanna 93
Brady, Julie Marie 62
Bran, E. 140
Brazee, Dianne 54
Brazelton, Cheryl 58
Breinin, Betty Ryen 21
Breuers, Georgie 155
Brewer, Barbara 187
Brierly, Patricia 180
Brimm, Mark 11
Brinkey, Samantha 130
Britnell, Jane 119
Broach, Clarence 234
Broach, Connie L. 228
Brodbeck, Cammie 181
Brodsky, Ben 212
Bronakoski, Rachel M. 192
Brooks, Jaymes 122
Broshear, Jeremy 150
Brothers, Darryl E. 245
Brough, Mildred 165
Brown, Eric Leonhardt 127
Brown, Kim 163
Brown, Pamela R. 213
Brown, Patricia 159
Brown, Shane 61
Browning, Lindsay 193
Brozenec, Susan 37
Brubaker, James 12
Bruney, Joann 91
Brunin, Derek 143
Brunstad, Robert 164

Bruyning, Julie 60
Bryant, Richard 46
Buck, Everett H. 24
Bukowski, Larissa 187
Bularz, Cheryl 236
Bullock, Tonya 118
Bunce, Nicholas 193
Bunkley, Mary 103
Burch, Betty 220
Burdett, Dorothy 158
Burger, Jeslyn 151
Burney, Sheila 232
Burney, Shirley 63
Burns, Anthony C. 83
Burns, David 152
Burrell, Carla 163
Burrill, Jim 156
Burt, Natalie 42
Burt, Sarah 37
Burton, Thomas 105
Bushnell, Kelly L. 203
Butcher, Beau Tyler 225
Butler, Andrea 11
Butler, Marshall N. 20
Buzan, Doris 132
Byrd, Deserea L. 239

C

Cagney, Caitilin 14
Calande, Eugenia 62
Caldwell, Michelle 15
Caldwell, Ray 78
Calorel, Patricia 166
Campbell, Adam 54
Campbell, Charlotte 56
Campbell, Edward L. 249
Campbell, Eric 40
Campbell, Genevieve 24
Campbell, Ruth L. 33
Camus, Jeanne-Louise 136
Cannata, Paul 205
Cannon, Emily 135
Cantrell, Vicki L. 196
Capell, Robert 149
Cappello, Sarah 114
Caraway, Heather 178
Cardis, Jamie 181
Cardoso, Nuno 101
Carlson, Jonathan 60
Carmon, Patricia 108
Carnrike, Jason 44
Carpenter, Justine 7
Carr, Rosemary C. 196
Carreiro, Nancy Lee 239
Carrera, Ivan 70
Carroll, Kevin 17
Carswell, Ashley 133
Carter, Alison 97
Carter, Christa 120
Carter, Willie 73
Caruso, Richard 246
Carver, Crista 174
Cathey, Carol 147
Caudill, Elaine 162
Cave, Jennifer 147
Cavender, Barbara G. 156
Ceile, Jean 155
Chalke, Janet 116
Chamis, Ashley 25
Champ, Amy 10
Chapman Rodriguez, Karen 163
Chartier, Marie 117